Life Principles from Proverbs

Life Principles from Proverbs

A Devotional Expositional Commentary

Frank R. Shivers

LIGHTNING SOURCE
1246 Heil Quaker Blvd.
La Vergne, TN

Unless otherwise noted, Scripture quotations are from
The Holy Bible *King James Version*

Library of Congress Cataloging-in-Publication Data

Shivers, Frank R., 1949-
Life Principles from Proverbs / Frank Shivers
ISBN 978-1-878127-34-1

Library of Congress Control Number:
2018952723

Cover design by
Tim King of Click Graphics, Inc.

For Information:
Frank Shivers Evangelistic Association
P. O. Box 9991
Columbia, South Carolina 29290
www.frankshivers.com

Presented to

_____

By

_____

Date

_____

We have now before us... [a] new way of writing, in which divine wisdom is taught us by Proverbs, or short sentences, which contain their whole design within themselves and are not connected with one another. We have had divine laws, histories, and songs, and now divine proverbs; such various methods has Infinite Wisdom used for our instruction, that, no stone being left unturned to do us good, we may be inexcusable if we perish in our folly.[1] ~ Matthew Henry

Plato wrote on the door of his Academy, "Let no man unskilled in geometry come hither." Solomon writes the very reverse on the door of his school: "Let the simple man who is easily deceived come hither, and he shall learn that subtilty which is necessary to preserve him from the snares of the destroyer and is yet fully consistent with integrity. Let the young and inexperienced come and learn knowledge and discretion.[2] ~ George Lawson

[In the Book of Proverbs] God has condescended to become our Teacher on the practical affairs belonging to all the relations of life. He has adapted His instruction to the plain and unlettered and presented, in this striking and impressive method, the great principles of duty to Him and to our fellowmen.[3] ~ Jamieson, Fausset and Brown

The Book of Proverbs is not to be regarded simply as a collection of wise sayings, genial sentiments, prudent guesses, or affectionate exhortations. The book may be viewed, on the contrary, as representing the very science of practical philosophy. Proverbs are condensed philosophies. Sometimes proverbs are condensed histories.[4] ~ Joseph Parker

To

Kirk Johnson

Friend, helper and intercessor

Contents

Preface

The writing of this book was from the start like a "grappling hook" on my heart. I simply could not lay it down until it was completed. As it was with the disciples on the Emmaus Road, my 'heart burned within me' as I explored the deep caverns of Proverbs, discovering choice gold nuggets of wisdom and knowledge. Some of the choicest nuggets found were those deepest in the cavern, requiring diligence and grave care in excavation and extraction.

The journey in this composition began with uncertainty regarding its duration, destination or even the discipline that it would require to accomplish it. I was like Abraham who "went out, not knowing whither he went," trusting God to direct him (Hebrews 11:8). As surely as the Lord provided Abraham guidance, so He guided me in the undertaking of writing this volume (research, study, exegesis and exposition), as the "cloudy pillar" by day and "pillar of fire" by night led the Israelites in their wilderness wandering until they entered Canaan (Nehemiah 9:12). Frankly, I never envisioned at its start (departure from Egypt) that it would evolve into such a mammoth task (wilderness wandering) that would yield such bountiful fruit (Canaan). Hopefully the reader will discover, as did I, that the land of Canaan (Proverbs) is a land "flowing with milk and honey" (Ezekiel 20:15), in that it abundantly provides rich soul instruction, nourishment and guidance in dealing with the practical issues of life.

Living within the pages of Proverbs literally seven to eight hours a day, seven days a week (as a rule) for months enriched my life and walk with God in ways indescribable and unexplainable. We read of the "Proverbs 31 woman." I feel as if I am the "Proverbs 1 man," at least in knowledge, striving to be in practice (please chuckle!). Hopefully the time expended on the research and writing will be viewed by believers as time well spent, producing profit for their soul and the kingdom of God at large.

The "Land of Proverbs" awaits your entrance as Canaan awaited the Israelites. Because the report of the liberal crowd caused them to fear to conquer and possess the land, they refused to enter—to their own loss and hurt (Numbers 14). As one who has traversed the land (Proverbs), I testify with Caleb and Joshua, "The land, which we passed through to search it, is an exceeding good land. If the LORD delight in us, then he will bring us into this land, and give it us; a land which floweth with milk and honey" (Numbers 14:7–8). Don't listen to the gainsayers. Strap on the backpack, lace up the hiking shoes, grab the Bible and enter the land with me via this book. When you do so, you will say, as David said of the whole of Holy Scripture, "How sweet are thy words unto my taste! yea, sweeter than honey to my mouth!" (Psalm 119:103).

The King James Version of the Bible was used as the basis for this work, though other translations are referenced. Effort was made to soundly "dissect" the text, concisely summarize its truth and clearly state its pertinent application. The book, unlike others I reviewed, draws heavily from the church's most conservative theologians and ministers, citing their enlightening and inspiring interpretations, observations and comments. I encourage the reading of the Introduction, which presents an overview of the Book of Proverbs (and this volume), laying the foundation for its study, comprehension and application.

To borrow the words of the biblical expositor Geier, "If there should be anything here to please the reader, ascribe not the writing to the pen, but to the Writer; not the light to the lamp, but to the Fountain; not the picture to the pencil, but to the Painter; not the gift to the unfaithful dispenser, but to God the bountiful Giver."[5]

Introduction

George Lawson, in his preface to *Exposition of the Book of Proverbs,* encapsulates the thrust of the Book in saying, "In this little book there appears more wisdom than in the combined monuments of Greek and Roman learning. The wisest of men wrote it, and His object is to make us wise. But a greater than Solomon is here, for Wisdom speaks in her own person."[6]

Proverbs was written around 900 B.C., primarily by Solomon, the King of Israel and son of David. It contains over 800 of his proverbs (he wrote over 3,000—Ecclesiastes 12:9; 1 Kings 4:32). Other writers contributed to the Book as well (Proverbs 30:1; 31:1).

A proverb is a succinct saying or principle that conveys spiritual truth. The root for the Hebrew word translated "proverbs" means "to rule or govern."[7] Proverbs are wise, simple sayings (parables) intended to govern our lives in the way of the Lord. B. H. Carroll says, "The power of a proverb lies partly in its form; it is short, sharp, concise, and impressive. It assumes, attracts attention, and imprints itself upon the memory."[8]

Bullock remarks that the proverbs do not argue; they assume.[9] Their purpose is to pointedly express a matter, not explain it. Numerous proverbs are restated slightly differently on purpose. Alexander Maclaren observes, "Many strokes drive the nail home."[10] B. E. Nicholls says, "A proverb, strictly speaking, is a short moral sentence which means something further than what the words literally imply."[11]

The Book of Proverbs is divinely inspired scripture (2 Timothy 3:16). What seems to be a contradiction or absurdity in a proverb is often clarified when it is studied in context and understood in the light of other proverbs. As to its "canonical authority" or legitimacy as part of Holy Scriptures, Michaelis states "that no Book of the Old Testament is so well ratified [confirmed as authentic] by the evidence of quotations."[12] Proverbs is quoted in the New Testament in Romans 3:15 (Proverbs 1:16); Hebrews 12:5–6 and Revelation 3:19 (Proverbs 3:11–12); James 4:6 and 1 Peter 5:5 (Proverbs 3:34); Romans 12:20 (Proverbs 25:21–22); and 2 Peter 2:22 (Proverbs 26:11).

Regarding the Book of Proverbs, Angus says, "It is for practical ethics what the Psalms are for devotion."[13] Charles Bridges says that "while other Scriptures show us the glory of our high calling, this instructs us minutely how to walk in it."[14] Oetinger says, "The Proverbs exhibit

Jesus with unusual clearness."[15] John R. Rice states, "They are a collection of sharp ethical precepts about practical living."[16]

Chuck Swindoll, in *Overview of Proverbs,* states, "Proverbs accomplishes something no other biblical book does. It simply compiles numerous short instructions for living an effective life on earth. While other books articulate profound theological truths, lengthy narratives of triumph and failure, or prophetic preaching to a disobedient people, Proverbs concerns itself completely with instructing people in the path of wisdom."[17] J. I. Packer, in *Knowing God,* indicates that "wisdom" in Scripture always means knowledge of the course of action that will please God and secure life.[18]

B. H. Carroll says of wisdom in the Book of Proverbs that it "is very comprehensive in its meaning and application. It is contrasted with folly, simplicity and scorning. It covers the practical world as it does the intellectual."[19] Grymestone says, "Wisdom is the olive that springeth from the heart, bloometh on the tongue and beareth fruit in the actions."[20] Bruce Waltke, quoting M. Saebo, says it is "masterful understanding," "skill," "expertise."[21]

David Jeremiah says that "within the context of Proverbs it [wisdom] refers to the ability to live righteously and justly."[22] "It is related to the intellect and the control of human behavior. Through wisdom, God reveals what the values of life are and how they may be achieved."[23] Simply and concisely stated, wisdom is divine discernment or understanding that enables man to do that which is right and pleasing unto the Lord in every facet of life (morally, ethically and religiously).

Wisdom's source is Jesus Christ, for in Him alone "are hid *all the treasures of wisdom* and knowledge" (Colossians 2:3). Wiersbe says, "To yield your life to Christ and obey Him is true wisdom."[24] Waltke says, "Agur argues…that Creation teaches the impossibility of attaining wisdom apart from special revelation (Proverbs 30:1–6)."[25] Satan attempts to counterfeit God's wisdom, making it appear to be the same; but upon closer examination, its vast differences are revealed.[26]

"The wisdom of their wise men shall perish" (Isaiah 29:14). The Apostle Paul cautioned man to make sure "[t]hat your faith should not stand in the wisdom of men, but in the power of God" (1 Corinthians 2:5). Wisdom in Proverbs is personified; Jesus Christ, who is the very embodiment of wisdom, is instructing, advising, counseling, commanding, scolding, warning, guiding and comforting. The book will brim with new light, insight and inspiration if you will view Him as the "father and sage (profoundly wise teacher)" who is issuing the instruction and yourself as the "son" who is addressed (John 1:12). God is referred to in 100 verses of the book.[27]

In studying Proverbs, it will be helpful to keep in mind that although the book is applicable and beneficial to everybody, its targeted audience appears to be youth (Proverbs 1:1–4). Alexander Maclaren comments, "Youth, by reason of hot blood and inexperience, needs such portable medicines as are packed in these proverbs, many of them the condensation into a vivid sentence of worldwide truths."[28] "My son" or "ye children" is used 27 times, in places such as 2:1; 3:1, 11; 4:1, 10; 5:1; 6:1.

Proverbs therefore may be categorized as a "how-to" book or textbook (unlike any other in academic study) for youth on navigating the maze of life. It gives candid advice and admonition for coping with life's every aspect. Its path is that of righteousness—rightness with God and right conduct precipitated by right belief.

To be governed by Proverbs helps one achieve a full and meaningful life (Proverbs 14:27; Ecclesiastes 12:13–14). To stubbornly turn deaf ears to its instruction is to shipwreck life in utter ruin (Proverbs 1:31–32). Its principles and teaching, if applied, will protect from the consequences of sin, disastrous snares, stupid mistakes and decisions, and fools who attempt to lead the believer astray. They will shape godly character by building and forming right ethical and moral beliefs and traits which are the foundational blocks to a higher quality of life spiritually, emotionally, materially, and physically. Though primarily designed to benefit the righteous (the Christian), the Book certainly has an evangelistic undertone beckoning the fool, gullible, senseless and wicked to be reconciled to God (Proverbs 1:22–23; 11:30; 23:26; 28:13–14; 29:1).

Plumptre said, "The great hindrance to all true wisdom is the thought that we have already attained it."[29] Isaiah warned, "Woe unto them that are wise in their own eyes, and prudent in their own sight!" (Isaiah 5:21). Michaelis remarks that there is only one source of wisdom and that "is to trust in God; to trust in yourself and in your own wisdom is unwisdom."[30] William Law wrote nearly two centuries ago, "Man needs to be saved from his own wisdom as much as from his own righteousness, for they produce one and the same corruption."[31]

In Proverbs, Solomon masterfully, under divine inspiration, makes an all-out effort to rescue man from "human wisdom" by revealing its falsity, deception, corruption and inferiority to that of God (Proverbs 3:7, 16:25, 21:30). King Solomon was consulted by foreign sages, "[f]or he was wiser than all men; than Ethan the Ezrahite, and Heman, and Chalcol, and Darda, the sons of Mahol: and his fame was in all nations round about" (1 Kings 4:31). These sages were considered to possess great wisdom, yet even they realized that their wisdom did not surpass that of Solomon.[32]

Messengers or ambassadors from "all kings of the earth" sought out audience with Solomon to learn from his wisdom (1 Kings 4:34). His most renowned visitor was the Queen of Sheba (1 Kings 10:1–13; Matthew 12:42). She traveled from Sheba (modern Yemen, not Ethiopia) in excess of 1,200 miles over rugged terrain (the desert sands of Arabia, the coast of the Red Sea to Moab and then over the Jordan River) by camel back to Jerusalem (a four-month journey round trip[33]) to verify as truth all that she heard of his wisdom. And what she had heard was overwhelmingly confirmed (1 Kings 10:7). Solomon answered all her "hard questions," which included difficult ethical and diplomatic questions.[34]

You don't have to travel a thousand miles or traverse difficult terrain to sit at the feet of the wisest man who ever lived (1 Kings 3:11–14). All that is necessary is simply to open up the Book of Proverbs.

Life Principles from Proverbs is written from a conservative perspective and is an excellent resource for inspiration and self-instruction, parental instruction to children, student curriculum (church, private and homeschool), daily Bible meditation or devotion, and expositional commentary. As you embark upon the journey through the commentary and comments in its 367 entries, it is my prayer that your life will be enriched, enhanced, edified and encouraged, as mine has been in the study, research and writing of this book.

Several of the Proverbs are used in more than one entry due to their multiple meanings and applications. The format of each entry includes an exegesis of the Proverb (explanation of its various words), a concise exposition or commentary, an application of its teaching, and a summary statement (*The Bottom Line*). The reader will find the entries listed by subject in alphabetical order and text in the table of contents to facilitate easier and faster navigation.

Interwoven throughout the volume are clarifying, pertinent, challenging and inspiring words upon the textual entry from the pens of Matthew Henry, H. A. Ironside, W. J. Deane and S. T. Taylor–Taswell, J. C. Ryle, Alexander Maclaren, W. A. Criswell, John MacArthur, John Gill,

Bruce Waltke, Allen Ross, S. S. Buzzell, Charles Bridges, George Lawson, John R. Rice, C. H. Spurgeon, Adrian Rogers, Matthew Poole, Charles Simeon and others. Although in the attempt to be thorough in the research, numerous expositional commentaries were "mined" for choice nuggets of gold in interpretation and application, as the vast number of references reveal, this volume is by no means to be taken as an exhaustive work. Added knowledge and insight may be gleaned from the reading and study of the references cited.

I am indebted to the many contributors to this work from both the past and the present. In the event of failure to give rightful credit for an entry, such will be corrected in future publications. I have done due diligence in my research and study in the effort to present sound biblical interpretation and application. The reader is urged to ever keep in mind that it is the Word of God that is infallible, not the commentary written regarding it.

Abortion, the infanticide of the unborn
Proverbs 6:17
"Hands that shed innocent blood."

"Hands" (the instruments of murder[35]) that "shed" (the vicious killing, murder of another; to take away a person's life[36]) "innocent blood" (Deane and Taswell say "the blood of those who have done it no injury"[37]; the murder of the non-guilty is a greater crime and sin which usually is exacted by those in positions of power [2 Kings 21:16; Ezekiel 22:27];[38] Gill says "that of persons who have not been guilty of any capital sin, for which they ought to die by the laws of God or men, and yet shed or poured out as common water; such hands must be defiled, and such men must be hateful to God, they destroying his image, and being like to the Devil, who was a murderer from the beginning"[39]). Such murder is an "abomination" (abhorred, detested and disgusting[40]) to the Lord (Proverbs 6:16). See Genesis 9:6; Deuteronomy 19:13 and Proverbs 1:11.

Many are the murdered innocent. Chuck Swindoll said, "It has come to the time when the most dangerous place to be in America is not the inner city, where gangs threaten innocent lives; or in angry prisons, where only the fit survive; but in the womb of a mother who is being told that if she doesn't really want the baby, an abortion is the solution."[41]

There is no legitimate "pro-choice" position according to Scripture. The alternative to abortion (outside of giving birth to and rearing the child) is adoption.

All sins are forgivable by a loving God, including that of abortion (1 John 1:7–9; Isaiah 43:25–26). The Christian's response to women who have an abortion, men who encourage abortion, and the medical team who perform the abortion is disdain for what they did, yet with open arms to forgive, heal and restore in Jesus' name (Galatians 6:1).

Why doesn't the Bible specifically condemn abortion (i.e., "Thou shalt not abort a child")? One major reason is that its prohibition is enveloped in the sixth commandment: "Thou shalt not murder" (Exodus 20:13, JB2000).

Henry Morris states that the "Israelites clearly understood this command to include killing by sword, poison, strangulation, abortion and all other means."[42] The same punishment was to be inflicted upon a person who killed an unborn child as upon one who had killed an adult (Exodus

21:22–25), which shows again that God sees the unborn as a human being. The early church embraced the same view. "Thou shalt not slay the child by procuring abortion; nor, again, shalt thou destroy it after it is born."[43]

"One accurate way to describe abortion," writes John Piper, "is subtle infanticide—that is, child-killing done in a way that the people don't recognize it as child-killing. That reality is why the word *abortion* exists. Some words are created to cloak reality the same way procedures are created to cloak reality. "Abortion" is cloaked child-killing."[44]

Not only does the Bible condemn the practice of abortion, but it also exhorts the believer to intervene on behalf of the babies that are being aborted. "Rescue those who are being led away to death, and save those who stumble toward slaughter" (Proverbs 24:11 ISV).

Adrian Rogers suggests several things which the believer may do for the unborn. "Refuse to be swayed by high-sounding arguments of liberals, humanists, or social planners [that abortion is okay]. We must teach and preach biblical sexual morality at home, and yes, in the church. We need to speak out clearly. We dare not be silent. We need to work for and pray for a constitutional amendment that will make abortion on demand illegal. But above all, keep your knees on the floor and pray to Almighty God."[45] "Rescue those who are being led away to death."

The Bottom Line: Francis Schaeffer said, "Certainly every Christian ought to be praying and working to nullify the abominable abortion law. But as we work and pray, we should have in mind not only this important issue as though it stood alone. Rather, we should be struggling and praying that this whole other total entity, [this godless] worldview, can be rolled back with all its results across all of life."[46]

2
Accountability, for personal sin
Proverbs 19:3

"A man's own folly ruins his life, yet his heart rages against the LORD." (NIV)

A man's "own" (personal) "folly" (foolish conduct; sin) "ruins" (overturns or subverts;[47] destroys and perverts[48]) his "life" (Reyburn and Fry say "refers to the person's life's situation, circumstances"[49]), YET his heart "rages against the LORD" (the person blames God for the consequences [the bitter fruit] of his own conduct).

Charles Bridges summarizes, "The fool rushes into the sin and most unreasonably frets for the sorrow; as if he could 'gather grapes of thorns, or figs of thistles' (Matthew 7:16). He charges his crosses [trouble], not on his own perverseness, but on the injustice of God. But God is clear from all the blame (James 1:13, 14). He had warned by His Word and by conscience. Man, deaf to the warning, plunges into the misery"[50] for which he blames God.

Years ago, comedian Flip Wilson made popular the saying "The Devil made me do it." He was wrong. Though Satan and friends may *persuade* man to sin, they can never *force* him to sin.

Man, however, from the beginning has sought to pass the blame for his actions onto another. Adam passed the blame to Eve. Eve passed the blame to the Devil. Aaron passed the blame for the golden calf to the flame. Murderers blame the influence of drugs for their crime. Other forms of deviancy or wrongdoing are blamed on one's genes, upbringing, circumstances and even God. Everybody wants to blame somebody or something else for his or her behavior. Don't play the blame game; assume personal responsibility for your behavior.

Jerry Falwell said, "I do not believe we can blame genetics for adultery, homosexuality, dishonesty and other character flaws."[51] In regard to wrong actions, say with Job, "And be it indeed that I have erred, mine error remaineth with myself" (Job 19:4). A man's own folly ruins his life. Man's choice to sin brings self-inflicted harm into his life for which he alone is to blame. Man can choose the road he travels but not its destination. See Galatians 6:7–8.

Daniel Webster, one of the greatest orators in American history, was asked to state the greatest thought that ever passed through his mind. He said, "My accountability to God." Since all are responsible for their behavior, all will give account to God regarding it (Romans 14:12; 2 Corinthians 5:10).

The Bottom Line: No man can evade personal responsibility or accountability to God for his conduct. Attempts to pass the buck are futile. Don't "blame" the "flame." Own up, "'fess" up and clean up.

3
Adultery, warning against
Proverbs 6:32–33

"But whoso committeth adultery with a woman lacketh understanding: he that doeth it destroyeth his own soul.

"A wound and dishonor shall he get; and his reproach shall not be wiped away."

"Thou shalt not commit adultery" (Exodus 20:14).

He that commits "adultery" (sleeps with another person's wife or husband) "lacketh" (is without; void of) "understanding" (Deane and Taswell say, "Lust has displaced right reason; devoid of judgment, without intelligence, senseless and stupid"[52]) and "destroyeth his own soul" (the act was punishable by death [Leviticus 20:10]; includes moral and spiritual loss[53]; a state of ruin[54]). A "wound" (blows and injuries from the husband[55] [Proverbs 6:34]) and "dishonor" (Reyburn and Fry say "to be held in contempt or scorn"[56]; loss of reputation[57]) shall he get; and his "reproach" (disgrace, shame [2 Samuel 13:13]) shall not be "wiped away" (Deane and Taswell say "to be blotted out"[58]; it always will remain as a stain upon the person).

Adultery is wrong for numerous reasons. It abuses the gift of sexuality God ordained to be exclusively between a husband and wife (Matthew 19:5). It degrades the temple of God which is within man (1 Corinthians 3:16–17). It diminishes fellowship with God (1 John 1:6). It devastates others (especially the adulterer's spouse and children). It is detrimental to the kingdom of God (2 Samuel 12:13–14; 1 Corinthians 10:32). It destroys the life and brings dishonor to the adulterer (Proverbs 6:32–33). God sees adultery as a hideous crime and promises to execute judgment upon those who practice it.

What is real is that adultery destroys tens of thousands of families every year across America. What is real is that adultery scars tens of thousands of children emotionally and psychologically every year. What is real is that adultery is an open wound in a relationship which more often than not overflows into domestic violence or worse.
Vice President Mike Pence

"Drink waters out of thine own cistern, and running waters out of thine own well" (Proverbs 5:15). W. A. Criswell explains, "In figurative language, Solomon counsels his son to find all his sexual satisfaction with his own wife in a life of pure married love."[59]

God says that marriage is highly honorable and must be kept pure. "Marriage should be respected by everyone. God will punish those who do sex sins and are not faithful in marriage" (Hebrews 13:4 NLV). The Bible says, "Stolen waters are sweet, and bread eaten in secret is pleasant" (Proverbs 9:17). "Stolen waters" refers to the act of adultery which brings pleasure, then pain (v.18).

Kent Hughes says: "The man who commits adultery says this to his children: 'Your mother is not worth much, and your father is a liar and a cheat. Furthermore, honor is not nearly as important as pleasure. In fact, my child, my own satisfaction is more important than you are.'"[60]

The Bottom Line: The grass isn't greener on the other side of the fence with another's spouse; it's deceitfully poisonous.

4
Age (Old), preparation for it
Proverbs 20:29

"The glory of young men is their strength: and the beauty of old men is the gray head."

The "glory" (pride; boasting[61]) of "young men" (prime of manhood) is their "strength" (Deane and Taswell say "unimpaired strength and vigor," which can be attained only by due exercise combined with self-control"[62]). In contrast the "beauty" (the splendor[63]; that which is greatly admired honorably by others[64]) of "old men" (aged; elderly) is their "gray head" (symbolic of honor, experience, wisdom, knowledge; represents all that is valuable about old age[65]).

Death and taxes are inevitable. But so is old age if we live long enough. It is therefore prudent to give the "golden years" thought and preparation long before their arrival.

God wants us to remember that life is short (James 4:14); that the beauty of youth is soon gone (Proverbs 31:30; 1 Peter 1:24); that all of life has its purpose (Psalm 92:12–14); that He will sustain His children in old age (Ruth 4:15); and that growing old is honorable (Proverbs 16:31; see also Proverbs 20:29). Paul Tournier states, "Your manner of life now is already determining your life in those years of old age and retirement, without your realizing it even, and perhaps without your giving enough thought to it. One must therefore prepare oneself for retirement."[66]

Max Lucado remarks, "Growing old can be dangerous. The trail is treacherous, and the pitfalls are many. One is wise to be prepared. You know it's coming. It's not like God kept the process a secret. It's not like you are blazing a trail as you grow older. It's not as if no one has ever done it before. Look around you. You have ample opportunity to prepare and ample case studies to consider. If growing old catches you by surprise, don't blame God. He gave you plenty of warning. He also gave you plenty of advice."[67]

Prepare for old age by developing an intimate relationship with God now through His Son Jesus Christ. The psalmist, in old age, said, "Thou art my hope, O Lord GOD: thou art my trust from my youth" (Psalm 71:5). The man knew God and rejoiced in his salvation (v. 23).

Second, spend quality time in the Word mediating upon and hammering out its teaching, expanding your knowledge of God and His instructions. The psalmist, in old age, could say, "O God, thou hast taught me from my youth" (Psalm 71:17). In youthfulness he learned that God was righteous (vv. 2, 19), Deliverer and Savior (verse 2), a strong refuge (vv. 3, 7), promise keeper (v. 3), Creator and sustainer of life (v. 6), victor over Satan (v. 13), doer of wondrous works (v. 17); that He is a God of great power and strength (v. 18), doer of great things (v. 19); that He quickens—revives, renews, restores (v. 20); and that He is a Redeemer (v. 23). He also discovered in youth that God desired him to live a righteous, clean life opposite of that of the wicked (v. 4).

Third, speak out for the cause of Christ with passion and fortitude. Be a soul winner. The psalmist declared, "Hitherto [from my youth] have I declared thy wondrous works" (Psalm 71:17).

Fourth, endure hardships triumphantly by leaning on the everlasting arms of God. Learn how to confront and conquer conflict and difficulties in His strength alone now so that in old age when they greatly surface you will not stumble. The psalmist declared, "Thou, which hast shewed me great and sore troubles, shalt quicken me again, and shalt bring me up again from the depths of the earth" (Psalm 71:20).

In the fifth place, prepare for old age now by developing the godly habits of prayer (Psalm 71), trust (v. 1), hope (v. 5), praise (vv. 8, 14, 22), worship (v. 23), witnessing (v. 24), service (v. 18) and singing (v. 22). "Habit formation is the process by which new behaviors become automatic."[68] Aristotle was so correct when he said, "Good habits formed at youth make all the difference."[69]

Jeremy Taylor said, "Habits are the daughters of action, but then they nurse their mother and produce daughters after her image, but far more beautiful and prosperous."[70] The way to replace a bad habit is by hammering a new *nail* (new habit) on its top, driving it out. "Experience tells me," states J. C. Ryle, "that people's hearts are seldom changed if they are not changed when young. Seldom indeed are men converted when they are old. Habits have deep roots. Once sin is allowed to settle in your heart, it will not be turned out at your bidding. Custom becomes second nature, and its chains are not easily broken."[71]

The Bottom Line: "God's plan is that old age be the crowning glory of a person's lifetime. The Word of God and the experience of the elderly righteous show that old age can have promise, productivity, vitality, confidence and a great deal of happiness, providing that spiritual preparation has taken place during the younger years."[72]

5
Alcohol, its destructive harm
Proverbs 20:1
"Wine is a mocker, strong drink is raging: and whosoever is deceived thereby is not wise."

"Wine" (MacArthur says "grape juice mixed with water to dilute it"[73]) is a "mocker" (its consumer scoffs at the holy and reproof, and it mocks at the consumer in its deceit) and "strong drink" (Reyburn and Fry say, "It denotes not just barley beer but any alcoholic beverage prepared from either grain or fruit;"[74] R. K. Harris says contained about 7–10 percent alcohol content, by comparison with today's[75]) is "raging" (i.e. a brawler, one who is loud, belligerent, violent, uncontrollable[76]). He that is "deceived" (deluded; fooled) into its consumption is "not wise" (foolish; not smart).

Adrian Rogers said, "The most dangerous drug in America is beverage alcohol. It is dangerous, number one, because of its availability. It is dangerous, number two, because of its acceptance. It is dangerous, number three, because of its horrible effect that it has on those who drink it and those who are affected by those who drink it. Drinking produces one contradiction after another. Drink for friendship and make an enemy. Drink for sleep and awaken without rest. Drink for strength and feel weak. Drink medicinally and acquire health problems. Drink for relaxation and get the shakes. Drink for bravery and become afraid. Drink for confidence and become doubtful. Drink to converse easier and get slurred speech. Drink to feel 'heavenly' and end up feeling 'hellish.' Drink to forget and be forever haunted. Drink for freedom and become slaves. Drink to erase problems and see them multiply. Drink to cope with life and invite death. What a mockery alcohol makes of this society!"[77]

Solomon states the danger and harm of alcohol consumption. *Alcohol is like the fangs of a rattlesnake* full of venomous poison awaiting an unexpecting passerby. Once alcohol is consumed, its poison is released into the body to do its deadly, destructive work. It kills the brain cells, deadens the senses, retards the reflexes, damages glands and vital organs, and initiates the process of death.

Alcohol is like the robber who steals all one possesses, leaving him in deep poverty. "For the drunkard and the glutton shall come to poverty: and drowsiness shall clothe a man with rags" (Proverbs 23:21).

Alcohol is like Mr. Hyde taking over Dr. Jekyll's speech leading him to say unruly and embarrassing things. "Thine heart shall utter perverse things" (Proverbs 23:33).

Alcohol is like a man in the ocean under its control being tossed to and fro, unaware of what's happening. "Yea, thou shalt be as he that lieth down in the midst of the sea" (Proverbs 23:34).

Alcohol is like a mule whose blinders are removed; his eyes are free to roam the terrain (the forbidden), resulting in impure conduct. Alcohol retards mental rationality and deteriorates walls of sexual restraint. "Thine eyes shall behold strange women" (Proverbs 23:33).

Alcohol is like a man getting beat up in a fight, unaware of the harm received; he denies the hurt that alcohol produces in his life. "And you will say, 'They hit me, but I didn't feel it. I didn't even know it when they beat me up.' (Proverbs 23:35 NLT).

Alcohol is like the tyrant that enslaves a person to serve him alone; the drunkard can't wait until he sleeps off his intoxication so he can drink again. "When will I wake up so I can look for another drink?" (Proverbs 23:35 NLT).

Alcohol is like a pretender, pretending to give a person gusto in life only to give sorrow. "Wine is a mocker, strong drink is raging: and whosoever is deceived thereby is not wise" (Proverbs 20:1).

Alcohol is the mother of sorrows and the father of trouble. "Who has anguish? Who has sorrow? Who is always fighting? Who is always complaining? Who has unnecessary bruises? Who has bloodshot eyes? It is the one who spends long hours in the taverns, trying out new drinks" (Proverbs 23:29–30 NLT).

H. A. Ironside says, "Wine has its place. Scripture recognizes its medicinal virtue, and a lawful use of it also when needed (1 Timothy 5:23). But how easily it becomes a snare that destroys the will and wrecks the life."[78] Underscore, its place in the early church was for medicinal use, not recreational.

The Bottom Line: Alcohol pleases; then it squeezes. It delights; then it bites. McGee says, "Intoxicants are condemned in the Word of God."[79] The wise avoid its consumption altogether.

6
Anger, its "comeback" in conversation
Proverbs 15:1

"A soft answer turneth away wrath: but grievous words stir up anger."

A person's "soft answer" (Deane and Taswell say, "Gentle and conciliatory, the injured person should not wrap himself in sullen silence"[80]; McKane says "an answer that restores good temper and reasonableness"[81]) "turns" (turns back; thwarts the disposition of the angry; cools it down) away "wrath" (anger): BUT "grievous words" (harsh and pain-inflicting words[82]) "stir up" (incite, spur) "anger" (to infuriate).

The proper uses of words (speech) comprise much of Proverbs. In Proverbs 15 alone they are referenced 12 times (vv. 1–2, 4, 7, 10, 14, 23, 26, 28, 31–33). Solomon in Proverbs 15:1 gives wisdom in dealing with the angry. The proverb cites the wrong and right responses to the insults, accusations and criticisms hurled harshly upon you by the angry: the irritating and agitating kind (escalates the person's wrath) and the pacifying and soothing kind (defuses, extinguishes, calms).

To answer the angry tit for tat ("grievous words") only fuels the fire, intensifying it. However, the response of calm, gentle words ("soft answer") throws buckets of water upon the raging flame, extinguishing it.

A good translation of the full text therefore is: "A reconciling answer cools down anger, but a hurtful word heats it up" (GECL). Gideon's answer to the men of Ephraim illustrates the proverb, showing how a "soft answer" quells anger (Judges 8:1–3). Jephthah's reply later to the same people pictures the opposite (Judges 12:1–6).

The Bottom Line: Keep your "cool" in dealing with the angry. Don't allow them to pull you down to their level in terms of rash and harsh intonation. "Let your speech be alway with grace, seasoned with salt, that ye may know how ye ought to answer every man" (Colossians 4:6).

7

Anger, management of it
Proverbs 14:17

"He that is soon angry dealeth foolishly: and a man of wicked devices is hated."

The person who is "soon angry" (quick-tempered; flying off the handle; hot-headed) "dealeth foolishly" (says and does things that in a calmer moment are regretted but may not be fixable): AND a man of "wicked devices" (schemes to do what is wrong[83]; plans to act underhandedly with others [Proverbs 12:2]) is "hated" (for his deceitfulness in his dealings with and his plotting against others, and for untrustworthiness[84]).

To be dominated by rash, unjustified anger instead of sound reason is utterly foolish and destructive. "When you are quick to get angry," states Adrian Rogers, "you can lose so much—your job, friends, children, wife, health and testimony. There is nothing more debilitating to your Christian testimony than for you to fly off the handle."[85] He says, "Anger is an acid that destroys its own container."[86]

John Piper remarks, "Think about how you do not want to give place to the Devil, because harbored anger is the one thing the Bible explicitly says opens a door and invites him in. Ponder the folly of your own self-immolation, that is, the numerous detrimental effects of anger to the one who is angry—some spiritual, some mental, some physical and some relational."[87] Mark Twain says, "Anger is an acid that can do more harm to the vessel in which it is stored than to anything on which it is poured."[88]

Not all anger is bad. Paul said, "Be ye angry, and sin not" (Ephesians 4:26). Shana Schutte explains, "Telling a child she is not allowed to become angry will create an emotionally unhealthy adult who suffers from guilt and who does not know how to accept her feelings or how to work through what's hurt her. However, just because it's okay to get angry [justifiable anger that the Lord approves], it's not okay to handle anger inappropriately, and your child needs to know that."[89]

If you are a parent, don't ignite anger in your children. Don't take the wind out of their sails by showing favoritism, depreciating their worth, setting unrealistic goals, criticism, excessive discipline, unfairness, resentment and failure to take care of them rightly (clothes, personal possessions, place to play, good meals, etc.), which only serves to 'provoke them to anger.'

Helping children understand the source of their anger will help in managing it. Is it biological or "stressors" (expectations of school achievement, athletic performance, competition overload, personal issue with another)? The same is true regarding fits of rage by adults. The underlying causes for the angry outbursts must be discovered, acknowledged and treated.

The Bottom Line: Adrian Rogers says an essential to controlling anger is, instead of repressing it, confess it unto the Lord, asking for help to keep it in check.[90] The Bible teaches that a man who controls his temper is a greater warrior than he who conquers armies (Proverbs 16:32). "The measure of a person is the size of the thing that makes him angry."[91]

8
Animals, give caring kindness
Proverbs 12:10
"A righteous man regardeth the life of his beast: but the tender mercies of the wicked are cruel."

The "righteous" (godly; upright) "regardeth" (proper and humane care) of his "beast" (domestic animal). The "tender mercies" (compassion) of the "wicked" (ungodly) are "cruel" (even the "compassions" of the wicked are shown in a cruel, mean way[92]).

The righteous or good man's very character prompts proper care for and treatment to "beasts" (domestic animals) in the form of food, water, medical attention, shelter and rest. To treat them otherwise is cruel and abusive, like the behavior of the wicked whose "tenderest" mercy is harsh toward people, as illustrated by Balaam (Numbers 22:23–31).

God values man above all creation, yet He values a sparrow that is worth less than a penny (Matthew 10:29). He cares for animals and watches over their treatment. My father taught me early in life by example and word that ownership of a pet included caring for it (humane treatment), something I have always practiced regardless of cost incurred.

The barbarous treatment of animals is yet practiced. For example, dog fighting continues although outlawed in all fifty states. The ASPCA says, "Dogfighting is a type of blood sport in which dogs are forced to fight one another for the entertainment and/or profit of spectators. Dogfighting is one of the most heinous forms of animal cruelty."[93] Estimates based upon underground dogfighting publications and on animals entering shelters with injuries that bear evidence of fighting suggest that in the United States alone there are tens of thousands of people that practice it.[94]

Charles Bridges says that the infliction of pain to animals by children for entertainment, "if not early restrained, will mature them in cruelty, demoralize their whole character, and harden them against all the sympathies of social life."[95] Locke observed, "They who delight in the suffering and destruction of inferior creatures will not be apt to be very compassionate and benign to those of their own kind."[96] George Lawson summarizes, "A righteous man's mercy…will not deprive his beast of its food and rest, nor oppress it with unreasonable toil, nor sport himself with the misery and pain of those creatures which God hath subjected to his power. Are they animals good for food? Even in depriving them of life, he shews his humanity by inflicting upon them no unnecessary degree of pain."[97]

The Bottom Line: Put heart (and purse) into caring for pets which are dependent upon you to supply their need (Proverbs 27:23; Genesis 24:32). It's the honorable and humane thing to do.

9
Anxiety, a calming antidote for it
Proverbs 12:25
"Heaviness in the heart of man maketh it stoop."

"Heaviness" (anxiety and fear, i.e., "anxious fear"[98]) in the heart of man "maketh" (causes) it to "stoop" ("bows it down," or weighs it down with despair, dejection, depression [effects documented by psychologists]). The condition interrupts life's tasks and robs it of peace, contentment, purpose and happiness.

C. H. Spurgeon remarks, "Anxiety does not empty tomorrow of its sorrows but only empties today of its strength."[99] Anxiety is symptomatic of mistrust in God to adequately care for you. Paul counsels, "Be anxious for nothing, but in everything by prayer and supplication, with thanksgiving, let your requests be made known to God; and the peace of God, which surpasses all understanding, will guard your hearts and minds through Christ Jesus" (Philippians 4:6–7 NKJV). Just ask God for what is needed; don't panic or worry.

Matthew Henry counsels, "When anything burdens our spirits, we must ease our minds by prayer; when our affairs are perplexed or distressed, we must seek direction and support."[100] In bringing challenges, difficulties, fears and troubles to the Lord, peace will rule the heart. "The peace of God, which surpasses all understanding, will guard your hearts and minds" (CSB). Isaiah gives affirmation to the truth, "Thou [God] wilt keep him in perfect peace, whose mind is stayed on thee: because he trusteth in thee" (Isaiah 26:3). "This peace," states Matthew Henry, "will keep our hearts and minds through Christ Jesus. It will keep us from sinning under our troubles and from sinking under them, keep us calm and sedate without discomposure of passion [disturbed; distressed] and with inward satisfaction."[101] As M. R. Vincent puts it: "Peace is the fruit of believing prayer."[102]

William Barclay summarizes, "When we pray, we must always remember three things: we must remember the love of God, which ever desires only what is best for us; the wisdom of God, which alone knows what is best for us; the power of God, which alone can bring to pass that which is best for us. He who prays with a perfect trust in the love, wisdom and power of God will find God's peace. The result of believing prayer is that the peace of God will stand like a sentinel on guard upon our hearts."[103]

Pray about everything. Fenelon explains, "Tell God all that is in your heart, as one unloads one's heart, its pleasures and its pains, to a dear friend. Tell Him your troubles, that He may comfort you; tell Him your joys, that He may sober them; tell Him your longings, that He may purify them; tell Him your dislikes, that He may help you conquer them; talk to Him of your temptations, that He may shield you from them; show Him the wounds of your heart, that He may heal them; lay bare your indifference to good, your depraved tastes for evil, your instability. Tell Him how self-love makes you unjust to others, how vanity tempts you to be insincere, how pride disguises you to yourself as to others."[104]

Spurgeon offers godly counsel to the anxious, "Away, then, with dark suspicions and anxieties! Is it care about past sin? 'The blood of Jesus Christ, God's dear Son, cleanses us from all sin.' Is it present temptation? 'There has no temptation happened to you but such as is common to men, but God who is faithful will not suffer you to be tempted above what you are able but will with the temptation also make a way to escape that you may be able to bear it.' Is it future peril? Oh, leave that with Him, for neither 'things present, nor things to come, nor height, nor depth, nor any other creature, shall be able to separate us from the love of God, which is in Christ Jesus our Lord.'"[105] *God doesn't want us to be careless* (negligent, complacent or compassionless), *simply carefree* (unanxious; unworried; relaxed).

The Bottom Line: "The cure of it [anxious fear or worry]," says Matthew Henry, is "a good word from God, [which] applied by faith makes it glad. Such a word is that: 'Cast thy burden upon the Lord, and he shall sustain thee'; the good word of God, particularly the Gospel, is designed to make the hearts glad that are weary and heavy laden."[106] Max Lucado says, "Become a 'worry-slapper!' Treat frets like mosquitoes! Do you procrastinate when a bloodsucking bug lands on your skin? Do you say, 'I'll take care of that in a moment'? Of course you don't! You give the critter the slap it deserves. Be equally decisive with anxiety. The moment a concern surfaces, deal with it. Don't dwell on it. Head it off before it gets the best of you."[107]

10
Apologetics, readiness to defend the faith
Proverbs 22:21

"That I might make thee know the certainty of the words of truth; that thou mightest answer the words of truth to them that send unto thee?"

"Be ready always to give an answer to every man that asketh you a reason of the hope that is in you with meekness and fear" (1 Peter 3:15).

That "I" (the sage [teacher of profound wisdom]) make "thee" (the student) know the "certainty" (reliability) of the "words of truth" (the "excellent things" [teachings of the Book of Proverbs], verse 20) so that the righteous can "answer the words of truth" (give credible evidence for its truthfulness and intelligent defense of its claims) "to them that send unto thee" (to one and all who ask; Septuagint: "That thou mayest answer words of truth to those who put questions to thee"[108]).

Though the Proverb has to do with the teachings (instructions of wisdom) in the Book of Proverbs, it certainly applies to the entire of the Word of God. Evidence for their truthfulness or the divine authority for their inclusion in Holy Scriptures of the Book of Proverbs is found in their quotation by Jesus (Luke 14:6–8); Paul (Romans 12:19–20); the author of Hebrews (Hebrews 12:5–6); James (James 4:6); Peter (1 Peter 5:5; 2 Peter 2:22) and Jude (v. 12).

The twofold breakdown of apologetics is clearly stated in 1 Peter 3:15. Peter clearly admonishes *all* believers to be *apologists,* ready at all times to give public defense of their faith. It follows that for a believer to declare the reason for his faith to the unbeliever in an effort to evangelize him, and to the doubting Christian to recover/restore him, he must first know what he believes and the why of that belief. Indoctrination ("church told me so") or emotional reasoning for one's belief is not sufficient. The intellect must be engaged to combat all forms of skepticism and unbelief.

Wise instruction in "true and reliable" (biblical) words solidifies the believer's faith and provides *good footing* in the refutation of skeptics, agnostics and atheists. "A wise man will hear [God's Word and instruction], and will increase learning; and a man of understanding shall attain unto wise counsels" (Proverbs 1:5). Mastery of the Holy Scriptures is essential to the success of the Christian apologist. "The word must come with 'power, and in the Holy Ghost' if it is to come 'in much assurance'" (1 Thessalonians 1:5).[109]

George Lawson summarizes, "So if we live as befits saints and seek after the knowledge of the truth, we will be useful members of the church of Christ, ready to give an answer to everyone who asks us a reason of our faith and hope, to instruct the ignorant, to satisfy the doubts of the scrupulous, and to fix those who waver."[110]

The Bottom Line: "An intelligent Christian," writes Clark Pinnock, "ought to be able to point up the flaws in a non-Christian position and to present facts and arguments which tell in favor of the Gospel. If our apologetic prevents us from explaining the Gospel to any person, it is an inadequate apologetic."[111]

11
Approval, harmful effects of seeking to please others
Proverbs 29:25

"The fear of man bringeth a snare: but whoso putteth his trust in the LORD shall be safe."

The "fear" (trembling; self-paralysis, fearing) of "man" (person or persons) bringeth a "snare" ("a susceptibility to be easy prey to the desires of another"[112]). Deane and Taswell summarize, "He who through fear of what man may do to him, think or say of him, does what he knows to be wrong, lets his moral cowardice lead him into sin, leaves duty undone—such a man gets no real good from his weakness, outrages conscience, displeases God"[113]: BUT whoso "putteth" (in contrast to fearing man places trust in the Lord, lives for His approval and not man's) his "trust" (confidence) in the Lord shall be "safe" ("the image of being *set on high* comes from the military experience of finding a defensible position, a place of safety and security"[114]).

"Most people are other people. Their thoughts are someone else's opinions, their lives a mimicry [act of mimicking], their passions a quotation."[115] Too many children (and adults) live their lives under the umbrella of another's approval. Actions, attitudes and aspirations are directly linked to how another thinks their lives should be lived; if they do as this person thinks, good feelings result, while failure to do so results in feeling miserable.

This manipulative type approval leads to an emotional roller coaster of ups and downs, an unhealthy view of one's own self-worth, an eroding confidence in one's own abilities and often into various types of sinful activities. The ultimate source of authoritative approval is God; it's what He thinks that counts most. All other sources of approval bow in subjection to His. The foundational question then is not how others approve of one's life but how God does.

A young violinist, in ending his first concert, was applauded by a standing audience. Amid the approval of the crowd, his eyes stayed fixed the entire time upon an elderly man in the balcony. The young violinist showed no emotion of joy until that man stood and applauded. You see, that elderly man was the young violinist's instructor, and he was concerned only with pleasing him.

Such was the attitude of the Apostle Paul with regard to Christ, for he testifies, "Obviously, I'm not trying to win the approval of people, but of God. If pleasing people were my goal, I would not be Christ's servant" (Galatians 1:10 NLT). Live life before an audience of ONE. Pleasing God with one's life is what matters, whether or not others approve. The psalmist declares, "I will give thanks to You, for I am fearfully and wonderfully made; Wonderful are Your works, And my soul knows it very well" (Psalm 139:14 NASB). You are an original, incredible design of God. Fully grasp that and rejoice in that!

The Bottom Line: Don't succumb to the pressure to become a duplicate of someone else or live under the umbrella of another's approval. Like Paul, live for the approval of the Lord Jesus Christ. He says, "Do you think I am trying to make people accept me? No, God is the One I am trying to please. Am I trying to please people? If I still wanted to please people, I would not be a servant of Christ" (Galatians 1:10 NCV).

12
Associations, with the bad or good
Proverbs 13:20

"He that walketh with wise men shall be wise: but a companion of fools shall be destroyed."

"And have *no fellowship* with the unfruitful works of darkness, but rather reprove them."—Ephesians 5:11.

He that "walketh with" (associates with; "stresses continual, durative action"[116]) "wise men" (persons that possess biblical knowledge and understanding [discerment] and live uprightly) "shall be wise" (like produces like-kind; the example and instruction of the wise encourage the pursuit of wisdom to all who join their company): BUT a "companion of fools" (he that keeps company with the ungodly) shall be "destroyed" (come to moral ruin; devastation).

To summarize, a person takes on the *image and lifestyle* of him with whom he associates. A Dutch proverb says, "He that lives with cripples learns to limp"; and the Spanish say, "He that goes with wolves learns to howl." To be wise, associate with the wise. Matthew Henry remarks, "He that would be himself wise must walk with those that are so, must choose such for his intimate acquaintance and converse with them accordingly, must ask and receive instruction from them and keep up pious [spiritual] and profitable talk with them."[117]

George Lawson says, "Friendship is the balm of life when it is entered into with discretion—but it is a plague and a snare when it is injudiciously contracted."[118] Friends or associates are either the "basement" kind that ever pull us down to their immoral and ungodly lifestyle or the "balcony" kind that ever lift us to the higher plane of life morally and spiritually.

The Bottom Line: A man's friends can be his most helpful allies or his most destructive enemies. "Tell me with whom you walk, and I will tell you who you are" (Spanish proverb).

13
Atheism, its contempt for God
Proverbs 14:2

"He that walketh in his uprightness feareth the LORD: but he that is perverse in his ways despiseth him."

The man that "walketh" (walking as a way of life) in his "uprightness" (righteously, justly, virtuously, according to biblical principles) "feareth" (shows reverential respect for and is obedient to) the Lord. In contrast, the person that is "perverse" (devious) in his conduct "despiseth" (shows contempt; considers as worthless; has scorn for[119]) the Lord. "A man is evil in his actions because he has cast off the fear of God, and such wickedness is a proof that he has lost all reverence for God and care to please him."[120] "The fear of the LORD is the beginning of knowledge: but fools despise wisdom and instruction" (Proverbs 1:7).

The bottom line for atheism or any disdain for God is man's desire to live according to the dictates of the flesh without accountability. Paul explains, "When people's thinking is controlled by [or outlook/mind is set on] the sinful self [sinful nature; flesh], they are against [hostile to] God, because they refuse to obey [submit to] God's law and really are not even able to obey [submit to] God's law" (Romans 8:7 EXB). Ray Comfort states, "Atheists hate God because of His righteous requirements, and the greatest form of contempt they can have for God is to deny His obvious existence."[121]

Aldous Huxley, renowned atheist of the last century, stated that his atheism stemmed from desire to sin. He wrote, "I had motives for not wanting the world to have a meaning and consequently assumed that it had not and was able without any difficulty to find satisfying reasons for this assumption. The philosopher who finds no meaning for this world is not concerned exclusively with the problem of pure metaphysics; he is also concerned to prove that there is no valid reason why he personally should not do as he wants to....For myself...the philosophy of meaninglessness was essentially an instrument of liberation, sexual and political."[122]

"The froward [wicked] is abomination [detestable] to the LORD: but his secret is with the righteous" (Proverbs 3:32). Unto them that show contempt for God it will be said, "Behold, ye despisers, and wonder, and perish" (Acts 13:41). Matthew Henry comments, "Note, it is the ruin of many that they despise religion; they look upon it as a thing below them and are not willing to stoop to it. Second, 'take heed lest the judgment come upon you which was spoken of in the prophets: that you shall wonder and perish, that is, wonderfully perish; your perdition shall be amazing to yourselves and all about you.' Those that will not wonder and be saved shall wonder and perish."[123] In contrast, the righteous walk in the fear (respect; acknowledgment of God's authority and supremacy) of the Lord. George Lawson says, "The good man not only receives Christ but walks in him. He not only enters in at the strait gate but continues travelling in the narrow way till he comes to the end of his faith and holiness in the heavenly world."[124]

The Bottom Line: At the root of the unbeliever's denial, thus rejection of God, is sin. "And this is the condemnation, that light is come into the

19

world, and men loved darkness rather than light, because their deeds were evil" (John 3:19). Leon Morris explains, "It is not God's sentence with which [John] is concerned here. He is telling us rather how the process works. Men choose the darkness, and their condemnation lies in that very fact....They refuse to be shaken out of their comfortable sinfulness."[125]

14
Attitude, its effect upon soul and body
Proverbs 17:22
"A merry heart doeth good like a medicine: but a broken spirit drieth the bones."

A "merry heart" (cheerful, positive disposition mentally) doeth "good" (brings "good" healing[126]) like a "medicine" ("healing," "relief" medicinal[127]) to the body: BUT a "broken spirit" (crushed; depressed) "drieth the bones" (brings the opposite; it impedes and worsens health). Allen Ross summarizes, "One's psychological condition affects one's physical condition: a healthy attitude fosters good health, but a depressed spirit ruins health."[128]

Attitudes are important, for they impact actions. Solomon states that a good (positive, healthy) attitude is like healing medicine to the body, but a bad (negative) one is like poison to it. Jesus said, "Either make the tree good, and his fruit good; or else make the tree corrupt, and his fruit corrupt: for the tree is known by his fruit. O generation of vipers, how can ye, being evil, speak good things? for out of the abundance of the heart the mouth speaketh. A good man out of the good treasure of the heart bringeth forth good things: and an evil man out of the evil treasure bringeth forth evil things" (Matthew 12:33–35).

Chuck Swindoll writes, "This may shock you, but I believe the single most significant decision I can make on a day-to-day basis is my choice of attitude. It is more important than my past, my education, my bankroll, my successes or failures, fame or pain, what other people think of me or say about me, my circumstances, or my position. Attitude is that 'single string' that keeps me going or cripples my progress. It alone fuels my fire or assaults my hope. When my attitudes are right, there's no barrier too high, no valley too deep, no dream too extreme, no challenge too great for me."[129]

Rid the mind of that stuff that robs joy, peace, hope, contentment and a healthy outlook and chokes out God's perspective and promises. Peter admonishes, "Wherefore *gird up the loins of your mind,* be sober, and hope to the end for the grace that is to be brought unto you at the revelation of Jesus Christ" (1 Peter 1:13). Hebrews 12:1–3 urges the believer not to *faint in his mind.*

"Wherefore seeing we also are compassed about with so great a cloud of witnesses, let us lay aside every weight, and the sin which doth so easily beset us, and let us run with patience the race that is set before us,

"Looking unto Jesus the author and finisher of our faith; who for the joy that was set before him endured the cross, despising the shame, and is set down at the right hand of the throne of God.

"For consider him that endured such contradiction of sinners against himself, lest ye be wearied and faint in your minds. "

The Bottom Line: Zig Ziglar said, "Your attitude, not your aptitude, will determine your altitude."[130]

15
Attributes, a divine mirror reflecting God
Proverbs 15:3
"The eyes of the LORD are in every place, beholding the evil and the good. "

The "eyes of the Lord are in every place" (that is, there is nothing hid from Him; nothing of which He is not aware, both with man personally and the world at large), beholding the "evil and the good" (He sees man's "private" and public sin, as well as his good, moral deeds). See Hebrews 4:13. The Proverb "underscores God's unrestricted presence in space and His unrestricted moral assessment of every individual."[131] See Psalm 139:1–12.

Although Proverbs is purposed to be a book of the governing principles of life, it is chock-full of theology. Its treatment of the deity of God in detailing God's wondrous attributes, while being superb, is simply stated. Knowledge and understanding of His attributes are foundational to Christian belief and practice. "Nothing will so enlarge the intellect," states C. H. Spurgeon, "nothing so magnifies the whole soul of man as a devout, earnest, continued investigation of the great subject of the Deity. And whilst humbling and expanding, this subject is eminently *consolatory*. Oh, there is, in contemplating Christ, a balm for every wound; in musing on the Father, there is a quietus for every grief; and in the influence of the Holy Ghost, there is a balsam for every sore. Would you lose your sorrows? Would you drown your cares? Then go, plunge yourself in the Godhead's deepest sea; be lost in His immensity; and you shall come forth as from a couch of rest, refreshed and invigorated. I know nothing which can so comfort the soul, so calm the swelling billows of grief and sorrow, so speak peace to the winds of trial as a devout musing upon the subject of the Godhead."[132]

The Omniscience of God. "The eyes of the LORD are in every place, beholding the evil and the good" (Proverbs 15:3). God is all-knowing. There is nothing of which God is unaware. Has it ever occurred to you that nothing has ever occurred to God? Matthew Henry says, "Secret sins, services and sorrows are under his eye."[133] To know that God's all-seeing eyes encompass our every step brings consolation, confidence, cheer and courage. The writer of Hebrews expresses this same thought: "And not a creature exists that is concealed from His sight, but all things are open and exposed, and revealed to the eyes of Him with whom we have to give account" (Hebrews 4:13 AMP).

The Omnipotence of God. "The king's heart is in the hand of the LORD, as the rivers of water: he turneth it whithersoever he will" (Proverbs 21:1). God is all-powerful. God can do anything He wants to do, and no man or nation can stop Him. C. H. Spurgeon stated, "God's power is like Himself, self-existent, self-sustained. He is Himself the great central source and originator of all power." The sovereignty of God speaks of His absolute control of all that happens.

The Omnipresence of God. "The eyes of the LORD are in every place" (Proverbs 15:3). God is present everywhere at the same time. "For thus saith the high and lofty One that inhabiteth eternity, whose name is Holy; I dwell in the high and holy place, with him also that is of a contrite and humble spirit, to revive the spirit of the humble, and to revive the heart of the contrite ones" (Isaiah 57:15). This knowledge benefits the believer in temptation, anxiety, trouble and trial, sickness and suffering, service, persecution, and witnessing. To heartily embrace God's constant companionship erases fear and instills hope. "Fear not: for I am with thee" (Isaiah 43:5). David realized God's personal presence (not just His power or help) was constantly with him. He declared, "Whither shall I go from thy spirit? or whither shall I flee from thy presence? If I ascend up into heaven, thou art there: if I make my bed in hell, behold, thou art there. If I take the wings of the morning, and dwell in the uttermost parts of the sea; Even there shall thy hand lead me, and thy right hand shall hold me" (Psalm 139:7–10).

The Immutability of God. "There are many devices in a man's heart; nevertheless the counsel of the LORD, that shall stand" (Proverbs 19:21). God remains ever the same. "Jesus Christ the same yesterday, and to day, and for ever" (Hebrews 13:8). C. H. Spurgeon, in the sermon "The Immutability of God," states that God is changeless with regard to His essence, attributes, promises, plans, threatening and in the objects of His love. He is the unchangeable changeable One.[134] C. S. Lewis remarked, "Though our feelings come and go, God's love for us does not."[135]

The Love of God. "He loveth him that followeth after righteousness" (Proverbs 15:9). God loves man and desires him to enter into a personal relationship with Him through Jesus Christ (John 3:16; Romans 5:1) that he might be saved from the penalty of sin, walk in holiness and obedience, experience abundant and eternal life and share constant communion with Him (John 3:16, 10:10; Romans 5:1). The love of God is uninfluenced by anything man has done or may do and is never ending. "We love him, because he first loved us" (1 John 4:19). "The sin underneath all our sins," states Martin Luther, "is to trust the lie of the serpent that we cannot trust the love and grace of Christ and must take matters into our own hands."

The Holiness and Righteousness of God. "God, who is always right, watches the house of the wicked and brings ruin on every evil person" (Proverbs 21:12 NCV). God is *holy* and *righteous,* incapable of doing wrong or failing to do as He declares (Isaiah 6:3; Titus 1:2). God in His holiness is intolerant of sin, hating what it does to the person who commits it and the impact it has upon others and the world. "The Lord is righteous in all His ways, Gracious in all His works" (Psalm 145:17 NKJV). "Holy, holy, holy, Lord God Almighty, which was, and is, and is to come" (Revelation 4:8).

The Mercy of God. "He that covereth his sins shall not prosper: but whoso confesseth and forsaketh them shall have mercy" (Proverbs 28:13). God is *merciful,* ever ready to forgive the sinner, reconciling him unto Himself (2 Corinthians 5:18–19; Ephesians 2:4). "Let us therefore come boldly to the throne of grace, that we may obtain mercy and find grace to help in time of need" (Hebrews 4:16 NKJV). T. Dewitt Talmage writes,

"Oh, this mercy of God! I am told that it is an ocean. Then I place four swift-sailing crafts with compass and charts and choice rigging and skilled navigators, and I tell them to launch away for me and discover the extent of this ocean. That craft puts out in one direction and sails to the north, this to the south, this to the east and this to the west. They crowd on all their canvas and sail ten thousand years and one day come up the harbor of Heaven, and I shout to them from the beach, 'Have you found the shore?' They answer, 'No shore to God's mercy.' Swift angels dispatched from the throne attempt to go across it. For a million years they fly and fly; but they come back and fold their wings at the feet of the throne and cry, 'No shore! No shore to God's mercy.'"[136]

The Creation of God. "The LORD by wisdom hath founded the earth; by understanding hath he established the heavens" (Proverbs 3:19). God is *Creator, Owner* and *Sustainer* of all that exists (Colossians 1:16–17). *"Creatio ex nihilo"* (creation out of nothing)—the best and only reasonable explanation for the existence of the universe and all within it is that an intelligent Designer created it. The Bible, God's authoritative Word, repeatedly declares that the world and all within it were made by God (Revelation 14:7; Psalm 33:6; 1 Timothy 2:13).

The Transcendence of God. "The heaven for height, and the earth for depth, and the heart of kings is unsearchable" (Proverbs 25:3). "For My thoughts are not your thoughts, Nor are your ways My ways," declares the LORD. "For as the heavens are higher than the earth, So are My ways higher than your ways And My thoughts than your thoughts" (Isaiah 55:8–9 NASB). "Transcendence refers to the fact that God is unlike any other being in our experience and so no analogy or comparison can come close to perfectly describing Him. His ways are so other than our ways that we cannot predict Him, categorize Him or comprehend Him with any sort of accuracy. All that we truly know of God comes solely through what He has chosen to reveal about Himself to us through His Word."[137]

The Bottom Line: J. I. Packer says there are four effects of the attributes of God: "Those who know God have great energy for God....Those who know God have great thoughts of God....Those who know God show great boldness for God....Those who know God have great contentment in God." Packer went on to say, "A little knowledge *of* God is worth more than a great deal of knowledge *about* Him."[138]

16
Avoiding Sin, restraint through fearing the Lord
Proverbs 16:6
"By the fear of the LORD men depart from evil."

In manifesting a "fear" (reverential respect for the Lord and obedience to His "law," "commands" and "statutes"; Waltke says it "also entails a nonrational aspect, an emotional response of fear, love and trust"[139]) of the Lord men "depart" (avoid; NASB says "keep away from") "evil" (sin, wrongdoing and thereby its hurtful consequence; "Faithfulness to the LORD brings freedom from sin"[140]).

The fear of the Lord has restraining and abstaining power with regard to sin and unsound doctrine. Proverbs 14:27 corroborates Proverbs 16:6 in saying, "The fear of the LORD is a fountain of life, to depart from the snares of death." He that embraces the fear of God identifies with Paul's goal "to have always a conscience void of offence toward God, and toward men" (Acts 24:16). Matthew Henry states, "Those will not dare to sin against God who keep up in their minds a holy dread and reverence of Him."[141]

Buzzell explains, "One cannot gain knowledge of spiritual things if he begins at the wrong point, refusing to fear the Lord (i.e., to recognize God's character and respond by revering, trusting, worshiping, obeying and serving Him). [Beginning] also means 'the capstone or essence.' The essence of true knowledge is in fearing God."[142] See Proverbs 1:7. Man ought to fear the present and eternal wrath of God upon sin. Sadly, this generation is one that does not believe that "it is a fearful thing to fall into the hands of the living God" (Hebrews 10:31). Pray for a spiritual awakening with regard to "the fear of the LORD."

The Bottom Line: The fear of the Lord is man's preventative against sin. Charles Bridges says, "The fear of the Lord is at once a bridle to sin and a spur to holiness."[143]

17
Backsliding, the cause and cure
Proverbs 14:14
"The backslider in heart shall be filled with his own way."

"I have gone astray like a lost sheep: seek thy servant; for I do not forget thy commandments."—Psalm 119:176.

The "backslider" (means "to move away; to move backwards; to depart;"[144] one who has turned away from the righteous path to do wrong) will be "filled" ("to be repaid;"[145] his sensual appetite and lifestyle will bear adverse consequence) with his "own way" (sinful, evil conduct and its bitter consequences).

The word *backslider* appears in only Proverbs 14:14 in the entirety of the Bible. The word *backsliding* is used by only Hosea and Jeremiah. Neither word is used in the New Testament. See Isaiah 57:17; Jeremiah 3:12; Hosea 11:7; 14:4. John R. Rice summarizes, "A backslider is a saved person who falls into sin. It may be outrageous and gross sin known to everyone, or it may be merely coldness of heart, a lukewarmness of heart instead of the burning fire of love for God. But when a Christian loses any of his joy or loses part of his sweet fellowship with God or falls into sin, then he is a backslider."[146]

Backsliding is not to be equated with a spiritual stumble that is only momentary. It is a spiritual relapse that continues indefinitely. "The backslider in [his] heart" purposely has decided to abandon the Lord to walk in "his own way." Clovis Chappell explains, "Whenever you make up your mind to refuse to go where God wants you to go and to do what God wants you to do, you must make up your mind at the same time to renounce the friendship of God. You cannot walk with Him and at the same time be in rebellion against Him. God has no possible way of entering into fellowship with the soul that is disobedient to His will. Believe me, it is absolutely useless, it is mere mockery, to say, 'Lord, Lord' and then refuse to do the things that He commands you to do."[147] J. C. Ryle states, "Men fall in private long before they fall in public."[148]

The Bible waves several "red flags" regarding that which prompts backsliding. These include improper associations, justification of a sinful activity, loss of first love for Jesus, neglect of spiritual disciplines (prayer, Bible study, church attendance, witnessing, worship), a pleasure that entangles (not necessarily sinful), and change in priorities (no longer spiritual but materialistic). The "backslider in heart" has the mindset of the prodigal son who departed from his father to go "into a far country, and there wasted his substance with riotous living" (Luke 15:13). Backsliding is departure from the Father to satisfy the worldly, lustful desires of the heart ("filled with his own way"). The wretched consequence of backsliding is that it is injurious to the Lord, the backslider, the church which he attends and the church at large, and the non-Christian world.

Charles Bridges says the backslider's hideous, corrupt behavior is a warning to the church; all must take heed lest he fall.[149] The rod of his punishment is "his own way"; it will become the fountain of his own misery and ruin.[150] Jeremiah 2:19 says, "Thine own wickedness shall correct thee, and thy backslidings shall reprove thee: know therefore and see that it is an evil thing and bitter, that thou hast forsaken the LORD thy God, and that my fear is not in thee, saith the Lord GOD of hosts." See Hebrews 12:5–6 (the believer's chastisement for sin).

Backsliding's only remedy is to 'repent and return' (Revelation 2:5). It was when the prodigal son "came to himself," remembered the good he received at his father's hand, and became dissatisfied with the "far country" that he acknowledged his woeful sin and returned to the father (Luke 15:17–18). When the backslider remembers the mercies of the Lord and His sweet communion, as the prodigal did, he will become so sickened in his sin that it will prompt repentance and return. "Go and proclaim these words toward the north, and say, Return, thou backsliding Israel, saith the LORD; and I will not cause mine anger to fall upon you: for I am merciful, saith the LORD....Only acknowledge thine iniquity, that thou hast transgressed against the LORD thy God" (Jeremiah 3:12–13). Say with the psalmist, "I have gone astray like a lost sheep; seek thy servant; for I do not forget thy commandments" (Psalm 119:176).

The Bottom Line: C. H. Spurgeon remarks, "Remember that if you are a child of God, you will never be happy in sin. You are spoiled for the world, the flesh and the Devil. When you were regenerated, there was put into you a vital principle which can never be content to dwell in the dead world. You will have to come back if indeed you belong to the family."[151] Woodrow Kroll provides simple but poignant advice: "The best way to avoid going downhill is to stay off the slope."[152] See 2 Chronicles 7:14 and Hosea 7:9.

18
Beauty, its downside without discretion
Proverbs 11:22
"As a jewel of gold in a swine's snout, so is a fair woman which is without discretion."

As a "jewel of gold" (nose ring made of gold [Ezekiel 16:12]) in a 'pig's snout' (nose) is disgusting, just so is a "fair" (beautiful) woman who lives without "discretion" (without modesty; says and does things out of bounds morally; "she has no moral sensibility, no propriety, no good taste—she is unchaste"[153]). "The external beauty of such a woman is as incongruous as a precious ring in the snout of a pig."[154] The proverb applies not only to "beauty" but "to all other bodily endowments and accomplishments; it is a pity that those should have them who have not discretion to use them well."[155]

A gold nose ring was acceptable jewelry worn by women in Old Testament times (Geneses 24:47; Ezekiel 16:12). Disgusting as a gold nose ring is in a filthy pig's snout, the lack of discretion (abandonment of discretion) by a beautiful woman is even more repulsive. Beauty is not to be flaunted or put on parade. It is not to be accentuated by immodest dress, loose morals, seductive speech or charm. Beauty is honorable unto the Lord for He is the One who gave it (a trait not personally acquired, so no reason to boast); however, it becomes an abomination when used for selfish and indiscreet purposes.

Indiscretion in dress by beautiful women, intentional or not, has generated erotic passions in men. "And it came to pass in an eveningtide, that David arose from off his bed, and walked upon the roof of the king's house: and from the roof he saw a woman washing herself; and the woman was very beautiful to look upon" (2 Samuel 11:2). And the next thing Scripture records is that "David sent messengers, and took her; and she came in unto him, and he lay with her" (verse 4). The indiscreet woman has caused the downfall of many righteous men. Matthew Henry comments, "It is lamented that beauty should be so abused as it is by those that have not modesty with it. It seems ill-bestowed upon them; it is quite misplaced, as a jewel in a swine's snout with which he roots in the dunghill. If beauty be not guarded by virtue, the virtue is exposed by the beauty."[156]

The woman of indiscretion does herself a disgrace and shame. She is a fool. The beauty in which she trusts to attract attention, allure men and attain worldly pleasure and possessions fades away. "Favour [charm] is deceitful, and beauty is vain [fades away]: but a woman that feareth the LORD, she shall be praised" (Proverbs 31:30). Charles Bridges advises, "Dear lady, learn to value far beyond beauty of face the inner 'ornaments' of grace, 'which are in the sight of God of great price' (1 Peter 3:4)."[157]

The Bottom Line: The woman that fears the Lord (loves Him; adheres to biblical precepts and principles; lives uprightly, modestly, honorably) possesses and manifests *true beauty.* External charm and beauty are temporary. Internal beauty does not erode or decay. The indiscreet are fools that will face the judgment of God. The entirety of Proverbs seeks to rescue fools from their wicked and injurious path. See 1 Samuel 16:7.

19
Beliefs, refrain from altering what you believe
Proverbs 22:28
"Remove not the ancient landmark, which thy fathers have set."

"Remove" (Pfeiffer says, "Removing landmarks meant falsifying the survey and stealing land"[158]) not the "ancient" (those that have been there for a long time[159]) "landmark" (boundary marker such as a stone; they were sacred, for God apportioned the property to the tribes[160]) which your "fathers" (ancestors) have "set" (to make or place). Therefore, it might be rendered, "Do not steal or diminish another's longstanding legal property by discreetly and deceitfully moving its marker."

Though the Proverb definitely is intended to protect property owners from property theft, I see also a spiritual application with regard to the sneakiness of theological liberals in their effort to *move back* the ancient, time-tested, God-authorized boundary markers of the tenets of the Christian faith. God takes seriously any *tampering with the boundary marker of biblical doctrine and scriptural standard* to govern life that He established nearly 4,000 years ago. He says, "For I testify unto every man that heareth the words of the prophecy of this book, If any man shall add unto these things, God shall add unto him the plagues that are written in this book: And if any man shall take away from the words of the book of this prophecy, God shall take away his part out of the book of life, and out of the holy city, and from the things which are written in this book" (Revelation 22:18–19).

One of America's leading newspapers at the turn of the twentieth century addressed the following question to many notable people of that time: "What in your opinion is the chief danger, social or political, that confronts the coming century?" William Booth, who was invited to reply to this question, responded: "The chief danger that confronts the coming century will be religion without the Holy Ghost, Christianity without Christ, forgiveness without repentance, salvation without regeneration, politics without God, Heaven without Hell." No more prophetic utterance has ever been spoken, for it depicts this century. Jude exhorts the believer to "earnestly contend for [apprehend and defend] the faith which was once delivered unto the saints" (Jude 3). The basic tenets (benchmarks) of the faith include the existence of a Sovereign God (Creator, Sustainer of all that exists); divine inspiration and infallibility of the Bible; man's fall and separation from God by sin; Jesus as the divine Savior (His deity, virgin birth, virtuous life, vicarious death, victorious resurrection, verifiable ascension, and visible return to earth); salvation by grace alone through faith freely expressed in Jesus Christ; literal eternal abode of punishment in Hell and reward in Heaven; the person and work of the Holy Spirit and the Holy Scriptures as the governing standard for human behavior (morality, ethics), worship, relationships, attitudes and all other matters of life. These eternal truths form a firm foundation for faith and life.

> Give me that old time religion;
> Give me that old time religion;
> Give me that old time religion;
> It's good enough for me.

The Bottom Line: Not everything that looks the same is the same. This is certainly true with regard to religious faith and the church. Stay clear of "religions" that push back the "ancient landmark" by preaching another doctrine, compromising biblical truth and morality, and negating the importance of evangelism and missions.

20
Bias, its harmful deception
Proverbs 18:17

"He that is first in his own cause seemeth just; but his neighbour cometh and searcheth him."

He that is "first in his own cause" (the first man to testify) "seemeth just" (appears to be right; Lawson says, "An eloquent speaker will make his own cause appear a great deal better, and that of his adversary a great deal worse, than it really is."[161]); BUT his "neighbour" (the person with whom he has the dispute) "cometh and searcheth him" (questions him in an attempt to prove inconsistencies or contradictory statements[162]).

Judicial bias. The man who speaks first (in court) appears innocent and just, but when the "neighbour" (opposing party or prosecutor) cross-examines ("searcheth him"), he is proven wrong. Wisdom instructs the righteous not to exhibit bias or prejudice by refusing to listen to all sides in a dispute. Truth and justice are ascertained by exhibiting fairness through listening with *open ears* to all involved.

Personal bias is the stubborn inclination to think your views are right even when they are not (close-minded to consideration of another's perspective, whether that of God, parents or teacher). The Bible addresses the fallacy. Jeremiah says, "The heart is deceitful above all things....who can know it?" (Jeremiah 17:9 AKJV). The heart is not the infallible guide to rightness or wrongness of a matter. Only God is, for He knows the heart (verse 10). Solomon warns, "There is a way which seemeth right unto a man, but the end thereof are the ways of death" (Proverbs 14:12). Even Paul understood he could not trust human inclinations to determine right from wrong. He said, "For my conscience is clear, but that does not vindicate me. It is the Lord who examines me" (1 Corinthians 4:4 ISV). A clear conscience and peaceful heart do not necessarily prove that one is right. The fallacy of bias is no more evident than with regard to the rejection of the Christian faith without definitive investigation and examination. To say "I know I am right; there is therefore no need to search it out" is the epitome of foolishness.

Upon running to the top of the mountain, I had the bright idea of making the return trip through its heart. Not too difficult—I just had to follow the yellow markers posted on the trail. All went great until the yellow markers disappeared, prompting me to think that I didn't need them anyway. To me, the way I was running seemed to be toward the mountain's base. The farther I ran, the more "lost" I became—something I finally acknowledged. I backtracked up the mountain to the last sighting of the yellow marker. Once I was back on the trail, the markers led me safely to the base of the mountain. That day the teaching of Proverbs 14:12 was clearly illustrated. "The way of a fool is right in his own eyes: but he that hearkeneth unto counsel is wise" (Proverbs 12:15). Jonathan Edwards remarks, "The way to Heaven is ascending; we must be content to travel uphill, though it be hard and tiresome and contrary to the bias of our flesh."

31

The Bottom Line: Personal bias (counting oneself right and correct when the evidence indicates otherwise) is prejudicial to your best and highest good in life spiritually and otherwise. You may be sincere in what you believe but sincerely wrong. C. H. Spurgeon stated, "Satan will make your own principles and inclinations to betray you."[163] The safest and best course is to base right and wrong upon the Holy Scripture.

21
Bible, a powerful restraint to sin
Proverbs 5:12–14

"And say, How have I hated instruction, and my heart despised reproof;

"And have not obeyed the voice of my teachers, nor inclined mine ear to them that instructed me!

"I was almost in all evil in the midst of the congregation and assembly."

"And say, How" (Reyburn and Fry say "as in 'how bad for me'"[164]) that "I" (a young man) "hated" (scorned) "instruction" (the Torah; teachings of the Lord[165]) and my heart "despised" (scorned—similar to "hated"; rejected) "reproof" (godly correction). The confession of the immoral man begins what Robert Alden calls a long litany of "if only's."[166] He laments not listening to the wise instruction that would have prevented the painful price of infidelity. Charles Simeon cites the Proverb as "The Sinner's Retrospect."[167]

Biblical instruction from teachers, parents and preachers, *if heeded,* prevents sin and its awful consequences. The man of Proverbs 5 states he was not without godly instructors (preachers, parents and teachers); he simply refused to hearken to their counsel and advice. "I hated instruction, and...despised" correction (scorned it, detested it). "Bereft of all that sustains life—self-esteem and material goods—he is left with nothing to do but to 'mourn,' literally 'groan' or 'growl' like a beast mortally wounded, flesh and body 'consumed.'"[168] In retrospect, the man says he acted senselessly and foolishly, that he lamented the audacity and shamelessness of his disobedience and failure to "listen and heed" biblical instruction. Such honest acknowledgement is admired.

George Lawson summarizes, "It is not in vain for ministers and parents and tutors to use means for acquainting young people with the Scripture and imprinting it upon their hearts. The confession of profligates, when arrived at the end of their career, makes it evident that if anything would have proved effectual to preserve them from ruin, it would have been the instructions and reproofs of parents and teachers."[169] Deaf or defiant ear or not, godly instructors must not lose heart in the proclamation of God's truth, for it has power to preserve life from harm and havoc.

Despite the pigheadedness of some not to listen and obey, they nevertheless must be continuously warned by biblical teaching of what awaits them on the path chosen, in hope of their turnabout (Jeremiah 23:29). Thankfully, some that rebel against godly instruction, as this youth of the Proverb did, "wake up" upon experiencing the misery and heartache that accompanies such a life and return to observing the teaching. Thus the Proverb offers hope to every parent who has a child in the "far country," that he or she can be divinely awakened to realize the error of that way and its only remedy. Never lose heart or hope in the prodigal's return. Always look and pray toward that end.

The Bottom Line: "Get wisdom, get understanding: *forget it not*; neither *decline* from the words of my mouth....Hear, O my son [God calls him that is saved by the blood of Christ 'son.' See John 1:12; 1 John 3:2], and receive my sayings; and the years of thy life shall be many" (Proverbs 4:5, 10). Wisdom (from the lips of the godly wise) encourages man to weigh the temporary pleasure of sin against its painful consequences and ask, "Is it worth it?"[170] Understanding the horrendous price for a sinful act may restrain one from indulging in it. The man that listens to godly and biblical instruction is spared shame, misery, guilt, trouble and personal loss (possessions, money, relationships, and position).

22
Bible, admonition to retain its truth
Proverbs 3:3
"Let not mercy and truth forsake thee: bind them about thy neck; write them upon the table of thine heart."

Do not let "mercy" (loyal love[171]) and "truth" (Reyburn and Fry say "trustworthiness, dependability"[172]) "forsake" (depart from) "you" ("you" is the subject of the admonition, as in "You don't let..."[173]). "Bind them about thy neck" (figuratively, as a necklace [Proverbs 1:9]); the thrust is to always keep them forefront) and "write them upon the table of thine heart" (as God chiseled into the two stone tablets the Ten Commandments [Deuteronomy 5:22] chisel your faithful love ("mercy") for Him personally and His holy Word ("truth") entirely upon the tablets of the heart to be remembered forever); Deane and Taswell say, "Inscribe them, mercy and truth, deeply there; impress them thoroughly and indelibly upon thine heart, so that they may never be forgotten and may form the mainspring of your actions"[174]). See Proverbs 6:21.

Love, loyalty and faithfulness (trustworthiness, dependability) are holy virtues to fulfill man's duty and commitment to man and God born in the heart at salvation. God's *Word* is the truth by which lives are to be ordered and governed. Moses declared, "Hear, O Israel: The LORD our God is one LORD: And thou shalt love the LORD thy God with all thine heart, and with all thy soul, and with all thy might. And these words, which I command thee this day, shall be in thine heart: And thou shalt teach them diligently unto thy children, and shalt talk of them when thou sittest in thine house, and when thou walkest by the way, and when thou liest down, and when thou risest up. And thou shalt bind them for a sign upon thine hand, and they shall be as frontlets between thine eyes. And thou shalt write them upon the posts of thy house, and on thy gates" (Deuteronomy 6:4–9). Allow them to order thy steps in every facet of life, and you will "find favor [graciousness; kindheartedness] and good understanding [a good name; reputation for prudence[175]] in the sight of God and man" (Proverbs 3:4).

Warren Wiersbe states, "God's will is found in God's Word (Colossians 1:9–10). It is not only the mind, but also the heart that should remember and consider the Word. We must ask the Spirit to write the Bible on our hearts (2 Corinthians 3:1–3). We must receive the Word every opportunity we have—in class, in church services, through reading. The better you know your Bible, the better you will know God's will for your life."[176] And I add, the better you know Holy Scripture, the better you will know God, fulfill His purposes and navigate the mazes of life successfully.

The hymn "Break Thou the Bread of Life" refers not to the Lord's Supper but to the Holy Scriptures. It is good to sing it but better to pray it.

Break Thou the Bread of Life,
  Dear Lord, to me,
As Thou didst break the loaves
  Beside the sea.
Beyond the sacred page
  I seek Thee, Lord;
My spirit pants for Thee,
  O Living Word. ~ Mary Artemesia Lathbury (1841–1913)

The Bottom Line: Keep God and His Word central in both the heart and the affairs of life constantly, lest you shipwreck. The Word of God in you must be manifested through you to impact others (Matthew 5:14–16). "Let the Word of Christ dwell in you [be at home in you] richly in all wisdom" (Colossians 3:16). It "must be an integral and permanent living force in them [the believer], not just an outward performance or routine activities."[177]

23
Bible, affirmation and credibility of Scripture
Proverbs 30:5
"Every word of God is pure."

"Every" (emphasis on *every*,[178] "each and every") "word" (Ironside says, "The Scriptures, as a whole, are called the Word of God. Any portion taken separately is a word or saying of God. Now just as 'all Scripture is God-breathed,' so is every part of it, yea, every jot and tittle, divinely inspired"[179]) is "pure" (flawless, without mixture of error, tested and proven true; Deane and Taswell say, "God's words are true, sincere, with no mixture of error, certain of accomplishment"[180]). Similarly, David declared, "As for God, his way is perfect: *the word of the Lord is tried [proved true]:* he is a buckler to all those that trust in him" (Psalm 18:30). See 2 Samuel 22:31; Psalm 12:6; 119:140. Agur states the certitude of Holy Scriptures without attempting to validate it by human reason, for such would be futile effort.[181] Waltke explains, "The finite mind can neither derive nor certify infinite truth."[182] Holy Scripture substantiates itself as truth in a multiplicity of ways.

Totally true in fact and doctrine, the Bible contains no contradictions and is thoroughly trustworthy. "Through the Holy Spirit's agency," states

W. A. Criswell, "God is involved in both the production and interpretation of Scripture. Men of God in antiquity spoke as they were moved by the Holy Spirit (2 Peter 1:20–21). 'Moved' means literally 'to bear along.' Scripture is infallible precisely because the Holy Spirit 'bore along' the prophets who spoke and wrote."[183] While the Bible validates itself through an array of internal supports of its reliability—consistency, multiple witnesses, verifiable history—the Bible is also validated by many external evidences. For instance, it has been confirmed by more than one hundred archeological finds. R. A. Torrey stated, "Every Word is pure and sure, in spite of the Devil, in spite of your fear, in spite of everything."[184]

W. A. Criswell, in *Why I Preach That the Bible Is Literally True,* stated, "Jesus believed and taught the infallibility of Scripture. He regarded it as divine authority and as the final court of appeal concerning all questions. He sets His seal to its historicity and its revelation from God. He supplements it but never supplants it. He amplifies it, but He never nullifies it. He modifies it according to His own divine prerogative, He fulfills it according to His divine mission, but He never lessens its divine authority. His attitude toward the Scripture was one of total trust. It was the direct written Word of God to man."[185]

> All of this Book I believe. Not some of it, not most of it, not part of it, but ALL of it—inspired in totality, the Miracle Book of diversity and unity of harmony and infinite complexity!
> R. G. Lee

Of the Bible, Solomon says, "Add thou not unto his words" (Proverbs 30:6). The same admonition is thundered in the final book of the Bible wherein the Lord states, "For I testify unto every man that heareth the words of the prophecy of this book, If any man shall add unto these things, God shall add unto him the plagues that are written in this book: And if any man shall take away from the words of the book of this prophecy, God shall take away his part out of the book of life, and out of the holy city, and from the things which are written in this book" (Revelation 22:18–19). The liberal theologian or pastor who claims that portions of Scripture are lies will be himself revealed as the liar, while that which was denounced will be proven true. Holy Scripture is the sound, safe and sure foundation on which to build the superstructure of life. To build life upon any other foundation is to suffer sure and swift ruin (2 Timothy 2:19; Matthew 7:24–27).

The Bottom Line: When Solomon says, "Every word of God is pure," it means that the Bible as a whole, as well as any portion therein, is without error. It is trustworthy and reliable. It is a shield of protection to those who "put their trust in" God (Proverbs 30:5). Matthew Henry says, "Every word of God is pure; there is not the least mixture of falsehood and corruption in it."[186]

24
Bitterness, the heart's private sorrow
Proverbs 14:10

"The heart knoweth his own bitterness; and a stranger doth not intermeddle with his joy."

The "heart" (here more than the seat of the emotions, includes the whole person[187]) "knoweth" (awareness, knowledge) "his own" (personally and privately, for no one can completely empathize with another's anguish of soul) "bitterness" (sorrow, grief, sadness, pain); AND a stranger doth not "intermeddle with his joy" (there are joys and sorrows that cannot be shared; no one can "understand the deepest feelings of another"[188]). R. E. Murphy says, "It does not deny that one can identify to some extent with another's sorrows and joys, but it does imply that such sensitivity has its limits."[189]

Bitterness in the Proverb refers not to its general meaning of resentment but inner pain and suffering. The Proverb reveals what all have experienced with regard to sorrow and sadness ("bitterness"), that the emotional trauma (hurt, pain, despair, anxiety) is impossible to convey or fully convey even to choicest and closest friends. It is indescribable, inexpressible and incomprehensible, hard for the person himself to understand, much less for others, even though they try the best they can. "No person stands in such intimate relation to us, or can put himself so entirely in our place, as to feel that which we feel."[190] "There is many a dark spot, many a grief, of which our best friend knows nothing; the skeleton is locked in the cupboard, and no one has the key but ourselves."[191] Or, as Paul states, "For what man knoweth the things of a man, save the spirit of man which is in him?" (1 Corinthians 2:11). Job's friends failed to understand his sorrows and distraught condition. John Foster, in the essay *On a Man's Writing Memoirs of Himself,* said, "Each mind has an interior apartment of its own into which none but itself and the Divinity can enter."[192]

Be mindful that the inner hurt of another is always *heavier* and more *horrendous* than communicated or conceived. As Matthew Henry puts it, "Their stroke perhaps is heavier than their groaning."[193]

BUT the Christian finds great comfort and consolation in knowing that though man is inapt to empathize with the "bitterness" of soul experiences, Jesus Christ can and does. He is 'acquainted with our deepest grief' (Isaiah 53:3); "surely he hath borne our griefs, and carried our sorrows" (verse 4). "No one knows the troubles I've seen; nobody knows but Jesus." Glory, hallelujah!

> Are you weary; are you heavyhearted?
> Tell it to Jesus; tell it to Jesus.
> Are you grieving over joys departed?
> Tell it to Jesus alone.
>
> Tell it to Jesus; tell it to Jesus.
> He is a Friend that's well-known.
> You've no other such a friend or brother.
> Tell it to Jesus alone.
>
> Do the tears flow down your cheeks unbidden?
> Tell it to Jesus; tell it to Jesus.
> Have you sins that to men's eyes are hidden?
> Tell it to Jesus alone.   ~ Jeremiah Eames Rankin (1855)

Simeon says, "None but the person feeling it can tell 'the bitterness' which is occasioned [prompted] by a sense of sin, with all its aggravations [worry] by the prospect of death and judgment whilst the soul is unprepared to meet its God, and by temptations to despondency and perhaps to suicide itself. Job's friends could not at all appreciate his sorrows, as depicted by himself."[194] Neither is it possible for the non-Christian to empathize with the Christian when God grants him a *peace that passes all understanding* during horrendous sorrow and pain.[195]

The Bottom Line: "Sometimes the prettiest smiles hide the deepest secrets, the prettiest eyes have cried the most tears, and the kindest hearts have felt the most pain."[196] Appearances are deceitful, especially with regard to the crucible of pain others bear. Learn to see through the facade.

25
Boasting, being presumptuous about tomorrow
Proverbs 27:1
"Boast not thyself of to morrow; for thou knowest not what a day may bring forth."

"Boast" (don't be arrogantly presumptuous in planning for the future) not thyself of "to morrow" (the future) for "thou knowest not" (ignorant; uncertain; beyond man's knowledge to know) "what a day may bring forth" (Murphy says, "If anything is certain, it is human ignorance of what will happen—this is a sphere that belongs to God"[197]). William McKane summarizes the Proverb the best in saying a person "must live from day to day, grateful for the life which he has from God, with the awareness that it may be withdrawn at any time and that he must not speak or plan as if himself had full disposal of his destiny and power over the future."[198]

H. A. Ironside remarks, "To defer until the morrow what should be attended to today is the sad mistake which has destroyed untold thousands."[199] Mexicans have a word for putting off until tomorrow what should be done today. It is *mañana*—tomorrow. A Spanish proverb says, "The road of by-and-by leads to the house of never." Procrastination ("By-and-by I will do it") often means *never*. It is presumptuous ignorance and arrogance that banks on doing something tomorrow that ought to be done today. Why? James explains, "Whereas ye know not what shall be on the morrow. For what is your life? It is even a vapour, that appeareth for a little time, and then vanisheth away" (James 4:14).

No man is a prophet or the son of a prophet. Tomorrow and what it will bring is hidden until it is unraveled minute by minute. The man in choicest of health may meet *tomorrow* with cancer, a heart attack, paralysis due to an automobile accident, or breathe his final breath. Further, loss may be incurred from a stock market crash or job dismissal. There are a host of unforeseen things that may happen on the morrow that would hinder a person from doing what he should have done today. "Boasting" spurs overconfidence, which in turn produces carelessness in fortifying oneself from unexpected and unforeseen calamities that tomorrow may bring.

The sin of presumptuous delay *until tomorrow* is manifested much with regard to salvation. God calls man to an instant decision (Hebrews 3:7–8; 2 Corinthians 6:2; Isaiah 1:18). But many, such as Festus, delay until a more "convenient season," which never arrives. If unsaved, delay the matter no longer. Tomorrow may be too late. Several reasons why it is dangerous to delay: The Danger of a Hardened Heart; The Danger of Losing the Soul (Mark 8:36); The Danger of Going to Hell (Luke 16:22–23); The Danger of Missing Heaven; The Danger of Not Participating in the Rapture; The Danger of Sudden Death.

The Bottom Line: Don't delay until tomorrow that which should be done today. Give that hug, write that note, send those flowers, witness to that friend, express that gratitude, spend time with that child, heal somebody's hurt, tell that special friend how much he or she is loved, and above all, be saved. As the song goes, "Live like you're dying."

26
Borrowing, its downside
Proverbs 22:7

"The rich ruleth over the poor, and the borrower is servant to the lender."

"Give to him that asketh thee, and from him that would borrow of thee turn not thou away."—Matthew 5:42.

The "rich" (wealthy) "ruleth" (the NJB says, "lords over" or controls) the "poor" (the needy who are dependent upon the "rich"), AND the "borrower" (he that receives loans or credit) is "servant" (as a "slave" in the sense he is in subjection, under obligation, without freedom) to the "lender" (Reyburn and Fry say "one who causes to borrow"[200]). The text is correctly summarized by Matthew Henry: "Those that have little will be in subjection to those that have much, because they have dependence upon them; they have received, and expect to receive, support from them."[201]

In the 2,350 verses in the Bible that deal with money, not once is borrowing or accruing debt forbidden.[202] It does, however, cite the downside of indebtedness, urging caution and prudence as in Proverbs

22:7. The Scripture makes crystal clear that although borrowing or debt is not in violation of a commandment, it is not in the best interest for the believer to borrow. Why? Borrowing places trust in man (the means of borrowing) instead of God to meet a need.

David warns of this danger in Psalm 20:7: "Some trust in chariots, and some in horses: but we will remember the name of the LORD our God." Borrowing robs God of an opportunity to provide a pressing need, bolstering faith, stimulating spiritual growth through increased trust in Him (Philippians 4:19). Borrowing may also have a negative impact upon unbelievers especially when the money borrowed is not repaid or is delayed (Psalm 37:21). Borrowing places the borrower in *bondage* to the *lender* (chains of debt). The saying "he that goes a-borrowing goes a-sorrowing"[203] is often true. Borrowing *may* remove divinely placed obstacles that prevent acquisition of items that will bring harm to our spiritual walk or physical well-being and transfer the obligation of repayment to family members in the event of an unexpected circumstance.[204]

Megan Pacheco warns of the danger of borrowing and lending. She says, "Greed hides behind both foolish borrowing as well as behind predatory lending. We borrow out of greed for more, bigger, better…and we lend to get more, faster and at a higher interest."[205]

Paul emphasizes that one's debts must not be left unpaid, but paid in full promptly. In Romans 13:8 (NIV) he states, "Let no debt remain outstanding, except the continuing debt to love one another, for whoever loves others has fulfilled the law." The Greek present imperative indicates continuous force: "Don't continue owing. Pay your debts."[206] If you borrow, *pay back every penny* according to the agreed time frame (sooner if possible, to save on interest, enhance credit score, liberate from its bondage and gain the ability to give more to Christian causes). See Psalm 37:21.

The Bottom Line: While in some cases it's justifiable to borrow (house, medical emergencies, job loss, etc.), clearly in others it is certainly wrong. The Bible does not count borrowing as "wise." Borrowing is permissible but not commendable. Obviously, *paying as you go* is ideal.

27
Bribery, its crime and condemnation
Proverbs 6:35

"He will not regard any ransom; neither will he rest content, though thou givest many gifts."

"He" (the husband whose wife had the adulterous affair as cited in the previous verses) will not consider any "ransom" (offered to "buy him off" from demanding full punishment which could include death[207]); neither will he be "content" (appeased) though you offer him "many" (multiple) "gifts" and bribes (suggest a lot of money the adulterer is willing to pay the husband as compensation for his immoral, despicable act to appease his anger and perhaps avoid a lawsuit; "hush money"[208]).

The context indicates that the man who has an adulterous affair will seek to *bribe* the woman's husband not to press charges or exact retribution. It is stated that the husband will not bend to the offer.

Bribery, according to *Webster's Dictionary,* is "money or favor given or promised in order to influence the judgment or conduct of a person in a position of trust." The *Cambridge Dictionary* says something similar: "the act of giving someone money or something else of value, often illegally, to persuade that person to do something you want."

Bribery is condemned in Proverbs 6:35, 15:27, 17:8; Exodus 23:8; Deuteronomy 16:19; 27:25; Job 36:18; Psalm 15:5; Ecclesiastes 7:7 and Isaiah 33:15. John Piper said, "To make the heinousness of bribery clear, God ordained that the worst sin in the universe would involve bribery—the betrayal of the Son of God to death for 30 pieces of silver."[209]

In essence, bribery is wrong because "a bribe blinds the clear-sighted and subverts the cause of those who are in the right" (Exodus 23:8 ESV). Samuel's sons took bribes to pervert judgment (1 Samuel 8:3). Jezebel bribed "two worthless men" (1 Kings 21:10 ESV) to testify against honorable Naboth to take possession of his vineyard that Ahab her husband desired. The bribery that led to the false witness led to the death of the good man Naboth (verses 4–16). Judas' bribery to betray Jesus (Matthew 26:14–16) led to Jesus' horrendously tormenting crucifixion at Calvary. Following the betrayal, Judas realized the taking of the bribe (30 pieces of silver) was wrong and sought to return it but in vain (Matthew 27:3–5).

Alexandra Wrage in her column *Bribery Is Bad* states, "The social arguments against bribery are compelling. Bribery of government officials constitutes theft from the public. Bribery undermines security when police, military, customs officials and border guards can be bought. Bribes are paid to ensure building inspectors look the other way, health officials approve unsafe products, toxic waste is disposed of inappropriately, and government contracts are awarded for inferior products at inflated prices."[210] Bribery among students is payment for unethical favors for getting a preview of an exam, selection to the team, copying another's answers on a test, getting the job or promotion, receiving a higher grade, or getting the award. These favors are purchased by a gift given or act performed (bribe).

C. H. Spurgeon said, "He who gives bribes is every way as guilty as the man who takes them, and in the matter of our parliamentary elections the rich villain who gives the bribe is by far the worse. Bribery, in any form or shape, should be as detestable to a Christian as carrion to a dove or garbage to a lamb. Let those whose dirty hands are fond of bribes remember that neither death nor the Devil can be bribed to let them escape their well-earned doom."[211]

The Bottom Line: Biblically and morally, bribery is wrong because it is an unethical, fraudulent and dishonest practice. Christians ought to view it as a great wickedness and reproach to God. See Proverbs 15:27; Ecclesiastes 7:7; Isaiah 33:15.

28
Bullying, generated by fear of man
Proverbs 29:25
"The fear of man brings a snare, But he who trusts in the LORD will be exalted." (NASB)

The "fear" (afraid of offending someone[212]; cowering down to another's wishes, expectations) "of man" (people) "brings a snare" (it precipitates trouble; ensnared or trapped in the sense his actions are controlled or dictated by the person that is feared), BUT he who "trusts" (places confidence) in the Lord will be "exalted" (kept safe, protected; Walvoord and Zuck say, "Security in the Lord removes intimidation by man"[213]). Garrett says the text's solution to cowardice is to do "what is right and trust the outcome to Yahweh."[214]

Solomon says that bullying ("fear of man") always leads to entrapment to humiliation, intimidation, accusation and deflation. Annually, in excess of 3.2 million students are victims of bullying.[215] It is approximated that 160,000 teens skip school *every day* because of bullying.[216] While physical bullying reaches its peak in middle school and declines in high school, verbal abuse remains unchanged.[217]

Bullying wounds the heart. It's not a harmless passage into adulthood or a means to make a person stronger. "And children," states Paul Coughlin "who were bullied as kids suffer more depression and low self-esteem than kids who were not bullied. For many, the problem doesn't "go away."[218] Bill Mayer states, "The emotional scars that result from bullying can last a lifetime. Children who have been bullied may sink into patterns of antisocial behavior such as vandalism or even look to drugs and alcohol as sources of relief. Constant bullying in school can interfere with a child's education and mental and physical health."[219]

Often bullying is concealed by its victims. Parents must ever be alert to its telltale signs which include "unexplainable injuries; lost or destroyed clothing, books, electronics or jewelry; frequent headaches or stomachaches; feeling sick or faking illness; changes in eating habits, like suddenly skipping meals or binge eating (kids may come home from school hungry because they did not eat lunch); difficulty sleeping or frequent nightmares; declining grades; loss of interest in schoolwork or not wanting to go to school; sudden loss of friends or avoidance of social situations; feelings of helplessness or decreased self-esteem; and self-destructive behaviors such as running away from home, harming themselves or talking about suicide."[220]

Caring confrontation of your child about the bullying and intervention in his behalf is expedient. It is important that he is not "put down," counted a weakling or punished for allowing the bullying to occur. "The thief's purpose is to steal and kill and destroy. My purpose is to give them a rich and satisfying life" (John 10:10 NLT). Behind the bullying is the power of darkness at work seeking to rob children of peace, hope, joy, self-worth and life itself. Urge them not to give place to Satan, realizing that in Jesus Christ they are more than able to overcome the sneers, mocking and ridicule.

Bullying is not just an elementary or high school thing. It happens in the workplace among adults. Bullying may come from colleagues, supervisors or the boss. It may include belittling or degrading remarks, nitpicking (constant criticism), verbal abuse (possibly shouting), embarrassing comments, setting one up to fail, passing up one for earned promotion or salary increase, overloading one with work deliberately, and exclusion from breaktime fellowship.[221]

It is fear of man (cowardice) that leads to emotional, physical and even spiritual captivity. In contrast, the person who trusts in the Lord is literally "set on high." That is, he is safe and out of danger, being protected by the Lord, having his cowardice transformed into courage. The *Pulpit Commentary* elucidates: "We are to find a refuge from the ensnaring fear of man by putting our trust in the Lord. God is mightier than the whole world. A howling mob hounding its victims to death cannot shake the confidence of one who has made the Lord his Refuge. It was trust in God that saved Shadrach, Meshach and Abednego from cowardice when threatened by cruel Nebuchadnezzar and cast into the burning fiery furnace."[222]

The Bottom Line: Refuge from and victory over bullying is found in Jesus Christ who makes us "more than conquerors" (Romans 8:37) over man's vicious ridicule and slams. Trust in Him enables one to say with David, "The LORD is on my side; I will not fear: what can man do unto me?" (Psalm 118:6).

29
Business, operate it prudently
Proverbs 27:23
"Be thou diligent to know the state of thy flocks, and look well to thy herds."

Be thou "diligent" (heart attentiveness) to "know" (know well) the "state" (condition; health) of thy "flocks" and thy "herds" (sheep and goats); "look well" (i.e., "put your heart into it" since it is for your livelihood[223]) to thy herds. Allen Ross summarizes the text's meaning: "Take care of your livelihood [because] riches do not last long."[224]

Be determined and disciplined to know exactly the state of your business, lest expenses erode profit or lead to bankruptcy. Solomon states the best way to assure the "books" are examined correctly for assets and deficits is by *looking at* (managing) them personally. The most successful businesses are those in which the owner continuously is abreast of their inventory, operation and financial status. A second lesson the text suggests is that it is wise to constantly know your financial state so that a crisis will never catch you off guard. Matthew Henry advises, "We must be discreet and considerate in the management of our business, know the state of things, and look well to them, that nothing may be lost, no opportunity let slip, but everything done in proper time and order, and so as to turn to the best advantage."[225]

The Bottom Line: Know what you have in the bank (balance the checkbook), as well as stocks and investments, and manage them well. Work hard in business, keeping up with its inventory ("state of thy flocks") and personally double-check company books.

30
Buying, keep from living above your means
Proverbs 24:27
"Prepare thy work without, and make it fit for thyself in the field; and afterwards build thine house."

"Prepare" (Reyburn and Fry say "'establish,' 'make firm,' 'make ready,' or 'accomplish'"[226]) thy "work without" (get your fields ready for sowing[227]), making it "fit for thyself" (the actual planting of the crop[228]). "Afterwards" (only after that) "build" (construct) your "house" (personal or family lodging).

The wise instruction is not to live beyond your means by building a house without first having established a sure plan to pay for it (job). Work hard, save judiciously and live within an established budget to the end that one day (sooner or later) you may "build thine house." Live contently in an *acceptable* abode until the more *desirable* is financially feasible.[229]

Luke 14:28–30 may well be the New Testament Proverbs 24:27: "Is there anyone here who, planning to build a new house, doesn't first sit down and figure the cost so you'll know if you can complete it? If you only get the foundation laid and then run out of money, you're going to look pretty foolish. Everyone passing by will poke fun at you: 'He started something he couldn't finish'" (MSG).

During the last recession some seven million Americans lost their homes. Various reasons are to blame, but one that tops the list is that many had a "Cadillac appetite with a Volkswagen budget." They failed to apply the wisdom of Proverbs 24:27 and Luke 14:28–30. Obviously the teaching of the Proverb spans every area of purchase (autos, entertainment devices, furniture and clothing). Don't buy what you can't afford. The use of credit cards only delays the payment (and accrues interest).

A second interpretation is similar. R. E. Murphy states that it indicates "a certain priority of values for a young man. Preparation for the material needs involved in marriage and establishing a family should be attended to first."[230] Allen Ross concurs, "A man should be financially secure before he starts a family."[231] There is no conflict with accepting and applying both views. S. S. Buzzell remarks, "Whether house should be taken literally (constructing a house) or figuratively (getting married and having a family), the principle is the same: it is important to have one's priorities straight."[232]

A spiritual application may also be made. The building of a strong, sound and stable spiritual house (heart) in which to live life happily and successfully requires first the removal of the weeds, thorns, thistles of sin (repentance) and receptivity to the "seeding" of the Word of God (Matthew 13:7, 8).

The Bottom Line: "Don't spend what you don't have for things you don't need." Plan before you purchase. Insofar as it is feasible, pay as you go. Do first things first.

31
Calamity, the winners and losers
Proverbs 10:25

"As the whirlwind passeth, so is the wicked no more: but the righteous is an everlasting foundation."

When the "whirlwind" (catastrophe, adversity, trouble; Deane and Taswell say "the idea is the speed with which, under God's vengeance, the sinner is consumed"[233]) "passeth" (comes to a conclusion, end) the "wicked" (unrighteous, evil) will be "no more" (destroyed; overcome by its trouble). See Psalm 1:4.

Sir Francis Bacon said, "It is a reverent thing to see an ancient castle or building not in decay, or to see a fair timber tree sound and perfect. How much more to behold an ancient and noble family which hath stood against the waves and weathers of time." In Matthew 7:24–27, Jesus tells of the kind of house that is able to withstand "the waves and weathers of time" in the story about two house builders. One of these builders built his house upon the sand, while the other built his upon the rock. In time, a storm came and blew against these two houses. The house built upon the sand was destroyed, while the house built upon the rock stood. A home or life built upon the shifting sands of irreligion and anti-God values in time will collapse (great will be the fall of it), whereas one built upon the Solid Rock (Jesus Christ and biblical values) will stand firm regardless of the storms encountered. "The righteous possess an everlasting foundation."

How firm a foundation, ye saints of the Lord,
Is laid for your faith in His excellent Word!
What more can He say than to you He hath said—
To you who for refuge to Jesus have fled?

"Fear not, I am with thee; oh, be not dismayed,
For I am thy God and will still give thee aid.
I'll strengthen thee, help thee, and cause thee to stand,
Upheld by My gracious, omnipotent hand.

"When through the deep waters I call thee to go,
The rivers of sorrow shall not overflow;
For I will be with thee thy trouble to bless
And sanctify to thee thy deepest distress.

"When through fiery trials thy pathway shall lie,
My grace, all-sufficient, shall be thy supply.
The flame shall not harm thee; I only design
Thy dross to consume and thy gold to refine.

"The soul that on Jesus doth lean for repose,
I will not, I will not, desert to his foes;
That soul, though all Hell should endeavor to shake,
I'll never, no, never, no, never forsake."   ~ Unknown (1787)

The Bottom Line: Ving Rhames said, "Since God is the foundation of my life, anything that streams from that can only be positive."[234]

32
Caution, man's careful, watchful guardian
Proverbs 14:16

"A wise man feareth, and departeth from evil: but the fool rageth, and is confident."

A *wise* (spiritually wise and sensible) person is *cautious* (Reyburn and Fry say, "careful," "alert," "on guard"[235] regarding conduct) and "departeth from" (takes preventive steps to avoid) *"evil"* (ethical, social or moral wrong): BUT "the fool rageth" (Garrett says "to be 'hot-headed and reckless'"[236]) and is "confident" (fools are overconfident, incautious and show no fear for the consequences of their actions[237]). See Proverbs 14:15; 28:14. Matthew Henry summarizes, "A wise man, for fear of harm, keeps out of harm's way, and starts back in a fright when he finds himself entering into temptation."[238]

In stark contrast, the fool, being arrogant and conceited, disregards caution and discards restraint to live "recklessly and carelessly" to satisfy the appetite of the carnal flesh. The wicked fool manifests no fear or respect for God, rushing headlong into sin without pondering the serious consequences. Charles Bridges states, "The *fool*, however stout and stubborn in his mind, never fears till he falls. Bravely independent, he sits amid the threatening of God as unalarmed as Solomon amid his brazen lions, carried by his rash will and blind passion, without apprehending the end and issue of things."[239]

The scars of others should teach us caution.
Jerome

The renowned London pastor of the nineteenth century, C. H. Spurgeon, in the sermon "A Caution to the Presumptuous" provides the believer with direction for caution so that he stumbles not. "Oh, ye, my beloved, ye, my brethren, think not that ye stand, lest ye should fall. My brother, stumble not. There lieth the gin, there the snare. I am come to gather the stones out of the road and take away the stumbling blocks. But what can I do unless, with due care and caution, ye yourselves walk guardedly. Oh, my brethren, be much more in prayer than ever. Spend more time in pious adoration. Read the Scriptures more earnestly and constantly. Watch your lives more carefully. Live nearer to God. Take the best examples for your pattern. Let your conversation be redolent of Heaven. Let your hearts be perfumed with affection for men's souls. So live that men may take knowledge of you that you have been with Jesus and have learned of Him; and when that happy day shall come when He whom you love shall say, 'Come up higher,' let it be your happiness to hear Him say, 'Come, My beloved, thou hast fought a good fight, thou hast finished thy course, and henceforth there is laid up for thee a crown of righteousness that fadeth not away.' On, Christian, with care and caution! On, with holy fear and trembling! On yet, with faith and confidence, for thou shalt not fall."[240]

The Bottom Line: Goethe was right when he stated, "Every step of life shows much caution is required." The *negative cautions* of Holy Scripture are *positive checkpoints* for conduct.

33
Chains, the binding effect of sin
Proverbs 5:22

"His own iniquities shall take the wicked himself, and he shall be holden with the cords of his sins."

A man's "own" (personal doing) "iniquities" (sin) "shall take the wicked himself" (victim of his own sin, it ensnares him) and he shall be "holden with the cords of his sins" (the net of captivity his sins have made; like a bird trapped in a net).[241] R. E. Murphy summarizes, "His sin comes back upon him, as it were—an application of the deed-consequence connection."[242]

The ungodly forge chains which hold them in bondage with the sins they commit. They are prisoners (captives) to their own wicked affections and actions. Ignoring and rejecting godly instruction, the sinner weaves constantly about his life the thread of ruin, havoc and heartache that leads to eternal damnation ("die without instruction" but not because it was not offered). Note that it is "his own iniquities" (personal sin; not the fault of another and certainly not of God) that shall ensnare him (trapped with no way out), preventing peace, joy, contentment and hope. The epitaph of the wicked is: "For that they hated knowledge, and did not choose the fear of

50

the LORD: They would none of my counsel: they despised all my reproof" (Proverbs 1:29–30). In the absence of biblical instruction and reproof man falls prey to hopeless remorse and helpless bondage. It is the *light* alone that shows the way out of the *dark*. An old proverb states, "You are not free if you carry your chains with you." Freedom from the chains of bondage await all at the foot of the cross. Charles Wesley, upon the first anniversary of his conversion (1739), wrote the hymn "O for a Thousand Tongues to Sing."

> O for a thousand tongues to sing
> My great Redeemer's praise,
> The glories of my God and King,
> The triumphs of His grace.
>
> He breaks the power of canceled sin;
> He sets the prisoner free.
> His blood can make the foulest clean;
> His blood availed for me.
>
> He speaks, and, listening to His voice,
> New life the dead receive;
> The mournful, broken hearts rejoice;
> The humble poor believe.

Jesus is your bondage breaker. "If the Son therefore shall make you free, ye shall be free indeed" (John 8:36). You don't have to bear those chains anymore. He is the great emancipator and liberator from Satan's prison camp. Look to Him, and in being set free you will sing with Chris Tomlin, "My chains are gone; I've been set free."

The Bottom Line: Charles Dickens is correct: "We forge the chains we bear in life."[243] A person bears chains for failure to receive that glorious liberty proclaimed and provided by Jesus Christ. See Luke 4:18.

34
Chastisement, the method and motive
Proverbs 3:11–12
"My son, despise not the chastening of the LORD; neither be weary of his correction: For whom the LORD loveth he correcteth; even as a father the son in whom he delighteth."

My "son" (a father's instruction to his son or those of a teacher [sage] to a student using the parental address; "My son(s)" occurs 27 times in the book) "despise not" (don't reject, resent or refuse) the "chastisement" (punishment or discipline by means of trials, difficulty, suffering) of the Lord; neither be "weary" (don't loathe, be disgusted with or hate it[244]) of "correction" (rebuke[245]). For whom the Lord "loveth" (exhibits affection) he "correcteth" (reproves; punishes the mistakes); just as a son who brings "delight" (pleasure; well-pleasing) to his father is disciplined (as a father "punishes the son that is dear to him"). See Job 5:17.

My son is the sinner's new position in the family of God upon experiencing the new birth (John 3:3). John says, "Beloved, now are we the sons of God, and it doth not yet appear what we shall be: but we know that, when he shall appear, we shall be like him; for we shall see him as he is" (1 John 3:2). A Great Awakening preacher, William Romaine, explains, "You are a pardoned sinner, not under the law but under grace, freely, fully saved from the guilt of all your sins. There is none to condemn, God having justified you. He sees you in His Son, washed you in His blood, clothed you in His righteousness; and He embraces Him and you, the Head and the members, with the same affection."[246] The Book of Proverbs is about an affectionate and concerned "Father" instructing His "sons" (primarily the young and immature) in the way of wisdom and righteousness that they may live rightly, abundantly and successfully unto His good pleasure.

About divine discipline the psalmist states, "Blessed is the man whom thou chastenest, O LORD, and teachest him out of thy law" (Psalm 94:12). In prosperity and adversity (and youthfulness) man tends to forget God, therefore punishment is administered to correct and instruct. Job is a classic example of one on the whole who does not "despise it" (loathe, feel disgust, give way to despondency) but submits to its purpose (Job 1:21; 2:10). Jonah on the other hand pictures the opposite.

H. A. Ironside summarizes, "The chastisement of the Lord must invariably follow departure from the ways that be in Christ. It is important to remember that the moment a poor sinner trusts the Lord Jesus as his Savior, his responsibility as a criminal having to do with the Judge is over forever. 'There is therefore now no condemnation to them that are in Christ Jesus' (Romans 8:1). But, that very moment, his responsibility as a child having to do with his Father begins; and that Father, 'without respect of persons, judgeth according to every man's work' (1 Peter 1:17)."[247]

Charles Bridges states, "Nowhere, indeed, are our corruptions so manifest, or our graces so shining, as under the rod. We need it as much as our daily bread."[248]

C. H. Spurgeon states, "The chastening must answer its purpose, or it cannot be brought to an end."[249] He also said, "God will never have great chastisements in store for those who are quick confessors of sin."[250]

The Bottom Line: God's chastisement (discipline) is done in love and for our good (even as fathers discipline their children) to gain our reconciliation, submission, protection and realignment of path.

35
Church, warning about neglect of the oxen
Proverbs 14:4
"Where no oxen are, the crib is clean: but much increase is by the strength of the ox."

Where no "oxen" (bulls as work animals) are, the "crib" (feedbox) is "clean" (without grain, thus empty). But "much increase" (grain, crops, food) comes by the "strength of the ox" (the might of the *work oxen* to pull a plow). To summarize, without the strength of laborers to assist the church and/or other ministries, the financial resources required for their continuation will be absent (the crib will be empty; destitute of what is needed to survive).

In attempts to resolve trouble in the church, sometimes members cast out the ox. The liberal Bible crowd throw out the fundamental Bible crowd who are the ox (giving the tithe, paying the bills, funding missionaries and evangelists). J. Vernon McGee cautions, "So before one tries to do any [church] cleaning, it is very important to find out who are the oxen in the Lord's work."[251] By the way, most oxen are found in the senior adult classes in the church, not in the young adult.

A second application is implied. Members can keep the church "clean" but "empty" and without "strength" through refusal to allow the undesired (the physically dirty, shabbily dressed, foul smelling, ungroomed, outcast) entrance. The church sanctuary may be "clean" on Sunday, without the dirty "ox," but it will be so to her impotency and decline. Strong work oxen start out as calves. A church known for its exclusiveness had a sign in the yard that read "Jesus Only." A windstorm blew away three letters, leaving the sign to read *Us Only*. Enough said.

In the Great Commission (Matthew 28:18–19) there is no exception clause as to whom the church is to win, baptize and disciple. "All" includes everyone regardless of face, race or place. "I was a stranger and you welcomed me" (Matthew 25:35 ESV). The movie *In His Steps* visualizes this lesson and would be an invaluable family viewing.

A third application has to do with the saints that engage in "serious" sin and wrongdoing. Ironside comments, "Too often it is taken for granted that the great object of discipline in the house of God is to get rid of the offender; whereas the truth is just the opposite. Earnest endeavor to recover the erring one should be the first thing thought of. Much crying to God and identifying ourselves with the sin of one who has misbehaved will accompany this if we are before Him about it as we should be."[252] Ironside concludes, "How much better is it to cleanse by leading an erring brother to repentance, thus covering his sin, than by excommunicating him before all possible means have been exhausted in seeking his restoration to God!"[253]

The Bottom Line: Retention of oxen is imperative to a ministry's success, but not at any price. Retain the righteous oxen that pull the Gospel's plow with you. Maintain an open-door policy in the church though it may mean getting the "stall" dirty; the little time required to clean the church is more than adequately reimbursed with the lives that are gloriously saved.

36
Clothing, the biblical code for women
Proverbs 7:10

"And, behold, there met him a woman with the attire of an harlot, and subtil of heart."

There "met" (intentional or chance meeting) "him" (young man) a "woman" (adult female) with the "attire of a harlot" (dressed like a prostitute, Genesis 38:14–15) that was "subtil of heart" (crafty or concealed of heart; she keeps her intentions with the young man locked up in her heart[254] awaiting the right moment to spring the trap).

Pointedly and plainly the Bible condemns provocative and indecent dress. All girls, especially those who are Christians, should dress modestly, appropriately and with propriety. The older godly women in the church are to instruct the young women with respect to dress. "Likewise also that women should adorn themselves in respectable apparel, with modesty and self-control" (1 Timothy 2:9 ESV).

The exhortation, though seriously needed, continuously goes unheeded. Girls should learn from the godly lady how to dress for school, work, church, dates, beach or pool, and the day-to-day activities. Sad as it is, young girls see poor examples among some women in the church and at school as to how a godly woman is to dress.

The key to modest attire is not a legalistic standard but rather a godly heart. It's what's in the heart that determines the type of dress (as it does behavior). The woman of Proverbs 7 dressed seductively ("attire of a harlot") because of wanton, lustful desires ruling the heart. Immodest attire will be a mute issue if one walks in fellowship with the Lord. The state of one's heart is manifest in dress.

The principle of "modest" dress is also addressed in the Old Testament when it forbids transvestitism (cross-dressing). "A woman must not wear men's clothes, and a man must not wear women's clothes. The Lord your God hates anyone who does that" (Deuteronomy 22:5 NCV). Man and woman must dress in clothing designed for their gender (masculine for men and feminine for women). Matthew Henry observes, "The purity of the heart will show itself in the modesty of the dress."[255]

The Bottom Line: Girls should be instructed to dress modestly, calling attention to their face, not their bust—not dress *to impress but to bless.* Intentional or not, girls should not so dress as to cause a boy to stumble (2 Samuel 11:2–4). Likewise, boys must avoid dress that evokes lust in girls. With Hollywood influence and teen pressure on children to dress "seductively," they will need godly help in navigating their dress standard until spiritually mature.

37
Comfort, inappropriate consolation
Proverbs 25:20
"As he that taketh away a garment in cold weather, and as vinegar upon nitre, so is he that singeth songs to an heavy heart."

As he that "taketh away a garment in cold weather" (steals a man's warm clothing when it is cold), and as "vinegar upon nitre" (pouring vinegar on soda is counterproductive, causing "a violent reaction"[256]). Walvoord and Zuck summarize, "Trying to perk up by songs a person who is discouraged or depressed (a heavy heart) is as cruel as stealing his garment in cold weather...[and] like pouring vinegar on soda; it is useless."[257] See 1 Samuel 19:9–10 (David's serenading King Saul when he was depressed almost got himself killed).

The way to help a cold man is not by taking his coat, nor is the way to help a wound (open cut) to pour vinegar (will only irritate) upon it. Just so, the way to comfort the heavy heart is not by singing "cheerful" songs in an effort to make it merry. The sad and depressed ("heavy heart") need sympathizing, not insensitive singing that fails to comfort and console.

There will be a time for cheerful and jolly singing, but certainly not at the first. Console the heavy heart by reaching out to it with a gentle, loving touch or hug, allowing your spirit and theirs to communicate without the use of words (when you know not what to say).

Charlie Walton in his book *When There Are No Words* explains the power of a hug in the hour of grief. "Pain doesn't come in pounds or ounces or gallons. You just feel like you are standing before a mountain that you are going to have to move one spoonful at a time. It is a task you can never hope to complete...a mountain that you can never hope to finish moving. But...as you stand surveying that mountain of grief...a loved one steps forward with a hug that communicates clearly. You can almost picture that person stepping up to your mountain of grief with a shovel and saying, 'I cannot move the mountain for you...but I will take this one shovelful of your grief and deal with it myself.'"

Walton continues, "Every hug helps to dilute the pain...to move the mountain. Don't be selfish with your mountain. Don't be a martyr about your grief. There is plenty of mountain to keep you busy the rest of your life...and...if your friends hadn't been willing to help...they wouldn't have showed up with those spoons, shovels and hugs."

Help the sad and depressed by shoveling some of their grief away from their mountain by showing care, love and concern—sometimes without words.

The Bottom Line: In the wilderness, a man became lost. He was met by a man who approached him, and the following conversation ensued. "Sir, I am lost. Can you show me the way out of this wilderness?"

"No," said the stranger, "I cannot show you the way out of the wilderness; but maybe if I walk with you, we can find it together." Though you may be unable to tell the hurting the way out of sorrow, walk with them one small step at a time until they find the way.

38
Comfort, sure source in sorrow
Proverbs 7:1
"My son, keep my words, and lay up my commandments with thee."

"My son" (instruction from the sage to his pupil or father to his son), "keep" (to heed, obey; live by) "my" (the sage's or father's, those of a teacher of profound wisdom) "words" (instructions, teachings, commands, warnings), and "lay up" (store up, treasure) my "commandments" (the "Torah" but also the entirety of God's Word) with thee.

Upon the death of the only son of Sir Harry Lauder (world-famed Scottish singer and comedian), he remarked, "I had three choices. One, I could drown my sorrow in drink. Two, I could drown my sorrow in the grave; I could take my own life. Or three, I could find hope and comfort in God." And he said, "I turned to God."[258] Wise and wonderful choice that he made!

W. A. Criswell states, "Sorrow will always do one of two things. It will warp your mind, embitter your soul, destroy your life, or else it will bring you closer to God."[259] By God's enabling hand, determine that sorrow will do the latter for you when you are within its grip.

Believers have always found strength and comfort in life's storms knowing that they have an "Anchor" that holds them safe and secure. The Anchor is the sure promises of God recorded in the Holy Scripture. "So God has given both his promise and his oath. These two things are unchangeable because it is impossible for God to lie. Therefore, we who have fled to him for refuge can have great confidence as we hold to the hope that lies before us. This hope is a strong and trustworthy anchor for our souls" (Hebrews 6:18–19 NLT).

The text is an analogy of olden days when most ships had sails. When such a ship approached a harbor that was difficult to navigate, the captain would send a seaman ahead in a small boat with the anchor attached to a rope that extended back to the ship. Once in the bay, the seaman would drop the anchor. The captain then would give orders to the crew to pull the rope little by little, drawing the ship safely into the harbor.

In the Christian life, Christ has gone before us to drop the anchor within the harbor of Heaven. The anchor is Scripture, God's promises, all of which ensure security, strength and stability amidst life's storms until life's journey ends in the harbor of the Celestial City. Hold fast to the Anchor's rope, for it is the griever's indispensable source of strength and comfort and prevents you from drifting off course, continually drawing you Heavenward.

The Bottom Line: Treasure the Word of God. To find comfort and hope in time of sorrow, meditate upon and claim continuously the promises of Jesus which He spoke to troubled, broken hearts.

39
Commandments, wisdom of accepting and adhering to
Proverbs 10:8

"The wise in heart will receive commandments: but a prating fool shall fall."

"A wise man will hear, and will increase learning; and a man of understanding shall attain unto wise counsels" (Proverbs 1:5).

The "wise in heart" (open to instruction, willingness to learn[260]) will "receive" (heed; apply) "commandments" (scriptural; note, *commandments* is plural, meaning all of its directives[261]): but a "prating fool" ("foolish of lips"—deceitful talking; not disposed to listening due to conceit,[262] thinks himself already wise) shall "fall" (rejection of God's Word always results in ruin, destruction).

One of the most valuable benefits of wisdom is not in what it gives, but in what it receives.[263] At the very heart of the wise is an openness and receptivity to instruction (Divine Law; Holy Scripture). He is teachable and moldable. He hungers and thirsts for the heavenly manna that alone nurtures the soul while instilling divine Truth. He who possesses wisdom declares with David, "Thy testimonies also are my delight and my counsellors" (Psalm 119:24) and testifies with Jeremiah, "Thy words were found, and I did eat them; and thy word was unto me the joy and rejoicing of mine heart: for I am called by thy name, O LORD God of hosts" (Jeremiah 15:16).

The absence of such longing indicates the absence of Christ (Wisdom) in a person's life. The Scripture says, "He that is of God heareth God's words: ye therefore hear them not, because ye are not of God" (John 8:47), and, "He that hath my commandments, and keepeth them, he it is that loveth me: and he that loveth me shall be loved of my Father, and I will love him, and will manifest myself to him" (John 14:21).

In contrast, "the prating fool" (foolish talker; empty head) is too conceited to receive God's instruction. These fools "will not be governed nor endure any yoke, will not be taught nor take any advice."[264] God says to him, "He that turneth away his ear from hearing the law [Ten Commandments], even his prayer shall be abomination" (Proverbs 28:9). And without biblical guidance, the fool will not turn from sin but will fall more into it, ending up in an eternal Hell ("shall fall").

The Bottom Line: He is wise who is teachable about and compliant to the Word of God.

40
Commending Others, show appreciation and admiration
Proverbs 12:8
"A man shall be commended according to his wisdom."

A "man" (youth or adult) shall be "commended" (praised) according to his "wisdom" (sound judgment; prudence[265]; knowing and doing what pleases God). R. E. Murphy says, "The point of the saying is that personal wisdom wins the attention and approval of neighbors."[266] "Let another man praise thee" (Proverbs 27:2). To praise one's self is the epitome of arrogance and conceit.

It is a character flaw to neglect to give the commendation deserved by others. Examples of biblical commendation are plenteous. Jesus offered commendation. Through John He commended the churches in Asia Minor who deserved it with expressions such as: "I know thy works, and thy labour, and thy patience, and how thou canst not bear them which are evil"; "thou holdest fast my name, and hast not denied my faith"; and "I know thy works, and charity, and service, and faith, and thy patience, and thy works; and the last to be more than the first." And to the Sardis church Jesus commended certain believers, saying: "Thou hast a few names even in Sardis which have not defiled their garments; and they shall walk with me in white: for they are worthy" (Revelation 2:2, 13, 19; 3:4). Jesus commended the widow for the sacrificial and heartfelt offering she placed in the offering box (Luke 21:1–4). Paul commended Timothy. "I hope in the Lord Jesus to send Timothy to you soon, so that I too may be cheered by news of you. For I have no one like him, who will be genuinely concerned for your welfare" (Philippians 2:19–20 ESV). Barnabas commended Paul to the disciples (Acts 9:27). Luke spoke words of commendation to the Berean Christians for their searching the Scriptures daily (Acts 17:11).

Charles Bridges makes a poignant observation. He states, "The ordinary judgment of this world is to "put darkness for light" (Isaiah 5:20), and therefore to commend according to folly rather than *according to wisdom.* And yet even hated *wisdom* often carries its voice of conviction both to conscience and judgment, and *a man is commended according to it.*"[267] Such is seen in the elevation of Joseph and Daniel, honor given to David, our Lord's wisdom commended by friends and enemies (John 7:46).[268] A word of approval, praise, commendation and thank you is fuel to the heart of every man.

Hebrews 10:24 says, "And let us consider one another to provoke unto love and to good works." Imitate Jesus, Paul, Barnabas and Luke by looking for the good in others that is commendable and then "commend" them. Richard Steele (1672–1729) advised, "Whenever you commend, add a compelling reason for doing so; it is this which distinguishes the approbation of a man of sense from the flattery of sycophants [someone who seeks gain by flattery] and the admiration of fools."[269]

When being praised, handle it gracefully, not arrogantly. Solomon warns that praise tests man's spiritual "mettle." "Fire tests the purity of silver and gold, but a person is tested by being praised" (Proverbs 27:21 NLT).

The Bottom Line: Mary Kay Ash reminds us of man's need of commendation in saying, "Everyone has an invisible sign hanging around his neck saying, 'Make me feel important.'"[270] Make it your business to make others feel important, appreciated and valued—not for personal gain but for their profit.

41
Concealed, God's secrets prove His power
Proverbs 25:2

"It is the glory of God to conceal a thing: but the honour of kings is to search out a matter."

"O the depth of the riches both of the wisdom and knowledge of God! how unsearchable are his judgments, and his ways past finding out! For who hath known the mind of the Lord? or who hath been his counsellor?" (Romans 11:33–34).

It is the "glory" (honor or greatness) of God to "conceal" (to keep hidden what it is not meant for man to know—Deuteronomy 29:29) a "thing" (physical or spiritual).

In contrast to man's government (kings, prime ministers, presidents), Allen Ross states, "God's government of the universe is beyond understanding—human understanding cannot fathom the divine intentions or operations."[271] R. E. Murphy says, "God's secret, or unsearchability, is proof of divine power—these are secrets that humans cannot even guess. What God does not reveal demonstrates who God really is. In contrast, the king is transparent, obvious."[272] William McKane suggests that "when it is supposed that everything is known about God, it is no longer possible to worship Him."[273] H. A. Ironside elucidates, "As the heavens are high above the earth, so, we are told, are His thoughts above ours. It therefore becomes Him to conceal from prurient curiosity His wondrous purposes."[274] God's ways are mysterious, for which man gives Him honor.

Often God chooses to reveal that which is hidden without disclosure of all the details. For example, God *reveals* the truth of the Second Coming but conceals its time; that all man will die but conceals the circumstances, day and hour. Much that was hidden He has revealed with regard to His Person, the Trinity, the incarnation of Christ, the last judgment, Heaven and Hell, the atonement, the resurrection of Christ, evil, Satan, suffering. God's will for man is concealed, but upon divine inquiry will be revealed (Jeremiah 29:11).

Admittedly, presently we know only in part, for to know in full would make us God or jeopardize spiritual growth in faith which is based upon things not seen and unknown (Hebrews 11:1). "Now we see but a dim reflection as in a mirror; then we shall see face to face. Now I know in part; then I shall know fully, even as I am fully known" (1 Corinthians 13:12 BSB).

Thomas G. Selby shares several reasons why God conceals: "*God is glorified by mystery*, because mystery has its place in the discipline and exaltation of human character. The veiled truth *sometimes calls out a higher faith,* a more chastened resignation, a more childlike obedience in God's people, than the truth that is unveiled. God conceals many things so that *He may be magnified through His people's trust during darkness and uncertainty.* God conceals many things, so that He *may protect us from needless pain and fear and magnify His own gentleness.* Many a thing must be hidden from a child; and the more sensitive he is, the stricter must be the concealment. God conceals some things from us *to excite us to nobler and more strenuous endeavor in our search after the truth.* And He conceals some things from us, so that He *may impress us with the solemnities of the unknown.* God never conceals what may be necessary to furnish His people for the work and service of life."[275]

God moves in a mysterious way
His wonders to perform;
He plants His footsteps in the sea
And rides upon the storm.

Deep in unfathomable mines
Of never failing skill
He treasures up His bright designs
And works His sov'reign will.

Ye fearful saints, fresh courage take;
The clouds ye so much dread
Are big with mercy and shall break
In blessings on your head.

Judge not the Lord by feeble sense,
But trust Him for His grace;
Behind a frowning providence
He hides a smiling face.

His purposes will ripen fast,
Unfolding every hour;
The bud may have a bitter taste,
But sweet will be the flower.

Blind unbelief is sure to err
And scan His work in vain;
God is His own interpreter,
And He will make it plain.
~ William Cowper (1774)

"The secret things belong unto the LORD our God: but those things which are revealed belong unto us and to our children for ever, that we may do all the words of this law" (Deuteronomy 29:29). T. Cartwright rightly observes, "He reveals enough of His blessed nature and counsels for faith to rest upon, not to satisfy the curiosity of irreverent self-conceit. He hath none to whom He is bound to render an account of His ways. Hence appears the audacity of those who permit God to do nothing except what falls under the comprehension of their petty minds; whereas He would not be God if His counsels and works did not transcend human intelligence."[276] This truth is seen in Psalm 36:6 and 77:19. Some think the Proverb additionally speaks to God's covering (pardoning; concealing) of sin upon the believer's confession. "I, even I, am he that blotteth out thy transgressions for mine own sake, and will not remember thy sins" (Isaiah 43:25).

The Bottom Line: "Can you understand [discover] the secrets [deep things] of God? Can you search [discover] the limits of the Almighty [Shaddai]? His limits are higher than the heavens; you cannot reach them [what can you do?]! They are deeper than the grave [Sheol]; you cannot understand them! His limits are longer than the earth and wider than the sea" (Job 11:7–9 NCV). What a mighty God we serve! With David the saint declares, "Who is so great a God, as our God?" (Psalm 77:13).

42
Concentration, admonition to focus on goals
Proverbs 4:25

"Let thine eyes look right on, and let thine eyelids look straight before thee."

"Brethren, I count not myself to have apprehended: but this one thing I do" (Philippians 3:13).

Let thine "eyelids" (fluttering eyelashes) "look straight" (to have "tunnel" vision without any blinking[277]; "The eyes must be focused on proper goals"[278]) before thee. Allen Ross says, "The wise person will have *an unswerving directness*, but the fool will be easily distracted (Proverbs 17:24)."[279]

George W. Truett, in the sermon *The Threefold Secret of a Great Life* based upon the words of Paul (Philippians 3:13), emphasizes the value of singleness of focus with regard to pursuit in life. He states, "This one thing I do—not a dozen things, not even two things, but 'this *one* thing I do.'" No life can be very great or very happy or very useful without this element of concentration. Everyone should have a work to do and know what it is and do it with all his might. Many a man in life has failed, not from lack of ability, but from lack of this element of concentration. One of the world's most successful businessmen was waited upon by a group of young men who sought his counsel about how to succeed, and he gave them this laconic advice: 'Young gentlemen, get all your eggs into one basket and then watch that basket.' It was his way of giving emphasis to the tremendous value of concentration."[280]

Not only is the concentrated focus needful in secular matters but also in spiritual ones. Truett continues, "When we come to the highest realm of all—the realm religious—this element of concentration there holds sway just as in these other realms. No man can serve two masters. Many a Christian man follows Christ afar off and limps and grovels in the Christian life because he is seeking to adjust himself in life to giving Christ some secondary place, and Christ will not have it. *Concentration is a prime requisite in the victorious life* anywhere."[281]

While a student in seminary, I pastored a church 220 miles away from campus. The only way I could do justice to both was by fully concentrating on each when I was in its arena. At seminary I focused on my books, and at the church I focused upon my ministry. Alexander Graham Bell advised, "Concentrate all your thoughts upon the work at hand. The sun's rays do not burn until brought to a focus."[282] My experience certainly reveals that counsel most beneficial. Publilius Syrus stated, "To do two things at once is to do neither."[283] It's always best, when feasible, to do one thing well instead of two things in a mediocre manner.

The Bottom Line: Vince Lombardi said, "Success demands a singleness of purpose."[284] Concentrate. The wise say with Paul, "This one thing I do," refusing to be sidetracked.

43
Confession, effectual repentance
Proverbs 28:13
"He that covereth his sins shall not prosper: but whoso confesseth and forsaketh them shall have mercy."

He that "covereth" (conceals; refusal to confess wrong) his "sins" (wrong, evil deeds) shall not "prosper" (be unsuccessful): but whoso "confesseth" (acknowledgement, admittance of wrong done; it is to say the same thing about them as God does) and "forsaketh" (abandonment of the wicked deeds) "them" (the wrong committed) shall have "mercy" (God's loving-kindness and forgiveness is extended. "But God, *who is rich in mercy*, for his great love wherewith he loved us."—Ephesians 2:4). Allen Ross points out that this verse is "unique in the Book of Proverbs; it captures the theology of forgiveness found in passages such as Psalm 32:1–5 and 1 John 1:6–9."[285]

Man adds sin upon sin when after sin he tries to conceal it instead of rightly confessing it unto the Lord Jesus Christ. "He that covereth his sins shall not prosper." A man who hides his sin from God eventually will be found out. *Be sure your sin will find you out* (Numbers 32:23). David sought to conceal his sin of adultery for thirteen months, but it was finally detected (2 Samuel 12:7). Psalm 32:3–4 records the bitter consequence both of the sin and its cover-up. "When I kept silent about my sin, my body wasted away through my groaning all the day long. For day and night Your hand [of displeasure] was heavy upon me; my energy (vitality, strength) was drained away as with the burning heat of summer" (AMP). Man's refusal to confess and renounce sin blocks God's forgiveness of it. "But whoso confesseth and forsaketh them shall have mercy." See 1 John 1:9–10. Gunther Plaut comments, "Confession must be coupled with true return in order to assure God's mercy."[286] The remedy for sin is return, renunciation and repentance (godly remorse that involves a change in direction). To the repentant, God's mercy (loving-kindness; forgiveness) will be extended. "I, even I, am he that blotteth out thy transgressions for mine own sake, and will not remember thy sins" (Isaiah 43:25). "I have wiped out your transgressions like a thick cloud and your sins like a heavy mist" (Isaiah 44:22 NASB). Matthew Henry says, "When we set sin before our face (as David said, "My sin is ever before me."—Ps. 51:3), God casts it behind his back."[287]

"Come now, and let us reason together, saith the LORD: though your sins be as scarlet, they shall be as white as snow; though they be red like crimson, they shall be as wool" (Isaiah 1:18).

The Bottom Line: Sin that is concealed *always* is revealed. Jesus said, "There is nothing covered up that will not be revealed, and hidden that will not be known. Accordingly, whatever you have said in the dark shall be heard in the light, and what you have whispered in the inner rooms shall be proclaimed upon the housetops" (Luke 12:2–3 NASB). Waltke says, "People may smash their consciences to avoid humbling themselves, but they cannot avoid the reality that God knows and will punish sin."[288] But sin revealed (confessed unto the Lord) is *always* concealed (God thrusts it into the sea of forgetfulness, to remember it against us no more—Micah 7:19).

44
Confidence (Faith), to be placed in Christ
Proverbs 3:26
"For the LORD shall be thy confidence, and shall keep thy foot from being taken."

For the Lord shall be "thy" (the righteous') "confidence" (trust; reliability; hope; Deane and Taswell say, "The sense of his all-encircling protection will render you undismayed"[289]), AND shall "keep thy foot from being taken" ("from the consequences of sin (snares) that afflict the wicked"[290]).

But not only is Jesus the believer's confidence in life's threatenings, troubles and satanic assaults, but also in salvation itself. Paul states, "I pray with great faith for you, because I'm fully convinced [confident] that the One who began this glorious work in you will faithfully continue the process of maturing you and will put his finishing touches to it until the unveiling of our Lord Jesus Christ!" (Philippians 1:6 TPT). David expressed a similar confidence in declaring "The LORD will perfect that which concerneth me" (Psalm 138:8). *Confidence* is the established and unquestionable trust in Christ's all-encircling hand of protection, provision, pardon and promises. C. H. Spurgeon, commenting on Psalm 138:8, writes, "The confidence which the Psalmist here expressed was a divine confidence. He did not say, 'I have grace enough to perfect that which concerneth me; my faith is so steady that it will not stagger; my love is so warm that it will never grow cold; my resolution is so firm that nothing can move it.' No, his dependence was on the Lord alone. If we indulge in any confidence which is not grounded on the Rock of Ages, our confidence is worse than a dream. It will fall upon us and cover us with its ruins, to our sorrow and confusion."[291]

God's arms are underneath me;
How can I fall?
I'll trust in Him completely;
He is my all.

God's arms support me ever;
How can I fall?
His promise faileth never;
Trust Him for all. ~ Barney E. Warren (1900)

"He [Christ] has done it all, must do it all, and will do it all. Our confidence must not be in what we have done nor in what we have resolved to do, but entirely in what the Lord will do. We can never be too confident when we confide in him alone, and never too much concerned to have such a trust."[292] The man who puts confidence in Jesus Christ for salvation (abundant and eternal life) and His Word for godly instruction (Proverbs 2:6) gains many benefits which include life (Proverbs 3:22; John 10:10), safety (Proverbs 3:23), restful and tranquil sleep (Proverbs 3:24), anxiety-free disposition (Proverbs 3:25), spiritual and physical health (Proverbs 3:8), escape of traps (snares) set by the wicked (Proverbs 22:5), certainty about the future (Proverbs 3:25–26) and the evasion of many troubles and trials (Proverbs 3:7–8).

The Bottom Line: Martin Luther said, "Faith is a living, daring confidence in God's grace, so sure and certain that a man could stake his life on it a thousand times."[293] Matthew Henry says, "When I cannot *feel* the faith of assurance, I live by the *fact* of God's faithfulness."[294]

45
Confidence, the soul's secure anchor in trouble
Proverbs 3:25–26

"Be not afraid of sudden fear, neither of the desolation of the wicked, when it cometh. For the LORD shall be thy confidence, and shall keep thy foot from being taken."

"Let him trust in the name of the LORD, AND STAY UPON HIS GOD" (Isaiah 50:10).

Be not "afraid" (fear thou not) of "sudden" (unexpected; ambush of bad news) "fear" ("sudden terror"[295]; that which excites terror or panic; Reyburn and Fry say "the nature of the fright is not indicated"[296]) for the Lord shall be thy "confidence" (trust, hope, assurance, security; high tower of refuge), and shall keep thy foot "from being taken" (the phrase in the Hebrew only occurs here in Proverbs[297]; Jehovah will protect the righteous from the hidden snares—like traps set for animals that the impious and ungodly lay for them[298]). Deane and Taswell explain, "Jehovah in the presence of the 'sudden fear,' and of 'the desolation of the wicked,' the evils and calamities which overwhelm the wicked, shall be thy confidence. The sense of His all-encircling protection will render you undismayed."[299])

In times of trouble God will be your "confidence" (trust, reliability, refuge). Confidence in God instills courage, hope, safety, surefootedness and serenity ("restful sleep") in the midst of the storms of life. An unshakable confidence in God is ascertained by faith. This faith is developed through abiding fellowship with Jesus (1 John 2:28) and saturation of the Holy Scriptures (Romans 10:17). Paul explains, "According to the eternal purpose which he purposed in Christ Jesus our LORD: in whom we have boldness and access with confidence *by the faith of him*" (Ephesians 3:11–12). But to fully know Jesus—His sinless life, miraculous works, atoning death on the cross, resurrection, His heart of love and compassion and sovereign control—is to completely trust Him with every affair of life, including the dark times. "In the fear [wisdom, knowledge] of the LORD is strong confidence: and his children shall have a place of refuge" (Proverbs 14:26).

"Because God directs our path," writes Warren Wiersbe, "He is able to protect our path."[300] Wiersbe however states, "The Lord isn't obligated to protect His children when they willfully go their own way."[301]

Like a river glorious is God's perfect peace;
Over all victorious in its bright increase;
Perfect, yet it floweth fuller every day;
Perfect, yet it groweth deeper all the way.

Hidden in the hollow of His blessed hand,
Never foe can follow, never traitor stand.
Not a surge of worry, not a shade of care,
Not a blast of hurry touch the spirit there.

Every joy or trial falleth from above,
Traced upon our dial by the Sun of Love.
We may trust Him fully all for us to do;
They who trust Him wholly find Him wholly true.

Stayed upon Jehovah, hearts are fully blest,
Finding, as He promised, perfect peace and rest.
~ Francis Havergal (1876)

John Ortberg says, "There is something you can't fix, can't heal or can't escape; and all you can do is trust God. Finding ultimate refuge in God means you become so immersed in His presence, so convinced of His goodness, so devoted to His lordship that you find even the cave is a perfectly safe place to be because He is there with you."[302] Knowing He is there with me, wherever the "there" is, gives peace like a river to my soul and lionlike courage to face the trial or trouble triumphantly.

Jesus Christ is our hiding place in the times of storm. "A man shall be as a hiding-place from the wind, and a covert from the tempest" (Isaiah 32:2 ASV). C. H. Spurgeon says, "A shelter is nothing if we stand in front of it. The main thought with many a would-be Christian is his own works, feelings and attainments; this is to stand on the windy side of the wall by putting self before Jesus. Our safety lies in getting behind Christ and letting Him stand in the wind's eye. We must be altogether hidden, or Christ cannot be our hiding place. Foolish religionists hear about the hiding place but never get into it. How great is the folly of such conduct! It makes Jesus to be of no value or effect. What is a roof to a man who lies in the open or a boat to one who sinks in the sea? Even the Man Christ Jesus, though ordained of God to be a covert from the tempest, can cover none but those who are in Him. Come then, poor sinner, enter where you may; hide in Him who was evidently meant to hide you, for He was ordained to be a hiding place and must be used as such, or the very aim of His life and death would be missed."[303]

The Bottom Line: The Lord is trustworthy. He is reliable. He is your ready Helper in the hour of deepest need. Place confidence not in thyself, religion, church, man or the government, for they will disappoint and fail you (Psalm 118:8; Philippians 3:3). Place utter confidence and trust in Him who alone is worthy of it, the Lord Jesus Christ. Declare with David, "Some trust in chariots, and some in horses: but we will remember the name of the LORD" (Psalm 20:7). In the time of trouble say with David, "For in the time of trouble he shall hide me in his pavilion: in the secret of his tabernacle shall he hide me; he shall set me up upon a rock. And now shall mine head be lifted up above mine enemies [personal or those of calamity and crisis] round about me: therefore will I offer in his tabernacle sacrifices of joy; I will sing, yea, I will sing praises unto the LORD" (Psalm 27:5–6).

46
Confidence, warning about relying on the undependable
Proverbs 25:19
"Confidence in an unfaithful man in time of trouble is like a broken tooth, and a foot out of joint."

"Confidence" (trust, reliance) in an "unfaithful man" (a traitor,[304] he that betrays trust) in time of "trouble" (time of need) is like a "broken tooth" (perhaps a decaying, rotten tooth[305]) and a "foot out of joint" (crippled foot[306]). To place trust in the time of adversity ("trouble") in a person proven (or that proves) to be untrustworthy (betrayer of trust) is as painful as chewing with a broken tooth and walking on a dislocated foot.

In time of crisis, how often has it been said, "I know I shouldn't have, but I trusted him again and was disappointed again. And now I have to pay for it." Some of life's greatest anguish of soul has come from the hands of an unfaithful friend in the hour of deepest need. Wisdom says stop trusting him; place trust in someone trustworthy who will not let you down. Why repeat the bitter cycle that only disappoints and despairs again and again? Use prudent discretion in selecting the one to trust in the hour of adversity.

The crisis itself will prove whether it was a wise choice or not, for it is only in the midst of the fire that a friend's faithfulness is really tested. Some will fail while a few will pass. Prize highly all proven of trustworthiness. In reverse, be a trustworthy, faithful, dependable, caring and confidential friend to him in adversity. Prove yourself reliable. Bear the burdens of others heartily and compassionately even as you would have them bear yours. At all costs maintain the reputation of being a friend that may always be counted upon.

The Bottom Line: Obviously our first resort in the time of trouble is the Lord who has numerous times proven to be trustworthy to help. In turning to friends, don't become a victim of misplaced confidence. "Make sure thy friend" (Proverbs 6:3). "A friend loveth at all times, and a brother *is born for adversity*" (17:17).

47
Conscience, formed by God for a purpose
Proverbs 20:27

"The spirit of man is the candle of the LORD, searching all the inward parts of the belly."

The "spirit of man" (conscience; Reyburn and Fry say, "Spirit is literally 'breath,' which was said to be breathed into the body by God so that 'man became a living being' (Genesis 2:7). Here it seems to refer to the moral and intellectual understanding, which is often expressed by the term 'conscience' in English"[307]) is "the candle of the LORD" (searchlight) that "searches" (illuminates) all the "inward parts of the belly" (inmost being).

The human conscience is God's searchlight that reveals man's sin by the Holy Spirit. Upon the revelation and conviction of sin, the believer is to repent, making things right with God. It is imperative to maintain a "clean conscience," which is only possible by prompt and complete confession of sin (Hebrews 10:2; 1 Timothy 3:9). The conscience also is a divine instrument in decision-making. The sanctified conscience enables the believer to differentiate right from wrong, moral from immoral, truth from error. "A good conscience," states Adrian Rogers "is like a warning system that can keep us on course in the rough seas of our lives. If we choose to steer past its waving red flags, then we can expect to become shipwrecked."[308] As long as it has not been "seared [defiled] with a hot iron" (1 Timothy 4:2) by repetitive acts of sinful disobedience or wrong theology, it is highly effectual in its divine task. Titus 1:15 says, "Unto the pure all things are pure: but unto them that are defiled and unbelieving is nothing pure; but even their mind and conscience is defiled." The defiled conscience is not to be trusted or followed, only the one that is controlled by the Lord.

The highest component in the formation of conscience is the Holy Word of God. Scripture must not only be believed as the inerrant Word of God, but also internalized through personal and corporate instruction. This is a lifelong process. The conscience never has veto power over the Word of God.

The Bottom Line: The formation of a godly conscience is immeasurably important to success, happiness and godliness.

48
Conscience, its effect on sinner and saint
Proverbs 28:1

"The wicked flee when no man pursueth: but the righteous are bold as a lion."

The "wicked" (ungodly, evildoer) "flee when no man pursueth" (guilt over sin makes him afraid of his own shadow[309]; suspicious of every person; edgy at every sound). But the righteous are "bold as a lion" (a clear conscience provides rest and peace, bolstering trust in God whatever may happen. Young David stood courageous against the giant Goliath—1 Samuel 17:32[310]). To summarize, Kidner says that the sinner flees imagined pursuers prompted by a guilty conscience while the righteous have a clear conscience with no need to look over their shoulders.[311]

The wicked flees when he is not pursued, that is, not pursued by man; but he is chased after by his own indicting, accusatory, haunting and condemning conscience. The wicked learns the convicting conscience is inescapable, for he can never elude himself (though he makes the attempt through drugs, alcohol and prescription medication). Chrysostom says well, "Such is the nature of sin that it betrays while no one finds fault; it condemns whilst no one accuses; it makes the sinner a timid being, one that trembles at a sound—even as righteousness has the contrary effect. How doth the wicked flee when no man pursueth? He hath that within which drives him on, an accuser in his own conscience; and this he carries about everywhere; and just as it would be impossible to flee from himself, so neither can he escape the persecutor within; but wherever he goeth, he is scourged and hath an incurable wound."[312]

The conscience is a treasured gift from God to alarm about an encroaching temptation that it may be avoided and to torment with accusatory guilt in the event of sin to prompt immediate confession and forgiveness. An immature set of values or a conscience that has been "seared" with repetitive wrongdoing fails to provide a scripturally sound and strong *conscience* (1 Timothy 4:1–2; Acts 23:1). The conscience's divinely designed role to be the gatekeeper into the domain of one's heart is made stronger as the person matures spiritually in the Word of God and fellowship with God. Oswald Chambers remarks "Conscience is that ability within me that attaches itself to the highest standard I know and then continually reminds me of what that standard demands that I do. It is the eye of the soul which looks out either toward God or toward what we regard as the highest standard. This explains why conscience is different in different people."[313]

The Bottom Line: Maintain a clear and sensitive conscience by walking in harmony with God and His Word and immediately turning to God for cleansing of sin through confession upon doing wrong (instead of fleeing from it) and by instantly listening to it without debate. He that maintains a clear conscience is bold as a lion. Gregory said, "The lion is not afraid in the onset of beasts, because he knows well that he is stronger than them all. Whence the fearlessness of a righteous man is rightly compared to a lion, because when he beholds any rising against him, he returns to the confidence of his mind and knows that he overcomes all his adversaries because he loves Him alone whom he cannot in any way lose against his will."[314]

49
Consequence, the law of sowing and reaping
Proverbs 11:17–18
"The merciful man doeth good to his own soul: but he that is cruel troubleth his own flesh. The wicked worketh a deceitful work: but to him that soweth righteousness shall be a sure reward."

The "merciful man" (kind, good, loyal, loving) doeth "good to his own soul" (benefits himself by blessing others[315]): BUT he that is "cruel" (fierce, angry, violent[316]) "troubleth his own flesh" (cruelty and "anger brings trouble…raging works against a person as a part of divine justice"[317]). Whybray interprets, "The point of the proverb is that one's behavior towards others, whether good or bad, has unintended or unexpected consequences for oneself."[318] The "wicked" (foolish) worketh a "deceitful work" (unrighteous works) which has its own reward of divine judgment. But to him that "soweth righteousness" (lives an upright, just, chaste, holy life) shall be a "sure reward" (the divine approval of God: "Well done" and His favor).

A person that shows mercy and compassion to the needy is benefited from the deed; if he is cruel and mean toward them, he reaps troublesome consequences. The law of sowing and reaping is inescapable. What a man sows, that shall he reap now or at the Judgment or in both (Galatians 6:7). Man must make no mistake in understanding ("be not deceived") that his actions (like a farmer's seed) good or bad bear consequences (like a farmer's crop) that are inescapable. The saying is true that a man may choose his path but not its destination (you cannot walk the path of the wicked and expect it to give you the blessing of the righteous). He that sows wheat will reap wheat; he that sows briers and thistles will reap briers and thistles. The reaping is not divorced from the sowing. "The quality of the harvest is determined by the quality of the seed sown."[319]

The truth is well illustrated in "The Law of Small Potatoes." Years ago, Chinese farmers in the harvest of potatoes chose to keep the big ones to eat while using the small ones for reseeding. The practice in time resulted in the decrease in the size of the potatoes harvested to the size of marbles! Bitterly these farmers learned a valuable lesson not only about the sowing of seed for potatoes but also for life. A person cannot keep the best things for himself and use the leftovers for seed. Nature's law of sowing and reaping decrees that you get what is sown in kind. God's law decrees the same regarding attitudes and actions. Selfishness will never produce blessing. If you plant small potatoes, all that you may expect to reap is small potatoes. The law applies to every aspect of life.[320]

We sow a thought and reap an act;
We sow an act and reap a habit;
We sow a habit and reap a character;
We sow a character and reap a destiny. —Selected.

A man asked his servant to sow barley. The servant sowed oats. The master asked why he sowed oats. The servant replied, "I hoped to grow barley." The master said, "What a foolish idea! Who ever heard the like!" The servant replied, "You yourself constantly sow seeds of evil and yet expect to reap the fruits of virtue."[321]

The Bottom Line: The law of sowing and reaping states that you reap *what* you sow, reap *more* than you sow and reap *later* than when you sow. You get what you plant.

50
Control, the sovereignty of God
Proverbs 16:33

"The lot is cast into the lap; but the whole disposing thereof is of the LORD. *"*

The "lot" (the physical appearance is unknown [perhaps marked pebbles[322]], but its purpose was to ascertain the will of God about a decision, direction, etc. R. E. Murphy says, "The underlying belief is that the Lord, who determines all things, also determines the way the lots turn out."[323]) is "cast into the lap" (the fold of a person's garment when seated[324]); BUT the whole "disposing" (decision, outcome) is of the "LORD" (it was the Lord, not mere chance, that determined the outcome, how the "lots" would fall).

There is no such thing as luck or chance, for God is in total control (sovereign). John Gill, in his exposition of Proverbs 16:33, states, "This is to be ascribed not to blind chance and fortune, to the influence of the stars, or to any invisible created being, angel or devil, but to the Lord only. There is no such thing as chance or events by chance; those events which seem most fortuitous or contingent are all disposed, ordered and governed by the sovereign will of God."[325] H. A. Ironside concurs, saying, "There is no such thing as chance, though it seems so to the man who looks only 'under the sun' (Ecclesiastes 9:11). But a supreme Intelligence is over all things, controlling even when unseen and unrecognized."[326]

Haman cast lots to determine the day for the Jewish holocaust, but God overruled the lots (Esther 3:7). Billy Graham explains, "Christians don't believe their lives are ruled by luck or chance; they believe God is in control. Think about it. If life is random or ruled by chance, then it doesn't really have any higher purpose. In fact, if you take it to its logical conclusion, it means we are here by accident and everything that happens to us is strictly accidental and has no meaning. Or we may decide we are ruled by fate and have no control over our destiny."[327]

Deane and Taswell state, "The lot was employed religiously in cases where other means of decision were not suitable or available. It was not to supersede common prudence or careful investigation; but, for example, in trials where the evidence was conflicting and the judges could not determine the case, the merits were ascertained by lot (Proverbs 18:18). After the effusion [outpouring] of the Holy Spirit, the apostles never resorted to [the practice], and the Christian church has wisely repudiated the practice of all such modes of discovering the Divine will."[328] The last time the practice was used in Scripture was in the selection of Matthias to replace Judas as an apostle (Acts 1:26).

The Bottom Line: The words *lucky* and *unlucky* are void of meaning, having nothing to do with happenings in a person's life. It is God alone, not superstition, astrology or chance, that determines the course of man's life. Maclaren says, "Nothing happens by accident. Man's little province is bounded on all sides by God's, and the two touch. There is no neutral territory between [the two] where godless chance rules."[329]

51
Cordiality, expressing it enhances life
Proverbs 27:9

"Ointment and perfume rejoice the heart: so doth the sweetness of a man's friend by hearty counsel."

"Oil and perfume" (perhaps olive oil used cosmetically on the skin, and incense, a scented smoke[330]) make the heart "glad" (happy, jolly), and the "sweetness of a friend comes from his earnest counsel" (the caring, loving advice of a friend *sweetens the soul*[331]). Plöger translates, with many others, "the sweetness of a friend strengthens the spirit."[332]

That was so sweet of you. Though not very masculine, it expresses the effect of caring, loving advice from a friend. It sweetens life with exuberant joy, a healthier outlook and a stronger mental and spiritual disposition. Few things are treasured more than the sincere cordiality of a friend. *Cordiality* is defined by *Merriam-Webster Dictionary* as "sincere affection and kindness." It is expressed through giving a person "the time of day" without interruption, undivided attention, empathy, and viewing him or her as a person of worth and significance. Hearts and lives are lifted by the cordial but often hurt by the uncordial. The writer of Hebrews instructs, "Do not forget or neglect or refuse to extend hospitality to strangers [in the brotherhood—"being friendly, cordial, and gracious, sharing the comforts of your home and doing your part generously], for through it some have entertained angels without knowing it" (Hebrews 13:2 AMPC). Chuck Swindoll suggests four basic ingredients for projecting cordiality: *A warm smile; a solid handshake; direct eyeball-to-eyeball contact* (reflects the heart's deep feelings); *a word of encouragement* [compliment, commendation, uplifting word using their name].[333]

Interactions with classmates, fellow employees, students or John Doe at Dollar General should reflect the fruit of the Spirit that abides in you. "But the fruit of the Spirit is love, joy, peace, longsuffering [patience], gentleness, goodness, faith, meekness, temperance [self-control]" (Galatians 5:22–23). In the love chapter (1 Corinthians 13), Paul says that Christian love is never rude or arrogant but ever cordial (kind, respectful, interested, concerned). What about people with whom you disagree theologically or politically? The Christian is nevertheless to exhibit cordiality, not rudeness, making every effort not to "throw the baby out with the bathwater."

The Bottom Line: "Kindness is the language which the deaf man can hear and the blind can see."[334]

52
Counsel, divine guidance in the affairs of life
Proverbs 19:21
"There are many devices in a man's heart; nevertheless the counsel of the LORD, that shall stand."

There are "many devices" (plans) in a man's "heart" (mind; used here for the center of thoughts, plans, and reasoning[335]); nevertheless the "counsel of the Lord" (guidance, rule, advice; Criswell and Patterson say, "God's counsel is immutable [Hebrews 6:17], faithful [Isaiah 25:1], wonderful [Isaiah 9:6; 28:29], great [Jeremiah 32:19], sovereign [Daniel 4:35], and eternal [Ephesians 3:11]"[336]) shall "stand" ("win out"; God's plan will overrule man's). See Proverbs 16:1.

Matthew Henry states that God knows all of man's schemes or devices—devices against His counsel, devices without His counsel and devices unlike His counsel. But he says, "His counsel often breaks men's measures and baffles their devices; but their devices cannot in the least alter His counsel, nor disturb the proceedings of it, nor put Him upon new counsels."[337] See Proverbs 16:1, 9; Isaiah 14:24; 46:11.

There are many "devices" for success, pleasure, marriage, vocation, salvation, health, retirement and satisfaction of *appetites* in a man's heart. These contrivances, schemes and plans, however cleverly designed, will meet with grave disappointment if they be outside the "counsel of the

Lord." Whatever man plans or designs that contradicts God's counsel and Word is overruled, destined to utter failure.

It is biblical to plan, but only with God's direction, for His counsel is the one "that shall stand" (certainty, bring to pass His desires). See Jeremiah 44:28. "Man's device will not have success unless God governs it, whose purpose is unchangeable."[338] David said, "The steps of a good man are ordered by the LORD: and he delighteth in his way" (Psalm 37:23). Again he says, "I cry out to God Most High, to God who fulfills his purpose for me" (Psalm 57:2 ESV). God's divine plan ("counsel") always meets with success, fulfillment, happiness and peace.

W. A. Criswell summarizes, "Man's own way is marked by selfishness, folly and uncertainty (Proverbs 1:30, 31; 3:5; 12:15; 14:12, 14; 16:2, 9, 25; 21:2; 30:12). Though man devises his own way, his steps ultimately are not under his control (Psalm 2; 33:10, 11). The person who refuses to follow the Lord's counsel as it is found in Scripture pursues foolishness (Deuteronomy 32:28, 29). Godly counsel is built upon the foundational premise that there is an infinite and personal God who has revealed Himself through His written Word, the Bible, and through the living Word, Jesus Christ. Godly counsel is not man-centered (i.e., doing things one's own way, controlling one's behavior by one's own feelings or thoughts) but rather is God-centered (i.e., going God's way regardless of what one wants or thinks)."[339]

The Bottom Line: "O LORD, I know that the way of man is not in himself: it is not in man that walketh to direct his steps" (Jeremiah 10:23). "I will guide thee with mine eye" (Psalm 32:8). C. H. Spurgeon remarks, "As servants take their cue from the master's eye, and a nod or a wink is all that they require, so should we obey the slightest hints of our Master, not needing thunderbolts to startle our incorrigible sluggishness, but being controlled by whispers and love-touches."[340]

53
Counselors, the benefit of multiple advisors
Proverbs 11:14
"Where no counsel is, the people fall: but in the multitude of counsellors there is safety."

"Plans go wrong for lack of advice; many advisers bring success" (Proverbs 15:22 NLT).

Where no "counsel" (steermanship[341] or steerings; "spiritual guidance is like steering a ship"[342]; direction) is, the "people" (inhabitants of a city or land) "fall" (meet with ruin or disaster[343]): BUT in the "multitude" (numerous) of "counselors" (advisors) there is "safety" ("victory or success"[344]). See Proverbs 15:22; 20:18; 24:6. To summarize, "Two eyes see more than one, and mutual advice is in order to mutual assistance."[345]

George Lawson stated, "Wisdom teaches us not only to trust in God, but to take advantage of that wisdom which God has granted to other men, not merely for their own benefit."[346] President Woodrow Wilson remarked, "I not only use all the brain I have but also that I can borrow." As in Robert Frost's poem *The Road Not Taken,* all men face "forks" in life's highway, requiring decisions for which counsel is needed.

Major reasons why counselors should be consulted include one's spiritual immaturity (1 Corinthians 3:1); influence by this evil age and culture (Ephesians 4:18); a seared conscience (1 Timothy 4:2; Isaiah 5:20); gaining clear and sound, untainted advice about a decision or direction or its confirmation (Proverbs 24:6); receiving the perspective of another who is outside the situation; revealing personal "blind spots"; and drawing upon another's spiritual maturity and experience.

The time to seek advice is when it is seriously warranted, not about the petty things. David candidly states that counselors shouldn't be selected indiscriminately, but thoughtfully, based upon their godliness. "Blessed is the man that walketh not in the counsel of the ungodly, nor standeth in the way of sinners, nor sitteth in the seat of the scornful" (Psalm 1:1). The apostle Paul states one's advisor should be "full of goodness, filled with all knowledge, able also to admonish [teach]" (Romans 15:14).

Receive the advice cautiously. Matthew Henry explains, "In our private affairs we shall often find it to our advantage to advise with many. If they agree in their advice, our way will be the more clear; if they differ, we shall hear what is to be said on all sides and be the better able to determine."[347] Take what is shared, weigh it in the scales of Holy Scripture and personal discernment of God's leadership, then decide the issue. "The way of a fool is right in his own eyes, But a wise man is he who listens to counsel" (Proverbs 12:15 NASB). Elizabeth Elliot writes, "The disciplined Christian will be very careful what sort of counsel he seeks from others. Counsel that contradicts the written Word is ungodly counsel. Blessed is the man that walketh not in that."[348]

The Bottom Line: H. A. Ironside comments, "To weigh a matter in the presence of God, to invite the counsel of those whose experience and spirituality evidence ability to try the things that differ, is the course of wisdom. Rehoboam lost the major part of his kingdom by neglect of this important truth, and many a one has suffered grievous loss for the same disdain of counsel and help."[349]

54
Counselors, the competent
Proverbs 12:5
"The thoughts of the righteous are right: but the counsels of the wicked are deceit."

"Without counsel purposes are disappointed: but in the multitude of counsellors they are established" (Proverbs 15:22).

The "thoughts" ("refers not to just random thoughts, but to what is planned"[350]) of the "righteous" (the upright) are "right" (fair and honest): but the "counsels" (advice) of the "wicked" (foolish, ungodly) are "deceitful" (Buzzell says, "dishonest, self-serving and warped"[351]).

Not all are competent to counsel. Righteous counselors ("thoughts of the righteous") are a benefit, whereas the wicked kinds are detriments ("deceitful"). Endeavor to discern the difference between the good and bad, godly and ungodly counsel. John advises, "Beloved, believe not every spirit, but try the spirits whether they are of God" (1 John 4:1). And a major way to "test the spirits" is by weighing what is said on the scales of the Word of God. Does the counsel mesh with what God says, or does it seem to contradict? Francis Bacon identifies the person who is qualified to counsel: "He that gives good advice builds with one hand, he that gives good counsel and example builds with both, but he that gives good admonition and bad example builds with one hand and pulls down with the other."[352] Jesus said the blind cannot lead the blind (Luke 6:39).

Make reasonably sure the person(s) from whom you seek counsel is a godly, devout Christian who embraces biblical convictions morally, ethically and spiritually. Proverbs emphasizes the great value of righteous and wise counsel, "multitudes" of them. Airing thoughts, questions, doubts and hurts to the right sort of people is medicinal (spiritually and emotionally), insightful, soul-edifying, and clarifying. Ultimately however, advice rendered must bow in submission to that of the Lord who alone is the "Wonderful Counselor" (Isaiah 9:6). Listen to the godly wise, but place trust in God, not in them (Psalm 20:7).

The Bottom Line: The godly wise may be used of the Lord to direct our feet on the path of righteousness safely, soundly and steadfastly.

55
Counterfeit, warning about deception
Proverbs 26:23

"Burning lips and a wicked heart are like a potsherd covered with silver dross."

"Burning lips and a wicked heart" (not burning with affection but the appearance of affection—hypocrisy; *worn* by the wicked to deceive, as a disguise to conceal evil intentions, hatred; Henry says "a wicked heart disguising itself with burning lips, burning with the professions of love and friendship"[353]) are like a "potsherd covered with silver dross" (MacArthur says, "A cheap veneer of silver over a common clay pot hiding its commonness and fragility is like the deception spoken by evil people"[354]). H. A. Ironside summarizes, "His burning words are only uttered to cover the corruption of his purposes. Hating the object of his attentions, he will endeavor to deceive by fair speech; but his heart is full of abominations, and he is not to be trusted. He endeavors to cover his malice by falsehood and for a time may succeed, but eventually his true character shall be manifested openly."[355] See Matthew 26:14–16; Luke 22:48 (Judas' pretense of affection [kiss] and betrayal of Jesus).

Solomon states that many people are like a valueless clay pot that is covered with a coating of silver dross to give the impression they are something that they are not. Matthew 23:27–28 is the Old Testament Proverbs 26:23. In the passage Jesus says, "Woe unto you, scribes and Pharisees, hypocrites! for ye are like unto whited sepulchres, which indeed appear beautiful outward, but are within full of dead men's bones, and of all uncleanness. Even so ye also outwardly appear righteous unto men, but within ye are full of hypocrisy and iniquity." Be wary of hypocritical professions. Watch out for religious pretenders who say or do anything to win acclaim, influence, power, position, prestige or money. They look genuine ("covered with silver dross") but are counterfeit ("a valueless clay pot"). Man's outward appearance and actions can be deceitful ("appear beautiful outward"), therefore look beyond it to the inner chamber of the heart for truth.

The Christiano Brothers Christian film *The Pretender* is the story of a worldly teenager who pretends to be a Christian in order to date an unsuspecting Christian girl. He jumps through all the right hoops, even standing before the youth group bearing testimony of how he was "saved." But it all was a façade in order to date the girl. Ultimately the pretender's true character will be manifested, as it was with the worldly teen in the movie. That which is concealed will be revealed openly.

The Bottom Line: The wise and godly man is not taken in by another's outward appearance. He looks to see if profession and practice mesh on a consistent level. Albert Barnes cautions, "Lips glowing with affection uttering warm words of love, joined with a malignant heart, are like a piece of broken earthenware from the furnace, which glitters with the silver drops that stick to it but is itself worthless."[356]

56
Courage, its divine infusion and manifestation
Proverbs 28:1
"The righteous are bold as a lion."

"Be strong and of a good courage, fear not, nor be afraid of them: for the LORD thy God, he it is that doth go with thee; he will not fail thee, nor forsake thee" (Deuteronomy 31:6).

The "righteous" (upright, godly, honest) are "bold" ("means 'to trust; to be secure; to be confident'"[357]) as a "lion" (confidence in God gives the believer a lionlike courage, boldness to face any danger).

Jesus said, "People will insult you and hurt you. They will lie and say all kinds of evil things about you because you follow me. But when they do, you will be blessed. Rejoice and be glad, because you have a great reward waiting for you in heaven. People did the same evil things to the prophets who lived before you" (Matthew 5:11–12 NCV). Billy Graham said, "Courage is contagious. When a brave man takes a stand, the spines of others are often stiffened."[358] Mark Twain said of courage, "Courage is resistance to fear, mastery of fear, not absence of fear."[359] Courage is a holy confidence in Almighty God that He is greater than any enemy that you may encounter, that He will grant your feet stability and life success in every battle.

As Hugh Latimer and Nicholas Ridley were both about to be burned as heretics for their teachings and beliefs outside Balliol College, Oxford (October 16, 1555), Latimer exclaimed, "Be of good comfort, Master Ridley, and play the man! We shall this day light such a candle, by God's grace, in England, as I trust shall never be put out."[360] In facing persecution for mirroring Christian values and proclaiming the faith, *"play the man,"* lighting a fire on campus, athletic field, the political arena and job site for Christ that no man can extinguish. Don't cower down. Never be ashamed of Christ. Take the ribbing and rejection. Never recant your beliefs (Romans 1:16).

At the beginning of the twentieth century, Christians taking the Gospel to China met violent resistance from Chinese rebels (Boxer Rebellion). A mission school housing students studying for the ministry was attacked. The rebels offered freedom to every student who would trample over a cross laid at the school's only unblocked exit; the others would be shot. The first six students who walked out trampled over the cross to their freedom. The seventh student, a teenage girl, walked up to the cross and knelt down by it as if to pray for added strength, and then walked around it, only to meet her death in refusal to sell out. The remaining ninety-two students, infused with her faith and courage, did the same. Oh, the power of a righteous and courageous life to incite others to stand their ground for Christ regardless of cost or consequence!

Whence comes courage? The Holy Scriptures answer.

A righteous life

"The wicked flee when no man pursueth: but the righteous are bold as a lion" (Proverbs 28:1).

Exhibiting trust in the Lord

"Be of good courage, and he shall strengthen your heart, all ye that hope in the LORD" (Psalm 31:24).

The infilling of the Holy Spirit

"They were all filled with the Holy Ghost, and they spake the word of God with boldness" (Acts 4:31).

God's promises

"Be strong and of a good courage; be not afraid, neither be thou dismayed: for the LORD thy God is with thee whithersoever thou goest" (Joshua 1:9).

Knowledge that God is greater than the foe

"Greater is he that is in you, than he that is in the world" (1 John 4:4).

Waiting before the Lord

"Wait on the LORD…and he shall strengthen thine heart: wait, I say, on the LORD" (Psalm 27:14).

Examples of the courageous

"And many of the brethren in the Lord, waxing confident by my bonds, are much more bold to speak the word without fear" (Philippians 1:14).

The Bottom Line: C. S. Lewis said, "Courage is not simply one of the virtues but the form of every virtue at the testing point."[361] Socrates remarks, "He is a man of courage who does not run away but remains at his post and fights against the enemy."[362] *Roar loudly like a lion* in stemming the enemy's tide, knowing that "greater is he that is *in you,* than he that is in the world" (1 John 4:4).

57
Creation, the wisdom of God on display
Proverbs 3:19–20

"The LORD by wisdom hath founded the earth; by understanding hath he established the heavens. By his knowledge the depths are broken up, and the clouds drop down the dew."

The "Lord" (Jehovah) by "wisdom" (Ross says, "The wisdom that directs life is the same wisdom that created the universe"[363]) hath "founded the earth" (God is the Architect and Builder of the earth).

By His sovereign wisdom God *founded the earth,* when there was nothing, upon nothing (Job 26:7). *"Creatio ex nihilo"* (creation out of nothing)—the best and only reasonable explanation for the existence of the universe and all within it is that an intelligent Designer created it.

The divine Designer (God) *established the heavens,* setting the stars, planets, moons and suns in place. "He hath made the earth by his power, he hath established the world by his wisdom, and hath stretched out the heavens by his discretion" (Jeremiah 10:12).

By His *knowledge the depths are broken up* (formation of oceans and rivers). "Who laid the foundations of the earth, that it should not be removed for ever. Thou coveredst it with the deep as with a garment: the waters stood above the mountains. At thy rebuke they fled; at the voice of thy thunder they hasted away. They go up by the mountains; they go down by the valleys unto the place which thou hast founded for them. Thou hast set a bound that they may not pass over; that they turn not again to cover the earth. He sendeth the springs into the valleys, which run among the hills....He watereth the hills from his chambers: the earth is satisfied with the fruit of thy works" (Psalm 104:5–10; 13). The Architect of the world designed the clouds to soak up moisture, only to return it to the earth ("the clouds drop down the dew"). "Every particle of the universe glitters with infinite skill."[364]

Matthew Henry summarizes, "God has likewise established the heavens and directed all the motions of them in the best manner. The heavenly bodies are vast, yet there is no flaw in them; numerous, yet no disorder in them; the motion rapid, yet no wear or tear. The depths of the sea are broken up; and thence come the waters beneath the firmament; and the clouds drop down the dews, the waters from above the firmament, and all this by the divine wisdom and knowledge. Christ is that Wisdom by whom the worlds were made and still consist."[365] In considering God's handiwork in the world, we can only exclaim with the Psalmist, "O LORD, how manifold are thy works! in wisdom hast thou made them all: the earth is full of thy riches" (Psalm 104:24).

The Bottom Line: The foundation of wisdom is embracing God as Creator and Sustainer of all that exists, and His Son Jesus Christ as personal Lord and Savior.

58
Criticism, give it well that it be taken well
Proverbs 25:12
"As an earring of gold, and an ornament of fine gold, so is a wise reprover upon an obedient ear."

"The ear that heareth the reproof of life abideth among the wise" (Proverbs 15:31).

As an "earring of gold" (golden earring) and an "ornament of fine gold" (perhaps a valuable necklace to complement the earrings to further beautify[366]), so is a "wise reprover" (one who corrects, reprimands and hopefully convinces another of wrong conduct[367]) upon an "obedient ear" (a listening ear; "a person who is open to correction and change"[368]).

A listening ear ("obedient ear") is one that is open to constructive criticism for the purpose of correction. Not all reproofs are worthy, but such that are must be received graciously and heeded. Most of us have learned by personal experience that not all reprovers are good at the task; it's most difficult to hearken to correction when it is administered harshly, rashly and angrily. It is the "wise reprover" (gracious, gentle, tender, loving) that gains the "obedient ear." He chides with discretion, making every effort to see that the reproof which is *well given may well be taken*, that the spirit of the person will not be wounded. His choice words of criticism are beautifully and aptly framed "like apples of gold in pictures of silver" (Proverbs 25:11).

Winston Churchill remarked, "Criticism may not be agreeable, but it is necessary. It fulfils the same function as pain in the human body. It calls attention to an unhealthy state of things."[369] Learning to "take correction like a man" (hearing and applying it) is better than obtaining the finest of gold rings or necklaces, for it will save the person from shipwreck of life and soul. Matthew Henry states with regard to the reprover and the reproved, "Both will have their praise, the righteous for giving it so prudently and the reproved for taking it so patiently and making a good use of it. Others will commend them both, and they will have satisfaction in each other."[370] Elbert Hubbard wisely said, "The final proof of greatness lies in being able to endure criticism without resentment."[371]

Parents are to be *wise in the criticism or correction* of their children, lest they provoke them to anger (Ephesians 6:4). Reproof that puts them down; laughs *at* them rather than *with* them; makes hateful, detestable "looks" toward them; and withholds affection and gentleness wounds their spirits and exacts excessive punishment, harming more than it helps.

The Bottom Line: The goal of the reprover is to make the correction *acceptable* though indicting and convicting. Charles Bridges well remarks, "From its (reproving's) extreme difficulty, no duty calls for more delicacy of feeling and more 'meekness of wisdom.'"[372] The wise hear and hearken to correction eagerly and willingly to their own good.

59
Cursing, biblically prohibited and punished
Proverbs 20:20

"Whoso curseth his father or his mother, his lamp shall be put out in obscure darkness."

"Whoso" (children of any age) "curseth" (speech that dishonors, disdains, is disrespectful; "to take lightly; to treat as worthless; to treat contemptuously"[373]) his father or mother, his "lamp" (the very breath of life) shall be put "out" (refers to death [Proverbs 13:9; 24:20; Job 18:5–6]) in "obscure darkness" (i.e., pitch blackness as that which occurs when a candle is snuffed out in the darkest of night; ruin and destruction is final[374]). To summarize, to divorce or abandon oneself by contemptuous speech and behavior from parents that provide wise instruction for life (light) is to be thrust into darkness (without their light) to reap devastation and destruction. Deane and Taswell say, "He shall suffer in body and soul, in character, in fortune. He will find himself surrounded on all sides by midnight darkness, without escape, with no hope of Divine protection."[375] See Deuteronomy 27:16.

Cursing was not taken lightly in Old Testament days. A rebellious child who cursed his parents ("to give them scurrilous [gross, offensive] and opprobrious [defamatory] language"[376]) would lose honor, reputation, peace of mind; experience a shortened life; and the lamp of happiness would be forever extinguished.[377] Though the law stated a child who violated the fifth commandment was to be put to death (Exodus 21:17; Leviticus 20:9; Matthew 15:4), it was something seldom, if ever, carried out, due to the parents' mercy.[378] Cursing is not only forbidden for children toward parents, but for adults as well.

God wants every believer to use *only* words that are kind, loving, truthful and wholesome, never demeaning or deflating or derogatory (Colossians 4:6). Hear the Word of the Lord: "But now ye also put off all these; anger, wrath, malice, blasphemy, filthy communication out of your mouth" (Colossians 3:8). "Neither filthiness, nor foolish talking, nor jesting, which are not convenient: but rather giving of thanks" (Ephesians

5:4). First Peter 4:11 says, "If anyone speaks, they should do so as one who speaks the very words of God" (NIV).

Cursing or cussing negatively impacts reputation, injures the cause of Christ, deflates the opinion others have of the speaker, expresses lack of self-control, shows disrespect for others within hearing, hurts or influences others with its poison, exhibits poor and limited vocabulary and reveals grave disdain for God who forbids it. Despite the many (teachers, coaches, friends, actors, employees, other "believers") that speak profanely, it remains a detestable and punishable sin. George Washington said, "The foolish and wicked practice of profane cursing and swearing is a vice so mean and low that every person of sense and character detests and despises it."[379]

C. H. Spurgeon said, "I would to God that every blasphemer would abandon that vile, inexcusable, useless habit, which lowers men in society, defiles them before God, and ensures their condemnation. Filthy speech puts those who are guilty of it among the chief of sinners, and to them will certainly be meted out a terrible vengeance in that day when God shall solemnly curse those who have so glibly cursed themselves."[380]

I remember with deep regret that as a youth I picked up some bad words from friends. I vividly recall the time when their ugliness and wrongness brought conviction. The method I used to break the habit was to immediately ask God's forgiveness upon using a profane word (regardless whose presence I was in) and replace the bad word with a wholesome one. The effort paid off quickly and permanently. Personally, I do not watch television shows or movies that are laced with profanity. In fact, I seldom watch any television shows at all (unless occasionally reruns of the old, clean shows) opting to stick with movies from the forties, fifties and sixties on YouTube, Amazon or Netflix. Closely check ratings of movies to determine if they contain obscenities prior to viewing them. The Christian, among all people, has no business cursing or cussing or using any form of unclean and indecent speech.

James summarizes, "Doth a fountain send forth at the same place sweet water and bitter? Can the fig tree, my brethren, bear olive berries? either a vine, figs? so can no fountain both yield salt water and fresh" (James 3:11–12). The words that flow from your lips reveal what's in the heart. The Christian ought to gently rebuke fellow believers who practice this sin.

The Bottom Line: C. H. Spurgeon advises, "Keep clear of the man who does not value his own character. Beware of everyone who swears [cursing]; he who would blaspheme his Maker would make no bones of lying or stealing."[381] The mouth is a mirror of the soul. If Jesus is living and reigning within a person, it certainly will be manifest in his vocabulary.

60
Death, end-of-life consolation
Proverbs 4:11

"I have taught thee in the way of wisdom; I have led thee in right paths."

"I" (sage to pupil or father to son) "taught" (instruction) "thee" (son or pupil) in the "way of wisdom" (wisdom is divine discernment or understanding that enables man to do that which is right and pleasing unto the Lord (which is for his best good) in every course of action); I have "led thee in right paths" (Reyburn and Fry say, literally, "I have made you walk in the tracks of uprightness"[382]).

Deathbed consolation is found in several recollections. Primarily it is experienced in knowledge of salvation. To recall the time of entering into a personal relationship with Jesus Christ through the new birth instills hope, comfort and assurance as one embarks into eternity. There is consolation in remembering that throughout life one endeavored to use time, talent and treasure wisely in Christian service. It was not squandered in wantonness. Consolation is found in memories of souls won to Christ. It is also gained in memories of good done unto others in the name of Christ and that which awaits the believer in Heaven with Christ.

But to say upon the deathbed to one's children, "I have taught thee in the way of wisdom; I have led thee in the right paths" is by far the greatest consolation outside that of personal salvation. The sweet recollection of rearing children in the "way of wisdom" (salvation; uprightness; godliness; biblical instruction; right over wrong) and in the "right paths" (prayer; church; Christian service; stewardship; Bible study) relieves much of the "sting" of death. To be able to truthfully claim Proverbs 4:11 as a consolation at death, you need to instill its principles in parenting now. What horror and sorrow it is for parents on their deathbed to recall with

89

tearful regret their neglect of teaching their children to walk in the ways of the Lord through spiritual discipline, instruction and example!

The Bottom Line: Rearing children to walk in the right paths is challenging and at times difficult, but extremely fruitful for time and eternity. Upon departure from life here on earth, it will be of immeasurable consolation to know that your children are saved and walk in the right paths, that you failed not to "declare unto them the whole counsel of God" that forever transformed their lives.

61
Deceit, braggadocious promises unkept
Proverbs 25:14
"Whoso boasteth himself of a false gift is like clouds and wind without rain."

The man that "boasteth" (brags; "full of hot air") himself of a "false gift" (a gift promised but not given) is like "clouds and wind without rain" (as clouds that are "promising" of rain but don't deliver; they get attention but disappoint;[383] Indians of yesterday would say of him, "Heap big wind—no rain."[384]).

Some people brag about sizeable charitable gifts they never give or gave. They speak lies having man believe they are generous when in reality they are stingy and greedy. "They are like clouds and wind that give no rain." These arrogant, detestable pretenders parade about with false promises to give "rain" (financial support; assist financially in some big undertaking in a ministry) but never do. Boasting of gifts never given was the sin of Ananias and Sapphira which resulted in their premature deaths. Ananias laid only a part of the money from the sale of his property at the apostles' feet while giving the pretense of having given it all (Acts 5:1–11). It is noteworthy that Peter states the deceit was not only a sin against man but also against "the Holy Spirit" (Acts 5:3). The story indicates that God takes *truth speaking* seriously with regard to financial giving. Sadly, churches and other ministries have those who make financial promises without performing them.

An application may be made of the proverb with regard to *spiritual gifts.* William McDonald remarks, "A man may pretend to be a great teacher or preacher, but it is disappointing when he cannot live up to people's expectations."[385] Outside of the fact that deceitfully arrogant bragging about *giftedness* is nauseating, it's despicable and utterly dismaying. Never have I encountered as many "conceited" young ministers as in this generation. Pray that the haughty will be "brought down" (Luke 1:52) so as to hearken unto James' admonition to "humble yourselves in the presence of the Lord, and He will exalt you" (James 4:10 NASB). See Micah 6:8; 1 Peter 5:6. John Maxwell says, "There are two kinds of pride, both good and bad. 'Good pride' represents our dignity and self-respect. 'Bad pride' is the deadly sin of superiority that reeks of conceit and arrogance."[386]

The Bottom Line: Don't make false promises. Maintain an honorable reputation as a person who follows through with his checkbook on that which is pledged. Don't engage in idle, arrogant ("Look at me!") chatter about gifts never given.

62
Decisions, navigating by wisdom
Proverbs 2:6
"For the LORD giveth wisdom: out of his mouth cometh knowledge and understanding."

"Whether therefore ye eat, or drink, or whatsoever ye do, do all to the glory of God" (1 Corinthians 10:31).

For the "LORD" (Jehovah God who is "divine wisdom" and its source—Daniel 2:21; Job 28:23) "gives" (*will give it* only to him who seeks it wholeheartedly—James 1:5–7) "wisdom" (wisdom is divine discernment or understanding that enables man to do that which is right and pleasing unto the Lord—and which is for his best good—in every course of action). FROM His "mouth" (Holy Scripture is God's medium to impart wisdom; its every word is God-breathed or mouthed—2 Peter 1:21) comes "knowledge and understanding" (biblical and spiritual insight and instruction and know-how for living life successfully from God's perspective).

The Holy Scripture is God's *mouth* speaking instruction and direction (wisdom). You have on occasions asked, as have I, "Should I do this or not do this?" In such times how are you to decide what to do? Look to God's Word to provide navigation by asking several questions.

Does it violate Scripture? "All scripture is given by inspiration of God, and is profitable for doctrine, for reproof, for correction, for instruction in righteousness" (2 Timothy 3:16). The Bible clearly identifies things that are wrong and always will be wrong and from which we must abstain. When a matter is directly addressed in the Word of God, one's decision regarding it should be automatic without further debate or discussion.

Can I do this in Jesus' name? "And whatsoever ye do in word or deed, do all in the name of the Lord Jesus, giving thanks to God and the Father by him" (Colossians 3:17). This is a principle that is most helpful in determining questionable things. Simply put, Paul is stating that whatever action is being considered, whether by lip or in life, it must be done in Jesus' name (under His authority, with His blessing, as His representative) or be left undone.

Will it hurt others? "'We are allowed to do all things,' but not all things are good for us to do. 'We are allowed to do all things,' but not all things help others grow stronger" (1 Corinthians 10:23, NCV). The weaker-brother principle stated in 1 Corinthians 8:7–13) states that one ought to refrain from activities (even things that are okay to do) that would cause a spiritually immature Christian to stumble. Love for others overrules personal liberty (Romans 15:2–3).

How does it appear to others? "Abstain from all appearance of evil" (1 Thessalonians 5:22). The appearance of wrong ought to be avoided inasmuch as possible, for malicious gossip can enable a lie to do damage as much as a wrongful act. Additionally, the appearance of wrong injures the believer's testimony and damages the reputation. Apply this principle to places you go, people with whom you associate, and pleasures in which you engage.

Will it be a temptation? "Brothers and sisters, if someone in your group does something wrong, you who are spiritual should go to that person and gently help make him right again. But be careful, because you might be tempted to sin, too" (Galatians 6:1 NCV). Decisions about conduct should be based upon one's level of spiritual maturity and strength and weaknesses. Sadly, many well-meaning believers, in an attempt to help others with a sinful habit they once embraced, have been pulled back down into the same captivity. Avoid settings which pose a potential moral or spiritual threat.

Will it wound my conscience? "Cling to your faith in Christ, and keep your conscience clear. For some people have deliberately violated their consciences; as a result, their faith has been shipwrecked" (1 Timothy 1:19 NLT). The conscience is a wonderful "Checkpoint Charlie" regarding right and wrong if saturated with the Word and mind of God and not seared [a spiritually cauterized conscience] by repetitive sinning (1 Timothy 4:2). Often the Holy Spirit will speak about an activity or attitude through the conscience, prodding restraint. Oswald Chambers stated, "If I am in the habit of continually holding God's standard in front of me, my conscience will always direct me to God's perfect law and indicate what I should do. The question is, will I obey?"[387] Paul disciplined himself to "have always a conscience void of offence toward God, and toward men" (Acts 24:16), and so must every believer.

Will it stand at the judgment? "Every one of us shall give account of himself to God" (Romans 14:12). Decisions made will be judged at the Judgment Seat of Christ. Make sure your decisions will meet His approval at that hour.

Does it jettison or jeopardize my spiritual growth? "But all things are not expedient" (1 Corinthians 6:12). Many things are acceptable, but are they spiritually beneficial to growth in Christ? Ask, "Will this activity be a help or hindrance in my pursuit of holiness, intimacy with God, and building up in the faith?"

The Bottom Line: God promises "to give" wisdom to navigate life's maze to the earnest seeker (James 1:5). He dispenses it through several channels: from the Holy Spirit into man's heart, from saints in which He has instilled wisdom, and from the Holy Scriptures. But He is the only ultimate Source.

63
Deliberation, sound advice
Proverbs 20:18
"Every purpose is established by counsel: and with good advice make war."

Every "purpose" (plans or thoughts, ideas which someone intends to act upon[388]) is "established" (be firmly intentional in seeking advice to decide the proper course of action) by "counsel" (advice, but not just "advice"): AND with "good advice" (sound and scriptural advice; deliberation with the godly wise and experienced) make "war" (literally "war"[389] but figuratively may be applied to life's struggles, spiritual warfare). It is foolhardy and arrogant to count no one else worthy to advise you. "Without counsel purposes are disappointed [fail]: but in the multitude of counsellors they are established [successful]" (Proverbs 15:22). See Proverbs 11:14.

The Proverb, by referencing "war" envelops all plans ("every purpose"). Some theologians interpret the reference to war simply as an example of the need of planning to be successful in any undertaking.[390] Reyburn and Fry offer a different opinion: "There may therefore be a progression of thought in the whole saying: 'While it is necessary to get sound advice when making all kinds of plans, it is most necessary in the case of going to war.'"[391] The more serious the plans to be devised, the more far-reaching should be the counsel derived (Luke 14:31 in matters of war; Proverbs 25:8 in legal issues).

The best of sound and godly advice profits nothing unless it is heeded. King Rehoboam, the son of the wisest man that ever lived (Solomon), consulted with the old men that advised King Solomon. "And king Rehoboam consulted with the old men, that stood before Solomon his father while he yet lived, and said, How do ye advise that I may answer this people?" (1 Kings 12:6). The advice which they rendered was rejected. "But he forsook the counsel of the old men, which they had given him" (v. 8). Failure to heed the wise and godly old men's advice proved destructive to his reign (vv. 16–19). Amaziah was counseled by King Jehoash but "would not hear" (2 Kings 14:11). As a result, "Judah was put to the worse before Israel; and they fled every man to their tents" (v. 12).

Go to God first for direction. Beg and plead thy case with Him. Cry out in desperation for direction. Seek out godly, mature, experienced, knowledgeable and wise friends and associates for advice. H. A. Ironside implores, "Rashness and unthinking precipitation are to be deplored. Before beginning what may not readily be ended, it is well to count the cost, and to counsel with some who are known to be wise and prudent."[392] Bounce your ideas off others, listening receptively to their advice prior to executing your plans.

Matthew Henry advises, "It is good in everything to act with deliberation and to consult with ourselves at least, and, in matters of moment, with our friends too, before we determine, but especially to ask counsel of God and beg direction from Him and observe the guidance of this eye."[393]

The Bottom Line: Thwart arrogance and pride. Exhibit humility and seek advice from the godly, wise and experienced. Sit down with them face to face, as did Amaziah with Jehoash, to deliberate the wisest *move.* And upon receiving counsel, if deemed as of the Lord, heed it.

64
Diligence, secret to success
Proverbs 12:24

"The hand of the diligent shall bear rule: but the slothful shall be under tribute."

The "hand of the diligent" (Reyburn and Fry say "a hard working person, energetic"[394]) shall bear "rule" (attain positions of authority over others; upper hand): BUT the "slothful" (lazy) shall be under "tribute" (compulsory hard work; they will be placed in work that requires harder labor). Allen Ross summarizes, "Diligence at work determines success and advancement."[395]

Horace described Lucilius (*Satires 1.4 and Lucilius*) as "garrulous and lazy—lazy in the hard work of writing, that is; as for quantity—I'll say no more."[396] That is, "Lucilius," states Gregson Davis, "was lazy about writing—not too lazy to write too much, too lazy to write it well."[397] Diligence may be defined as "steady, earnest, and energetic effort: persevering application" *(Merriam-Webster)*; "constant, careful effort; perseverance; painstaking" (yourdictionary.com). A person may be disciplined to undertake a task (going to work, doing homework, daily devotional, writing) but not be "diligent" in its execution, as was the case with Lucilius. The diligent invest the necessary hard work (pay attention to even the "small details") and time in a task that it be done thoroughly and rightly. Regrettably, we find too many "Luciliuses" in the workplace and schoolhouse who are too lazy to do their work or studies well.

The principle of Proverbs 12:24 is that it's not only ability or academic prowess that brings success. It must be accompanied with quantitative work. H. A. Ironside remarks, "There must be earnest endeavor, otherwise talent and brilliancy count for nothing. The slothful, however much he may have the advantage of another in natural gifts and intelligence, will in the end be inferior to the patient [diligent] plodder."[398]

The Bottom Line: Take the measures necessary to do all that is assigned thoroughly and with excellence. "Write it well."

65
Direction, effect of wrong thinking, morally and theologically
Proverbs 14:12
"There is a way which seemeth right unto a man, but the end thereof are the ways of death."

There is a "way" (manner of life, conduct, belief system, world-view) which "seemeth" (the appearance of) "right" (upright, moral, ethical), BUT the "end" (results of; leads to) thereof are the "ways of death" (Murphy says, "By death is meant a broad range of unhappy experiences, from simple adversity to one's [premature?] departure from this world"[399]). John R. Rice cautions, "I do not deny that the Devil has some pretty apples; I just say that all of them are fakes and that after you bite into them, you will find they have worms. All Satan's apples have worms."[400]

Not only "a way" but many ways seem right unto man (abortion; homosexuality; dishonesty; theft; alcohol and drugs; sexual immorality; vulgar and profane speech; retaliation; disrespect and dishonor to God, etc.). The eyes of him who sees no wrong or harm in these paths are deceived by the master deceiver, Satan (Revelation 12:9; John 8:44; 2 Corinthians 4:4). *What they see is not all that is to be seen.* Hidden from view is the devastating, destructive and damning "end" of such ways (presently and eternally). H. A. Ironside summarizes, "A way there is— yes, many such; but none can rightly be designated *the* way save Jesus only. The end of a way that seemeth right is death—death moral, death spiritual, death eternal, yet death conscious forever!"[401] Jesus is the only "way" that is right (John 14:6). The narrow way (Jesus) is neither as popular nor crowded as the broad way, but it leads not to destruction and Hell but to abundant life and Heaven (Matthew 7:13–14). The wages of sin is still separation from God (Romans 3:23; 6:23). The supreme gift of

God remains reconciliation to Him through Jesus' death at Calvary and subsequent resurrection (Romans 5:10).

Many ignorantly and sincerely believe that they are walking in the right direction (by right standards, rules, etc.), while in actuality they are not. "The way of a fool is right in his own eyes" (Proverbs 12:15).

Matthew Henry explains, "It seems right to themselves; they please themselves with a fancy that they are as they should be, that their opinions and practices are good and such as will bear them out. The way of ignorance and carelessness, the way of worldliness and earthly-mindedness, the way of sensuality and flesh-pleasing seem right to those that walk in them, as well as the way of hypocrisy in religion, external performances, partial reformations, and blind zeal. This they imagine will bring them to Heaven; they flatter themselves in their own eyes that all will be well at last."[402] But disaster awaits. Pray for the sinners' spiritual illumination to the truth that their fallacy be revealed before it's everlastingly too late. "To open their eyes, and to turn them from darkness to light, and from the power of Satan unto God, that they may receive forgiveness of sins, and inheritance among them which are sanctified by faith that is in me" (Acts 26:18).

The Bottom Line: The sinner is following the wrong light (though it seems to be the right light in his rationale) down the wrong path. Though the path is sprinkled with pleasure and fun, it is short-lived, for soon its destination is reached—Hell (Proverbs 5:5; 1 Timothy 4:2). "All Satan's apples have worms."

66
Direction, keep your eyes on the light
Proverbs 4:18

"But the path of the just is as the shining light, that shineth more and more unto the perfect day."

"The steps of a good man are ordered by the LORD: and he delighteth in his way" (Psalm 37:23).

"But" (about to make a contrast of the way of the righteous with that of the wicked) the "path of the just" (righteous, honorable, right) is as a "shining light" (the sun at sunrise) that "shineth more and more" (the sun as the day progresses shines brighter, more brilliantly) unto the "perfect day" (the sun shines ever brighter until it is "full" day or "high-noon." Imagery is of high noon and not after because the father or sage desired to "indicate the full knowledge which the just attain in God, and which can know [has] no decline"[403]).

It is said of Moses that "he forsook Egypt, not fearing the wrath of the king: for he endured, as seeing him who is invisible" (Hebrews 11:27). Moses left Egypt not because of fear but because of divine guidance. Barclay observes, "For Moses to withdraw to Midian was not an act of fear; it was an act of courage. It showed the courage of the man who has learned to wait."[404] Obviously he would have preferred to stay to lead the Israelites out of horrendous bondage, but at that moment they were not ready.[405] It wasn't God's ordained timing for the Exodus. So Moses "goes" when in his heart he wants to "stay." Barclay remarks, "If he had gone on recklessly, he would simply have thrown his life away, and the deliverance from Egypt might never have happened. He was big enough and brave enough to wait until God said: 'Now is the hour.'"[406] A. S. Peake says, "The courage to abandon work on which one's heart is set and accept inaction cheerfully as the will of God is of the rarest and highest kind and can be created and sustained only by the clearest spiritual vision."[407]

The principle of Proverbs 4:18 teaches that God illuminates the path of the righteous continuously. As we walk that path in faith, the divine Light shines "more and more," clarifying and confirming God's perfect plan and will. Sometimes the hardest task in doing God's will is abandoning what is a successful and enjoyable work to venture out at His direction to attempt one with grave uncertainty.

The Bottom Line: With the words of A. C. Palmer, based upon 2 Samuel 15:15, declare:

Ready to go, ready to stay,
Ready my place to fill,
Ready for service lowly or great,
Ready to do His will.

67
Discernment, for victorious living
Proverbs 2:9

"Then shalt thou understand righteousness, and judgment, and equity; yea, every good path."

"Then" (points back to what previously was stated in Proverbs 2:1–8) shalt "thou" (the one being discipled) "understand" (learns, develops mental and spiritual capacity to discern right from wrong) "righteousness" (rightness), "judgment" (just) and "equity" (fair) [408]); yea, "every good path" (comprehensive in its widest decree; Deane and Taswell say "every course of action of which goodness is the characteristic"[409]).

Then shalt thou understand. Knowledge of and a righteous fear for God, and discernment and direction for living life happily and successfully are based upon *receiving* biblical instruction and applying it—*hiding* it in the heart (v. 1); *inclining the ear* unto wisdom—manifesting an insatiable hunger for God's Word (v. 2); *crying out* for more knowledge—"as one that is ready to perish for hunger begs hard for bread. Faint desires will not prevail; we must be importunate, as those that know the worth of knowledge and our own want of it. We must cry, as newborn babes, after the sincere milk of the word"[410] (v. 3); *seeking biblical knowledge* as he that searches for hid treasures—paying the price in discipline to dig (mine) out of God's Word nuggets of pure gold (v. 4).

Reception of and response to biblical instruction from the godly wise coupled with a man's own appetite for and studious discipline in Bible study will lead him in "every good path," for Scripture is "a lamp unto my feet, and a light unto my path" (Psalm 119:105). Holy Scripture will govern the entirety of life, providing discernment and discretion to walk securely, safely and happily, avoiding life's evil snares, always pleasing unto the Lord. Knowledge of the Holy One and Holy Scripture is never exhausted, nor is man's need ever lessened for both. The more knowledge possessed and applied, the surer the footing. "Fear of the Lord is the foundation of true wisdom. All who *obey his commandments will grow in wisdom*" (Psalm 111:10 NLT).

Traveling life's journey, a person needs a map that marks the safest way to Heaven, lest he become shipwrecked along the way. The Bible is such a map.

The Bottom Line: Allen Ross summarizes, "The disciple will develop the intellectual capacity and moral insight [based upon biblical knowledge] to discern what is 'right,' 'just,' and 'fair.' [This makes possible] a lifestyle that regularly leads in the direction of what is morally good."[411] Buzzell comments, "Wisdom gives positive, health-inducing moral benefits. It keeps one from evil and contributes to holiness."[412]

68
Discernment, provides protection
Proverbs 20:8
"A king that sitteth in the throne of judgment scattereth away all evil with his eyes."

A king that sitteth in the "throne of judgment" (as judge, the king renders just verdicts, seeing through the "smokescreens") "scattereth" (winnows) away all evil with his "eyes" (upon seeing evil, he issues a guilty verdict).

The text references him who rules upon judicial cases ("king") with keen discernment, rendering decisions between that which is true or false, right or wrong. Nothing wrong is allowed to remain in their presence. However, it is applicable to all, for everyone needs wisdom in winnowing (sifting) the chaff (bad) from the wheat (good) that he may 'keep his heart clean' and be 'pure from all sin' (Proverbs 20:9). The chief end of "discernment" is to discriminate or differentiate between good and evil. It is not based upon culture, what's trending or personal preference, but upon the Word of God. The writer of Hebrews declares, "But solid food is for those who are grown up [mature]. They are mature enough [...who through practice/exercise have trained their faculties/senses] to know the difference between good and evil" (Hebrews 5:14 EXB). The overarching teaching of Proverbs is the necessity of "wisdom" that one might "discern" dangerous people, places, pursuits and pleasures so that he might avoid harm.

The ability of the wise to *see through* the deceptive costume of evil and also weigh the rightness or wrongness of an issue comes from theological knowledge, Holy Spirit illumination (discernment) and experience. Truth should be so ingrained that when wrong or a questionable issue arises, it is easily seen ("with his eyes") and thus avoided. A. T. Robertson states, "Few things are more needed by modern Christians than precisely this intelligent moral insight."[413]

The Bottom Line: Sin blurs the moral, ethical and spiritual senses. The Holy Spirit, through God's Word, dispels the *blur* so that one is able to see clearly.

69
Discretion, its preventing power
Proverbs 2:11
"Discretion shall preserve thee, understanding shall keep thee."

"To give subtilty to the simple, to the young man knowledge and discretion" (Proverbs 1:4).

"Discretion" (knowledge to make the right decisions and choices; derived from wisdom; conduct based on godly precepts and principles) shall "preserve" (guard and protect from wicked behavior) thee, "understanding" (Deane and Taswell say "in the case of conflicting interests to decide what's the best"[414]) shall "keep thee" (the knowledge to make right choices "will protect him from blunders and their consequences"[415]).

Biblical *discretion* is God's wisdom in man at work preventing harm. "It tests what is uncertain and avoids danger."[416] Biblical *understanding* is godly discernment between that which is right and wrong, true and false. The text may therefore read, "The Truth of God controlling the heart (mind) of man will enable correct and honorable decisions, reactions and actions, guarding him from the enemy who ever seeks to lure him onto the wicked path."

> Great ability without discretion comes almost invariably to a tragic end.
> Leon Gambetta

Obviously for wisdom (wisdom is divine discernment that enables man to do that which is right and pleasing unto the Lord—which is for his best good—in every course of action) to protect, it must not only be received but also applied. George Lawson remarks, "This wisdom entering into their souls furnishes them with understanding to see their way and discretion to manage their affairs with prudence and judgment to the end.

This understanding with prudence is an antidote against the poisonous infection of evil men and strange women. It is, first, a means of preserving us from the snares of bad men."[417]

Simeon summarizes the development of discretion: "When once religion occupies the soul, it implants a principle there which thenceforth regulates the whole man. No longer does an anxiety about earthly things distract the mind. Pleasure, riches and honor are all subordinated to the welfare of the soul, and the will of God is the one and only rule of conduct to him. A regard for God's honor, too, will then operate, so as to give to all circumstances, whether of time or place, their legitimate influence, and to secure to him who is under its influence the approbation of the wise and good."[418]

Andrew Murray writes, "Discretion has its root in self-knowledge. The deeper my knowledge of my impotence and the sinfulness of my flesh, the greater is the need of watchfulness. Discretion has its power in faith. The Lord is our Keeper, and He does His keeping through the Spirit, keeping us in mind. It is from Him that our discretion comes."[419]

The Bottom Line: "Judgment is not upon all occasions required, but discretion always is" (Philip Stanhope, 4th Earl of Chesterfield).[420] Walter Scott comments, "Discretion is the perfection of reason, and a guide to us in all the duties of life."

70
Disputes, listen to both sides
Proverbs 18:17

"He that is first in his own cause seemeth just; but his neighbour cometh and searcheth him."

The man that is "first" (to give testimony to what occurred) in his "own cause" (personal dispute) "seemeth just" (to be the one wronged) *until* his "neighbor" (the other party involved in the dispute) "cometh" (to the courthouse, principal's office, parents' bedroom, boss's office) and "searcheth him" (cross-examination; fingers error in what the man stated).

There are always two sides to an issue. The person who testifies first presents facts favoring his side in the best possible convincing manner (truthful or not). However, judgment must be withheld until the "neighbor" (other party) has 'searched him' (cross-examined). Attorneys utilize this principle in the courtroom, but all would do well to use it in handling disputes between friends, children or acquaintances. Don't make rash or hasty judgments upon hearing only one side of a matter. Let your children see you pattern this principle in handling their disputes and behavior (when they are accused of wrongdoing).

The Bottom Line: H. A. Ironside summarizes the Proverb: "To decide a case on one-sided testimony is almost certain to result in a miscarriage of justice."[421]

71
Distractions, beware of the squirrels
Proverbs 4:25
"Let thine eyes look right on, and let thine eyelids look straight before thee."

"This one thing I do" (Philippians 3:13).

"Let" (fix) "thine" (the son whom the father instructs) "eyes look right on" (Deane and Taswell say it "is to fix the eyes steadily and unswervingly upon an object before them, not to allow the gaze to deflect either to the right hand or to the left"[422]). The second part of the verse virtually means the same, "Don't be distracted off the righteous path." Hubbard and Ogilvie summarize, the son must retain the words of the wise parent (v. 20). The "eyes" must be riveted to them in their written form, a reminder of the literacy of Israel's aristocracy (v. 21), and must at the same time be fixed on the path to spot any obstacle or deviation (v. 25)."[423]

Squirrels! Shep, my German shepherd, was obsessed with chasing squirrels. The moment he saw a squirrel, he immediately and completely was distracted from play, sleep, petting, obeying or even eating. The distraction caused loss of focus which led to straying from the issue at hand. Sound familiar?

You may not be distracted by literal *squirrels* but may often have your focus interrupted by squirrels of a different nature in your walk with and service to the Lord. Your *squirrels* may include entertainment (athletic and social events); Xbox; media (television, Netflix, radio); money (obsession with making more, having more); relationships (family, friends, boyfriend/girlfriend, fellow believers); job (fatigue from working long days and nights); hobbies and the cell phone (rings, chimes or talks, stealing spiritual focus). All know so well that good intentions often go awry due to a "momentary distraction." The allowed interruption blurs focus just long enough to negate desire to do the task. The intentional spiritual discipline or task is defeated by an insignificant *squirrel*.[424]

The name the author of Hebrews gave to distractions (squirrels) is "weights." He says, "Wherefore seeing we also are compassed about with so great a cloud of witnesses, let us lay aside every weight, and the sin which doth so easily beset us, and let us run with patience the race that is set before us" (Hebrews 12:1). Weights are things that are not bad in and of themselves but which become grave hindrances to living the Christian life to its fullest when they are indulged (or overindulged) in. The believer is to "lay aside EVERY weight" (remove it that it no longer harms his spiritual walk).

Some squirrels may require total abstinence; others only moderation. Getting distracted is a choice. An African proverb says, "The lion does not turn around when a small dog barks." You are a lion in pursuit of godliness and holiness of life; don't "turn around" (get distracted) when the small dog barks.

The Bottom Line: Stay focused. Don't chase the squirrels. Follow through on your intentions regarding daily quiet time, witnessing, praying, church, ministry, stewardship and living righteously. "The moral gaze is to be steadily fixed, because if it wanders indolently, lasciviously, aimlessly, it imperils the purity of the soul."[425]

72
Education, the wise never stop learning
Proverbs 18:15
"The heart of the prudent getteth knowledge; and the ear of the wise seeketh knowledge."

"It is senseless to pay tuition to educate a fool, since he has no heart for learning" (Proverbs 17:16 NKJV).

The "heart" (mind, the inner organ for reception of instruction[426]) of the "prudent" (wise; discerning) getteth knowledge; and the "ear" (the outer organ by which instruction is received[427]) of the wise "seeketh" (in Proverbs, biblical knowledge, discernment and understanding are continually sought by the wise[428]). Allen Ross summarizes, "The verse stresses the full acquisition of knowledge: the ear of the wise listens to instruction, and the heart of the wise discerns what is heard to acquire knowledge."[429]

Knowledge is ascertained through diligent discipline ("seeking"), and its possession enables and enhances success in every facet of life. Henry Ward Beecher said, "Education will not come of itself; it will never come unless you seek it; it will not come unless you take the first steps which lead to it; but, taking these steps, every man can acquire it."[430] The highest knowledge to gain is the knowledge of God, His divine Word and will, and His assignments.

The search for and acquisition of knowledge are continuous. Derek Kidner says, "Those who know most know best how little they know."[431] Aristotle wisely said, "Educating the mind without educating the heart is no education at all." Paul declares, "Study to shew thyself approved unto God, a workman that needeth not to be ashamed, rightly dividing the word of truth" (2 Timothy 2:15). Joshua said, "This book of the law shall not depart out of thy mouth; but thou shalt meditate therein day and night, that thou mayest observe to do according to all that is written therein: for then thou shalt make thy way prosperous, and then thou shalt have *good success*" (Joshua 1:8).

"Book" knowledge of the core subjects of math, science, history, geography and English is invaluable. Solomon states, "Get all the advice and instruction you can, so you will be wise the rest of your life" (Proverbs 19:20 NLT). Again he says, "If you become wise, you will be the one to benefit. If you scorn wisdom, you will be the one to suffer" (Proverbs 9:12 NLT). Dr. Thomas J. DeLaughter, one of my Old Testament professors in seminary, shared a contrast between the educated and the uneducated that has stuck with me through life. He said the man without an education looks into a well and sees its refreshing water but has no means to reach it. The educated, on the other hand, has a bucket attached to a rope to lower into the well and draw up all the water desired. Education (religious and secular) gives a person the tools necessary to get to what is needed for highest achievement and success in life.

The Bottom Line: Abigail Adams, mother of John Quincy Adams, said "Learning is not attained by chance; it must be sought for with ardor and attended to with diligence."[432] Henry David Thoreau said of the value of education, "What does education often do? It makes a straight-cut ditch of a free, meandering brook."[433]

73
Elderly, display respectfulness for
Proverbs 20:29

"The glory of young men is their strength: and the beauty of old men is the gray head."

The "beauty" ("splendid adornment"[434]) of old men is the "gray head" (white or gray hair is symbolic of a long life, experience, wisdom). Waltke says, "Though weak, the aged lay down the tracks along which immature youth through their power advance the faithful community's rich inheritance in everlasting life."[435] See 2 Corinthians 4:16–18.

The Lord expects the young to honor the aged. He said, "I command you to show respect for older people" (Leviticus 19:32 CEV).

The aged are oft misunderstood. Their loneliness and brokenness due to the death of most, if not all, of their friends is not comprehended or granted sympathy. Theirs is the buried generation; and among the buried are those by whom they were admired, appreciated, loved and even embraced dearly, and with whom they worshipped, served, and fellowshipped. Their lingering grief and sorrow for their deceased spouse and friends, their physical frailty and/or sickness that inhibits activity, their fixation upon one day at a time, their anxiety over making ends meet and their fear of facing the unknown are all often met with misapprehension, especially among the young.

Besides being often misunderstood, the elderly are often forgotten and forsaken. Children abandon them, friends desert them, society at large ignores them, the young overlook them, and employers don't want them, while others would euthanize them. How strange it is that relationships radically change simply by our growing older. Certainly not all relationships change drastically, but all will experience change to one degree or another.

The Bottom Line: Look out for the aged. Treat them with the respect and decency they deserve. Splash out sunshine and love upon them. Interact with them. Lower the bucket into the deep well of their wisdom. Do unto them as you would have others do unto you at their age.

74
Emotions, healing medicine for depression
Proverbs 17:22

A merry heart doeth good like a medicine: but a broken spirit drieth the bones."

A "merry" (cheerful; glad) "heart" (disposition of the soul) is like a "medicine" (here is the only place the Hebrew word for medicine is used[436]; refers to healing, relief[437]) that doeth "good" (betters the emotional state; defends the mind against satanic attack). In contrast, a "broken spirit" (crushed, depressed, disheartened) "drieth" (saps life's strength; to "go downhill in health" and even "to die slowly"[438]) the "bones" (the entire body is impacted). "The chariot's wheels," writes Charles Bridges, "are taken off, so that we drag 'heavily.' External things act upon the body, and through the body, upon the mind."[439] Deane and Taswell summarize, "A cheerful, contented disposition enables a man to resist the attacks of disease, the mind, as everyone knows, having most powerful influence over the body."[440]

George Lawson states, "The joys of God's salvation will be a mighty antidote against every grief and strengthen the body and soul against those bad impressions which the multiplied calamities of life too often make."[441] "Peace of mind [A healthy mind/heart] means a healthy body" (Proverbs 14:30 EXB).

The Bottom Line: The righteous possess healing medicine to cope with every emotional distress. It is the joy of the Lord which resides in the heart that is manifested in a cheerful disposition. This joy and gladness are ever springing up from the fountain of the soul in response to the great things God has wrought in its behalf. It's not faked (thus beneficial), as it is with the ungodly (thus unbeneficial). What's on the inside affects the mental and physical aspects of life. *Don't allow the joy to be suppressed when depressed, or you will be oppressed.*

75

Employers, whom you hire can make or break you
Proverbs 26:10

"As an archer that woundeth all, So is he that hireth a fool and he that hireth them that pass by" (ASV).

As an "archer" (he who shoots arrows indiscriminately, wildly[442]) that "woundeth all" (injures everyone), SO is "he" (employer) that "hireth" (employs) a "fool" (the unwise, insensible and perhaps unsuited for the position) and he that "hireth" ("pays wages to"[443]) them that "pass by" (Reyburn and Fry say "people who come and go in a public place"[444]). Walvoord and Zuck summarize, "The absurdity of an employer hiring a fool or any passerby is like a berserk archer indiscriminately shooting without aiming."[445]

Translators of Proverbs (Hebrew language) count this the most difficult verse in Proverbs to interpret. John MacArthur and others understand it to mean that a good leader (vision, discipline, charisma, knowledge, skill) is only as good (successful) as the people that he hires to assist in the work. Great potential leaders or bosses have failed, not due to their own inabilities, but because of those of the woeful workers employed. The principle is clear: don't hire (necessarily) the first person that walks through the door ("them that pass by"), for he is likely to "wound all" (the boss, other employees, church, business). "The king's favour is toward a wise servant: but his wrath is against him that causeth shame" (Proverbs 14:35).

Proceed cautiously and prayerfully when in search of a staff member, business associate or employee. Organize from top to bottom to maximize potential and profitability. A leader would do well not only to look to be surrounded with people of common vision and skill (who can do the work) but with those that supplement his weaknesses with their strengths (especially in Christian service). A church or business would be wise to allow their pastor or CEO latitude in staff or employee selection.

The Bottom Line: A person may possess the ability to be a successful boss, pastor or leader (accomplish what is undertaken), only to miserably fail if he hires the foolish.

76
Employment, the righteous work ethic
Proverbs 10:4

"He becometh poor that dealeth with a slack hand: but the hand of the diligent maketh rich."

"The desire of the slothful killeth him; for his hands refuse to labour" (Proverbs 21:25).

"Poor" (poverty stricken; to be in want of food and other necessities of life) is he who "works" (labors) with a "slack hand" (lazily and slothfully): BUT the hand of the "diligent" (the industrious and hardworking person[446]) makes "rich" (rich in contrast to being poor; Whybray says not wealthy but "sufficient prosperity to confer an economic security...."[447]; be without want [Proverbs 14:3]).

Don't serve your employer with a "negligent hand" (too lazy to do the work; deceptive as to how much work is done; "sleeping on the job"). The Christian, of all people, ought to give a full day's work for a full day's pay. It's *stealing* when he does otherwise. The Christian employee is to work with a *diligent hand* (industrious, hardworking, honorable and dependable). Godly work ethic pays off financially, with job security and to the glory of God.

The Bottom Line: Oswald Chambers said, "The proof that our relationship is right with God is that we do our best whether we feel inspired or not."[448] A godly work ethic is founded in a commitment to *excellence* in whatever is assigned. "And whatsoever ye do, do it heartily, as to the Lord, and not unto men" (Colossians 3:23).

77
Endurance, caution about straying as a bird
Proverbs 27:8

"As a bird that wandereth from her nest, so is a man that wandereth from his place."

As a "bird" that "wandereth" (strays; "flees the coop" without intending to return) from her "nest" (strays from the place of safety, its home, to the dangerous), just so is a "man" (any person; but is applicable especially to a young person that leaves home too soon unprepared to care for himself as with the prodigal of Luke 15:11–32[449]) that "wandereth" (intentional straying) from his "place" (sphere of duty).

The bird that wanders from its nest is exposed to danger and hardship. Just so, Solomon states, is the person who strays from God's designed sphere of service. "But now hath God set the members every one of them in the body, as it hath pleased him" (1 Corinthians 12:18). Kyle Yates remarks, "The highest form of obedience is to continue to remain at our post of duty when we cannot see why we are kept there."[450]

In God's appointed place is man's highest and richest benefit. To stray from it for whatever cause is to be as a homeless bird that deserts its nest.[451] See Jonah 1:3 and 2 Timothy 4:10. Matthew Henry explains, "Those that thus desert the post assigned to them are like a bird that wanders from her nest. It is an instance of their folly; they are like a silly bird; they are always wavering, like the wandering bird that hops from bough to bough and rests nowhere. It is unsafe; the bird that wanders is exposed; a man's place is his castle; he that quits it makes himself an easy prey to the fowler."[452]

"Let every man abide in the same calling wherein he was called" (1 Corinthians 7:20). Stick with the work God has assigned. Don't forsake its nest though the grass may appear greener on the other side of the fence. Not only may the principle of the Proverb be applied to one's place of work and life but also to the spiritual sphere.

C. H. Spurgeon remarks "We know that at the first our only comfort came from simply depending upon the finished work of Jesus, and yet we are so mad that we try to get comfort from that poor flesh of ours which has already been our encumbrance and will be our plague till it dies. Now the moment that a Christian wanders away from his place—that is, from the simplicity of his faith in Jesus—the moment he departs from that standing upon the solid rock of what Christ did and what Christ is and what Christ has promised, that moment he is like a bird that wanders from her nest. The bird away from her nest has no comfort; the instincts of nature make her feel during her incubation that the nest is her proper place. And when the Christian gets away from the cross, the newborn instincts within him make him feel that he is out of his proper position. The cross is the true rest of a Christian."[453] Spurgeon continues, "Are you not like a bird that has wandered from her nest? Believe me, there is no solid joy, no seraphic rapture, no hallowed peace this side of Heaven, except by living close under the shadow of the cross and nestling in the wounds of Jesus.

Oh! That we should be so foolish! The bird doth not forget her nest, but we do forget our Lord."[454]

The Bottom Line: Don't wander from intimate fellowship with Jesus Christ or the assigned place of service as "the wandering bird." To borrow Paul's words addressed to the captain of the sinking ship regarding its crew, I caution, "Except these [you] abide in the ship, ye cannot be saved" (Acts 27:31). Stay aboard the ship [God's ordained place of service] even in time of furious storm lest you experience shipwreck. Instruct youth to delay departure from the "nest" of parental guidance until their wings are "ready to fly" without assistance.

78
Enemies, treat with kindness
Proverbs 25:21–22
"If thine enemy be hungry, give him bread to eat; and if he be thirsty, give him water to drink: For thou shalt heap coals of fire upon his head, and the LORD shall reward thee."

If your "enemy" (one who hates you) be "hungry" (without food), give him "bread" (food) to eat; and if he be "thirsty" (without water), give him water to drink. In doing this you shall "heap coals of fire" (not actually, but figuratively; in showing kindness you heap hot embers or fiery coals made from burning wood upon his head, which "refers not to taking vengeance but most probably to producing a feeling of contrition, that is, causing the enemy to feel shame and thus to regret his actions or thoughts"[455]).

The Christian's response to one who is an "enemy" (literally, "one who hates you") is not to get even or do the person harm, but to exhibit love and kindness toward him while praying for his conversion and good. Our Lord instructs, "Love your enemies, bless them that curse you, do good to them that hate you, and pray for them which despitefully use you, and persecute you" (Matthew 5:44). In such display of kindness, the Christian is "heaping coals of fire upon his head" (Proverbs 25:22).

John MacArthur comments, "As metals are melted by placing fiery coals on them, so is the heart of an enemy softened by such kindness."[456] Matthew Henry further elucidates its meaning: "It will be a likely means to win upon them and bring them over to be reconciled to us; we shall mollify them as the refiner melts the metal in the crucible, not only by putting it over the fire, but by heaping coals of fire upon it. The way to turn an enemy into a friend is to act towards him in a friendly manner. If it do not gain him, it will aggravate his sin and punishment. Whether he relent towards thee or no, the Lord shall reward thee; He shall forgive thee who thus showest thyself to be of a forgiving spirit."[457]

A further insight is shared by Deane and Taswell: "It implies that though the sinner is benefited by the clemency shown to him, the requital of evil by good brings the offender to a better mind and aids his spiritual life. 'Coals of fire' are a metaphor for the penetrating pain of remorse and repentance. The unmerited kindness which he receives forces upon him the consciousness of his ill doing, which is accompanied by the sharp pain of regret."[458]

Edwin Markham (1852–1940), in the poem "Outwitted," reveals the believer's pursuit to win an enemy.

He drew a circle that shut me out—
Heretic, rebel, a thing to flout.
But Love and I had the wit to win:
We drew a circle that took him in!

The Bottom Line: Our exhibiting (with the right motive) the exact opposite of what an enemy expects may be the means of his repentance and conversion. Jesus Christ certainly acted accordingly toward us, "for while we were yet sinners, Christ died for us" (Romans 5:8).

79
Entanglements, frantically fight to be freed
Proverbs 6:5
"Deliver thyself as a roe from the hand of the hunter, and as a bird from the hand of the fowler."

"Deliver thyself" (nothing was to interfere with the matter's resolution being accomplished before another day dawned[459]) as a "roe" from the "hand" (grasp that results in captivity, bondage) of the "hunter" (the "neighbor" for whom a note was cosigned or debt underwritten [see Proverbs 6:3–4 for background]), and as a bird (any small bird[460]) from the hand of the "fowler" (bird hunter, sets traps for birds).

As birds struggle to be freed from the fowler's *net,* relentlessly the man who cosigned or underwrote a debt for a friend at an exorbitant interest rate must without delay desperately fight to be set free (Proverbs 6:1–5). It is a snare that has injured the reputation, financial stability and spiritual walk of many. Matthew Henry advises, "If we have been drawn into this snare, it will be our wisdom by all means, with all speed, to get out of it. This is a care which may well break thy sleep, and let it do so till thou hast got through. *Give not sleep to thy eyes till thou hast delivered thyself.* Strive and struggle to the utmost, and hasten with all speed, as a roe or a bird delivers herself out of this snare of the hunter or fowler. Delays are dangerous, and feeble efforts will not serve."[461]

Paul cautioned Timothy, "No man that warreth entangleth himself with the affairs of this life; that he may please him who hath chosen him to be a soldier" (2 Timothy 2:4). To be 'entangled with the affairs (business; occupation; pursuits) of life' is to give place to things that restrict and impede one's devotion and duty to God. "For if after they have escaped the pollutions of the world through the knowledge of the Lord and Saviour Jesus Christ, they are again entangled therein, and overcome" (2 Peter 2:20). To paraphrase Peter, since Christ has delivered you from the entanglements of this life, don't be entangled again; but should that happen and you are "overcome" again, be delivered immediately (fight to be set free as the gazelle and bird).

Many Christians that were *entanglement free* have shipwrecked by gradually becoming entangled with a sinful pleasure (pornography; alcohol; gambling; immorality) or secular pursuit (perhaps "innocent" and "acceptable" but done in excess). Let that not happen to you. "Let us lay aside every weight [entanglement], and the sin which doth so easily beset us, and let us run with patience the race that is set before us" (Hebrews 12:1).

The Bottom Line: "Stand fast therefore in the liberty wherewith Christ hath made us free, and be not entangled again with the yoke of bondage" (Galatians 5:1).

80
Enticement, allurement to wrong
Proverbs 16:29

"A violent man enticeth his neighbour, and leadeth him into the way that is not good."

A man of "violence" (cruel behavior, acts of dishonesty, high-handed in dealings[462]) "enticeth" (tempts, lures) "neighbors" (misery always loves company of friends) into "the way" (conduct—life of crime and wrongdoing) that is "not good" (offensive to God, injurious to others, and dishonorable and destructive to self).

The "violent" are cohorts of Satan that 'compass sea and land to make the righteous twofold more the child of hell than themselves' (Matthew 23:15). To state that these "lead" the upright and innocent into a way that "is not good"—forgetfulness of and disobedience to God, captivity to sin, abandonment of the church, possibly imprisonment, calamity and grave spiritual loss—is an understatement. An example of the enticement of the ungodly is stated in Proverbs 1:10–14. The righteous, in foreseeing the danger of enticing bait to do evil, must abstain, ever avoiding him who *dangles* it. Parents need to exhibit wisdom regarding with whom their children come in contact.

The Bottom Line: Inconceivable as it may seem, there are people that seek your physical and spiritual harm in the guise of friendship, fun and material gain. These are good at wearing masks (frauds), preventing the supreme motivation of the enticement to sin from being revealed until their purpose is achieved. Don't act foolishly or rashly. Don't be naive. Ponder the path's ending prior to its beginning. Watch out for the "Judas kiss."

81
Envy, caution against emulating the wicked
Proverbs 3:31
"Envy thou not the oppressor, and choose none of his ways."

Envy thou not the "oppressor" (wicked; unscrupulous), AND "choose none of his ways" (don't emulate the wicked fool in any manner). See Proverbs 24:1.

Asaph was envious of evildoers upon seeing their *apparent* prosperity. He said, "For I was envious at the foolish, when I saw the prosperity of the wicked. For there are no bands in their death: but their strength is firm. They are not in trouble as other men; neither are they plagued like other men. Therefore pride compasseth them about as a chain; violence covereth them as a garment" (Psalm 73:3–6).

Your faith may be tested by the example of evil men (Psalm 73:2). The psalmist says, "Therefore his people return hither: and waters of a full cup are wrung out to them" (verse 10). Matthew Henry remarks, "God's people are drawn away from him by the evil example of prosperous sinners, and in their infatuation seek to drink from the flowing stream of sinful pleasure."[463] Henry explains, based on Psalm 73:20, why envy of the wicked by the godly is foolish. He says, "What their prosperity now is—it is but an image, a vain show, a fashion of the world that passes away; it is not real, but imaginary, and it is only a corrupt imagination that makes it a happiness. It is not substance but a mere shadow; it is not what it seems to be, nor will it prove what we promise ourselves from it. It is as a dream which may please us a little while we are asleep, yet even then it disturbs our repose; but howsoever pleasing it is, it is all but a cheat, all false. When we awake we find it so."[464]

Asaph found the mind of God about the matter through wrestling in prayer in *the sanctuary of God* (Psalm 73:17–19). Deeply ashamed and grieved over his erroneous perception of the evildoer and desire to be as them, he confesses that he acted as a fool (Psalm 73:21–22).

The Bottom Line: Look not upon the wicked from earth's perspective, but from the eternal God's. At times the believer has to struggle and wrestle in prayer and meditation to clearly see *true truth* about the "prosperity" of the wicked.

82
Envy, it's rottenness to the bones
Proverbs 14:30
"Envy [is] *the rottenness of the bones"*

"Envy" (see below) is the "rottenness of the bones" (like a cancer, it ravages life from the inside out, bringing despair and turmoil and ultimately death).

James Stalker defines envy as "grief or displeasure at the good of another—the good consisting of wealth or fame or any other possession which men prize."[465] "Envy is rebellion," states Erwin Lutzer, "against God's leading in the lives of His children. It's saying that God has no right to bless someone else more than you."[466] Envy is an ugly-spirited attitude and action toward others. Abel's murder by Cain, Joseph's bitter treatment by his brothers, David's forced exile by Saul, Daniel's night in the den of lions, Jesus' arrest and trial all were precipitated by the rottenness of envy.

Envy prompts men to do some of the most vicious, malicious, and meanest things imaginable in efforts to make themselves appear better than others (Romans 1:29). Oswald Chambers says, "How do I know when I am envious of someone's being what I am not? When I am secretly rather glad, though my lips say the opposite, when that one stumbles."[467]

None are exempted from the poison of envy, not even the clergy. Ministers must not despise their counterparts who possess superior ability, talents, position and success in the work of the Gospel. James Stalker well says, "What! Do we grudge that humanity should be served and God glorified by powers superior to our own? Would we impoverish the cause of progress or of the Gospel by restricting it to the support of those inferior to ourselves? We cannot love the good cause very passionately if we do not welcome every talent consecrated to His service."[468]

The sin of envy, says Solomon, leads to "rottenness of the bones" (Proverbs 14:30). "The envious man is impoverished by another's riches and tormented by another man's happiness."[469] Envy literally eats away at the person, resulting in dire physical consequences.

In an old castle where Martin Luther spent one of his most eventful years one will find etched upon the wall a poem that reveals the cure to envy.

I love a thing that's fine,
Ev'n when it is not mine;
And though it never mine can be,
Yet it delights and gladdens me.

An ancient Greek legend depicts envy. A large statue honoring the winner of a race was erected in the town square to the chagrin of him who came in second. The man was so overcome with envy and jealousy that he plotted to destroy it. Nightly, while others were sleeping, he chipped away at the statue's foundation, intending that it would collapse while he was away. However, one night he chipped away more than was intended, which caused the giant marble to fall upon him. He died (as he lived) beneath the crushing weight of the man envy brought him to hate.

Envy can be thwarted. Paul discovered peace and tranquility with little or much, based upon an intimate relationship with the Lord

116

(Philippians 4:11–13). And so will every man. C. H. Spurgeon said, "The cure for envy lies in living under a constant sense of the divine presence, worshiping God and communing with Him all the day long, however long the day may seem. True religion lifts the soul into a higher region where the judgment becomes clearer and the desires are more elevated. The more of Heaven there is in our lives, the less of earth we shall covet. The fear of God casts out envy of men."[470]

Humility also cures envy. "The humble man," declares Andrew Murray, "looks upon every, the feeblest and unworthiest, child of God and honors him and prefers him in honor as the son of a King. The spirit of Him who washed the disciples' feet makes it a joy to us to be indeed the least, to be servants one of another. The humble man feels no jealousy or envy. He can praise God when others are preferred and blessed before him. He can bear to hear others praised and himself forgotten, because in God's presence he has learnt to say with Paul, 'I am nothing.' He has received the spirit of Jesus, who pleased not Himself and sought not His own honor, as the spirit of his life."[471]

The Bottom Line: "The cure for the sin of envy and jealousy," writes Jerry Bridges, "is to find our contentment in God."[472] Vance Havner said the eleventh commandment is "thou shalt not compare."

83
Ethics, moral code for conduct
Proverbs 22:17–19

"Bow down thine ear, and hear the words of the wise, and apply thine heart unto my knowledge. For it is a pleasant thing if thou keep them within thee; they shall withal be fitted in thy lips. That thy trust may be in the LORD, I have made known to thee this day, even to thee."

"Bow down thine ear" (be attentive; NCV says "to listen carefully;" NIV says "pay attention to"); and "hear" (listen; "He that hath ears to hear, let him hear"—Matthew 11:15); "the words of the wise" ("wise" is plural[473]; wisdom gathered from the wise), and "apply" (pursue, ponder, study and obey) thine heart unto my "knowledge" (instruction that he had ascertained from the wise—the Thirty Sayings that are shared [Proverbs 22:17–24:34]). "For" (motives for listening and obeying) it is a "pleasant thing" (delightful, joy) if thou "keep" (possess) "them" (points back to the words of the wise and "my knowledge") "within thee" ("the casket of the belly"[474]; mind and memory); they shall withal be "fitted in thy lips" ("be not ashamed to profess them openly; let them regulate thy words, teach thee wisdom and discretion"[475]; memorize to quote to others). That thy "trust" (confidence) may be in the "LORD" (the instruction in wisdom will bolster complete confidence in the Lord to enable the righteous, once aware of His will (divine plans), to do it at any cost or consequence, leaving the outcome in God's hand[476]). To summarize, the teacher instructs the student or disciple to soak in (allow permeation) biblical knowledge and understanding gained from the godly wise, fasten it as a nail in a sure place within the mind and memory, allow it to govern the affairs of life, and share it verbally with others for their edification and encouragement.

The Thirty Sayings of the Wise (Proverbs 22:17–24:34) as Proverbs at large imparts biblical ethics.

Ethics is defined as "moral principles that govern a person's behavior or the conducting of an activity."[477] Biblical ethics and morality are framed by God for all humanity and communicated through Holy Scripture. The man who embraces God's moral code by walking within its boundaries is counted wise (successful, happy, godly, and spared from destruction); he who ignores or detests it is counted foolish (failure, defeated and wicked, headed toward destruction). The contrast is made numerous times in Proverbs. Man's moral code is not to be culture, the conscience, the crowd or even the church. It is the unalterable holy standard of God set forth in Holy Scripture.

With Solomon I say, "Hear me now therefore, O ye children, and depart not from the words of my [God's] mouth" (Proverbs 5:7), and, "Turn not to the right hand nor to the left [don't get sidetracked; stay away from straying]: remove thy foot from evil" (Proverbs 4:27). Stick with God's moral compass to navigate life's treacherous waters. "The light of the righteous rejoiceth: but the lamp of the wicked shall be put out" (Proverbs 13:9).

Solomon teaches, "Incline thine ear unto wisdom, and apply thine heart to understanding [learn God's moral and ethical code and order life accordingly]" (Proverbs 2:2) and you will "understand righteousness, and judgment, and equity; yea, every good path" (v. 9), which is the key to a successful, happy and meaningful life. The psalmist declared, "Blessed are the undefiled in the way, Who walk in the law of the LORD! Blessed are those who keep His testimonies, Who seek Him with the whole heart!

They also do no iniquity; They walk in His ways" (Psalm 119:1–3 NKJV). Violation of or disregard for God's moral code brings devastation and ultimately destruction of life. (The same is true for a nation.) "There is a way which seemeth right unto a man, but the end thereof are the ways of death" (Proverbs 14:12). "He that trusteth in his own heart is a fool: but whoso walketh wisely, he shall be delivered" (Proverbs 28:26).

The Bottom Line: J. I. Packer comments, "God's laws, and the actions which they prescribe and prohibit, have fixed, intrinsic values."[478]

84
Etiquette, "table" manners for guests
Proverbs 25:6
"Put not forth thyself in the presence of the king, and stand not in the place of great men."

Don't honor or claim honor for yourself ("put not forth thyself") in the presence of high-ranking people by engaging in unrequested talk and seeking attention. "Stand not" refers to the place a person stood or sat determined by rank or the king's wishes.[479] The principle simply means that when in the presence of important people, don't try to pretend to be or act important by standing where they stand and sitting where they sit. The rule of etiquette is to sit in the "lower seat" furthest from the king (the important one), allowing him the choice to have you move to a place of honor if so deserved or desired.[480] H. A. Ironside remarks, "He who places his own estimate upon his importance and takes his place accordingly will likely rate himself far higher than others would and so be forced in shame to give place to abler and better men. The man who is content with the lowly seat may be called to a higher one if found to be deserving of such recognition."[481]

The principle is similar to that Jesus set forth in Luke 14:7–11. "And he put forth a parable to those which were bidden, when he marked how they chose out the chief rooms; saying unto them, When thou art bidden of any man to a wedding, sit not down in the highest room; lest a more honourable man than thou be bidden of him; And he that bade thee and him come and say to thee, Give this man place; and thou begin with shame to take the lowest room. But when thou art bidden, go and sit down in the lowest room; that when he that bade thee cometh, he may say unto thee,

Friend, go up higher: then shalt thou have worship in the presence of them that sit at meat with thee. For whosoever exalteth himself shall be abased; and he that humbleth himself shall be exalted." Pride prompts a man to rudely claim undeserved attention, to the disgust and disfavor from the very important people he seeks to impress.

The Bottom Line: Table manners are especially important when in the presence of those who are *important*. But more important is the denial of selfish desire and pride so you do not push yourself upon them as though you were one of them. That decision is for the king (the important one) to make. Exhibit genuine humility and modesty in behavior in the presence of all men, whether they are important or not.

85
Evil Plots, devisers of wrongdoing
Proverbs 14:22

"Do they not err that devise evil? but mercy and truth shall be to them that devise good."

Do "they" (the instigator of sinful deeds) not "err" (commit wrong, sin; stray from the righteous path) who "devise" (plot, plan, scheme; Trapp says "that plough it and plot it, that dig it and delve it, that whet their wits and beat their brains about it."[482]) "evil" (wrong, sinful)? BUT "mercy and truth" ("loyal-love and truth"[483]) shall be to them that "devise good" (plan or plot good actions [kindness] toward others[484]).

The question posed is one of the few in Proverbs and is rhetorical. He that doth evil certainly "errs," but he that formulates plans for others and himself to do wrong is an even greater sinner. David describes the ungodly to which Solomon refers: "They lie awake at night, hatching sinful plots. Their actions are never good. They make no attempt to turn from evil" (Psalm 36:4 NLT).

Deviseth evil against the righteous

Documentation exists stipulating the intrinsic, detailed and exhaustive time-consuming planning that the ungodly invested, thinking such would give them the edge in wrongdoing. Haman's devised plan to kill Mordecai came to naught (Esther 7:10). The Jews' conspiracy to kill Paul was thwarted (Acts 23:12, 23–24). The scheme of Sanballat, Tobiah and Geshem to lure Nehemiah into hiding was frustrated (Nehemiah 6:10–12).

Matthew Henry remarks, "They think that by sinning with craft and contrivance and carrying on their intrigues with more plot and artifice than others, they shall make a better hand of their sins than others do and come off better. But they are mistaken. God's justice cannot be outwitted."[485] The ungodly ought to take to heart Job 5:12: "He [God] disappointeth the devices of the crafty, so that their hands cannot perform their enterprise," and Psalms 21:11: "For they intended evil against thee: they imagined [plotted; devised] a mischievous device, which they are not able to perform [without success]." Believers take to heart the words of Isaiah: "No weapon that is formed against thee shall prosper" (Isaiah 54:17).

The Proverb principle also is applicable to the devising or planning of willful, wrong and wanton conduct (the unethical, immoral, illicit and dishonorable). Despite meticulous planning, that which is wrong ultimately will not succeed. George Lawson explains, "Whatever profit wicked men propose to themselves, they shall find to be loss; and if they should triumph in the accomplishment of their devices, a moment will put an end to their boasting."[486]

May the righteous be as industrious and energetic in devising good as the wicked are in devising bad. Good conduct always procures the favor and blessing of the Lord ("mercy and truth"). Oh, that we might lie *awake at night hatching out plans to achieve that which is good, holy, honorable and just* in relationships, ministry, missions, witnessing and every other needful undertaking!

The Bottom Line: A. B. Evans remarks, "The wicked 'err' egregiously in imagining for a moment that any man is placed here to be independent of God and of His commandments."[487]

86
Existence, from everlasting to everlasting thou art God
Proverbs 30:4
"Who hath ascended up into heaven, or descended? who hath gathered the wind in his fists? who hath bound the waters in a garment? who hath established all the ends of the earth? what is his name, and what is his son's name, if thou canst tell?"

"Who hath ascended up into heaven, or descended?" ("No man hath ascended up to heaven, but he that came down from heaven, even the Son of man which is in heaven" (John 3:13). Only Jesus has done both. At His incarnation He came down to earth; forty days after His resurrection He ascended back into Heaven.) "Who hath gathered the wind in his fists?" (See Amos 4:13.) "Who hath bound the waters in a garment?" (Clouds are the *garment* in which God wraps water [Job 26:8; 38:37].) "Who hath established all the ends of the earth?" (the extreme limits of the earth). The answer to the questions is clearly Almighty God. "What is his name, and what is his son's name?" (reference to *name* indicates understanding that the Creator of the universe is a "who" rather than a "what"; a person).

Such questions as Agur's man ponders due to his incapacity to fully comprehend the nature and attributes of the Creator and Sustainer of the world, God. God understands, for He says, "My thoughts are not your thoughts, neither are your ways my ways, saith the LORD. For as the heavens are higher than the earth, so are my ways higher than your ways, and my thoughts than your thoughts" (Isaiah 55:8–9). David, who was a 'man after God's own heart' (Acts 13:22), said, "Great is our Lord, and of great power: his understanding is infinite [beyond comprehension]" (Psalm 147:5).

This being true, one nonetheless can *touch the hem of His garment* regarding His existence, power and creation of all that exists. There has to be an explanation for all that begins to exist; nothing just exists (since God has always existed, He needed no cause; only things that begin to exist require a cause). It follows to say that if there is a cause for all that begins to exist, then there has to be a "First Cause" to set things in motion.

"If there is no First Cause, then the universe is like a railroad train moving without an engine. Each car's motion is explained, proximately, by the motion of the car in front of it. The caboose moves because the boxcar pulls it; the boxcar moves because the cattle car pulls it, etc. But there's no engine to pull the first car and thus the whole train. That would be impossible, of course. But that's what the universe is like if there is no *First Cause*. Dependent beings cannot cause themselves. They are dependent on their causes. If there's no Independent Being, then the whole chain of dependent beings is dependent on nothing and could not exist. But they do exist. Therefore, there is an Independent Being."[488] This "first cause" is God. He is the originating "domino" (Creator) that has set the world in motion.

There are three primary arguments of natural reasoning for God's existence. Stephen Olford explains each: *"the cosmological argument,* the cause-and-effect argument for God's existence (everything that exists outside of God Himself demands a cause); *the teleological argument,* the argument of design which states that whatever consists of parts requires a designer (God); *the anthropological argument,* man's moral nature gives argument of a moral governor to whom man is accountable (God). The sense of right and wrong and moral responsibility suggests the intuitive recognition of a moral ruler in the universe."[489]

The Bottom Line: The best and only reasonable explanation for the existence of the universe and all within it is that an intelligent designer created it. The Bible, God's authoritative Word, repetitively declares that the world and all within it were made by God.

87
Experience, it's a great teacher
Proverbs 24:32
"Then I saw, and considered it well: I looked upon it, and received instruction."

"Wisdom is with aged men, With long life is understanding" (Job 12:12 NASV).

Serious reflection ("considered it well") upon that which is experienced by others and yourself ("looked upon it") provides invaluable instruction. Having observed an ill-kept vineyard and a broken down wall, the proverb man, upon pondering what was seen, gained instruction— laziness, slothfulness, lack of discipline to work, and overindulgence in sleep lead to "poverty" (financial or material loss).

President Calvin Coolidge well said, "Knowledge comes, but wisdom lingers. It may not be difficult to store up in the mind a vast quantity of facts within a comparatively short time, but the ability to form judgments requires the severe discipline of hard work and the tempering heat of experience and maturity."[490] Wisdom is not attained in an instant, nor is her graduate diploma ever earned; it is developed in solitude with the Lord through the insight He instills through Holy Scriptures over a lifetime. Job concurs. He says, "Wisdom is with aged men, With long life is understanding" (Job 12:12 NASV). Leonardo da Vinci said, "Wisdom is the daughter of experience." But I add that experience is what is meshed out in daily life that was received from the Lord in the secret chamber.

I certainly am wiser with regard to ministry than I was at age 16 when I started. Knowledge gained in college and seminary and personal study was and is of immense value, but its *hammering* out into everyday life (experience) has been the best instructor. This "hands-on" instruction at times comes with a great price. I agree with Vernon Law, "Experience is a hard teacher because she gives the test first, the lesson afterward."[491] Don't take the test and miss the lesson. The godly or biblical lesson derived from the experience must be contemplated, ingested and digested to gain knowledge. "What is God teaching me through this? How might the experience or encounter better me? How might I apply it to my Christian life or ministry? What cautions or warnings does it present? In what way was my action wrong or injurious? How might it be done more profitably, spiritually and/or otherwise?"

The Bottom Line: Experience is a good teacher, provided she has a good student.

88
Eyes, the "rolling eyes" toward parents
Proverbs 30:17
"The eye that mocketh at his father, and despiseth to obey his mother, the ravens of the valley shall pick it out, and the young eagles shall eat it."

"He winketh with his eyes" (Proverbs 6:13).

The "eye" ("the index to the inner feeling"[492]) that "mocketh" (makes fun of, ridicules) at his father, and "despiseth" (shows scorn, contempt for) to "obey" (unheeding; disobeying) his mother, the "ravens of the valley shall pick it out, and the young eagles shall eat it" (at death the child's body left unburied will be devoured by flesh-consuming birds which first prey on the eyes).

R. E. Murphy says, "The precise implication of winking the eyes is not clear (Proverbs 6:13). It can be understood as a hostile gesture, perhaps like the magical spell of the "evil eye."[493] Hubbard and Ogilvie state, "The set of the eye can convey volumes of disrespect."[494] The eye is at times the "mind's instrument for expressing scorn and insubordination."[495] It can do its "mocking" (sneering resentment; to make fun of; refusal to obey) work without the assistance of the mouth. Were the Proverb written today, Agur may have worded it, "The eye that rolleth at his father and mother…" Parents often tell their defiant child, "Don't you roll those eyes at me?"

Inasmuch as the lustful eye is counted as the sin of sexual immorality (Matthew 5:27–28), the sneering or rolling eye is counted as the sin of actual contemptuous disobedience to parents. The eyes are the spout of the heart, displaying its inner feelings. "The eyes reveal what the heart conceals." Jesus said, "The light of the body is the eye: therefore when thine eye is single [without corruption, sinfulness], thy whole body also is full of light; but when thine eye is evil, thy body also is full of darkness" (Luke 11:34). You say more with the eyes (good and bad; positive and negative) than imaginable.

The severest of punishment is assigned to the disobedient child. Charles Bridges observes, "Certainly if the fifth commandment is 'the first…with promise' (Ephesians 6:2), it is also the first with judgment."[496] "The ravens [crows] of the valley shall pick it out [eyes], and the young eagles [vultures] shall eat it." A violent and horrific death will be the lot of the contemptuous child. His body shall be left unburied only to be devoured by the birds of the air.

In time past criminals testified upon the scaffold that what led them to such an end was the scorning of parental authority. Upon death their unburied bodies would hang from the gallows exposed to the birds of the air or be thrust into a valley. The eyes that showed contemptuous mockery toward his father were the first to be plucked out by the birds.[497] What a horrific picture of divine retribution that awaits the disobedient child, either literally or figuratively.

H. A. Ironside summarizes, "The disobedient mocker shall come to grief in a similar way to what is here described. Suddenly, but surely, he shall be bereft of the power of vision and stumble in the darkness, vainly trying to beat off the foes that have destroyed his happiness and would further ruin his life. It is the law of retribution which all have to bow to."[498]

The Bottom Line: Children cannot violate the fifth commandment without serious repercussion. Matthew Henry remarks, "Many who have come to an ignominious [disgraceful; shameful] end have owned that the wicked courses that brought them to it began in a contempt of their parents' authority."[499]

89
Fainting, the cause and effect of spiritual relapse
Proverbs 24:10
"If thou faint in the day of adversity, thy strength is small."

If thou "faint" (to falter; to show weakness and/or cowardice[500]) in the day of "adversity" (Reyburn and Fry say "trouble or distress"[501], pressure), thy "strength is small" (God, in His authority, grants man strength to withstand that which is encountered). Limited strength that leads to spiritual fainting is caused by man's failure to "grow in grace, and in the knowledge of our Lord and Saviour Jesus Christ" (2 Peter 3:18). To summarize, faintheartedness or *cowardice* to fulfill responsibilities and/or to cope successfully in pressing times of trouble or distress ("adversity") manifests spiritual immaturity or weakness. Many righteous that outwardly attest *strong strength* reveal in trouble or sorrow that it is not possessed.

Adversity tests the mettle of perceived and proclaimed strength, and sometimes we are found lacking. Elijah, the champion of the morning at Mt. Carmel became the coward of the evening when threatened by Jezebel. He fled to the wilderness in Beersheba. "But he himself went a day's journey into the wilderness, and came and sat down under a juniper tree: and he requested for himself that he might die; and said, It is enough; now, O LORD, take away my life; for I am not better than my fathers" (1 Kings 19:4). In stark contrast, when threatened with death, David's strength proved strong. "And David was greatly distressed; for the people spake of stoning him, because the soul of all the people was grieved, every man for his sons and for his daughters: but David encouraged [strengthened] himself in the LORD his God" (1 Samuel 30:6).

The Proverb indicates times of adversity will be everyone's lot ("If *thou* faint in the day…"). Its "day" of arrival is an unknown, as is its challenging crisis. We must do due diligence to prepare, lest our strength prove to be too "weak" or insufficient to withstand, resulting in collapse. The ship must be built for the storm, not just the calm.

We learn from Peter that perceived strength may be hollow. Boasting of strength, he professed that he would never deny the Lord; yet, upon facing the test, he failed it three times. "Jesus said unto him, Verily I say unto thee, That this night, before the cock crow, thou shalt deny me thrice. Peter said unto him, Though I should die with thee, yet will I not deny thee" (Matthew 26:34–35). The holiest of saints must confess they live in danger of overestimating their strength and faith as Peter did.

Prepare so as not to faint, by "growing" your faith. Faith, as the muscles in the body, may be strengthened. "When your faith is increased" (2 Corinthians 10:15); "your faith groweth exceedingly" (2 Thessalonians 1:3); "follow righteousness, *faith,* charity, peace" (2 Timothy 2:22); "increase our faith" (Luke 17:5). The primary way that faith is increased and strengthened is through the study and meditation upon Holy Scripture. "Faith cometh by hearing, and hearing by the word of God" (Romans 10:17). Dig deeper; go deeper in the Book that you might be "stedfast, unmoveable, always abounding in the work of the Lord" (1 Corinthians 15:58).

Trust God (faith) to envelop you in the midst of the storm with His *presence:* "The eternal God is thy refuge, and underneath are the everlasting arms" (Deuteronomy 33:27); His *promise:* "And call upon me in the day of trouble: I will deliver thee, and thou shalt glorify me" (Psalm 50:15); His *peace:* "Thou wilt keep him in perfect peace, whose mind is stayed on thee: because he trusteth in thee" (Isaiah 26:3) and His *provision:* "Blessed [gratefully praised and adored] be the God and Father of our Lord Jesus Christ, the Father of mercies and the God of all comfort, who comforts and encourages us in every trouble…For just as Christ's sufferings are ours in abundance [as they overflow to His followers], so also our comfort [our reassurance, our encouragement, our consolation] is abundant through Christ [it is truly more than enough to endure what we must]" (2 Corinthians 1:3–5 AMP).

An experienced old seaman told Richard Fuller, "In fierce storms, we must put the ship in a certain position and keep her there." Said Fuller, "This, Christian, is what you must do.…You must put your soul in one position and keep it there. You must stay upon the Lord; and, come what may—winds, waves, cross seas, thunder, lightning, frowning rocks, roaring breakers—no matter what, you must hold fast your confidence in God's faithfulness and His everlasting love in Christ Jesus."[502] "Even the youths shall faint and be weary, and the young men shall utterly fall: But they that wait upon the LORD shall renew their strength; they shall mount up with wings as eagles; they shall run, and not be weary; and they shall walk, *and not faint*" (Isaiah 40:30–31).

The Bottom Line: Past victories in adversity bear no proof of victories in your tomorrows. The holiest and strongest saint must *brace* steadfastly upon the Lord today, gathering strength to withstand tomorrow's storm. *If thy strength is small* (weak), now is the time to grow it. "He giveth power to the faint; and to them that have no might he increaseth strength" (Isaiah 40:29). With the resources God has made available for inner soul strengthening and stamina, there is no excuse for fainting.

90
Fake News, warning not to believe all that is heard
Proverbs 14:15
The simple believeth every word: but the prudent man looketh well to his going."

The "simple" (Deane and Taswell say, "The credulous fool believes all that he hears without proof or examination; having no fixed principles of his own, he is at the mercy of any adviser, and is easily led astray"[503]) "believe every word" they hear (open to all influences, gullible, swallows all he hears without checking or verifying its correctness, thus is easily led astray): BUT the "prudent" (clever, wise) "looketh well to his going" (deliberates, ponders, weighs the advice given based upon biblical teaching; Reyburn and Fry say "so not to be misled by untruth"[504]; whatever he hears is examined for accuracy and correctness). See Proverbs 13:16.

Italy's newest high school class is "Detecting Fake News." "Fake news drips drops of poison into our daily web diet, and we end up infected without even realizing it," Laura Boldrini, an Italian journalist and politician who helped launch the project, told the *Times*. "It's only right to give these kids the possibility to defend themselves from lies."[505] *Fake news* simply is the incorporation of untruths (lies) to accomplish the desired end. And it's not always easily detectable. *Fake news* dates back to the Garden of Eden when Satan altered what God stated. It was deceptively dangerous then, resulting in man's disobedience against God, and remains so today.

Sanballat was the bearer of *fake news* regarding Nehemiah, whom he opposed vehemently. He said, "The fifth time Sanballat sent his helper [servant; assistant] to me (Nehemiah), and in his hand was an unsealed [open] letter. This is what was written: A report is going around to all the nations, and Geshem [Gashmu; the same person as in 2:19] says it is true, that you and the Jewish people are planning to turn against the king [rebel; revolt] and that [therefore] you are rebuilding the wall. They say you are going [intending; planning; wishing] to be their king and that you have appointed [anointed; established] prophets to announce [proclaim] in Jerusalem: "There is a king of Judah!" (Nehemiah 6:5–7). Nehemiah debunked the *fake news* in responding, "Nothing you are saying is really happening. [We are not doing what you are saying.] You are just making it up [inventing/imagining them] in your own mind [heart]" (Nehemiah 6:8 EXB).

Fake news has the power to wreck marriages and lives; ruin reputations; bring down leaders (political and pastoral); negatively alter ethical and moral standards; create distrust, doubt and disdain; negatively impact a nation economically, politically and socially; injure financially; imprison the innocent; change public opinion against what is right; divide and spiritually harm a nation or church.

Sadly, the day of *fake news* is far from over. It is reported that by 2022 the majority of people in mature economies will consume more false information than true information (Gartner Research).[506] It is most expedient therefore for youth and adult alike to differentiate the one from the other.

Solomon cautions us not to be "fools," believing everything that is heard (spiritually, politically or otherwise). John advises, "My dear friends, don't believe everything you hear. Carefully weigh and examine what people tell you" (1 John 4:1 MSG). It is foolish to believe something simply because CNN, NBC, ABC, Fox News, Google, or a minister reports it as factual. Check it out personally; don't rely upon secular news networks or liberal theologians for the telling of the truth, the whole truth and nothing but the truth. This principle cuts across political and religious lines. Ralph Waldo Emerson has given us the solution to the fake news problem in saying, "The highest compact we can make with our fellow is 'let there be truth between us two forevermore.'"

C. H. Spurgeon well said, "A lie can travel halfway around the world while the truth is putting on its shoes." The same goes for *fake news. Real truth gets buried beneath the headlines given to fake news, to our personal and national hurt.*

The Bottom Line: Ask God for added wisdom (divine insight, understanding) and discernment in the detection of *fake news.* "Wise people," Solomon says, "think carefully about everything" they hear prior to believing it and adhering to it.

91
Family, its killjoy and ruin
Proverbs 19:13
A foolish son is the calamity of his father: and the contentions of a wife are a continual dropping."

A "foolish son" (a child that lives in disregard for God and His teachings and that of parents; walks the path of the ungodly) is the "calamity" (heartache, grief, pain) of his father: and the "contentions" (Reyburn and Fry say "refers to the contention, strife or trouble stirred up endlessly by a woman"[507]; bickering, quarrelsome) of a wife are a "continual dropping" (a constant irritation and disturber of peace and joy in the home).

"Calamity" (ruin; suffering) in the Hebrew is in the plural, indicating many and continual sorrows a rebellious son brings upon his father.[508] "He that begetteth a fool doeth it to his sorrow: and the father of a fool [rebellious, evil child] hath no joy" (Proverbs 17:21). A son that is lazy (will not keep a job), unteachable (will not study or be instructed), profane (makes mockery of the Christian faith), disrespectful (without honor for parents), sexually immoral (without restraint sexually), and lives riotously as the prodigal son in the "far country" is the grief of his father and likely will become the devastation of the family.

A quarrelsome wife is like a continual dripping of rain. The foolish-son problem is exacerbated when the wife sides with him (the foolish son), playing down the seriousness of the wrongs committed while undermining the punishment to be rendered. The refusal to join her husband in a united front in exacting godly and biblical discipline creates contention between them that further leads to the breakdown or ruin of the family. Many homes united in holy matrimony have become hellish messes all because of an obstinate, wicked child that pivoted his mother against his father. Either family problem (the foolish son or the quarrelsome wife) alone erodes the foundation of the home. Together they intensify the trouble, unhappiness and misery in the home, leading to its demise. It is unendurable without remedy.

The Bottom Line: A father's son ought to be the joy of his life, adding to the happiness of the home. "A wise son maketh a glad father" (Proverbs 10:1). Foolish sons must be rescued from Satan's strangle grip to keep it from tightening (prayer; pastor; Christian counsel therapist; church; Bible). Love must be tough. A father must never allow the wayward child to bring about the disintegration of their home. The wife that relentlessly nags, complains and quarrels makes life miserable for all the family. She must discipline and control the use of the tongue like the Proverbs 31 virtuous wife who "openeth her mouth with wisdom; and in her tongue is the law of kindness" (Proverbs 31:26).

92
Fear (of man), effect of intimidation
Proverbs 29:25

"The fear of man bringeth a snare: but whoso putteth his trust in the LORD shall be safe."

"Fear of man" (subjection to another's approval and expectations; cowardice to oppose another) bringeth a "snare" (a deceptive trap whose design conceals its danger and purpose) set to catch and captivate fowls and animals; a trap that is designed by the evil one to imprison a person emotionally and spiritually, sapping joy, peace, self-worth, and often purity. Fear masters the heart (man is controlled by what or whom he fears): BUT whoso "putteth" (places) his "trust" (confidence; see Proverbs 18:10; 28:18, 26) in the Lord shall be "safe" (Walvoord and Zuck say, "Security in the Lord removes intimidation by man"[509]; Deane and Taswell say, "Man safe through all dangers; fearing to offend God, living as always under His eye, he feels Divine protection and knows that whatever happens is for the best"[510]).

The fear of man's rejection, ridicule, disapproval or disdain immobilizes (hinders what should be done), demoralizes (participate in wrong activities to please), paralyzes (silences the tongue when we ought to speak up), and jeopardizes (relationship with God and man; happiness). Allowing the opinion of man to govern life (conforming to their preferences, dictates, whims) is not only unhealthy emotionally but highly destructive to the whole of life.

Spurgeon remarks, "Fear of man deadens conscience, distracts meditation, hinders holy activity, stops the mouth of testimony, and paralyzes the Christian's power. It is a cunning snare which some do not perceive, though they are already taken in it."[511] In *Two Ancient Proverbs,* he further elucidates upon the Proverb: "It was the fear of man that caused Pilate's name to become infamous in the history of the world and of the Church of God, and it will be infamous to all eternity. The fear of man led him to slay the Savior; take care that it does not lead you to do something of the same kind. Truly, 'the fear of man bringeth a snare,' even to the best of men. God save us from it and make us so brave that we shall never fear any man so as to do a wrong action!"[512]

But Solomon says the person who puts his trust in the Lord shall be safe. Spurgeon continues, "There is nobody living that any one of us, if he is a Christian, has any right to be afraid of. Trusting in God, we become safe not merely from fear, but from the consequences of defying fear. 'Whoso putteth his trust in the LORD shall be safe.' By trusting in the Lord and doing that which is right, he may be a great sufferer, but he shall be safe. A Christian man need never be afraid of anybody. If you are doing right, you have no cause to fear the greatest man who is serving the Devil."[513]

The Bottom Line: Fear is the sin of misplacing approval and authority in the creature instead of the Creator. "No man can serve two masters" (Matthew 6:24). "One fire puts out another. Nothing so effectually kills the fear of man as abundance of the fear of God. Faith is armor to the soul; and clothed with it, men enter the thick of the battle without fear of wounds."[514]

93
Fear (of sin), its safeguard against wrongdoing
Proverbs 28:14

"Happy is the man that feareth alway: but he that hardeneth his heart shall fall into mischief."

"Happy" (blessed, fortunate) is the man that "feareth alway" (fears his own weakness toward sin[515]; horrified over the possibility of moral failure; dreads the consequence of sinning): BUT "he" (the fool) that "hardeneth his heart" (stubborn, hardheaded who refuse to listen to biblical instruction) shall "fall into mischief" (calamity, trouble). Allen Ross summarizes, "The one who is always apprehensive about sin and its results will be more successful at avoiding it and finding God's blessing."[516]

The Christian is to continuously "fear" doing wrong (sinful; evil deeds). Without "fear" of spiritual or moral failure, the believer becomes self-confident in his own strength not to waver or suffer shipwreck. Paul bears out the principle of the Proverb in saying, "Wherefore let him that thinketh he standeth take heed lest he fall" (1 Corinthians 10:12).

It is wholesome, holy and healthy to fear moral or spiritual slippage that grieves the Holy Spirit; injures testimony, reputation and family; and brings disgrace unto the name of God. Fear of falling prompts dependence upon God to sustain us; avoidance of likely "snares"; accountability to others; and the disciplines of prayer, Bible meditation and worship. Righteous fear of doing wrong serves as the believer's strong ally and guardian in its prevention. Wilson remarks, "There is no sin which a man ought not to fear or to think himself capable of committing, since we have in our corrupt will the seeds of every sin."[517] The believer that, in contrast, "hardeneth his heart" (acts stubbornly) toward walking in the fear of doing wrong is riding for a fall (calamity; bad end). "Pride goeth before destruction, and an haughty spirit before a fall" (Proverbs 16:18). It is foolish to think that you are beyond relapse.

The Bottom Line: "Thou standest by faith. Be not highminded, but fear" (Romans 11:20). Spiritual giants greater than yourself have been slain (King David; Samson; Peter; Demas). Happiness will be the estate of the man who applies the principle (it is joyous not to suffer shipwreck of soul and life upon the rocks of sin).

94

Fear (of the Lord), prerequisite to true knowledge
Proverbs 1:7

"The fear of the LORD is the beginning of knowledge: but fools despise wisdom and instruction."

The "fear of the LORD" (Ross says, reverential attitude "that ultimately expresses reverential submission to the Lord's will"[518] [trusting and obeying]; includes obedience to His Word) is the "beginning" (starting point is with God for He alone is the source of true knowledge and

133

understanding) of "knowledge" (spiritual truths that are revealed in God's works, ways and Word): BUT "fools" (the ungodly, incorrigible; Waltke says, "They are blockheads because, deaf to wisdom, from their distorted moral vision, of which they are cocksure, they delight in twisting values that benefit the community;"[519] "idoits"[520]) "despise" (treat biblical knowledge and instruction as worthless and with grave disdain; no desire to know how they might live unto the Lord "all pleasing" [Colossians 1:10]).

John MacArthur remarks about the "fool," "While the unbeliever may make statements about life and truth, he does not have true or ultimate knowledge until he is in a redemptive relationship of reverential awe with God."[521] Solomon emphasizes that the foundation of all wisdom and knowledge is the fear of the Lord. This fear is twofold in its nature. First, the fear is a deep-seated reverence for the thrice holy God (Isaiah 6:3) who is the Creator and Sustainer of all that exists. "The Lord of Hosts, him you shall regard as holy; let him be your fear, and let him be your dread" (Isaiah 8:13 RSV).

Holy, holy, holy, merciful and mighty!
God in three Persons, blessed Trinity

Holy, holy, holy! though the darkness hide Thee,
Though the eye of sinful man
Thy glory may not see;
Only Thou art holy; there is none beside Thee,
Perfect in power, in love, and purity.   ~ Reginald Heber

The second aspect of the *fear of the Lord* is the heart manifestation of love, honor and loyalty for His person and obedience to His law and counsel. Wardlaw summarizes, "We truly fear God just in proportion as we truly love him."[522] "How blessed is everyone who fears the LORD, Who walks in His ways" (Psalm 128:1 NASB). They that fear the Lord will have their names written in the Book of Remembrance. Malachi states, "Then those who feared the LORD spoke to one another, and the LORD gave attention and heard it, and a book of remembrance was written before Him for those who fear the LORD and who esteem His name. 'They will be Mine,' says the LORD of Hosts, 'on the day when I prepare My own possession, and I will spare them as a man spares his own son who serves him'" (Malachi 3:16–17 NASB).

It is notable that Solomon says that to fear the Lord is the *foundation* ("beginning") of true wisdom and knowledge. Paul hits a similar note in saying, "For other foundation can no man lay than that is laid, which is Jesus Christ. Now if any man build upon this foundation gold, silver, precious stones, wood, hay, stubble; Every man's work shall be made manifest: for the day shall declare it, because it shall be revealed by fire; and the fire shall try every man's work of what sort it is" (1 Corinthians 3:11–13). Jesus taught the importance of a firm foundation for the building of the edifice of life in the parable of two houses (Matthew 7:24–27).

The Bottom Line: God is to be submissively reverenced, wholeheartedly worshipped, obediently served and devotedly loved. S. S. Buzzell remarks, "One cannot gain knowledge of spiritual things if he begins at the wrong point, refusing to fear the Lord (i.e., to recognize God's character and respond by revering, trusting, worshiping, obeying, and serving Him)."[523]

95
Flattery, it will get you somewhere (but the wrong "where")
Proverbs 26:28
"A flattering mouth worketh ruin."

"Watch out for anyone who tells lies and flatters—they are out to get you" (Proverbs 26:28 CEV).

A "flattering mouth" (deceptive talk to achieve devious ends) works "ruin" (destruction).

Flattery simply is insincere praise. Flattery sets man up for ruin unexpectedly because of its very nature; it touches man's "sweet spot," ego. When it is given, it is eagerly and wholeheartedly believed and treasured without thought of harm. Flattery harms in several regards. It puffs up the overestimation of self that leads to the attempt of a task beyond one's capability or competency.[524]

The witty London pastor C. H. Spurgeon remarks, "I dare say that if any cautious flatterer will assure me that I am a very wise person, I shall before long come to the conclusion that he is a remarkably sensible and far-seeing individual. If anyone should accuse you of a virtue which you never possessed, if he would but persevere long enough with his pleasing insinuation, you will begin to smile inwardly and hint to your conscience that there are latent excellencies about you which this man with prophetic glance has discovered."[525] It engenders a false estimation of self that is counter to the teaching "not to estimate and think of himself more highly than he ought [not to have an exaggerated opinion of his own importance], but to rate his ability with sober judgment, each according to the degree of faith apportioned by God to him" (Romans 12:3 AMPC).

It endangers man's spiritual and material estate. With the former it promotes spiritual decline and decay; with the latter it leads to perilous decisions financially or otherwise.

Watch out for the flatterer, refusing to give place to harmful words dressed in appealing apparel. Spurgeon said, "Soft, smooth, oily words are most plentiful where truth and sincerity are most scarce."[526]

The Bottom Line: Abraham Lincoln was correct in stating that "knavery [untrustworthy, dishonest trickery] and flattery are blood relations." Commend but don't flatter (Proverbs 12:8).

96
Focus, spiritual tunnel vision
Proverbs 4:26
"Ponder the path of thy feet, and let all thy ways be established."

"Sensible people keep their eyes glued on wisdom, but a fool's eyes wander to the ends of the earth" (Proverbs 17:24 NLT).

"Ponder the path" (Reyburn and Fry say "consider; be careful as you go"[527]; to make straight; remove from life every impediment to walking righteously, morally, holy) of thy feet, and let "all thy ways be established" ("fixed and steadfast"[528]). Robert Alden summarizes, "Proverbs provides both a goal and route. The goal is successful living, and the route is the way of wisdom."[529] See Proverbs 4:11.

Giving serious consideration to one's conduct (righteous, godly) will result in life being happily and successfully established. R. E. Murphy comments, "The youth is to have 'tunnel' vision, without any blinking, as described in Proverbs 17:24: the perceptive person looks straight ahead at wisdom, but the eyes of a fool are on the ends of the earth."[530] "As the plowman," remarks H. A. Ironside, "cuts a straight furrow when the eye is on a distant point directly before him, so the Christian's path will be that of the just when the eye of the heart is fixed on the Lord Jesus, now ascended to Glory. But this involves likewise earnest concern about one's ways, that all may be established in accordance with the truth. Evil is to be judged and departed from, the foot turning neither to the right hand nor the left."[531]

Examine ("ponder") the path you are presently upon. Is it worldly or Christian? Is it agreeable or disagreeable with God? Are its governing "rules" those of culture or Holy Scripture? Is its goal selfish pleasure or God's glory? Are you deriving from it heartache or happiness? "The longer you walk in the wrong path, the harder it will be to get out of it into the right (the awful law of habit; the binding power of bad companionships, etc.)."[532] If you are upon the wrong path, now is the time to switch.

The Bottom Line: Farmers place blinders on mules to force their focus on the furrow being plowed. This device prohibits the mule from looking to the left or right, keeping him on course. Constantly pray on spiritual blinders, asking God to keep you plowing a straight furrow with regard to life.

97
Fool, an invitation to salvation
Proverbs 1:23
"Turn you at my reproof: behold, I will pour out my spirit unto you, I will make known my words unto you."

"Turn" (repentance, change of direction) you at "my" (Wisdom, which is God speaking) "reproof" (correction, reprimand): "behold" ("listen, what I am about to tell you is very important") I will "pour out" (wisdom is like a fire hydrant that is connected to great reservoirs of water ready to *gush out* upon all who "repent" and "listen" to biblical knowledge) "my" (again Wisdom, the Lord Almighty) "spirit" (the Holy Spirit; "And the spirit of the LORD shall rest upon him, the spirit of wisdom and understanding, the spirit of counsel and might, the spirit of knowledge and of the fear of the LORD" [Isaiah 11:2]), I will "make known" (reveal

clearly, expound) my "words" (teachings, doctrines, precepts, commandments) unto you.

The Proverb teaches the "fool" (foolish, unwise, sinner), regardless
of woeful estate, may be saved; if not, he would not be told to "turn"
(repent). The timing of the fool's conversion is not at his discretion or that
of others, but at the very moment of "reproof" (God's correction,
conviction, command) which has been clearly sounded to man's heart time
and again. God not only invites the sinner to be partaker of His grace,
mercy and love that cleanses and covers sin and saves the life presently
and eternally, but also enables the coming and acceptance ("I will pour out
my Spirit unto you").

Charles Spurgeon clarifies the point. "'No man can come, except he
be drawn, and I cannot.' Yes, but you may put a truth into such a shape
that it is a lie. Will you let me put that into the right shape? Every time
when a sinner *cannot,* the real reason is that he *will not.* All the *cannot*s in
the Bible about spiritual inability are tantamount to *will not*s. But when
you say, 'I cannot repent,' you mean, 'I will not—I will not seek; I will
not believe.' Now put it honestly to your own soul, for that is what you
mean, for if you would, you could. If the will were conquered, the power
would be sure to come with it. But the first difficulty is you will not; and
this is it—you will not seek eternal life; you will not escape from Hell; you
will not have Heaven; you will not be reconciled to God; you will not come
into Christ that you might have Christ. 'Do you want to come?' 'Yes, but
there is much I cannot do.' 'Aye! But there are means provided to help
you.' God the Holy Spirit helps you, yea, works mightily in you."[533]

John Ross McDuff, in *Sunsets on the Hebrew Mountains,* remarks,
"We have a glorious testimony, in the case of Manasseh, that no sinner
need despair. Manasseh is now stooping over the walls of Heaven in
company with Saul the blasphemer, Zacchaeus the extortioner, the
Magdalene…, the dying felon of Calvary, and proclaiming that for the
vilest sinner there is mercy. Yes, although this man had defied his God,
had scorned pious counsels, had added bloodshed and cruelty to rampant
unbelief and lawless lust, yet when the blast of God's trumpet sounded
over the apparently impregnable citadel of his heart, it fell to the dust; and
from that hour in which grace triumphed, its walls became 'Salvation and
[its] gates praise' (Isaiah 60:18). And that grace which saved Manasseh
can save every one of us—the poorest, the vilest, the most desponding."[534]

The Bottom Line: Ultimately the reason why men end up in Hell is faulty choosing. Jesus said, "And ye will not come to me, that ye might have life" (John 5:40). Oh, hear and hearken to the words of the Lord today as He once again speaks saying, "I call heaven and earth to record this day against you, that I have set before you life and death, blessing and cursing: therefore choose life, that both thou and thy seed may live" (Deuteronomy 30:19). All may be saved who will be saved.

98
Fool, close-minded to the truth
Proverbs 23:9

"Speak not in the ears of a fool: for he will despise the wisdom of thy words."

"Speak not in the ears" (don't waste time trying to instruct him; he will not listen) of a "fool" (the fool here is he that is completely closed-minded to truth): for he will "despise" (scorn, show contempt for) the "wisdom of thy words" (possesses no appetite for spiritual knowledge from you). See Matthew 7:6. R. E. Murphy summarizes, "Do not waste words on such a person who has no ear for what is said."[535]

Don't speak wisdom (wise words that proceed from biblical knowledge and understanding from a life of learning and experience) to "fools" that will despise it outright. The New Testament Proverbs 23:9 is Matthew 7:6, which states, "Give not that which is holy unto the dogs, neither cast ye your pearls before swine, lest they trample them under their feet, and turn again and rend you." In both, the advice is to avoid contentious arguments with the unreasonable and unconvincible. It's a waste of time, for regardless of the irrefutability of the argument presented, they will "trample them under their feet." Christians are to declare the Good News to all that will *hear* it, including "fools" (scorners, scoffers, mockers). At the outset in a witnessing encounter, it will be evident if the person will *receive* it; if not, don't shove it down their throats nor waste your time.

The Bottom Line: At the outset of a gospel presentation or that of a moral issue, make sure that you are not casting pearls before swine. Only those open-minded to truth will receive, not "despise," your words.

99
Fool, senselessness about sin
Proverbs 15:21

Folly is joy to him that is destitute of wisdom: but a man of understanding walketh uprightly. "

"Folly" (sin, wrongdoing; the absence of discipline to live right) is "joy" (happiness; there is pleasure in sin for a season [Hebrews 11:24–25]) to "him" (the foolish, perverse) that is "destitute" (senseless; "one who has not developed the ability to make proper choices"[536]): BUT a man of "understanding" (in contrast to the fool, the righteous have true knowledge and understanding of biblical teaching, which he appropriates) walketh "uprightly" (the fool walks the broad road of wickedness, while the righteous travels the narrow road of godliness [Matthew 7:13–14]). Reyburn and Fry summarize, "The person who has no thinking is always happy in his own stupid behavior."[537]

Sin, instead of being despicable, is delightful; and being loathed is loved by the fool (ungodly; wicked; lacking wisdom). In contrast, to the righteous ("upright") sin is abhorred and avoided, remorseful (grievous) and regretful. "The lost leap into sin and love it; the saved lapse into sin and loathe it." To the man who doesn't think *rightly,* sin is "fool's gold," prompting senseless conduct. Matthew Henry remarks, "It is the character of a wicked man that he takes pleasure in sin; he has an appetite to the bait and swallows it greedily and has no dread of the hook nor feels from it when he has swallowed it. Folly is joy to him—the folly of others is so, and his own much more."[538]

A teenager, in responding to my inquiry as to why he wasn't a Christian, said, "I guess I love my sin too much." All unbelievers like him have an insatiable appetite for sin which prevents their salvation. Why? Jesus said, "Ye are of your father the devil, and the lusts of your father ye will do" (John 8:44). A heart bent on doing wrong to satisfy its wanton lusts without regard to its disobedience toward God and consequence is indicative of Satan's occupancy and control. "And this is the condemnation, that light is come into the world, and men loved darkness rather than light, because their deeds were evil" (John 3:19).

The person instructed in the Word of God gains "understanding" of right and wrong, God and Satan, righteousness and sinfulness, Heaven and Hell, real happiness and *false joy,* and the way of abundant and eternal life through a personal relationship with Jesus Christ (John 14:6). Oh, that the "fool" might receive it as has the "wise." May the fool's eyes be opened to the discovery that "they that observe lying vanities forsake their own mercy" (Jonah 2:8).[539] And may the wise ever increase in knowledge of the Holy One and His Word that they may stand more solidly in the truth.

Evidence of salvation (God's grace wrought in man by faith that transforms life) is seen in change of attitude and action toward sin. He "walketh uprightly" (not only shuns it but 'hates the very garments spotted by it'—Jude 23) pleasing unto the Lord. The upright are not sinless, but they endeavor to be less sinful. A *bona fide* tackle for a football team misses a block occasionally but not ordinarily. The Christian aims at making every "block" but occasionally falters.

The Bottom Line: The fool engages in sin shamelessly and joyfully, while the Christian does so distraughtly and remorsefully.

100
Fools, find fun in doing wrong
Proverbs 10:23

"It is as sport to a fool to do mischief: but a man of understanding hath wisdom."

"Fools make a mock at sin: but among the righteous there is favour" (Proverbs 14:9).

It is as "sport" (laughter; "refers to what is exhilarating and pleasurable"[540]) to a "fool" (one that acts with stupidity bent on doing wrong) to do "mischief" ("to carry out a plan" to do wickedness[541]; sin, wrongdoing; Henry says, "Ungodly men bestow more pains to do mischief than would be needful to do good"[542]): BUT a man of "understanding" (he with godly discernment) hath "wisdom" (wisdom is divine discernment that enables man to do that which is right and pleasing unto the Lord— which is for his best good—in every course of action) and counts it a great pleasure or joy.

It is a "sport" (laughter, fun, amusement, favorite pastime) for a fool to do wickedly. "It is," remarks Matthew Henry, "as natural to him, and as pleasant, as it is to a man to laugh."[543] The foolish takes his sinful conduct as lightly as a joke and the threat of punishment the same. Seemingly he fears no consequences for evil behavior. H. A. Ironside elucidates, "What the wise man would shrink from with horror, the fool will practice, not only with complacency, but with positive fiendish delight."[544]

The nature of the fool's "mischief" (wrongdoing) is alarming and horrifying. The word translated "mischief" or "to do wrong" is used in Scripture to refer to blatant, serious crimes such as incest, adultery and idolatry (Leviticus 18:17; Job 31:11; Jeremiah 13:27). "Mischief" may be translated "lewdness."[545] "Fools make a mock of sin" (Proverbs 14:9). Maclaren interprets, "Sin tempts men into its clutches and then gibes and taunts them."[546]

Sin mocks us by its broken promises. It promises what it cannot deliver. It promises good, pleasure, prosperity, happiness, popularity for wrongdoing, which may momentarily be attained only to disappear. It is always foolish to attempt to buy happiness or any of these other things by doing wrong.

Sin mocks us by making us its slaves. It tells us that one sin won't hurt us, that it can be stopped at will anytime desired. But it is mocking us, for it well knows the inescapable web that sin weaves one strand at a time. Years ago, in the cruel day of slavery, men were overheard on the African coast tempting the natives to board their ship with wonderful promises; but once aboard, sadly came the hatches and, if needed, the chains.

Sin mocks in its unforeseen consequences. Man will reap that which was sown. The train he put in motion in the far distant past or yesterday will arrive at the station. "We are what we are because we were long ago what we were."[547]

He that is flippant with regard to iniquity must be warned that it is a fearful thing to mock God, that suddenly He will execute judgment upon him without remedy. The fool who refuses to repent had better enjoy (if you can say that) the thrills of sin as long as possible, for a day is coming in outer darkness in Hell where the mocking smile and laughter will be eternally erased. The fool may scoff at the idea of future punishment, but that doesn't in any wise dismiss its reality.

"I fear that in too many places," remarks C. H. Spurgeon, "the doctrine of future punishment is rejected and laughed at as a fancy, but the day will come when it shall be known to be a reality. The men of Noah's generation laughed at the foolish old man, as they thought him, who told them to take heed, for the world should be drowned. But when they were climbing to the treetops and floods were following them, did they then say that the prophecy was untrue?"[548]

The Bottom Line: The fool only sees foolishness in the counsel of God. He hard-headedly embraces the hedonistic philosophy to "eat, drink and be merry" without thought or worry of divine retribution. He knows not that sin mocks all its consumers.

101
Forgiveness, divine cleansing and concealing
Proverbs 25:2
"It is the glory of God to conceal a thing."

It is the "glory of God" (Reyburn and Fry say "honor or greatness"[549]) to "conceal" (hide, not disclose) a "thing" (whatever "thing" He desires, counts best, including man's inordinate and sinful conduct, upon repentance).

Adam Clarke understands the text: "This has been understood as referring to the revelation of God's will in His Word, where there are many things concealed in parables, allegories, metaphors, similitudes, etc. And it is becoming the majesty of God so to publish His will, that it must be seriously studied to be understood, in order that the truth may be more prized when it is discovered. Prophecies are partially concealed, and we cannot fully know their meaning till their accomplishment, and then the glory of God's wisdom and providence will be more particularly evident when we see the event correspond so particularly and exactly with the prediction. I know not, however, that there are not matters in the Book of God that will not be fully opened till mortality is swallowed up of life. For here we see through a glass darkly; but there, face to face. Here we know in part, but there we shall know as we also are known."[550]

Matthew Poole explains the text as meaning "to keep His counsels and the reasons of His actions in His own breast, that He needs not to impart them to any other for their advice and assistance, as being self-sufficient both for the contrivance and execution of whatsoever pleaseth Him, and accountable to none for any of His matters."[551]

A second application may be made with regard to the forgiveness of sin; Christ Jesus conceals it when it is confessed. What happens to man's sin upon its confession to Jesus Christ (1 John 1:9)? Through the atoning blood of Jesus, God removes them all, making the heart "whiter than snow."

- Jesus takes them away (John 1:29)
- He forgets them (Hebrews 10:17)
- He washes them away (Isaiah 1:17–18)
- He blots them out (Isaiah 43:25)
- He wipes them out like a cloud (Isaiah 44:22)
- He pardons them (Isaiah 55:7)
- He buries them in the depths of the sea (Micah 7:19)
- He separates them from us as far as the east is from the west (Psalm 103:12)

Whiter than snow, yes, whiter than snow,
Now wash me, and I shall be whiter than snow. ~ James L. Nicholson

Martin Luther well said, "To be convinced in our hearts that we have forgiveness of sins and peace with God by grace alone is the hardest thing." See Ephesians 2:8–9. Forgiveness is freely given by God, though undeserved, through His Son Jesus Christ to all that confess sin.

The Bottom Line: Immediately upon doing wrong, lay it at the foot of the cross so that Jesus may not only "cleanse" it but "conceal" it. It's the glory of God to conceal it. Let the soul that has been so cleansed and had his sin concealed exalt the Lord in praise and thanksgiving. He now should endeavor to be like his Lord and "conceal" the sins of others upon their repentance, not expose them.

102
Foundation, the sure and the shaky
Proverbs 12:3
"A man shall not be established by wickedness: but the root of the righteous shall not be moved."

A man's life shall not be "established" (foundation of stability [Proverbs 10:25], as that of a king upon the throne) by "wickedness" (sinful, ungodly conduct). Wrong behavior rather causes life to be built upon shifting sand (Matthew 7:26–27) and slippery places (Psalm 73:18) that fail to provide man with stability and success (Psalm 1:3–4). The wicked are "rootless." See Job 8:17–18. In contrast, the righteous are "rooted" deeply in the sod of God's way and Word, always immovable ("will not totter [or slip]"[552]). See Ephesians 3:17. "As the whirlwind passeth, so is the wicked no more: but the righteous is an everlasting foundation....The righteous shall never be removed: but the wicked shall not inhabit the earth" (Proverbs 10:25, 30). Matthew Henry summarizes, "The root of the righteous shall not be moved, though their branches may be shaken. Those that by faith are rooted in Christ are firmly fixed; in Him their comfort and happiness are so rooted as never to be rooted up."[553] See Psalm 62:2; Micah 7:8; Romans 8:31–39.

> Glory hallelujah, I shall not be moved.
> Anchored in Jehovah, I shall not be moved.
> Just like the tree that's planted by the waters,
> I shall not be moved.
>
> In His love abiding, I shall not be moved;
> And in Him confiding, I shall not be moved.
> Just like the tree that's planted by the waters,
> I shall not be moved.
>
> Though all Hell assail me, I shall not be moved.
> Jesus will not fail me; I shall not be moved.
> Just like the tree that's planted by the waters,
> I shall not be moved.
>
> Though the tempest rages, I shall not be moved.
> On the rock of ages, I shall not be moved.
> Just like the tree that's planted by the waters,
> I shall not be moved.
>
> I shall not be, I shall not be moved;
> I shall not be, I shall not be moved.
> Just like the tree that's planted by the water,
> I shall not be moved.
> ~ Alfred H. Ackley[554] (1906, based on Psalm 16:8; 62:6)

The Bottom Line: The Christian alone is rooted and grounded in a sure foundation. "Rooted and built up in him, and stablished in the faith, as ye have been taught, abounding therein with thanksgiving" (Colossians

2:7). All other ground is sinking sand. See Jeremiah 17:8–9; 1 Corinthians 15:58.

103
Fraud, its short- and long-term effects
Proverbs 20:17
"Bread of deceit is sweet to a man; but afterwards his mouth shall be filled with gravel."

"Choosing rather to suffer affliction with the people of God, than to enjoy the pleasures of sin for a season" (Hebrews 11:25).

"Bread" (food or "means of livelihood"[555]) of "deceit" (fraud; what is gained by immoral or unethical means) is "sweet" (delightful, or as the CEV says, "delicious"; "Wickedness is sweet in his mouth" [Job 20:12 WEB]) to a "man" (the foolish); BUT afterwards his "mouth shall be filled with gravel" (the ill-gotten gain is distasteful; the pleasure turns to poison, bringing discomfort, dissatisfaction, disturbance [contrast with its beginning delight]; "like food turning into sand and dirt"[556]). Job testifies of this very thing happening: "But that evil will turn sour in his stomach. It will be like a snake's bitter poison inside him" (Job 20:14 ERV). To summarize, Allen Ross states, "Good things that were acquired dishonestly will not bring [ultimate] satisfaction."[557] See Lamentations 3:16.

Fraudulent acts (dishonesty, cheating) are, as any sin, "sweet" (pleasurable, enjoyable). That is in its beginning. Upon the conscience's being awakened to the wrong committed and its impending judgment of God, the pleasure of the sin quickly devolves into pain and disappointment ("mouth shall be filled with gravel"). The text therefore may read, "Bread gained by dishonest means tastes sweet (enjoyable) only to end up tasting horrible (like a mouthful of 'sand' or 'grit')." Buzzell says, "This contrasts the short-range pleasure of sin with its long-range consequences."[558] Sophocles said, "Things gained through unjust fraud are never secure."[559] The Holy Scriptures say, 'The pleasures (enjoyment) of sin are for a season'—fleeting, passing, and momentary (Hebrews 11:25). Maclaren says, "A momentary pause to ask ourselves when tempted to do evil, 'And what then?' would burst not a few of the painted bubbles after which we often chase."[560]

In contrast, *true bread* is a personal relationship with and obedience to Him who is the "bread of life" (John 6:35), Jesus Christ. In relationship to the text it is man's good and honorable deeds. "The roll may be bitter to the lips, but eaten, becomes sweet as honey; whereas the world's bread is sweet at first but bitter at last."[561] Say with the disciples, "Lord, evermore give us this bread" (John 6:34).

The Bottom Line: Sophocles advises, "Rather fail with honor than succeed by fraud."[562] The kind of bread eaten bears serious consequences upon well-being.

104
Freedom, the indebtedness bondage
Proverbs 24:4

"And by knowledge shall the chambers be filled with all precious and pleasant riches."

And by "knowledge" (wisdom instilled in man that enables him to act prudently, skillfully, industriously) shall the "chambers" (rooms in a house) be "filled" (possessed with many things) with all "precious and pleasant" (desirable, splendid, beautiful) "riches" (refers to either "furnishings" in the rooms or "treasures" kept in the storerooms of the house[563]). To summarize, wisdom (biblical knowledge and understanding, discernment) that God gives man to order life (practically and theologically) right and pleasing unto Him in every course of action contributes to the financial prosperity and security of a home or business.

To be in debt is to be enslaved, for it controls to what or to whom your money is to be expended. Freedom to utilize it for the Lord's work, assist the poor, benefit your children or better your own life is *stolen*. Ron Blue suggests four guiding principles when considering taking on debt, which I summarize and expand.[564]

Common Sense: Debt can only make sense if what is purchased will yield in time greater dividend than the amount borrowed.

A Guaranteed Way to Repay: You need to have a way out of the debt (selling what the debt was incurred for or another asset or acquiring additional money by other means).

Peace of Heart and Mind: Make sure the debt decision is necessary, ethical and in compliance with your conscience (no reservations, hesitations). Clay Smith says, "The question is not is it wrong, but is it wise."[565]

Unity: Personal agreement with your spouse about the debt decision. "A house divided against itself shall not stand." Presented with all the facts, your spouse is a good *Checkpoint Charlie.*

To these four principles I add a fifth: *Rely upon God's Wisdom.* The bottom line is that all debt-related decisions must be based upon God's will. You can be confident that God will give guidance when it is diligently sought (Proverbs 3:5–7; James 1:5).

The Bottom Line: Andy Stanley reminds us, "'I want' is better than 'I owe.'"[566] Some debt is necessary, but make sure it's *affordable.* If in debt bondage, take steps toward financial freedom. God desires your financial freedom and will lead you to it, provided that you are "leadable" (Psalm 32:8).

105
Fretting, blaming God instead of self
Proverbs 19:3
"The foolishness of man perverteth his way: and his heart fretteth against the LORD."

The "foolishness of man" ("the folly of a man"[567]) "perverteth" ("subverts"[568] or undermines his moral, spiritual foundation, resulting in trouble, calamity) his way: AND his "heart fretteth" ("heart raging"[569]; in furious outrage man accuses God for the adversity that his own conduct precipitated) against the Lord.

Man blaming God for the *bitter fruit* of personal wrongdoing dates back to Adam. W. F. Adeney comments, "It is monstrous to charge the providence of God with the consequences of actions that He has forbidden."[570] But man often does charge God for that which is not His doing. Isaiah makes plain that it is man's foolish actions, not God, that bring trouble and distress (Isaiah 50:1). It is a solemn injustice and sin to lash out at God angrily for the painful consequences of personal choices sowed. God has shown man the better way; man chooses the worst.[571] He warns of the cost of wrong, but man ignores. He gives man a moral and ethical compass to navigate life safely, only to see it abused, misused or not used. He provides man with a remedy for sin and its eternal consequence (Hell), but man blasphemously tramples upon it in ridicule and rejection. The case before the tribunal of Heaven seeking the prosecution of God for man's own conduct is unfounded. It is man that is proven guilty and responsible for the consequences of his own foolish actions.

Matthew Henry remarks, "In fretting, we are enemies to our own peace and become self-tormentors. In fretting against the Lord we affront Him and His justice, goodness, and sovereignty; and it is very absurd to take occasion from the trouble which we pull upon our own heads by our willfulness or neglect, to quarrel with Him, when we ought to blame ourselves, for it is our own doing."[572] If we are mad or angry with anyone over the consequences of wanton conduct, it should be entirely with ourselves.

But even in self-inflicted trouble or adversity resulting from unethical or immoral conduct, God will readily assist in its resolution. If you walk into difficulty or trouble following the Lord, He is there to lead you out. *But* if you walk into it on account of personal sin, He yet is there to lead you out. God is our "Mighty Deliverer" (Psalm 18:2).

The Bottom Line: A mature relationship with God shifts blame for the bitter fruit of personal sin away from God (and others) to oneself. "Be not deceived; God is not mocked: for whatsoever a man soweth, that shall he also reap" (Galatians 6:7). See Psalm 51:3–4. Simeon comments, "Whatever we suffer, we should not 'charge God foolishly.' Under the darkest dispensations [difficulties, trials, troubles], we should say [what the psalmist said in] Psalm 22:2–3. If we wait, we shall see the wisdom of many things which now seem utterly inexplicable; we may rest assured that David's assertion shall be verified."[573]

106
Fretting, the futility of worrying
Proverbs 24:19
"Fret not thyself because of evil men."

"Fret not" thyself (don't get angrily upset) because of "evil men" (about people who do evil, wicked, sinful things). Deane and Taswell say, "The anger would arise on account of the apparent inequitable distribution of blessings"[574] [the wicked would prosper better than the righteous].

Be careful not to allow the estate of the wrongdoer or events of the day or personal circumstances to enrage ("fret") you. John MacArthur defines worry as "the sin of distrusting the promise and providence of God."[575] He continues to say, "And yet it is a sin that Christians commit perhaps more frequently than any other."[576] Thomas à Kempis said, "Oh, how great peace and quietness would he possess who should cut off all vain anxiety and place all his confidence in God."[577]

"Worry is a thin stream of fear trickling through our minds. If encouraged, it cuts a channel into which all other thoughts are drained."[578] Jesus says, "Don't worry, but trust." *Worry* is used only 13 times in the Bible, whereas *trust* is used 126 times, and *faith* 226 times. Worry slanders every promise of God to the believer. "Worry," states Adrian Rogers, "doesn't take the sorrow out of tomorrow; it takes the strength out of today. There are two days that can steal joy from today. One is yesterday, and the other is tomorrow. Both are days in which we as Christians should refuse to live."[579]

"What is the use of worrying?" says Darlow Sargeant. "It never made anybody strong, never helped anybody do God's will, never made a way of escape for anyone out of perplexity. Worry spoils lives which would otherwise be useful and beautiful. Restlessness, anxiety and care are absolutely forbidden by our Lord, who said: 'Take no thought,' that is, no anxious thought."[580] You are to live without anxiety controlling your life. Jesus said, "Therefore I say unto you, Take no thought for your life, what ye shall eat, or what ye shall drink; nor yet for your body, what ye shall put on. Is not the life more than meat, and the body than raiment?" (Matthew 6:25). Again, He says, "Take therefore no thought for the morrow: for the morrow shall take thought for the things of itself. Sufficient unto the day is the evil thereof" (v. 34). And this is possible if we "seek...first the kingdom of God and His righteousness" (v. 33).

With David confidently say, "What time I am afraid, I will trust in thee. In God I will praise his word, in God I have put my trust; I will not fear what flesh can do unto me" (Psalm 56:3–4). "Only the Holy Spirit," says Billy Graham, "can give us peace in the midst of the storms of restlessness and despair. We should not grieve our Guide by indulging in worry or paying undue attention to self."[581]

The Bottom Line: In casting all your care upon the Lord in prayer, "the peace of God, which passeth all understanding, shall keep your hearts and minds through Christ Jesus" (Philippians 4:7). Peter Lord advises, "Glance at your needs but gaze upon the Lord."[582]

107
Friends (Bad), avoid wicked companions
Proverbs 1:15

"My son, walk not thou in the way with them; refrain thy foot from their path."

"Enter not into the path of the wicked, and go not in the way of evil men. Avoid it, pass not by it, turn from it, and pass away" (Proverbs 4:14–15).

"My son" (a father to his son, or teacher to his student), "walk" (travel not down the path of the unrighteous; "don't associate"[583] with them) "with them" (the wicked, foolish, immoral); "refrain" (avoid or resist their companionship) "thy foot from their path" (like signage that reads "Keep Off" or "Do Not Enter"; be intentional about not joining them in fellowship or partnership in sinful behavior).

Solomon admonishes strenuously, without reservation, that a person refrain from fellowship with the wicked ("walk not; enter not; go not; avoid it; turn from it"). Due to the horrendous danger lurking on the evil path (Proverbs 4:16), he warns the believer not even to put one foot on it ("enter not"); but if that has happened, to immediately get off it ("turn from it") and stay off it ("avoid it"). A key to staying off the unrighteous path is not to "pass by it" (don't allow Satan the chance to lure you onto it; avoid people and places that entice unto wrong).

Proverbs 13:20 says, "He who walks with wise men will be wise, *But* the companion of fools will be destroyed [suffer harm]" (NKJV). Paul states, "Do not be deceived: "Bad company corrupts good morals [conduct; convictions]" (1 Corinthians 15:33 NASB). If by happenstance you find yourself near the wicked path, then at all speed "flee" (2 Timothy

2:22) to safety as Joseph did in being approached by Potiphar's wife (Genesis 39:12). Never "give place to the devil" (Ephesians 4:27).

To pray "lead us not into temptation, but deliver us from evil," only to choose to ignore the Scriptures' command to avoid wicked companions which seek to steal our purity, reputation, righteousness and fellowship with God, all in the guise of fun and pleasure, is a vast contradiction.[584]

The Bottom Line: Satan deceives you into thinking that in joining the wicked you can *pull him up,* while in reality most often he *pulls you down.* The safer and most prudent course is to persuade the wicked to depart the wicked path. "Turn ye again now every one from his evil way, and from the evil of your doings, and dwell in the land that the LORD hath given unto you and to your fathers for ever and ever" (Jeremiah 25:5).

108
Friends (Bosom), an enhancement to life's happiness
Proverbs 27:9
"Ointment and perfume rejoice the heart: so doth the sweetness of a man's friend by hearty counsel."

"Ointment" (refers perhaps to olive oil used as a cosmetic rub[585] [Psalm 104:15]) and "perfume" (Reyburn and Fry say "a scented smoke sometimes used in rituals"[586]) "rejoice the heart" (make happy due to their pleasantness): so doth the "sweetness" (as ointment and perfume joy the heart, so does the loving and sweet advice of a friend that speaks wisely[587]) of a man's friend by "hearty counsel" (wise, sound advice spoken from a caring heart). John Gill summarizes, "Common oil or ointment used at entertainments…which were very delightful, pleased the senses and so exhilarated the heart; so doth the sweetness of a man's friend by hearty counsel; so the sweet and pleasant words, the wise and cordial counsel of a man's friend, rejoice his heart."[588] See Exodus 18:17–24 (Jethro's helpful counsel to Moses).

Loving advice from a friend's heart is likened to a person's being anointed with soothing and invigorating oil and perfume that makes him happy. "It is the counsel of his soul. He puts himself in our case and counsels as he would wish to be counselled himself."[589] Close friends enhance life's purpose and happiness by splashing out *holy perfume* through conversation, consultation (soul issues), and consolation. Cicero wrote, "A friend is, as it were, a second self."[590] Paul told Philemon regarding Onesimus that in "sending him back to you [it] is like sending you my own heart" (Philemon 1:12 NLV). D. W. Thomas suggests, "Counsels of a friend make sweet the soul."[591]

To say, "My friend is to me as my own soul" is indeed exhilarating and invigorating. David and Jonathan had such *oneness* in friendship. "The soul of Jonathan was knit with the soul of David, and Jonathan loved him as his own soul" (1 Samuel 18:1). To clutch the hand or heart of another in *soul oneness* sharing life's ups and downs, successes and failures, joys and sorrows and the good and bad adds a gusto and peace without which the journey would be less doable and happy. Such a relationship is to be valued highly, yea prized beyond gold and silver.

The Bottom Line: God has given us *bosom* friends to walk with in the journey. He never intended for us to walk it alone. Treasure such friends. Forever cultivate the friendship. Express gratitude for the friendship. Rely readily upon such friends as instruments of the Lord to bless your life.

109
Friends, caution about the fake ones
Proverbs 19:4
"Wealth maketh many friends; but the poor is separated from his neighbour."

"Wealth" (riches) "maketh many friends" (people gravitate to those with wealth to become their friends—often for personal gain); BUT the "poor is separated from his neighbor (in contrast, the poor person is deserted by his friends[592]).

Wealth attracts and gains many friends with its ability to give gifts, entertain, support and provide an overall good time. See Proverbs 14:20. In contrast, the poor are abandoned by friends, being unlikely to benefit them financially. The lesson is that in life not all whom we count "friends" are that in reality. Some are *false friends* who befriend us for what they can get from us, not give to us. In discovering the money, good time, and free ride are gone, they quickly depart. What it takes to gain some friends, it will take to keep them. Popularity, position and prestige also attract friends. But once such is gone, they are as well. All are victimized (though perhaps not rich or popular) by people who for ulterior motives become "friends." The discovery of the *fakeness* of the friendship is always hurtful and disappointing.

The Bottom Line: Genuine friendship is not based upon materialistic stuff but upon *soul-oneness, commonality, concern* and *affection.* Few people measure up to such criteria. Few are truly friends.

110
Friends, clutch tightly or lose forever
Proverbs 27:10
"Thine own friend, and thy father's friend, forsake not."

Thine "own friend" (personal), and thy "father's friend" (friends of the family), "forsake not" (do not abandon or allow the relationship to decay).

Over time strangers may become friends, but also friends may become strangers unless the relationship is cultivated. One needs to work hard at maintaining abiding friendships. "A friend," states Jerry White, "is a trusted confidant to whom I am mutually drawn as a companion and ally, whose love for me is not dependent on my performance, and whose influence draws me nearer to the Lord." Aristotle defined friendship as a "single soul, dwelling in two bodies."

General Westmoreland, when reviewing a platoon of paratroopers during the Vietnam War, asked each one as he walked passed him, "How do you like jumping, son?" Each responded, "I love it, sir!" When he came to the last soldier in line and asked how he liked jumping, the man replied quietly, "I hate jumping, sir." Westmoreland then asked, "Then why do you jump?" The paratrooper replied, "Because I want to be around guys who jump."

A person is a friend because in his eyes you are a person that "jumps" and he wants to be around you. Friends enhance each other's life for the better. "Ointment and perfume delight the heart, and the sweetness of a man's friend gives delight by hearty counsel" (Proverbs 27:9 NKJV). "As iron sharpens iron, so a man sharpens the countenance of his friend" (v. 17).

Someone has said, *"A friend lives to make life less difficult for another."* A false friend will abandon you in time of trouble. "Confidence in an unfaithful man in time of trouble is like a bad tooth and a foot out of joint" (Proverbs 25:19 NKJV). A friend exhibits unquestionable loyalty. He has your back when the rumor mill begins churning and the slander/criticism is splattered everywhere! He is gladdened when he is passed up so that you may receive the prize, the position, the popularity, the praise.

C. H. Spurgeon declares the value and blessing of a good friend: "Friendship is one of the sweetest joys of life. Many might have failed beneath the bitterness of their trial had they not found a friend."[593] "A friend loves at all times" (Proverbs 17:17 NKJV). "Jonathan loved David as himself" (1 Samuel 18:1 ERV). It is possible for a friend's love and concern to surpass that of family. David found far greater loyalty, affection and care from Jonathan than from his own brothers. With so many dysfunctional families in America, it's uplifting to know there are Jonathans in the world waiting to become "a friend that sticketh closer than a brother" (Proverbs 18:24).

When Jim Bakker, founder of PTL, was asked about the fall of PTL and the scattering of all the people close to him, including his friends, he commented, "I didn't lose any friends. I just discovered who my true friends are." Friends are not fair-weather comrades but are loyal come what may. He is one who will pursue you in order to encourage you. A friend strengthens our spiritual walk. Jonathan, in a time of grave difficulty for David, helped him strengthen his grip on God (1 Samuel 23:16). Strengthening another's grip on God is an essential to friendship.

Old family friends

But whom may these include? (1) the Sabbath, (2) the Sanctuary, (3) the Savior, (4) the Scriptures,[594] (5) the Saints. *Forsake them not,* for their profit to our "father" (parents) certifies they likewise will be to our benefit in navigating the maze of life happily and successfully.

The Bottom Line: Cultivate and retain close-knit friendships for life. However, keep in mind that even the best of friendships cannot fully satisfy. Hugo Black remarks, "The human heart has ever craved for a relationship deeper and more lasting than any possible among men."[595] An affectionate and caring bond with another simply cannot substitute for the divine bond needed with God.

111
Friends, it's the quality, not quantity
Proverbs 18:24

"A man that hath friends must shew himself friendly: and there is a friend that sticketh closer than a brother."

A man that hath "friends" (numerous friends; Buzzell says "chosen indiscriminately"[596]) "must show himself friendly" (the Hebrew meaning "to break in pieces,"[597] "may come to ruin or destruction"). There is a "friend" (a true friend who loves you; a close friend) that "sticketh" (clings to you; loyal, faithful despite what happens) "closer than a brother" (the first friends mentioned are the *casual sort*; these are the *close sort*). To summarize, the person that indiscriminately, without wise discretion, makes a lot of "friends" does so to his own potential harm (prove unreliable, take advantage of him for selfish purposes, abandon in trouble or crisis, talk ill of him behind his back and/or entice into sin). It is far better to have one or two reliable, true and loving friends than a dozen of the *nominal, casual kind*.

Solomon gives much advice about friends—the good, the bad and the ugly (Proverbs 12:26; 13:20; 17:17; 18:24; 22:24–25; 27:5–6). George Lawson remarks, "A well-chosen friend sweetens the present life and assists us in our progress to a better self. An unworthy friend will bring on us disappointment, vexation and remorse."[598]

Friendships are so powerful an influence that they impact life in at least three ways. First, a person *becomes like them*. Goethe said, "Tell me with whom thou art found, and I will tell thee who thou art." People become like those with whom they associate. Pure and clean water passing through a dirty pipe will become dirty.

Second, they become *known as them*. A man is known by the company he keeps. People are prone to judge a person based upon the company he or she entertains.

Third, a person's future will be *affected by them*. Go to any prison, reformatory or drug rehab center, and it is doubtful that you will find any who wouldn't say a friend played a role in his being there. Visit the graves of the young in the cemeteries of the world, and an honest epitaph etched upon the tombstones of far too many would include the words: "I'm here due to a friend." François Mauriac could not have spoken any truer words than when he said, "No love, no friendship, can cross the path of our destiny without leaving some mark on it forever."

It is not the quantity of friends one possesses, but their quality. "Number counts for little in friendship."[599] Man in a lifetime may develop only several *true* friends—those not fickle (in and out) or shallow or temporary or fleeting or distant or corrupt or spurious, but who 'stick closer than a brother' (Proverbs 18:24) and enhance instead of injuring life. The Message elucidates the text, "Friends come and friends go, but a true friend sticks by you like family." George Lawson remarks, "There is a friend that sticks closer than a brother, and we do him honor by placing an entire confidence in him when we need his assistance."[600]

The classic example of friendship is portrayed between Jonathan and David. The Bible states that Jonathan's soul was knit with David's and David's to Jonathan's (1 Samuel 18:1). *Knit* literally means knotted, tied together firmly by indissoluble bonds.[601] Matthew Henry, in wondrous and theologically sound fashion, remarks, "The friendship of David and Jonathan was the effect of divine grace, which produces in true believers one heart and one soul and causes them to love each other. This union of souls is from partaking in the Spirit of Christ. Where God unites hearts, carnal matters are too weak to separate them."[602]

Ordinary friendships (the run-of-the-mill type) are based on natural affinities, interests, hobbies, pursuits and personality, whereas *sacred friendships (though these factors may play a role) are supernaturally established and based upon the spiritual dimension* of being brothers or sisters in the family of God. It is for this reason Solomon states that there is "a friend that sticketh closer than a brother" (spiritual blood-brothers may be closer, more united and more knit together than those who are only physically kin). Such friends are a rare find.

G. Campbell Morgan writes, "All consideration of this great verse leads us at last to one place, to one Person. He is the Friend of sinners. There comment ceases. Let the heart wonder and worship."[603]

There's not a Friend like the lowly Jesus,
No, not one! no, not one!
None else could heal all our souls' diseases,
No, not one! no, not one!

Jesus knows all about our struggles;
He will guide 'til the day is done.
There's not a Friend like the lowly Jesus,
No, not one! no, not one!

No friend like Him is so high and holy,
No, not one! no, not one!
And yet no friend is so meek and lowly,
No, not one! no, not one!

There's not an hour that He is not near us,
No, not one! no, not one!
No night so dark but His love can cheer us,
No, not one! no, not one!

Did ever saint find this Friend forsake him?
No, not one! no, not one!
Or sinner find that He would not take him?
No, not one! no, not one! ~ Johnson Oatman (1895)

The Bottom Line: Focus on cultivating a few true friends (close) instead of merely possessing many that are only casual friends that may over time forsake or harm you. Prized friendship is that which is divinely orchestrated and sustained by the Lord. Man's best friend is the lowly Jesus.

112
Friends, keeping confidentialities
Proverbs 11:13

"A talebearer revealeth secrets: but he that is of a faithful spirit concealeth the matter."

A "talebearer" (he who gossips; betrayal of trust; untrustworthy) "revealeth" (to disclose, make known openly) "secrets" (confidentialities; Murphy says, "The confidences are the 'secret' that must be honored"[604]): BUT he that is of a "faithful spirit" (trustworthy spirit) "concealeth the matter" (retains the secret, keeps confidences). To summarize, silence is golden with regard to the secrets another entrusts. Bear them in the casket of the soul, concealed from public view, treating them as if they were your own. See Proverbs 20:19.

Friends bring disappointment, heartache and remorse through an unrestrained tongue. Make your choice of them therefore carefully. A key trait of a faithful friend is the ability to restrain the tongue, to keep confidentialities. He ought to be one in which the trials, sorrows,

158

challenges and burdens of life are unloaded without worry they will be blabbed to the world. Most assuredly a true friend will never divulge publicly that which is told in private which would bring hurt or disgrace to him who shared it. I, as others, have concealed in my heart matters shared in confidence that I will take to my grave without their ever being divulged.

The tongue has the power to strengthen, weaken or destroy the "best of friends." "Gossip separates the best of friends" (Proverbs 16:28 NLT). Envy and jealousy of others (talebearers) undermine close friendships. H. A. Ironside states, "There is no question that whispering and backbiting is one of the greatest curses among Christians. By means of this detestable vice the dearest friends are alienated, misunderstandings of all kinds are created, and many are defiled by the recital of tales which a godly person would seek to cover and forbear ever to repeat."[605]

Charles Bridges says, "Who entrusts a secret to his friend goes thither as to a sanctuary, and to violate the rites of that is sacrilege and profanation of friendship. Never let us think this to be a trifle. Never let us undertake a trust without the most resolute determination of Christian faithfulness."[606] Bridges cautions, "Would we have our friend rest his anxieties on our bosom (Proverbs 17:17), let him not see the results of misplaced confidence dropping out of our mouth."[607]

The Bottom Line: Be a person who merits the honor of friends in keeping their secrets.

113
Friends, proven by consistency of love and loyalty
Proverbs 17:17
"A friend loveth at all times, and a brother is born for adversity."

A "friend" ("one attached to another by affection or esteem" *[Merriam-Webster]*) "loveth" (caring affection) at "all times" (in the good and the bad), and a "brother" (same person as the friend) is "born for adversity" ("is born"—Wordsworth fancifully remarks, "Adversity brings him forth. He comes, as it were, out of the *womb of calamity and seems to be born for it.*"[608]).

A friend is somebody who cares ("loveth") and shows it consistently. A friend is somebody who sharpens us (Proverbs 27:17). He edifies, encourages and enriches our life (v. 6). A friend is somebody who sticks (Proverbs 17:17; 27:10) with us; he walks in when others walk out. He is genuinely loyal despite adversity or calamity. A note in D. L. Moody's Bible says, "A true friend is like ivy—the greater the ruin, the closer he clings."[609] A friend is someone that renders hearty and godly counsel (Proverbs 27:9) and remains sensitive to our hurts and needs. Friends watch over us with continuous care and concern, ever seeking to lighten our burden and uplift our spirit (Hebrews 10:24). Timothy Keller writes, "Friends voluntarily tie their hearts to one another. They put their happiness *into* their friends' happiness, so they can't emotionally flourish unless their friends are flourishing too."[610]

The "upper tier" type of friends are always in our corner rooting for our success and utmost happiness. They believe in us when we don't. Barnabas was that kind of amazing friend to Paul. He kept saying, "Paul, keep going; you can do this. I believe in you. I will help you." The spread of the Gospel to the whole world and the writing of more than one third of the books of the New Testament are attributable in reality not just to Paul who was the penman under the inspiration of the Holy Spirit but also to Barnabas' encouragement and friendship. Who sits in the "upper tier" in your life? Who is life's "difference maker" (your Barnabas)? In whose "upper tier" do you sit?

> Thank you for giving to the Lord.
> I am a life that was changed.
> Thank you for giving to the Lord.
> I am so glad you gave. ~ Ray Boltz

A true friend leaves *unerasable, life-enhancing footprints upon our lives*. Based upon this criterion for true friendship, a person is blessed to have two or three in life. A David-Jonathan type friendship is extremely rare but should always be sought. And once found, it should be maintained through communication, demonstration and cultivation. Express affection and appreciation for your *Jonathans* verbally and tangibly. Harriet Beecher Stowe (1811–1896), author of *Uncle Tom's Cabin,* said, "The bitterest tears shed over graves are for words left unsaid and deeds left undone."[611]

The Bottom Line: William Penn summarizes, "A true friend unbosoms [unloads] freely, advises justly, assists readily, adventures boldly, takes all patiently, defends courageously, and continues a friend unchangeably."[612]

114
Friends, the dangers of "overexposure"
Proverbs 25:17
"Withdraw thy foot from thy neighbour's house; lest he be weary of thee, and so hate thee."

"Withdraw" ("be *seldom* in a friend's house"; seldom means to "make precious," that is "valuable," by its rarity[613]) thy "foot" ("'make your foot precious'—do not overdo your visiting, or overstay it"[614]); lest he be "weary" (grows tired of you), and "hates" (continual intrusion without consideration for a friend's need for *privacy* can shove that friend away).

A healthy friendship hinges much on the frequency yet infrequency of contact or visitation. Respect for a friend's privacy, family life and pursuits must be exhibited, or else even the best of friendships will deteriorate. Don't evolve into a burden or a nuisance. Matthew Henry remarks, "He that sponges upon his friend loses him."[615] A true friend does not have a *suction tube* attached to a friend demanding too much attention. He that does needs a therapist, not a friend. Make "visits, emails, phone calls and texts" *precious* to a friend by not intruding too often. Even the most intimate of friendships may suffer harm (weariness and setback) due to overexposure. A keen sensitivity in friendship is imperative about knowing when to push forward and when to back off. "Familiarity breeds contempt."

In contrast, a person cannot too frequently enter into the Holy chambers of the best of Friends. Jesus never tires or grows weary with a *friend's* much coming. In fact, He desires it much. See Daniel 6:10; Matthew 11:28–29; Hebrews 10:19; Ephesians 3:12.

The Bottom Line: Cultivate, don't suffocate friends.

115
Friends, warning about "friendly fire"
Proverbs 12:26

"The righteous is more excellent than his neighbour: but the way of the wicked seduceth them."

The "righteous" (godly wise, upright, honorable) is more "excellent than his neighbor" (literally means more *cautious* ["searches out, spies out"] in the selection of friends[616]): BUT the "way" (path of unrighteousness) of the "wicked" (the ungodly, foolish) "seduceth them" (the wicked lead the wicked further astray). To summarize, Allen Ross remarks, "The righteous cautiously avoid dangerous friendships."[617]

The wicked further induce others who are wicked to do wrong, while the godly associate only with those who lead them to do that which is right. Despite the most cautionary steps the Christian undertakes in developing spiritually healthy relationships, there exists the danger of "friendly fire."

In 1982, in the war between England and Argentina, the Royal Navy's 3,500–ton destroyer *HMS Sheffield* was destroyed by a single missile shot from an Argentine fighter jet. Investigation later revealed that the Sheffield's computer did pick up the incoming missile correctly, identifying it as a French-made *Exocet* which it had been programmed to ignore as "friendly." The Sheffield was sunk by a missile it saw coming and could have evaded.

That's how most have programmed the computer in their mind regarding "friends." In being vigilantly defensive against the obvious missiles of assault on one's purity and holiness, the unwise lower their guard against the less obvious, their friends. And the result is that the "wicked" friend "leads them astray." They are "sunk" by a missile which they have seen coming and could have evaded. Gravestones of multitudes across the world could bear the epitaph, "Destroyed by 'friendly fire.'"

Who encouraged Amnon to rape Tamar? "But Amnon had a friend, whose name was Jonadab" (2 Samuel 13:3). Jonadab helped plot the hideous act (v. 5). Of King Ahaziah it is recorded that "he did evil in the sight of the LORD like the house of Ahab: for they were his counsellors after the death of his father to his destruction" (2 Chronicles 22:4). Friends, due to their influence and access, can generate or instigate far greater harm and hurt than enemies.

The Bottom Line: "Friendly fire" must be recognized as destructive and averted.

116
Friends, wounding for love's sake through rebuke
Proverbs 27:6

"Faithful are the wounds of a friend; but the kisses of an enemy are deceitful."

"He who [appropriately] reprimands a [wise] man will afterward find more favor than he who flatters with the tongue" (Proverbs 28:23 AMP).

"Faithful" (the friend's words are "reliable, sure, trustworthy—can be trusted"[618]; Reyburn and Fry say "a true friend's criticism or frank speaking"[619]) are the "wounds" (infliction of pain) of a friend; BUT the "kisses of an enemy" (the numerous Judas kisses of insincerity) are "deceitful" (CEV says, "they are 'nothing but lies'"). Deane and Taswell summarize, "The wounds which a real friend inflicts by his just rebukes are directed by truth and discriminating affection. An enemy is lavish with his Judas kisses to hide his perfidy [deceitfulness] and hatred."[620]

"Faithful" friends are they that out of a heart of genuine love, without criticism or disdain privately, constructively reprimand (rebuke) you upon erring. Such confrontation from a "faithful" friend will hurt ("wound") initially but in the end be of great help. "The teaching of the wise is a fountain of life, to depart from the snares of death" (Proverbs 13:14 MEV). Granted, this task is not an easy one. It may require great wrestling within the soul to execute. It may even diminish or destroy the friendship. But love dictates it be done regardless of consequence. The hope is that it will enhance the relationship. Much hinges upon how the *wounds* are inflicted or administered as to its outcome.

Receive rebuke from a friend graciously

Paul reprimanded Peter for refusing to eat with the Gentiles, which he graciously received without ill feeling (Galatians 2:11–21). Where love truly abounds between people, the one is not afraid to offer rebuke; the other is unafraid to receive it. Love makes rebuke, though piercingly painful, acceptable and bearable. "It is a great proof of wisdom to take a rebuke well, as to give it well."[621] So-called *friends* are they who, instead of honestly approaching you about a wrong, condone, excuse or encourage it, lavishing out an abundance of affection ("kisses of an enemy"). All their "kisses" are deceptive and unreliable, failing to keep your best interest at heart (Joab's kiss was deceitful as was that of Judas). "Few people have the wisdom to like reproofs which will do them good better than praises that do them hurt."[622]

> The true friend reveals faults in an effort to edify and protect but conceals them from all others in a spirit of loyalty and genuine love.
> W. A. Criswell

"Open rebuke is better than secret love" (Proverbs 27:5). H. A. Ironside comments, "Reproof in grace is better far than love kept concealed, which forbids my drawing his attention to his faults."[623] "The true friend," states W. A. Criswell, "reveals faults in an effort to edify and protect but conceals them from all others in a spirit of loyalty and genuine love. God's standard shows 'secret love,' which refuses to risk rebuke or correction, to be in actuality hatred (Leviticus 19:17)."[624] Criswell continues to say that open rebuke does not mean public exposure.[625] Have the attitude of David toward reproof. He declared, "Let the righteous smite me; it shall be a kindness: and let him reprove me; it shall be an excellent oil, which shall not break my head" (Psalm 141:5).

The Bottom Line: Though reprimand is not what is desired, if it be given lovingly, rightly and constructively, receive it. If a friend falters, address it with him or her. "But speaking the truth in love, may grow up into him in all things, which is the head, even Christ" (Ephesians 4:15). Charles Bridges remarks, "Rebuke kindly, considerately and prayerfully administered cements friendship rather than loosening it."[626]

117
Future, embraced with peace and laughter
Proverbs 31:25
"She shall rejoice in time to come."

It was the godliness and uprightness of the Proverbs 31 woman that enabled her to laugh ("rejoice") at the "time to come" (future; look toward it without fear, with confidence and happiness).

This is true for all the righteous. Isaiah declares, "Thou [God] wilt keep him in perfect peace, whose mind is stayed on thee: because he trusteth in thee" (Isaiah 26:3). John said, "There is no fear in love; but perfect love casteth out fear" (1 John 4:18). Ralph Waldo Emerson well remarked, "What lies behind us and what lies before us are tiny matters compared to what lies within us." With Jesus Christ at the helm of our life, there is no need to worry about or fear the future.

> I don't worry o'er the future,
> For I know what Jesus said;
> And today I'll walk beside Him,
> For He knows what lies ahead ~ Alison Krauss

Conversely, the unrighteous and he who lives in constant controversy with the Lord should fear and tremble what tomorrow may bring (divine punishment and eternal Hell). Of the wicked, Isaiah says, "But the wicked are like the troubled sea, when it cannot rest, whose waters cast up mire and dirt" (Isaiah 57:20). David warns, "God judgeth the righteous, and God is angry with the wicked every day. If he turn not, he will whet his sword; he hath bent his bow, and made it ready" (Psalm 7:11–12). Hasten to God, turning from sin in godly repentance before it's too late. "It is a fearful thing to fall into the hands of the living God" (Hebrews 10:31).

The Bottom Line: For the upright in heart (Christian), explicit trust in God banishes fear regarding the future. "Fear thou not; for I am with thee: be not dismayed; for I am thy God: I will strengthen thee; yea, I will help thee; yea, I will uphold thee with the right hand of my righteousness" (Isaiah 41:10).

118
Gambling, its devastating effects upon teens
Proverbs 13:11
"Wealth gotten by vanity shall be diminished: but he that gathereth by labour shall increase."

"Wealth" (abundance of money) gotten by "vanity" (obtained by dishonest or illegitimate means[627]) shall be "diminished" ("run out"; "quickly got, quickly gone"; Proverbs 10:2): BUT he that "gathereth by labor shall increase" (the gain of money that comes honestly, though little by little, will increase).

The principle "wealth gotten by vanity shall be diminished" is echoed by a gambling addict who said, "The paradox with gambling is that if you win, you lose. If you lose, you lose. If you win, the high consumes your mind until you're back in action. If you lose, you crash and chase your losses to regain that high." What is gambling? John MacArthur stated, "Gambling is an activity in which a person risks something of value, usually money…to forces of chance completely beyond his control or any rational expectation, in hope of winning something of greater value, usually more money. But it is an appeal to sheer chance."[628] Adrian Rogers says, "Gambling is based primarily on covetousness."[629] In another article Rogers states, "Risk is not what makes gambling wrong. We take risks every day, like when we get in a car. Greed and gain without mutual benefit is the issue that makes gambling a sin."[630]

Although the legal age for gambling is over 18, many teens pawn possessions, borrow money, steal, prostitute themselves, falsely use credit cards and lie to gamble. The Internet has opened wide the door for teens to gamble. There are an estimated 7.9 million teens who are problem and pathological (compulsive) gamblers (5.7 million problem and 2.2 million pathological).[631] Problem gambling is not based on how often one gambles or the amount of money one loses, but on the disruption to life (like use of money designated for car payment or tuition payment; sleep deprivation due to staying up too late gambling on the Internet or in a club; failing grades; missed classes; relationships injured). Pathological gamblers are defined by criteria set forth by the American Psychiatric Association. "The three cardinal signs of PG are (1) preoccupation with gambling and obtaining money with which to gamble; (2) loss of control of one's gambling, that is, not following reasonable limits of time and money spent on gambling; and (3) continuation of gambling despite adverse consequences, such as continuing to gamble in spite of losing large sums of money."[632] However, the term *problem gambling* is a general term used for both categories.

Consequences for teen gambling addictions include: declining grades, habitual money problems, less time for friends and family, temptation to engage in illegal behavior to get money to pay off gambling debts—leading to possible jail time and associations with unsavory characters who could make life difficult if they are not paid.[633] This addiction takes priority over friends, family, classes and God. It often leads to severe desperation for an "out" and depression that leads to suicide. One of the most salient risk factors with gambling is substance use, abuse and dependence. The link between gambling and alcohol, illicit drugs, and tobacco use is strong.[634] Timothy Keller summarizes that gambling "is an 'end run' around the hard work, due diligence, and time investment that ordinarily is required to make wealth grow."[635] And that is futile. The second part of the principle in Proverbs 13:11 states the key to happiness and money sufficiency: "He that gathereth by labor shall increase."

The Bottom Line: Wilson Mizner said, "Gambling: The sure way of getting nothing for something."[636]

119
Generosity, its blessing to others and reward to self
Proverbs 11:25
"The liberal soul shall be made fat."

"Honour the LORD with thy substance, and with the firstfruits of all thine increase: So shall thy barns be filled with plenty, and thy presses shall burst out with new wine" (Proverbs 3:9–10).

The "liberal soul" (generous person) shall be made "fat" (enriched financially; prosper; "to become rich, prosperous"[637]). To summarize, the generous will be rewarded for their benevolent and charitable gifts. See 2 Corinthians 9:6.

Honor God not only with the body, heart and mind but with possessions (stewardship). Ultimately, the sacrifice Christ made for man's salvation is the believer's impetus and inspiration for generous giving. How generous was Christ?

Paul answers, "For ye know the grace of our Lord Jesus Christ, that, though he was rich, yet for your sakes he became poor, that ye through his poverty might be rich" (2 Corinthians 8:9). He was the most generous Person who ever lived. "He was rich in possessions, power, homage, fellowship, happiness. He became poor in station, circumstances, in His relations with men. We are urged to give a little money, clothing, and food. He gave Himself."[638] John MacArthur remarked, "He laid aside the independent exercise of all His divine prerogatives, left His place with

167

God, took on human form, and died on a cross like a common criminal, *that you...might become rich.* Believers become spiritually rich through the sacrifice and impoverishment of Christ. They become rich in salvation, forgiveness, joy, peace, glory, honor and majesty. They become joint heirs with Christ."[639]

> Faith's way of gaining is giving.
> C. H. Spurgeon

God wants you to be "fat" and flourishing in soul through generous and sacrificial giving to God's causes and the poor. Captain Levy was asked how he could give so much to the Lord's work and still possess great wealth. The Captain replied, "Oh, as I shovel it out, He shovels it in; and the Lord has a bigger shovel." C. H. Spurgeon testified, "In all of my years of service to my Lord, I have discovered a truth that has never failed and has never been compromised. That truth is that it is beyond the realm of possibilities that one has the ability to outgive God. Even if I give the whole of my worth to Him, He will find a way to give back to me much more than I gave."

If you are married and have children, lead the way for them by giving generously to the Lord. It's healthy and expedient to let children know what you give and why (without boasting), for this sows seeds of generosity in their hearts. One way to do this is by baking a cake, allowing it to represent your weekly or monthly paycheck. Cut a portion that represents how much you gave to the Lord, discussing why.[640] Such a word picture not only indicates the size of the gift given but the amount left over for personal and family use. Catherine Wilson, associate editor for Focus on the Family, states, "We empower our kids when we teach them that they can be generous not only with their belongings but also with their energy (performing chores and tasks for others); their time (spending time with those who are hurting); and their interests, creativity and skills (creating handcrafted gifts, coaching or tutoring others, entertaining others through music, song and drama, or offering design, construction or car maintenance skills, etc.)"[641]

"Much food is in the tillage of the poor" (Proverbs 13:23). The poor man must not judge the little he has to give financially, materially, in labor or in counsel as too meager an offering. He must not adopt the attitude: "What I might do is insignificant in contrast to what others do; therefore, I will take my 'talent' and bury it in the sand and do nothing" (Matthew 25:18). He is to "make the most of his little patch of ground."[642] If you are

among the "one-talented," refuse to use that as an excuse for doing nothing to advance the cause of Christ. Rather, be diligent and prayerful in looking for ways you might "enlarge" your gifts and opportunities for service. "Industry applied to small natural capacity will do far more than larger power rusted away by sloth."[643]

The Bottom Line: God blesses the cheerful and generous giver to Kingdom causes. "Little is much when God is in it."

120
Gifts, influence for bad and good
Proverbs 17:8
"A gift is as a precious stone in the eyes of him that hath it: whithersoever it turneth, it prospereth."

A "gift" (bribe; Google Dictionary says to "persuade someone to act in one's favor, typically illegally or dishonestly, by a gift of money or other inducement") is as a "precious stone" (a charm or amulet[644]) in the "eyes of him that hath it" (the owner, he who gives it): "whithersoever it turneth, it prospereth" (in the eyes of the giver, giving gifts is the means to get people to do whatever he wants; it works like a charm—magical stone[645]).

The Proverb may apply not only to the giving of bribes to influence unjust favor but also to appease anger or to prove friendship.[646] "A precious stone" is literally "a stone of grace" (Proverbs 1:9).[647] Gifts are influencing, bonding, commending, grateful, reconciling, or proving *stones* freely given (grace) out of affection and concern. The merit of the gift is dependent upon its motivation. Obviously gifting gifts to bribe is wrong, as is giving them to bring attention to self (impress others). H. A. Ironside comments, "A gift presented as a token of pure affection and esteem will be highly valued by its possessor and will pave the way for much that is of value. He who would find love should be a giver—not a mere receiver."[648]

Jonathan's gifts to David not only strengthened but "cemented their friendship by expressing the love that was in his heart."[649] "Then Jonathan and David made a covenant, because he loved him as his own soul. And Jonathan stripped himself of the robe that was upon him, and gave it to David, and his garments, even to his sword, and to his bow, and to his girdle" (1 Samuel 18:3–4). Friendship entails more than engaging in social outings, correspondence and dialogue. It involves giving. Jonathan gave David his robe (symbolic of David's claim to the throne) and sword (one of the only two in Israel—1 Samuel 13:22). See Proverbs 18:24; 27:19; 1 Samuel 23:16.

God is the great example of the gifting of gifts—providing for both the temporal and eternal. James attests this in saying, "Every good gift and every perfect gift is from above, and cometh down from the Father of lights, with whom is no variableness, neither shadow of turning" (James 1:17). The supreme gift God has given to man is that of His only Son, Jesus Christ, to make atonement for sin to procure his salvation (Romans 10:9–13). God's grace gifts ought to influence man unto salvation. "Despisest thou the riches of his goodness and forbearance and longsuffering; not knowing that the goodness of God leadeth thee to repentance?" (Romans 2:4).

Whithersoever it turneth, it prospereth. Rarely do gifts given legitimately, scripturally and affectionately falter in good works. Unethical or otherwise improper gifts seldom fail to produce evil works. The seed sowed in giving, be it good or bad, determines the fruit of the gift.

The Bottom Line: Giving with honorable motivation has a powerful influence in the cultivation of friendship.

121
Gifts, none required to enter God's presence
Proverbs 18:16
"A man's gift maketh room for him, and bringeth him before great men."

A man's "gift" (not a "bribe;"[650] Deane and Taswell say, "The term here signifies the present which duty or friendship offers to one whom one wishes to please"[651]) "maketh room" (opens the door; enables access[652]) for him, and "bringeth" (grants entrance unto) "great men" (the important).

Gifts are required to gain the audience of many that are of great stature in the eyes of the world. But He who is above them all, being the

King of kings and Lord of lords, the Alpha and Omega, and the Savior of the world, graciously receives all without price (Isaiah 55:1).

Nothing in my hand I bring;
Simply to Thy cross I cling.
Naked, come to Thee for dress;
Helpless, look to Thee for grace;
Foul, I to the fountain fly;
Wash me, Savior, or I die. ~ Augustus M. Toplady, 1776

C. H. Spurgeon well states the way to genuine salvation: "And what thou hast to do with it is this: believe the Father's Word and trust thyself wholly to what Christ has done for sinners. May the Divine Spirit take thee off from all other ways of salvation and bring thee to trust to this alone and make thee abhor and loathe even to detestation anything like confidence in thy prayers or thy tears, thy doings, thy sufferings, thy preparings, thy repentings, or anything else; for it is none but Jesus who can bring a sinner near to God. All that you spin, you will have to unravel; all that you build will have to come down; all that you can bring to God, you will have to take back again. You must come to him empty-handed, with nothing of your own, and simply rest where God Himself doth rest—in the blessed Person and the finished work of the Lord Jesus who is all in all."[653]

Jesus said, "Freely ye have received, freely give" (Matthew 10:8). Salvation is absolutely free for the taking (Romans 10:9–13) and trusting (Acts 16:31). As Jesus gives good gifts to man (James 1:17), even so should the believer. The crowning gift to share is the "unspeakable gift" (2 Corinthians 9:15) of the Person and work of Jesus Christ in provision of salvation.

The Bottom Line: You have *free* access into the throne room of Almighty God, 24/7 (Hebrews 4:16). Enter frequently and bring others. To know Christ and His full forgiveness of sin, come with "empty hands" but a "sorrowful, repentant heart," inviting Him to be Lord and Savior of your life. See Ephesians 2:8–9 and Isaiah 55:1.

122
Gloating, callous insensitivity to misfortunes of others
Proverbs 24:17
"Rejoice not when thine enemy falleth, and let not thine heart be glad when he stumbleth."

"Rejoice not" (don't be gleeful secretly or openly) when thine "enemy" (one that hates you) "falleth" (meets with disaster, hardship), AND let not thine heart be glad when he "stumbleth" (gloating even is forbidden with regard to his problems).

Gloating is contrary to the believer's nature in Jesus Christ and the Word of God. The Bible instructs: "Rejoice with them that do rejoice, and weep with them that weep" (Romans 12:15). Manifesting a heart of sorrow (not joy) over what happened to an enemy fulfills the law of love. In the love chapter Paul states, "Love does not brag and is not arrogant" (1 Corinthians 13:4 NASB). Jesus taught that we are to love even our enemies (and love does not rejoice in the hurt of another). He said, "If you love those who love you, what credit is that to you? Even sinners love those who love them" (Luke 6:32 HCSB). John MacArthur remarks, "Gloating over a fallen enemy can be more serious than the sin the enemy committed."[654]

"The maxim," expositor John Gill states, "refers to private enemies. The overthrow of public enemies was often celebrated with festal rejoicing...But private revenge and vindictiveness are warmly censured and repudiated."[655] Examples of such celebration include Moses' triumph over the Amalekites and Pharaoh's host at the Red Sea.

The Bottom Line: If guilty of the infraction of gloating over the hurts another experiences, acknowledge and confess it unto the Lord as sin. Pray for grace to love those who persecute and offend you, and to be restrained from gloating in[656] their defeat, failure, sorrow or loss (even if deserved). "'I told you so,' is never appropriate."[657]

123
Gluttony, to master or be mastered
Proverbs 23:2
"And put a knife to thy throat, if thou be a man given to appetite."

"Be not among winebibbers; among riotous eaters of flesh: For the drunkard and the glutton shall come to poverty: and drowsiness shall clothe a man with rags" (Proverbs 23:20–21).

"Put a knife" (Hubbard and Ogilvie say "is a hyperbole that means take whatever drastic steps are necessary to curb your urges"[658]) to thy "throat" (doesn't mean to kill yourself but to stop gorging[659]), if a man "given to appetite" (one prone to overindulge in food, a glutton).

Use moderation and strong self-restraint with regard to eating so you do not overindulge. Second, the principle is to be applied when dining with "kings" (and other people of prominence). Be mindful of table etiquette (manners and consumption) and the "royal" presence so you do not offend. Such times are opportunities to learn and impress (in the best of senses).[660] A religious professor in college advised ministerial students to eat something prior to partaking a meal with a church member. I never understood that counsel. Now I do.

The Bottom Line: Don't allow stomach appetite to master the entire body. Curb the appetite by the most stringent means necessary. Beat your body into submission to eating only that which is healthy and needful for sustenance (1 Corinthians 9:27).

124
God, His divine sovereignty
Proverbs 16:33

"The lot is cast into the lap; but the whole disposing thereof is of the LORD. *"*

The "lot" (type of "dice") is cast into the "lap" (fold of the garment); BUT the "whole disposing thereof" (God determines the outcome, "the roll of the dice") is of the Lord.

God's sovereignty means He can do whatever, whenever, however He chooses. He is limitless in power, supreme in authority, and autonomous in rule. No man or nation can thwart the plan of God. Arthur W. Pink stated, "To the one who delights in the sovereignty of God, the clouds not only have a "silver lining," but they are silver all through, the darkness only serving to offset the light!" Thomas Brooks says, "The sovereignty of God is that golden scepter in his hand by which he will make all bow, either by His Word or by His works, by His mercies or by His judgements."

Kyle Yates remarks, "It is good to be reminded that the eternal God is still in active control of the affairs of the world. His sovereign will is to hold sway to the ends of the earth."[661] Deane and Taswell state, "Events seem to be tossed about in the lap of chance. Yet just as surely as laws of motion govern the slightest movement of all the leaves that are blown by an autumn wind, divine purposes control all human events, in the midst of their seeming confusion. This must be so if God is God."[662] C. H. Spurgeon well said, "If the simple casting of a lot is guided by Him, how much more the events of our entire life? It would bring a holy calm over your mind if you were always to remember this. It would relieve your mind from anxiety, that you might be the better able to walk in patience, quiet and cheerfulness as a Christian should."[663]

The Bottom Line: God is in absolute control not only of the world, but also of our lives individually.

125
Godliness, the highway to holiness
Proverbs 16:17

"The highway of the upright is to depart from evil: he that keepeth his way preserveth his soul."

"Highway" refers to a road that is built higher than the land that surrounds it and is free of obstacles.[664] The "upright" (virtuous, godly) travel the highway, avoiding "exits" that would lead to sin. They are careful to heed the counsel of God: "Do not enter the path of the wicked and do not proceed in the way of evil men. Avoid it, do not pass by it; turn away from it and pass on" (Proverbs 4:14–15 NASB). The godly love not the world, nor the things that are of the world, and live differently from the world (1 John 2:15–17; 2 Corinthians 6:17). They refrain their feet from "evil" (wickedness). This is why Isaiah calls this highway "the highway of holiness" (Isaiah 35:8 NLT).

Right and holy conduct "preserves" (guards, protects, keeps safe) the believer's life from harm, ruin, death, blight on God, and shame. The way of right always leads to man's highest and best good. Proverbs 13:6 (NLT) says, "Godliness guards the path of the blameless, but the evil are misled by sin." "Keep the rules and keep your life; careless living kills" (Proverbs 19:16 MSG). "Thorns and traps are in the way of the sinful. He who watches himself will stay far from them" (Proverbs 22:5 NLV).

The Bottom Line: A. J. Gossip challenges, "You will not stroll into Christlikeness with your hands in your pockets, shoving the door open with a careless shoulder. This is no hobby for one's leisure moments, taken up at intervals when we have nothing much to do and put down and forgotten when our life grows full and interesting....It takes all one's strength and all one's heart and all one's mind and all one's soul, given freely and recklessly and without restraint."[665]

126
Good, extension of kindness to others
Proverbs 11:27

"He that diligently seeketh good procureth favour: but he that seeketh mischief, it shall come unto him."

"And Jesus increased in wisdom and stature, and in favour with God and man" (Luke 2:52).

He that "diligently" (to seek early or earnestly; works hard at being and doing good[666]) seeketh "good" (to do what is right in conduct) procureth "favor" (acceptance by and respect of people[667]): BUT he that seeketh "mischief" (evil, wickedness), it shall "come unto him" (he will find in evil conduct more than he wants—"misfortune, difficultly, trouble"[668]).

He that diligently and constantly looks for opportunities to help others (friends, the poor, orphan, widow, sick, down-and-outers) is highly esteemed, appreciated, respected, well spoken of, and loved ("procureth favor"). The good which is done unto others is reciprocated (Proverbs 11:17) and rewarded by God. The exact opposite is true for him that seeks opportunities to do mischief regardless of the harm it brings unto others.

For the Lord Jesus Christ's sake,
Do all the good you can
To all the people you can
In all the ways you can
As long as ever you can.
~ Inscription on a tombstone at Shrewsbury, England

Be authentic; don't *fake* concern in the good done.

The Bottom Line: Adoniram Judson encourages believers to "embrace every opportunity of exercising kind feelings and doing good to others, especially to the household of faith."[669]

127
Gossip, its destructiveness
Proverbs 20:19

"He that goeth about as a talebearer revealeth secrets: therefore meddle not with him that flattereth with his lips."

He that "goeth about" ("house to house") as a "talebearer" (gossip) "revealeth secrets" (betraying trusts, confidentialities): therefore "meddle not" (don't associate) with him that "flattereth" (speaks foolishly, deceitfully; a babbler) with his lips.

An up-and-coming young evangelist years ago made the mistake of counseling a young girl in private upon her insistence following a revival service. She made advances toward him that were not reciprocated, evoking fury and untruthful accusations from her. The revival was cancelled immediately while the church leaders investigated the matter. The preacher honestly testified and asked to face his accuser. The leaders thought such was justified and called for the girl along with her parents to meet with the committee and the preacher. The accused pleaded with the girl to tell the truth, citing that his reputation and ministry were on the line, that both would be irreparably jeopardized. In time, the girl in tears confessed to the injurious lie that was fabricated. A revival was shut down (no telling how many souls might have been won had it not been interrupted) and a young evangelist's reputation scarred and his ministry damaged (at least temporarily, if not permanently) all because of a lie that masqueraded as truth.

Chuck Swindoll offers timely counsel to those who are spreading rumors, lies and slander against another. He states, "There is nothing more treacherous you could be doing than that—nothing. If you claim to be a follower of Christ, that must stop—now. You hurt the body. You disease the church. You ruin the testimony of Christ. There is nothing the lost world loves to hear and see more than the family of God fighting each other."[670]

The Bottom Line: Hopefully you agree with A. B. Simpson, who said, "I would rather play with forked lightning or take in my hand living wires with their fiery current than speak a reckless word against any servant of Christ or idly repeat the slanderous darts which thousands of Christians are hurling on others."[671]

128
Government, its effect for good or evil
Proverbs 29:16
"When the wicked are multiplied, transgression increaseth: but the righteous shall see their fall."

"As they were increased, so they sinned against me: therefore will I change their glory into shame" (Hosea 4:7).

When the "wicked" (godless, especially when in authority positions) are "multiplied" (increased time and again; Bridges says that the increase in sin will not only be in number but also in power[672]), "transgression" (evil, sinful, corrupt) "increaseth" (Garrett says, "Literally, when the wicked increase, rebellion increases"[673] [When the godless are many, sins become many]): BUT the "righteous" (the upright, godly, he that does what is honorable and just) shall see "their fall" (God will exhibit vengeance, display divine wrath upon them, for He is not to be mocked; experience a great fall into ruin, destruction). Allen Ross summarizes, "When the 'wicked thrive,' then sin thrives."[674] See Psalm 37:34–36.

Ungodly government increases "transgression" (lawlessness; wickedness) through the wrong it sanctions, legalizes and encourages. The hearts of the righteous are crushed, oppressed and depressed in the rampage of evil that stalks the land; they groan for deliverance (Proverbs 29:2). Wickedness in high and low places, though it flourishes, will suddenly flounder. Its end will be witnessed by the righteous ("shall see their fall"). "Wait on the LORD, and keep his way, and he shall exalt thee to inherit the land: when the wicked are cut off, thou shalt see it" (Psalm 37:34). "The triumphing of the wicked is short, and the joy of the hypocrite but for a moment" (Job 20:5). The time will come when "the earth shall be filled with the knowledge of the glory of the LORD, as the waters cover the sea" (Habakkuk 2:14).

Matthew Henry offers encouragement to the righteous in an era of great sin. "Let not the righteous have their faith and hope shocked by the increase of sin and sinners. Let them not say that they have cleansed their hands in vain or that God has forsaken the earth, but wait with patience. The transgressors shall fall. The measure of their iniquity will be full; and then they shall fall from their dignity and power and fall into disgrace and destruction; and the righteous shall have the satisfaction of seeing their fall, perhaps in this world, certainly in the judgment of the great day when the fall of God's implacable enemies will be the joy and triumph of glorified saints."[675]

The Bottom Line: Noah saw the fall of wickedness (Genesis 7:23), Moses witnessed the fall of Egyptian captivity (Exodus 14:30), and Abraham likewise witnessed the fall of Sodom and Gomorrah (Genesis 19:28). God promises the believer that he too will witness the fall of wicked government and wickedness. And He keeps His Word. Don't lose hope, for "redemption draweth nigh" (Luke 21:28). A day is coming when "the kingdoms of this world are become the kingdoms of our Lord, and of his Christ; and he shall reign for ever and ever" (Revelation 11:15). Glory, hallelujah! Hasten such a day, O Lord. All of creation groans for its arrival (Romans 8:22).

129
Government, the righteous rule brings rejoicing
Proverbs 20:8

"A king that sitteth in the throne of judgment scattereth away all evil with his eyes."

A "king" (judicial judges) that sitteth in the "throne of judgment" (place of authority to render legal binding decisions[676]) "scattereth" (sifts out the lies from the truth, not easily fooled[677]) away all evil with "his eyes" (ability to "see" through the deceit, falsehood, to uncover the truth regardless who the accused may be [Proverbs 20:26]).

The principle stated is true; righteous judicial leaders have the desire and power to remove from government the corrupt. The righteous rules with "his eyes" (not having his eyes closed to wrongdoing), ever seeking the exposure and punishment of the wicked. And such righteous rule brings rejoicing to the people. "When it goeth well with the righteous, the city rejoiceth: and when the wicked perish, there is shouting. By the blessing of the upright the city is exalted: but it is overthrown by the mouth of the wicked" (Proverbs 11:10–11). The righteous are placed in office by their constituency, as are the wicked. The Christian's vote at the ballot box helps ensure "righteous rule" locally and nationally. The righteous have certainly experienced *sorrowing*, grieving with regard to unrighteous judicial leaders from the White House down to the city mayor's office, time and again through the ages. But they have also known times of *rejoicing* when the righteous were in rule.

The Bottom Line: Matthew Henry summarizes, "The happy effect of a good government: the presence of the prince goes far towards the putting of wickedness out of countenance; if he inspect his affairs himself, those that are employed under him will be kept in awe and restrained from doing wrong. If great men be good men and will use their power as they may and ought, what good may they do and what evil may they prevent!"[678]

130
Grandchildren, the "pride and joy" of the old
Proverbs 17:6

"Children's children are the crown of old men; and the glory of children are their fathers."

"Children's children" (grandchildren) are the "crown" ("reward," "honor," "pride"[679]) of "old men" (elders, the aged); AND the "glory" (similar to "crown"; pride) of "children" (Joseph was a crown to his aged father [Genesis 47:11–12]; Jacob was the glory of his son Joseph [vv. 7–10]).

To live long enough to see "children's children" is the "crown" (honor, cause for joy) of parents. What ecstasy it is to see grandchildren walking in the way in which their parents as children were reared spiritually. Grandchildren add a dimension to the life (splash out sunshine, fill the room with sweet fragrance, enhance happiness) of their grandparents that is indescribable. Every grandparent without doubt says, "If I'd known grandchildren were so much fun, I'd have had them first." Jay Kesler said, "Grandparents have always played an important role in providing stability and support for families."[680] Kesler further states that the family in ancient times had the involvement of the extended family, especially grandparents, for such was crucial to the survival of the children.[681] The same is no less true today.

Dr. Karl Pillemer, who studies aging and intergenerational relationships, underscores the importance of the relationship between children and their grandparents. He notes that, "Research shows children need four to six involved, caring adults in their lives to fully develop emotionally and socially" and that "the grandparent/grandchild relationship is second in emotional importance only to the parent/child relationship."[682] So you have good reason to "spoil" the grands. By the way, grandparenting has a boomerang effect. As you invest in the grandchildren, they enhance your life emotionally and socially. The bottom line is that grandparenting is good medicine.

"The glory of children are their fathers." Fathers and grandfathers must so order their lives in the path of the Lord that their children and "children's children" will have reason to be proud of them (godly and righteous life). What a worthy challenge this is for every father. Billy Graham said, "The greatest legacy one can pass on to one's children and grandchildren is not money or other material things accumulated in one's life, but rather a legacy of character and faith."[683] Work tirelessly to carve into the hearts of those whom you love godly affirmations, convictions and values by example and precept. Remember, a godly legacy won't just happen. It must be tediously and prayerfully built. The "honor" of "children's children" to their grandparents and that of children to their parents all is contingent upon a life of devoted commitment to God. Moses elucidates, "That thou mightest fear the LORD thy God, to keep all his statutes and his commandments, which I command thee, thou, and thy son, and thy son's son, all the days of thy life; and that thy days may be prolonged" (Deuteronomy 6:2).

The Bottom Line: Grandparents' purpose in life, if none other, is to enrich the lives of their grandchildren spiritually, emotionally and socially. And they get to have fun doing it! I say with David, "May you live to see your children's children" (Psalm 128:6 NIV).

131
Greed, leads to gloom and doom
Proverbs 1:19
"So are the ways of every one that is greedy of gain.

"The love of money is the root of all evil" (1 Timothy 6:10).

So are the "ways" (paths; manner of life) of every one that is "greedy" (stinginess) for "gain" (unjust).

Greed is an insatiable desire for *always more* of the world's material goods, primarily money. What the greedy may not gain by honest means he does by chicanery or overwork to the neglect of family. Jesus gave warning about the deadly, destructive sin of greed: "Take heed, and beware of [watch against, preserve yourself from] covetousness" (Luke 12:15). Greed's motto is: "He who dies with the most toys wins." John D. Rockfeller was America's first billionaire. When a reporter asked him, "How much money is enough?" he responded, "Just a little bit more." The greedy never have quite enough. He who learns to live with less lives best (contentment instead of covetousness), "for a man's life consisteth not in the abundance of the things which he possesseth" (Luke 12:15). Happiness and meaning in life are not contingent upon accumulation of wealth or the world's "toys" ("abundance of the things") but rather is found in a personal relationship with Jesus Christ (John 10:10). Among the poor are found some of the happiest people, while among the wealthy are some of the most miserable. It's not what man possesses externally that grants peace, hope and joy, but that which is within him. Jesus said, "He that believeth on me, as the scripture hath said, out of his belly shall flow rivers of living water" (John 7:38).

The Bottom Line: Dr. David Myers, a psychologist whose research includes hundreds of studies on happiness, concludes, "Making more money—that aim of so many graduates and other American dreamers...does not breed bliss."[684] Many, after climbing the ladder to happiness, discover it was leaning against the wrong wall (greed, covetousness).

132
Grief, helping children cope with sorrow
Proverbs 15:13
"By sorrow of the heart the spirit is broken."

By the "sorrow of the heart" (heartache, pain, grief) the "spirit" (the "inner man being"; morale[685]) is "broken" (crushed, depressed, despair).

See Proverbs 15:4; 17:22; 18:14. H. A. Ironside summarizes, "A burdened heart is the portion of the one who tries to carry his own sorrows and daily cares and fails to turn all over to Him who so delights to bear them for us. Nothing breaks the spirit like hidden grief, but such need not be the portion of any saint who will allow the Lord Jesus to be not only his Sin-bearer but his Burden-bearer too."[686]

Children take their cues about death from you. Well-intentioned people often say to a parent in times of horrendous grief, "You must be strong for your children." They are wrong. In all reality, seeing how you handle heart-wrenching grief is what they most need for the present hour and future ones. By parental example, children learn that it's acceptable (and healthy) in their times of grief for Christians to weep, mourn, cry out for help, be distraught, experience sleepless nights and lonely days, and at times even question God about why the family member or friend died when and how he did.

Helpful guidelines from the writing of Dr. James Dobson (revamped and expanded with several of my own) will help your child deal with grief.[687]

Children should not only be permitted to cry but encouraged to cry as long as there is need. "Don't cry" should not be uttered by parents to their children.

Children must never be told they are acting "babyish" for crying.

Children must never feel ashamed for crying.

Children should be allowed their private time to grieve, if needed; if not, physical contact with others will be healing medicine.

Children should be told the truth about death. Saying simply, "Daddy has gone on a vacation," or, "Mommy has taken a trip," or, "Brother has moved away" only confuses the child more and delays the inevitability of explaining what has really happened. The use of such language to young children speaks of a soon return of their loved one which will never happen. "We can say," states Dr. James Dobson, "'Your mother is gone for now, but thank God, we'll be together again on the other side!'" How comforting for a grieving child to know that a family reunion will someday occur from which there will never be another separation! I recommend that Christian parents begin acquainting their children with the gift of eternal life long before they have need of this understanding."[688]

Children should be encouraged but not forced to view the body of daddy or mommy, etc. Such will help in understanding the finality of the loss of physical life. Children are prone to feel guilty for a parent's or sibling's death if they were angry or disobedient prior to the time of departure—they tend to believe it was their anger or disobedience that caused mommy or sister to leave (die). Assure them such is not the case.

Children should be allowed to ask questions, some of which you may not be able to answer. Remember that young children take what you say literally. The mentality of very young children is not mature enough to understand that everyone and everything will die, that death is certain and final. It is beyond their limited comprehension to understand that since daddy died, daddy will not be home from work tomorrow as usual.

Children should be taught that death is part of life for everyone.

A father's business required him to take a long walk through the Alps early in the morning and back home after dark. As his son grew up, he begged to be taken on these trips, but the father thought his little legs too weak to make the journey. Finally, after years of refusal, the father gave in and agreed to take him on the next trip.

In the early morning walk they crossed a valley on a high rope bridge with a few missing slats. With daylight and dad leading the way, it posed no problem for the young boy to cross. Once completing their business in the city, they set out for home. The boy began to worry about crossing the rope bridge after dark and shared that fear with his father. The missing slats, the deep gorge, the thick darkness all were of grave concern.

Unable to cross the bridge until they came to it, the father was unable to give the boy assurance everything would be just fine. With strong arms and a loving heart he placed his son on his back, seeking to assure him. The next thing the boy remembered was awakening to early rays of sunlight and seeing a silhouette of his father standing in the doorway. "Dad, what happened?" the boy inquired. "What about the bridge?" he worried out loud. "Well, Son, you fell asleep with your arms around my neck. I carried you across the bridge and laid you safely in your own bed. You've just awakened on the other side."[689] What a beautiful picture of the death of a child of God!

The Bottom Line: Sorrow is part and parcel of life, something from which parents cannot protect their children. Your proper response to death and teaching from you will benefit them more than volumes written in

183

books upon the subject. A wounded, crushed spirit is manifested on the face, just as is a joyous disposition.

133
Grudges, shrug off insults and hurts
Proverbs 10:12
"Hatred stirreth up strifes: but love covereth all sins."

"It is his [man's] honor and glory to overlook a transgression or an offense [without seeking revenge and harboring resentment]" (Proverbs 19:11 AMP).

"Hatred" ("extreme dislike or disgust" for another *[Merriam-Webster]*) "stirreth up" (to incite, spur) "strifes" ("refers to discord, conflict, disharmony, quarrels, and fighting between people"[690]): BUT "love" (affectionate concern) "covereth" (not only means to conceal [tomb of the soul] but to "forgive"[691]).

William McDonald interprets Proverbs 10:12 as follows: "A hateful spirit isn't satisfied to forgive and forget; it insists on raking up old grudges and quarrels. A heart of love draws a curtain of secrecy over the faults and failures of others. These faults and failures must, of course, be confessed and forsaken, but love does not gossip about them or keep the pot boiling."[692] Jesus portrays this covering of love in His atonement for our sins upon the cross (1 Peter 2:21–24).

Forgiving is not an erasure. "When we grant forgiveness, does that entail a promise to forget the offense completely?" John MacArthur answers, "Yes and no. There is obviously no way to purge the memory of an offense. And the more severe the offense, the more difficult it may be to keep the memory from coming to mind."[693] Therefore what is involved in forgiveness is not the promise to forget but rather not to ever bring the offense up again. Jay Adams characterizes this promise as threefold: "You promise not to remember his sin by bringing it up to him, to others or to yourself. The sin is buried."[694] Lewis B. Smedes states, "Forgiving does not erase the bitter past. A healed memory is not a deleted memory. Instead, forgiving what we cannot forget creates a new way to remember. We change the memory of our past into a hope for our future."[695]

The Bottom Line: Instead of being *hateful,* ever fueling the flames of old grudges, manifest the grace of God to forgive and *forget.* Thanks be unto God that He does not hold grudges toward us! John Chrysostom said, "As a spark falls into the sea and doesn't harm the sea, so harm may be done to a loving soul and is soon quenched without ever disturbing that soul." His words picture the effect of forgiveness over against that of holding grudges and resentment.

134
Guilt, freedom from haunting guilt
Proverbs 16:6
"By mercy and truth iniquity is purged."

By "mercy and truth" (God's love and loyal faithfulness has provided a way for man's justification; His Word promises it; His mercy secures it) "iniquity" (sin and its guilt) is "purged" (banished, covered, forgiven, and atoned for through the blood of the Lord Jesus Christ [Jesus "by himself purged our sins"—Hebrews 1:3]).

Arthur Conan Doyle, author of the Sherlock Holmes mysteries, played a practical joke on twelve famous friends, all of whom were virtuous and greatly respected. He sent each the same telegram: "Fly at once; all is discovered!" Within twenty-four hours, the men were on a plane out of the country. Guilt plagues all, regardless of honorable reputation or status. Adrian Rogers comments, "Guilt brings anxiety. It brings depression. The soul becomes a window covered with the dirt and grime of guilt. Everything we look at is colored or discolored by the guilt within. Guilt can make you sick. If you carry around a load of guilt, it can make you emotionally, spiritually and even physically ill."[696]

Upon doing wrong, with godly repentance you confessed it to God and were forgiven. Then why still the heart-crushing, soul-accusing guilt? Why the humiliating shame? The bottom line is that guilt and shame are Satan's insidious robbers of our happiness, peace of mind and self-worth which are spurred by him continuously in the heart. Jesus said, "The thief cometh not, but for to steal, and to kill, and to destroy: I am come that they might have life, and that they might have it more abundantly" (John 10: 10).

There are two kinds of guilt mentioned in the Bible. The first is that produced by the Holy Spirit when a wrong has been committed (John 16: 8). When one expresses godly sorrow unto God over the sin (confession) and resolves not to engage in the act again (repentance), the sin is forgiven (2 Corinthians 7:10). The second kind is false guilt (accusations, condemnation) that originates with Satan. Satan will seek to sabotage God's promise to forgive every sinful act. He seeks to steal our peace and happiness, cause us to feel dirty and unworthy (shameful), by feeding the mind the lie that God did not forgive when asked or that we must pay more for the wrong committed to satisfy God. The key to victory over haunting, hurting guilt is in recognizing its source (Satan, the father of lies) and steadfastly, stoutly rejecting giving any place to it (John 8: 44). Don't go rummaging through the cemetery of past sins that long have been forgiven and buried (Ephesians 4:27).

To summarize, healthy (legitimate) guilt originates with God through conviction of wrong; unhealthy (illegitimate) guilt originates with Satan through condemnatory accusation. Far too many Christians, despite this knowledge, yet are in bondage to false guilt. Satan has a "stronghold" in their life that they cannot seem to break. The Apostle Paul said that "the weapons of our warfare are not carnal [of a fleshly or earthly nature], but mighty through God to the pulling down of strong holds" (2 Corinthians 10:4). The stronghold of false, unhealthy guilt is torn down by counteracting what Satan says with that which God says ("renewing of the mind"—Romans 12:2).

A. W. Tozer stated, "Are you still afraid of your past sins? God knows that sin is a terrible thing—and the Devil knows it, too. So he follows us around; and as long as we will permit it, he will taunt us about our past sins. As for myself, I have learned to talk back to him on this score. I say, 'Yes, Devil, sin is terrible—but I remind you I got it from you! And I remind you, Devil, that everything good—forgiveness and cleansing and blessing—everything that is good I have freely received from Jesus Christ.'" Tozer continues, "Why do we claim on one hand our sins are gone and on the other act just as though they are not gone? Brethren, we have been declared, 'Not Guilty!' by the highest court in the universe....Now, on the basis of grace as taught in the Word of God, when God forgives a man, He trusts him as though he had never sinned."[697]

Reread that last sentence until it soaks into your mind. God so forgives the sin committed the moment it is confessed in godly repentance (Acts 20:21; 1 John 1:9) that it is *just as if you had never sinned* (justification). Yes, such forgiveness is undeserved and certainly unmerited. Yes, we should be required to pay more for the hideous sin committed mentally and physically. But because of God's awesome, all-enveloping love for man and graciousness, He overrules these and every other reason why we shouldn't be forgiven and says, "I, even I, am he that blotteth out thy transgressions for mine own sake, and will not remember thy sins" (Isaiah 43:25). "Guilt of sin," states Matthew Henry, "is taken away from us by the mercy and truth of God—mercy in promising, truth in performing, the mercy and truth which kiss each other in Jesus Christ the Mediator."[698] That is, the only lasting solution to a guilty conscience is the forgiveness of Jesus Christ through His rich mercy and grace.

The Bottom Line: Refuse to give place to the haunting memories of forgiven sin that would sow false guilt, through fortification of the mind with the Word of God and prayer.

135

Gullibility, its cause, consequence and cure
Proverbs 14:15

"The simple believeth every word: but the prudent man looketh well to his going."

The "simple" (the gullible; witless; clueless) "believeth every word" (accepts as truth what he hears without examination): BUT the "prudent" (the godly wise, righteous) man "looketh well to his goings" (checks out what he hears for validity or ponders advice proffered with regard to its help or harm). Deane and Taswell summarize, "The credulous fool believes all that he hears without proof or examination; having no fixed principles of his own, he is at the mercy of any adviser and is easily led astray."[699] Waltke states that the gullible are not said to be godless or wicked, but until they exhibit repentance toward God, "they must be grouped with morally culpable fools and mockers."[700]

The "simple," or fool, has no one to blame but himself for being gullible. Wisdom, biblical instruction, and understanding are available to him for the receiving, as they are to all. R. E. Murphy comments, "The whole purpose of the wisdom enterprise [Book of Proverbs] is to make the naive aware of reality and its complications, to enable them to make the right judgment and follow the right path."[701]

Don't swallow everything you hear. There are no "free lunches," despite the advertisement or sales pitch. No credible company will notify you by email requesting personal information in order that you might "claim" the prize. A friend will not text from another country requesting money be sent to a hotel due to robbery (obviously he would call). The "free three-day vacation" isn't really free. The gift card to Amazon or Burger King that only takes a click to receive free is just a baiter (Amazon and Burger King did not authorize it) to get you to enter their website. The foolish and naive believe what they hear at face value.

It is the wise that request proof, documentation and verification prior to making a decision. "A prudent [wise] man foreseeth the evil, and hideth himself: but the simple pass on, and are punished" (Proverbs 22:3). The successful man in life understands that if something sounds too good to be true, it most likely is, so he backs away. The pithy saying of Solomon is especially applicable to spiritual things. Don't believe everything spoken from pulpits or podiums. John cautions, "Beloved, believe not every spirit, but try the spirits whether they are of God: because many false prophets are gone out into the world" (1 John 4:1). Don't be hoodwinked into believing a "lie." John is saying that the truly wise, prudent person will test all he hears with the Word of God prior to embracing it.

Christians are not gullible with regard to their faith. We didn't check our brain at the door at conversion. Intellectually and honestly we evaluated the validity of the Bible, existence of God, person and work of Jesus Christ, doctrine of salvation by grace through faith alone, and other doctrines, determining they were true, completely worthy of acceptance. George Lawson summarizes the principle of the Proverb wondrously, "Multitudes have been seduced into the most dangerous errors and damning sins by seducers whom they believed, either from an implicit faith or from want of care in searching the oracles of Truth [Holy Scripture]. A prudent man will therefore look well to his goings. He will not risk his fortune and happiness, his life and soul, *by believing groundless reports or receiving doctrines that are destitute of sufficient proof.* He considers the Scriptures to be his only rule, and the Spirit that dictated them is their great Interpreter. He searches the Scripture and seeks wisdom from God by daily prayer."[702]

The Bottom Line: This Proverb is deserving of memorization and frequent meditation, for it is an essential principle to be applied to avoid shipwreck spiritually, financially and physically. Adhering to it leads to truth, success, security and happiness. Murphy says, "The caution of the prudent or clever will preserve them from missteps."[703] See Proverbs 13:16.

136
Happiness, found in a "who," not a "what"
Proverbs 3:13

"Happy is the man that findeth wisdom, and the man that getteth understanding."

"Happy" (blessed, fortunate) is the man that "findeth" ("to reach and possess"[704]; resultant of seeking, not by accident is wisdom acquired) "wisdom" (wisdom is divine discernment that enables man to do that which is right and pleasing unto the Lord—which is for his best good—in every course of action), and the man that "getteth understanding" (*draws out* understanding from the wise).

Happiness is not found by chance but by earnest search of truth and knowledge which always ends at the foot of the cross. God promised, "You will seek me and find me when you seek me with all your heart" (Jeremiah 29:13 NIV). A drunkard was staggering along the city sidewalk looking for his wallet when a stranger stopped to assist. "Where did you lose it?" he inquired. "Over there in the alley," came the reply. "Then why are you looking for it here on the sidewalk?" The drunkard answered, "Cause there ain't no light over there." People in their quest for happiness are looking in all the wrong places and obviously, therefore, will never find it. Happiness is found in a Person, not a possession; in Christianity, not a creed; in regeneration, not reformation. Jesus said, "I am come that they might have life, and that they might have it more abundantly" (John 10:10).

C. S. Lewis summarizes my point: "God made us—invented us as a man invents an engine. A car is made to run on petrol, and it won't run properly on anything else. Now God designed the human machine to run on Himself. He Himself is the fuel our spirits were designed to burn, or the food our spirits were designed to feed on. There isn't any other. That's why it's just no good asking God to make us happy in our own way without bothering about religion. God can't give us happiness and peace apart from Himself, because it isn't there. There's no such thing."[705]

Octavius Winslow, in *The Sympathy of Christ,* states, "The believer in Jesus is essentially a happy man. The child of God is, from necessity, a joyful man. His sins are forgiven; his soul is justified; his person is adopted; his trials are blessings; his conflicts are victories; his death is immortality; his future is a Heaven of inconceivable, unthought-of, untold and endless blessedness. With such a God, such a Savior, and such a hope, is he not, ought he not to be, a joyful man?" "Happy are the people who are in such a state; Happy are the people whose God is the Lord!" (Psalm 144:15 NKJV). Edward Stieglitz says, "The important thing is not how many years are in your life but how much life in your years." Jesus provides "life" in your years.

The Bottom Line: You will find happiness, peace of mind and significance in entering into a personal relationship with Jesus Christ (Romans 10:9–13).

137
Hardship, its endurance
Proverbs 15:15
"All the days of the afflicted are evil."

"All the days" (sum and total of) of the "afflicted" (the unfortunate; downtrodden; miserable[706]) are "evil" (refers to a difficult, hard life[707]). R. E. Murphy encapsulates the text: "The afflicted can and must cultivate a happy heart. Their lot is hard, but their interior attitude can help them attain some joy in life."[708]

Chuck Swindoll comments, "Words can never adequately convey the incredible impact of our attitude toward life. The longer I live, the more convinced I become that life is ten percent what happens to us and ninety percent how we respond to it."[709] With God's grace, Paul, who suffered many hardships, maintained a right attitude. In 2 Corinthians 11:25–27, he says, "Thrice was I beaten with rods, once was I stoned, thrice I suffered shipwreck, a night and a day I have been in the deep; In journeyings often, in perils of waters, in perils of robbers, in perils by mine own countrymen, in perils by the heathen, in perils in the city, in perils in the wilderness, in perils in the sea, in perils among false brethren; In weariness and painfulness, in watchings often, in hunger and thirst, in fastings often, in cold and nakedness." Paul then says in Philippians 3:8, "Yea doubtless, and I count all things but loss for the excellency of the knowledge of Christ Jesus my Lord: for whom I have suffered the loss of all things, and do count them but dung, that I may win Christ." Despite multiple hardships, Paul states he learned that the secret of endurance with joy was to be content with whatever he had and the circumstances, trusting God for care (Philippians 4:11–12).

While waiting patiently for your hardship to improve or pass, don't complain, grumble or grow embittered; instead, be content knowing God is in control and somehow, someway it will be for *gain,* even as it was for Paul and Job. The Lord blessed the latter part of Job's life more than the first (Job 42:12). "Job found his legacy through the grief he experienced. He was tried that his godliness might be confirmed and validated. In the same way, my troubles are intended to deepen my character and to clothe me in gifts I had little of prior to my difficulties, for my ripest fruit grows against the roughest wall. I come to a place of glory only through my own humility, tears and death, just as Job's afflictions left him with a higher view of God and humbler thoughts of himself. At last he cried, 'Now my eyes have seen you' (Job 42:5). If I experience the presence of God in His majesty through my pain and loss so that I bow before Him and pray, 'Your will be done' (Matthew 6:10), then I have gained much indeed."[710]

A. W. Pink said, "Faith endures as seeing Him who is invisible, endures the disappointments, the hardships, and the heartaches of life by recognizing that all comes from the hand of Him who is too wise to err and too loving to be unkind." C. H. Spurgeon writes, "What an encouraging thought that Jesus—our beloved Husband—can find comfort in our lowly feeble gifts! Can this be? For it seems far too good to be true! May we then be willing to endure trials or even death itself if through these hardships we are assisted in bringing gladness to Immanuel's heart."[711]

The Bottom Line: "When something bad happens, you have three choices: you can let it define you, let it destroy you, or you can let it strengthen you."[712]

138
Hasty, the downside of impulsive decisions
Proverbs 21:5
"The thoughts of the diligent tend only to plenteousness; but of every one that is hasty only to want."

The "thoughts" (plans) of the "diligent" (NJB says "hard-working") tend only to "plenteousness" (profit; "abundance and prosperity"[713]); BUT of everyone that is "hasty" (REB says "rash haste"; the hurried, careless ones; *acts fastly thus rashly* in developing plans or making decisions) only to "want" (poverty; "lacks thing needed"[714]).

He that engages in "Get rich quick" schemes (lying, deceit, robbery, dishonesty) discovers in its wake is sorrow, shame and discontent. In contrast, the person who works honestly to earn "riches" will prosper bountifully in peace, pleasure and provision. See Proverbs 28:6.

The principle is also applicable to that which is done in a hurry without serious consideration as to its merit, ethicalness and consequence. Much havoc and heartache may be spared throughout life simply by pondering an action prior to its performance. Impulsive decisions or hasty speech often are regretted. The more serious a matter the action is and the more difficult it would be to undo, the more thought it requires before undertaking. (Granted, some impulsive decisions spare one from danger; but by and large they place one in jeopardy of trouble, financial or otherwise).

As I write, four teenagers sit in a jail in Indiana, the result of an impulsive decision to rob some houses, that tragically went awry. Not sitting with them is Danzele, who was killed by a homeowner. It wasn't supposed to go down like that. As one of the teens later told *ABC News*, "It was never the plan to hurt anyone or even confront anyone." Sadly, these students learned the hard way that impulsive decisions can lead to serious consequences, even life-ending ones.[715]

Esau's impulsive decision to sell his birthright to Jacob for food was ludicrous and costly (Genesis 25:29–34; 27:34). The author of the book of Hebrews fills in the blanks where Genesis leaves off. "And afterwards, when he wanted those rights back again, it was too late, even though he wept bitter tears of repentance." Then he cautions the believer, "So remember, and be careful" (Hebrews 12:17 TLB). A riot erupted in Ephesus that threatened the very lives of Paul, Gaius and Aristarchus. The town clerk suppressed the crowd, prompting its dispersion and sparing the lives of these three innocent men. In part, he said, "You ought to be quiet (keep yourselves in check) and do nothing rashly" (Acts 19:36 AMP). Thankfully, they listened. May we heed the same appeal.

The Bottom Line: Impulsive speech and decision-making can lead to unintended and harmful consequences.

139
Hatred, seven things God hates
Proverbs 6:16–19

"These six things doth the LORD hate: yea, seven are an abomination unto him: A proud look, a lying tongue, and hands that shed innocent blood, An heart that deviseth wicked imaginations, feet that be swift in running to mischief, A false witness that speaketh lies, and he that soweth discord among brethren."

The seven sins that God abhors and detests depict the utter depravity of man. There is absolutely no evil thing of which man apart from God's grace and power is incapable. Matthew Henry comments, "God hates sin; he hates every sin; he can never be reconciled to it; he hates nothing but sin. But there are some sins which he does in a special manner hate, and all those here mentioned are such as are injurious to our neighbor."[716]

A Proud Look. Solomon condemns a "haughty look" (arrogant, self-inflated, pride) throughout Proverbs. In contrast, it is the humble man in whom God delights, for He states, "To this man will I look, even to him that is poor [or lowly] and of a contrite spirit, and trembleth at my word" (Isaiah 66:2). Live humbly and lowly before the Lord that you may be able to say with the psalmist "LORD, my heart is not haughty, nor mine eyes lofty: neither do I exercise myself in great matters, or in things too high for me" (Psalm 131:1).

A Lying Tongue. "The getting of treasures by a lying tongue is a vanity tossed to and fro of them that seek death" (Proverbs 21:6). In order to gain possessions, popularity and friends, or to avoid punishment for acts committed, lies often are told. Always speak the truth, despite the consequence. H. A. Ironside remarks that "false words bespeak a deceitful heart."[717] Pray continually, "Deliver my soul, O LORD, from lying lips, and from a deceitful tongue" (Psalm 120:2).

Malicious Murder. God values life and condemns the cruelty and viciousness of murder.

Wicked Imaginations. The generator for all unholy deeds is the heart (mind). Of the heart Jesus said, "For out of the heart proceed evil thoughts, murders, adulteries, fornications, thefts, false witness, blasphemies" (Matthew 15:19). Proverbs 4:23 is the Old Testament Matthew 15:19: "Keep and guard your heart with all vigilance and above all that you guard, for out of it flow the springs of life" (AMPC).

Eagerness to Do Wrong. "Their feet run to evil, and they make haste to shed innocent blood: their thoughts are thoughts of iniquity; wasting and destruction are in their paths" (Isaiah 59:7). The wicked, without hesitation, rush into that which is wrong, seeking pleasure, only to find the path taken leads to waste and destruction. "The heart blazes the trail that their feet will follow."[718]

Slanderous Tongue. A slanderer is a person who gives an evil or untrue report (verbal, gestures, writing, pictures, etc.) about another. The Old Testament condemns slandering: "Do not spread false reports. Do not help a guilty person by being a malicious witness" (Exodus 23:1 NIV), as does the New Testament: "Brothers and sisters, do not slander one another. Anyone who speaks against a brother or sister or judges them speaks against the law and judges it. When you judge the law, you are not keeping it, but sitting in judgment on it" (James 4:11 NIV).

An old writer has said about slander, "This is an accursed thing! It works oftentimes by other means than words: by a look or a shrug of the shoulders it levels its poisoned arrows. It has broken many a virtuous heart and stained many a virtuous reputation. It has nodded away many a good name and winked into existence a host of suspicions that have gathered round and crushed the most chaste and virtuous of our kind. It often works in the dark and generally under the mask of truthfulness and love."[719]

Divisiveness. God hates the sowing of discord period. Believers are to be peacemakers, not troublemakers. "Talebearing, untrue stories, half-truths, subtle insinuations produce the disruption of friendships and the breakup of fellowship."[720]

Allen Ross wisely observes that these seven hated things have a contrasting parallel with the seven Beatitudes in Matthew 5. He states, "It [Matthew 5] has seven blessed things to answer for these seven hated things."[721]

The Bottom Line: The seven things God hates picture the anatomy of possible wickedness in man (an unhealthy spiritual body): the eyes, the tongue, the hands, the heart, and the feet. Are you in good health? If not, Jesus stands ready to heal (1 John 1:9).

140
Headstrong, it's my way or the highway
Proverbs 18:1

"Through desire a man, having separated himself, seeketh and intermeddleth with all wisdom."

Through "desire" (pleasure; selfish ends) a man, having "separated" (estranged; divorced himself from the religious community/church[722]) "himself" (not excommunicated, personal choice to isolate from it), "seeketh and intermeddleth" ("burst out in contention"—to "snarl," "show the teeth"[723]; defiant, contemptible) with all "wisdom" (sound biblical instruction and divine understanding that comes from God into the deep things of life that enable man to live pleasing in His sight; the man is quarrelsome, in disagreement with the judgment and decision-making of the righteous wise in the church and opposes them).

In the church are unquestionably Christians who are gifted spiritually that are extremely headstrong with regard to their opinions and leadership. These are congenial and cooperative with the brethren as long as their mandate is *bowed* to and authority recognized. In the case where either is broached, the man's pride surfaces with a demand for adherence to his opinion implicitly, or else he will depart ("separated himself") the church.[724] The principle boils down to the same meaning of the secular proverb that says, "If you don't do it my way, I will take my marbles and play with somebody else." Sadly, there is a segment of the church that makes an exodus not due to theological grounds or for the sake of God's glory, but for their own pleasure and whims. In the path of their departure is left injury to people and the church at large. H. A. Ironside wisely says, "To separate from apostasy is right and scriptural. To separate from what is of God is schism and heresy."[725]

The headstrong are often destructive to the church, as were Hymenaeus and Alexander the coppersmith (1 Timothy 1:20), and need excommunication. Specifically of Alexander the coppersmith Paul said, "Alexander the coppersmith did me much harm, but the Lord will judge him for what he has done. Be careful of him, for he fought against everything we said" (1 Timothy 4:14–15 NLT). People who get in the way of kingdom work by fighting "tooth and nail" with the brethren over how it ought to be done need to repent or be removed so as not to hinder the work of others.

The Bottom Line: Foes to growth in especially "small churches" are the Alexander the coppersmiths. Fear often prevents people from opposing or removing them. Ideally, when the brethren stand firm against their implicit mandates, they will do as the Proverb states: "separate themselves" (excommunicate themselves instead of the church needing to do it).

141
Health, righteousness is medicinal
Proverbs 3:8
"It shall be health to thy navel, and marrow to thy bones."

"For length of days, and long life, and peace, shall they add to thee" (Proverbs 3:2).

"It" (the teaching, instruction and fear of the Lord and abstinence from wrongdoing [Proverbs 3:1–7]) shall be "health" (healing medicine) to thy "navel" (flesh or body) and "marrow" (refreshing the body[726]) to thy bones.

Adherence to the Word of the Lord and His will, by its very nature, tends to preserve man's days (and be medicinal to his health), even as the opposite (unrighteous living) hastens its end. Solomon is promising the righteous "length of days" on earth, as God plans, and in Heaven as well. "Long life" is properly translated "years of life," which conveys the idea of material prosperity.[727]

"Without dispute it is agreed that man's moral and spiritual estate has a close connection upon the physical. It is believed that up to sixty percent of illnesses are caused by emotional stresses (resentment, fear, sorrow, envy, hatred and guilt). Additional illnesses are spurred by alcohol (cirrhosis of the liver); tobacco (emphysema, cancer, heart disease) and immorality (venereal diseases, AIDS)."[728] Exhibiting trust in God for guidance ("not wise in your own eyes"), walking in obedience to God, and avoiding sin are game changers not only spiritually but physically (Exodus 15:26).

Peace is also the benefit of godly living (Proverbs 3:3). God's kind of peace grants rest, security and a sure, safe foundation in spite of whatever may be encountered. "Thou wilt keep him in perfect peace, whose mind is stayed on thee: because he trusteth in thee" (Isaiah 26:3).

The Bottom Line: Godly living benefits spiritually, physically, morally and emotionally. It's a *win-win* life.

142
Heart, an appeal to surrender to the Lordship of Christ
Proverbs 23:26
"My son, give me thine heart, and let thine eyes observe my ways."

"My son" (father's instruction to his son or teacher to a student [God]) give me "thine heart" (mind; the center of thoughts, intelligence, value determinations), AND let thine "eyes observe" (watch my godly example; Reyburn and Fry say "learn from what I do"[729]) "my ways" (lifestyle; manner of life).

Though the proverb presents advice from a father to his son as to how he might avoid the sexual snares placed in his path, it is pertinent to the believer in regard to surrendering to the Lordship of Jesus Christ. God wants the believer's heart fully committed to Him so that He might enrich it (1 Peter 2:1–3), empower it (Hebrews 13:6; 1 Corinthians 10:13), encourage it (Deuteronomy 31:6), establish it (2 Corinthians 1:21), enlighten it (Ephesians 1:17) and enlist it (Matthew 28:18–19).

> Take my poor heart, and let it be
> Forever closed to all but Thee.
> Take my love, my Lord; I pour
> At Thy feet its treasure store. ~ John Wesley

H. A. Ironside explains, "If the young man would be preserved from impurity and ensnarement of soul, God must have his heart. None are safe who allow their affections to be fixed on objects "under the sun." Everywhere are there to be found those who would decoy from the paths of truth and virtue. In the Lord alone is there strength and deliverance."[730] Romans 12:1–2 is the New Testament Proverbs 23:26. In the passage Paul instructs the believer: "I beseech you therefore, brethren, by the mercies of God, that ye present your bodies a living sacrifice, holy, acceptable unto God, which is your reasonable service. And be not conformed to this world: but be ye transformed by the renewing of your mind, that ye may prove what is that good, and acceptable, and perfect, will of God." A living sacrifice is a total presentation of oneself (its members, plans, desires, thoughts, conduct) in devotion to God. This is but man's "reasonable" (logical) response to the supremacy of God, who is Maker, Sustainer and Owner of all that exists.

> Give Thee mine heart? Lord, so I would,
> And there's great reason that I should,
> If it were worth the having;
> Yet sure Thou wilt esteem that good
> Which Thou hast purchased with Thy blood
> And thought it worth Thy craving.
>
> Lord, had I hearts a million
> And myriads in every one
> Of choicest loves and fears,
> They were too little to bestow
> On Thee, to whom I all things owe;
> I should be in arrears.
>
> Yet, since my heart's the most I have
> And that which thou dost chiefly crave,
> Thou shalt not of it miss.
> Although I cannot give it so
> As I should do, I'll offer it though.
> Lord, take it; here it is. ~ Christopher Harvey, Schola Cordis

The Proverb is also applicable to external religious practice apart from internal devotion to the Lord. During the persecution of the Papists by Queen Elizabeth, some wealthy Catholics sought to save their lives by outward compliance with the intolerant laws while remaining Romanists at heart. The Pope, upon being asked for direction as to how to handle them, replied, "Only let them give me their hearts, and they may for this time do as they are compelled to do." Regardless of the validity of the story, we do know for truth that if Satan can "keep the heart," it matters little to him what outward religion is practiced.[731] Outward conformity to religious observances, rules, rituals and traditions does not equate to right standing with or acceptance by God. "This people draweth nigh unto me with their mouth, and honoureth me with their lips; but their heart is far from me" (Matthew 15:8).

The Bottom Line: Cultivate a surrendered and devoted heart to God. See Romans 12:1–2.

143
Heart, its devious plotting schemes
Proverbs 6:18
"An heart that deviseth wicked imaginations."

The "heart" (thought and reasoning center of the body) that deviseth (fabrication) "wicked imaginations" (thoughts of iniquity, evil, wrongdoing) is a hideous and grievous sin unto God. See Isaiah 59:7. To summarize, to allow the heart to be a workshop for the mental fabrication of inordinate, immoral, unethical and indecent behavior is an abomination to God. God condemns it and pledges to punish it.

Stephen Charnock (1628–1680) states, "Let me add this too, that sin in thoughts is more simply sin—outward acts are but the sprouts; the sap and juice lie in the wicked imagination or contrivance, which has the strength in it to produce a thousand fruits [just] as poisonous." John Flavel (1630–1691) said, "Thy thoughts are vocal to God." Adam Clarke remarks (1760–1832), "It is the earnest wish or desire of the soul which in a variety of cases constitutes the good or evil of an act. If a man earnestly wish to commit an evil but cannot because God puts time, place and opportunity out of his power, he is fully chargeable with the iniquity of the act." Matthew Henry (1662–1714) writes, "There is such a thing as *heart-adultery*—adulterous thoughts and dispositions which never proceed to the act of adultery or fornication."

Solomon declares that evil thoughts that produce wicked actions are born in the heart (Proverbs 4:23; 12:20; 14:22). Keep your heart (no entrance to unholy, corrupt and lustful imaginations) therefore with all diligence. Abstain from that which *feeds* the heart with fuel for devious thinking (indecent or obscene movies, books, magazines, Internet websites); and likewise avoid the people, places and pleasures that incite them. Saturate the mind with the Word of God in reading and hearing. *Darkness cannot abide where Light resides.* Martin Luther King well said, "Darkness cannot drive out darkness; only light can do that."[732]

The Bottom Line: "Finally, brethren, whatever things are true, whatever things are noble, whatever things are just, whatever things are pure, whatever things are lovely, whatever things are of good report, if there is any virtue and if there is anything praiseworthy—meditate on these things" (Philippians 4:8 NKJV).

144
Heart, its divine weight scales
Proverbs 21:2
"Every way of a man is right in his own eyes: but the LORD pondereth the hearts."

"Every way" (actions, behavior, conduct) of a man is "right" (morally right, pure, correct) in his own "eyes" (opinion, perspective): BUT the Lord "pondereth" (weighs, tests, judges conduct and motives[733]) the hearts (see 1 Samuel 16:7). C. H. Spurgeon summarizes that "He knows all things, but He is pleased to show us the strictness of His examination by the use of the metaphor of weighing. He takes nothing for granted; He is not swayed by public opinion or moved by loud profession; He brings everything to the scale, as men do with precious things or with articles in which they suspect deception. The Lord's tests are thorough and exact."[734]

Scripture indicates the various type hearts that God weighs. The natural man's heart is weighed in God's balances and found wanting of salvation (1 Corinthians 2:14). The perverse man's heart is tested only to reveal rebellion and defiance (Proverbs 16:28). The proud man's heart is examined and discovered to be filled with godless arrogance and conceit (Isaiah 2:11). The hard man's heart is judged guilty of stubbornness and obstinacy to God's invitation to repent (Romans 2:5). The wishy-washy heart placed upon the divine scales is revealed as inconsistent, unstable and undependable spiritually (James 1:8). The indecisive man's heart is checked and ruled unacceptable (1 Kings 18:21). The deceived man's heart, though convinced of its purity and moral uprightness, is judged as being in error (Proverbs 21:2). In the case of all such hearts, God's judgment is thorough, true and inescapable.

The way to an *acceptable heart* unto the Lord begins with a *humbled heart*. David declares, "The sacrifices of God are a broken spirit: a broken and a contrite heart, O God, thou wilt not despise" (Psalm 51:17). Solomon says, "By humility and the fear of the LORD are riches, and honour, and life" (Proverbs 22:4), and, "The fear of the LORD is the instruction of wisdom; and before honour is humility" (Proverbs 15:33).

The Bottom Line: Fear being weighed and found wanting, as Belshazzar was (Daniel 5:27). Judgment fell upon him and will likewise fall upon all "found wanting." Weigh your heart upon Heaven's scale (Holy Scripture) to see if you meet with divine approval.

145
Hedonism, the pursuit of pleasure ends in want
Proverbs 21:17
"He that loveth pleasure shall be a poor man: he that loveth wine and oil shall not be rich."

He that "loveth" (lives to have a good time; "an excessive or uncontrolled indulgence in pleasure"[735]) "pleasure" (enjoyment; reason for life) shall be a "poor man" (impoverished, in want): he that loveth "wine and oil" (habit of a lifestyle of "unbridled luxuries"[736]; "costly indulgences"[737]) shall not be "rich" (never have money; impoverished).

Hedonism defined by the *Merriam-Webster Dictionary* is "the doctrine that pleasure or happiness is the sole or chief good in life." Google dictionary states hedonism is "the ethical theory that pleasure (in the sense of the satisfaction of desires) is the highest good and proper aim of human life." Its synonyms include self-indulgence, pleasure-seeking, self-gratification, debauchery.

> We have had enough, once and for all, of hedonism—the gloomy philosophy which says that pleasure is the only good.
> C. S. Lewis

Proverbs states that hedonism, "loveth pleasure [and] wine" (excessive feasting, sinful folly and its constant pursuit), is a cause for poverty (21:17) and shipwreck of life for time and eternity (2:22). Adopting the mindset to do what comes naturally (Matthew 15:19), withholding nothing that is desired (Ecclesiastes 2:10) and doing what is right in your own eyes (Judges 21:25) is sinful, wanton foolishness (Proverbs 10:23; 12:15; 14:19; 28:26; Romans 1:22). Just ask Solomon (Ecclesiastes 2:4–15). The meaning and purpose of life is not found in the endless pursuit of pleasure (eat, drink and be merry). Rather, it is discovered in a personal relationship with the Creator and Sustainer of life through Jesus Christ (John 10:9–10).

The Bottom Line: "There is a way which seemeth right unto a man, but the end thereof are the ways of death. Even in laughter the heart is sorrowful; and the end of that mirth is heaviness" (Proverbs 14:12–13). He with the most "toys" in the end doesn't *win.*

146
Hell, the eternal doom of sinners
Proverbs 24:20

"For there shall be no reward to the evil man; the candle of the wicked shall be put out."

"Hell and destruction are never full" (Proverbs 27:20).

For there shall be no "reward" (future hope; no happy future in store[738]) to the "evil man" (the wicked, foolish); the "candle shall be put out" (the light of physical life will be snuffed out[739]).

The Proverb stops with the wicked man's judgment physically. His judgment spiritually is revealed in Revelation 21:8: "But the fearful, and unbelieving, and the abominable, and murderers, and whoremongers, and sorcerers, and idolaters, and all liars, shall have their part in the lake which burneth with fire and brimstone: which is the second death." The ungodly that mock God with their lips, profane Him with their conduct, and abhor His Word with disdain had better extract from life on earth all joy possible, for a day is approaching when they will be cast into eternal Hell to suffer indescribable torment and anguish forever and forever. It has been said that eye hath not seen, nor ear heard, nor hath it entered into the heart of men what awaits a man in Hell. The narrative of the rich man and Lazarus told by Jesus reveals Hell's sordid nature (Luke 16:19–31).

Hell is a *place of Pain* (vv. 23–24). Physical and mental torment unimaginable will be experienced in Hell. Scripture makes clear that there will be varying degrees of punishment inflicted in Hell (Matthew 10:15; 11:22, 24; Mark 6:11; Hebrews 10:29).

Hell is a *place of Passion* (v. 24). Insatiable appetites and desires plague the inhabitants of Hell forever and ever.

Hell is a *place of Parting* (v. 26). The unsaved are forever separated from the redeemed.

Hell is a *place of Prayer* (v. 27). The eternally damned will come to see the need of God but woefully too late. Hell is a domain in which men with weeping, wailing and gnashing of teeth cry out to God for salvation, but in vain.

Hell is a *place of Permeating Darkness.* Jude describes Hell as "the blackness of darkness for ever" (Jude 13). Utter blackness makes relationships impossible in Hell. C. S. Lewis declared Hell is a place of "nothing but yourself for all eternity!" The inhabitants of Hell know only isolation and utter loneliness; there are no friendships or fellowship.

Hell is a *place of Permanence* (v. 26). Hell has no "Exits." There is no way out of Hell, so there is no hope for its inhabitants. This is one of the worst things about Hell. It is a place where you will be absolutely without hope, for not even God can grant deliverance from one already there. One can purchase a shirt in the country store in Hell, Michigan, that states, "I've been to Hell and back"; but a person cannot purchase such a shirt in Satan's domain of eternal darkness.

To go to Hell, a person must walk around the cross in rejection of Jesus Christ. You ask, "How can a loving God send someone to Hell?" It is man's doing. Hell was made for the Devil and his demons, not man. Man goes to Hell by personal choice. If a person dies and ends up in Hell, he will go there over the warnings of God, the prayers of the saints, the preaching of the minister, the wooing of the Holy Spirit, and the Holy Bible. God has done all He can to keep man out of Hell. All must choose not to go there by repenting of sin and submitting to Christ as Lord and Savior.

The Bottom Line: Hell is a choice. C. S. Lewis said, "There are only two kinds of people in the end: those who say to God, 'Thy will be done,' and those to whom God says, in the end, 'Thy will be done.' All that are in Hell choose it."

147
Helpers, the holders of the "ropes"
Proverbs 11:25

"The liberal soul shall be made fat: and he that watereth shall be watered also himself."

"She [Phebe] herself also hath been a helper of many, and of mine own self" (Romans 16:2 ASV).

The "liberal soul" (generous, charitable; the person who gives generously to the blessing of others) shall be made "fat" (he that gives receives bountifully from the Lord blessings of prosperity). To be a helper of them in the "harvest," financially and otherwise, will be rewarded graciously and bountifully by the Lord.

In 1792, William Carey challenged his brethren to obey their responsibility to take the Gospel to unreached lands. *The Particular Baptist Society for Propagating the Gospel Amongst the Heathen* was formed. At its meeting, Andrew Fuller remarked, "There is a gold mine in India, but it seems as deep as the center of the earth. Who will venture to explore it?" An answer came from Carey: "I will venture to go down; but remember, you must hold the ropes." Fuller afterward said, "We solemnly engaged to do so, pledging ourselves never to desert him as long as we should live." William Carey spent forty years in India and translated the Bible into forty languages. The need is great for more people to "hold the ropes" for missionaries, evangelists and church planters. Though you may not be able to go to the "regions beyond" with the Gospel, you can facilitate that undertaking of others.

In a fishing village that was located at the mouth of a turbulent river, a scream was heard: "Boy overboard!" The strongest swimmer in the village tied one end of a rope around his waist and threw the other end among the crowd gathered and plunged into the river. He gallantly fought the tide until he reached the young boy, and a great cheer went up when he grasped him into his arms. He then shouted, "Pull in the rope!" Each upon the shore looked one to the other, inquiring, "Who is holding the rope?" Sadly, no one was. In the excitement of watching the rescue effort, they allowed the rope to slip into the water. Unable to help, they watched two lives drown because no one made it his business to hold the other end of the rope. Make it your business to hold the shore end of the rope for God's chosen servants through intercessory prayer, encouragement and financial support as they seek to rescue the unsaved locally and globally. Many yet would go, as did Carey, if they but knew someone would "hold the ropes."

The Bottom Line: Every Christian ought to have rope in hand that is attached around the waist of a servant of God. To whom will you be a "Phebe"?

148
Hold Fast, tightly grasp God's Word
Proverbs 4:13

"Take fast hold of instruction; let her not go: keep her; for she is thy life."

Take "fast hold" (to grasp tightly like a drowning man would take hold of a piece of floating driftwood) of "instruction" (biblical knowledge and its understanding that leads man to live pleasing unto the Lord; divine insight, discernment); "let her not go" (don't loosen your grip upon biblical instruction; whatever you do be sure to keep, observe that which Holy Scripture teaches): "keep her" (guard); for she is "thy life" (the foundation of all of life). Deane and Taswell summarize, "Just in proportion as Wisdom is retained and guarded, so is life secured; and so far as the hold upon her is lost, so are the hopes of life diminished. Life depends upon the observance of her precepts."[740]

Instead of vacillating spiritually, saints are exhorted to "hold fast." The New Testament version of the Proverb is 1 Corinthians 15:58, wherein Paul says, "Therefore, my beloved brethren, be ye stedfast, unmoveable, always abounding in the work of the Lord, forasmuch as ye know that your labour is not in vain in the Lord."

C. H. Spurgeon summarizes Proverbs 4:13: "We are to take fast hold of instruction, and the best of instruction is that which comes from God; the truest wisdom is the revelation of God in Christ Jesus. Of that therefore we are to take fast hold. The best understanding is obedience to the will of God and a diligent learning of those saving truths which God has set before us in His Word, so that in effect we are exhorted to take hold of Christ Jesus our Lord, the incarnate Wisdom in whom dwelleth all the treasures of wisdom and knowledge. We are not to let him go but to keep him and hold him, for he is our life."[741]

The author of Hebrews emphasizes the same: "Therefore we ought to [must] give the more earnest heed to the things which we have heard [biblical truth], lest at any time we should let them slip [drift away from them]" (Hebrews 2:1). The easiest thing in the world to do is to drift; it requires no effort at all. To drift spiritually, all one has to do is simply do nothing with his or her faith. Many who were giants for God no longer are, due to spiritual carelessness. They fail to "hold fast" to biblical instruction and the Lord.

Drifting occurs due to religious surfing. Allowing heretical religious seeds to be sown in the mind will result in devastating spiritual shipwreck (2 Timothy 1:13–14).

Drifting occurs due to wrong friends. Proverbs gives many warnings in this regard (Proverbs 13:20; 18:24; 22:24–25).

Drifting occurs due to living on past spiritual highs. The spiritual emotional high experienced at summer camp or revival won't last long. You can't live on it—it can't be done. A fresh encounter with God daily is an absolute imperative if you are to progress rather than digress spiritually. The Israelites in the wilderness were to gather manna daily. If they sought to save the manna for the next day, spoilage would occur. In this I see the principle of disciplined quiet time. Spiritual manna awaits the believer who is hungry enough to come to the table daily to receive it. Spiritual life is sustained by feasting regularly upon God's Word.

Drifting occurs due to a favorite sin. If you are to live for Christ without wavering, the coattails of former sin must be severed permanently. The sin that you are unwilling to forsake will be the sin that brings you down.

Believers drift due to neglect of God's house. Forsake the church, and your boat is adrift (Hebrews 10:25).

Drifting occurs due to spiritual laziness. In Proverbs 24:30–31, Solomon portrays a towering, strong wall that, due to neglect by its owner (laziness), fell to the ground. Failure to care for the "strong wall" of your walk with Jesus through the disciplines of prayer, Bible study, worship, confession and witnessing will likewise lead to its collapse.

Drifting occurs due to distractions. School, sports, work, dating, relationships and entertainment are potential distractions in living for Jesus. Demas failed to successfully handle the distractions he faced and drifted from his first love for Christ (2 Timothy 4:10). Recognize potential distractions and carefully protect your walk with Christ, lest your end be like that of Demas.

In the time of wooden ships, one was attacked by a wounded whale until it began to sink. Sailors took what possessions they could while trying to escape. As the ship was sinking, two men were seen plunging into the waters' depth in a frantic search for something. Upon surfacing, one embraced an object. Despite the voracious vortex the sinking ship developed, the man in peril of his life held tightly to the object. What was the treasure that incited such a heroic feat? It was the ship's compass, without which it would have been impossible for the sailors to navigate the dangerous sea to safety. The compass prevented their death. It was their lifeline. The Word of God is the same to the believer. It is his compass of life, and he must be willing to *risk all for its preservation.*

The Bottom Line: Take hold firmly and steadfastly of Jesus Christ primarily, then to biblical instruction, prayer, godliness, Bible study and the church, not allowing them to "slip" from your grasp. Their value and benefit are incalculable to all of life.

149
Honesty, better than hypocrisy
Proverbs 13:7
"There is that maketh himself rich, yet hath nothing: there is that maketh himself poor, yet hath great riches."

There is that "maketh himself rich, yet hath nothing" (pretends to be wealthy although poor, for personal gain or acceptance): there is that "maketh himself poor, yet hath great riches" (pretends to be poor although wealthy, for selfish reasons). Allen Ross summarizes Proverbs 13:7: "People may not be what they seem to be."[742]

The ungodly often play the role of the hypocrite. The poor pretends to be rich (for acceptance; impression; avoid embarrassment), and the rich pretends to be poor (to conceal greed; to gain advantage; to avoid solicitation from the truly poor; uncharitableness). Such hypocritical pretense bears a great price. The poor always incurs more and more debt and defrauds more and more people to move in the circles of the rich, to his own ruin. The rich, in concealing their wealth, smites the hand of God who in His providence gave it to him for relief of the poor, care for the widows and orphans, and expansion of His kingdom work. Both types of hypocrites are guilty of grievous sin against Almighty God that will not go unpunished. George Lawson remarks, "Divine providence makes us either rich or poor, and it is our duty cheerfully to acquiesce in its disposal and to suit our appearance and way of life to our circumstances, which are appointed for us by infinite wisdom."[743]

The Proverb makes inference regarding similar hypocrites in the church. Many count themselves to be rich spiritually and present themselves so, when in reality they are bankrupt in soul. To them Jesus declares, "Because thou sayest, I am rich, and increased with goods, and have need of nothing; and knowest not that thou art wretched, and miserable, and poor, and blind, and naked: I counsel thee to buy of me gold tried in the fire, that thou mayest be rich; and white raiment, that thou mayest be clothed, and that the shame of thy nakedness do not appear; and anoint thine eyes with eyesalve, that thou mayest see" (Revelation 3:17–18).

Maclaren says, "If you do not know your need, you will not go to look for supply of it. If you fancy yourselves to be quite well, though a mortal disease has gripped you, you will take no medicine nor have recourse to any physician. If you think that you have enough good to show for man's judgment and for God's, and have not been convinced of your dependence and your sinfulness, then Jesus Christ will be very little to you, and His great work as the Redeemer and Savior of His people from their sins will be nothing to you. And so you will condemn yourselves to have nothing unto the very end."[744]

Likewise, there are spiritually rich believers in the church (Ephesians 3:8) that live *like* the spiritually poor, ignorant of their true position in Christ Jesus.[745] "And if children, then heirs; heirs of God, and joint-heirs with Christ" (Romans 8:17).

The Bottom Line: Be honest and unpretentious. Be what you are, not that which you want others to think you are. "Woe unto you, scribes and Pharisees, hypocrites! for ye are like unto whited sepulchres, which indeed appear beautiful outward, but are within full of dead men's bones, and of all uncleanness. Even so ye also outwardly appear righteous unto men, but within ye are full of hypocrisy and iniquity" (Matthew 23:27–28).

150
Honesty, character trait of the righteous
Proverbs 11:1

"A false balance is abomination to the LORD: but a just weight is his delight."

"Thou shalt not have in thy bag divers weights, a great and a small. Thou shalt not have in thine house divers measures, a great and a small. But thou shalt have a perfect and just weight, a perfect and just measure shalt thou have: that thy days may be lengthened in the land which the LORD thy God giveth thee" (Deuteronomy 25:13–15).

"What shall I say about the homes of the wicked filled with treasures gained by cheating? What about the disgusting practice of measuring out grain with dishonest measures?" (Micah 6:10 NLT).

A "false balance" (false weights used by merchants to jack the price up; fraudulent, deceitful) is "abomination" (abhorable, revolting and disgusting to God): BUT a "just weight" (accurate, honest weights) is his "delight" (pleasing unto the Lord).

Dishonesty (cheat, defraud or swindle, misrepresentation, lying) in any form is forbidden, detested and abhorred ("abomination") by God. He vehemently states displeasure with it. Dishonesty will catch up with you. The story is told of four high school boys who couldn't resist the temptation to skip morning classes. Each had been smitten with a bad case of spring fever. After lunch they showed up at school and reported to the teacher that their car had a flat tire. Much to their relief, she smiled and said, "Well, you missed a quiz this morning, so take your seats and get out a pencil and paper." Still smiling, she waited as they settled down and got ready for her questions. Then she said, "First question—which tire was flat?"[746]

> No legacy is so rich as honesty.
> William Shakespeare

In casting out the dishonest moneychangers in the Temple, Jesus showed His displeasure with those who cheat and swindle others. "And Jesus went into the temple of God, and cast out all them that sold and bought in the temple, and overthrew the tables of the moneychangers, and the seats of them that sold doves, And said unto them, It is written, My house shall be called the house of prayer; but ye have made it a den of thieves" (Matthew 21:12–13). Rationalization never can justify doing something dishonest.

The Bottom Line: Nathaniel Hawthorne encapsulates the difference between honesty and dishonesty in stating, "Accuracy is the twin brother of honesty; inaccuracy, of dishonesty."[747] Christians, of all people, ought to be fair and just in all their personal and business transactions. To be otherwise is gross hypocrisy and a disgrace to their Savior Jesus Christ.

151
Honesty, transacting business honorably
Proverbs 11:1

"A false balance is abomination to the LORD: but a just weight is his delight."

A "false" (dishonest, deceptive) "balance" (weight scale) is "abomination" (detestable) to the Lord: BUT a "just" (accurate, honest) weight is his "delight" (pleasing to Him). See Deuteronomy 25:13–15.

A "false weight scale" is that which the merchant *rigs* to overcharge customers without their knowledge. The dishonest practice is such an "abomination" (repulsive, hated, and abhorred) to the Lord that it incites His indignation. Throughout Scripture dishonesty in business is condemned.

Exodus 20:15: "Thou shalt not steal."

Leviticus 19:35–36: "Ye shall do no unrighteousness in judgment, in meteyard, in weight, or in measure. Just balances, just weights, a just ephah, and a just hin, shall ye have: I am the LORD your God, which brought you out of the land of Egypt."

Deuteronomy 25:13–16: "Thou shalt not have in thy bag divers weights, a great and a small. Thou shalt not have in thine house divers measures, a great and a small. But thou shalt have a perfect and just weight, a perfect and just measure shalt thou have: that thy days may be lengthened in the land which the LORD thy God giveth thee. For all that do such things, and all that do unrighteously, are an abomination unto the LORD thy God." See Proverbs 20:10, 23.

The Christian businessperson should practice honesty, but that sadly is not always the case. Testimonies abound of those *taken in* by crooked and deceitful "Christians." Matthew Henry says, "He is not a godly man that is not honest."[748] Dishonest and deceitful business practices are not always manifest to the customer, causing the fraudulent businessman to think he has gotten by with the thievery. But he is mistaken. See Micah 6:10–13. God will judge harshly and severely the Christian and non-Christian alike who defrauds another for personal gain (Proverbs 20:17).

As a young boy, the preacher Harry Ironside worked for a Christian named Dan Mackay in a cobbler shop.[749] He had the tiring task of hammering water out of wet leather that had soaked in a tub of water all night, until it was dry enough to use as a sole. Ironside one day noticed a cobbler in another shop attaching "wet leather" to shoes and inquired why he did not first pound the water out of the leather. The dishonest cobbler replied, "They come back all the quicker this way, my boy!" Young Ironside conveyed what this cobbler said to his boss, who instantly stopped his work and explained to him that as a preacher was called to preach, he was called to repair shoes and that only as he did this to the best of his ability would God receive glory. Further, he told Ironside that he imagined a scene at the Judgment Seat of Christ when all the shoes he made would be heaped into one pile and Jesus would examine each. "Dan," He would say, holding up a pair of shoes, "that's not up to par. You didn't do a very good job there." But with others He would say, "Dan, that was a splendid job." He continued by telling Ironside that he wanted to make shoes that would pass the inspection of Christ at the Judgment. Whatever the business, so engage in it that at the Judgment it will pass the inspection of Christ.

The Bottom Line: "A just weight is His delight." God is pleased with honest transactions. Honesty is an imperative trait of the child of God. Thomas Jefferson said, "Honesty is the first chapter in the book of wisdom." Build your business upon the reputation of honesty, and there will be no lack for customers.

152
Hope, the believer's certainty of Heaven
Proverbs 14:32
"The wicked is driven away in his wickedness: but the righteous hath hope in his death."

The "wicked" (ungodly) is "driven away" (Fausset and Brown say "thrust out violently"[750]; cast down) by his "wickedness" (the ungodly conduct of the wicked brings them to their own destruction): BUT the "righteous" (the godly wise, upright, honorable; "Christian") hath "hope in his death" (Reyburn and Fry say, "The Hebrew form of the text may be taken as an expression of belief in personal immortality"[751]).

The Christian has *hope* (confidence) that at life's end a better world awaits. Paul pointedly states that to be absent from the body is to be present with the Lord (2 Corinthians 5:8). At the moment that Lazarus died, angels escorted him into the presence of God in Heaven (Luke 16:22). The saint shuts his eyes in death and opens them instantly in Heaven. The epitaph on the tombstone of Solomon Peas, London, England, expresses this biblical truth.

Beneath these clouds and beneath these trees
Lies the body of Solomon Peas.
This is not Peas; it is only his pod.
Peas has shelled out and gone Home to God.[752]

At death, the believers' hope is for *gain*. Paul said, "For to me to live is Christ, and to die is gain" (Philippians 1:21). Christians hope (confident trust; assurance) to gain freedom from sin, sorrow and suffering; fellowship supreme with Jesus and Heaven's citizens; incomparable joy and peace and rest from service and spiritual warfare. Jonathan Edwards comments, "To go to Heaven, fully to enjoy God, is infinitely better than the most pleasant accommodations here."[753] Matthew Henry states, "The righteous then have the grace of hope in them; though they have pain, and some dread of death, yet they have hope. They have before them the good hoped for, even the blessed hope which God, who cannot lie, has promised."[754] In contrast, the wicked will meet death in his sin (its guilt, shame, judgment) and be cast into outer darkness for it ("The wicked is driven away in his wickedness"). His estate at death only moves from bad to worse, whereas for the saint his estate changes from good to far better.

The Bottom Line: John R. Rice said, "Those who go to Heaven ride on a pass and enter into blessings that they never earned, but all who go to Hell pay their own way."[755] John Knox remarks, "When the wicked is paid in his own coin, there is an end of him; at death's door, the just still hope."[756]

153
House, its building blueprint
Proverbs 24:3

"Through wisdom is an house builded; and by understanding it is established."

"Through" (by the means of) "wisdom" (biblical knowledge and understanding [discernment] from God—insight as to how to live pleasingly unto the Lord) is a "house" (home, family) "builded" (constructed on a sure, secure and firm foundation). See Matthew 7:24–27.

Specific instruction is given in the building of a "safe" house in Deuteronomy 22:8: "When thou buildest a new house, then thou shalt make a battlement for thy roof, that thou bring not blood upon thine house, if any man fall from thence." Ancient homes were built with flat roofs where family members would resort for leisure. The command was given for a protective railing to be constructed about it lest a child or guest accidentally fall to his or her death. Figuratively, God commands parents to erect a spiritual barrier or wall about the home for its protection and preservation from evil.

Erect the battlement of marital fidelity. Infidelity leads to divorce, which leads to the breakup of the home and dysfunctional children. Keep your marital vows.

Erect the battlement of moral sanction. Don't allow the corrupt, profane, irreligious or scoffer entrance personally or electronically. Post the signs in front of your house: "No solicitation to evil allowed" and "Posted: Keep Out" to pornography, alcohol, drugs, immorality and gambling.

Erect the battlement of measured discipline. Children *learn* through discipline that there are consequences to disobedience and wrongdoing. Solomon says, "A youngster's heart is filled with foolishness, but physical discipline will drive it far away" (Proverbs 22:15 NLT). Again, he says, "Punishment that hurts chases evil from the heart" (Proverbs 20:30 TLB).

Erect the battlement of modeled example. Austin Sorenson said, "A child is not likely to find a father in God unless he finds something of God in his father." Parents are the example for how children should live their lives. Building the battlements is to be part of the original plan. The house is not complete without it.

Application may be made of the Proverb to the construction of the spiritual house. "For ye are the temple [house] of the living God; as God hath said, I will dwell in them, and walk in them; and I will be their God, and they shall be my people (2 Corinthians 6:16 WBT). The spiritual house is built upon the rock-solid foundation of personal faith in Jesus Christ; its every room, with the lumber of compliance to the Holy Scriptures and the permeation of godliness in its whole. See 2 Peter 1:3. The construction is never ending (2 Peter 3:18). It is a "work in progress." "He's still working on me [as I also am], to make me what I ought to be."[757]

The Bottom Line: A home built upon the shifting sands of irreligion and anti-God values in time will collapse (great will be the fall of it), whereas one built upon the Solid Rock (Jesus Christ and Biblical values) will stand firm regardless of the storms encountered (Matthew 7:24–27). Deane and Taswell state, "By prudence, probity [uprightness], and the fear of God, a family is supported and blessed, maintained and prospered."[758]

154
House, the spiritual house the Divine Architect made
Proverbs 9:1
"Wisdom hath builded her house, she hath hewn out her seven pillars."

"Wisdom" (the fullness and excellences of Wisdom, the Lord God) hath "builded her house" (as a carpenter), she hath "hewn out her seven pillars" (see explanation following). B. H. Carroll paraphrases Proverbs 9:1–6: "Come to a decision; your present neutral position is not tenable. Your choice lies between wisdom and the scorner. Therefore, break altogether with the scorner and the wicked man, and become the guest of wisdom."[759]

In the homes of the rich in ancient Israel *seven pillars* (luxurious) were used to beautify and support the portico (porch or walkway with a roof leading into the house's main entrance).[760] The house (temple) that wisdom (God) has built is perfectly constructed and all sufficient ("seven pillars": the number seven pictures perfection in Scripture) to supply man with bountiful provision for living life meaningfully, knowledgeably, happily and successfully solely based upon the Holy Scriptures. Her "furnished" table fully spread is never exhausted for all to sit and dine, to thereby be enriched spiritually and mentally (Proverbs 9:2–5; 18:4) and find guidance (Proverbs 3:23) to navigate the mazes of life. It is easily accessable (John 14:6).

Come, eat of my bread, and drink of the wine which I have mingled (Proverbs 9:5). Wisdom (God) invites us to 'come and dine' at His table. Jesus offered a similar invitation (John 21:12). In Luke 14:23, the believer is instructed to issue the invitation to the ungodly with urgency ("compel them to come in"). We are to urge the eternally damned to "forsake the foolish" way of life and turn to Christ (Proverbs 9:6). At wisdom's banqueting table awaits Jesus Christ to give him who comes "the bread of life" ("my bread") and "the living water" ("drink of the wine") freely (Proverbs 9:5). See John 6:51 and John 4:14.

Theologians see in Proverbs 9:1 two pictures of Jesus Christ: His incarnation (built Himself a house to live in on earth via the virgin birth) and His formation of the church which is His *body* (1 Peter 2:5). Matthew Henry views it as the saints' eternal abode in saying, "Heaven is the house which Wisdom has built to entertain all her guests that are called to the Marriage Supper of the Lamb; that is her Father's house where there are many mansions and whither she has gone to prepare places for us."[761] With regard to the *seven pillars,* it is viewed by some to be symbolic of the sevenfold gift of the Holy Spirit that rested upon Jesus (Isaiah 11:2)[762] or the sevenfold fruit of wisdom cited in James 3:17.[763]

The Bottom Line: Primarily there stand but two invitations, two paths, two destinies and two choices. Man may heed the call of folly, only to walk the path of foolishness in wickedness to punishment presently and eternally. Or he may receive God's call to salvation through His Son Jesus Christ to walk the path of righteousness to blessing presently and Heaven hereafter. Choose folly and "die." Choose Jesus and "live." The "house" that God built provides nothing but the best for its residents. "Jesus saith unto them, Come and dine" (John 21:12). "O taste and see that the LORD is good: blessed is the man that trusteth in him" (Psalm 34:8). See Revelation 22:17. As the Lord's "maidens," we are commissioned with the task to give *loud* and *immediate* issuance of the invitation to salvation's table (Proverbs 9:3–6).

155
House, the vast treasure of the righteous
Proverbs 15:6

"In the house of the righteous is much treasure: but in the revenues of the wicked is trouble."

In the "house" (abode) of the "righteous" (upright, honorable, just) is much "treasure" (prosperity, if not financially, most certainly spiritually): BUT in the "revenues" (income) of the "wicked" (the unwise godless) is "trouble" (calamity; experience the retribution of God).

The Christian home possesses a treasure chest of wealth (salvation, peace, comfort, contentment, hope, love, God's blessing) which never fades away. Physically and materially it may be meager, but its value spiritually is incalculable.

Oh, the unsearchable riches of Christ,
Wealth that can never be told!
Riches exhaustless of mercy and grace,
Precious, more precious than gold!

Precious, more precious,
Wealth that can never be told!
Oh, the unsearchable riches of Christ,
Precious, more precious than gold!

Oh, the unsearchable riches of Christ!
Who shall their greatness declare?
Jewels whose luster our lives may adorn,
Pearls that the poorest may wear!

Oh, the unsearchable riches of Christ,
Freely, how freely they flow,
Making the souls of the faithful and true
Happy wherever they go!

Oh, the unsearchable riches of Christ!
Who would not gladly endure
Trials, afflictions, and crosses on earth,
Riches like these to secure?   ~ Fanny Crosby (1882)

Though poor on this earth, oh, why should I care,
Since glorious things for me God doth prepare?
Though trials abound, yet, still I may sing:
All glory to God; I'm a child of the King.   ~ Harriet E. Buell (1877)

Not so with the wicked whose "revenues" (income from a life of sin) is trouble. Matthew Henry explains, "There is guilt and a curse; there is pride and passion and envy and contention; and those are troublesome lusts, which rob them of the joy of their revenues and make them troublesome to their neighbors."[764]

The Bottom Line: The believer (whatever his financial state) is far richer than the evil man that has dungeons of silver and gold. See Romans 11:33. The psalmist testifies, "A little that a righteous man hath is better than the riches of many wicked" (Psalm 37:16).

156
Houses, the two kinds; the two outcomes
Proverbs 14:11
"The house of the wicked shall be overthrown: but the tabernacle of the upright shall flourish."

The "house" (residence) of the "wicked" (ungodly) shall be "overthrown" (destroyed; come to ruin): BUT the "tabernacle" (abode) of the "upright" (the wise righteous, honorable) shall "flourish" (prosper).

The house of the godless (evil life and its goods), though luxurious and well-constructed, is built upon a foundation of shifting sand (Matthew 7:26; Proverbs 12:7). It is thought to be permanent, but its suitors will be surprisingly and suddenly "overthrown" (destroyed; suffer ruinous collapse).[765] "Their inward thought is, that their houses shall continue for ever, and their dwelling places to all generations; they call their lands after their own names" (Psalm 49:11).

In contrast, the "tabernacle" (tent; humble abode of the righteous), though inferior to that of the godless externally, is properly built upon a sure foundation (the Solid Rock, Jesus Christ). Its stability is permanent, and all its residents "flourish" (spiritual riches and sometimes others as well). "Great wealth is in the house of the righteous" (Proverbs 15:6 NASB). See Isaiah 33:5–6; Ephesians 1:7–8; 2:7; Philippians 4:19.

The tabernacle of the righteous is "moveable." Tents are designed to be easily disassembled, packed and moved from one place to another. It pictures believers as *sojourners* traveling to a far better place. The world is not their home, so they refuse to drive tent pegs deep into its sod (1 Peter 2:11). "For here have we no continuing city, but we seek one to come" (Hebrews 13:14).

H. A. Ironside summarizes, "The house [of the wicked] might seem by far the more stable, but it shall be overthrown; for its foundations shall be destroyed because built upon sinking sand. The pilgrim's tent wherein the upright tabernacles as he journeys through a foreign scene—foreign to the new nature within him—will abide and flourish till tenting days are over."[766]

I'm but a stranger here;
Heaven is my home.
Earth is a desert drear;
Heaven is my home.
Danger and sorrow stand
'Round me on every hand.
Heaven is my fatherland;
Heaven is my home. ~ Thomas Rawson Taylor (1895)

The Proverb may even have application to the posterity of the ungodly. John Gill remarks, "Their families shall become extinct, none to be their heirs and inherit their estates and transmit their name to posterity; or the substance of their house, their riches and wealth, especially that gotten dishonestly, shall waste away."[767]

The Bottom Line: Don't be deluded by the *appearance* of the estate of the godless (Psalm 37:35–36). Better it is to live in a tent pleasing unto the Lord than to dwell in a mansion in His disfavor. The unbeliever is blinded by Satan to the transitory and destructive nature of his prosperous estate.

157
Humility, the way up is down
Proverbs 18:12
"Before destruction the heart of man is haughty, and before honour is humility."

Before "destruction" (that which leads to ruin; Reyburn and Fry say "the crushing, shattering of man"[768] [Proverbs 16:18; 29:23]) the heart is "haughty" (arrogant, proud), AND before "honor" (respect from others) "humility" (abasement of self; opposite of pride; 'lowliness of mind' [Colossians 3:12]).

Andrew Murray in *Humility* defines *humility* as "the displacement of self by the enthronement of God."[769]

He continues, "It is to expect nothing, to wonder at nothing that is done to me, to feel nothing done against me. It is to be at rest when nobody praises me and when I am blamed or despised."[770]

John the Baptist manifested true humility. Regarding his life and work he said of Jesus, "He must increase, but I must decrease" (John 3:30). The humble defer all glory and praise unto the Lord and honor unto others, preferring to back up into the shadows. In *Mere Christianity*, C. S. Lewis states that the cure for pride is humility. "If anyone would like to acquire humility, I can, I think, tell him the first step. The first step is to realize one is proud—and a biggish step, too. At least nothing whatever can be done before it. If you think you are not conceited, it means you are very conceited, indeed."[771]

The Bottom Line: Andrew Murry states, "Until a humility that rests in nothing less than the end and death of self, and which gives up all the honor of men as Jesus did to seek the honor that comes from God alone (which absolutely makes and counts itself nothing) that God may be all, that the Lord alone may be exalted—until such a humility is what we seek in Christ above our chief joy, and welcome at any price, there is very little hope of a faith that will conquer the world."[772]

158
Husband, wife honoring
Proverbs 31:11–12

"The heart of her husband doth safely trust in her, so that he shall have no need of spoil. She will do him good and not evil all the days of her life."

A godly wife instills "trust" (confidence) in her husband in her capacity as a manager of the household. He has no reason to fear that she will "spoil" (waste; squander that which his labor secures) due to her prudence and discipline. She *always* works diligently to bring him good, never harm, throughout their marriage. The wife that honors her husband seeks his advancement and success in business and elevation in influence among others (Proverbs 31:23). Additionally, a wife honors her life-mate by treasuring him (as a prize catch; greatly loved), respecting him (in contrast to belittling or degrading him and treating him as a child instead of an adult), submitting to him (authority; position as spiritual head of the home), trusting him (until he gives reason of untrustworthiness), praising him (exhibit proudness) and forgiving him ("seventy times seven"). Stand by your man, and in so standing you not only honor him but also God (Romans 12:10–11).

Ruth Graham said, "It is the woman's job to love her husband; it's God's job to make him good."[773] And she certainly did that for the 64 years in marriage to Dr. Billy Graham before her death in 2007.

I read of a three-day retreat for pastors and their wives. In one of the sessions the wives were asked to bear testimony of how the Lord had blessed their lives and ministries. One young wife stood and said, "The Bible promises that 'no good thing does the Lord withhold from them that walk uprightly.' Well," she said, "my husband is one of those 'no good things.'"

I don't think what she said came out like she intended. Let's at least think not. However, if you count your husband a "no good thing" in the negative sense, nurture the relationship with love, honor and submission (within the boundaries of God's Word) until he becomes a "good thing."

The Bottom Line: Holy Scripture instructs, "Give each other more honor than you want for yourselves [or Outdo one another in showing honor; or Be eager to show honor to one another]" (Romans 12:10 EXB).

159
Hypocrisy, parental inconsistencies between faith and practice
Proverbs 20:7
"The just man walketh in his integrity: his children are blessed after him."

It is the parents who walk in integrity (moral uprightness; honesty; walk matches talk) that beget children that are "blessed" (happy; fortunate;

"fare the better for his sake"[774]). Abraham well illustrates the truth (Genesis 17:1–9).

But the opposite equally is true. The parents who continuously fail to match *walk with talk* (practice with profession) are a curse to their children. *Hypocritical parents* turn their children "off" to the church and away from the Christian faith.

C. H. Spurgeon said, "Do you not think that in many families, where the parents are worldly and conformed to the world, it would be a great wonder if the sons and daughters were not ungodly?"[775] Likeness begets likeness. Apples don't fall too far from the tree. To beget ungodly children certainly is a deplorable and despicable sin against God and injurious to the children for time and eternity.

Charles Bridges summarizes, "Christian parents—let integrity, as before God, be the broad stamp of our family religion. Walk not according to the maxims of the world yourselves, nor allow them in your children. Let us make God's Word—His whole Word—our universal rule; His ways, however despised, our daily portion. 'Let us seek first' for our children as for ourselves 'the kingdom of God and His righteousness.'"[776] When we do this, the blessing of which the Proverb speaks shall be conferred upon our children.

The Bottom Line: Don't be a parent that's like a pin, pointing one way but heading the other. "Do not sin against the child" (Genesis 42:22). Kids can spot a fake in an instant. Be their role model by sincerely making the effort to live out the faith not only at church and in the workplace, but also in the home.

160
Hypocrisy, with regard to being a Christian
Proverbs 26:11
"As a dog returneth to his vomit, so a fool returneth to his folly."

As a "dog returneth to his vomit" (dogs disgustingly lap up their vomit; see 2 Peter 2:22), so a "fool" (the unwise, ungodly) "returneth" (fails to learn from wanton mistakes and sins, for he continuously repeats them) to his "folly" (sinful conduct). Allen Ross summarizes, "No matter how many times a fool is warned, he never learns, not even from experience, but "repeats his folly.'"[777]

The disgusting practice of a dog returning to and eating that which he ejected is picturesque of a person returning to an old sinful habit ("folly") with delight and eagerness. A fool continuously repeats the same mistakes. He commits a sinful act with delight, then abhors and detests what he did. Guilt sickens him (mental and spiritual nausea) to the point of "vomiting" it up (abstains from it), but he returns to do the same horrible thing. It is a vicious, continuous cycle. Peter states such is the lifestyle of the hypocrite. "But it is happened unto them according to the true proverb, The dog is turned to his own vomit again; and the sow that was washed to her wallowing in the mire" (2 Peter 2:22).

The hypocrite has enough "religion" to *convince* him of wrong, but not enough to *convert* him. The hypocrite is for a *season* involved in the church and its manifold aspects, outwardly presenting the *impression* of being a Christian. Reformed, not regenerated, in time he slips back into the old sinful habits.

Peter, in addition to the dog, uses the pig to picture hypocrisy. Take a pig from the mud and filth of the pigpen, bathe it in the finest of shampoo, apply a sweet-smelling fragrance, tie a beautiful ribbon about its neck, and let it reside inside a beautiful home. Given the first opportunity, the pig will return to its natural habitat. Such is true with hypocrites. Changing their "habitat" won't change them. It's their *nature* that must be changed (Romans 3:23; 6:23).

John testifies to the reality of hypocrites in the church. "They went out from us, but they were not of us; for if they had been of us, they would no doubt have continued with us: but they went out, that they might be made manifest that they were not all of us" (1 John 2:19). The departure of a church member back into the world and its sinfulness, there to remain, indicates he was never saved. Are you a hypocrite? With Paul, I exhort, "Examine yourselves, whether ye be in the faith; prove your own selves. Know ye not your own selves, how that Jesus Christ is in you, except ye be reprobates?" (2 Corinthians 13:5).

The Bottom Line: Don't be a fool, a hypocrite. Enter into a personal relationship with Jesus Christ.

161
Hypocrite, destroyer of others with his mouth
Proverbs 11:9

"An hypocrite with his mouth destroyeth his neighbour: but through knowledge shall the just be delivered."

A "hypocrite" (profane and godless;[778] estranged from God) with his "mouth" (insinuations, lies, falsehoods, slander[779]; Henry says "decoying him into sin or into mischief by the specious pretenses of kindness and goodwill"[780]) "destroys" (harm, ruin) his "neighbor" (Reyburn and Fry say, "Your neighbor may be another person, someone you interact with, a fellow citizen, or, more intimately, a friend or companion"[781]).

Potiphar's wife is an example of the hypocrite, for with her mouth false accusations were uttered regarding Joseph (Genesis 39:11–19) which led to his imprisonment. See also Haman (Esther 3:8–13); Ziba (2 Samuel 16:1–4). The "just" (righteous, upright, godly) through "knowledge" (of God, of Holy Scriptures, of truth) and spiritual discernment (Philippians 1:9–10; Psalm 119:66) will be "delivered" (escape; be vindicated; survive). See Romans 16:18–19. The climate of the day necessitates preventive measures (accountability to others; avoidance of the appearance of wrong; alertness to the hypocrites' ambush and the arsenal of spiritual weaponry) against the hypocrite's effort to destroy one's good name, reputation, family and ministry.

The Bottom Line: George Lawson comments, "Many souls have been ruined by the mouth of the hypocrite, whilst the servants of Satan have artfully disguised themselves in the dress of the ministers of righteousness and by fair words and saint-like speeches, deceived the hearts of the simple."[782]

162
Immortality, its promise to the believer
Proverbs 12:28

"In the way of righteousness is life; and in the pathway thereof there is no death."

"For surely there is an end; and thine expectation shall not be cut off" (Proverbs 23:18).

"But the righteous hath hope in his death" (Proverbs 14:32).

In the "way" (path) of "righteousness" (right living based upon Holy Scriptures and relationship with Jesus Christ) is "life" (abundant and meaningful [John 10:10]); AND in the "pathway" (the person is on *the* path that leads to Heaven) thereof there is "no death" (immortality; eternal life). Solomon affirms the existence of life after death. Waltke says, "Commentators often reject this interpretation to uphold modern dogma that there is no afterlife, not for exegetical reasons."[783]

The second text (Proverbs 23:18) simply affirms the first. With Maclaren, I believe we are entitled to see here "a dim anticipation of a future life beyond the grave."[784] "Newberry suggests, 'Verily there is a hereafter' as an adequate rendering of the original."[785] For surely "there is an end" (Maclaren says, "The word so translated literally means 'something that comes after'"[786]); AND thine "expectation" (hope of future life) shall not be "cut off" (Deane and Taswell say, "The prosperity of sinners is not to be envied, for it is transitory and deceptive"[787]).

The third text (Proverbs 14:32) substantiates the teaching of the first two. The "righteous" (the upright, honorable, God-fearing and obeying, i.e., the Christian) hath "hope" (certitude—Job 19:25–26; Psalms 31:5; 49:14–15; 73:24; Ecclesiastes 11:9; Isaiah 26:19; Daniel 12:1–2) "in his death" (of future life in Heaven with Jesus and all the saints while the wicked experience eternal death in the Lake of Fire). "In hope of eternal life, which God, that cannot lie, promised before the world began" (Titus 1:2).

In all three texts Solomon answers Job's question: "If a man die shall he live again?" (14:14) emphatically in the positive. In Christ Jesus there is an abundant life free from sin's condemnation that in the end leads into His glorious presence in Heaven (John 10:10; Romans 8:1). The Apostle Paul declares, "For this corruptible must put on incorruption, and this mortal must put on immortality. So when this corruptible shall have put on incorruption, and this mortal shall have put on immortality, then shall be brought to pass the saying that is written, Death is swallowed up in victory. O death, where is thy sting? O grave, where is thy victory?" (1 Corinthians 15:53–55). Paul further states about death: 'To be absent from the body, and to be present with the Lord' (2 Corinthians 5:8). Death to the Christian is not a dead-end but a thoroughfare. See Proverbs 12:28.

George Lawson well says, "Christ hath abolished death and secured an uninterrupted life to them that believe in him."[788] "The grave," states Alexander Maclaren, "has a door on its inner side."[789] The Christian enters grave's door on earth's side momentarily only to exodus through its unseen door to Heaven. The only Christian that goes to a cemetery is he who mourns the death of another.

The Bottom Line: The only way to possess immortality (life beyond the physical realm) with Jesus Christ is to enter into a personal relationship with Him through repentance and faith (Acts 20:21; 1 John 5:11–13).

163
Inexcusable, failure to rescue the eternally damned
Proverbs 24:11–12

"If thou forbear to deliver them that are drawn unto death, and those that are ready to be slain; If thou sayest, Behold, we knew it not; doth not he that pondereth the heart consider it? and he that keepeth thy soul, doth not he know it? and shall not he render to every man according to his works?"

If thou "forbear" (hold back) to "deliver" (rescue; intervene in behalf of) them that are "drawn unto death" (people being "dragged"[790] to their execution or death), and those that are "ready to be slain" (hauled off to be slain[791]); If thou sayest, Behold, "we knew it not" (to say that you were unaware of their state; atrocity against them); doth not "he" (the Lord God) that "pondereth the heart" (God "weighs the heart"; knows the heart inside out, its truthfulness or deceit) "consider it?" (takes note of your inaction to help). And He that "keepeth thy soul" (the Guardian of your life, its Protector, Sustainer), doth not He know it? And shall "render to every man according to his works?" (payback man for intervening or for withholding help). Alexander Maclaren summarizes, "The wholesome truths which it utters apply to our duties in regard to Christian missions because they apply to our duties in regard to every misery within our reach. They speak of the murderous cruelty and black sin of negligence to save any whom we can help from any sort of misery which threatens them."[792]

It is the Christian's duty to rescue people who are unjustly being executed (the oppressed; innocent) and those whose lives stand in deadly peril from evildoers. Queen Esther, at risk to her own life, intervened in behalf of the Jews (Esther 4:16). Reuben rescued Joseph from death (Genesis 37:20–22). Jonathan saved David from the sword of King Saul (1 Samuel 19:1–6). Ebed-melech and Ahikam rescued Jeremiah from the deep miry pit of death (Jeremiah 26:24; 38:11–13). Paul's sister's son saved Paul's life in telling the Roman chief captain of a murderous plot to kill him (Acts 23:16–22). These rescuers 'kept back them that are drawn unto death, and those that are ready to be slain' (Proverbs 24:11) at risk of personal peril.

The Christian must not claim pretented ignorance ("We knew it not") to the atrocities inflicted upon others (Christian martyrdom; the murder of the unborn; sex trafficking [child prostitution slave trade]; oppression of the poor; the innocent's execution for political, social or religious reasons; etc.). "Our ignorance, so far as it is real, is the result of a sinful indolence [avoidance of exertion, laziness]."[793] Ignorance of the woeful estate of others also is attributable to preoccupation and absorption with selfish concerns.[794] We just don't want to be bothered, so we ignore.

In Nazi Germany, during the Holocaust, death trains occupied by screaming, terrified Jews passed weekly by a Christian church. A member of that fellowship said, "Their screams tormented us....If some of their screams reached our ears, we'd just sing a little louder." That's what many Christians do in hearing the screams of the innocent marching to the slaughter; they just "sing a little louder" so as not to be disturbed or involved.

A judgment will fall upon all (Christians and unbelievers alike) who could have done something to relieve the misery and suffering of others but did not.

But as imperative as is the rescuing of the socially, religiously and politically maltreated from the hands of injustice, *the saving of immortal souls from eternal damnation* in Hell is even more so. To plead ignorance ("We knew it not") as to man's eternal plight and peril without Christ, and therefore to "forbear" in soliciting his soul for Jesus, is inexcusable. His blood will be required "at your hand" (Ezekiel 3:18). Always keep in the conscious mind what it means for a soul to be lost to God.

L. R. Scarborough says to be lost "means separation from God. It means eternal dwelling in the land of eternal punishment. It means the opposite of Heaven. It means the extreme opposite of righteousness. It means Hell. It means no peace. It means no happiness, no joy. It means separation from the good and companionship with evil. It means all there is that is wrapped up in darkness into which no sun shines. It means the starless night of eternity. It means sunless day forever and ever. It means all there is in the punishment of sin, in the wrath of God, in the indignation of a wrathful sovereign."[795]

Paul says, "Knowing therefore the terror of the Lord, we persuade men [to be reconciled to God]" (2 Corinthians 5:11). "And of some have compassion, making a difference: And others save with fear, pulling them out of the fire" (Jude 22–23). Regarding God's mandate to win the unsaved, no Christian will be able to say at the Judgment, "We knew it not."

The Bottom Line: Maclaren appeals, "If there is one tear we could have dried and didn't, or one wound we could have healed and didn't, that is a sin; if we could have lightened the great heap of sorrow by one grain and didn't, that is a sin; and if there be one soul that perishes which we might have saved and didn't, the negligence is not merely the omission of a duty but the doing of a deed which will be 'rendered to us according to our works.'"[796]

164
Inheritance, the believer's
Proverbs 8:21

"That I may cause those that love me to inherit substance; and I will fill their treasures."

"That I" (the embodiment of Wisdom, the Lord Jesus Christ) give to all who "love me" (love Him; walk in the path of the righteous, obeying instructions and in submission to His will; if sin is involved in the walk then wisdom has not been followed[797]) an "inheritance" (valuable possessions that include abundant and eternal life; success) that is imperishable (1 Peter 1:4). Matthew Henry states, "Their inheritance hereafter is *substantial*; it is a weight of glory; it is substance (Hebrews 10:34). All their happiness they have as heirs; it is grounded upon their sonship. In Wisdom's promises believers have goods laid up, not for days and years, but for eternity; her fruit therefore is better than gold."[798]

I will fill their treasures. John Gill comments, "The treasures of their hearts (Matthew 12:35); Christ now fills their understandings with spiritual knowledge, their souls with grace, their minds with peace and joy, and their hearts with food and gladness; and hereafter he will fill them to full satisfaction with knowledge, holiness, and joy, and will be all in all to them."[799] Jesus forthrightly and clearly in the Proverb is stating, "They that love me shall not be losers by me."[800] Take heart, weary pilgrim; you are on the winning team.

Alexander Maclaren writes, "He who finds God, as every one of us may find Him, in Christ, has found a Good that cannot change, pass or grow stale. His blessedness will always last. We can never exhaust God. We need never grow weary of Him. We grow weary of most good things, and those which we have had a long time, we generally find get somewhat faded and stale. Habit is a fatal enemy to enjoyment. But it only adds to the joy that springs from the possession of God in Christ. Everything outside the substance of the soul can be withdrawn, but the possession of God in Christ is so intimate and inward, so interwoven with the very deepest roots of the Christian's personal being, that it cannot be taken out from these by any shocks of time or change. The Christian's good is the only good which cannot be taken away." [801]

A hotel bellboy in Toledo, Ohio, was taking a nap when two attorneys knocked on the door of his room. In response to the knocking, the boy yelled out, "Get away from that door!" However, they continued to knock until the boy opened the door only to discover he had inherited $25,000. Lost men often respond to the knocking of Jesus at their heart's door in similar fashion. Believers must inform them of the "inheritance" that waits outside the door.

The Bottom Line: Believers are "joint heirs" with Christ Jesus by divine relationship, inheriting every possession that belongs to Him (Hebrews 1:2; 2 Peter 1:3–4; 2 Corinthians 1:20; Ephesians 1:11–12). The believer is "heir of God," all else included in the believer's inheritance (permanence, peace, position, provision, promises) pales in light of this fact.

165
Instruction, its benefit
Proverbs 15:32
"He that refuseth instruction despiseth his own soul: but he that heareth reproof getteth understanding."

He that "refuseth" (not open to it; closed-minded) "instruction" (to learn what is an unknown spiritually, morally and practically; its foundational source is biblical knowledge and the experience of the wise. In context it encompasses the entirety of the Book of Proverbs) "despiseth" (disdain; to show contempt; to treat as worthless and without value[802]): BUT he that "heareth reproof" (heeds godly admonition) "getteth" (gains) "understanding" (wisdom; divine knowledge on which to base life successfully and live pleasingly unto the Lord).

Man's refusal to receive instruction and correction results in moral suicide because of failure to follow the path of the Lord. He is like a sick man that thrusts away the antidote which is his only hope and cure.[803] Intellectual arrogance must be crucified and humility exhibited with regard to instruction and reproof to avoid shipwreck. He that does this loves himself (for in receiving instruction and applying it he is protected from many snares of the enemy—Proverbs 19:8) and is honored (Proverbs 15:33). "The ear that heareth the reproof of life abideth among the wise" (v. 31).

> If you plan to build a tall house of virtues, you must first lay deep foundations of humility.
> Augustine

Charles Bridges, commenting on Proverbs 24:7 ("Wisdom is too high for a fool"), comments, "The *fool,* destitute of wisdom, is debarred from this honor. The simple and diligent prove that the treasure [wisdom] is not out of reach. But it is too high for the fool. His groveling mind can never rise to so lofty a matter. He has no apprehension of it, no heart to desire it, no energy to lay hold of it."[804]

The Bottom Line: Spiritual and moral well-being depends upon receiving instruction. Man never outgrows the need of instruction and correction. Knowledge and wisdom are freely accessible to all.

166
Instruction, lessons from four wise creatures
Proverbs 30:24–28

"There be four things which are little upon the earth, but they are exceeding wise: The ants are a people not strong, yet they prepare their

meat in the summer; The conies are but a feeble folk, yet make they their houses in the rocks; The locusts have no king, yet go they forth all of them by bands; The spider [lizard] taketh hold with her hands, and is in kings' palaces."

Solomon, in these four wise things, beautifully preaches the Gospel.

The Ant is wise in the preparation it makes

The ant works hard gathering food in the summer in preparation for the future (the cold winter). Man likewise must *store up* material necessities in the summer of prosperity in preparation for the winter of ill-health, calamity, financial loss, and old age. The greater lesson seen, however, is man's need to make preparation now for the eternal future, Heaven or Hell. For many, Jeremiah's words sadly ring true when he states, "The harvest is past, the summer is ended, and we are not saved" (Jeremiah 8:20).

H. A. Ironside observes, "In material things, man readily shows the same wisdom as this tiny creature. He, too, provides against the coming days when ill health or old age will forbid his going forth to labor. But is it not an amazing thing that men who display remarkable foresight in regard to matters that pertain to this life will yet forget altogether to make due preparation for that unending eternity to which every moment bears them nearer? Forgetful of the ages to follow this short life on earth, they allow golden opportunities to slip by, never to return, and rush carelessly on, ignoring the need of their souls and the fearful danger that lies just beyond death."[805]

The Coney (perhaps rock badger or marmot) is wise in the protection it enjoys

The marmot is a defenseless animal that takes refuge among the rocks (unable to burrow or dig). It is vulnerable in the plains but finds security in the rocks from predators and inclement weather. He pictures the Rock of Ages (Jesus Christ) to whom all sinners (unclean, defenseless, helpless) must flee for refuge from the wrath of God (judgment, condemnation, Hell). Salvation is available to the man who flees to the Rock. "And did all drink the same spiritual drink: for they drank of that spiritual Rock that followed them: and that Rock was Christ" (1 Corinthians 10:4).

Over a century ago a ship sank off the coast of England. Many lives were lost. Clinging to a rock all night, a sixteen-year-old boy was saved from the turbulent sea. Upon being rescued, he was asked, "Didn't you shake as you were clinging all night to that rock?"

The boy replied, "Yes, of course. But the rock never shook once."

Rock of Ages, cleft for me,
Let me hide myself in Thee;
Let the water and the blood,
From Thy riven side which flowed,
Be of sin the double cure—
Cleanse me from its guilt and pow'r. ~ Augustus Toplady (1776)

The Locust is wise in the partnership it shares

The locust without a leader (king or president or general) travels methodically and orderly in bands as a regiment of soldiers. It functions (discipline, duty) as if under supervision, taking orders of another. Christians are to be like the locust in being harmonious in fellowship and united in service, totally submissive to our invisible Head, the Lord Jesus Christ (Colossians 1:15). Paul says, "Now ye are the body of Christ, and members in particular" (1 Corinthians 12:27). This one "body" must be free from schisms and divisions (1 Corinthians 3:3). Paul insists believers are to walk in fellowship, building up one another and extending the kingdom of God. In 1 Corinthians 1:10 he states, "Now I beseech you, brethren, by the name of our Lord Jesus Christ, that ye all speak the same thing, and that there be no divisions among you; but that ye be perfectly joined together in the same mind and in the same judgment." If the church, the body of Christ, would function as the locusts (partnership, comradery), Christ would be glorified, morality issues would be rectified, and the lost world notified of who Jesus is and their need of Him (Matthew 28:18–20).

As sweet strains of heav'nly music
Blend in one harmonious sound,
So the members of Christ's body
In blest unity are found—

One in mind and one in spirit;
One in doctrine, faith, and love;
One in name—oh, precious union,
Like the angel hosts above!

Blood-washed pilgrims on the highway
Chant the sweet, melodious strain
Of their freedom from confusion;
Angels join the glad refrain.

One with all the hosts of Heaven;
There their names are written down.
Jesus only, Jesus ever,
In their hearts as King they crown.

Love, the theme of all their praises,
Doth in holy bond unite
All their hearts, in Him made perfect,
Turned from darkness unto light.

Thus the saved in Christ together
Dwell in sacred unity,
In the secret of His presence—
Hid away, dear Lord, in Thee. ~ Clara M. Brooks (1907)

The Spider (house lizard) is wise in the position it occupies

The lizard (like the Geico lizard), using the liquid-filled spongelike sac on its toes, is able to attach to any surface. In this may we see faith, the means whereby the believer is able to take hold (adhere, fasten) "with his hand" to the precious truth of God's Word and to dwell in the heavenlies with Him. For "God, who is rich in mercy, for his great love wherewith he loved us, Even when we were dead in sins, hath quickened us together with Christ, (by grace ye are saved;) And hath raised us up together, and made us sit together in heavenly places in Christ Jesus: That in the ages to come he might shew the exceeding riches of his grace in his kindness toward us through Christ Jesus" (Ephesians 2:4–7).

The Bottom Line: Happy will be the man and greater will be the church that follows the instructions materialistically and spiritually taught by these four small, wise creatures.

167
Instruction, warning about wrong teaching
Proverbs 19:27
"Cease, my son, to hear the instruction that causeth to err from the words of knowledge."

"Cease" (desist; stop listening to), my son, to "hear" (receive and follow) the "instruction" (teaching; guidance) that "causeth" (incites; leads to) to "err" (to stray away[806]) from the "words of knowledge" (God's holy counsel; Holy Scriptures).

The Proverb is straightforward, leaving no room for misunderstanding or misinterpretation. The believer (young and old alike) is not to give ear to any teaching (from minister, theologian, teacher or friend) that is countercurrent to the Word of God. Shipwreck awaits the heedless.

H. A. Ironside provides timeless advice: "When another gives out what is contrary to God's revealed Word, it is time to refuse him and his teaching. You cannot afford to trifle with unholy doctrine. To dabble with it is to expose yourself to its powerful influence. Therefore, refuse to hear it."[807] It is the height of intellectual naivety and spiritual immaturity to think one might listen to every wind of adulterated and profane doctrine without being negatively impacted. Proverbs 6:28 is applicable: "Can one go upon hot coals, and his feet not be burned?"

Perhaps as with the "son" in the text, you are giving ear to heretical (unsound, unbiblical) teaching. If so, then the mandate is directed to you: 'Cease, my son, to hear *corrupt* instruction.' Assess the damage done by comparing present belief with the "standard gauge" which judges all belief, the Holy Scriptures. Accordingly, adjust belief to conform to the standard, discarding the perverted. Henceforth, sit at the feet of those teachers and preachers who embrace the Bible as the infallible, inerrant and eternal Word of God.

John admonishes, "If there come any unto you, and bring not this doctrine, receive him not into your house, neither bid him God speed" (2 John 10). Avoid people who twist God's Word, calling "sweet bitter and bitter sweet" (they rationalize or theorize that what was wrong yesterday is not today). Paul warned, "Beware lest any man spoil you through philosophy and vain deceit, after the tradition of men, after the rudiments of the world, and not after Christ" (Colossians 2:8).

Regrettably, a time arrived when Solomon failed to "practice what he preached" in this Proverb (1 Kings 11:1–10). Waltke remarks, "Let it be noted that he constructed his own gibbet on which he impaled himself (Proverbs 19:27)—that is, he ceased listening to his own instruction. Spiritual success today does not guarantee spiritual success tomorrow."[808]

Deane and Taswell observe that the proverb may be taken as an "injunction warning against listening to wise teaching with no intention of profiting by it: 'Cease to hear instruction in order to err,' etc.; i.e., if you are only going to continue your evildoings. You will only increase your guilt by knowing the way of righteousness perfectly while you refuse to walk therein."[809] See James 4:17.

The Bottom Line: You have the truth in the Christian faith; there is no need to look elsewhere. If the ears start to itch ("itching ears"—2 Timothy 4:3) for a religion that is more *palatable,* always bear in mind that such are deceptive and deadly (like drinking in spiritual poison). Just ask Solomon (1 Kings 11:11). He that was the wisest man that ever lived died as one of the most foolish. Starting well is important, but finishing well is just as vital.

168
Insult, the prudent man's response
Proverbs 12:16

"A fool's wrath is presently known: but a prudent man covereth shame."

A "fool's" (the unwise, unrighteous) "wrath" (anger) is "presently known" (people know he is quick to fly off the handle, short-fused; McKane says that the fool's reaction is "like an injured animal and so his opponent knows that he has been wounded"[810]): BUT the "prudent" (wise) man "covereth" (conceals, ignores) "shame" (insults).

Harsh, insulting words are but an invisible sharp razor that cuts and deeply pains its recipient (Psalm 52:2). I have been on the receiving end of venomous words from a friend while other "friends" sat by without intervention. Though what was said hurt, the manner in which it was spoken and its condoning by friends exacted a pain indescribable. A physical stabbing with a knife would have been less painful. My spirit was wounded, and my heart broken. I learned that day, "Careless words stab like a sword, but wise words bring healing" (Proverbs 12:18 NCV).

Rick Warren remarks, "People need to know that their words have consequences."[811] Chuck Swindoll comments, "Regardless of the level of maturity you've reached in your walk with Christ, you are not immune to hurt. Sharp words strike like shrapnel, and they get imbedded in the brain.

The result is the inflicting of a wound that's slow to heal. Sometimes, regrettably, it never heals."[812]

Frankly, it's hard, though not impossible, to "shrug off" a piercing insult (dishonoring, humiliating assault), as Proverbs 12:16 advises (sensible, calm response). Matthew Henry elucidates the wise man's response to insult: "He covers the passion that is in his own breast; when his spirit is stirred and his heart hot within him, he keeps his mouth as with a bridle and suppresses his resentments by smothering and stifling them. He covers the provocation that is given him, the indignity that is done him, winks at it, covers it as much as may be from himself, that he may not carry his resentments of it too far. It is a kindness to ourselves, and contributes to the repose of our own minds to extenuate and excuse the injuries and affronts that we receive instead of aggravating them and making the worst of them, as we are apt to do."[813]

It helps in diffusing the desire to strike back and/or bear resentment when insulted if we understand its source (the immaturity and/or temperament of the person) and God's counsel (Matthew 5:39). Paul exhorts, "Let all bitterness, and wrath, and anger, and clamour, and evil speaking, be put away from you, with all malice" (Ephesians 4:31). "If they attack, the wise course is to stay cool and conceal the insult. Anger will only lead one to play into the hands of an opponent."[814] Matthew Henry is right on target in saying that covering the insult is "a kindness to ourselves, and contributes to the repose of our own minds." This I know to be true from personal experience.

The Bottom Line: The wise man will ignore (control his response to) injurious insult, being careful not to exacerbate it, by forgiving it.

169
Integrity, press hard to possess a good reputation
Proverbs 20:11

"Even a child is known by his doings, whether his work be pure, and whether it be right."

"A good name is better than precious ointment; and the day of death than the day of one's birth" (Ecclesiastes 7:1).

Even a "child" (children) makes himself "known" (reputation) by his "doings" (conduct; lifestyle), whether his work be "pure" (clean, upright), and whether it be "right" (righteous; upright).

Oxford Dictionary defines *integrity* as "the quality of being honest and having strong moral principles." It is the manifestation of internal and external consistency in doing what is right (honest, moral, just) in a reliable and ethical way.

To understand what a child really is like, it's best to use the ears to hear what he says and the eyes to see what he does (Proverbs 20:12). A child's conduct serves as a good prognosticator of his future.[815] Such was true of the child Samuel who served God in the tabernacle. "And Samuel grew, and the LORD was with him, and did let none of his words fall to the ground. And all Israel from Dan even to Beer-sheba knew that Samuel was established to be a prophet of the LORD" (1 Samuel 3:19–20). The distance from Dan to Beersheba covers the whole of Israel. Samuel's reputation was well known as a child. Children and adults alike ought to so walk with the Lord in integrity of heart that their godly and honorable reputation is known *from Dan even to Beersheba* (work, school, athletic arena, church, political office). Do those who know you best count you a person of integrity above all else?

Paul pressed hard to be a person of integrity. He declared, "We are trying hard [taking pains] to do what the Lord accepts as right and also what people think is right" (2 Corinthians 8:21 NCV). We, like Paul, must exert intense effort and energy to live honorably, beyond reproach. Integrity is not automatic. It is not developed overnight. It is nourished from childhood throughout life.

The Bottom Line: A godly reputation before classmates, employees, friends and strangers spreads like wildfire, revealing trustworthiness, dependability, holiness and honesty. And, "a good reputation and respect are worth much more than silver and gold" (Proverbs 22:1 CEV).

170
Jealousy, the deadly venom
Proverbs 6:34
"For jealousy is the rage of a man."

For "jealousy" (see below) is the "rage" (furious anger; refers to a man whose outrage leads him to act violently[816]) of man. The Proverb's context is with regard to a husband's outrage with the man who has an adulterous affair with his wife (v. 32).

Jealousy is defined by the *KJV Bible Dictionary* as "that passion of peculiar uneasiness which arises from the fear that a rival may rob us of the affection of one whom we love, or the suspicion that he has already done it; or it is the uneasiness which arises from the fear that another does or will enjoy some advantage which we desire for ourselves. In short, jealousy is awakened by whatever may exalt others or give them pleasures and advantages which we desire for ourselves." See Proverbs 27:4.

Jealousy and envy, though connected, are not the same. Envy mourns for that which it doesn't have, while jealousy is threatened and disturbed by the loss of what it does have.[817] "Jealousy," Chuck Swindoll remarks, "will decimate a friendship, dissolve a romance and destroy a marriage. It will shoot tension through the ranks of professionals. It will nullify unity on a team…it will ruin a church…it will separate preachers…it will foster competition in a choir, bringing bitterness and finger-pointing among talented instrumentalists and capable singers."[818] As Solomon states, it is "the rage of man."

What can you do to defeat it? Recognize its presence and impact in your life; renounce it as sin to God and yourself. As long as jealous desires are allowed to roam freely in your mind, they will imprison, control and destroy. Manifest an "enough is enough" attitude. Ask God to remove it. He has the power to extract the seed that gave birth to the "green-eyed monster." Give no place to it. When jealousy seeks to show its ugly head, refuse and reject it. Pray for the good of the person of whom you are jealous (helps extinguish it). Remember God's goodness to you (positive traits, abilities, blessings). Rest in the knowledge that God is in control; be content with His plan and provisions.

Don't be jealous when another gets the promotion, award, position, accolade, relationship or win. Instead of viewing such experiences through the lenses of jealousy, look at them through the lenses of Romans 8:28 and Genesis 50:20. Our disappointments are often His appointments intended for our highest good.

The Bottom Line: "The jealous," states William Penn, "are troublesome to others, but a torment to themselves." C. H. Spurgeon remarks, "Self-love is, no doubt, the usual foundation of human jealousy…the fear lest another should by any means supplant us."[819]

171
Jesus, He is more than enough
Proverbs 13:25

"The righteous eateth to the satisfying of his soul: but the belly of the wicked shall want."

The "righteous" (upright, honorable, just, Christian) "eateth" (partakes) to the "satisfying" (fullness; contentment) of his "soul" (bodily appetite; hunger quenched): BUT the "stomach" (belly) of the "wicked" (ungodly) shall "want" (will lack for food; be hungry). Matthew Henry summarizes, "It is the happiness of the righteous that they shall have enough and that they know when they have enough."[820]

The believer has *more than enough* in Christ Jesus to satisfy every need. The Apostle Paul wrote, "My God shall supply all your need according to his riches in glory by Christ Jesus" (Philippians 4:19). H. A. Ironside remarks, "The portion of the righteous may be small, but enjoyment is with it, for heart and conscience are at rest. But the lawless, though he riot in pleasure and plenty for a time, finds no real satisfaction; and his recklessness shall bring him to want at last."[821]

The prophet Isaiah exclaims with a triumphant note, "Ho, every one that thirsteth, come ye to the waters, and he that hath no money; come ye, buy, and eat; yea, come, buy wine and milk without money and without price" (Isaiah 55:1). F. C. Jennings has written, "Let us listen then as if we had never heard the melody of this tender and gracious invitation before. Who are the guests here invited? All who thirst! All that is needed to be welcome then is not to *need* (for that is true of all), but to *want* what is offered. Am I utterly dissatisfied with myself? I thirst! Am I dissatisfied with all the world can offer me and of which I have tasted? I thirst! Is my spirit altogether dissatisfied with all the formalism of religion? Then do I thirst! Blessed thirst! It is the only prerequisite to enjoyment!"[822]

Are you as the woman at Jacob's well, thirsting for that which the world and its carnal pleasures and pseudoreligions cannot satisfy? Then as she did, *come, come, come* to the Fountain of Living Waters (Jesus) and drink. You will not be disappointed. Jesus said "But whosoever drinketh of the water that I shall give him shall never thirst; but the water that I shall give him shall be in him a well of water springing up into everlasting life" (John 4:14). Matthew Henry states, "Those that feed on the Bread of life, that feast on the promises, meet with abundant satisfaction of soul."[823]

And Jesus said, "Come to the water; stand by My side.
I know you are thirsty; you won't be denied.[824]

C. H. Spurgeon states that in coming to Jesus you will find "His wisdom is our direction; His knowledge, our instruction; His power, our protection; His justice, our surety; His love, our comfort; His mercy, our solace; and His immutability, our trust. He makes no reserve but opens the recesses of the Mount of God and bids us dig in its mines for the hidden treasures. 'All, all, all are yours,' saith he. 'Be ye satisfied with favor and full of the goodness of the Lord.'"[825]

The Bottom Line: Jesus wants to meet your innermost need for this life and the life which is to come. And He will if you but *drink* of the cup of salvation (Romans 10:9–13). "O taste and see that the LORD is good: blessed is the man that trusteth in him" (Psalm 34:8).

172
Joking, the serious effects of practical jokes
Proverbs 26:19
"So is the man that deceiveth his neighbour, and saith, Am not I in sport?"

So is the man that "deceiveth" (makes a person to believe something not true) his "neighbor" (see Luke 10:29–37), and saith, "Am not I in sport?" (after the deceit the person says he was only joking, just kidding; that, however, is not acceptable, for his action in the name of "joking" was injurious[826]). Deane and Taswell summarize, "When a man has injured his neighbor by lies or malice, the plea that he was only in joke is not allowed. The injury is not less real because he excuses it by alleging it was done not seriously, but playfully, no more than the fatal effects of the use of murderous weapons are lessened by their being employed by the hands of a maniac. Practical joking is often a most serious matter."[827]

Ephesians 5:4 is the New Testament Proverbs 26:19. In the text Paul states categorically that the Christian shouldn't engage in "foolish talking, nor jesting, which are not convenient [suitable or becoming of a believer]." The jesting which Solomon and Paul condemn consists of off-colored jokes, foul or obscene talk, crude joking and dirty stories. Such speech is unbecoming of the child of God.

An example of crude joking comes from the *Andy Griffith Show* episode "Man's Best Friend." Opie and Tommy are having fun with miniature walkie-talkies. As a practical joke, they hide one of the walkie-talkies in the collar of Goober's dog and deceive him into thinking he has a talking dog. All the while the boys are laughing at him. When Andy learns of their cruel jesting and humiliation of Goober, he teaches them a lesson in what it feels like to be the butt of such insensitive fun at the expense of another's suffering.

After engaging in an act like that of the two boys, saying afterwards, "I was only joking" doesn't make it right or undo the harm it caused. H. A. Ironside comments, "To want to only perpetrate unkind tricks upon one, and then, after having caused serious inconvenience, and perhaps heavy loss, to attempt to laugh it off as mere amusement, is to act like a man pretending to madness and finding his sport in working injury upon others."[828]

The Bottom Line: It is never right to have fun at the expense of another's humiliation and hurt. The problem with practical jokes is that they are often not practical but painful.

173
Joy, splash out sunshine everywhere you go
Proverbs 12:25
"Heaviness in the heart of man maketh it stoop: but a good word maketh it glad."

"Heaviness" (anxiety, worry, fear) in the heart of man "maketh it stoop" (depression,[829] dejection, mourning sorrow): BUT a "good word" (uplifting, encouraging word[830]; "The 'good word' here would include encouragement, kindness and insight—the person needs to regain the proper perspective on life and renew his confidence"[831]) "maketh it glad" (cheerful).

Job said to his friends, "How forcible are right words!" (Job 6:25). The right word spoken exactly at the right time lifts and gladdens the heart. Lives everywhere are hurting, depressed, downtrodden, sorrowing, despondent and discouraged. This is true of the drugstore clerk, the postal employee, the grocery cashier, the classmate, the fellow employee, the church member, the friend. The Christian's task daily is to splash out the love of Jesus upon such people, bringing comfort, cheer and encouragement through the words they speak. "A good word maketh it glad." The "good word" is any word that is spoken truthfully that makes the distraught and sick feel better, if only for the moment. It is ultimately a word based upon God's Word, which is healing medicine to the hurting heart.

The "good word" may be communicated verbally in person (the best means), by phone, texting, through cards and letters (far better than emails), or emails. I am fond of the use of greeting cards to instill joy in others, for they continuously impart our "good word" long after their initial reception (emails and texts are erased; the phone conversation cannot be "replayed," but the paper card continues to speak).

Teresa of Calcutta said, "Spread love everywhere you go. Let no one ever come to you without leaving happier."[832] It's the Christian's duty to relieve the heavy-hearted and down-trodden.

The Bottom Line: Make it your business to brighten another's day every day. "Spread a little sunshine every day. Help someone along life's way. Spread a little sunshine every day."

<h1 style="text-align:center">174</h1>

Judgment, the day of divine accounting
Proverbs 11:4

"Riches profit not in the day of wrath: but righteousness delivereth from death."

"Riches" (wealth) "profit not" (without value) in the "day of wrath" (God's divine judgment): BUT "righteousness" (to be right and do right) "delivereth" (rescues) from "death" (from a "premature and unhappy death"[833]). In keeping with the *whole* of Scripture, deliverance from death also includes "spiritual death" or the "second death" (Lake of Fire). "And death and hell were cast into the lake of fire. This is the second death" (Revelation 20:14).

In the day of divine judgment when all must give an account of the life lived and the faith embraced, riches wrought by our works will bear no influence and have no value (Zephaniah 1:18; Luke 12:16–21). Riches will not lessen the sentence to be rendered nor the pain and suffering to be experienced in Hell. Money never has and never will provide man with an escape from the consequences of sin (only Jesus can do that). Dives, the rich man that "was clothed in purple and fine linen, and fared sumptuously every day" (lived in luxury), despite great wealth, 'died and went to Hell' (Luke 16:19, 23). In the day of the *wrath of God,* though the rich seek shelter, it will be in vain. "The rich men…hid themselves in the dens and in the rocks of the mountains; And said to the mountains and rocks, Fall on us, and hide us from the face of him that sitteth on the throne, and from the wrath of the Lamb: For the great day of his wrath is come; and who shall be able to stand?" (Revelation 6:15–17). Job states, regardless of the sum of the ransom, it will not deliver the rich from the judgment (wrath) of Almighty God (Job 36:18).

It is "righteousness" (God's *imputed righteousness* to man through Jesus Christ—Romans 4:22) that "delivereth [saves; rescues] from death" (eternal separation from God in Hell). "For he hath made him to be sin for us, who knew no sin; that we might be made the righteousness of God in him" (2 Corinthians 5:21). The word *impute* means "to attribute to another, to pass to one's account." Simply put, that means that when we trust Christ Jesus as Lord and Savior, God places His righteousness in Heaven's ledger next to our name, to our account. From that moment forward, when He looks at us, He sees Christ's righteousness, not any righteousness that we might claim.

The Bottom Line: At the Judgment Bar of God, all the gold and silver in the world will not purchase a ticket into Heaven. Peter explains, "Forasmuch as ye know that ye were not redeemed with corruptible things, as silver and gold, from your vain conversation [sinful conduct; disobedience to God] received by tradition from your fathers; But with the precious blood of Christ, as of a lamb without blemish and without spot" (1 Peter 1:18–19). "Weigh" yourself upon the scales of Holy Scriptures to see if you are "found wanting" while there is time for salvation (Romans 10:9–13).

175
Kings, sins of the prominent
Proverbs 16:12

"It is an abomination to kings to commit wickedness: for the throne is established by righteousness."

It is an "abomination" (abhorrence) to kings to commit "wickedness" (deeds of evil): FOR the "throne is established by righteousness" (monarchs are to rule righteously, but this does not always happen).

All who commit sin, regardless of status or position, grieve the Lord, harming others and self. "But sin," states George Lawson "*is greatly aggravated by the place that a man holds in society*—and what is pernicious to one individual in a private man is mischievous to a kingdom in a sovereign."[834] King David's sin brought reproach, shame to the name of God, scandal to the church and reason for unbelievers to blaspheme Judaism (Christianity) throughout the whole nation of Israel (2 Samuel 12:14). King Jeroboam not only sinned, but no less than twenty-one times caused the nation of Israel to sin (1 Kings 14:16). Matthew Henry states, "There is this great evil in the sins of those who profess religion and relation to God that they furnish the enemies of God and religion with matter for reproach and blasphemy."[835]

When the "mighty" do wickedly, their notoriety exacerbates the evil done; the greater the person's prominence, the more far-reaching is the impact of his sin. *Kings and presidents* (all in positions of authority and trusted leadership) must work hard to establish their "throne" (entrusted position) in righteousness (free from corruption and scandal). The blessing and favor of God rests only upon leaders who live and rule by the moral and ethical teachings of the Bible. The righteousness of godly leaders influences a nation to honor God and His teachings, just as wicked leaders influence it toward grave abomination. *Kings* need to remember the words of Daniel: "He [God] removeth kings, and setteth up kings" (Daniel 2:21). That is, God put leaders on the *throne;* He can likewise easily facilitate their removal.

As believers, we are to pray "for kings, and for all that are in authority; that we may lead a quiet and peaceable life in all godliness and honesty" (1 Timothy 2:2). Pray specifically that all in authority will rule in righteousness, not by underhanded, shady and wicked means.

The Bottom Line: Leaders must guard their hearts from wickedness and the nation from evil, anti-God principles of governing and lifestyle.

176
Knowledge, flaunting what is known
Proverbs 12:23
"A prudent man concealeth knowledge."

The "prudent" (Buzzell: "shrewd [in a good sense]"[836] or intelligent) "concealeth" (covers, keeps hidden) their knowledge. That is, he does not show it off,[837] flaunt or brag about it, remaining humble [not "self-inflated" over it]). Knowledge is to be revealed or displayed discreetly, not arrogantly.

Theologian Matthew Henry summarizes about the prudent or wise man: "He communicates his knowledge when it may turn to the edification of others, but he conceals it when the showing of it would only tend to his own commendation."[838] The wise do not "parade" their academic achievements, accolades or accomplishments for praise. Arrogance is detrimental to all, but especially to ministers. An old secular proverb states, "He that blows much smoke is full of hot air."

The Bottom Line: Abstain from saying anything that even *smells* like ostentation. Always apply the principle of Proverbs 27:2 in communicating with others: "Let another man praise thee, and not thine own mouth; a stranger, and not thine own lips."

177
Knowledge, its effective communicator
Proverbs 16:23
"The heart of the wise teacheth his mouth, and addeth learning to his lips."

The heart of the "wise" (godly righteous) "teacheth his mouth" (judiciously controls, guides his mouth in what is spoken; careful; cautious[839]), AND "addeth learning to his lips" ("increases persuasiveness"[840]; "increases reception of what he says"[841]; Murphy says, "Intelligence and wisdom are requisite for wise speech"[842]).

What's in the heart comes out the mouth. The godly wise, in acquiring head knowledge of biblical truth, absorbs it, allowing it to work itself out experientially. It is he who has experienced that which he "teacheth with his mouth" that communicates it passionately, persuasively, understandably and effectively. We all note the difference between him who speaks of what he has only read or heard and the man who speaks of what he has personally "felt and tasted."[843] The one possesses biblical knowledge, *dry and dead*; the other, *powerful and invigorating* (2 Corinthians 2:14).[844]

Knowledge must be ingested, digested and manifested in life and lip. It is the "heart of the wise" that testifies, "Come and hear, all ye that fear God, and I will declare what *he hath done for my soul*" (Psalm 66:16). The greatest schoolhouse of learning is that of experience. "That which was from the beginning, which we have heard, which we have seen with our eyes, which we have looked upon, and our hands have handled, of the Word of life; (For the life was manifested, and we have seen it, and bear witness, and shew unto you that eternal life, which was with the Father, and was manifested unto us;) That which we have seen and heard declare we unto you, that ye also may have fellowship with us: and truly our fellowship is with the Father, and with his Son Jesus Christ" (1 John 1:1–3).

Be cautious of preachers, teachers and others who *intelligently* declare God's counsel but who themselves have not *experienced* it. Avoid all who cannot testify, "That which we have seen and heard declare we unto you" (v. 1). Only he that speaks of what has been instilled from instruction in God's Word *and* experienced it can do so with passion and the power of the Holy Spirit.

The Bottom Line: "Learning lips" are those that speak from the wellspring of theological and practical knowledge that has been proven from personal experience.

178
Knowledge, spreading the good news
Proverbs 15:7
"The lips of the wise disperse knowledge: but the heart of the foolish doeth not so."

The "lips" (teaching) of the "wise" (godly righteous, biblically literate) "disperse" (spread, scatter, extend) "knowledge" (biblical knowledge; the wise "help others to learn biblical truth"[845]): BUT the heart of the "foolish" (the ungodly) "doeth not so" (cannot due to lack of instruction and learning).

Matthew Henry remarks that the wise "must take pains to spread and propagate useful knowledge, must teach some that they may teach others, and so it is dispersed."[846] Knowledge and truth are not to be hoarded or reserved for a select group but made available (scattered) to all for their benefit and blessing. Never is this truer than with regard to the Gospel of Jesus Christ. Believers must no longer be silent but "take pains" to proclaim the Good News from "pillar to post" to all.

> We have endless treasure found;
> We have all things and abound.
> Rich abundance and to spare,
> Shall we not the blessing share?
> For while we are feasting here,
> Starving millions, far and near,
> Call us with the bitter cry,
> "Come and help us, or we die!"

> In this day of full increase,
> Shall we, can we, hold our peace?
> Staying here we do not well;
> Now then, let us go and tell
> How He hath set us free,
> How He leads triumphantly,
> How He satisfies our need,
> How His rest is rest indeed.[847] ~ Annie W. Marston

The Bottom Line: Scatter the "good news" everywhere. Teach it; preach it; sing it; write it "till the whole world knows" Jesus.

179
Knowledge, when to conceal or reveal
Proverbs 12:23

"A prudent man concealeth knowledge: but the heart of fools proclaimeth foolishness."

A "prudent" (Buzzell says, "shrewd [in a good sense],"[848] sensible person) man "concealeth" (withholds it; keeps it in the casket of the soul until the right moment to reveal it) "knowledge" (biblical truth): BUT the heart of "fools" (the ungodly, unwise) "proclaimeth foolishness" (Buzzell says they that "blurt out folly"[849]; Deane and Taswell say, "A foolish man cannot help exposing the stupid ideas that arise in his mind, which he considers wisdom"[850]).

He that is prudent withholds what he knows until it is most expedient. He is not a "show-off." He ever stores what is learned from the study and meditation of Holy Scriptures in the heart for personal edification and only when appropriate shares it (Ecclesiastes 3:7). The wise know it is better to be silent than to "cast [their] pearls before swine, lest they trample them under their feet" (Matthew 7:6). A word spoken in season is pleasant. "A man hath joy by the answer of his mouth: and a word spoken in due season, how good is it!" (Proverbs 15:23). But spoken untimely (out of season), it is unprofitable, undesirable and may prove detrimental to the speaker and the recipient. By contrast, reticence to speak at times is sinfully wrong.[851] The godly wise so walk in stride with the Lord that they discern when speaking is justified and necessary. They do not use silence as a cloak for cowardice or apathy.

The Bottom Line: The godly wise don't flaunt their knowledge (in contrast to the arrogant, conceited). It is ever stored up in their heart awaiting the timing of the Lord to be communicated.

180
Knowledgeable, sit at the feet of the wise and learn
Proverbs 20:15
"There is gold, and a multitude of rubies: but the lips of knowledge are a precious jewel."

There is "gold, and a multitude of rubies" (that of vast value): BUT the "lips" (mouth that utters biblical knowledge, wisdom) are a "precious jewel" (more valuable than the gold and multitude of rubies).

The lips of a knowledgeable person (wise speech; comprehension of knowledge and ability to share it in understandable fashion, making personal application) are a far better possession (to him who utters it and him whom receives it) than a treasure chest full of gold and rubies. Though the Proverb is absolutely true, most fail to avail themselves of the treasure chest of jewels of knowledge that the wise possess. People in King Solomon's time understood the value of wisdom, for they went to great expense and effort to sit at his feet to receive it. "And all the earth [whole world] sought to Solomon, to hear his wisdom, which God had put in his heart" (1 Kings 10:24). Life would be enriched and greatly enhanced by going out of the way to sit at the feet of the truly wise to receive godly instruction and counsel about family life, marriage, leadership, finances, spiritual growth/discipline, biblical doctrine, God's will and parenting.

The Bottom Line: "A wise man will hear, and will increase learning; and a man of understanding shall attain unto wise counsels" (Proverbs 1:5 NKJV). A man of godly wisdom is a rarity, as he was in King Solomon's day. Upon finding him and availing oneself of his knowledge and understanding (especially that of the spiritual sphere), one finds a treasure chest, yea, a bank vault full of precious jewels that benefit and bless their life.

181
Landmarks, don't tamper with what God has established
Proverbs 22:28
"Remove not the ancient landmark, which thy fathers have set."

"Remove not" (don't touch it) the "ancient landmark" (boundary markers set long ago) which thy fathers have "set" (forefathers put in place, established).

This directive was given to the Israelites centuries ago regarding property boundaries between neighbors. Its application today is to be taken spiritually regarding moral and ethical boundaries God has established for man's protection and best good. The removal of or tampering with a property landmark skews what belongs to whom, whereas removal of or tampering with God's spiritual landmarks results in havoc and heartache. Removal or adjustment of a property landmark can be done legally with permission of its owner. The same is true with spiritual landmarks. However, without consent of God, liberal clergy, psychologists, scholars, teachers and politicians have moved and are constantly moving the marker stakes further to the left. The ancient boundary markers now are blurred due to man's continual tampering.

> Ancient words ever true,
> Changing me and changing you,
> We have come with open hearts;
> Oh, let the ancient words impart. ~ Michael W. Smith

Clearly defined boundary markers God has erected regarding issues such as abortion, homosexuality, premarital sex, gambling, alcohol, drugs, suicide, tobacco, parental submission, dating, marriage and divorce must be honored and preserved. The great London pastor C. H. Spurgeon challenges parents and children alike to be proactive in maintaining these landmarks. He states, "We are not to expect to win victories for the Lord Jesus by a single blow. Evil principles and practices die hard. In some places it takes years of labor to drive out even one of the many vices which defile the inhabitants. We must carry on the war with all our might, even when favored with little manifest success. Our business in this world is to conquer it for Jesus. We are not to make compromises but to exterminate evils. We are not to seek popularity but to wage unceasing war with iniquity. Infidelity, drink, impurity, oppression, worldliness, error—these are all to be 'put out.' The Lord our God can alone accomplish this. He works by His faithful servants. Let us never sheathe the sword till the whole land is won for Jesus. Courage, my heart! Go on little by little, for many littles will make a great whole."[852]

H. A. Ironside observes about the believer's landmark, "Their inheritance is in the precious truth which He has committed to us. To remove the landmarks—the great distinguishing doctrines of Scripture—will be to incur the divine displeasure. Yet, alas, this is the wretched business in which many learned doctors and wiseacres are engaged today. Nothing is too sacred for their irreverent handling. Precious truths like those of atonement and justification by faith—yea, even the mystery of the Holy Trinity and the Person of the Lord Jesus Christ—are, in their eyes, but common things which they may dismiss or ignore as they please. But a day of reckoning is coming when God will judge them in righteousness and when those who have been misled by their removal of ancient and venerable landmarks will curse them for the loss of their souls. Terrible will be the accounting of men who, while posing as instructors of the flock of Christ, have all the while been Satan's instruments for overthrowing the saving truths of Scripture."[853]

The Bottom Line: To tamper with God's definitive Landmarks set forth in Holy Scripture solicits His wrath and judgment and always is the purveyor of personal havoc and heartache. See Revelation 22:18–19.

182
Laughter, smiling depression
Proverbs 14:13

"Even in laughter the heart is sorrowful; and the end of that mirth is heaviness."

Even in laughter the "heart" (center of man's emotions or feelings) of the foolish sinner is "sorrowful" (pain; aches; sad) and the end of "that" ("carnal," fleshly, worldly) "mirth" (joy; happiness) is "heaviness" (grief).

That which is advocated by the world and sinful flesh as the secret to meaning and happiness is a lie, for the "joy" which it produces is empty and fictitious (outward laughter while inward restlessness, sadness and heartache). Psychologists' name for the malady is *smiling depression*; the Bible calls it *sinful delusion* and *deception* (Proverbs 14:12). Man parades a face of happiness and contentment to mask the emptiness inside. Suicides of the famous and not as famous sadly substantiate this truth. Even the world gives testimony to this, as seen, for example, in the lyrics of such songs as the 1960s "Tracks of My Tears" by Smokey Robinson. The song speaks of being inwardly sad, even while laughing and joking outwardly.

In Ecclesiastes 2:10–11, Solomon testifies from experience of the hollowness of laugher and carnal joy derived from worldly pleasure: "And whatsoever mine eyes desired I kept not from them, I withheld not my heart from any joy; for my heart rejoiced in all my labour: and this was my portion of all my labour. Then I looked on all the works that my hands had wrought, and on the labour that I had laboured to do: and, behold, all was vanity [void of meaning; empty] and vexation of spirit [grief; sorrow], and there was no profit under the sun." Joy produced by the evil pleasures of life is *transient* (fleeting; momentary; temporal); *counterfeit* (appears genuine but is a fake) and *hollow* (void of real fulfillment; empty of peace and purpose). Maclaren says, "The laughter that echoes through the soul is the hollower the louder it is, and reverberates most through empty spaces."[854]

Its end is sadness and heaviness. "He feedeth on ashes: a deceived heart hath turned him aside, that he cannot deliver his soul, nor say, Is there not a lie in my right hand?" (Isaiah 44:20). As the woman at Jacob's Well, all sinners drink from a fountain that cannot satisfy (John 4:13). In their much drinking their heart is empty, sorrowful and sad despite "laughter and mirth." Evil or sinful conduct cannot replace the deep need of the soul, regardless of its amount. "They being ignorant of God's righteousness, and going about to establish their own righteousness, have not submitted themselves unto the righteousness of God" (Romans 10:3). Jesus informed the woman at the well of the source of true and lasting joy and peace. "But whosoever drinketh of the water that I shall give him shall never thirst; but the water that I shall give him shall be in him a well of water springing up into everlasting life" (John 4:14). If you are empty of inner peace, joy and purpose, say, as did the woman in response to His words, "Sir, give me this water, that I thirst not" (John 4:15).

The *heaviness* of sin (if the conscience is not spiritually calloused) inflicts great pain, disgust and sorrow. In its final end however, the heaviness will become even heavier as the sinner is judged for the evil deeds committed (Romans 14:12; 2 Corinthians 5:10; Matthew 12:36).

The Bottom Line: There is sadness under the sinner's smile. Gaiety often conceals grief. Happiness and meaning are elusive apart from a personal relationship with Jesus Christ (John 10:10).

183
Laziness, the sin of wasted time and neglected work
Proverbs 6:9–11

"How long wilt thou sleep, O sluggard? when wilt thou arise out of thy sleep? Yet a little sleep, a little slumber, a little folding of the hands to sleep: So shall thy poverty come as one that travelleth, and thy want as an armed man."

"How long will you lie there, O sluggard?" (the lazy waste away the day just lying there as if there is nothing else to do; the harvest is waiting, but he is sleeping). "When will you arise from your sleep?" ("how much longer are you going to stay in bed?") A "little sleep, a little slumber, a little folding of the hands to rest" (sarcastically the lazy man is told that all he needs is just a little more sleep and rest): SO "poverty" (lack of support;

no money or food) will come upon you like a "robber" (vagabond, no one to support you), and an "armed man" (bandit). Laziness has its consequences.

A sluggard is a lazy man. He sleeps when he should be working as others are. "Go to the ant, O sluggard; consider her ways, and be wise" (Proverbs 6:6 ESV). Solomon tells the lazy to examine the work ethic of the ant that works diligently and prepares for the winter. "Without having any chief, officer, or ruler, she prepares her bread in summer and gathers her food in harvest" (v. 7).

The point is that the sluggard shouldn't have to be told to work and store up goods for hard times. The Apostle Paul frankly said, "For even when we were with you, this we commanded you, that if any would not work, neither should he eat" (2 Thessalonians 3:10). Solomon portrays another example of laziness in Proverbs 24:30–31 in picturing a towering strong wall that due to neglect of its owner's care (laziness) fell to the ground.

Work and *toil* are mentioned over 480 times in Scripture, revealing that God counts work important. Work ethic begins in childhood with family responsibilities (cleaning up the bedroom, taking the trash out, cutting the grass, washing the car, feeding the dog, washing dishes) and continues throughout life with regard to livelihood and necessary home chores.

> He also that is slothful in his work is brother to him that is a great waster.
> Proverbs 18:9

The Bottom Line: Henry Ward Beecher said, "When God wanted sponges and oysters, He made them and put one on a rock and the other in the mud. When He made man, He did not make him to be a sponge or an oyster; He made him with feet and hands, and head and heart, and vital blood, and a place to use them; and He said to him, 'Go work.'"[855] There are no "free lunches."

184
Leadership, traits of godly leaders
Proverbs 20:7
"The just man walketh in his integrity: his children are blessed after him."

The "just" (godly righteous, honorable, fair) man "walketh" (manner of conduct) in his "integrity" (walks uprightly; walk and talk agree): his children are "blessed" (made happy) after him.

Proverbs offers numerous principles on effective leadership.

Life and work divinely governed. "The king's [leader's] heart is in the hand of the LORD, as the rivers of water: he turneth it whithersoever he will." (Proverbs 21:1).

Work ethic is honorable. "Go to the ant, thou sluggard; consider her ways, and be wise: Which having no guide, overseer, or ruler, Provideth her meat in the summer, and gathereth her food in the harvest. How long wilt thou sleep, O sluggard? when wilt thou arise out of thy sleep?" (Proverbs 6:6–9).

Counsel is godly. "Without counsel purposes are disappointed: but in the multitude of counsellors they are established" (Proverbs 15:22).

Character is credible. "Righteous lips are the delight of kings; and they love him that speaketh right" (Proverbs 16:13).

Criticism is tempered. "A wise heart instructs its mouth and increases learning with its speech. Pleasant words are a honeycomb: sweet to the taste and health to the body" (Proverbs 16:23–24 CSB).

Motivation is honorable and effective. "A good leader motivates, doesn't mislead, doesn't exploit" (Proverbs 16:10 MSG).

Humble instead of arrogant. "Pride goeth before destruction, and an haughty [arrogant] spirit before a fall." (Proverbs 16:18).

Correction is accepted and applied. "Whoso loveth instruction loveth knowledge: but he that hateth reproof is brutish [stupid]" (Proverbs 12:1).

Critics are ignored. "He that reproveth a scorner getteth to himself shame: and he that rebuketh a wicked man getteth himself a blot" (Proverbs 9:7).

Wisdom is coveted and pursued. "Forsake her not [wisdom], and she shall preserve thee: love her, and she shall keep thee. Wisdom is the principal thing; therefore get wisdom: and with all thy getting get understanding." (Proverbs 4:6–7).

The Bottom Line: John Maxwell says, "A leader is one who knows the way, goes the way, and shows the way."[856]

185
Learning, readiness to be taught
Proverbs 1:5–6

"A wise man will hear, and will increase learning; and a man of understanding shall attain unto wise counsels: To understand a proverb, and the interpretation; the words of the wise, and their dark sayings."

"I will open my mouth in a parable: I will utter dark sayings of old" (Psalm 78:2).

"A wise man" (Carroll says, "The Jewish concept of a perfectly *wise man* is 'that he is one who, in his whole being, lives and thinks and acts in right relationship to the all-wise God. His wisdom commences emotionally in the fear of God, is manifested intellectually in his acquaintance with the manifestations of the divine nature in Word and work, is active volitionally in obedience to the will of God as revealed in Word and work"[857]) "will hear" ("an active listening; an obedience"[858]; specifically, Reyburn and Fry say "hear" in the text "means being open and obedient to the teaching and thoughts that the Proverbs contain"[859]) and "will increase learning" (godly instruction increases knowledge and enhances the understanding of "dark sayings"—the obscure, hard, difficult, deep doctrinal or practical truths).

Additionally, "the words of the wise prod us to live well. They're like nails hammered home, holding life together. They are given by God, the one Shepherd" (Ecclesiastes 12:11 MSG). The overarching purpose of Proverbs is to get man to seek godly counsel (biblically based) regarding the discourse of life (the path to avoid; the one to follow), decision-making, discretionary choices, discernment (right or wrong; for his best good or not) and clarification of theological doctrine and practice that he may increase in understanding and knowledge of God's Word, will and way which will enable him to walk pleasing unto the Lord and prosper in every dimension (Proverbs 1:2–6; 3:19–26).

The Bottom Line: Readiness to learn is a character trait of the godly. All men are ignorant when it comes to the deep things of God, whether he is a theologian, Bible scholar or seminary professor. Of all men, the man who pompously says, as the "old and foolish king" of Ecclesiastes did, that there's nothing more to learn about God, is egoistical, prideful and blinded to his own ignorance. In fact, Solomon says, "Better is a poor and a wise child" than he (Ecclesiastes 4:13).

186
Life, the creator of us all
Proverbs 22:2

"The rich and poor meet together: the LORD is the maker of them all."

The "rich and poor" (regardless of status all are created equally[860]) "meet together" ("live side by side"[861]): the Lord is the "maker of them all" (God made everyone of "us"—through His creation of man we are related one to another and called "mankind").

Despite *place* (rich or poor), *race* or *face,* all mankind have commonality. God is their giver of life ("the Lord is the maker of them all"). All are *stamped* in God's image (Genesis 1:27) and therefore bear the same significance ("fearfully and wonderfully made"—Psalm 139:14) and purpose ("for I have created him for my glory, I have formed him; yea, I have made him"—Isaiah 43:7). God is not only man's Maker but also his Sustainer ("upholding all things by the word of his power"—Hebrews 1:3). "He maketh his sun to rise on the evil and on the good, and sendeth rain on the just and on the unjust" (Matthew 5:45).

As people made by God, in God's image and for God's purpose, we should manifest mutual respect, dignity and love one for another (Mark 12:31) despite religious, philosophical, political or social differences. In Scripture we are exhorted to refrain from acts of violence (infliction of bodily harm), theft, discrimination, fraud and anything else that brings harm or injustice to another. All mankind share in common not only their *creation* but also their need of *conversion.* "All have sinned, and come short of the glory of God" (Romans 3:23). It is God's desire for "all men to be saved, and to come unto the knowledge of the truth" (1 Timothy 2:4). Every Christian is his "brother's keeper," especially with regard to bringing him to the knowledge of the truth in Christ Jesus (Christ's death and resurrection alone make possible man's salvation).

The Bottom Line: Jesus in His high priestly prayer said, "Neither pray I for these alone, but for them also which shall believe on me through their word; That they all may be one; as thou, Father, art in me, and I in thee, that they also may be one in us: that the world may believe that thou hast sent me. And the glory which thou gavest me I have given them; that they may be one, even as we are one: I in them, and thou in me, that they may be made perfect in one; and that the world may know that thou hast sent me, and hast loved them, as thou hast loved me" (John 17:20–23).

187

Listening, don't listen to heretics
Proverbs 19:27

"Cease, my son, to hear the instruction that causeth to err from the words of knowledge."

"Cease" (desist), my son, to "hear" (listen, heed) the "instruction" (teaching, advice) that "causeth" (incites, prompts) to "err" (stray away) from the "words of knowledge" (biblical truth).

Since the Holy Scriptures instill principles, precepts and commandments for righteous living, any and all things that undermine them must be ignored and avoided. The believer is to be cautious not to even sit at the feet of a professor or teacher that distorts and diminishes the Word of God (Psalm 1:1).

He is but a self-deluded "fool" who overly estimates his strength (maturity) to march into "Enemy's Headquarters" to "listen" to their point of view undaunted. Paul's directive (Ephesians 4:27) that believers are to give no place to the Devil is applicable not only to a physical place (opportunity for sin) but to the intellectual as well (opportunity for doubt and apostasy). In the parable of the sower, Jesus warns of Satan's power to "steal" the good seed sown in a person's life. He says, "And these are they by the way side, where the word is sown; but when they have heard, Satan cometh immediately, and taketh away the word that was sown in their hearts" (Mark 4:15). Never underestimate Satan's deceptive and manipulative ability to either "uproot" the gospel seed or create doubt as to its legitimacy and truthfulness.

Dr. B. H. Carroll boldly and candidly said, "The prevalent evil of today arises from the fact that the children of Belial occupy many pulpits and many chairs in theological seminaries and Christian schools. Always they are the advance courier of disaster to God's cause." Sounds like a description of our day, doesn't it? Yet these words were spoken nearly 100 years ago. What he pronounced has certainly come to pass and continues to do so. The Christian finds no delight or benefit in listening to the ungodly and scorners of God and His Holy Word. Thus they are avoided.

John MacArthur advised the best way to deal with those who peddle another gospel when they knock on your door simply is not to allow them entrance. The same advice applies to listening to liberal and lost teachers, professors and preachers; don't give them the chance to sow corrupt seeds into your life in the classroom, church or lecture hall.

The Bottom Line: Don't give the devil a "foothold" to sow seeds of religious doubt and/or heresy. Stay out of the enemy's camp.

188
Listening, stop listening to the wicked
Proverbs 17:4
"A wicked doer giveth heed to false lips; and a liar giveth ear to a naughty tongue."

The bad ("wicked") listen to (pay attention; follow) the advice (counsel) of others who are sinful ("false lips"), for they are like-minded (justify each other's wrong). To summarize, the sinner does not want correction or condemnation but commendation and justification for wicked behavior. He wants counsel that coincides with his own devious desires and schemes, as in the case of Amnon (2 Samuel 13:2–5).

Bad people occasionally listen to the righteous, but often they *do not hear* (allow godly instruction to be ingested but not digested). They give deaf ears to the Gospel of the Lord Jesus Christ that has the power to transform (Revelation 22:17) while giving receptive ears to the wicked that corrupt, ruin and destroy (Proverbs 16:27). The gist of Proverbs is to show the foolishness and folly of listening to the wrong people and the benefit and blessing of listening to the godly wise. To continue to listen to the ungodly precipitates foolish conduct; listening to the godly initiates change (transformation) in heart and habit (2 Corinthians 5:17).

The Bottom Line: Change in lifestyle (actions, attitudes, aspiration) starts with a change in whom you listen to. "Evildoers do not understand what is right, but those who seek the LORD understand it fully" (Proverbs 28:5 NIV).

189
Loneliness, the painfulness of isolation
Proverbs 18:1
"Through desire a man, having separated himself..."

"I am like a pelican of the wilderness: I am like an owl of the desert. I watch, and am as a sparrow alone upon the house top." (Psalm 102:6–7).

Through "desire" (earnest, strong appetite for) a man, having "separated" (withdraws) himself.

The person Solomon describes is an "unsociable man," for he chooses to live aloof from friends and others, pursuing personal pleasures. "The one who looks only to his own interest isolates himself from others." We may also translate, for example, "A person who thinks only of himself does not make many friends."[862]

Sadly, many people choose to be alone, like the man described here—a state that easily turns to one of loneliness. They break away from the church, friends and colleagues for personal issues (quarrels, disagreements), not the glory of God, to live in solitary confinement in their home, cabin, library or study, only in time to discover what they did not expect to intrude: loneliness.

Loneliness is certainly no respecter of persons. Aloneness is not to be equated with loneliness. Solitude is "a life-giving practice that enriches our hearts with the powerful gifts of clarity, cleansing, and strength."[863] Jesus engaged in times of solitude (Mark 1:12; 3:7, 13). Paul Tillich shares a helpful distinction between solitude and loneliness. "Loneliness expresses the pain of being alone and solitude expresses the glory of being alone."[864]

Covet, crave *to be alone* with God. Joshua was alone with God when called to ministry (Joshua 1:1). Moses was alone when the bush burned in the wilderness (Exodus 3:1–5). Gideon was alone when God raised him up to save Israel (Judges 6:11). John the Baptist was alone in the wilderness (Matthew 3:1). John, the Beloved of the Lord, was exiled upon the Isle of Patmos when under divine inspiration he wrote the book of Revelation (Revelation 1:9). We must dare to be alone with God. Only in doing so will "the print of Heaven" be stamped upon us and "the power of God" infuse us. Many that are alone are not lonely.

Loneliness, on the other hand, is "a painful sense of being unwanted, unneeded, uncared for, maybe even unnecessary," states Adrian Rogers.[865] And I add unloved. Loneliness also is a feeling of being invisible to others. James Dobson says, "Most loneliness results from insulation rather than isolation. In other words, we are lonely because we insulate ourselves, not because others isolate us."[866] The psalmist likens the lonely to the "pelican of the wilderness" and the "owl of the desert." "Wilderness" and "desert" refer to waste places or abandoned ruins, places where people do not live.[867] Further, he states the lonely are like "a sparrow...upon the house top" (lonely bird that for hours moans, laments the loss of its mate on a housetop).[868]

Oh, the pain of being lonely, to be as the pelican, owl and sparrow in a place where there are none to socialize or care about you! The person who never receives a letter, never hears a word of encouragement, never feels the handclasp or hugs of another and never receives a visit knows the pain loneliness spurs.

Lord Byron described the agony and heartache of his loneliness. He said, "What is the worst of woes that wait on age? What stamps the wrinkle deeper on the brow? To view each loved one blotted from life's page and be alone on earth, as I am now."[869] Perhaps you identify with him; if so, know there is reason to hope in God.

Psychologists inform us that man has the basic need for inclusion in community and close relationships. God wired us that way. It is when social relationships break down that the enemy enters, sowing the seed of loneliness. And loneliness brings or may bring sadness, emptiness, depression, anxiety and despair. It has a crippling impact upon us emotionally. One survey reveals that a whopping eighty percent of psychiatric patients sought help due to loneliness.[870]

Jesus Understands Loneliness

He experienced the ultimate pain of loneliness upon the cross when making possible man's salvation from sin. The Bible states that Jesus cried, "Eli, Eli, lama sabachthani? that is to say, My God, my God, why hast thou forsaken me?" about the ninth hour (Matthew 27:46). John MacArthur states, "The Father forsook the Son because the Son took upon Himself "our transgressions,...our iniquities" (Isaiah 53:5).[871] The disciples also forsook Him, along with the crowd gathered at the cross. Jesus died alone. But in His loneliness He rested upon God's promises and won the day. So Jesus has empathy with the lonely and is able to bring healing to their wounded soul. He cares for you. He loves you. He stands ready to help you.

> No one ever cared for me like Jesus;
> There's no other friend so kind as He.
> No one else could take the sin and darkness from me;
> Oh, how much He [cares] for me! ~ Charles Weigle

Isolation from God due to sin is the root of all loneliness. But it is fixable easily. He says, "Come unto me, all ye that labour and are heavy laden, and I will give you rest. Take my yoke upon you, and learn of me; for I am meek and lowly in heart: and ye shall find rest unto your souls. For my yoke is easy, and my burden is light" (Matthew 11:28–30).

The Bottom Line: In order to know the healing of loneliness, you must know its Healer personally. As long as you remain outside the family of God, loneliness will be inescapable. Jesus compassionately invites you to bring your sin and loneliness to the cross to experience the life-changing transformation found only in Him. He has said of some, but may He not say it of you, "And ye will not come to me, that ye might have life" (John 5:40).

190
Love, it covers all wrong and sin
Proverbs 10:12

"Love covereth all sins."

"Love" ("refers to harmonious and affectionate relations with positive feelings toward others"[872]) "covereth" (pardons, forgives) "all" (without exception) "sins" (to miss the mark; transgression of the law; wrongdoing). Charles Bridges summarizes, "Love covers, overlooks, speedily forgives, and forgets."[873]

Note several applications of the Proverb. It first suggests that upon being offended by a friend (insulted or harmed), out of love it be "covered" (*kāsâh*, pardoned), lest strife be kindled and the relationship damaged. Out of love it's best to forgive and forget the hurts inflicted by a friend. Do it "yet for love's sake" (Philemon 9). Matthew Henry remarks, "Love, instead of proclaiming and aggravating the offence, conceals and extenuates it as far as it is capable of being concealed and extenuated."[874]

The second application has to do with a brother's faltering into sin. Love dictates that you confront him that he might confess it and be restored (Galatians 6:1). The love of Jesus Christ exhibited at Calvary "covereth all sins." And that's the end of the matter as far as the Lord, the friend and you are concerned, for love conceals that which God cleanses (1 Peter 4:8). That which God conceals, out of love we do not reveal.

However, *the overarching lesson and application* of the Proverb is with regard to the atoning work at Calvary by Jesus Christ who out of love for the world freely laid down His life that all might be saved (John 3:16). He *covered* our sins upon the cross in His precious blood. "Who his own self bare our sins in his own body on the tree, that we, being dead to sins, should live unto righteousness: by whose stripes ye were healed" (1 Peter 2:24). You have not prayed the last time for forgiveness. It's good to know that God's love will never run out on you. He always is ready to forgive (cover) your sin (1 John 1:9). That's what true love does.

The Bottom Line: C. S. Lewis said, "Though our feelings come and go, God's love for us does not."[875] Christian's are to mirror 1 Corinthians 13 (the love chapter).

191
Love, wisdom's love for its lovers
Proverbs 8:17

"I love them that love me; and those that seek me early shall find me."

"I" (Wisdom) "love them that love me" (mutual affinity); AND those that "seek" (search for) me "early" (early in life) shall "find" (discover and be benefited by) me.

The Proverb refers specifically to wisdom, not God. Kayatz cites that "the formula of reciprocity is never found in the Old Testament in the mouth of the Lord."[876] H. A. Ironside concurs stating that it would be extremely faulty to limit God's love only to those who returned it.[877] John states, "We love him, because he first loved us" (1 John 4:19). See John 3:16; Jeremiah 31:3.

Wisdom (wisdom is divine understanding [discernment] that enables man to do that which is right and pleasing unto the Lord—which is for his best good—in every course of action) is *only* acquired by him that *loves* it. The foolish *loathe* it, therefore never know it. Wisdom loves them that love it, assuring it will be found upon diligent search ("shall find me"). See Proverbs 2:1–4. We are to "seek" wisdom early—earnestly, speedily, strenuously, above all else—at the outset of life, for it is foundational to a happy and successful life lived for God.

In Ecclesiastes 12:1, Solomon sounded a similar note in reference to God: "Remember now thy Creator in the days of thy youth, while the evil days come not, nor the years draw nigh, when thou shalt say, I have no pleasure in them." Not only is it expedient to seek wisdom early in life, but also Him who is the personification of wisdom, the Lord Jesus Christ. Man ought to seek the Lord early for many reasons: life without Him is empty and meaningless; to stave off sin and its ruinous effects; to prevent the hardness of heart toward Him (salvation, surrender and service); to safeguard the heart against heresy; to gain forgiveness of sin and eternal life; to live pleasing unto the Lord.

Now is the time to seek the Lord Jesus Christ. "Seek ye the LORD while he may be found, call ye upon him while he is near" (Isaiah 55:6). A time will come when you may seek the Lord too late (He will not be found). The invitation to seek the Lord comes with a promise. "And ye shall seek me, and find me, when ye shall search for me with all your heart" (Jeremiah 29:13).

The Bottom Line: "Just as Wisdom offers great treasure to those who seek her, so Jesus makes all who come to him spiritually rich, at great cost to himself (2 Corinthians 8:9; Matthew 6:19–20; Revelation 3:18). In him we have an imperishable heavenly inheritance (1 Peter 1:4–5)."[878]

192
Lust, warning to avoid its trap
Proverbs 6:25
"Lust not after her beauty in thine heart."

"Lust" (same word for "covet" in Exodus 20:17: "Thou shalt not covet thy neighbour's wife"; restrain from unchaste and immoral thoughts, imaginations, desires) not after her "beauty" (don't be captivated by her seductive charms; physical attraction) in thine "heart" (the thoughts of the mind). See Matthew 5:28. To summarize, a person is not to hesitate to repress wanton sexual desires when they are triggered.

Sexual lust may be described as a sexual craving, longing or desiring. Its sources of stirring are people, movies/videos, books, photos and music from without, and impure memories from within—all spearheaded by the demons of Hell. Lust is manifested when the mind allows sexual imaginations to be entertained (sexual fantasies). It might be said that "lust" is the sensual salt that causes a person to thirst for sexual gratification.

James states quite bluntly that man "is drawn away of his own lust, and enticed. Then when lust hath conceived, it bringeth forth sin: and sin, when it is finished, bringeth forth death" (James 1:14–15). The word *lust* here carries the picture of a fish being drawn out of its hiding place (the safety of the deep or the brush pile). The word translated *entice* means "to bait, to catch a fish with bait or to hunt with snares." James thus presents the modus operandi of lust. Satan begets immoral, perverted desires in the heart (if there is a conception there has to be a father, and in this case it has to be the ruler of darkness). These cravings of sexual desire draw a person from the place of safety with the Lord only to be "baited" to partake of its forbidden pleasure. Ultimately lust results in sin, and the sin in death. Some want to blame God, blame friends, blame their genes or blame circumstances for their sin. This text clearly reveals man's personal responsibility for sin, that it is his own evil desire that prompts it.

Jesus not only forbids immoral sexual activity physically, but also mentally. He said, "You have heard that it was said, 'You must not be guilty of adultery.' But I tell you that if anyone looks at a woman and wants to sin sexually with her, in his mind he has already done that sin with the woman" (Matthew 5:27–28, NCV). In addition to sexual fantasies, lust stimulates and fuels sexual acts forbidden by God, including premarital sex (1 Thessalonians 4:3), adultery (Exodus 20:14), homosexuality (Leviticus 18:22), and sexual rape (Exodus 20:15). Lust soils the soul with sin, steals allegiance from God, stunts growth spiritually, saturates the mind with deviant desires, spoils relationships, sickens the mind and body, sorrows with remorse for its indulgence, shackles with almost unbreakable chains, and spurs immoral acts.

The apostle Paul tells us not to sow unto the flesh (Galatians 6:8). To sow to the flesh is to stroke it mentally or physically instead of renouncing and crucifying it. A person sows to the flesh by the planting of its sensual seeds in the mind. The reason so many fall into sexual sin is that they sow to the flesh, positioning themselves for defeat. The key to the defeat of lust is to sow unto the Spirit (Bible study, prayer, submission to the Holy Spirit's prompting, Scripture memory, godly obedience, worship, moral restraint); in so doing you will reap the fruit of the Spirit (Galatians 6:8) which is self-control, godliness, kindness, love, patience, gentleness, faith, meekness and moral goodness (Galatians 5:22–23). In essence, Paul summarizes that the secret to victory over the flesh is to give no place to it (Ephesians 4:27), mentally or physically.

The Bottom Line: The sin in thought is equated by Jesus as the sin in deed (Matthew 5:28). Thomas Fuller offers excellent advice: "Hold not conference, debate or reasoning with any lust; 'tis but a preparatory for thy admission of it. The way is at the very first flatly to deny it."[879]

193
Lying, its abomination and condemnation
Proverbs 12:22

"Lying lips are abomination to the LORD: but they that deal truly are his delight."

"Wherefore putting away lying, speak every man truth with his neighbour: for we are members one of another" (Ephesians 4:25).

"Lying lips" (liars; they who utter untruths) are "abomination" (abhorred, hated) to the Lord: BUT they that "deal" (act or talk) "truly" (speak truthfully [Proverbs 12:17, 19]; trustworthy) are His "delight" (pleasure; gain His approval).

Dictionary.com defines *lying* as "a false statement made with deliberate intent to deceive; an intentional untruth; a falsehood…[As] something intended or serving to convey a false impression." The text may be rendered: "Liars are disgusting to the Lord."[880] The lies in question are not unintentional ones (unknowingly untrue) but intentional deceit (Hebrews 4:12). Be careful not to accuse another of lying who was *innocent* in heart in what was spoken.[881] As others, you too have said what you thought to be truth only later to discover it wasn't.

H. A. Ironside remarks, "One is often pained to hear good men recklessly charge others with lying because they have uttered an untruth in the innocence of their hearts. A statement may be false as to fact, which is true as to intent; just as a statement may be true as to fact, which was uttered with the intent to deceive. It is the deceit in the heart that causes the lips to utter a lie."[882] According to research by Pamela Meyer, the average person gets lied to 10 to 200 times a day.[883] Meyer states there are six types of lying—straight-out lying, lying by vagueness or ambiguity, lying by omission, lying by withholding information, lying by appearance and actions, and tacit ["understood or implied without being stated"— *Oxford Dictionary*] lying.[884] Warren Wiersbe summarizes, "The truth will deliver souls (Proverbs 14:25), but lies only lead to bondage and shame. Proverbs 17:4 indicates that liars enjoy listening to liars. People who enjoy listening to gossip will turn around and gossip themselves. The heart controls the ear as well as the lips. But all liars will be punished (Proverbs 19:5, 9); and when they 'eat their own words,' it will be like gravel (Proverbs 20:17). Hell is waiting for the one who 'loves and practices a lie' (Rev. 22:15, NKJV)."[885] A lying tongue may be attempting to conceal sin in the heart, as was the case with Ananias and Sapphira (Acts 5:1–10) and Judas (John 12:1–8).[886] Harry Ironside again said, "Honest speech manifests integrity of heart; falsity declares unerringly the lack of truth in the inward parts."[887] "A lie has no legs," and, "truth may be blamed but shall ne'er be shamed."[888]

Lying is a problem that all parents face with their children. Dr. James Dobson states an effective way to help children tell the truth is through Bible devotionals that address the issue. Dobson advises, "Memorize the passage in Proverbs [Proverbs 6:16–19] together so it can be referred to in other contexts. Use it as a springboard to discussions of virtues and behavior that will please God. Each verse can be applied to everyday situations so that a child can begin to feel accountable for what he does and says. Returning to the specific issue of lying, point out to the child that in a list of seven things the Lord hates most, two of them deal with dishonesty. Telling the truth is something God cares about, and therefore it should matter to us. This will explain why you are going to insist that your son or daughter learn to tell the truth even when it hurts to do so. Your goal is to lay a foundation that will help you underscore a commitment to honesty in the future." [889]

The Bottom Line: J. Vernon McGee said, "One of the things that should characterize a child of God is his truthfulness."[890] "Let us," says

George Lawson, "always speak truth one to another—and if we lose anything by it, our gain shall counterbalance the damage."[891]

194
Malice, its unanticipated effects
Proverbs 26:27
"Whoso diggeth a pit shall fall therein: and he that rolleth a stone, it will return upon him."

Whoso "diggeth" (prepares a trap) a "pit" (snare or trap for an animal) shall "fall" (stumble or slip into traps of their own making) therein: AND he that "rolleth a stone" (a huge stone that is pushed down a hill to inflict injury on another[892]), it will "return" (it will "reverse," striking him). The Proverb teaches the law of retributive justice.

He who sets a snare for another, seeking the injury of that party, will himself be the victim. Haman's gallows for Mordecai claimed him. "And Harbonah, one of the chamberlains, said before the king, Behold also, the gallows fifty cubits high, which Haman had made for Mordecai, who had spoken good for the king, standeth in the house of Haman. Then the king said, Hang him thereon" (Esther 7:9). Likewise, the men who induced King Darius to make a decree that would harm Daniel were themselves destroyed by it (Daniel 6:24). Chrysostom speaks of the blindness of malice: "Let us not plot against others, lest we injure ourselves. When we supplant the reputation of others, let us consider that we injure ourselves; it is against ourselves that we plot. For perchance with men we do him harm, if we have power; but ourselves in the sight of God, by provoking Him against us. Let us not, then, injure ourselves. For as we injure ourselves when we injure our neighbors, so by benefiting them we benefit ourselves" ("Homily XIV on Philippians," Oxford translation).[893]

Hypocritical friends conceal their plot for your destruction. Therefore, walk wisely and cautiously lest they succeed. Be not such a friend to another. Paul admonishes, "Let all bitterness, and wrath, and anger, and clamour, and evil speaking, be put away from you, [along] with all malice" (Ephesians 4:31).

The Bottom Line: Do unto others like you would have them do unto you (Luke 6:31). Don't allow malice to rule life, for it in the end brings ruin. Stop "rolling large stones" upon others with the tongue.

195
Marriage, its sacredness and blessedness
Proverbs 18:22

"Whoso findeth a wife findeth a good thing, and obtaineth favour of the LORD."

"Who can find a virtuous and capable wife? She is worth more than precious rubies" (Proverbs 31:10 NLT).

Whoso "findeth" a wife (gets married) findeth a "good thing" ("that which is pleasing to God, beneficial to life, and abundantly enjoyable"[894]), AND obtaineth "favour" (approval [Proverbs 8:35]) of the Lord.

Obviously, it is not God's will for everyone to marry. In 1 Corinthians 7, the Apostle Paul, in counseling the unmarried, makes clear they were not unspiritual because they were single. One version translates verse 1: "It is perfectly proper, honorable, morally befitting for a man to live in strict celibacy" (WUEST). It's okay to remain single (v. 8) provided the person has been given the "gift" (v. 7) of celibacy, which Paul possessed. Marriage was divinely instituted by God (Matthew 19:3–4) to be a sexually exclusive lifetime relationship (Matthew 19:9) between one man and one woman (Matthew 19:4).

It has been said, "Before you remove a fence, you need to ask why that fence was erected in the first place." Over 6,000 years ago God erected the fence of marriage between a man and woman for good reason, and now an attempt is afoot to remove it (1 Corinthians 7:3–48; Romans 7:1–4; Ephesians 5:22–33; Colossians 3:18–19; 1 Timothy 3:2, 11–12; 5:14; Titus 1:6; 2:4–5; 1 Peter 3:1–7). Teach your children that same-sex marriage is simply a counterfeit of God's heavenly design for marriage that cheapens and degrades the real thing.

Here are seven keys to selecting a husband or wife.

Walk in harmony with God and His Word. When Abraham's servant sought a wife for Isaac, God led him to Rebekah. Upon meeting her, the servant explained himself to Rebekah, saying, "I being in the way, the LORD led me" (Genesis 24:27). It is essential that your children spend time "in the way"—in obedience and intimate communion with God—to be led by God. Max Lucado states, "We learn God's will by spending time in His presence. The key to knowing God's heart is having a relationship with Him—a personal relationship."[895]

Pray for wisdom. Wisdom and discernment are acquired through prayer: "But if any of you needs wisdom, you should ask God for it. He is generous to everyone and will give you wisdom without criticizing you" (James 1:5 NCV). In other words, James says that the believer who wants to know God's will should go to Him saying, "God, I do want to fulfill your plan regarding my lifemate, but I need divine wisdom to know that plan." Theologian J. I. Packer, in *Knowing God,* indicates that "wisdom" in Scripture always means knowledge of the course of action that will please God and secure life.[896] Solomon, too, insisted that believers rely wholly on insights from God: "Trust the Lord with all your heart, and don't depend on your own understanding. Remember the LORD in all you do, and he will give you success. Don't depend on your own wisdom. Respect the Lord and refuse to do wrong." (Proverbs 3:5–7 NCV). Wisdom also comes through experience in walking with the Lord.

Set aside personal preference. It's not uncommon for a person to ask God for guidance only to hear what they want to hear instead of the real voice of God. John Wesley said, "I find that the chief purpose in determining the will of God is to get my will in an unprejudiced state about the issue at hand."[897] Children must do exactly the same when seeking divine guidance regarding a marriage mate.

Take in the Word of God. A fourth key to making the right decision about whom to marry is absorption of Holy Scripture. Mark this down: God will never lead anyone to do something that violates His Word. "The statutes of the LORD are right, rejoicing the heart: the commandment of the LORD is pure, enlightening the eyes." (Psalm 19:8). Holy Scripture transmits light (divine knowledge) to the soul. J. I. Packer states that "the fundamental mode whereby our rational Creator guides His rational creatures is by rational understanding and application of His written Word."[898]

Consult others. Solomon states, "The way of a fool is right in his own eyes, but a wise man is he who listens to counsel" (Proverbs 12:15 NASB). Hopefully your children will seek and listen to your counsel.

Vetting. Politicians are known for vetting potential candidates for public office prior to nomination to make sure that they are actually what they appear to be. It is not only sensible to vet a potential mate, but imperative. Far too many have said, "I do," only to discover later that the person lying in bed next to them was a stranger.

Base it on love, not infatuation. Infatuation is based on fleeting feeling; love, on emotion and the will. Infatuation is for a moment in time; love is forever. Infatuation is self-serving, seeking personal pleasure; love is selfless. Infatuation fades with separation; love grows. Infatuation is something one falls into; with love, one grows into it (1 Corinthians 13:4–8).

The Bottom Line: Allen Ross summarizes, "A good marriage is a good gift from God."[899] But a bad marriage is heartbreaking. Someone humorously (but I fear sorrowfully) wrote, "I married for the ideal, got a bad deal, now want a new deal." To marry in the Lord prevents the desire or necessity of wanting a "new deal."

196
Marriage, the working wife and mother
Proverbs 31:24

"She maketh fine linen, and selleth it; and delivereth girdles unto the merchant."

"She" (the Proverbs 31 wife and mother) "maketh" (industrious) "fine linen" (garments; possibly "linen shirts"[900]; Toy suggests "night dress"[901]), and "selleth it" (enterprising; she markets what she sews); AND "delivereth" (supplies to distributers[902]) "girdles" (belts [2 Samuel 18:11]) unto the "merchant" (tradesmen, shop owners[903]).

The Bible is replete with women who worked (in addition to working at home). The Proverbs 31 wife had a linen business (Proverbs 31:24); Lydia worked with purple cloth (Acts 16:14); Pricilla worked as a tentmaker with her husband (Acts 18:1–3); Ruth worked to support Naomi and herself (Ruth 2:1–3). Women in the workforce have contributed much to society and the advancement of the kingdom of God.

Abigail Dodds in an article for *Desiring God* states, "God's Word is not silent in regard to the priorities that women in particular should have. We are made as helpers, coworkers (Genesis 2:18), with the home as a priority (Titus 2:5) and a place of industry, hospitality and respite (Proverbs 31:10–31). Women are to be fearless in the face of frightening things and submissive to their own husbands, to cultivate inward beauty over outward (1 Peter 3:1–6). We are to be examples of generous patrons, selfless service and spiritual mothering (Romans 16:1–13)."[904]

The religious (biblical) education and training of one's children in godliness must be viewed as a priority (Deuteronomy 6:5–7; Proverbs 22:6; Ephesians 6:4; 2 Timothy 3:15). Make due diligence to insure that outside work does not interfere with it. Many godly women have learned to balance workload and motherhood so that neither is hindered or injured, while many others choose not to work until their children are raised.

The Bottom Line: Ladies, consult God on the matter of work outside the home. It is essential that in every aspect of life He directs our steps. It doesn't take a village to raise a child, only godly parents committed to the task.

197
Meddling, it's none of your business
Proverbs 26:17

"He that passeth by, and meddleth with strife belonging not to him, is like one that taketh a dog by the ears."

He that "passeth by" (a person happening by two people he does not know having a quarrel) and "meddleth" (interferes) with "strife" (quarrel) "belonging not to him" (none of his business), is like one that taketh a "dog by the ears" (provokes the dog to act aggressively in defense, leading to the man's injury).

A man who meddles in another's business (unless invited to intervene) is like a man that grabs the ears of a wild dog. He often will be hurt. Dogs in ancient Israel were considered "unclean," thus never kept as pets.[905] To grab their "ears" would generate furious reaction from the animal. Interference in another man's quarrel may result in a similar reaction.[906]

I learned the truth of this Proverb while young. Two of our beagles (rabbit hunting dogs) got head to head in a bitter fight. Unthinkingly, I grabbed their collars to pull them apart, only to be severely bitten. It was a quarrel I should have left alone.

Matthew Henry provides guidance as to when interference is appropriate: "If we can be instrumental to make peace between those that are at variance, we must do it. We are cautioned against it because of the danger it exposes us to."[907] Note the condition he set forth for inserting ourselves in the fray of others. Do so only if you might be instrumental to their reconciliation. Otherwise you may simply exacerbate it and bring harm to yourself.

The Bottom Line: Avoid interfering in the disputes of others that are none of your business unless invited by either of the parties involved or clearly prompted by the Lord. Sometimes the best action is inaction in entering a fray.

198
Medicinal, strong drink and wine
Proverbs 31:6–7

"Give strong drink unto him that is ready to perish, and wine unto those that be of heavy hearts. Let him drink, and forget his poverty, and remember his misery no more."

Give "strong drink" (beer) unto him that is "ready to perish" (in emergencies give to him that is about to die to use as a drug to relieve the pain of suffering; in contrast to today's it had about 7–10 percent alcohol content[908]) and "wine" (MacArthur says "grape juice mixed with water to dilute it"[909]) unto those that are of "heavy hearts" (mental distress).

The principle may refer to strong drink for medicinal use, "as anesthetics or drugs to deaden physical pain or deep emotional bitterness (and the pain of those who were dying)."[910] Paul prescribed it for Timothy's "infirmities" (1 Timothy 5:23). Medicinal ways of treating such things have improved in many nations and become more available, negating the need to use strong drink in this manner. Such is certainly the case in the United States.

C. F. Pfeiffer remarks, *"This is not an allowance of moderate drinking.* It may recommend alcohol as a drug (Toy). Regardless of others, you should not take it."[911] I agree with Pfeiffer's assessment and application of the Proverb.

H. A. Ironside comments, "Earnestly Bathsheba warns her son of the evil effects that follow intemperate indulgence in wine and strong drink."[912] She says to him, "It is not for kings, O Lemuel, it is not for kings to drink wine; nor for princes strong drink" (Proverbs 31:4). And what's good for the goose is good for the gander. Oh, that every mother would instruct her children likewise.

The Bottom Line: The Proverb grants place to the personal use of strong drink medicinally (prescribed by a physician) not recreationally or socially or for any other purpose. Alcohol is a drug. Solomon describes the devastating effect of strong drink in Proverbs 23:20, 29–35.

199
Medicine, the antidote of laughter
Proverbs 17:22
"A merry heart doeth good like a medicine."

A "merry heart" (cheerful, happy, glad) doeth "good" (brings about that which is good) like a "medicine" (brings healing, relief). Deane and Taswell summarize, "A cheerful, contented disposition enables a man to resist the attacks of disease, the mind, as everyone knows, having most powerful influence over the body."[913]

Adrian Rogers stated, "A merry heart is the sign of happiness. Now, happiness and joy are not the same thing, but they are first cousins. Joy is that constant presence of God no matter what happens, but a merry heart is the ability to capture and enjoy those wonderful times of life and let them turn to laughter."[914] Abraham Lincoln said, "God must have meant for us to laugh, or else he would not have made so many mules, parrots, monkeys and human beings. God wants us to laugh." Dr. Marvin E. Herring of New Jersey's School of Osteopathic Medicine said, "The diaphragm, thorax, abdomen, heart, lungs and even the liver are given a massage during a hearty laugh."[915]

Laughter is medicine prescribed by the Great Physician for a broken, crushed spirit. Solomon says, "A cheerful heart is good medicine, but a broken spirit saps a person's strength" (Proverbs 17:22 NLT). At times in life the pain is horrendous, making it really difficult to even want to laugh. But laugh anyway. Laughter is like the prescribed medicine the doctor orders for a physical ailment. It may not be desired, but it certainly will speed up the healing.

Research indicates that laughter produces endorphins in the body that produce the sense of well-being. Other physical benefits of laughing noted by health care professionals include:

Decrease in stress hormone levels
Strengthening of the immune system

Muscle relaxation
Pain reduction
Lowering of blood pressure
Cardiovascular conditioning
Natural antidepressant[916]

So laugh. It's a gift from God. "Then was our mouth filled with laughter, and our tongue with singing" (Psalm 126:2). Neuroscientist Jodi Deluca, Ph.D., of Embry-Riddle Aeronautical University, said, "It doesn't matter why you laugh. Even in small doses, it improves our overall quality of life."[917] Personally I turn to the *Hogan's Heroes* television show for laughter therapy. It's impossible to watch without laughing. Follow the Doctor's advice and daily take your laughter medication.

Charles Bridges admonishes, "If then, Christian, you believe the Gospel to be 'glad tidings,' show that you believe it by lighting up your face with a smile, not by 'bowing down the head as a bulrush' and as it were "spreading sackcloth and ashes under you.' Show that it is the daylight of your soul, that you really find its ways to be 'pleasantness and peace,' that you believe their joys, not because you have read and heard of them, but because you have tasted them. If they are happy, be happy in them."[918]

The Bottom Line: The source of the believer's joy is internal, based upon a personal relationship with Jesus Christ, not external happiness, which is *based upon what happens* (Galatians 5:22–23). Abraham and Sara laughed (in being overwhelmed with joy) when blessed with the son Isaac (the name means "laughter"). See Genesis 21:6.

200
Memorization, merits of Scripture memory
Proverbs 3:1

"My son, forget not my law; but let thine heart keep my commandments."

"He taught me also, and said unto me, Let thine heart retain my words: keep my commandments, and live" (Proverbs 4:4).

My son, "forget not" ("remember!" don't be guilty of willful forgetfulness or neglect of what I have taught you[919]) "my" (God's) "law"

("Torah"; teaching, doctrine); BUT let thine "heart keep" (let the casket of the soul be the keeping place of God's commandments; its treasure chest [Jeremiah 31:33]; and put them into "practice, obey them"[920]) my "commandments" (precepts; the law and commandments).

Etch the Word of God into the heart both by meditation and memorization. David testifies, "Thy word have I hid in mine heart, that I might not sin against thee" (Psalm 119:11). Scripture was the weapon Jesus used to defeat Satan in the wilderness and likewise is the able defense for you. Chuck Swindoll explains the merit of Scripture memorization: "I know of no other single practice in the Christian life that's more rewarding, practically speaking, than memorizing Scripture. That's right. No other single discipline is more useful and rewarding than this. No other single exercise pays greater spiritual dividends! Your *prayer life* will be strengthened. Your *witnessing* will be sharper and much more effective. Your *counseling* will be in demand. Your *attitudes* and outlook will begin to change. Your *mind* will become alert and observant. Your *confidence and assurance* will be enhanced. Your *faith* will be solidified."[921] Fanny Crosby, blinded at six weeks old due to an incompetent doctor, yet memorized Scripture. By the age of 15, Fanny could quote the first five books of the Bible, Proverbs, Song of Solomon and the four Gospels. And she mastered that blind!

The Bottom Line: Store up the Word of God in your heart, as Fanny Crosby did, for ready recall at any time, anywhere and to anyone.

201
Memory, of the righteous and wicked
Proverbs 10:7
"The memory of the just is blessed: but the name of the wicked shall rot."

"When a wicked man dieth, his expectation shall perish: and the hope of unjust men perisheth" (Proverbs 11:7).

The "memory" (not what the righteous remember but their memory by others[922]; the person's reputation of godliness, saintliness, holiness) of the "just" (righteous, just, fair, honest, upright) is "blessed" (a blessing to those who knew them): BUT the "name" (memory of) of the wicked shall "rot" (decay; be forgotten[923]).

A good man will be remembered long after death for his good to family, friends, and even foes. Matthew Henry is correct to say, "Blessed men leave behind them blessed memories."[924] Solomon said, "A good reputation is more valuable than costly perfume. And the day you die is better than the day you are born" (Ecclesiastes 7:1 NLT). David adds, "A good man sheweth favour, and lendeth: he will guide his affairs with discretion. Surely he shall not be moved for ever: the righteous shall be in everlasting remembrance....his righteousness endureth for ever; his horn shall be exalted with honour." (Psalm 112:5–6, 9).

Good people, through memories of them, live on long after death, impacting lives. Matthew Henry states that it is noble and right to make "honorable mention of good men that are gone, bless God for them, and for His gifts and graces that appeared in them, and especially be followers of them in that which is good."[925] Everyone ought to desire and endeavor to leave behind a good opinion of himself at death.

> Don't forget the godly and faithful that dies, but use their memory as an example and encouragement.
> Matthew Henry

The name of the wicked in contrast shall "rot." The unrighteous and their deeds will soon be forgotten upon their death. As their bodies rot in the grave, just so will memory of them decay.[926] In living, the wicked may have gained more possessions, wealth, notoriety and "success" than that of *good men,* but in death their names will fade away as the morning fog, while the memory of the just will live on forever.

King Jehoram is an example of one whose memory rots in death. He was such a bad person that the people refused to give him a funeral like unto his predecessors. "And after all this the LORD smote him in his bowels with an incurable disease. And it came to pass, that in process of time, after the end of two years, his bowels fell out by reason of his sickness: so he died of sore diseases. And his people made no burning for him, like the burning of his fathers" (2 Chronicles 21:18–19). Lawson says, "As Jeroboam made Israel to sin after he was dead, so the good man helps to make others holy whilst he is lying in the grave."[927]

Or I shall live your epitaph to make,

Or you survive when I in earth am rotten;
From hence your memory death cannot take,
Although in me each part will be forgotten.
                              ~ from Shakespeare's Sonnet LXXXI.

The truth of the Proverb is witnessed to in this volume. The lives of men like Matthew Henry, George Lawson, W. A. Criswell, H. A. Ironside, C. H. Spurgeon, Charles Bridges, John Gill and Albert Barnes, long in Heaven, yet are remembered for their honorable, righteous and holy lives, and serve yet to bless, despite their absence, through their reputation and writings. But the names of the wicked such as Nero, Al Capone, Tom Horn, Andrew Kehoe, John Wayne Gacy and Ted Bundy have decayed with their bodies in the grave.

The Bottom Line: Every man will leave behind a memory. There are memories that do *rot while others will not be forgotten* but flourish. Which kind are you *weaving* for yourself? Live an honorable and good life unto the Lord and before others, and in death blessed memories of you will continue to bear impact for ages to come. Who is it that is deceased whom you might honor for their service to God and benefit to you?

202
Mentoring, the sharpening of another's iron
Proverbs 27:17

"Iron sharpeneth iron; so a man sharpeneth the countenance of his friend."

Iron "sharpeneth" ("steel whetted against a knife sharpens the edge"[928]) iron; so a man sharpeneth the "countenance" (the result of two people of common mindset [iron to iron] interaction (collision of wits) is that both are *bettered* mentally, spiritually and biblically; the *face* of his friend "refers to his personality or character"[929]) of his "friend" (note the sharpening, mentoring is between two "objects" of like-mindedness, nature).

Augustine said, "One loving heart sets another on fire." When iron sharpens a blade (iron), it gives it an "edge," making it more useful, productive and powerful. Mentoring is the sharp iron of another rubbing across one's life spiritually and intellectually in conversation and example, refining it, refreshing it, renewing it, reinforcing it, and at times restoring it.

The benefits of being mentored are many.

Promotes spiritual growth. Mentoring will help you be a spiritual man by instilling the adaptation and application of spiritual disciplines (Bible study, prayer, quiet time, solitude and fasting, witnessing) which are the building blocks of the Faith.

Provides a worthy role model. Seeing a godly life lived out is an invaluable benefit. Seneca said, "The road to learning by precept is long, but by example short and effective." Spiritual growth is "caught" as well as "taught." Timothy learned much by watching Paul. The example of what a godly man looks like and acts like in every "season" of life is invaluable.

Provides accountability that serves as spiritual and moral safeguards. "Stay alert! Watch out for your great enemy, the devil. He prowls around like a roaring lion, looking for someone to devour" (1 Peter 5:8 NLT). Many and manifold are Satan's hidden landmines designed to destroy your life, career and future family (pornography, gambling, alcohol and drugs, sexual immorality, and humanism). Having a mentor accountability partner is an invaluable benefit for heading off danger and avoiding shipwreck.

Provides encouragement. In the New Testament the word used most for encouragement is *parakalein.* This word is derived from two Greek words which mean "to come alongside." It is when people come *alongside* us instructing, comforting, challenging and at times correcting us that we are encouraged. Therefore, a *parakletos* (encourager), states William Barclay, is "one who puts courage into the fainthearted, one who nerves the feeble arm for fight, one who makes a very ordinary man cope gallantly with a perilous and dangerous situation."[930] Timothy was pumped [encouraged] by Paul to be the best Christian and servant of God possible. Sadly, you won't find much "encouragement" from the world, but thankfully you will from a mentor.

Provides a confidant/advisor in times of crisis. In times of storms mentors provide counsel and help navigate to safety and the comfort of a stable, caring relationship on which to lean.

Gain trusted counsel in life decisions. "Plans are established by seeking advice" (Proverbs 20:18 NIV). You will face major decisions that are not clear-cut, and in such times a godly mentor can pray and talk and walk with you through it.

> We live by encouragement, and we die without it, slowly, sadly and angrily.
> Celeste Holm

Provides affirmation. Paul felt confident about and affirmed Timothy's faith, gifts and call. Mentor's will believe in you when no one else will; they will see your potential when others or even you cannot. Barnabas saw Paul's potential when the church didn't. They were wrong, and Barnabas was right. Most get denunciation, not affirmation; are downed, not uplifted; are criticized, not commended. It is invaluable to have a mentor to support you in your dreams and plans.

Witnessing empowerment. Most are fearful or timid in talking to others about their relationship with Jesus Christ. A mentor will dispel the hesitations.

Disciplinary compulsion. Tom Landry, coach of the Dallas Cowboys for three decades, said, "The job of a football coach is to make men do what they don't want to do in order to achieve what they have always wanted to be." A mentor will be like a coach helping your child do what he doesn't want to do in order to grow in godliness. As a football coach pushes players to engage in certain disciplines that are necessary to play their best, the mentor emphasizes the practice of spiritual disciplines to grow the best.

Reveals blind spots, prejudices and weaknesses which impede spiritual progress.

The Bottom Line: Mentoring is like a group of men scaling a mountain. If a guy is linked to the guy above him and that man is linked to other men further up the cliff, then together they have stability, safety and strength. If a man slips and begins to fall, the men he is linked to absorb the impact and pull him back from disaster. While a lone climber without such a support system may achieve great heights, by one wrong move he could fall to his death without having anyone hear his cry for help.

203
Mentoring, the transferral of knowledge
Proverbs 31:15

"She riseth also while it is yet night, and giveth meat to her household, and a portion to her maidens."

"She" (the Proverbs 31 woman) "riseth also while it yet night" (prior to dawn), and "giveth meat to her household" (prepares breakfast[931]), AND a "portion to her maidens" (feeds the servants also[932]).

Everyone, including older children, can *mentor* others in the things of God. The task is simple in that you simply help another understand spiritual things at whatever level possible. *Chok,* "portion," may apply either to tasks or food.[933] With this understanding the godly woman of Proverbs 31 may have arisen early in the morning (prior to daybreak) to prepare breakfast for her household and give godly instruction to the servants. Mentoring is the rewarding process of taking another under one's protective and provisional wings to edify, educate, embolden, emancipate, enlighten, establish, excite and equip in spiritual matters. A mentor is a guide, instructor and model to his mentee.

Mentoring is first mentioned in Scripture in God's command to parents to instill in their children the commandments of the Lord. "Hear, O Israel: The Lord our God, the Lord is one. Love the Lord your God with all your heart and with all your soul and with all your strength. These commandments that I give you today are to be on your hearts. Impress them on your children. Talk about them when you sit at home and when you walk along the road, when you lie down and when you get up. Tie them as symbols on your hands and bind them on your foreheads. Write them on the doorframes of your houses and on your gates" (Deuteronomy 6: 4–9 NIV).

The injunction still stands. In the New Testament the writer of Hebrews underscores the practice in stating, "And let us consider how we may spur one another on toward love and good deeds, not giving up meeting together, as some are in the habit of doing, but encouraging one another [mentoring]—and all the more as you see the Day approaching" (Hebrews 10:24–25 NIV). Solomon wrote, "Iron sharpeneth iron" (Proverbs 27:17). Christians are to *sharpen the iron* of others doctrinally, devotionally and dutifully until they then can do the same for another.

The Bottom Line: Transferal of what you have gained from experience and study in life to another will make an eternal impact. As the godly woman of Proverbs 31, make room on your plate to provide biblical instruction and guidance to others on a regular basis.

204
Mercy, showing empathy and kindness
Proverbs 11:17

"The merciful man doeth good to his own soul: but he that is cruel troubleth his own flesh."

"Blessed are the merciful: for they shall obtain mercy" (Matthew 5:7).

The "merciful" (see below) man doeth "good" (mercy, kindness is reciprocal; it is returned to him by those to whom it is extended[934]) to his own soul: BUT he that is "cruel" (mean, hateful to others) "troubleth" (the trouble he dishes out, he receives[935]) his own flesh.

Theologian Charles Hodge states, "Mercy is kindness exercised toward the miserable, and includes pity, compassion, forbearance, and gentleness, which the Scriptures so abundantly ascribe to God."[936] William Barclay remarks that the Hebrew word for "mercy" (*chesedh*) is untranslatable. He says, "It does not mean only to sympathize with a person in the popular sense of the term; it does not mean simply to feel sorry for someone in trouble. [It] means the ability to get right inside the other person's skin until we can see things with his eyes, think things with his mind, and feel things with his feelings."[937] Mercy is to identify with the person from the inside out (understand his hurt and pain), not outside in.

Don't be too harsh with the man that sins
Or pelt him with words, or stone, or disdain,
Unless you are sure you have no sins of your own
And it's only wisdom and love that your heart contains.

Just walk a mile in his moccasins
Before you abuse, criticize and accuse.
If just for one hour you could find a way
To see through his eyes instead of your own muse.

~ Mary T. Lathrap, (1895)

God did this on the first Christmas: He got into the skin of man and identified with him from the inside out by viewing life through human "lenses." Matthew 9:36 says, "But when he [Jesus] saw the multitudes, he was moved with compassion on them, because they fainted, and were scattered abroad, as sheep having no shepherd." To show genuine mercy (compassion, love, sympathy, forgiveness), place yourself in that person's skin. He that shows mercy to the undeserving shall receive it.

By the way, Matthew 5:7 has nothing to do with the foundation of salvation; salvation is not determined by man's work of extending mercy. Failure to extend mercy blocks the mercy of others toward you. The believer, in showing mercy, points to Jesus Christ who manifested the supreme mercy for all men through His death, burial and resurrection.

"Gospel riches," writes C. H. Spurgeon, "are sent to remove our wretchedness, and mercy to remove our misery."[938] Ever give thanks for God's abiding, unspeakable grace and mercy. Mercy must be given gladly or cheerfully (Romans 12:8). The merciful man is rewarded with personal gratification that he has done that which is proper and biblical (Proverbs 11:17). The merciful is benefited by mercy's reciprocation (as he gives it, he receives it from others). The merciful also will be manifested mercy by God at the Judgment, unlike "he that is cruel" in his heart that withholds mercy. James explains, "For he shall have judgment without mercy, that hath shewed no mercy; and mercy rejoiceth against judgment" (James 2:13). Indeed, the person who is merciful doeth his soul much good!

The Bottom Line: So long as we are the receivers of God's and people's undeserved mercy, we must keep giving it. He that has been mercifully forgiven much overflows with mercy toward others.

205
Messengers, trustworthy to bear the King's message
Proverbs 25:13
"As the cold of snow in the time of harvest, so is a faithful messenger to them that send him: for he refresheth the soul of his masters."

"A wicked messenger falleth into mischief: but a faithful ambassador is health" (Proverbs 13:17).

As the "cold of snow in the time of harvest" ("it does not mean a snowfall in harvest [March–September], which did not happen and would have been disastrous. It refers to a cool drink from the snowy mountains or a cooling trip to them"[939] or "the refreshing breeze that comes from the snow-capped mountains"[940]), so is a "faithful messenger" (a trustworthy representative for a person) to them that "send him" (the messenger fulfils the assignment to the great pleasure of the one who commissioned it): FOR he "refresheth the soul" (Ross beautifully frames the phrase in this manner: "to 'refresh in spirit' is the idea that someone who sends the messenger entrusts his life (i.e., his soul) to him; and a mission faithfully accomplished 'restores' it to him"[941]). See Acts 10:4–5, 25 (the refreshed spirit Cornelius received upon the return of his messengers with Peter); Genesis 24:63–64 (the refreshed spirit of Isaac upon the return of the servant sent to find him a bride); 2 Timothy 1:16 (Paul was oft refreshed in spirit by Onesiphorus).

Note three applications. All people ought to be receptive to God's authorized, divinely ordained and commissioned messenger sent to share the *greatest Message of all*, that of the glorious Gospel of the Lord Jesus Christ. In unison at their arrival man should cry, "Blessed be he that cometh in the name of the LORD" (Psalm 118:26). But many servants instead of being met with honor are met with horror, as is illustrated in the parable of the wicked husbandmen (Mark 12:2–8). Note that the master at the last sent the *message* by his only son, whom they maliciously murdered. See 1 Thessalonians 2:15.

The second application is with reference to the messengers personally. All Christians are ambassadors for Christ, bearing His message, and they ought to do so as the Proverb indicates, faithfully and thoroughly to the delight of the Lord. But specifically I make application to the clergy, vocational ministers of the Gospel who have been entrusted with the proclamation of the King's message. To them pungently I declare with Paul, 'Woe be unto you if you fail to preach the Gospel—the whole counsel of God' (1 Corinthians 9:16). Discharge God's calling and duty faithfully that upon your return to Him (at the Judgment) it will be as "the cold of snow in the time of harvest" to Him.

Woe be unto the unfaithful messenger who distorts and adulterates the message. As God's "messenger boys," we have no discretionary authority to alter the message in any fashion. May the "man of God," with Paul, ever say truthfully and frankly, "For I have not shunned [shrunk;

avoided; hesitated] to declare unto you all the counsel of God" (Acts 20:27). J. C. Ryle exhorts the minister, "You preach the Gospel of Jesus Christ so fully and clearly that everybody can understand it. If Christ crucified has not His rightful place in your sermons, and sin is not exposed as it should be, and our people are not plainly told what they ought to be and do, your preaching is no use."[942]

A third application is suggested. Under the employment (business) of another, determine to be a "faithful" laborer. Perform that which he orders ("sends") with utmost care and thoroughness as if it were your own business. Such integrity in duty brings great satisfaction and gratitude from your employer ("his masters"). The Christian who performs his job with integrity brings honor to the Lord; he that doesn't, brings disgrace to His church and cause.

The Bottom Line: May God's messengers be wardrobed in holiness, committed to His Word as infallible, abandoned to His will, passionate to win the lost and ever in a hurry to fulfil His divine errand.

206
Mirror, the mirror in the heart tells what kind of person one is
Proverbs 27:19
"As in water face answereth to face, so the heart of man to man."

As in "water face answereth to face" (the face is reflected in clear water), so the heart of "man to man" (the heart of man is a reflector of his thoughts or personality, his true nature[943]). To summarize, Allen Ross states, "Thoughts reflect one's true character."[944]

Clear water reflects the person's face it beholds as a mirror. (Probably the earliest mirror in time.) It does not lie; what you see is what you are. In like fashion, Solomon states that the conscience, desires, affections, values and pursuits of man reflect his true character. The heart (mind) reflects without error the kind of person one is. It shows the ugliest sin and most offensive acts against God and man. Every man must look into this *looking glass* regularly in examination so that any alteration of godly conduct may be corrected. See Psalm 139:23–24.

Another way to know one's character is the meditation upon Holy Scripture. Romans 7:7 states, "What shall we say then? Is the law sin? God forbid. Nay, I had not known sin, but by the law." The law (Ten Commandments) is a mirror that reflects man's *identity* before God. It is essential to make changes regarding wrong and sinful attitudes and actions that are reflected in the looking glass. James warns, "The man who simply hears and does nothing about it is like a man catching the reflection of his own face in a mirror. He sees himself, it is true, but he goes on with whatever he was doing without the slightest recollection of what sort of person he saw in the mirror. But the man who looks into the perfect mirror of God's law, the law of liberty (or freedom), and makes a habit of so doing, is not the man who sees and forgets. He puts that law into practice and he wins true happiness" (James 1:23–24 Phillips).

The Bottom Line: "A person's heart is the true reflection of that person. It is in looking at the heart, the will, the choices, the loves, the decisions, the attitudes, that people come to self-awareness."[945] Most refuse to look into the *mirror* because they don't want to see what it truly it reflects.

207
Money, parental instruction about financial savings
Proverbs 21:20
"There is treasure to be desired and oil in the dwelling of the wise; but a foolish man spendeth it up."

"The thoughts of the diligent tend only to plenteousness; but of every one that is hasty only to want" (Proverbs 21:5).

There is "treasure" (something of immense value "stored up") to be "desired" (that is "precious treasure" which means "all kinds of valuables"[946]) and "oil" (refers perhaps to "luxury" as the NLT has it) in the "dwelling" (abode, home) of the "wise" (righteous, upright, honorable); BUT a "foolish man" (the ungodly, wicked, void of biblical knowledge and understanding, without fear of the Lord) "spendeth it up" (devours all that he owns or exhausts its supply; unlike the wise who store up possessions and valuables, the fool wastes his in riotous living, as the prodigal in the far country in Luke 15).

William McDonald illustrates the proverb in telling the story of an alcoholic who sold his furniture and other household goods to have a means to buy whiskey. Upon becoming a Christian, he was asked, "You don't really believe that stuff about Jesus' turning water into wine, do you?" His answer was, "I don't know about turning water into wine, but I know that in my house He turned whiskey into furniture!"[947]

The wise live within their means, storing up "treasure" (saves and invests), while the foolish devour ("spendeth") it upon materialistic and sensual desires. The prodigal son "wasted his substance with riotous living" (Luke 15:13). Even children need discipline to lay aside (store up) a percentage of their allowance and income for unforeseen needs, financial stability, retirement, and for "wants." Ron Blue advises, "Children should be trained to see the value and importance of *delayed gratification*."[948]

Aesop's fable of *The Ant and the Grasshopper* illustrates the futility of undisciplined spending and the wisdom of putting aside money in savings.

In a field one summer's day a Grasshopper was hopping about, chirping and singing to its heart's content. An Ant passed by, bearing along with great toil an ear of corn he was taking to the nest.

"Why not come and chat with me," said the Grasshopper, "instead of toiling and moiling in that way?"

"I am helping to lay up food for the winter," said the Ant, "and recommend you to do the same."

"Why bother about winter?" said the Grasshopper; "we have got plenty of food at present." But the Ant went on its way and continued its toil.

When the winter came, the Grasshopper found itself dying of hunger, while it saw the ants distributing, every day, corn and grain from the stores they had collected in the summer.

Then the Grasshopper knew...

It is best to prepare for the days of necessity.[949]

Help your child understand that financial maturity simply means "giving up today's desires for future benefits."[950] Jumpstart their savings discipline through the use of a piggy bank. Every child has one dust-ladened in the closet. Encourage its use by personally pledging to "pay interest" on every penny they place in it.

Dave Ramsey provides counsel, "There's an old Native American proverb that goes, 'Tell me, and I'll forget. Show me, and I may not remember. Involve me, and I'll understand.' Our kids are going to imitate our habits of handling money. Don't just make them work; let them see you working. Better yet, have them work alongside you. Let them know that work is how money is earned. When it comes to saving, spending and giving, let them sit at the table with you when you work on the budget. Show them how you figure out where the money goes and what's most important."[951]

The Bottom Line: The work and savings ethic of the ant (as displayed in the fable) must be embraced, or else that of the grasshopper (spendthrifts on the latest fashion trends, delicious candies, newest toys, electronic gadgets, entertainment, etc.) most assuredly will be.

208
Mother, in her old age show how much you care
Proverbs 23:22
"Despise not thy mother when she is old."

"Despise not" (don't reject your mother's instruction; honor her with obedience) thy "mother" (she who begot you through childbearing) when she is "old" (in the elderly years, as age takes its toll with sickness and adversity, don't abandon her; care for her). See Ephesians 6:2.

"Exuberant youth, self-confident and resourceful," states H. A. Ironside, "is likely to forget the reverence due to parents when age enfeebles the once bright and active mind."[952] Therefore, the admonition is given not to "despise" mom or her advice when she grows old. Matthew Henry remarks, "Scornful and insolent young men will make a jest, it may be, of the good advice of an aged mother and think themselves not concerned to heed what an old woman says; but such will have a great deal to answer for another day, not only as having set at nought good counsel, but as having slighted and grieved a good mother."[953]

Make time for her; she needs *you*, not just the stuff you supply. Don't infringe on her personal rights. Treat her as an adult, not as a child. Care for her needs (don't wait for her to tell you). Provide for her security; help her feel safe. Listen to her counsel. Exhibit expressions of love continuously (flowers, meals, gift cards, being handyman, cards). Try to identify with her world (the sorrow; grief; loneliness and isolation; struggles, financial and otherwise) and never let your "world" totally eclipse hers. Obey her; she's still your mom. Include her on special occasions like Thanksgiving, Christmas, birthdays and school events for your children. Discover what makes her happy and do it. Do not hide behind lame excuses (work, children, spouse, etc.) for neglecting the very lady who went to the brink of death to give you birth, sacrificed that you might have the best possible (clothing, education, possessions, medical help) and was always there for you to resort to in times of trouble, heartbreak and need. The love of a mother has never been penned. It defies description and definition.

Adrian Rogers certainly was correct in stating that "the closest thing to God's love is the love of a mother."[954] When you see mom's empty chair, it's sadly too late to show you care.

The Bottom Line: The child who neglects his or her godly elderly mother, for whatever reason, is most detestable and despicable.

209
Murder, capital punishment authorized
Proverbs 28:17
"A man that doeth violence to the blood of any person shall flee to the pit; let no man stay him."

The man guilty of murder ("violence to the blood of any person"; one who takes the life of another), though he flees for his life, will be haunted by a tormenting conscience and hunted vigorously by the law until he pays for the crime with his own life ("the pit" is a metaphor for the world of the dead). "Let no man stay him" (the person who aids and abets the criminal in his escape will be punished). Contrast the Proverb with the law given to Noah regarding capital punishment. "Whoso sheddeth man's blood, by man shall his blood be shed" (Genesis 9:6).

Adrian Rogers, in a weekly news column in *The Commercial Appeal* entitled "Is Capital Punishment Contrary to the Word of God?" stated, "The government is ordained of God, and one thing that the government does is to bear the sword. Look if you will in Romans 13:4, 'He beareth not the sword in vain.' He is talking about the instrument of death. Is capital punishment, therefore, ordained of God? May I say it is. Exodus 21:12 says, 'He that smiteth a man, so that he die, shall be surely put to death.' When the Bible says, 'Thou shalt not kill,' it is literally translated, 'thou shalt do no murder.' It does not mean that you should not execute a murderer. The Bible is quite clear on this point. We need to understand that the Bible does not forbid capital punishment. As a matter of fact, God has ordained capital punishment because He loves us."[955]

The Bottom Line: The Christian in affirming capital punishment desires to extend mercy as God chooses to extend that mercy (delay for the sake of possible repentance and salvation).[956] The mercy and forgiveness of Jesus Christ are to be extended compassionately in an attempt to rescue their eternal souls from eternal death in Hell.

210
Name, the good name obtained by being upright
Proverbs 22:1

"A good name is rather to be chosen than great riches, and loving favour rather than silver and gold."

"A good name is better than precious ointment" (Ecclesiastes 7:1).

A "good name" (well respected, highly esteemed, honored, reputation beyond repute) is rather to be "chosen" (refers to the reason for wanting a good name—it is "more desirable, preferable, worth much more"[957]) than "great riches" (wealth and possessions), AND "loving favor" (Kidner says that man's joy is "not in the power we wield, but in the love in which we are held"[958]) rather than "silver and gold" (same meaning as "great riches").

Names like Herodias, Jezebel, Judas Iscariot, Stalin and Hitler certainly bear an ill reputation because of the evil conduct of the people who bore them—and forever will. The lapse of time does not erase a bad name. The Proverb instruction is that we obtain and maintain a "good name" (honorable; reputable for good and right conduct; godly). Note that the good name it commends is not necessarily synonymous with that which the world attributes as good. Jesus warned, "Woe unto you, when all men shall speak well of you! for so did their fathers to the false prophets" (Luke 6:26).

The *good name* that is to be desired more than great riches is derived from a godly and holy life lived consistently privately and publicly. It is an untarnished name, being blameless, having "a good report of them which are without" (1 Timothy 3:7). It is to so live that what was said of Demetrius may be ascribed to you: "Demetrius hath good report of all men, and of the truth itself" (3 John 12). Charles Bridges says, "The good name is gained by godly consistency."[959]

To flippantly say that man's opinion of our life has little value is mere foolishness and goes against the entirety of God's Word. While we certainly must not overvalue it, neither should we carelessly underrate it.[960] It is only when the world takes note that we are different (not hypocrites) that it will be impacted by our witness. A godly reputation benefits our authority, influence, reproof and counsel, not only to the ungodly but to the righteous as well.

A good name is to be preferred over the accumulation of great wealth or prestigious position or the company of worldly friends and associates. Don't sell your good name to any of the Devil's bidders, for its value far exceeds all they may offer. Likewise is the "loving favor" (affection, honor, love and kindness) of God and man to be chosen above silver and gold (Luke 2:52).

The Bottom Line: Harry Ironside summarizes, "No name is more lasting and enduring than that won by him who lives for God, and for the sake of the Lord Jesus Christ counts all earth has to offer as dung and dross."[961] A good name is sustained, as is loving honor from others, by wise choices (biblically based).

211
Neighbors, a friend in need is a friend indeed
Proverbs 3:27–28
"Withhold not good from them to whom it is due, when it is in the power of thine hand to do it. Say not unto thy neighbour, Go, and come again, and to morrow I will give; when thou hast it by thee."

"Withhold not" (don't refuse) "good" (Henry says "to do justly and show mercy,"[962] see explanation following) "from them to whom it is due" (people who need the help), when it is in the "power of thine hand" (opportunity and the means to do good) to do it. Say not unto thy "neighbor" (any person), "Go, and come again, tomorrow I will give; when thou hast it by thee" (Reyburn and Fry say "an encouragement to give promptly and willingly"[963]). The Apostle Paul summarizes, "As we have therefore opportunity, let us do good unto all men" (Galatians 6:10). Wuest, in *Wuest's Word Studies from the Greek New Testament,* says that "do good" means "to labor, to be active, to perform," with the idea of continued exertion being included. It is not merely what may be good in character as judged by anybody's standards, but the good spoken of in the context, *good which is the product of the work of the Holy Spirit through the saint.*"[964]

Who is our neighbor? Perhaps the parable of the Good Samaritan answers best (Luke 10:30–37). A neighbor is anyone in *legitimate* need (don't be a sucker). Jesus clarifies the duty to our neighbor in saying, "As ye would that men should do to you, do ye also to them" (Luke 6:31). In the parable, the thieves said, "What's thine is mine, and I am going to take it." The priest and Levite said, "What's mine is mine, and I am going to keep it." But the Samaritan (whom we are to imitate) said, "What's mine is thine, and I am going to give it." Martin Luther King, Jr., said, "The first question which the priest and the Levite asked was: 'If I stop to help this man, what will happen to me?' But the Good Samaritan reversed the question: 'If I do not stop to help this man, what will happen to him?'"[965]

Hurriedness often prevents involvement in the lives of the hurting. John Ortberg says, "Love and hurry are fundamentally incompatible. Love always takes time, and time is the one thing hurried people don't have."[966] The Samaritan was just as busy as the priest and Levite. He just chose not to allow hurriedness to interfere with helping a neighbor in need. Be careful not to be like Martha who, due to hurriedness in the kitchen, missed "that good part" (Luke 10:42), as did the priest and Levite. Hurriedness is a sin when it impedes the believer's spiritual walk inwardly toward self and outwardly toward others. "He that hasteth with his feet sinneth" (Proverbs 19:2).

The Bottom Line: Do not to be selfish with possessions; be generous to those in need. Paul said, "Because of this, we should do good to everyone. For sure, we should do good to those who belong to Christ" (Galatians 6:10 NLT). If too hurried to help someone that is hurting, slow down.

212
News, refreshing good news
Proverbs 25:25

"As cold waters to a thirsty soul, so is good news from a far country."

As "cold waters" (refreshing, renewing, restoring water) to a "thirsty soul" (Murphy says a "dry throat";[967] NASB says a "weary soul"; thus it refers to a person who has become "weary and faint" as a result of the lack of water, as one in the desert where no water may be found; parching thirst), SO is "good news" (probably what constitutes good news for us did likewise for them) from a "far country" (in Solomon's day news traveled at a snail's pace from territory to territory and town to town so much so that when good news did arrive it was as refreshing to the heart as cold water was to a parched throat).

All identify with the Proverb's truth, for all know what it is to wait eagerly and expectantly at the mailbox (computer or phone) for a *good word* from a family member or friend from a "far country" (locally or globally) until it arrives. The jubilation and refreshment such news brings to the heart is likened to one with parched lips having his thirst satisfied with "cold waters" (plural, i.e. all that he desires). Who might be looking to you for some good news to refresh his soul and renew his spirit? Dispense some "cold waters" to his parched lips today.

Multitudes in bondage to sin living in *the far country* away from God are "thirsty" for deliverance, as with the prodigal son. They await the *Good News* of salvation from someone, anyone, but often no one bothers to make its delivery to their address. H. A. Ironside comments, "The glorious Gospel of the blessed God is, above all else, that good news from a far country, which is to the thirsty soul like a draught of clear sparkling water from a cold spring. When weary, famished and ready to perish, the poor sinner quaffs [heartily drinks] the living water, it becomes in his inmost being a fountain springing up unto everlasting life."[968] See John 4:14. It's the Christian's duty to deliver the glorious Good News to the thirsty, proclaiming with Isaiah, "Ho, every one that thirsteth, come ye to the waters, and he that hath no money; come ye, buy, and eat; yea, come, buy wine and milk without money and without price" (Isaiah 55:1).

We have heard the joyful sound:
Jesus saves! Jesus saves!
Spread the tidings all around:
Jesus saves! Jesus saves!
Bear the news to every land;
Climb the steeps and cross the waves;
Onward!—'tis our Lord's command:
Jesus saves! Jesus saves! ~ Priscilla J. Owens (1829–1907)

C. H. Spurgeon, in the sermon *Good News,* gives appeal to the unsaved, saying, "If thou art spiritually thirsty, this good news will be to thee as a draught of cold water; but if thou art not thirsty, thou wilt not partake of it. It is little use to praise cold water to a man who is already drunk with the world's intoxicating draughts, or to those who have no thirst and who will despise it. Cold waters are for the thirsty, and the good news of mercy and salvation is for the guilty. Oh, that the Holy Spirit would make you feel your deep need and give you intense spiritual thirst, for then Jesus Christ and the good news from the far country would be precious to you!"[969]

Not only is good news from God like cold waters to a thirsty soul for sinners, but also for the saint. How is such good news transmitted from Heaven to man? Spurgeon says, "Our prayers and sighs and tears, our praises and thanksgivings get there all right; they are not lost en route. They reach the great heart of God, and messages come down to us from Him in response to them. How do they come? Well, they come by the Holy Spirit sealing home to the soul the promises of the Word."[970] The good news from the distant land of Heaven concerning the saint's divine protection, preservation, and provision for every need, trial and circumstance is as cold waters to a thirsty soul. But there is more. The good news of the preparation made for the saint's arrival in Heaven, the many loved ones that await his arrival, and the announcement that the King is soon to return to earth all are as good news from a far country, and are as cold waters to a thirsty soul.

The Bottom Line: For saint and sinner, good news from a far country is as cold waters to a parched throat.

"Tell the Good News; tell the Good News; tell the Good News to everyone" (Gene Bartlett).

213
Obedience, its value above religious observances
Proverbs 21:3

"To do justice and judgment is more acceptable to the LORD than sacrifice."

"And Samuel said, Hath the LORD as great delight in burnt offerings and sacrifices, as in obeying the voice of the LORD? Behold, to obey is better than sacrifice, and to hearken than the fat of rams" (1 Samuel 15:22).

To do "justice" (right and just behavior toward others) and "judgment" (righteousness; the doing of what is right or required in God's eyes[971]) is more "acceptable" ("chosen of the Lord; more pleasing"[972]) to the Lord than "sacrifice" (ceremonial rituals). Matthew Henry summarizes, "It is plainly declared that living a good life (doing justly and loving mercy) is more pleasing to God than the most pompous and expensive instances of devotion."[973] See Proverbs 15:8 and Psalm 40:6–8.

King Saul sought to excuse his disobedience by sacrifices rendered to the Lord (1 Samuel 15:19–21). The Proverb suggests that, like Saul, many that are religious erroneously believe that justification for wrong is derived from ceremonial, ritualistic and formalistic worship to God. External piety, however, is no substitute for internal purity, for "to obey is better than sacrifice" (1 Samuel 15:22). The prophets forthrightly state that God desires a good, obedient and devoted life above religious ritual or observance (Isaiah 1:11–27; Amos 5:21–24). Proverbs 21:3 echoes their teaching. God demands "justice" (righteousness—doing what is right and required in God's sight) for it outweighs religious observance and duty. The Pharisees of Jesus' day were condemned, as was King Saul, for religious observance without sincere devotion and obedience (Matthew 9:13; Luke 20:47). The transgression is likewise being repeated in the church today. The Christian must ever be careful not to base divine approval upon religious worship, monetary giving, or duty. It is to be based upon heart devotion (Romans 12:1–2).

The Bottom Line: Don't count religious observance as a substitute for uprightness. The practice of "religion" has as its foundation a heart devoted to Jesus Christ. All else must flow from that fountain or else be counted impotent and unacceptable to the Lord, void of meaning and blessing.

214
Obedience, teaching children to obey Holy Scripture
Proverbs 1:8

"My son, hear the instruction of thy father, and forsake not the law of thy mother."

"My son" (teachers of old often used the "parental" address to young students, and Deane and Taswell say it "marks that superintending, loving and fatherly care and interest which the former felt in and towards the latter"[974]) "hear" (listen) the "instruction" (the "torah"; the teaching of the Law) of thy father, and "forsake not" (don't forget, slip, waver from) the "law" (the "Torah"; Deuteronomy 6:4–7) of thy mother. [A second view is that the writer is Solomon addressing his two sons.]

Prophecy cited in Matthew 10:21 is being presently fulfilled. Children are rising up in opposition to parents, rebelling against their God-ordained authority by refusal to submit to instructions and show respect for their persons. And many are getting away with it, not only to their harm but to that of the home and society at large. It is assumed by Solomon, and rightly so, that a father and mother will instruct their children with regard to God, Holy Scripture, salvation, biblical ethics and morality, and other essentials.

Jesus loves me this I know,
For my mother and father tell me so.

Timothy certainly was so instructed. Paul wrote of Timothy's faith, saying, "And that from a child thou hast known the holy scriptures, which are able to make thee wise unto salvation through faith which is in Christ Jesus" (2 Timothy 3:15). All parents who value their children will be diligent in extolling the things of God meticulously and consistently to them. That's the parents' responsibility in capsule. The child's part is to hear and receive the instruction in honor and subjection.

Obedience to one's parents is to be coupled with submission to God, which is mandated throughout the Bible. The fifth commandment says, "Honour thy father and thy mother: that thy days may be long upon the land which the LORD thy God giveth thee." In Ephesians 6:1 we read, "Children, obey your parents in the Lord: for this is right." Colossians 3:20 sounds the note again in saying, "Children, obey your parents in all things: for this is well pleasing unto the Lord." In our day it appears the command has been reversed to say, "Parents, obey your children." Josh McDowell said that if your children have committed their lives to the Lordship of Christ, they have no other option but to show you honor at all times.[975]

The Bottom Line: The parents' instruction is to be Bible-based ("in the Lord") with insistence it be heard and obeyed. Parents must from *day one* set out to instruct their child in the things of the Lord, instilling a heart of obedience. The child, in response, is to submissively receive the instruction without grumbling, applying it to his life, "for this is right."

215
Obstinate, the effect of hardening of the heart
Proverbs 29:1
"He, that being often reproved hardeneth his neck, shall suddenly be destroyed, and that without remedy."

He, that being "often" (every time reproved) "reproved" (a reprimand; rebuked, corrected, or receives warning) "hardeneth his neck" (exhibits stubbornness; obstinate; Reyburn and Fry say the person "always says no"[976]), shall "suddenly" (without warning) be "destroyed" (a dreadful, fearful, tormenting end; even eternal darkness in Hell), AND that "without remedy" (no hope in the end for their restoration, healing or salvation due to their continual refusal to listen and be corrected and converted). *Baker's Evangelical Dictionary of Biblical Theology* states, "The heart represents the total response of a person to life around him or her and to the religious and moral demands of God. Hardness of heart thus describes a negative condition in which the person ignores, spurns or rejects the gracious offer of God to be a part of his or her life."[977]

"Hardening the neck" is a picture of an obstinate, stubborn bull that resists the yoke. H. A. Ironside remarks, "In this way, men, in their obstinacy, persistently refuse to heed reproof and set their wills stubbornly against what would be for their own best interests, thus insuring their destruction. [Though God is longsuffering, yet] even *His* patience with the unrepentant comes to an end at last. He will plead and strive and warn till it is manifest the heart is fully set upon having its own way. Then He leaves the hardened soul to its doom, giving it up to sudden destruction."[978] See Hebrews 3:8.

Examples in Scripture of hardening of the neck are numerous. The list includes Pharaoh (Exodus 9:34); Eli's sons (1 Samuel 2:25); Ahab (1 Kings 18:18); Korah, Dathan and Abiram (Numbers 16); Jezebel (2 Kings 9:32–37); Belshazzar (Daniel 5:22–23).

George Lawson comments, "But woe to that man who is stubborn and obstinate after many reproofs. He despises a merciful appointment of God for his recovery and tramples upon precious pearls. He refuses to bow before the Lord—and he shall be dashed in pieces like a potter's vessel! He perhaps designs to reform at some other time—but he is hardened in sin and puts off his intended repentance until judgment comes upon him unexpectedly and he is ruined forever! The reproofs which he received will then be like hot thunderbolts to him, and the remembrance of them will feed the worm that never dies."[979]

The Proverb states that upon man's "sudden" and "unexpected" end, he will be "without remedy." Charles Bridges elucidates: "No remedy— not even the Gospel—can remedy the case. As they lived, so they die; they stand before God *without remedy*. No blood—no advocate, pleads for them. As they sink into the burning lake, every billow of fire, as it rolls over them, seems to sound—*without remedy*."[980] They are without remedy, for they are without Christ. If the reader is unsaved, having been resistant to the invitation of the Lord to turn away from unrighteousness unto devotion to Him time and again, with grave earnestness I appeal for serious and hasty consideration of your most woeful and damnable estate and its only remedy. With all the passion and urgency that pen can express, I use the words of the two angels to Lot (with regard to Sodom and Gomorrah) to say, "Escape for thy life; look not behind thee, neither stay thou in all the plain; escape to the mountain, lest thou be consumed" (Genesis 19:17). While there is yet time, leave Sodom and Gomorrah (life of rebellion against God and sinful conduct) and come to the "mountain" (Mount Calvary) of deliverance. In coming to Christ, a new song will be birthed in the soul, a song of the Savior's intervention out of compassion and love to snatch you as "a brand plucked out of the fire." See Zechariah 3:2; Jude 23.

The Bottom Line: Stubbornly refusing to heed reproof (correction) *time and again* leads to sudden destruction without the possibility of restoration or salvation.

216
Opinion, preferred over instruction
Proverbs 18:2

"A fool hath no delight in understanding, but that his heart may discover itself."

A fool has no interest ("no delight") in instruction ("understanding"), preferring to express his own opinions. He is close-minded, having no willingness to learn from God or the godly. Derek Kidner says the fool has a "closed mind" and "open mouth,"[981] BUT that his "heart may discover itself" (the fool takes pleasure in "uncovering" his heart, making people think how "clever" he is;[982] McKane says the fool is in love with his own opinions and enjoys spewing them out[983]).

Conceit, bad conduct and bad companions fuel disdain for godly and biblical instruction. You can't tell the fool anything, for his continual opinionated talkativeness. "The tongue of the wise useth knowledge aright: but the mouth of fools poureth [gushes] out foolishness" (Proverbs 15:2). Garrett comments, "Profundity, not verbosity, is the mark of wisdom"[984] (Proverbs 17:27; 18:4; Ecclesiastes 10:12–14).

H. A. Ironside says, "The fool cares not for that which would build true character and draw him from his evil ways, but feeds on folly and vanity, thus becoming all the time more empty and foolish than before."[985] He knows not, or cares not, that wise words outweigh gold and precious rubies in value (Proverbs 20:15). The unteachable fool may pretentiously appear teachable to appease and/or gain favor with parents, teachers, ministers and even the police. Like the hearer in the parable of the sower, he receives the Word with joy, only later to abandon it (Luke 8:13).

Don't be fooled by such deception. The wise, in contrast, gladly and eagerly receive instruction. "The way of a fool is right in his own eyes: but he that hearkeneth [listens] unto counsel is wise" (Proverbs 12:15). May the fool see the fallacy and consequence of foolish thinking that he may heed the call to godly instruction in Proverbs 22:17: "Bow down thine ear, and hear the words of the wise, and apply thine heart unto my knowledge."

The Bottom Line: Be discerning. It is in vain to cast pearls before swine. Pray that the fool who ever delights in "airing his own opinions" and is closed-minded to instruction will come to his senses. The opinionated need to know that "poverty and shame shall be to him that refuseth instruction: but he that regardeth reproof shall be honoured" (Proverbs 13:18). See Proverbs 18:6–7.

217
Opportunity, the wise discern its knocking and open the door
Proverbs 10:5

"He that gathereth in summer is a wise son: but he that sleepeth in harvest is a son that causeth shame."

He that "gathereth" (harvests the crops) in "summer" (time of harvest) is a "wise" (prudent, "sound judgment"[986]) son: BUT he that "sleepeth" ("that snoreth"; lazy, slothful, undisciplined) in harvest is a son that causeth "shame" ("disgrace to his parents"[987]). To summarize, discipline and diligence must be exhibited to seize the opportunities of the "season" lest they forever pass, squandered to one's own loss and shame.

Opportunity is a divinely orchestrated conjuncture of happenings to facilitate and effectuate the plan of God. An ancient Greek sculptor entitled a piece of his work *Opportunity*. A visitor in this studio viewing the sculpture inquired, "Why is its face veiled?"

"Because men seldom know her when she comes to them," was the reply.

"And why does she stand upon her toes, and why the wings?"

"Because," said the sculptor, "when once she is gone, she can never be overtaken."[988]

This sculpture is never truer than in regard to witnessing. Delays in telling man about Jesus often result in irretrievably lost opportunities to win a person to Christ. Additionally, it is applicable with regard to education, service, ministry, family time, financial investment, giving encouragement, counsel, expression of gratitude and love. Recognize opportunities when they knock at the door, and immediately *jump* at them lest they depart as quickly as they came without being taken advantage of, to your loss and perhaps that of others.

"Opportunity is missed by most people because it is dressed in overalls and looks like hard work."[989] Don't become like Mark Twain, who stated, "I was seldom able to see an opportunity until it ceased to be one."[990]

The Bottom Line: "Redeem the time" should be emblazoned upon the mind and applied to life lest we suffer "shame" and forfeiture of reward at the Judgment Seat of Christ.

218
Orphans, their defender and provider
Proverbs 23:10–11

"Enter not into the fields of the fatherless: For their redeemer is mighty; he shall plead their cause with thee."

"In thee [Jehovah God] the fatherless findeth mercy." (Hosea 14:3).

"Enter not" (don't encroach[991]; take over) into the "fields" of the "fatherless" (the orphans; those without parents to protect their interests): For their "redeemer" ("kinsman redeemer"; here pictured as God Almighty) is "mighty" (strong); he shall "plead" ("act in their defense"[992]) "with thee" (against those who defraud the orphan).

God cares for orphans and opposes all who deal with them mischievously (Deuteronomy 10:18; Psalm 10:14, 17–18; 68:5; 82:3; 146:9). He is their defender ("pleads their cause") against injustice. He is their protector, watching over them lest they are taken advantage of in some way or mistreated (stealing their fields).

And how may the orphan know that God will so care for him? Solomon states that "their redeemer is mighty." He is the Almighty God, and "His omnipotence is engaged and employed for their protection, and their proudest and most powerful oppressors will not only find themselves an unequal match for this, but will find that it is at their peril to contend with it."[993] Be careful not to hurt orphans or invade their rights or steal their possessions. Pray for the orphans' welfare morally, physically and spiritually. Intervene in their behalf when they are being abused or misused or neglected.

Child sex trafficking is sickening and deeply horrifying. Annually in the United States 300,000 children are prostituted—two million across the globe. Obviously many of these are orphans void of a father's protection. Severe divine punishment will be levied upon all who enslave helpless orphans to the sexual slave trade. "He [God] is the Eternal Vindicator of downtrodden right."[994]

Martin Niemöller (1892–1984) was a Lutheran minister who was an outspoken critic of Adolf Hitler. His protest of Hitler resulted in his imprisonment in concentration camps for the last seven years of Nazi rule. He probably is known best for the following quotation that shows our need to "speak out" for the helpless and orphans.

> First they came for the Socialists, and I did not speak out—
> Because I was not a Socialist.
> Then they came for the Trade Unionists, and I did not speak out—
> Because I was not a Trade Unionist.
> Then they came for the Jews, and I did not speak out—
> Because I was not a Jew.
> Then they came for me—and there was no one left to speak for me.

The Bottom Line: Steven Curtis Chapmans says, "If only seven percent of the two million Christians in the world would care for a single orphan in distress, there would effectively be no more orphans. If everybody would be willing to simply do something to care for one of these precious treasures, I think we would be amazed by just how much we could change the world."[995]

219
Panic, coping with fearful anxiety
Proverbs 3:25–26

"Be not afraid of sudden fear, neither of the desolation of the wicked, when it cometh. For the LORD shall be thy confidence, and shall keep thy foot from being taken."

Be not "afraid" (don't live in panic mode) of "sudden" (without warning, surprise) "fear" ("the object which excites terror or fear"[996]), neither of the "desolation of the wicked" (their ruin). For the Lord shall be thy "confidence" (trust, hope, shield of protection), and shall keep thy foot from being "taken" (prevent you from falling into the snares which the sinful set for you).

All are but a phone call away from bad news. But there is no need to fear or panic about *possible harms* as long as the Lord is our "confidence" (trustworthy protector). He who walks uprightly and wisely with the Lord may courageously and victoriously (without stumbling) face whatever crisis or calamity that may be encountered. Neither is there cause for apprehension or anxiety regarding the coming judgment that is the lot of the wicked, for God knows who "are his and how to separate between the precious and the vile. Therefore be not afraid (Matthew Henry)."[997]

Choose not to allow *tomorrow* to rob joy, peace and productivity from life *today*. Upon being pressed to the core over "what may happen tomorrow," listen to the instruction of Jesus. He said, "Give your entire attention to what God is doing right now, and don't get worked up about what may or may not happen tomorrow. God will help you deal with whatever hard things come up when the time comes" (Matthew 6:34 MSG).

> I don't know about tomorrow;
> I just live from day to day.
> I don't borrow from its sunshine,
> For its skies may turn to gray.
> I don't worry o'er the future,
> For I know what Jesus said,
> And today I'll walk beside Him,
> For He knows what is ahead.
>
> I don't know about tomorrow;
> It may bring me poverty,
> But the One who feeds the sparrow
> Is the One who stands by me.
> And the path that be my portion
> May be through the flame or flood,
> But His presence goes before me,
> And I'm covered with His blood
>
> Many things about tomorrow
> I don't seem to understand,
> But I know who holds tomorrow,
> And I know who holds my hand. ~ Ira Stanphill (1950)

The Bottom Line: Don't live life in a state of fear over what may happen *tomorrow*. All is in the knowledge and hands of God in Whom you may trust explicitly. Choose not to be paralyzed by fear and anxiety. "Bridges" you worry about crossing may never arise.

220
Parent, directives on child discipline
Proverbs 29:15

"The rod and reproof give wisdom: but a child left to himself bringeth his mother to shame."

The "rod" ("symbol of punishment"; a slender, flexible cane used for punishment[998]) and "reproof" (verbal correction) give "wisdom" ("apply the board of education to the seat of wisdom"; discipline's purpose is instruction, biblical or otherwise; to instill in the child how to so live that his every course of action is pleasing unto the Lord): BUT a child "left" (same Hebrew word used in Job 39:5 of the wild donkey left to ramble free without any restraint[999]) to "himself" (a child allowed to freely do as he chooses will become uncontrollable, unruly) bringeth his mother to "shame" (cause his mother embarrassment, shame).

Note the Proverb couples "the rod" with verbal "reproof" with regard to parental discipline. You may reprove a child without the "rod," but never exert the "rod" without the reproof. In discipline, words of explanation and correction must always be conveyed. For example: "Dad is spanking you because of the way you mistreated your brother. You should never hit him when he upsets you. The next time he takes a toy from you, let me know, and I will handle it." Children learn through discipline that there are consequences to disobedience and wrongdoing. Solomon says, "A youngster's heart is filled with foolishness, but physical discipline will drive it far away" (Proverbs 22:15 NLT). Again he says, "Punishment that hurts chases evil from the heart" (Proverbs 20:30 TLB).

Discipline should be *measured discipline*. Paul warns about the sternness of discipline. He says, "Fathers, provoke not your children to anger, lest they be discouraged" (Colossians 3:21). Don't *exasperate* (cause to feel bitterness or resentment, prompt to anger) your child in discipline, for he will be "discouraged" (disheartened, listless, lose heart, disinterested). Make sure the punishment fits the "crime" and is administered calmly and lovingly, not angrily and bitterly. Integrate affirmations with discipline. Martin Luther's father was very strict, strict to the point of cruelty. Luther used to say, "Spare the rod and spoil the child—that is true; but beside the rod keep an apple to give him when he has done well."

Proverbs 23:13–14 states, "Withhold not correction from the child: for if thou beatest him with the rod, he shall not die. Thou shalt beat him with the rod, and shalt deliver his soul from hell." B. H. Carroll remarks in regard to this parental admonition to discipline a child, "There is a principle here enunciated, that life issues from obedience to law and one who has never learned the principle of obedience to the authorities, whether parent, government, or God, is not likely to yield himself to the Lordship of Jesus Christ, without which he can never escape Hell."[1000]

The Bottom Line: Through discipline parents teach children that wrong has consequences. Spare the rod; spoil the child.

221
Parent, the effect of integrity
Proverbs 20:7
"The just man walketh in his integrity: his children are blessed after him."

"But the mercy of the LORD is from everlasting to everlasting upon them that fear him, and his righteousness unto children's children" (Psalm 103:17).

The "just" (righteous, upright, honorable) man "walketh" (manner of conduct; lifestyle) in his "integrity" (practice matches profession in uprightness): his children are "blessed" (count their dad a blessing, a joy to them) "after him" (Buzzell says his children "seeing his example of integrity, are encouraged to be the same kind of people"[1001]).

The righteous ("just") man abhors and abstains from all that is morally wrong consistently. He is not only justified but "'just" before men and "devout" before God."[1002] His duty unto the Lord is exemplarily performed. The righteousness of the upright is manifested in heart (personally first) and walk (corporately to others—"walketh in his integrity"), testified to by all. The Shunammite woman, regarding Elisha, said unto her husband "Behold now, I perceive that this is an holy man of God, which passeth by us continually" (2 Kings 4:9).

The Proverb contains the promise that the "children" of the "just" who walk in his steps—follow his example ("after him")—will be blessed (highly favored by God). Moses cites the promise: "Obey his laws [statutes; ordinances; requirements] and commands that I am giving you today so that things will go well for you and your children. Then you will live a long time in the land that the Lord your God is giving to you forever" (Deuteronomy 4:40 EXB). David also shared the promise, saying, "The good man's children will be powerful in the land; his descendants will be blessed" (Psalm 112:2 GNT).

Upon Zacchaeus' salvation and transformation, he vowed that he would walk justly (renounced dishonesty and stealing). It was then that Jesus pronounced a blessing upon his children in saying, "This day is salvation come to this *house*" (Luke 19:9). Children will be *blessed by* godly parents during their life and after their death (pays dividends now and later). What a challenge the Proverb is for parents to be upright, just, honorable, holy and steadfast in their walk with the Lord!

The Bottom Line: C. Ridley Pearson, writing in 1881, summarizes the Proverb in stating, "God has by way of a spur and also a rein for parents made their children's happiness and prosperity to depend largely upon them, their example, their bringing up, the friends and connections they form. He will bequeath them, along with an inheritance of good principles and valuable friends, such a share in God's covenant blessings as is promised to the seed of the righteous" (Psalm 103:17)."[1003]

222
Parent, warning about "free-parenting"
Proverbs 22:6
"Train up a child in the way he should go: and when he is old, he will not depart from it."

There are various interpretations rendered for the Proverb, as also stated in the next entry. W. A. Criswell remarks, "It may be better, however, to understand the text as a warning to parents. The phrase "in the way he should go" is more literally "according to his way." In other words, the parent who continually allows a child to have his own way is laying a foundation for self-willed living, from which the child will not depart (cf. [compare] 3:5; 12:15; 14:12; 21:2; 29:15; Judg. 21:25; Is. 53:6). This would explain a child who, under the influence of a godly home, chooses to attend to the things of the Lord; whereas in his adult years he tires of the spiritual life and willfully turns to the way of the world, breaking the hearts of his parents and rejecting the training of his youth."[1004] Plaut says, "Dedicate a youth according to his foolish way, and when he grows old he will not depart from it."[1005]

"Free parenting" (taking a backseat approach) may make the task less taxing and more relaxing to parents, but it is devastating to the child. A child allowed to do what he pleases, when he pleases, and how he pleases ("according to his way") develops a hedonistic outlook on life and feels he is "entitled" to everything desired. Amy McCready, in the article "Avoid Raising an Entitled Child," states, "While these kids can be hard to live with now, overentitled kids eventually become high-maintenance employees and demanding spouses with the same childish attitudes, only on a greater scale. It's a big problem, because kids who feel entitled to call the shots all the time are unable to handle it when things don't go their way (like here in the real world)."[1006]

The Bottom Line: Children must be raised with parental restraint so as to etch within them traits of a holy saint that they will embrace the whole of life.

223
Parenting, training a child in the way he should go
Proverbs 22:6
"Train up a child in the way he should go."

"Train" (to dedicate the child to the Lord and morally train him to follow the Lord[1007]; to nurse a child[1008] through godly instruction; direction; guidance) up a "child" (infant up; from the first breath a child should be pointed toward God) in the "way" (in the way of the Lord by instilling biblical teachings and values; the path of righteousness and obedience to God's standards) he should "go" (MacArthur says, "There is only one right way, God's way, the way of life"[1009]; if parents don't instruct him in God's way, he will head in the way he shouldn't go).

Every home that has children is to have *a school for their spiritual instruction and training*. Deuteronomy 6:7 states, "And thou shalt teach them diligently unto thy children, and shalt talk of them when thou sittest *in thine house*." Timothy's house had a schoolhouse. Paul said of him, "And that from a child thou hast known the holy scriptures, which are able to make thee wise unto salvation through faith which is in Christ Jesus" (2

Timothy 3:15). Timothy's mother, Eunice, and grandmother, Lois, taught him to know and love the Lord. Samuel's house was a schoolhouse. Hannah's faith and godliness were instilled in young Samuel. John and Charles Wesley's house was a schoolhouse. Their mother, Susannah, devoted several hours a week with them (each alone) regarding spiritual things. Someone has said, "The Methodist Church began at Susannah Wesley's knee, when she rocked Charles in a cradle and held John on her lap while she patiently taught him to read, 'In the beginning God created the heaven and the earth.'" Homes like Timothy's, Samuel's and John and Charles Wesley's produce godly men and women who enhance the kingdom of God.

Expound the Word continuously within the home to your children (teach doctrines, attributes of God, commandments). Ingrain in them sound biblical principles to govern all of life (the book of Proverbs is an excellent resource). Teach them right from wrong. Clarify Christian beliefs and values. Instill good and honorable habits. Instruct them about prayer, daily devotions, Scripture memory and church attendance. Warn them about the dangers of wrong companions, dishonesty, disobedience to God, and immorality. Encourage them to witness to friends and serve the Lord regardless of cost or consequence.

The Bottom Line: Don't delay godly instruction; start immediately in infancy. Don't abrogate the parental responsibility of biblical instruction to your child by passing it on to a teacher, coach, school or church. Set the example for your child's own parenting in adulthood.

224
Parents, effects of a child's impact
Proverbs 10:1

"A wise son maketh a glad father: but a foolish son is the heaviness of his mother."

A "wise" (one who is sensible to make sound decisions based upon God's truth) son "maketh" (causes) a "glad father" (a happy, rejoicing father): BUT a "foolish son" (ungodly, imprudent, senseless; refusing to listen and heed instruction) is the "heaviness" (sorrow, bitter disappointment, grief) to his mother. To summarize, children bear grave impact upon their parents' happiness or heaviness, blessing or burden, health or hurt.

Deane and Taswell say, "Children should realize the great trust that is given to them. They are entrusted with the happiness of their parents. After receiving from them life, food, shelter, innumerable good things and a watchful, tender love throughout, they have it in their power to make bright the evening of their father's and mother's life, or to cloud it with a deep, dark gloom of hopeless misery."[1010]

How might you contribute to your parents' happiness? Obey their instructions explicitly and instantly. Treat them with respect and honor. Work hard at being the best student possible. Stand firm on your convictions (moral and ethical code). Do your best in whatever is undertaken (you don't have to excel or win a trophy). Do your chores without complaint. Don't quarrel with siblings. And above all, live continuously submissive unto the Lord.

In adulthood, what is done to enhance a parent's happiness changes. Stay in constant contact (phone calls, texts, emails, cards and especially visits). Involve them in your life and, if married, in that of your family (celebrations, special occasions, holidays, school events, vacations). Seek their counsel (they may be old but still are wise). Do things with them (shopping, movie, dinner out, walking, take them to a ball game). Treat them with dignity and respect (don't be their tyrant). And yet above all, they will be the most joyous in knowing you walk in obedience and service unto the Lord. The desire and delight of all children ought to be to enhance the disposition of joy and gladness in their parents out of love and gratitude for their parentage (if for no other reason). Regrettably, foolish children endeavor to make their parents miserable (exceptionally unhappy). These are a "heaviness of [their] mother" and father.

The Bottom Line: Children take for granted that which their parents do for their happiness while never entertaining a thought as to what they might do to contribute to that of their parents. The secular proverb is so often true, "When they're little, your children step on your toes; when they're grown, they step on your heart."

225
Parents, to honor and obey
Proverbs 19:26

"He that wasteth his father, and chaseth away his mother, is a son that causeth shame, and bringeth reproach."

"Honour thy father and thy mother" (Exodus 20:12).

"He" (a grown[1011] rebellious son) that "wasteth his father" (steals his father's goods; mistreats) and "chaseth away his mother" (drives off his mother from her home[1012]), is a son that "causeth" (brings) "shame" (this causes his parents to feel shameful) and bringeth "reproach" (disgrace). To summarize, the caring affections of parents all too often are repaid with cruel, crushing unkindness of rebellious children.

"You spend years wishing your parents would get off your back, only to realize they're the only ones who ever really had your back."[1013] Though unimaginable, some children actually steal from their parents stored up treasure through fraudulent acts. Some *rob* their money by playing upon their sympathy. But even worse and more hideous is the theft of their respect, authority, honor and dignity (Deuteronomy 21:18–21). God clearly instructs children: "Honour thy father and thy mother: that thy days may be long upon the land which the LORD thy God giveth thee" (Exodus 20:12). Note the promise that is coupled with the command. "While honor is an internal attitude of respect, courtesy and reverence, it should be accompanied by appropriate attention or even obedience. Honor without such action is incomplete; it is lip service (Isaiah 29:13)."[1014]

The greatest gifts children can give their parents are respect, obedience and affection. "Children, obey your parents in all things: for this is well pleasing unto the Lord" (Colossians 3:20). Plaster Proverbs 23:24–25 all over the house (figuratively speaking). "The father of the righteous shall greatly rejoice: and he that begetteth a wise child shall have joy of him. Thy father and thy mother shall be glad, and she that bare thee shall rejoice." Children should make their parents happy and proud, not sad and shamed.

> A child who is allowed to be disrespectful to his parents will not have true respect for anyone.
> Billy Graham

The Bottom Line: Submission to parental authority and exhibition of parental respect are foundational to a happy, honorable and prosperous life. See Proverbs 20:20.

226
Partiality, prejudicial attitudes and actions
Proverbs 24:23

"These things also belong to the wise. It is not good to have respect of persons in judgment."

"These things" (words of wisdom) also belong to the wise. It is "not good" ("This is a figure known as *tapeinosis*—a deliberate understatement to emphasize a worst-case scenario: 'it is terrible!'"[1015]) to have "respect for persons" (show partiality) in "judgment" (in judicial matters; rendering verdicts).

The Proverb is counsel to judges and magistrates who administer judgment based upon the law. Foundationally it is essential that they do not show favoritism or disfavor toward the accused. "Respect of persons [partiality] gives the sense of the Hebrew idiom 'to have regard for faces'; it means to give a decision or to act on the basis of who a person is rather than on the basis of his or her guilt or innocence."[1016] Fairness in judgment is jeopardized when based upon anything (politics, race, culture, religion, friendship, enmity) other than the truth. Additionally, justice must not be blinded to a person's innocence or guilt by courtroom theatrics, deceitful witnesses or highly skilled persuasive lawyers. Matthew Henry says that "a good judge will know the truth, not know faces, so as to countenance a friend and help him out in a bad cause, or so much as omit anything that can be said or done in favor of a righteous cause, when it is the cause of an enemy."[1017]

Though the principle is addressed to judges, it bears application for all, especially the church. Paul instructs young Timothy and all saints, "I charge thee before God, and the Lord Jesus Christ, and the elect angels, that thou observe these things without preferring one before another, doing nothing by partiality [favor]" (1 Timothy 5:21). Arichea and Hatton state, "*Favor* is literally 'partiality' or 'prejudice'; it describes the act of making a decision based on assumptions and prejudgments that are usually unjustified. The word for *partiality* is synonymous with *favor;* it describes

309

an unjustified preference for something or someone."[1018] Timothy is not to prejudge the accused elder nor allow himself to be prejudicial in the determination of his innocence or guilt (1 Timothy 5:19). He is to remain totally impartial that he might render a just verdict based upon truth and the Holy Scriptures.

The same *rule* applies to the church today. William Barclay comments, "Nothing does more harm than when some people are treated as if they could do no wrong and others as if they could do no right. Justice is a universal virtue, and the church must surely never fall below the impartial standards which even the world demands."[1019]

The Bottom Line: Court justices must not be prejudicial in dispensing justice, nor should leaders in the church.

227
Past, digging up the sin of others
Proverbs 16:27

"An ungodly man diggeth up evil: and in his lips there is as a burning fire."

An "ungodly man" (a "wicked scoundrel";[1020] Toy says the title "includes deep depravity and wickedness"[1021]) "diggeth up evil" (Henry says, "They take a great deal of pains to find out something or other on which to ground a slander, or which may give some color to it. If none appear above ground, rather than want it, they will dig for it by diving into what is secret, or looking a great way back, or by evil suspicions and surmises, and forced innuendos"[1022]): AND in his "lips there is as a burning fire" (Reyburn and Fry say his "words destroy like hot fire"[1023]).

He who is ever digging up "evil" (another's past failures, hurts, sins, misdeeds, mistakes) that should ever remain buried, to *broadcast* to the world is of all people a "wicked scoundrel" whose lips are set on fire of Hell (lips as a burning or scorching fire). Such a raging inferno constantly fueled from Hell (James 3:6) does vicious, cruel devastation to its target.

Themistocles was offered to be taught the art of memory, but he answered, "Ah, teach me rather the art of forgetting; for I often remember what I would not, and cannot forget what I would."[1024] It is the honorable trait of the godly to forget the wrongs and injuries of another, to allow the past to remain buried. Too many are as the frequent client to a barber shop who always shared slanderous stories. Finally, the barber, totally disgusted with the man's incessant and injurious talk, said to him, "You remind me of the dogs that licked Lazarus' sores, never allowing them to heal" (Luke 16:21). Don't lick "Lazarus' sores" by forever taking the bandage off, exposing them. Let them heal.

Corrie ten Boom states that when God forgives sin, He places it in the sea of utter forgetfulness and then posts a sign for the world to see that states: "No fishing allowed." *No person has the right to dredge up* that which God has cleansed and forgiven, even the person who committed the sin. Forget what ought to be forgotten. Don't be a "graverobber." "Those who plan evil are full of lies [deceit], but those who plan [advise] peace are happy" (Proverbs 12:20 EXB).

The Bottom Line: Stop hunting for stories to trouble, harm, destroy and shipwreck another. Act graciously unto others, as God has toward you in the forgiveness and covering of sin. Stop "licking" Lazarus' sores.

228
Paths, the good and the bad
Proverbs 4:18–19

"But the path of the just is as the shining light, that shineth more and more unto the perfect day. The way of the wicked is as darkness: they know not at what they stumble."

But the "path" (walk; lifestyle) of the "just" (righteous; saved) is as a "shining light" (sunrise), that "shineth more and more" (the sun rising gradually throughout the day gets brighter and brighter) unto the "perfect day" (until it is at its brightest point; Maclaren says, "What is meant is the point of time at which the day culminates, and for a moment, the sun seems to stand steady...in the very zenith, raying down 'the arrows that fly by noonday'"[1025]). The way of the "wicked" (ungodly) is as "darkness" (way is dark or pitch black, for they are without the LIGHT to illumine their way; experiences the dark night of the soul): they know not at what they "stumble" (to trip).

Salvation is in three tenses. *The believer has been saved* from the guilt and penalty of sin (1 Corinthians 1:18; Luke 7:50). Salvation occurs in an instant upon repentance and faith expressed to the Lord Jesus Christ.

The believer is being saved from the habit and dominion of sin (Romans 6:14; Philippians 2:12–13). Solomon pictures the believer's progression in sanctification to that of the sun (Proverbs 4:18). The Christian is saved in an instant (sunrise), but godliness is progressive (as the sun rises in the sky) until clothed with Christ's perfection in Heaven (sun reaches noonday). A grave contradiction exists when one states the fact of personal salvation and yet is content to continue in the old life of sin (2 Corinthians 5:17). Maclaren says, "The intention of every Christian life should be a life of increasing luster, uninterrupted, and the natural result of increasing communion with and conformity [continuous growth] to the very fountain itself of heavenly radiance."[1026]

The believer will be saved to absolute, total conformity to Christ— "the perfect day" (Proverbs 4:18; Romans 13:11). A day is coming when the saint's transformation into the likeness of Christ will be complete (1 John 3:2).

The Bottom Line: There are but two paths on which a person may choose to walk. One path is that which leads to the city of Zion (Heaven, v. 18); the other leads to eternal banishment from the presence of God (Hell, v. 19). The one is lit with the brilliancy of Christ; the other is enveloped in darkness. The saved in Heaven will be in a domain where there is no darkness, for God is the Light of the city (Revelation 21:23); the lost will be in Hell where there is nothing but the blackness of darkness forever (Jude 13).

229
Patience, trait of the effective soul winner
Proverbs 25:15

"By long forbearing is a prince persuaded, and a soft tongue breaketh the bone."

"A soft answer turneth away wrath: but grievous words stir up anger" (Proverbs 15:1).

A prolonged patience[1027] ("forbearing") with gentle words ("soft tongue") convinces ("persuades") a person of authority [like a judge] ("prince") to listen and change his mind ("breaketh the bone"). D. A. Garrett states, "The bones are the most rigid body parts inside of a person, and fracturing the bones here refers to breaking down the deepest, most hardened resistance to an idea a person may possess."[1028]

Deane and Taswell say, "The proverb says that such an officer is led to take a favorable view of an accused person's case when he sees him calm and composed, ready to explain the matter without any undue heat or irritation, keeping steadily to the point, and not seduced by calumny or misrepresentation to forget himself and lose his temper."[1029] H. A. Ironside summarizes, "Continued kindness and forbearance are powerful agents in overcoming obstinacy and angry passion, which seem as unyielding as a bone."[1030]

The Proverb offers keen insight into dealing with the most resistant of sinners set against salvation. Many a hardened heart has been penetrated and won by patient gentle persuasion regarding the truth. "Hard bones" are broken by "soft words."[1031] Winning souls sometimes is done in an instant. Other times it takes "long forbearing" (lengthy manifestation of winsome patience).

As a young minister I recall hearing the testimony of a man who stated it was on the fifty-first witness to him that he was converted to Christ. Never give up on winning the most stubborn opposed to Christ; patiently, gently keep sowing the seed in the sod of their soul, believing God for its germination to eternal life.

The New Testament version of the Proverb is 2 Timothy 2:24–26 in which Paul gives witnessing instruction to Timothy. "And the servant of the Lord must not strive; but be gentle unto all men, apt to teach, patient, In meekness instructing those that oppose themselves; if God peradventure will give them repentance to the acknowledging of the truth; And that they may recover themselves out of the snare of the devil, who are taken captive by him at his will."

The Bottom Line: Patience, gentleness and passionate persuasion are powerful weapons in winning the most hardened sinner to faith in Jesus Christ. Deane and Taswell say, "A soft answer (Proverbs 15:1), gentle, conciliating words, overcome opposition, and disarm the most determined enemy, and make tender in him that which was hardest and most uncompromising."[1032]

230
Peace, the anchor holds in spite of the storm
Proverbs 1:33

"But whoso hearkeneth unto me shall dwell safely, and shall be quiet from fear of evil."

But whoso "hearkeneth" (hears and heeds) unto "me" (wisdom; the Lord God) shall "dwell safely" ("with confidence, without danger"[1033]; securely, safely), AND shall be "quiet" (know peace, tranquility) from "fear" (worry, anxiety, troubled spirit) of "evil" (amidst adversity their heart will be at rest,[1034] knowing God is their refuge and strong tower).

Storms are forever brewing, striking life with unexpected turmoil, trouble or trial. The promise set forth in the Proverb is that in spite of the storm's devastating impact, the Lord will sustain the righteous, granting peace in its midst. The righteous possess what the fool does not to keep him safe in the calamities and crises of life: a sure and secure Anchor to which his ship is fastened (Hebrews 6:19).

C. H. Spurgeon, in the sermon "The Anchor," states, "What is our anchor? It has two great blades or flukes to it, each of which acts as a holdfast. It is made of *two divine things*. The one is *God's promise*, a sure and stable thing indeed! Jehovah's promise, what a certain thing it must be; if you had nothing but the Lord's bare word to trust to, surely your faith should never stagger! To this sure word is added another divine thing, namely, *God's oath*. I scarcely dare speak upon this sacred topic—God's oath, His solemn assertion, His swearing by Himself. Conceive the majesty, the awe, the certainty of this! Here then are two divine assurances which, like the flukes of the anchor, hold us fast. Who dares doubt the promise of God? Who can have the audacity to distrust His oath?"[1035]

The Anchor has been tried and tested for over 4,000 years through many and various storms that afflict life, only to be found reliable and sure. Corrie ten Boom said, "In order to realize the worth of the anchor, we need to feel the stress of the storm."[1036] Storms challenge the righteous' faith to trust the "worth" of the Anchor to sustain. It has been said that faith is like film. It's developed in the dark. It's in the dark times of life that we learn to trust God.

The anchor holds,
Though the ship is battered;
The anchor holds,
Though the sails are torn.
I have fallen on my knees as I face the raging seas;
The anchor holds in spite of the storm. ~ Ray Boltz

The Bottom Line: Although the righteous are not exempt from storms (John 16:33), they have been provided a sure and secure anchor to prevent their ship from capsizing or breaking apart. It's this Anchor that enables the believer to have "peace in the midst of the storm." "Thou wilt keep him in perfect peace, whose mind is stayed on thee: because he trusteth in thee" (Isaiah 26:3).

231
Peace, when enemies are turned into friends
Proverbs 16:7
"When a man's ways please the LORD, he maketh even his enemies to be at peace with him."

When a man's "ways" (conduct, manner of living) "please" (delight; acceptable) the Lord, He maketh even his "enemies" (those who hate and despise him) to be at "peace" (see explanation below) with him.

Categorically, the text states that if a man walks pleasing unto the Lord, though his enemy may hate him, they cannot discredit his godly character. This was true with Daniel's enemies. "Then the presidents and princes sought to find occasion against Daniel concerning the kingdom; but they could find none occasion nor fault; forasmuch as he was faithful, neither was there any error or fault found in him" (Daniel 6:4).

The Proverb cannot mean that if a person is righteous and godly that he will be reconciled to all that hate him. God Himself has many enemies. The text does indicate that God is able to reconcile the Spirit-filled believer with those that vehemently hate him and/or turn their evil (devious) intentions into his good. Joseph said to his brothers who sold him into slavery, "As for you, you meant evil against me, but God meant it for good, to bring it about that many people should be kept alive, as they are today" (Genesis 50:20 ESV).

"One thing," remarks H. A. Ironside, "that is very conducive to closing the mouths of enemies is just going on quietly through 'evil report and good report' (2 Corinthians 6:8), bent on pleasing One alone, wasting no time in self-vindication, but committing all to Him who judges righteously. A holy, humble walk must silence even my worst foes."[1037] Matthew Henry remarks that "the image of God appearing upon the righteous, and His particular lovingkindness to them, are enough to recommend them to the respect of all, even of those that have been most prejudiced against them."[1038]

W. A. Criswell interprets the text as follows: "Man can be most effectively reconciled to his enemies by his own reconciliation to God. God is the omnipotent Creator-Ruler of this universe, and no enemy can attack us except by His permission (Job 1:9–12). Though Laban followed Jacob as an enemy, he was constrained to make peace with him (Genesis 31:24). Esau reversed from adversary to brother under God's hand (Genesis 27:41; 33:1–4). Godly kings were delivered from their enemies (1 Kings 4:21–25; 10:23–29). Even when the enemies are permitted to attack, they, together with their harm, may be overruled for a greater good (Romans 8:28)."[1039]

The Bottom Line: God can change foes into friends. The believer's civility, impeccable lifestyle, forgiving spirit and godliness *may* be used of the Lord to restore broken relationships (the operative word is *may*).

This general rule (Proverbs 16:7), states John MacArthur, "does not preclude persecution for some." Paul said, "Yea, and all that will live godly in Christ Jesus shall suffer persecution" (2 Timothy 3:12).[1040]

232
Peer Pressure, resist the pull of the crowd to do wrong
Proverbs 1:10
"My son, if sinners entice thee, consent thou not."

"My son" (either Solomon addressing his sons or a teacher using the parental address to a student, as was oft the custom), if "sinners" (evildoers, the foolish and ungodly; immoral reputation; Smith says, "The Hebrew term points to those habitually addicted to crime, i.e., thugs, gang members"[1041]) "entice" (allure; tempt) you, do not "consent" (don't yield to the pressure to conform).

Surrounded by others at school and the neighborhood that do bad things, children will be tempted by their persuasive pressure "to do as they do." Solomon says to such a child, "Don't consent. Don't do what is contrary to God's Word, despite the ridicule, rejection or abandonment." The Apostle Peter said, "We must obey God rather than men" (Acts 5:29 ESV).

Pilate yielded to peer pressure in crucifying Jesus. "So Pilate, wishing to *satisfy the crowd*, released for them Barabbas, and having scourged

Jesus, he delivered him to be crucified" (Mark 15:15 ESV). Pilate had found no fault in Jesus, nothing worthy of death, but to *satisfy the crowd,* he went against his conscience and conviction. A *satisfying-the-crowd* demeanor always leads to conduct that violates biblical standards, dishonors the Lord and brings shame, havoc and heartache. The Christian is to live to satisfy *Christ,* not the *crowd.*

Alexander Maclaren says, "It is not enough to listen to the nobler voice. We have resolutely to stop our ears to the baser, which is often the louder. If we cannot say 'No' to the base, we shall not say 'Yes' to the nobler voice."[1042]

The Bottom Line: Sheep that do not follow the Good Shepherd are headed for a slaughter. Multitudes that walk the broad way of worldly pleasure and disgrace to God will face judgment. Stay on the narrow way, walking in conformity to God's expectations and standards, and be blessed beyond measure. See Proverbs 4:14–15.

233
Perjury, the injurious and punishable crime of lying
Proverbs 19:9
"A false witness shall not be unpunished, and he that speaketh lies shall perish."

A "false witness" (untruthfulness; bearing false testimony) shall not be "unpunished" (not be acquitted in court[1043]), and he that "speaketh lies" (tells untruth) shall "perish" (not escape due punishment).

Lying (private and public conversation) and perjury (judicial courtroom testimony) bear stiff consequences from man and God (Revelation 21:8). "They stand on the same footing and shall have one doom."[1044] God's Word is clear. "Thou shalt not raise a false report: put not thine hand with the wicked to be an unrighteous witness" (Exodus 23:1). "Be not a witness against thy neighbour without cause; and deceive not with thy lips" (Proverbs 24:28). Tell the truth, always the truth, and nothing but the truth, regardless of cost or consequence. A false statement when received as the truth bears much harm, even if perchance later it is detected and corrected. Damaged reputations, relationships, ministries and homes caused by a lie often cannot be reversed.

A family residing in a small town in North Dakota was happy despite the mother's lingering illness since the birth of her second child. It was a simple and loving family. Each evening the neighbors witnessed their abiding love for each other as the wife and children would meet their husband and father at the gate. Laughter filled the home and happy faces as the father played with the children on the back lawn.

Then a village gossip invented a story saying the husband was being unfaithful to his wife. Upon hearing the story, the young wife was devastated. Reason left her. In the evening as the husband returned home from work, there was no one to meet him at the gate. He heard no laughter in the house nor smelled any fragrant aroma coming from the kitchen. He felt a coldness that chilled his heart with fear. In frantic search for his beloved wife and children, he discovered them hanging from a beam in the basement. Heart-smitten, the young mother had taken the lives of her two children and then her own. The truth finally was revealed days later. A gossip's tongue precipitated a terrible tragedy.[1045]

The young wife is representative of myriads of people over the centuries (perhaps like you) whose life was turned upside down all due to the maliciousness of someone spreading an untruth (intentionally or unintentionally) about them or one they greatly loved or admired. Though vindication may come, irreparable damage is often already done. The scars of slander forever linger.

The Bottom Line: "An hypocrite with his mouth destroyeth his neighbour" (Proverbs 11: 9). "Good name in man and woman, dear my lord, is the immediate jewel of their souls. Who steals my purse steals trash. 'Tis something, nothing; 'twas mine; 'tis his, and has been slave to thousands. But he that filches from me my good name robs me of that which not enriches him, and makes me poor indeed" (William Shakespeare, *Othello*).

234
Persuasion, the sinner's proposal to sin
Proverbs 1:13

"We shall find all precious substance, we shall fill our houses with spoil."

"Consent thou not" (Proverbs 1:10).

"We" (the wicked includes the innocent; join us and "we") shall "find" (gain by robbery) all "precious substance" (greatly prized valuables[1046]; money and possessions), we shall "fill" (cram full[1047]) our houses with "spoil" (the money and valuables taken from their victims).

Sinners love company in their sinful conduct and misery. Do not therefore expect to escape their persuasion, solicitation and enticement. It is the pleasure of the sinner to destroy the innocent. This truth resoundingly struck home while I was yet a student in seminary. The *National Observer* reported research indicating that harlots targeted ministers for sexual encounters. Somehow the moral failure of a minister made them feel less guilty and dirty. When solicited to do wrong, keep in mind the solicitor's purpose may be to destroy you in order to appease personal guilt by pulling you down to his or her level.

A persuasion used by the sinner to solicit another to wrong is its gain. "We will take [find] all kinds of valuable things [precious wealth] and fill our houses with stolen goods [plunder]" (Proverbs 1:13 EXB). The sinner is wrong in his assessment (and knows that he is) but so speaks to draw another into his crime. Ill-gotten gain never is "precious substance or wealth," for it never may be enjoyed legally, morally or fearlessly (danger of apprehension ever a possibility).

Matthew Henry remarks, "It is as that which is not, which will give a man no solid satisfaction. It is cheap, it is common, yet, in their account, it is precious, and therefore they will hazard their lives, and perhaps their souls, in pursuit of it. It is the ruining mistake of thousands that they overvalue the wealth of this world and look on it as precious substance."[1048] The Lord declares, "There is no peace...unto the wicked" (Isaiah 48:22).

John Gill summarizes the appeal of Wisdom and the Lord in stating, "My son, if sinners entice thee—endeavour to seduce thee from thy parents and draw thee aside from them, from listening to their instructions, advice and commands—and make use of all plausible arguments to persuade thee to join with them in the sins they are addicted unto and are continually employed in, "do not consent."[1049]

The Bottom Line: In the wilderness temptations of our Lord, Satan offered Him the kingdoms and glories of the world, if only He would submit to his persuasions (Matthew 4:8–9). He forthrightly refused. All must do the same when confronted with various enticing persuasions to do wrong. As He did, use the Holy Scriptures to drive back the tempter and temptation.

235
Plagiarism, claiming another's work as one's own
Proverbs 10:9
"He that walketh uprightly walketh surely: but he that perverteth his ways shall be known."

He that "walketh" (manner of lifestyle) "uprightly" (walks in integrity; uprightness inside out) walketh "surely" (securely [Proverbs 2:7]): BUT he that "perverteth" (behaves crookedly and deceitfully[1050]) his "ways" (conduct) shall be "known" (shall be exposed and suffer the consequences).

Merriam-Webster defines *plagiarism* as "to commit literary theft: present as new and original an idea or product derived from an existing source." It is a form of thievery, for it's stealing the literary works of another, crediting it to oneself. The Bible is explicit in denouncing such offences (Matthew 19:18; Romans 2:21, 13:9; Leviticus 19:11). The righteous man walks in integrity (honesty, truthfulness, rightness) in all the affairs of life. It is the ungodly that scheme to benefit themselves through deceitful and dishonorable practices. The sin of plagiarism will come to light ("shall be known"), and when it does, devastating consequences will result.

In Tennessee some years ago, a prominent minister's plagiarism was made "known" with regard to a book he authored that contained another's writing. The discovery shocked the Christian world and led to his immediate dismissal. All authors, especially religious ones, must do double-duty insuring their work credits that of others used. Perhaps as an author I go overboard in citing documentation from material gained through research and study in my books, but I prefer to err on the "side of caution."

Unintentional plagiarism (ignorance that it's another's work or carelessness) happens in sermons that are preached, songs that are composed, lessons that are written, blogs that are posted, as well as in books that are written. All who do such works *must exhibit due diligence in crediting the original author or composer* (unless permission upfront has been granted that it is unnecessary, as Dr. Herschel Ford does for his *Simple Sermons* series[1051] and Dr. Adrian Rogers, former pastor of Bellevue Baptist Church in Memphis, Tennessee, said about use of his material, "If my bullet fits your gun, go ahead and shoot it."[1052] In the event that knowledge surfaces after the fact of committal of unintentional plagiarism, insofar as possible take steps to render proper credit.

The Book of Proverbs' purpose, at least in main part, is to instill in man divine wisdom, which includes righteous discernment for handling issues just like this one. Righteous discernment navigates man around the dangerous snare of plagiarism, that it may be avoided altogether (Proverbs 3:21).

The Bottom Line: To borrow Jesus' words about taxes, applying them to plagiarism, I say, "Render therefore unto Caesar the things which are Caesar's" (Matthew 22:21). Give credit, where credit is due.

236
Plan, the masterful blueprint for your life
Proverbs 3:5–6
"Trust in the LORD with all thine heart; and lean not unto thine own understanding. In all thy ways acknowledge him, and he shall direct thy paths."

"A man's heart deviseth his way: but the LORD directeth his steps" (Proverbs 16:9).

"Trust" (Deane and Taswell say "entire reliance upon Jehovah"[1053]) in the Lord with "all" (totality) thine "heart" (with the entire mind); and "lean" (depend upon) not unto thine own "understanding" (Murphy says, "Wisdom is a gift of God (2:6), but whoever claims to be wise is more foolish than the fool"[1054] [Proverbs 26:12; Jeremiah 9:22–23]); don't rely upon personal insights, discernment or impressions, impulsiveness). In "all thy ways" (entails every facet of life, spiritual and secular, public and private[1055]; plans, pursuits, decisions) "acknowledge him" (to recognize authority and rule; look to and depend upon Him), and he shall "direct thy paths" (order, guide your steps on a straight path, the righteous path that assures what is best for you; Buzzell says more than just guidance, but that God will remove obstacles from the path to enable the obedient righteous who walk by faith to reach the "appointed goal"[1056] or plan of God).

Alexander Maclaren summarizes that not only will God be our guide but "Roadmaker, showing us the way and clearing obstacles from it. Calm certitude follows on willingness to accept God's will, and whoever seeks only to go where God sends him will neither be left doubtful whither he should go nor find his road blocked."[1057]

Jeremiah states, "'For I know the plans I have for you,' says the Lord, 'plans for well-being and not for trouble, to give you a future and a hope'" (Jeremiah 29:11 NLV).

> God wants us to know His will, and He reveals it to us both through the Bible and through the guidance of His Holy Spirit. Seek God's will when you pray, and He will help you know it.
> Billy Graham

God has a masterful blueprint for all of life that is designed for best happiness, success, fulfillment and peace. To know and experience the plan, however, you must totally rely upon Him to 'direct your paths.' To 'lean unto your own understanding' thwarts the divine plan and shipwrecks life. The Christian must live under God's management and supervision in every detail (work, business, school, finances and church).

"*Acknowledge Him.*" Wait upon the Lord to grant direction; refuse to make knee-jerk reactions, and "he shall direct thy paths." God, by His Word, by the Holy Spirit, and at times by the godly, will prompt you in the right way to go and keep you on the right path.

The Bottom Line: Allowing God to guide your steps assures of a full and meaningful life.

237
Plans, committed to God, bring success
Proverbs 16:3

"Commit thy works unto the LORD, and thy thoughts shall be established."

"Commit thy way unto the LORD; trust also in him; and he shall bring it to pass" (Psalm 37:5).

"Commit" (roll your works on the Lord, pictures complete dependence upon Him[1058]) thy "works" (undertakings, deeds, plans) unto the Lord, and thy "thoughts" (plans) shall be "established" (successful; turn out well; be achieved[1059]). The Proverb isn't giving a blanket endorsement to every plan of man, only those that meet with God's approval. The man who trustingly commits ("rolls on God") his works (actions, endeavors, undertakings that are pleasing unto the Lord) will have all his plans established (achieved; turn out well). He will have "deep roots" (firmly established), unlike the ungodly that live unto themselves (Proverbs 12:3). "The plans and deliberations out of which the "works" sprang shall meet with a happy fulfillment, because they are undertaken according to the will of God and directed to the end by his guidance."[1060] Maclaren says, "'Commit thy works unto the LORD'—that is to say, do not be too sure that you are right because you do not think you are wrong. We should be very distrustful of our own judgments of ourselves, especially when that judgment permits us to do certain things."[1061]

Not only will the man that commits his "works" unto the Lord *possess confidence, but calmness.* The knowledge that sovereign God is in control of his deliberations, decisions and directions floods the heart and mind with peace (absence of anxiety and worry). Charles Bridges remarks, "The burden being now cast upon One who is better able to bear it (1 Peter 5:7), the mind is easy, the thoughts composed, quietly waiting the issue of things, knowing that all that is for our good and the glory of our God shall be brought to pass (Psalm 112:7)."[1062]

The promise of the Proverb applies only to him who trusts, relies upon the Lord, "rolling" upon Him all his deeds and affairs (Deuteronomy 20:20; Hebrews 4:3). H. A. Ironside cautions, "It must be borne in mind that if I thus commit all to Him, I no longer choose for myself as to what the outcome should be, but say with confidence, 'Thy will be done.'"[1063]

The Bottom Line: As the believer through prayer commits (rolls upon the Lord) ALL worldly and spiritual cares, concerns, challenges and choices, his goings are firmly established (successful, secure, satisfied and serene). To say with David, "The LORD will perfect that which concerneth me" (Psalm 138:8) takes the worry and stress out of life.

238
Political Correctness, resist the sellout
Proverbs 23:23

"Buy the truth, and sell it not; also wisdom, and instruction, and understanding."

"Buy" (get the truth regardless of the price; suggests "spending whatever energy or financial resources are necessary to acquire truth"[1064]) the "truth" (the one and only truth as revealed by God in Holy Scriptures), and "sell it not" (don't part with it for any reason[1065]); ALSO "wisdom" (wisdom is divine discernment that enables man to do that which is right and pleasing unto the Lord—which is for his best good—in every course of action), "instruction" (teaching about moral and ethical disciplines), and "understanding" (the ability of discernment; comprehension and application of knowledge). Deane and Taswell summarize, "Consider truth as a thing of the highest value, and spare no pains, cost or sacrifice to obtain it, and, when gotten, keep it safe; do not barter it for earthly profit or the pleasures of sense; do not be reasoned out of it or laughed out of it; "sell it not," do not part with it for any consideration."[1066]

Political correctness is defined as "disapproving of and avoiding language or behavior that any particular group of people might feel is unkind or offensive" *(Cambridge Academic Content Dictionary).* The key word in the definition is "offensive." Franklin Graham states that PC ("the maddening and prevailing public sentiment of offending no one [except Christians]") is one of the most sinister threats to society. Graham continues, "It has infected our schools, government, universities, and the marketplace, leaving no room for moral absolutes or the authoritative truth of Scripture."[1067] The Bible, God's divinely inspired Word, is not politically correct. It is offensive to those whose lifestyle and beliefs it condemns (1 Peter 2:8). In fact, the Scriptures condemn PC (political correctness): "Woe unto them that call evil good, and good evil; that put darkness for light, and light for darkness; that put bitter for sweet, and sweet for bitter!" (Isaiah 5:20).

Abraham Lincoln said, "What is morally wrong can never be politically correct."[1068] May his tribe in government, schools, universities and churches be praised and increased. Proverbs 23:23 exhorts us to obtain ("buy") the Truth (religious, moral, ethical knowledge based on Holy Scriptures), and upon getting it not to "sell" it at any price to those who peddle political correctness. Political correctness must never be allowed to dictate to the Christian or church its stance on moral, ethical, religious or relational issues. The Christian and church have the Holy Scriptures assigned by God to that purpose.

I belong to the Lamb of God;
He purchased me with his precious blood.

I don't need popularity;
I'd rather have what He gave to me.

Some sold convictions for compromise;
Some have sold the truth for a pack of lies.
Some have sold testimonies for fortune and fame;
I just want to glorify and magnify His name.

Well, if you're living for Jesus, friend, there'll come a day
That old Devil's gonna try to get you some way.
He'll try you and tempt you with his lies straight from Hell.
Just say, "I belong to Jesus, and, Devil, I'm not for sale."

Not for sale; Not for sale; No way, no sir.
~ Michael Combs (Not for Sale)

Tell the PC crowd you're not for sale!

The Bottom Line: Like Jesus, the Christian does not purposely "offend" unbelievers or naysayers. The apostles preached Christ and the resurrection though ordered to desist. They frankly said, "We ought to obey God rather than men" (Acts 5:29). Go and do likewise, not spurring needless offence, but not cowering down to avoid it.

239
Politics, when the righteous govern
Proverbs 29:2

"When the righteous are in authority, the people rejoice: but when the wicked beareth rule, the people mourn."

When the "righteous" (godly, just, honorable, upright) are in "authority" (rule, governing power), the people "rejoice" (are glad, happy): BUT when the "wicked" (ungodly) beareth "rule" (in power), the people "mourn" (sorrowful, distressful, grieved).

H. A. Ironside remarks, "In the measure that the principles of the New Testament control the minds of the men who administer civil government, peace and prosperity prevail—as none know better than the openly skeptical."[1069] Ironside continues, "The reign of a Josiah or a Hezekiah was much to be preferred to that of an Ahab or a Manasseh."[1070] "When it goeth

325

well with the righteous, the city rejoiceth: and when the wicked perish, there is shouting. By the blessing of the upright the city is exalted: but it is overthrown by the mouth of the wicked" (Proverbs 11:10–11).

The unrighteous rule brings reproach (disgrace). "Righteousness exalteth a nation: but sin is a reproach to any people" (Proverbs 14:34). They govern by lies and deceit and place in office *wicked* assistants. "If a ruler hearken to lies, all his servants are wicked" (Proverbs 29:12). They abuse their office and power. "A ruler with no understanding will oppress his people, but one who hates corruption will have a long life" (Proverbs 28:16 NLT). They show partially toward the unrighteous. "It is not good to accept the person of the wicked, to overthrow the righteous in judgment" (Proverbs 18:5).

The righteous governs with truth, honor and integrity. "Mercy and truth preserve the king: and his throne is upholden by mercy" (Proverbs 20:28). The rule of the righteous will be successful. "The king that faithfully judgeth the poor, his throne shall be established for ever" (Proverbs 29:14). The righteous reject bribes to alter decisions or the law. "A wicked man taketh a gift out of the bosom to pervert the ways of judgment" (Proverbs 17:23). They expose and punish the wicked. "Partiality in judging is not good. Whoever says to the wicked, 'You are in the right,' will be cursed by peoples, abhorred by nations, but those who rebuke the wicked will have delight, and a good blessing will come upon them" (Proverbs 24:23–25 ESV). The righteous refrain from appetites and activities which interfere with governing honorably. "It is not for kings, O Lemuel, it is not for kings to drink wine; nor for princes strong drink: Lest they drink, and forget the law, and pervert the judgment of any of the afflicted" (Proverbs 31:4–5). They defend the rights of the unfortunate. "Open thy mouth for the dumb in the cause of all such as are appointed to destruction. Open thy mouth, judge righteously, and plead the cause of the poor and needy" (Proverbs 31:8–9).

The Christian assists the ruler in governing righteously by electing and supporting the godly in office. "Take away the wicked from before the king, and his throne shall be established in righteousness" (Proverbs 25:5). Further, believers may influence governing officials toward godly principles and practices. "Righteous lips are the delight of kings; and they love him that speaketh right" (Proverbs 16:13). "When one is slow to anger, a ruler may be won over. A gentle tongue will break a bone" (Proverbs 25:15 NLV). To influence *rulers,* be cautious not to associate with radicals who bounce from *pillar to post* politically, morally and/or theologically. "My son, fear thou the LORD and the king: and meddle [associate] not with them that are given to change: For their calamity shall rise suddenly; and who knoweth the ruin of them both?" (Proverbs 24:21–22). A final thing which you ought to do to influence godly governing locally and nationally is to exercise the right to vote. Voting remains the one powerful means to replace the wicked with a righteous person.

The Bottom Line: Regardless who may be in rule, God is in still in control. "The king's heart is in the hand of the LORD, as the rivers of water: he turneth it whithersoever he will" (Proverbs 21:1). It is the duty of every Christian to pray "for kings, and for all that are in authority; that we may lead a quiet and peaceable life in all godliness and honesty" (1 Timothy 2:2).

240
Poor, closing the eyes to the needy
Proverbs 28:27
"He that giveth unto the poor shall not lack: but he that hideth his eyes shall have many a curse."

He that "giveth" (renders help financially or otherwise) unto the "poor" (destitute and hungry) shall not "lack" (not be in need of food for himself; God rewards or compensates the giver for the kind deed): BUT he that "hideth" (Reyburn and Fry say "closes his eyes"[1071]; purposefully refuses to be made aware of their need so he will not feel compelled to help or turns his head in happening upon them) his eyes shall have "many a curse" (the greedy will be punished by God "many" times over for their insensitivity and lack of compassion to help the hungry and likewise "the poor they mistreat"[1072]). To summarize, those who are generous to the poor are compensated with divine blessings of provision so that personal needs are not jeopardized, but those who are greedy and indifferent to the poor will experience the retributive justice of God.

The greedy avoid encounters with the poor (pass by on the other side of the road, as did the priest and Levite—Luke 10:25–37) that cry for assistance or upon seeing their miserable predicament pretend ("closes his eyes") they do not see for fear of being moved to generous response. "The unmerciful man meets with the curses of those whom he has neglected to relieve when he had the power."[1073] "Many a curse" (numerous curses from God and man in contrast to blessings the generous receive) the uncharitable will experience. The greatest of these is the divine retribution of God. He will say to the unmerciful, "When ye spread forth your hands, I will hide mine eyes from you" (Isaiah 1:15).

The benevolent giver to the poor and needy "shall not lack" (God sees to it that the aid given will not hurt or deprive the giver of what is needed). Not only will God pay back the giver for the gift given, but He will do so with high-interest yield. "He that hath a bountiful eye shall be blessed; for he giveth of his bread to the poor" (Proverbs 22:9). "There is that scattereth, and yet increaseth; and there is that withholdeth more than is meet, but it tendeth to poverty" (Proverbs 11:24).

The Bottom Line: You honor the Lord when you demonstrate mercy toward the poor (Proverbs 14:31).

241
Poor, don't hold back the corn from the hungry
Proverbs 11:25–26
"The liberal soul shall be made fat: and he that watereth shall be watered also himself. He that withholdeth corn, the people shall curse him: but blessing shall be upon the head of him that selleth it."

"Whoever is generous to the poor lends to the Lord, and he will repay him for his deed" (Proverbs 19:17 ESV).

The "liberal" (generous, charitable) "soul" (person) shall be made "fat" (will become "rich or prosperous"[1074]): AND he that "watereth" (gives assistance) shall be "watered" (giving or helping others boomerangs back to the giver; in giving, they will be given unto) also himself. He that "witholdeth" (refuses to give, holds back his giving) "corn" (people horded and stockpiled grain, making its price increase, then sold it at the more exorbitant price[1075]), the people shall "curse him" (Reyburn and Fry say to "speak badly against someone"[1076]): BUT "blessing" (God's favor and the poor's also) shall be upon the head of him that "selleth it" (the person that refuses to cheat the poor by the practice of stockpiling). See Amos 8:4.

Benevolence toward the poor and needy is expected. The enemy of benevolence is selfishness, which always clamors for more without regard to those who have little or none ("witholdeth corn"). To withhold (stockpile) corn to make it a scarcity in order to sell it at an inflated price[1077] is ethically, biblically and morally wrong. Such incurs the anger ("curse") of the people, whereas forgoing the high profits to assist in the emergency brings the blessing and reward of the Lord.[1078] "Whoever has a bountiful eye will be blessed, for he shares his bread with the poor" (Proverbs 22:9 ESV). Rewarded ("blessed") perhaps not by the recipient of the good done with their gratitude, but by God. He promises to bless works and gifts of benevolence ("he that watereth shall be watered"). In giving unto the needy, our life will be enriched by the gracious giving of God and others. It's a win-win situation. Nabal, a prosperous man, refused to give to David and his followers when persecuted by King Saul. Joseph, on the other hand, stored up grain to provide for the needy during time of famine. Don't be insensitive and greedy as Nabal, but compassionate and generous as Joseph.

The old epitaph teaches a biblical truth.

What we spent, we had.
What we saved, we lost.
What we gave, we have.

But not only must the redeemed of the Lord not "withhold corn" from the physically famished when it is within their means to give it; they (we) must not withhold the *Bread of Life* from the spiritually dying who will not only suffer havoc on earth but the torments of Hell without it. A spiritual famine exists for over five billion people. God commands and expects His people to supply their "thirst and hunger," lest they be consumed by sin and His wrath. We have the needed "corn"; how inhumane and selfish not to share it! The fields are white unto harvest (John 4:35), but the labourers are few (Matthew 9:38).

Bottom Line: We must not withhold our "corn" from the poverty-stricken or His "corn" from the spiritually impoverished, lost and damned.

242
Pornography, its danger and devastation
Proverbs 4:25

"Let thine eyes look right on, and let thine eyelids look straight before thee."

"Let" (fix) thine "eyes" (to focus without distraction; "to gaze; to look intently"[1079]) "right on" (straight ahead as you walk the path of the righteous; don't deviate from doing right things) and let thine "eyelids look straight before thee" (Deane and Taswell say, "Let thine eyelids direct thy way before thee;" i.e., do nothing rashly, but everything with premeditation; examine thy conduct and see that it is right'[1080]).

To summarize, fix your eyes to look at right things. Why? Wrong looks are destructive physically and spiritually. Pornography is just such a destroyer. Forty-seven percent of Christians say pornography is a major problem in the home. Ninety-three percent of boys and sixty-two percent of girls see porn before the age of eighteen. A recent study found that fifty percent of teenagers and approximately seventy-five percent of young adults come across pornography at least monthly.[1081] The average age for a child to first view pornography is now eight.[1082] A child with an email address is at great risk to be exposed to pornographic email. Research has revealed that forty-seven percent of school-aged children receive porn spam on a daily basis, and as many as one in five of them open the spam.[1083] Be proactive in protecting yourself (and family) from the seduction of pornography via the Internet by installing a filter (Covenant Eyes) to block its intentional or accidental viewing. Apply Job 31:1 ("I have made a covenant with my eyes" ESV) to the computer screen as a reminder of your vow to God not to look at deviant and perverted material. The viewing of pornography is not innocent but brings serious harm. Adrian Rogers says, "The Devil knows if he can get you to lusting, he can get you to sinning. And if he can get you to sinning, he has you. It is a form of spiritual suicide. 'The wages of sin is death.'"[1084]

What harm is pornography?

It *derails* your walk with God. You cannot serve two masters (Matthew 6:24). In serving pornography, intimacy with God decays, and your walk becomes cold and distant.

It *distorts* God's view of sex. Sex is intended to be shared between a husband and wife. Pornography distorts the mind into believing that any form of sex is acceptable at anytime.

It *devours* peace. Pornography leads to shame and deep guilt that robs one's inner peace and joy.

It *destroys* life. Pornography fuels the heart with such lustful passion that it can lead to acts of violence to satisfy its craving.

It *depreciates* women. Pornography degrades women into sex objects.

It *dupes* you. It deceives you into believing that what once was thought abominable is really acceptable.

It *disrupts* marriage. Pornography leads to an unhealthy expectation regarding sex in marriage. Its pictures, movies and magazines mar normal and healthy marital sexual expectations.

It *damages* one's reputation. Pornography injuries the believer's witness and testimony.

It *depletes* a person's time and energy. Endless hours and energy can be exhausted searching for that "right" picture on the Internet or in magazines. It robs one of time and energy that should be spent in wholesome activities with family and friends.

It *dominates* the mind. Pornography masters the will, taking you prisoner. Pornography will take you further than you want to go. It will keep you longer than you want to stay. It will cost you more than you want to pay. Freedom from the clutches of pornography takes serious action, beginning with a repentant heart unto God.

The Bottom Line: Be careful little eyes (and big ones too) what you see, for that which is seen impacts character, reputation, lifestyle and fellowship with God.

243
Possessions, the dishonestly acquired profit
Proverbs 10:2

"Treasures of wickedness profit nothing: but righteousness delivereth from death."

"Treasures" (material substance of value) of "wickedness" (ill-gotten gain from theft or deceit; Deane and Taswell say "treasures acquired by wrongdoing"[1085]) "profit nothing" (without benefit ultimately): BUT "righteousness" (that which is right, fair and just) "delivereth from death" (Ross says "mortal danger"[1086]; doing right bears the treasure of life abundant and eternal [John 10:10]).

Solomon is saying that treasures obtained from wrongdoing are of no profit to the soul or to one's standing with God. In time, God will strip from him that which is not his rightly. However, in contrast, "That which is honestly got will turn to a good account, for God will bless it."[1087]

The Bottom Line: It's never right to do wrong, regardless of personal loss. That which is acquired dishonestly is never profitable in the long run.

244
Praise, when the righteous commend the wicked
Proverbs 28:4

"They that forsake the law praise the wicked: but such as keep the law contend with them."

They that "forsake" (abandon) the "law" (God's law—"Mosaic law") "praise" (commend; honor) the "wicked" (the ungodly, foolish): BUT such as "keep" (obey) the "law" (God's law) "contend" (struggle with the wicked, combatting their evil ways) with them. To summarize, when the righteous forsake God's standards, straying into sin, they began siding with the wicked, defending and commending their hideous conduct. Kidner correctly states of these, "Without reservation, all is soon relative; and with moral relativity, nothing quite merits attack."[1088]

"Those who love sin naturally 'have pleasure in them that do' it (Romans 1:32). The world loves its own (John 15:19)."[1089] Evildoers speak well of the conduct (violation of God's Word) of evildoers. It just stands to reason that they do; don't expect otherwise. To justify, praise and/or give approval to those who do wickedly (engage in ungodly behavior and push agendas for unbiblical issues) places us in their camp. As hideous a sin as the ungodly backing up the ungodly is, it pales in its sordidness and abomination in comparison to that of a *righteous* man *praising the wicked.* The Christian is not to condone (defend the sinner's sin) the evil lifestyle of the wicked but "contend with it" (fight, battle, oppose). He that complies with "the law" (God's Word) will vehemently be in conflict with them that corrupt it. "Who will rise up for me against the evildoers? or who will stand up for me against the workers of iniquity?" (Psalm 94:16).

The Bottom Line: The godly consistent Christian that walks in compliance to God's Word convicts the wayward sinner of the need of repentance and salvation. "And such as do wickedly against the covenant shall he corrupt by flatteries: but the people that do know their God shall be strong, and do exploits" (Daniel 11:32).

245
Prayer, for a nation
Proverbs 14:34

"Righteousness exalteth a nation: but sin is a reproach to any people."

"Righteousness" (observance of what is just, godly and honorable based upon the sacred Word of God) "exalteth" (makes great) a nation: BUT "sin" (transgression of God's law; acts of injustice and immorality) is a "reproach" (disgrace and shame) to any "people" (the citizens of the nation).

A little girl heard the choir singing "God Is Still on the Throne." She didn't understand it quite correctly and told someone they were singing "God is still on the phone." Humorously but truthfully stated! God is still on the throne awaiting the petitions of His children. He is still the prayer-hearing and prayer-answering God. General George Washington issued a decree on March 6, 1776, calling upon all Americans to engage in a day of prayer and fasting on behalf of the nation: "Set apart...as a day of fasting, prayer and humiliation, to implore the Lord and Giver of all victory to pardon our manifold sins and wickedness, and that it would please Him to bless the Continental Arms with His divine favor and protection—all officers and soldiers are strictly enjoined to pay all due reverence and attention on that day to the sacred duties due to the Lord of hosts for His mercies already received and for those blessings which our holiness and uprightness of life can alone encourage us to hope through His mercy to obtain." Oh, that such a *decree* would be forthcoming from both sides of the political aisle and observed by all people!

Regardless of political association, the righteous are to pray for "all that are in authority; that we may lead a quiet and peaceable life in all godliness and honesty" (1 Timothy 2:2). Franklin Graham offers a pattern prayer for the believer in behalf of America. "Lord, we are thankful for the abundant blessings You have bestowed on America. Our forefathers looked to You as protector, provider and the promise of hope. But we have wandered far from that firm foundation. May we repent for turning our

333

backs on Your faithfulness. We pray that this great nation will be restored by Your forgiveness. From bondage, You grant freedom. Through Your own sacrifice, You offer salvation. From the state of despair, You offer peace. From the bounties of Heaven, You have blessed—not because of our goodness, but by Your grace. You have given us freedom to worship You in spirit and in truth as Your holy Word instructs. May our lives honor You in word and deed. May our nation acknowledge that all good things come from the Father above. Amen."[1090]

Our nation needs a return to God, biblical morality and ethics and the Christian faith before we slip any further down the slippery precipice of degradation and perversion. Such a return must be spurred by heartfelt confession and repentance by those in the White House, church house and our house.

See 2 Chronicles 7:14.

The Bottom Line: Andrew Murray wrote, "The coming revival must begin with a great revival of prayer. It is in the closet, with the door shut, that the sound of abundance of rain will first be heard."[1091]

246
Prayer, for personal renewal
Proverbs 30:8
"Remove far from me vanity and lies."

Often it is needful for the believer to get upon his knees in confession saying, "O Lord, remove far from me "vanity" (all types of sinful acts; inward spiritual hollowness and worthlessness) "and lies" (falsehood, deceit). I am distressed over my emptiness of that which is good and holy and the presence of that which is sinful and defiling. In mercy cleanse all that is impure from within me through Thy precious blood, making me "whiter than snow." With David, I beg, "Create in me a clean heart, O God; and renew a right spirit within me....Restore unto me the joy of thy salvation" (Psalm 51:10, 12). Lord Jesus, keep temptation far, far away from me and deliver me from Satan who desires to destroy both my life and soul. Amen."

The Lord graciously and lovingly awaits such prayer for renewal and/or restoration. He says, "Call unto me, and I will answer thee" (Jeremiah 33:3). And John declares, "If we confess our sins, he is faithful and just to forgive us our sins, and to cleanse us from all unrighteousness" (1 John 1:9). God's compassionate and merciful response will prompt praise and gratitude to His holy name. With David you will declare, "Gracious is the LORD, and righteous; yea, our God is merciful. The LORD preserveth the simple: I was brought low, and he helped me. Return unto thy rest, O my soul; for the LORD hath dealt bountifully with thee. For thou hast delivered my soul from death, mine eyes from tears, and my feet from falling. I will walk before the LORD in the land of the living" (Psalm 116:5–9). "He will not always chide: neither will he keep his anger for ever. He hath not dealt with us after our sins; nor rewarded us according to our iniquities. For as the heaven is high above the earth, so great is his mercy toward them that fear him. As far as the east is from the west, so far hath he removed our transgressions from us. Like as a father pitieth [compassionate] his children, so the LORD pitieth [compassionate] them that fear him" (Psalm 103:9–13).

The Bottom Line: Andrew Murray stated, "A true revival [personal or corporate] means nothing less than a revolution, casting out the spirit of worldliness and selfishness, and making God and His love triumph in the heart and life."[1092]

247
Prayer, it is pleasing unto the Lord
Proverbs 15:8
"The prayer of the upright is his delight."

The "prayer" (communicating with God) of the "upright" (the righteous, just, honorable) is "his" (God's) "delight" (pleases God).

Prayer is conversation with God. Jesus forthrightly issues the must of prayer in saying, "Men ought always to pray, and not to faint" (Luke 18:1). Believers live in an evil, polluted society. The only escape from its toxic fumes which promote spiritual fainting (drifting, backsliding, worldliness) is the intake of "pure air" from the atmosphere of Heaven which occurs in prayer. Prayer is to the believer what an oxygen mask is to those who work in hazardous waste facilities, an absolute essential to survival. Obviously, then, this oxygen mask for believers ought to be worn continuously ("always to pray"). The Apostle Paul similarly states, "Pray without ceasing" (1 Thessalonians 5:17).

Christians should pray scripturally (in accordance with God's Word and will), passionately (earnestly, fervently), specifically (without vagueness), and confidently (not doubting, but fully trusting God to answer). The only posture imperative in prayer is that of the heart. It must ever be kneeling in humility and submission in its approach to the throne room of a thrice holy God. Warren Wiersbe states, "Prayer should be the natural habit of our lives, the 'atmosphere' in which we constantly live."[1093]

Does prayer work? James states, "The earnest prayer of a righteous person has great power and produces wonderful results" (James 5:16 NLT). Sometimes prayer results are seen instantly, while at other times they are delayed. Sometimes we receive exactly that for which we pray, while at other times God provides something far better (though we may not think so at the time). Chuck Swindoll writes of the value of prayer. He said, "To be used of God—is there anything more encouraging, more fulfilling? Perhaps not, but there is something more basic: to meet with God, to linger in His presence, to shut out the noise of the city and, in quietness, give Him the praise He deserves. Before we engage ourselves in His work, let's meet Him in His Word...in prayer...in worship."[1094] The prophet Daniel prayed regularly at set times and in a set place (Daniel 6:10). Make an appointment to meet God in prayer, scheduling the time and place each day. This is your "closet" prayer time. Plan the day around prayer, not prayer around the day.

The Bottom Line: Prayer is to the believer's victory over sin and fellowship with God what oxygen is to our lungs. It is absolutely vital.

248
Prayer, prayers that God will not hear
Proverbs 28:9
"He that turneth away his ear from hearing the law, even his prayer shall be abomination."

He that "turneth away his ear" (Reyburn and Fry say "pay no attention"[1095] to God's Word; intentional spiritual deafness) from hearing the "law" (disobedience to the law of God—its commandments and mandates—is reason God refuses to listen to their praying), even his "prayer shall be abomination" (God will not hear it; his prayers become sin [Psalm 109:7]; counts it disgusting).

God has reached out to the unsaved often without success. He says, "Because I have called, and ye refused; I have stretched out my hand, and no man regarded" (Proverbs 1:24). In rejection of salvation (rightness with God through faith in Jesus Christ), man forfeits the privilege of prayer. The psalmist says, "If I regard iniquity in my heart, the Lord will not hear me" (Psalm 66:18). It is futile for the unrepentant to pray and vain to expect answers for what is prayed. Why? John says it is because "God heareth not sinners" (John 9:31). Don't waste time "praying," mouthing words from an insincere, unregenerate and unrepentant heart, regardless how eloquent, for it is but an abomination in the ears of God. The man that God hears is he that has renounced sin, repented of it and in heartfelt sincerity and faith entered into a personal relationship with His Son, the Lord Jesus Christ. "The LORD is far from the wicked: but he heareth the prayer of the righteous" (Proverbs 15:29).

The Bottom Line: "Now we know that God heareth not sinners: but if any man be a worshipper of God, and doeth his will, him he heareth" (John 9:31).

249
Prayer, the divine pattern
Proverbs 30:8–9

"Remove far from me vanity and lies: give me neither poverty nor riches; feed me with food convenient for me: Lest I be full, and deny thee, and say, Who is the LORD? or lest I be poor, and steal, and take the name of my God in vain."

Remove far from me "vanity and lies" (equivalent to "complete deception"[1096]): give me neither "poverty" (impoverishment, neediness) nor "riches" (abundant wealth); feed me with "food convenient for me" (literally "a set portion of food" [Genesis 47:22];[1097] Henry says "such bread as thou thinkest fit to allow me";[1098] the NLT says, "Give me just enough to satisfy my needs"): LEST I be "full, and deny thee and say, Who is the Lord? or lest I be poor, and steal" (too much prosperity tends to bolster forgetfulness of God[1099] or outright denial of God, as too little provision may compel thievery) and "take the name of my God in vain" (to do violence to God's name; Reyburn and Fry say to "bring into disrepute" or to "disgrace" or "dishonor"[1100]).

That which is requested in Agur's prayer is strikingly similar to several parts of the "Lord's Prayer" (Matthew 6).

First and foremost, it is asked that God remove his sin ("vanity and lies"). Confession and cleansing of sin is always the springboard to effective praying. See Matthew 6:12.

The second aspect of the first request is that not only would God cleanse all his sin but preserve ("remove far from me") him from it (its power, persuasion and presence). See Matthew 6:13. Desire for holiness of heart and life is evidence of genuine salvation. To say with David Brainerd "all I want is to be more holy, more like my dear Lord" is the heartthrob of the saint. He yearns for greater conquest over temptation's snare. He detests any form of darkness (sin) invading the *Light* within him.

John Gill remarks "This is the 'first' request, to be preserved from sin, in general, which is a vain, lying and deceitful thing, promising pleasure, profit, liberty and impunity, which it does not give. Agur desires to have vain thoughts removed out of his mind, vain words from his mouth, and vain actions from his life and conversation, to have his eyes turned from beholding vanity and his feet from walking in it, and his affections taken off from the vain things of the world, the lusts, pleasures, profits and honors of it, as well as to be kept from all errors and false doctrines, which are lies in hypocrisy with which men that lie in wait to deceive would, if it were possible, deceive the very elect. Agur, conscious of his own weakness and proneness to evil, desires the Lord would not lead him into temptation, but deliver him from all evil, doctrinal and practical."[1101]

Next is requested protection from too much ("riches") or too little ("poverty)." Matthew Poole's perspective regarding this request is that it bears reference to the first. He states "[P]overty [is] commonly the occasion and temptation to the sin of lying, and riches [are] the great occasions and enticements to vanity. Thus, as his first petition was against the sins themselves, so this latter is against the occasions of them."[1102] Therefore Agur is saying, "Lord, not only take sin from me, but that which facilitates or enables it (riches that promote independence from God, poverty that promotes thievery for food, the evil friend, lustful appetite, indecent magazine or DVD, alcoholic beverage in the cooler, etc.).

The final petition is that God would make provision for his needs as it but pleased Him ("feed me with food convenient for me"). Thus, "Lord, supply my needs according to Your determined will." Some relate this to the Lord's Prayer (Matthew 6:11); "but the idea is not the same. In the latter, bread for the needs of the coming day is meant; in our passage it is more indefinite, a casting one's self on the Divine love, in readiness to take what that love assigns."[1103] Believers can trust God to give unto them that which is sufficient. Paul argues the case, "And having food and raiment [clothing] let us be therewith content" (1 Timothy 6:8). *With what God is satisfied to give me, I will be satisfied to live.*

The Bottom Line: Pray that God will cleanse your sin, preserve you from sin, and provide only that which He deems necessary (lest too much or too little becomes the means of stumbling).

250
Praying, preventative praying
Proverbs 30:7–9

"Two things have I required of thee; deny me them not before I die: Remove far from me vanity and lies: give me neither poverty nor riches; feed me with food convenient for me: Lest I be full, and deny thee, and say, Who is the LORD? or lest I be poor, and steal, and take the name of my God in vain."

"Two things" (but he prays for three things) I "required" (ask, petition) of "thee" (God); deny me not before I "die" (as long as I live). "Remove" (take away) far from me (1) "vanity and lies" (falsehood; "By 'falsehood' is meant more than a casual lie; it designates deceit and pretense, whether before God as in the Decalogue, Exodus 20:7, or before humans"[1104]; keep me honest); (2) "give me neither poverty nor riches" ("wants a life of balanced material blessings"[1105]); (3) "feed me with food convenient for me" (provide only the food that is sufficient to my well-being): "Lest I be full, and deny thee, and say, Who is the LORD? Or lest I be poor, and steal, and take the name of my God in vain" (the motive for the prayer: "He reasons that if he has too much, he might become independent of God, and if he has too little, he might steal and thus profane God's name"[1106]).

Agur's prayer is an example of *preventative praying* ("keep from me anything and everything that might cause me to dishonor You, my Lord, injure others and cause spiritual shipwreck"). Vance Havner, at age 79, in the sermon "Home Before Dark," said, "Lord, I'd like to get Home before I make some big blunder along the way. I'd like to get Home before dark." In essence, that's what Agur prayed.

Chuck Swindoll remarks, "So few finish well—really well."[1107] It has been for many years that I have prayed, "Lord, take me home before dark." I want to finish well and strong. I certainly don't want to fall out on the last lap. I know that if I'm incautious, I can spoil and damage a lifetime of service and godly reputation in a moment's time. All can.

Paul was finishing the race victoriously. However, to his sorrow, one of his counterparts faltered in the race. Writing of Demas, Paul says, "Demas, in love with this present world, has deserted me and gone to Thessalonica" (2 Timothy 4:10 ESV). Demas anticipated finishing the race well like Paul, his mentor, but the stuff of the present world tripped him up. You and I could wind up as Demas if not careful. With Paul, come what may, let's finish the race well. It's always too soon to quit.

To finish life well requires that we "be strong in the Lord and in His mighty power" (Ephesians 6:10 NIV). How? The Bible scholar Matthew Henry states, "We have no sufficient strength of our own. Our natural courage is as perfect cowardice and our natural strength as perfect weakness, but all our sufficiency is of God. In His strength we must go forth and go on."[1108] Henry, in that one sentence, summarizes the single most important thing necessary for us to finish the race of life strong and well. It is a constant awareness of our utter spiritual weakness in battling Satan, and utmost reliance upon Jesus Christ for strength and mighty power. "In His strength we must go forth and go on."[1109] "Greater is he that is in you, than he that is in the world" (1 John 4:4).

The Bottom Line: Take me home, Lord, prior to any action of mine that will bring reproach unto Thy glorious name. Engage in *preventative praying*. 'O Lord enlarge my steps under me, that my feet do not slip' (Psalm 18:36). Strive for God's "Hall of Fame" so that you will stay out of man's "Hall of Shame."

251
Premature Judgment, jumping to conclusions too quickly
Proverbs 18:13

"He that answereth a matter before he heareth it, it is folly and shame unto him."

He that "answereth a matter" (replies to or about something) before he "heareth it" (prior to hearing the whole case or whole story; interrupting someone who is speaking, not allowing them to finish before you speak), it is "folly" (foolishness) and "shame" (disgraceful) unto him. Warren Wiersbe summarizes, "Too often we are slow to hear—we never really listen to the whole matter patiently—and swift to speak; and this gets us into trouble. A godly person will study to answer, but a fool will open his mouth and pour out foolishness (Proverbs 15:28)."[1110] See James 1:19.

Solomon condemns prejudging a matter prior to the hearing from all involved. Wiersbe reminds us that Potiphar failed to hear Joseph's side of the story and imprisoned him as a result (Genesis 39:19–20). Likewise, Jesus and the apostles were cut short on telling their whole story, and verdicts were rendered based only on their accusers' testimony.[1111] Ziba, Mephibosheth's servant, told David that Mephibosheth was in Jerusalem reclaiming the kingdom of his grandfather, Saul (2 Samuel 16:1–4). David jumped to wrong conclusions out of failure to hear Mephibosheth's side of the story (2 Samuel 19:24–30).[1112] When both sides were presented, David learned Ziba had lied.

How applicable to parents and children is this teaching! A secular proverb comes to mind: "No matter how thin you slice the bologna, there are always two sides." Hear both sides prior to casting judgment and punishment. Solomon certainly was wise to abide by this principle in ruling the nation of Israel. An example of the principle being applied is in his dealing with the two harlots who both claimed custodial rights of the same child (1 Kings 3:16–28).

Matthew Henry advises, "It is folly for a man to go about to speak to a thing which he does not understand or to pass sentence upon a matter which he is not truly and fully informed of and has not patience to make a strict inquiry into; and, if it be folly, it is and will be shame."[1113]

The Bottom Line: Partial truth or half the story results in drawing the wrong conclusion. Don't make hasty judgments, for insufficient knowledge often leads to decisions that inflict punishment upon the wrong person. Get all the facts before you act.

252
Pride, its effect
Proverbs 16:18

"Pride goeth before destruction, and an haughty spirit before a fall."

"Before destruction the heart of man is haughty, and before honour is humility" (Proverbs 18:12).

"Pride" (arrogance, self-conceited, egoistical) "goes before" (precedes) a "fall" (to stumble on the "face"; ruin). See Proverbs 18:12.

The apostle Paul said, "Give preference to one another in honor" (Rom.12:10 NASB) and '[Do] not think of *yourself* more highly than *you* ought to think' (Romans 12:3). Pride is doing the exact opposite. It is an ugly sin that goes neither unnoticed nor unpunished by God. It is counted an abomination unto the Lord (Proverbs 16:5). McKane says, "The nose is in the heavens, the seat is in the mire" (Arabic proverb).[1114]

Its nature

Pride is lofty with flattering thoughts of oneself often based upon education, intellect, talent, ability, appearance and/or possession. It is repulsive and detestable to man. Pride is fueled by debasing others to make self look better and gain more admirers.

Its consequence

The Bible states pride separates us from God, causes the disdain of others, harms others and leads to ruin. Charles Caleb Colton says, "Pride, like the magnet, constantly points to one object—self; but, unlike the magnet, it has no attractive pole, but at all points repels."[1115]

Its detection

Pride hides itself in man and is not easily detectable except as it appears in others. An indication that a man is haughty and arrogant is boastful talk, elevation of self above others (better-than-you attitude) and avoidance by man (most people can't stand to be around an arrogant person).

Insights on pride from others

C. H. Spurgeon said, "None are more unjust in their judgments of others than those who have a high opinion of themselves. He who is greedy of applause never gives a cheer for a rival."[1116]

William Law states, "You can have no greater sign of confirmed pride than when you think you are humble enough."[1117]

Watchman Nee remarks, "Often Satan injects pride into the believer's spirit, evoking in him an attitude of self-importance and of self-conceit. He causes him to esteem himself a very outstanding person, one who is indispensable in God's work. Pride springs from desire. Man aspires to obtain a place for himself that he may feel honored before men. He loves to hear praising voices and considers them just and true. He also attempts to elevate himself in his work, whether in preaching or in writing, for his secret self-motive goads him on. In a word, this one has not yet died to his desire of vainglory. He is still seeking what he desires and what can inflate him."[1118]

Augustine said, "It was pride that changed angels into devils."

John W. Stott declared, "Pride is your greatest enemy; humility is your greatest friend."[1119]

C. S. Lewis remarks, "According to Christian teachers, the essential vice, the utmost evil, is pride. Unchastity, anger, greed, drunkenness, and all that, are mere flea bites in comparison; it was through pride that the Devil became the Devil. Pride leads to every other vice. It is the complete anti-God state of mind."[1120]

A kite flying high in the sky moved as stately as a person of royalty. In looking down with contempt on that which was below, it said, "What a superior being I am now! Who has ever ascended so high as I have? What a poor groveling set of beings are all those beneath me! I despise them." And then the kite shook its head in sneers, wagged its tail, moving onward and upward, thinking everything must make way for it. Then suddenly the string broke, bringing the kite down with greater speed than that by which it had ascended. It was badly hurt in the fall.[1121] With pride, what goes up, always comes down, and what is inflated will always be deflated.

The Bottom Line: It is said, "Humility is not thinking less of yourself; it's just thinking of yourself less." That's a healthy dose of medicine for all. "Let another man praise thee, and not thine own mouth; a stranger, and not thine own lips" (Proverbs 27:2). Matthew Henry advises, "Men cannot punish pride, but either admire it or fear it; and therefore God will take the punishing of it into His own hands. Let him alone to deal with proud men."[1122]

253
Prodigals, Jesus will take you back
Proverbs 29:3

"Whoso loveth wisdom rejoiceth his father: but he that keepeth company with harlots spendeth his substance."

"But as soon as this thy son was come, which hath devoured thy living with harlots, thou hast killed for him the fatted calf" (Luke 15:30).

Whoso "loveth" (loves, embraces) "wisdom" (knowledge and understanding [discernment] from the Lord that enables man to please the Lord in all that he does and live life successfully) "rejoiceth" (makes glad, happy) his father: BUT he that "keepeth" (maintains) "company" with (associates with; befriends; "hangs out with") "harlots" (prostitutes) "spendeth" (wastes, squanders) his "substance" (wealth, as did the prodigal in the far country; brings untold grief to his father).

The Proverb is the Old Testament miniature version of the story of the prodigal son (Luke 15:11–32).[1123] The prodigal is the person who abandons God for worldly substance and its pleasure (sex, alcohol, drugs, gambling). Many that depart to the "far country" of wantonness never return to the Father's house, despite losing their "substance" (potential, possessions, self-respect, health, dignity). Perhaps failure to return is based on others; evil companions hold them back. Perhaps it's the feeling of inability; a change in lifestyle is thought impossible. Perhaps it's the fear of rejection by the Father; sins are too hideous to be forgiven by a righteous and holy God. Perhaps it's the inability to repent (to actually change the mind) though the person hungers to do so *deep down*. To radically say "I will arise and go to my father, and will say unto him, Father, I have sinned against heaven, and before thee" (Luke 15:18) seems too difficult, therefore it is continually delayed. He that stays in the pigpen of the world will never know the Father's love, compassion, forgiveness and deliverance. He forever will waste his life away only to be shut out of the Father's house for all eternity.

But in contrast, as with the prodigal son of Luke 15, some do return to the Father. Undoubtedly, they wrestled with the excuses for not returning that were mentioned above, only to discover they were futile, sown in their mind by Satan, who desired them to remain in the far country. These prodigals courageously moved toward God, only to find Him waiting all the time with arms outstretched for their return. He ran to meet them, embraced them, forgave them, and delivered them (Luke 15:20–24; John 8:36). Now instead of living ill-spent and meaningless lives, life is being lived to the fullest potential and satisfaction. The principle of the Proverb rings true with every prodigal who returns to the Lord. Though their life was devoured with "harlots" (or any other vice), causing their Father grave sorrow, now in their return they cause Him to rejoice and be glad. "Bring hither the fatted calf, and kill it; and let us eat, and be merry: for this my son was dead, and is alive again; he was lost, and is found. And they began to be merry" (Luke 15:23–24). "Likewise, I say unto you, there is joy in the presence of the angels of God over one sinner that repenteth" (Luke 15:10).

C. H. Spurgeon observes, "Not joy among the angels, as some read it, though no doubt that is a truth, but, 'joy in the presence of the angels of God.' And what can that mean but that God Himself rejoices, and rejoices so that angels perceive it! And no doubt they then join in the delight! But all this points out that it is the lost one that is the great object of consideration, that out of any congregation where the Gospel is preached, it is *the lost one who is the most important person in the whole place!*"[1124] May preacher and people never forget that!

Though all may, not many return from the far country of sin. We read that despite the many to whom the prodigal "joined himself" in that distant land of sin and sorrow, *only one chose to return* "home" to the Father. "*And he arose*, and came to his father" (Luke 15:20). Pray and labor for the multitudes yet in the "far country" to return.

The Bottom Line: God will always take the prodigal back upon his repentance, despite the reasons friends or oneself may give why He shouldn't and wouldn't.

254
Promises, the sin of unkept promises
Proverbs 25:14

"Whoso boasteth himself of a false gift is like clouds and wind without rain."

Whoso "boasteth" (brags about a gift he is going to give) himself of a "false gift" (a gift he has no intention of giving) is like "clouds and winds without rain" (such promised gifts are disappointing and deceitful like the arrival of clouds and winds but without rain[1125]).

Empty promises are disappointing to the promised and injurious to the reputation and trustworthiness of the promiser. Broken promises have resulted in broken friendships and partnerships, and in divorce. Always keep your word; do all that is promised (don't promise what you cannot deliver), when promised, and how promised. Norman Vincent Peale humorously said, "Promises are like crying babies in a theater; they should be carried out at once."[1126] Delay in performing a promise increases the likelihood of its abandonment.

The woods are lovely, dark and deep,
But I have promises to keep
and miles to go before I sleep.[1127] ~ Robert Frost

C. S. Lewis advised, "Always prefer the plain, direct word to the long, vague one. Don't implement promises, but keep them."[1128] The Proverb may have stimulated your memory to recall a forgotten promise, like that of the Chief Butler regarding Joseph (Genesis 40:14–15; 23). In Genesis 41:9 the Butler says to Pharaoh, "I do remember my faults this day." In remembering the forgotten promise, he makes good on it (Genesis 41:12–13). Inasmuch as it is reasonable and possible, make good on broken promises (including the ones made to God); where it is not, ask the forgiveness of God and make amends with the offended.

The Bottom Line: My dad taught me as a child that a man's word or handshake was his "bond," that to promise or agree to do something meant it was as good as done. That, in essence, summarizes the principle of the proverb.

255
Providence, the Lord's providential administration of life
Proverbs 10:29
"The way of the LORD is strength to the upright."

The "way of the LORD" (His "providential administration of life"[1129] and commandments, standards by which man is to order his conduct) is "strength" (a fortress; a strong tower; a mighty refuge [Psalm 31:2, 4; Nahum 1:7]) to the "upright" (integrity; righteous; Christian).

It is possible to mistake a season of darkness (barrenness, closed doors, God seems distant, all seems futile, etc.) as the judgment of God. Such a misunderstanding yields grave heartache and anguish of soul.

The prophet Isaiah declared, "Who is among you that feareth the LORD, that obeyeth the voice of his servant, that walketh in darkness, and hath no light? let him trust in the name of the LORD, and stay upon his God" (Isaiah 50:10). Isaiah observes that it is possible for believers who both fear and obey the Lord to experience times when darkness so envelopes their lives that they don't know what to do. The darkness referred to is not due to sin but is providential, an act of God. It is a darkness that encompasses the mind, not the heart.

Matthew Henry explains, "It is no new thing for the children and heirs of light sometimes to walk in darkness and for a time not to have any glimpse or gleam of light. This is not meant so much of the comforts of this life (those that fear God, when they have ever so great an abundance of them, do not walk in them as their light) as of their spiritual comforts, which relate to their souls. They walk in darkness when their evidences for Heaven are clouded, their joy in God is interrupted, the testimony of the Spirit is suspended, and the light of God's countenance is eclipsed."[1130]

Such truth surprises us. One would but think that he who walks in stride with the Lord, obeys the word of His servants, and fears the Lord would ever walk in the light of joy and laughter. But not so according to the divine Book. Job testifies of this. Why is this so? It certainly is not due to sinful conduct (though there is a "darkness of sin").

God allows the believer to experience "darkness" for manifold reasons, including to strengthen, increase faith (utter dependence upon Him); to show forth His ability to sustain when all props are taken away; "to let us see from whence spiritual comforts and refreshings come: that God alone has the keys of that cupboard";[1131] to prize the "light" God gives more highly when it returns; to train the believer to trust Him in the dark as in the light; to humble; to prompt earnest and frequent praying;[1132] to prepare the believer for a new assignment or adversity that will appear when the light returns; to help the believer understand that the Christian walk is one of faith, not feelings, things unseen, not seen.

What are you to do in the darkness? Pardington says, "The first thing to do is do nothing. This is hard for poor human nature to do. In the West there is a saying that runs thus: 'When you're rattled, don't rush'; in other words, 'When you don't know what to do, don't do it.' When you run into a spiritual fog bank, don't tear ahead; slow down the machinery of your life. If necessary, anchor your bark or let it swing at its moorings."[1133] In not knowing what to do, haste to do something is hazardous. It's best to wait until the light breaks through the overshadowing clouds, giving clarity of direction. Don't try to eliminate the darkness by building your own "fires."[1134]

The Bottom Line: If divine providence has placed you in the "darkness," don't fight to regain the "light." Once the purpose is accomplished for the darkness, the light will spring forth instantaneously. Until that moment arrives, be content in your blindness to walk hand in hand with God, allowing Him to control every step taken. He can do anything and everything but fail you. See Proverbs 10:25.

256
Prudence, taking precautions
Proverbs 22:3

"A prudent man foreseeth the evil, and hideth himself: but the simple pass on, and are punished."

A "prudent man" (wise, sensible, cautious) "foreseeth" (anticipates danger, therefore knows when, where and from whom it comes) the "evil" (danger), and "hideth" (take preventative measures not to be injured by it[1135]) himself: BUT the "simple" (the insensible, foolish, unwise) "pass on" (they walk headlong into the trouble, not foreseeing it[1136]), and are "punished" (suffer the consequences; "pays the fiddler").

Prudence dictates precautionary measures with regard to the future. He that has a *que sera, sera* attitude (whatever will be, will be) lives blindly (fails to see potential danger and take steps to avert it) and will suffer the consequences. The wise man will avail himself of health and life insurance, a last will and testament, a living will, estate planning, custodial care of children document (in the event of the death of both parents), and retirement planning (savings). Expert and godly advice is readily available in each of these matters.

Spiritually, the prudent foresees the coming judgment of God and hides himself from it in the Refuge of Jesus Christ. See Romans 10:9–13; Psalm 91:2.

The Bottom Line: Benjamin Franklin said, "By failing to prepare, you are preparing to fail."

257
Punishment, the inescapable consequence of sin
Proverbs 13:21
"Evil pursueth sinners: but to the righteous good shall be repayed."

"The righteousness of the upright shall deliver them: but transgressors shall be taken in their own naughtiness" (Proverbs 11:6).

"Evil" (trouble, misfortune, calamity; Deane and Taswell say includes "stings of conscience, remorse"[1137]) "pursueth" (like a "bloodhound" in chase of a criminal; is on their trail[1138]; follows them) "sinners" (the immoral and all who violate God's law): BUT to the "righteous" (the upright) "good" (prosperity, "good" conscience, happiness[1139]) shall be "repayed" (rewarded).

Intertwined throughout Proverbs is the principle of divine judgment upon sin presently and eternally. Regardless of sin's ("evil") secrecy, security, sanction or size ("red like crimson or a milder hue"), its consequences are inescapable ("pursueth"). Misfortune financially, sickness physically, and most assuredly shipwreck spiritually (broken fellowship with God; loss of reputation and character; stinging conscience of guilt) pursue (chases after) the sinner (one who "misses the mark") now and in eternal damnation later.

David declared, "Upon the wicked he [God] shall rain snares, fire and brimstone, and an horrible tempest: this shall be the portion of their [sinners'] cup" (Psalm 11:6). Matthew Henry remarks, "Unavoidable the destruction of sinners is; the wrath of God pursues them, and all the terrors of that wrath. Evil pursues them closely wherever they go. Whom God pursues He is sure to overtake. They may prosper for a while and grow very secure, but their damnation slumbers not, though they do."[1140] The punishment upon the Amalekites for their ill treatment of the Israelites during the wilderness journey was delayed but arrived many years later (1 Samuel 15:3–7). Achan's sin pursued and captured him (Joshua 7:20–26). The sin of Jezebel (the wickedest woman in the Bible) pursued and punished her (2 Kings 9:30–37), as did her husband's (1 Kings 21:18–19). Deane and Taswell say, "As the shadow attends the substance, so guilt is attached to sin and brings with it punishment."[1141]

In contrast, only "good" (happiness; divine blessing) at God's hand pursues the righteous. As the sinner will be punished for the bad done, the righteous will be rewarded for their good in this life and in the life which is yet to come. "Be sure your sin will find you out" (Numbers 32:23) sooner or later if it be not cleansed and thus covered by the precious blood of the Lord Jesus Christ (1 John 1:7). "He that covereth his sins shall not prosper: but whoso confesseth and forsaketh them shall have mercy" (Proverbs 28:13).

The Bottom Line: Don't think the sinner gets by with sin despite all that might indicate otherwise. The shadow of his sin looms heavy about him following hard. It is inescapable. Destruction presently and damnation later await.

258
Purging, sin in the church
Proverbs 20:26

"A wise king scattereth the wicked, and bringeth the wheel over them."

"That he might present it to himself a glorious church, not having spot, or wrinkle, or any such thing; but that it should be holy and without blemish" (Ephesians 5:27).

A "wise" (righteous, sensible) king "scattereth" (winnows; sifts; refers to the threshing wheel used for breaking grain away from the stalks which is followed by the wind blowing or winnowing the straw and chaff from the good grain[1142]) the "wicked" (the ungodly; sifts the good from the bad), and bringeth the "wheel over them" (the threshing wheel that assists in the sifting, winnowing out of the bad; possibly alludes to "the 'harsh' punishment"[1143] the wicked will receive at the judgment).

Leaders, pastoral or governmental, must be willing to *winnow* out the unrighteous, especially those in governing roles, for the good of the people. Simply to turn a blind eye to the "godly" wicked is not only cowardice but condonement of their corrupt lifestyle and theology. The New Testament substantiates this governing principle of leadership in saying, "For the time is come that judgment must begin at the house of God: and if it first begin at us, what shall the end be of them that obey not the gospel of God?" (1 Peter 4:17).

Believers are to be accountable for other followers of Christ, correcting them when they err. Scripture commands, "My brothers, if any of you should wander away from the truth and another should turn him back on to the right path, then the latter may be sure that in turning a man back from his wandering course he has rescued a soul from death, and his loving action will 'cover a multitude of sins'" (James 5:19–20 Phillips). Believers who will not repent and be restored to fellowship, insisting on continuation in their wanton lifestyle, are to be avoided (1 Corinthians 5:11–13).

Not even the wisest of kings (pastors, presidents, governors, mayors) are able to detect all that are corrupt. Some (tares) resemble wheat so closely that Jesus says let them remain until the judgment at the end of the age (Matthew 13:28–30). The prophet Malachi prophesied of a supernatural purge coming to God's house. "The Lord, whom ye seek, shall suddenly come to his temple,…But who may abide the day of his coming? and who shall stand when he appeareth? for he is like a refiner's fire, and like fullers' soap: And he shall sit as a refiner and purifier of silver: and he shall purify the sons of Levi, and purge them as gold and silver, that they may offer unto the LORD an offering in righteousness" (Malachi 3:1–3). Upon Christ's coming, He will purify the church from the inside out, holding responsible the leaders and people who condoned iniquity in its ranks.

The Bottom Line: Shepherds especially are responsible for the sanctity of the church. Lend support to their biblical effort to keep the church "without spot or wrinkle." Upon the church's compromise of conviction, standard and theology, she writes her on obituary.

259
Purity, its personal interrogation and negative answer
Proverbs 20:9

"Who can say, I have made my heart clean, I am pure from my sin?"

Who can say, I have "kept" (refrained from wrongdoing) my "heart" "pure" (clean; see explanation below); I am "clean" (pure) and "without sin" (without any trace of defilement of wrongdoing—transgression of God's law).

Solomon testifies to man's defilement, "There is no man that sinneth not" (1 Kings 8:46), and, "For there is not a just man upon earth, that doeth good, and sinneth not" (Ecclesiastes 7:20). The prophet Jeremiah testifies, "The heart is deceitful above all things, and it is desperately sick: who can know it?" (Jeremiah 17:9 ERV). And John warns, "If we say that we have no sin, we deceive ourselves, and the truth is not in us" (1 John 1:8).

But man, though warned of sin's continual presence, is yet prone to be deceived; undetected or unaware (presumptuous—Psalm 19:13) sins are overlooked by a "deceived" or "haughty" heart. Sinful habits dull the conscience, preventing their recognition. Alexander Maclaren cautions, "According to the old saying, the man that began by carrying a calf can carry an ox at the end and feel no burden. What we are accustomed to do, we scarcely ever recognize to be wrong, and it is these things which pass because they are habitual that do more to wreck lives than occasional outbursts of far worse evils, according to the world's estimate of them. Habit dulls the eyes."[1144]

In New Testament times, the Greeks used "purity" to refer to something physically clean, like a cloth free of dirt. To them, something was pure when it was free from additives, things that would hinder it from being used for its designed purpose. A substance that was contaminated could be free to do its intended work once the interference was removed. For example, a surgical cloth was pure when separated from deadly bacteria.

You are pure in heart when the sinful additives are removed, allowing life to be lived as God designed it to be lived. At the core of the meaning of heart purity is right motives in doing right, for wrong motives equally contaminate the heart. Accordingly, Matthew 5:8 may be rendered, 'Blessed is the man whose conduct and motive in thought and deed is unmixed with the contaminating agents of this world, for he shall see God.'

The Apostle Paul put it in this fashion: "But among you there must *not be even a hint* of sexual immorality, or of any kind of impurity, or of greed, because these are improper for God's holy people" (Ephesians 5:3 NIV, italics added). It is impossible to see God through heart lenses that are contaminated with sin. The promise to the pure in heart is that "they shall see God" (Matthew 5:8). A person sees only what he is able to see.

Two men view paintings in a famous art museum. One is an art connoisseur; the other is not. The art connoisseur sees priceless art, while the other fails to see any worth in the same paintings. One can see only what he *can* see. The unclean heart cannot clearly see God, know God, nor serve God successfully. In contrast, the clean heart presently sees God clearly and will have no trouble recognizing Him upon His return. The corruption of sin is removed from the heart by personal examination (Psalm 139:23–24) and repentance (1 John 1:9). Gold is pure when it has been separated by the refiner's fire from all foreign matter. The same is true for the heart.

The Bottom Line: No man can say that he is truly clean and without sin (Proverbs 20:9), which underscores the need for continual confession and cleansing. Maintain the attitude and heart of the Puritan who prayed, "My enemy is within the citadel. Come with almighty power and cast him out, pierce him to death, and abolish in me every particle of carnal life this day."[1145]

260
Reasoning, human reasoning is futile, leading to ruin
Proverbs 19:2

"Also, that the soul be without knowledge, it is not good; and he that hasteth with his feet sinneth."

The man ("soul") without "knowledge" (biblical insight as to how to live rightly) experiences ruin ("it is not good"); AND he that "hasteth" (hurriedness; fails to take time to think, ponder before acting) with his "feet" (always running, never slowing down to consider his ways; Kidner says, "How negative is the achievement of the man who wants tangible and quick rewards—he will miss the way"[1146]) "sinneth" (results in wrongdoing; missing the way).

Why? For philosophical reasoning, human intelligence and fleshly rationale are inapt, unfit guides to man's best in this life and that which is to come. Jeremiah testified of this truth, "O LORD, I know that the way of man is not in himself: it is not in man that walketh to direct his steps" (Jeremiah 10:23). Paul gives caution about the reliance upon human reasoning and philosophy. "Don't let anyone capture you with empty philosophies and high-sounding nonsense that come from human thinking and from the spiritual powers of this world, rather than from Christ" (Colossians 2:8 NLT). Emphatically Paul states that man's source of knowledge (wisdom) for life flows from Jesus Christ (relationship with and adherence to His Word).

Simeon summarizes, "Being ignorant of Christ, he cannot see what fullness there is in Him of wisdom and righteousness, and sanctification and redemption; or what necessity there is for the sinner to receive supplies from it by the daily exercises of faith and prayer. In a word, from a man ignorant of the Gospel, everything that constitutes vital godliness is concealed. He has no higher principle than that of fear, no better standard than that of heathen morals, no nobler end than that of saving his own soul."[1147]

Spiritual ignorance (absence of divine knowledge) opens the door to sin without restraint, condemnation without remedy (salvation), calamity without comfort, uncertainty without certainty, blindness without sight, and death without hope. "Fools die for want of wisdom" (Proverbs 10:21). "My people are destroyed for lack of knowledge: because thou hast rejected knowledge" (Hosea 4:6). "It is a people of no understanding: therefore he that made them will not have mercy on them, and he that formed them will shew them no favour" (Isaiah 27:11). The path of the ungodly (personal choice) ends in Hell. In the day of the Lord, "Jesus shall be revealed from heaven with his mighty angels, In flaming fire taking vengeance on them that know not God" (1 Thessalonians 1:7–8).

The ignorant are shrouded in a cloak of eternal darkness and blackness, blinded by Satan to the truth, groping through life without hope, for they are without God. They are of all people most miserable and are to be pitied (compassionate sympathy). The man who runs (hastily, speedily, rashly and thoughtlessly) on without knowledge errs in decisions that bring harm, distress and ruin. "Haste is opposed to knowledge, because the latter involves prudence and circumspection, while the former blunders on hurriedly, not seeing whither actions lead."[1148] H. A. Ironside remarks that the man bent on his own way, without biblical learning of the will of God, adds sin to sin.[1149]

The Bottom Line: Academic, experiential or philosophical knowledge bears but little benefit in contrast to biblical knowledge and godly wisdom that is solely man's infallible guide to abundant and eternal life. Escape from reason to reliance upon God's revelation (biblical truth and instruction and a personal relationship with Jesus Christ) to shape and govern life happily, meaningfully and successfully.

261
Rebellion, when teenagers rebel against parents
Proverbs 17:21
"He that begetteth a fool doeth it to his sorrow: and the father of a fool hath no joy."

"He" (father, but "parents" implicated) that "begetteth" (gives birth to) a "fool" (the unwise, ungodly and unruly) doeth it to his "sorrow" (grief, heartache): AND the father of a fool hath "no joy" (absence of gladness). Alexander Maclaren says, "The 'fool,' the name which, in Proverbs, is shorthand for mental stupidity, moral obstinacy, and dogged godlessness—a foul compound, but one which is realized oftener than we think."[1150]

The Proverb principle certainly was borne out with regard to Absalom who inflicted much trouble and heartache to his father, David. But nonetheless David loved him. Upon hearing of Absalom's death, David "broke into tears, and went up to his room over the gate, crying as he went. 'O my son Absalom, my son, my son Absalom. If only I could have died for you! O Absalom, my son, my son'" (1 Samuel 18:33 TLB).

A parent's love is so knitted and intertwined with their children that their joy and peace is disturbed by their foolish wicked lifestyle. Indeed, "the father of a fool hath no joy." David didn't. No parent of a troublesome child will. Children need to understand that as a baby they step on their parents' toes but in youth they step on their hearts upon erring from the path of the righteous.

The prodigal's father in Luke 15 loved his son enough to embrace him despite a rebellious lifestyle, keeping the door open for his return. Upon the boy's return, he granted mercy, forgiveness and complete restoration. In the event your child becomes rebellious, keep in mind this story and its happy ending. Never give up on your child's return, as exemplified by this father! The stress, heartache and frustration experienced over a self-willed, rebellious child and the grace exhibited will be more than worth it when you come out on the other side victoriously (and you will). Keep praying for the child's return to the Lord. Unload the heartache and pain they bring at Jesus' feet, for He will enable you to bear it.

The Bottom Line: "Don't panic; stay on your child's team," states Dr. James Dobson, "even when it appears to be a losing team; and give the whole process time to work itself out."[1151]

262
Refuge, the believer's strong tower in times of trouble
Proverbs 18:10–11
"The name of the LORD is a strong tower: the righteous runneth into it, and is safe. The rich man's wealth is his strong city, and as an high wall in his own conceit."

The "name of the LORD" (the name of the Lord reveals His character, nature, attributes) is a "strong tower" ("a high wall";[1152] place of safety in the storms of life): the "righteous" (upright; Christian) "runneth into it" (flees into it; escapes from the pursuit of the storm or trouble), and is "safe" (guarded, protected from harm).

God's name is "like a strong tower" that keeps us safe and secure from the enemy (Satan). A tower in biblical days provided protection for people in times of different types of emergencies. For example, when an enemy was about to attack, they would run into this strong tower and be kept safe. God's name is like that strong tower for us. In times of emergencies (all sorts of trouble or crisis or problems), call on God's name; and He will grant protection. This tower is so deep that no bomb can undermine it, so thick that no missile can penetrate it, so high that no ladder can scale it or arrow of Hell reach it (Psalm 27:5).

I have four names. My children call me "Dad"; grandchildren call me "Papa"; family members call me "Brother," and my given name is "Frank." Each of these names describes something about me and who I really am. "Dad" means I am a father; "Papa" means I am a grandfather; "Brother" means I have a brother and sister; and "Frank" means "mighty warrior." (I am still working on this one.) Although I have four names, I am still one person, and I answer to any of them.

God has many names, and each one tells us what He is like so we can love and follow Him better. Though He has a lot of names, He is still just one God.

In times of need, run into the Strong Tower of *Jehovah-Jireh,* who will provide.

In times of hurt or sickness, run into the Strong Tower of *Jehovah-Rapha,* who will heal.

In times of temptation or attack by Satan, run into the Strong Tower of *Jehovah-Nissi,* who will deliver.

In times of trouble, unrest or fear, run into the Strong Tower of *Jehovah-Shalom,* who will give peace.

In times of uncertainty about what to do or in need of comfort, run into the Strong Tower of *Jehovah-Raah,* who shepherds His sheep.

In times of wrongdoing, run into the Strong Tower of *Jehovah-Macoddeshem,* who makes holy.

In the time that you realize you need to be saved, run into the Strong Tower of *Jehovah-sidknue,* who through His Son, Jesus Christ, saves.

In times of doubt about the future and what is happening in your life, run into the Strong Tower of *El-El-Yon,* who is in total control.

"The rich man's wealth is his strong city, and as an high wall in his own conceit" (Proverbs 18:11). In contrast to the righteous, the rich man's fortress or "strong city" is his money ("all external and material goods"[1153]) and high wall of security is his own "conceit" (imaginations that his money can protect him[1154]). Foolishly he believes that which is possessed is a sure defense against life's storms and God's judgments. Blinded, he cannot see that the self-made castle is merely built with "cardboard" upon the sand that will but crumble upon the first shot. But, as Maclaren says, man has a hard time having them not to trust in them.[1155] He says, "I would urge you, young men, especially to lay this to heart—that of all delusions that can beset you in your course, none will work more disastrously than the notion that the *summum bonum*, the shield and stay of a man, is the 'abundance of the things that he possesses.'"[1156]

The Bottom Line: God's name (a personal relationship with Jesus Christ) is man's only "strong tower" (high wall) of protection. Man's attempt to erect castles of refuge is futile, regardless of the material used in their construction.

263
Repentance, its opportunity is not forever
Proverbs 1:28
"Then shall they call upon me, but I will not answer; they shall seek me early, but they shall not find me."

Then shall "they" (the foolish referenced in Proverbs 1:22) "call upon me" (only after the trouble, calamity and anguish occur, they call out to Wisdom to help, picturing suffering in Hell), but I will not "answer" (pay no attention to their cry for help); they shall "seek me early" (earnestly search for Wisdom), but they shall not "find me" (Wisdom hides its presence from them; Buzzell says, "When a fool who has earlier rejected wisdom attempts to start over and follow the wise path, his efforts are of no avail. Wisdom rejected cannot be reclaimed after she has withdrawn her invitation"[1157]). There comes a point at which it's too late to attain wisdom—in the eternal abode of Hell. See Proverbs 29:1.

The book of Proverbs teaches that it is God's desire that "the simple" return to Him (with love, duty, obedience, allegiance) in godly repentance that they might know salvation and restoration instead of damnation and destruction. That sounds a whole lot like what Peter stated in 2 Peter 3:9: "The Lord is not slack concerning his promise, as some men count slackness; but is longsuffering to us-ward, not willing that any should perish, but that all should come to repentance." It is not God's desire that any man live apart from Him presently or in eternity. Man's obstinacy against Holy God in embracing the Gospel and His Son, Jesus Christ, as Lord and Savior brings calamity presently and torment in Hell hereafter. The sinner, in deepest agony, fear and misery, will pray unto the Lord for deliverance, but He "will not answer," for their prayers are void of genuine confession and repentance.

"For the kind of sorrow God wants us to experience leads us away from sin and results in salvation. There's no regret for that kind of sorrow. But worldly sorrow, which lacks repentance, results in spiritual death" (2 Corinthians 7:10 NLT). Neither will the sinner's prayer in Hell be answered. The rich man in Hell prayed, but it was in vain (Luke 16:27–28). George Lawson correctly states, "Sinners miserably delude their own souls by proposing to live in the indulgence of their sins, and die in the exercise of repentance. True repentance is never too late, but late repentance is seldom true."[1158]

Matthew Henry explains, "Now God is ready to hear their prayers and to meet them with mercy, if they would but seek to Him for it; but then the door will be shut, and they shall cry in vain: 'Then shall they call upon me when it is too late, Lord, Lord, open to us. They would then gladly be beholden to that mercy which now they reject and make light of; but I will not answer, because, when I called, they would not answer'; all the answer then will be, 'Depart from me, I know you not.'"[1159]

The Bottom Line: God always hears the prayer of the genuine repentant. Approach God in an attitude of reverence, contrition and receptivity to His compassionate offer of salvation (forgiveness, justification) through His Son, Jesus Christ, and you will not be denied. Time is quickly elapsing to be reconciled to God. Do it today lest you wait until it's too late.

264
Reproof, biblical reprimand
Proverbs 28:23

"He that rebuketh a man afterwards shall find more favour than he that flattereth with the tongue."

He that "rebuketh" (reprimand, criticize) a man "afterwards" (it is only following the rebuke that the person sees it profit and appreciates it[1160]) shall find more "favor" (to find acceptance, approval[1161]) than he that "flattereth with the tongue" (praises him; Ross says, "The flattering tongue may be pleasing for the moment, but it will offer no constructive help like the rebuke"[1162]).

Dietrich Bonhoeffer said, "Reproof is unavoidable. God's Word demands it when a brother falls into open sin. The practice of discipline in the congregation begins in the smallest circles. Where defection from God's Word in doctrine or life imperils the family fellowship and with it the whole congregation, the word of admonition and rebuke must be ventured."[1163] In reproof oft time the right thing is stated in the wrong manner, resulting in spirit wounding either due to ego, anger or ignorance of how it is to be handled. Much heart wounding and its intensity would be lessened if Christians would exact reproof biblically.

Don't jump the gun on reproving someone of a matter which is simply based on assumption, opinion or hearsay. To have your actions misjudged by Christian brothers/sisters and to be on the end of sharp, compassionless and unjust rebuke because of it, is exceedingly painful. Reproof (reprimand) is necessary if the person who erred isn't repentant. Paul gives clear direction as to the method, manner and attitude of reprovers. "Dear brothers and sisters, if another believer is overcome by some sin, you who are godly should gently and humbly help that person back onto the right path" (Galatians 6:1 NLT).

Regrettably much reproof fails to take Paul's words into account, resulting in a wounded heart in the reproved. Paul makes clear that a major objective of reproof is not only to confront a believer's sin but to be restorative to the fallen brother spiritually. This dual objective of reproof can be accomplished only by those "who are godly." Solomon states, "As an earring of gold, and an ornament of fine gold, so is a wise reprover upon an obedient ear" (Proverbs 25:12). Wise reprovers lessen the possibility of wounding hearts, for the reproved are more likely to receive their precepts with a listening ear and wear them as a valued ornament.

How prone Christians are to gossip about a brother's fault and rebuke him publicly! This violates Jesus' teaching when He said, "If your brother sins against you, go and tell him his fault, between you and him alone. If he listens to you, you have gained your brother" (Matthew 18:15 ESV). Hearts are wounded, just as yours would be, when their dirty laundry is hung out on the line for the world to see. *Hearts are mended when they are gently and kindly dealt with in private personally.* If the offense is known only between the two or few of you, that's where it should stay if the person repents.

To reprove a fallen brother in love "afterwards" (emphasis on this word) will be greatly appreciated and honored. Nathan, in reproving King David, later ("afterwards") found his favor. David named a son after him (1 Chronicles 3:5) and allowed him to serve in his court until he died (1

Kings 1:32–34). The injured cry out in pain in being examined by the doctor, yet pay him well and extend gratitude to him upon healing.[1164]

The Bottom Line: More often than not the "flatterer" is desired, not the reprover. "Few people have the wisdom to like reproofs which would do them good better than praises that do them hurt." John MacArthur says, "Flattery has no value, but reproof does, so it leads to gratitude."[1165]

265
Resiliency, the righteous rebounds from sin and trouble
Proverbs 24:16
"For a just man falleth seven times, and riseth up again: but the wicked shall fall into mischief."

For a "just man" (righteous, upright, honorable) "falleth" (as a result of sin or adversity) "seven times" (plurality of times[1166]), and "riseth up again" (recovers; is restored): BUT the "wicked" (ungodly) shall "fall into mischief" (they in contrast will be "done in" by sin and calamity; meet with ruination and devastation). R. E. Murphy summarizes, "The 'optimism' of the Book of Proverbs should not be exaggerated. It is presumed that the just will not be without troubles, but there is also the belief that in the long run shalom will be restored."[1167]

The righteous man (honorable, moral, upright) though he fall into trouble (misfortunes) or sin (moral lapses) "seven times" (reference to completeness or plurality; "seventy times seven"), to the chagrin of the wicked rises (recovers; restored upon repentance), while the empty professor of the faith will return to sin like a dog to his vomit.[1168] The Christian may be knocked down by sin and adversity but never knocked out. He ever rises to fight another round by the grace and mercy of the Lord. Whybray says though the righteous fall they "will "rise," for virtue triumphs over evil in the end."[1169] The Christian is not immune to worldly cares, misfortune, infirmities, losses and the insidious attack of the wicked or spiritual failure (Job 5:19). The rain falls upon the just and the unjust (Matthew 5:45).

God forbid, but one may suffer moral or economic lapses multiple times with the opportunity to recover. The *frequency* of one's stumbling is not the emphasis of the Proverb, but God's ability to pardon and restore them who do. Knowledge that God forgives all sin, even if it's repetitive, is not a license to engage in it (Romans 6:1–2). The Bible makes clear that a true believer will not *habitually* sin as a matter of lifestyle (1 John 3:8–9). David was overtaken in moral failure, yet upon repentance of the act was restored (Psalm 32:1–5).

The Bottom Line: Holy Scripture affirms time and again that the depth of the fall of the righteous or its frequency in no wise affects God's love toward him (Isaiah 43:25–26; 1 John 1:9; Micah 7:18–19). "He brought me up also out of an horrible pit, out of the miry clay, and set my feet upon a rock, and established my goings" (Psalm 40:2). Never give up on restoration for others or yourself upon moral failure. God doesn't. Don't buy into the lie of Satan that another or you personally have passed the point of no return regarding restoration (1 John 1:9; Isaiah 41:13). As with the prodigal son, God awaits eagerly the opportunity to recover all from the snare of the Devil. See Luke 15:11–32.

266
Resistance, the peril of resisting God
Proverbs 1:25

"But ye have set at nought all my counsel, and would none of my reproof."

But "ye" (the foolish) have set at "naught" (ignored it as if it had no value[1170]; paid no attention to it) all my "counsel" (advice; instruction), and "would none" (you didn't want it; refused it) of my "reproof" (correction). See Proverbs 1:20–24.

Don't treat lightly the commandments, counsel or correction of the Lord, lest you bear serious consequences. It is dangerous to listen to the summons of temptation from Satan (Proverbs 1:10–19). But it is dangerous also to ignore and pay no attention to the summons of God to repent of one's wickedness and to live wisely, godly and morally (Proverbs 1:24–26). H. A. Ironside remarks, "Ah, dear unsaved reader, if into the hands of such a one these pages fall, remember there is not only a world in which you can say "No" to God, the God of all grace; there is also a world in which He will say "No" to you, if you meet Him as the God of judgment. What can be worse for a lost soul than to have to remember, in the abyss of woe, gospel messages once indifferently listened to, the Word of God once treated as a subject unfit for serious consideration; and then to have to cry in despair, "Jesus died, yet I'm in Hell! He gave Himself for sinners. He provided a way of salvation for me, but, like the fool that I was, I spurned His grace till grace was withdrawn, the door of mercy was closed, and now I am to be on the wrong side of that closed door forever!'"[1171]

There is a time, I know not when,
A place, I know not where,
Which marks the destiny of men
To Heaven or despair.

How long may men go on in sin?
How long will God forbear?
Where does hope end, and where begins
The confines of despair?

One answer from those skies is sent:
Ye who from God depart,
While it is called today, repent
And harden not your heart."
~ Author unknown

The wise will hearken to God's call to turn from sin while there is time. John Rice pleads "Poor lost sinner, is not your heart convicted of your terrible sin in crowding Jesus out? Will you go to Hell because you have no room in your heart for the Son of God? Will you spend eternity in torment because pleasure or self-will or sin in any form bars the door of your heart against Jesus? Oh! Let Him in! Let Him in today!"[1172]

The Bottom Line: To disregard and ignore the call of the Lord to shun evil and embrace righteousness is destructive presently and eternally.

267
Retaining, scattering to keep and keeping to scatter
Proverbs 11:24
"There is that scattereth, and yet increaseth; and there is that withholdeth more than is meet, but it tendeth to poverty."

There is he that "scattereth" (gives generously, liberally[1173] with his money to the poor and other good causes), and yet "increaseth" (gets richer, for he is blessed for the giving by the Lord [Proverbs 19:17; Psalm 112:9]); AND there is he that "withholdeth" (is greedy, stingy) more than is meet, but it "tendeth to poverty" (what he keeps fails to benefit him, for he grows poorer[1174]).

John Bunyan's quaint rhyme summarizes the Proverb.

A man there was, though some did count him mad,
The more he cast away, the more he had.
He that bestows his goods upon the poor
Shall have as much again, and ten times more.[1175]

Matthew Henry says, "God blesses the giving hand, and so makes it a getting hand."[1176] Paul states, "But this I say, He which soweth sparingly shall reap also sparingly; and he which soweth bountifully shall reap also bountifully" (2 Corinthians 9:6). Jesus said, "Give, and it shall be given unto you; good measure, pressed down, and shaken together, and running over, shall men give into your bosom. For with the same measure that ye mete withal it shall be measured to you again" (Luke 6:38). See Haggai 1:6, 9; Proverbs 11:25.

The Proverb is also applicable to spiritual sowing. The more one broadcasts the seed of the Gospel through witnessing, teaching, preaching, benevolent acts, missionary endeavors and other "good works" in blessing others, the more blessing is heaped upon him from the Lord and those whom he helps. God rewards faithful and sacrificial service as He does that of financial liberality to worthy causes.

The Bottom Line: The generous, though he "scatters" his money to Christian and humanitarian causes, obtains that which is scattered financially or otherwise. The greedy will not long prosper, for divine punishment is assured (Proverbs 11:17; 28:22).

268
Retirement, rethinking its purpose and possibilities
Proverbs 20:29

"The glory of young men is their strength: and the beauty of old men is the gray head."

The "glory" (pride; boasting [1177]) of "young men" (prime of manhood) is their "strength" (Deane and Taswell say "unimpaired strength and vigor," which can only be attained by due exercise combined with self-control"[1178]). In contrast, the "beauty" (the splendor[1179]; that which is greatly admired honorably by others[1180]) of "old men" (aged; elderly) is their "gray head" (symbolic of honor, experience, wisdom, knowledge; represents all that is valuable about old age[1181]).

Charles Bridges states, "Every stage of life has its peculiar honor and privilege. Youth is the glory of nature, and *strength is the glory of youth*. Old age is the majestic beauty of nature, and the *grey head* is the majestic *beauty* which nature hath given to old age. These pictures describe the use, not the abuse. It is their youth usefully exercised, especially consecrated to God and employed for his glory. Otherwise, as an occasion for wantonness or vainglorious boast, its *strength* is its shame and will end in vanity. The silver crown brings honor and reverence and authority—only "in the way of righteousness."[1182]

"Retirement age," writes Vance Havner, "is supposed to mean that I should sit in a rocking chair, wait for my social security check, and reminisce about the good old days. I have no thought of retiring. I would say with Caleb, "Give me this mountain!" (Joshua 14:12). I am not asking for molehills. Old soldiers need not fade away. I have asked, like Hezekiah, for an extension of time; like Jabez, for an enlargement of coast; like Elisha, for an enduement of power. Caleb did not suffer, like the ten frightened spies, from a grasshopper complex. Too many cowards are cringing before the giants of Anak. God give us Calebs looking for mountains to conquer!"[1183]

In 1546 Michelangelo consented to the role of chief architect of the Basilica of St. Peter's in Rome, Italy when he was more than seventy years old. In a letter to his nephew Buonarotti he wrote, "Many believe—and I believe—that I have been designated for this work by God. In spite of my old age, I do not want to give it up; I work out of love for God, and I put all my hope in Him."[1184]

With Michelangelo, in "old age" identify the mountain (ministry task) of God's designation and then exhibit faith in the mountain's acquisition. Don't stagger in unbelief. Don't look at the obstacles or difficulties. Rather, believe God will give it into your hands according to His will. Hebron (the mountain Caleb claimed) was yet in possession of giants, the Anakim. Nonetheless, Caleb fearlessly in faith says, "Give me this mountain!" Caleb's faith gives way to work, and the mountain is acquired.

The pivotal key to Caleb's success was that he wholeheartedly "followed the Lord" (v. 14). To make the best of the twilight years of life, you must do the same. John MacArthur states, "There's no value in being old if you're not godly. There's no value in being old if you're not a model or an example."[1185] And I add, there is no value in being old if you've given up, hung up your cleats, turned in the keys and posted the sign "Do Not Disturb."

Every season of life has its divine purpose, including that of the *golden years*. To simply *retire* to a rocking chair, bucket list, bingo at the recreational center, travel, or be a recluse is a tragic waste of the treasure of a lifetime in knowledge, experience and service that yet can be of great benefit to the kingdom of God. Arouse yourself to take hold of that which God would have you accomplish in these latter years and finish life well. Did Moses retire? Did David retire? Did Paul retire? Certainly not. Someone said, "God sends His servants to bed when they have done their work." Our journey is not done; our work is yet incomplete until God sends us to bed.

Does the road wind uphill all the way?
Yes, to the very end.
Will the day's journey take the whole long day?
From morn to night, my friend. ~ Christina Rossetti, 1830–1894

The Bottom Line: Remembering that God is Owner of every stage of life, resolve to submit joyfully and willingly to that which He wants you to do in "old age." There is no discharge or retirement in serving the Lord, only promotion to Heaven or desertion. Live life to the fullest for the Lord until the final buzzer sounds!

269
Revenge, the error of retaliation when wronged
Proverbs 20:22

"Say not thou, I will recompense evil; but wait on the LORD, and he shall save thee."

"Recompense to no man evil for evil....Dearly beloved, avenge not yourselves, but rather give place unto wrath: for it is written, Vengeance is mine; I will repay, saith the Lord" (Romans 12:17–19).

Say not thou, I will "recompense evil" (take revenge for a wrong ["evil"] done); BUT "wait on the LORD" (don't give in to the knee-jerk reaction to strike back, to get even, but trust the matter with the Lord who will handle it rightly; Deane and Taswell say "commit his cause to the

Lord, not in the hope of seeing vengeance taken on his enemy, but in the certainty that God will help him to bear the wrong and deliver him in His own good time and way"[1186]) and he shall "save thee" (help, deliver you).

"Don't repay evil for evil. Don't retaliate with insults when people insult you. Instead, pay them back with a blessing. That is what God has called you to do, and he will grant you his blessing" (1 Peter 3:9 NLT). Or, as The Message puts it, "That goes for all of you, no exceptions. No retaliation. No sharp-tongued sarcasm. Instead, bless—that's your job, to bless. You'll be a blessing and also get a blessing." When offended or injured by another's actions, restrain from striking back to get even. This is most difficult, for to the flesh "revenge is sweet" (settling the score).

Scripture teaches that "if someone does wrong to you, do not pay him back by doing wrong to him....My friends, do not try to punish others when they wrong you, but wait for God to punish them with his anger" (Romans 12:17–19 NCV). God exhorts the righteous to bless the people (extend forgiveness to them, speak well of them, extend kindness toward them, and pray for them) who inflict hurt.

David exemplifies Proverbs 20:22 in the dealing with Shimei who cursed and stoned him. Hear the Word of the Lord detailing the event: "Then said Abishai the son of Zeruiah unto the king, Why should this dead dog curse my lord the king? let me go over, I pray thee, and take off his head. And the king said, What have I to do with you, ye sons of Zeruiah? so let him curse, because the LORD hath said unto him, Curse David. Who shall then say, Wherefore hast thou done so? And David said to Abishai, and to all his servants, Behold, my son, which came forth of my bowels, seeketh my life: how much more now may this Benjamite do it? let him alone, and let him curse; for the LORD hath bidden him. It may be that the LORD will look on mine affliction, and that the LORD will requite me good for his cursing this day" (2 Samuel 16:9–12).

Bear in mind Shiemi acted on this occasion on behalf of Satan, not the Lord (2 Samuel 19:16–23). He lied about saying the Lord hath told him to stone and curse David. Of this incident H. A. Ironside in picturesque fashion remarks, "It is doubtful if, in all David's spiritual history, he ever reached a higher height of holy confidence in God than at this time of deep, deep trial. Shimei's spiteful cursing in so public a manner, and at so sorrowful a time, must have deeply lacerated his already wounded spirit. But he bows his head in submission; and instead of executing vengeance on Shimei and seeking self-vindication from the charges made, 'through evil report and good report' he holds on his way, in submissive confidence, saying, 'Let him curse,' and taking all from the Lord Himself."[1187] Later David extends royal clemency (forgiveness) to Shiemi (2 Samuel 19:22).

Pride prompts immediate *payback* for wrong incurred. However, don't strike back; rather, place utter confidence in God (as David did) that He will use the bad for good, the pain for great gain. Despite your circle of friends urging "payback," as did David's (2 Samuel 16:21), graciously forgive. See Romans 12:17, 19; Hebrews 10:30; Deuteronomy 32:35.

The Bottom Line: Don't allow your hurts to turn into hates.[1188] God turns the "sweetness of revenge" quickly into "sour grapes." The Proverb does not state "wait on the Lord, and he shall avenge thee" but that "he shall save thee." Matthew Henry admonishes, "We must refer ourselves to God, and leave it to Him to plead our cause, to maintain our right, and reckon with those that do us wrong in such a way and manner as He thinks fit and in His own due time."[1189]

270
Revival, its nature, need and necessity
Proverbs 1:23
"Turn you at my reproof: behold, I will pour out my spirit unto you, I will make known my words unto you."

"If my people, which are called by my name, shall humble themselves, and pray, and seek my face, and turn from their wicked ways; then will I hear from heaven, and will forgive their sin, and will heal their land" (2 Chronicles 7:14).

"Turn" (repent; change of direction that one is traveling spiritually) you at "my" (Wisdom, i.e. God) "reproof" (Wisdom's [God's] words of correction, reprimand): behold I will "pour out" (based upon your repentance I will *gusher* out the Holy Spirit) upon you. I will make known my "words" (God's thoughts, decrees, commandments, precepts) to you.

Although the *interpretation* of 2 Chronicles 7:14 clearly reveals it was a promise directed to King Solomon about the nation Israel, its *application* for the church is appropriate. In reference to the text, J. Vernon

McGee said, "There is an application. This verse has a message for me. I can't toss it aside just because God did not direct it to me."[1190]

Such is the case with all Scripture. Personal revival begins with the "reproof" of the Lord (conviction of wrong or sin) which in turn prompts expression of godly sorrow over the sin and its confession (repentance), resulting in forgiveness and Holy Spirit infilling (controlling, empowering). In capsule, revival fires are ignited in the heart upon the believer's cry unto Lord in deep contrition and repentance. "Some undeniable traits of revival," writes Melvin Worthington, "are a humble spirit, hatred of sin, hunger for the Scriptures, holiness in saints, honesty among servants, and a harvest of souls."[1191]

Charles Finney describes revival as "the renewal of the first love of Christians, conviction of sin and searching of hearts among God's people. Revival is nothing less than a new beginning of obedience to God, a breaking of heart and getting down in the dust before Him with deep humility and forsaking of sin. A revival breaks the power of the world and of sin over Christians. The charm of the world is broken, and the power of sin is overcome. Truths to which our hearts are unresponsive suddenly become living. Whereas mind and conscience may assent to truth, when revival comes, obedience to the truth is the one thing that matters."[1192] Jonathan Goforth states that if revival tarries, "it is because some idol remains still enthroned, because we still insist in placing our reliance in human schemes, because we still refuse to face the unchangeable truth that 'It is not by might, but by My Spirit.'"[1193] See 1 Kings 8:35; Amos 4:7; Zechariah 4:6.

An employee who worked for a city located in a valley was fired. In anger the man plugged the primary pipe that supplied water to the city from the reservoir in the mountain. People fully expecting water to flow upon turning the nozzle or knob were sorely disappointed when nothing happened. Efforts to ascertain the cause were unsuccessful. In time the distraught employee confessed to the act, indicating the place the channel or pipe was plugged. Upon removal of the plug, the water flowed freely again.

We wonder why we pray for revival and it doesn't "come." It is because the channel or pipe between God and man has been clogged with some form of sin. The sin must be acknowledged and removed for the power of God to flow freely into and through us.

The Bottom Line: J. I. Packer stated, "Christians in revival are accordingly found living in God's presence (*Coram Deo*), attending to His Word, feeling acute concern about sin and righteousness, rejoicing in the assurance of Christ's love and their own salvation, spontaneously constant in worship, and tirelessly active in witness and service, fueling these activities by praise and prayer."[1194]

271
Righteous, their song is one the wicked cannot sing
Proverbs 29:6
"In the transgression of an evil man there is a snare: but the righteous doth sing and rejoice."

In the "transgression" (sin; offense against God and man) of an "evil man" (wicked) there is a "snare" (Deane and Taswell say, "The snare is that the sinner is caught and held fast by his sin and cannot escape, as he knows nothing of repentance and has no will to cast off evil habits"[1195]): BUT the "righteous" (upright) doth "sing and rejoice" (Reyburn and Fry say "not due to the sinner's ensnarement but that he has no reason to fear the trap of sin"[1196]).

The evildoer forfeits peace and joy as a result of his sin. All the Devil's apples have worms. In contrast, the righteous, by virtue of abstinence from sin or deliverance from it, experiences great joy and jubilant song. The righteous are singing people. The psalmist testified, "But I will sing of thy power; yea, I will sing aloud of thy mercy in the morning: for thou hast been my defence and refuge in the day of my trouble" (Psalm 59:16).

It's a song of joy. "Happy day, happy day, when Jesus washed my sins away. He taught me how to watch and pray and live rejoicing every day. Happy day, happy day, when Jesus washed my sins away."

It's a song of peace. "I have peace like a river; I have peace like a river; I have peace like a river in my soul."

It's a song of praise. "Thank you, Lord, for saving my soul. Thank you, Lord, for making me whole. Thank you, Lord, for giving to me Thy great salvation so rich and free."

It's a song of hope. "When Christ shall come with shout of acclamation to take me home, what joy shall fill my heart! Then I shall bow in humble adoration and there proclaim, my God, how great Thou art!"

Keep silent ye mountains, ye fields and ye fountains,
For this is the time I must sing.
It's the time to sing praises to the Rock of the Ages,
For this is the time I must sing. ~ Bill and Gloria Gather (1975)

God even gives His children a song in the night, a truth which Paul and Silas may attest (Acts 16:25). "No one says, 'Where is God my Maker, who gives songs in the night'" (Job 35:10 NIV).

The Bottom Line: Christians sing a song the evildoer cannot sing, for it's a song reserved for the righteous, the song of a soul set free. See Revelation 5:9.

272
Rudeness, being insolent, brash and disrespectful
Proverbs 18:23
"The poor useth intreaties; but the rich answereth roughly."

The "poor" (needy, destitute) "useth intreaties" (plead with) the "rich" (wealthy) for assistance; BUT the rich "answereth" (responds "impolitely or rudely,"[1197] roughly and cruelly). John MacArthur summarizes, "The rich do not need favors from others, so they do not care how they treat people."[1198]

The rich not only do wrong by failure to help the poor, but also in responding to their requests harshly, roughly and sternly. Wealth may instill in the one who possesses it haughtiness, greed, impoliteness and an uncompassionate heart (Luke 16:19–31). The rich must always guard against such attitudes and action.

But rudeness is not just the sin of the "rich." It exists in every class of humanity. In the love chapter of the Bible, Paul states that love "is not rude [unmannerly]" (1 Corinthians 13 NCV). "Selfless love is never rude, does not offend but always has good manners and tactfully shows courtesy, politeness and sensitivity to others' feelings."[1199] Rudeness may be exhibited in what is said or unsaid, done or undone. Youth often are rude to their parents verbally (what is said and the tone in which it is said) and to others by display of poor manners (pushing self ahead of others in the line, interrupting others as they speak, demanding recognition, manifesting an air of self-inflated importance, and unkind speech.

Paula Deen says, "There was one thing my daddy wouldn't tolerate in any shape, form or fashion, and that was being unkind or rude to somebody. And as it turns out, that was a legacy that he left me that money can't buy...how to be able to treat people."[1200]

It is the common observance on Wednesdays in New Zealand not to be rude ("Don't be rude Wednesday"). They refrain from offending others on that day. Such an observance must be praised. But far better it would be if it were practiced daily, year-round.

The Bottom Line: Be caring, courteous and sensitive to the feelings of people with whom you make contact (store, church, home and work). Christians, regardless of social status, must never be rude and impolite. Treat others in like manner as you desire to be treated. See 1 Samuel 17:18.

273
Safety, the believer's security in battle
Proverbs 21:31
"The horse is prepared against the day of battle: but safety is of the LORD.*"*

The "horse" (horses in Solomon's day were "exclusively" used for military battle—not for agricultural purposes[1201]) is "prepared against the day of battle" (since it was a war horse it was always ready to carry a soldier into battle): BUT "safety" (victory in battle) is "of the LORD" (even with war horses that are ready for battle a people have no guarantee of victory, but with the Lord fighting the battle with them, they are assured of triumph). Matthew Henry says, "He [God] can save without armies, but armies cannot save without Him; and therefore He must be sought to and trusted in for success; and when success is obtained, He must have all the glory."[1202]

Prepare for the day of battle (ministry, witnessing, opposition and teaching), but as Elijah at Mount Carmel, rely not upon "it" but in the counsel and power of the Lord (1 Kings 18:33–38), for "safety (victory, success) is of the LORD." The believer's confidence in spiritual warfare and ministry, despite overwhelming odds, is in the Lord, the Mighty Deliverer. Asa serves as a biblical example. Upon conflict with the great army of Zerah, he "cried unto the LORD his God, and said, LORD, it is nothing with thee to help, whether with many, or with them that have no power: help us, O LORD our God; for we rest on thee, and in thy name we go against this multitude. O LORD, thou art our God; let not man prevail against thee" (2 Chronicles 14:11).

George Lawson remarks, "God is the keeper of our souls, and therefore we need not be afraid to risk our lives in obedience to His will. We cannot exist one moment without His kind providence—so why should we scruple to risk everything dear to us in the service of Him in whom we live, move and have our being? We are always safe in the way of duty—and we are never safe in neglect of it."[1203] I have held tightly to the belief that God can take better care of my family (and me) while I'm away doing His will than I can while staying home outside it. And for over forty years, He has done just that!

H. A. Ironside remarks, "The trusting soul rests on the fact that the counsel of the Lord will never be defeated. Therefore, he fears not the wisdom or understanding or the plots of his foes. What can man do to harm the one who is covered by the wings of Jehovah? 'Though a host encamp against me,' said David, 'my heart will not fear' (Psalm 27:3 NASB)."[1204]

Do you recall the story of the prophet Elisha in Dothan under siege by the Syrian army (2 Kings 6:8–18)? Elijah awoke early one morning only to see the city surrounded by chariots, horses and a host of enemy Syrian troops. Elisha's servant, seeing all this said, "Alas, my master! how shall we do?" Elisha responded, "Fear not: for they that be with us are more than they that be with them." The prophet then prayed for God to open the servant's eyes that he might see the grand host of *chariots of fire* upon the mountain that surrounded them.

Being out there in the trenches preaching, teaching, soul winning and ministering at times becomes frightful. In such times remember the *chariots of fire,* that there is no need to fear or panic for God has encompassed you on every side with an unseen heavenly host providing protection. In Christian ministry, foreign and at home, God backs the servant up to the hilt! To know it is Almighty God who fights our battles for us grants courage and confidence in their midst. "The LORD shall fight for you, and ye shall hold your peace" (Exodus 14:14).

I have found great comfort and confidence throughout my ministry in the thought that there is no demand upon my spirit that is not also a demand upon His Spirit within me. With trusting assurance, the believer may declare with Asa, "LORD, it is nothing with thee to help, whether with many, or with them that have no power: help us, O LORD our God; for we rest on thee, and in thy name we go against this multitude" (2 Chronicles 14:11). God can do anything but fail the believer as he undertakes a divine assignment; therefore, shrink not back from it, despite "apparent" defeat or failure.

The Bottom Line: Don't trust in "chariots or horses" (intelligence, skill, giftedness or talent, ability, education, training, experience) in ministry but in "the name of the LORD" (Psalm 20:7) for there is safety in the Lord. "The arm of flesh will fail you; you dare not trust your own." Deane and Taswell say, "The only safety against spiritual enemies is the grace of God."[1205]

274
Salvation, its must and means
Proverbs 10:16
"The labour of the righteous tendeth to life: the fruit of the wicked to sin."

The "labor" (wages, reward, and prize[1206]) of the "righteous" (upright) "tendeth to life" (it leads to a "good life"[1207]): the "fruit" (gain, profit) of the "wicked" (ungodly) "to sin" (what they gain is reinvested in deeds of wrongdoing).

The Proverb does not teach eternal salvation by works but rather that a good and noble life is the reward of righteous living, as is the "fruit (income, result) of the wicked" heartache, havoc and being lost. The Bible makes crystal clear that salvation is not earned by the good that is done (Titus 3:5). Man's best "righteousness" is as a filthy rag only fit to be discarded (Isaiah 64:6).

C. H. Spurgeon remarks, "If there be one stitch in the celestial garment of our righteousness which we are to insert ourselves, then we are lost."[1208] Salvation is received as a free gift by grace (God's Riches at Christ's Expense) through faith (Forsaking All I Trust Him) in the Lord

Jesus Christ (Ephesians 2:8–9). It is based upon His work for us upon the Cross, not our work for Him.

> Some day the silver cord will break,
> And I no more as now shall sing.
> But, oh, the joy when I shall wake
> Within the palace of the King!

> And I shall see Him face to face
> And tell the story—saved by grace;
> And I shall see Him face to face
> And tell the story—saved by grace. ~ Fanny Cosby

John Calvin said, "Since no man is excluded from calling upon God, the gate of salvation is open to all. There is nothing else to hinder us from entering but our own unbelief."[1209]

The Bottom Line: C. H. Spurgeon stated, "You will find all true theology summed up in these two short sentences: Salvation is all of the grace of God. Damnation is all the will of man."[1210]

275
Salvation, its Who, What and How
Proverbs 30:4

"Who hath ascended up into heaven, or descended? who hath gathered the wind in his fists? who hath bound the waters in a garment? who hath established all the ends of the earth? what is his name, and what is his son's name, if thou canst tell?"

The most educated and brightest unbeliever is inapt to answer the questions herein posed, "for they are foolishness unto him: neither can he know them, because they are spiritually discerned" (1 Corinthians 2:14). The first question posed was answered by Jesus in John 3:13: "And no man hath ascended up to heaven, but he that came down from heaven, even the Son of man which is in heaven." In Ephesians 4:9–10, Paul reveals that *Jesus likewise descended:* "Now that he ascended, what is it but that he also descended first into the lower parts of the earth? He that descended is the same also that ascended up far above all heavens, that he might fill all things." Here we discover the gospel proclaimed in the Old Testament.

What enormous, pregnant truth is found in Jesus' descent from and ascension to Heaven! In Jesus' own words the reason for His descent to earth was "to seek and to save that which was lost" (Luke 19:10). Man's salvation and reconciliation to God necessitated Jesus' agonizing and tormenting death upon the cross. Peter explains, "For Christ also hath once suffered for sins, the just for the unjust, that he might bring us to God, being put to death in the flesh, but quickened [made alive again] by the Spirit" (1 Peter 3:18).

Three days after His crucifixion and burial, He was raised from the dead, which was verified by many witnesses. Forty days later, *Jesus ascended* back into Heaven. "And when he had spoken these things, while they beheld, he was taken up; and a cloud received him out of their sight. And while they looked stedfastly toward heaven as he went up, behold, two men stood by them in white apparel; Which also said, Ye men of Galilee, why stand ye gazing up into heaven? this same Jesus, which is taken up from you into heaven, shall so come in like manner as ye have seen him go into heaven" (Acts 1:9–11).

H. A. Ironside summarizes Jesus' ascension: "Jesus, His work finished and His ministry on earth accomplished, ascended of His own volition, passing through the upper air as easily as He had walked upon the water. The fact of His having gone up and having been received by the Shekinah—the cloud of divine Majesty—testifies to the perfection of His work in putting away forever the believer's sins. When Jesus was on the tree, Jehovah 'laid on Him the iniquity of us all' (Isaiah 53:6). He could not be now in the presence of God if one sin remained upon Him. 'Wherefore he saith, When he ascended up on high, he led captivity captive, and gave gifts unto men' (Ephesians 4:8). He had destroyed 'him that had the power of death, that is, the devil' (Hebrews 2:14)."[1211]

"The great superiority of the sacrifice Jesus brought," writes William Barclay, "lay in three things: (1) The sacrifice of Jesus shows us a God whose arms are always outstretched and in whose heart is only love. (2) The sacrifice of Jesus brought eternal redemption. The idea was that men were under the dominion of sin; and just as the purchase price had to be paid to free a man from slavery, so the purchase price had to be paid to free a man from sin. (3) The sacrifice of Christ enabled a man to leave the deeds of death and to become the servant of the living God. That is to say, he did not only win forgiveness for a man's past sin; he enabled him in the future to live a godly life. The sacrifice of Jesus was not only the paying of a debt; it was the giving of a victory. What Jesus did puts a man right with God, and what He does enables a man to stay right with God. The act of the cross brings to men the love of God in a way that takes their terror of Him away; the presence of the living Christ brings to them the power of God so that they can win a daily victory over sin."[1212]

As to the remaining questions that are posed in the Proverb, answer is given by divine revelation. Isaiah 66:2 (ERV) says, "'I am the one who made all things. They are all here because I made them,' says the Lord." Paul states, "For by him were all things created, that are in heaven, and that are in earth, visible and invisible, whether they be thrones, or dominions, or principalities, or powers: all things were created by him, and for him" (Colossians 1:16). And Proverbs 8:29 (NIV) says, "He gave the sea its boundary so the waters would not overstep his command, and when he marked out the foundations of the earth."

The Bottom Line: Jesus' deity is proclaimed in Proverbs 30:4. He came down to earth to be the Mediator between man and God (1 Timothy 2:5). Upon completion of the work (procurement of salvation for man through the cross), He ascended back into Heaven (Acts 1:11). The church awaits His glorious return (John 14:2–3).

276
Scoffers, show contempt for the things of God
Proverbs 15:12
"A scorner loveth not one that reproveth him: neither will he go unto the wise."

"Knowing this first, that there shall come in the last days scoffers, walking after their own lusts" (2 Peter 3:3).

A "scorner" (scoffer or mocker is a person that shows contempt for [sneers at] God, the church and Bible) "loveth not" (resents) one that "reproveth" (rebukes, reprimands, corrrects) him: "neither will he go unto the wise" (totally unwilling to seek the advice, instruction or counsel of the godly wise). Deane and Taswell summarize that scoffers "are conceited, arrogant persons, freethinkers, indifferent to or skeptical of religion, and too self-opinionated to be open to advice or reproof"[1213]).

Scoffers are persons that bear great disdain and ridicule for the Christian faith. Though in need of "reproof" (correction), their conceit (attitude that they are right, everyone else is wrong) prompts its avoidance. "Neither will he go unto the wise." He avoids the minister, the Christian, the church, religious books, and evangelistic events for they serve to confront him about wrongdoing, heretical belief and its consequences. Darkness does not like exposure to the Light; therefore, it flees it. "For every one that doeth evil hateth the light, neither cometh to the light, lest his deeds should be reproved" (John 3:20).

But there is *One* whom the scoffer cannot shun. It is the unavoidable Christ, the inescapable Christ. H. A. Ironside comments, "With Him he must have to do, whether he will or not. Solemn indeed will be the accounting for opportunities refused, instruction neglected, and grace despised."[1214] All must either meet Christ now as Friend or later as Judge. There will be a day in which "every knee shall bow to [Jesus], and every tongue shall confess to God. So then every one of us shall give account of himself to God" (Romans 14:11–12). The scoffer faces serious consequences for sin. "Correction is grievous unto him that forsaketh the way: and he that hateth reproof shall die" (Proverbs 15:10). Not only will he suffer ruination presently but will also experience eternal damnation (2 Peter 3:3–8; Revelation 21:8).

Not only does the scoffer shun reproof, but he also hates the reprover ("loveth not"). He resents the person (parent, preacher, church member) that seeks to give godly advice, counsel and correction. "They hate him that rebuketh in the gate, and they abhor him that speaketh uprightly" (Amos 5:10). Why do scoffers resent Christians so vehemently? Paul explains, "For the preaching of the cross is to them that perish foolishness; but unto us which are saved it is the power of God" (1 Corinthians 1:18). Jesus was ridiculed, resented and rejected by the very ones He came to rescue from the jaws of eternal damnation (John 1:11; Matthew 21:37–39).

The scoffing fool seems to be a most hopeless case with regard to salvation. But yet he is not unreachable, unsalvageable or unsaveable through the power of the Gospel of the Lord Jesus Christ. He faces present and eternal peril, necessitating divine intervention. Paul's argument is that if Jesus could save the greatest of sinners (Paul), then anyone, regardless of spiritual mindset, can be saved (1 Timothy 1:15).

The Bottom Line: Scoffers are persons that disagree with Christian belief and practice and ridicule those who embrace it, while remaining too arrogant (conceited) to consider its validly. Yet there is hope for their salvation through Jesus Christ. Pray for the scoffers' spiritual illumination to the truth that sets man free.

277
Security, danger of possessing a false hope of salvation
Proverbs 11:28

"He that trusteth in his riches shall fall: but the righteous shall flourish as a branch."

He that "trusteth" (rests his hope, reliance for protection) in his "riches" (wealth) shall "fall" (Proverbs 11:5): BUT the "righteous" (upright; Christian) shall "flourish" (grow) as a "branch" (a green leaf is the symbol of prosperity and fertility throughout the Ancient Near East[1215]).

Security, defined by John MacArthur, is "the absence of threat, the absence of fear, the absence of danger, that comfortable freedom that says everything is under control."[1216] Further, he says, "And I think particular men also look for spiritual security—to be free from anxiety about death; to be free from apprehension about facing God, about divine judgment; to be free from the fear that your sins are going to be brought up and held against you."[1217]

In the quest for security, men often look in the wrong places. He who looks to fortune, position, religion, and charitable or humanitarian deeds for security is embracing a false hope of security for today, tomorrow and eternity.

Ponder the words of Arthur W. Pink: "It is greatly to be feared that there are multitudes in Christendom who verily imagine and sincerely believe that they are among the saved, yet who are TOTAL STRANGERS to a work of divine grace in their hearts. It is one thing to have clear intellectual conceptions of God's truth; it is quite another matter to have a personal, real heart acquaintance with it. It is one thing to believe that sin is the awful thing that the Bible says it is, but it is quite another matter to have a holy horror and hatred of it in the soul. It is one thing to know that God requires repentance; it is quite another matter to experimentally mourn and groan over our vileness. It is one thing to believe that Christ is the only Savior for sinners; it is quite another matter to really trust Him from the heart. It is one thing to believe that Christ is the sum of all excellency; it is quite another matter to love him above all others. It is one thing to believe that God is the great and holy One; it is quite another matter to truly reverence and fear Him. It is one thing to believe that salvation is of the Lord; it is quite another matter to become an actual partaker of it through His gracious workings."[1218] Pink continues, "It is exceedingly solemn to discover that there is a 'believing' on Christ by natural man, which is not a believing unto salvation."[1219]

Simply put, mere intellectual belief in Jesus Christ provides a person with a false, counterfeit security. Genuine salvation involves not only mental assent to the person and works of Jesus Christ, but also personal repentance with regard to sin and faith placed in Him alone as Savior and Lord (Acts 20:21). False security is based upon the external; the genuine, on the internal. The first is believed to be procured by what we do religiously; the latter, by what He has done (atonement at Calvary). William W. Hamilton summarizes, "The result of false teaching is false trusting, and the result of false trusting is false hope. No soul is safe unless its hope be based on nothing less than Jesus' blood and righteousness."[1220]

The Bottom Line: It's better to have no hope than to possess a false hope. Paul exhorts, "Examine yourselves, whether ye be in the faith; prove your own selves. Know ye not your own selves, how that Jesus Christ is in you, except ye be reprobates?" (2 Corinthians 13:5).

278
Security, the only anchor of hope for the soul
Proverbs 10:30

"The righteous shall never be removed: but the wicked shall not inhabit the earth."

"As the whirlwind passeth, so is the wicked no more: but the righteous is an everlasting foundation" (Proverbs 10:25).

The "righteous" (upright) shall "never be removed" ("overthrown, dislodged, shaken"[1221] from the land of Israel): BUT the "wicked" (ungodly) "shall not inhabit the earth" (will be forced to leave; perish). The Proverb seems to apply to the land of Israel. The righteous would never be driven out, while the wicked would be exiled. Though countries with greater military might than that of Israel have sought to dislodge the Jews from Israel, the Proverb has been proven true. See Proverbs 2:21–22.

Here I make a spiritual application of the text that is in keeping with the whole of Scripture. He that has anchored his soul upon the solid foundation of Jesus Christ shall remain steadfast amidst life's storms, persecution, evil assault, and loss. Evil and the cohorts of Hell may rage, but they will not prevail, for the Christian is enveloped in the omnipotent protective hands of Almighty God.

David, from experience, could easily say, "The Lord is with me; I will not be afraid. What can man do to me? The Lord is with me; he is my helper" (Psalm 118:6–7 BSB). Jeremiah joins him in affirming man's invulnerability in the Lord: "Blessed is the man who trusts in the Lord, whose trust is the Lord. He is like a tree planted by water, that sends out its roots by the stream, and does not fear when heat comes, for its leaves remain green, and is not anxious in the year of drought, for it does not cease to bear fruit" (Jeremiah 17:7–8 ESV). Henry Martyn said, "I am immortal until God's work for me to do is done." That's stability. All believers who live within the will of God may make the same attestation.

But such is not so for the wicked, for they will meet with God's judgment. Conversely, they will be *rooted out*. They will not inherit the earth in this life or Heaven in the life which is to come. The treasures of "wood, hay, stubble" they stored up in this life will be burned along with them in everlasting fire.

The Bottom Line: An anchor is only as secure as that to which it is attached. "So in this matter, God, wishing to show beyond doubt that his plan was unchangeable, confirmed it with an oath. So that by two utterly immutable things, the word of God and the oath of God, who cannot lie, we who are refugees from this dying world might have a source of strength, and might grasp the hope that he holds out to us. This hope we hold as the utterly reliable anchor for our souls, fixed in the very certainty of God himself in Heaven, where Jesus has already entered on our behalf" (Hebrews 6:19–20 Phillips). The Christian will never be "dislodged" from the "land" that is "flowing with milk and honey."

279
Self-control, guard the mind from wanton imaginations
Proverbs 4:23
"Keep thy heart with all diligence; for out of it are the issues of life."

"He that hath no rule over his own spirit is like a city that is broken down, and without walls" (Proverbs 25:28).

"Keep" (guard) thy "heart" (mind, the center of the thoughts and reason; MacArthur says, "The heart is the depository of all wisdom and the source of whatever affects speech [v. 24], sight [v. 25], and conduct [vv. 26, 27]"[1222]; Maclaren says, "The seat of will, moral purpose"[1223]) with all "diligence" ("guard above all guarding"[1224]; "keep thy heart more than any other keeping"[1225]; top priority in guarding); for out of it are the "issues of life" (the heart determines the conduct; it is the wellspring of all we do).

Deane and Taswell summarize, "The heart is here compared with a fountain. The same idea which is affixed to it in its physical sense is also assigned to it in its ethical or moral sense. Physically, it is the central organ of the body; morally, it is the seat of the affections and the center of the moral consciousness. From this moral center flow forth "the issues of life;" i.e., the currents of the moral life take their rise in and flow forth from it, just as from the heart, physically considered, the blood is propelled and flows forth into the arterial system, by which it is conveyed to the remotest extremities of the body. And as the bodily health depends on the healthy action of the heart, so the moral health depends on and is influenced by the state in which this spring of all action is preserved."[1226]

The fortress of our life (mind) must be ruled with a strong hand, lest traitors enter therein to influence with that which is wrong and destructive. *Sit tight* on your thoughts, for they determine the manner of person you become. It takes only one traitor to effect great harm. Therefore, exile them all forever. "Casting down imaginations, and every high thing that exalteth itself against the knowledge of God, and bringing into captivity every thought to the obedience of Christ" (2 Corinthians 10:5). Matthew Henry says, "God, who gave us these souls, gave us a strict charge with them: Man, woman, keep thy heart. We must maintain a holy jealousy of ourselves, and set a strict guard, accordingly, upon all the avenues of the soul; keep our hearts from doing hurt and getting hurt, from being defiled by sin and disturbed by trouble; keep them as our jewel, as our vineyard; keep a conscience void of offence; keep out bad thoughts; keep up good thoughts; keep the affections upon right objects and in due bounds."[1227]

Instructing man to guard his heart is like putting the fox in the henhouse to protect the hens. He is his own worst enemy, often caving to the sensual appetites of the flesh. Notwithstanding, Solomon is right; man is to keep (guard) his heart, but the means by which it is done is all-important for success. He must relinquish its control to that of the Lord

Jesus Christ. With Christ seated upon the throne in man's heart, the enemy of sinful thinking and planning is repelled, for such people "are kept by the power of God through faith unto salvation ready to be revealed in the last time" (1 Peter 1:5).

It is useless and futile to preach and practice self-keeping. Maclaren says, "Unless we can tell the beleaguered heart, 'The Lord is thy Keeper; He will keep thee from all evil; He will keep thy soul,' we only add one more impossible command to a man's burden."[1228] "Now unto him that is able to keep you from falling, and to present you faultless before the presence of his glory with exceeding joy, To the only wise God our Saviour, be glory and majesty, dominion and power, both now and ever. Amen." (Jude 24–25).

The righteous need a motive to rigorously guard the fountainhead (mind). It is the same motive that prompted Paul to guard his heart. "For the love of Christ constraineth us; because we thus judge, that if one died for all, then were all dead: And that he died for all, that they which live should not henceforth live unto themselves, but unto him which died for them, and rose again" (2 Corinthians 5:14–15). Jesus' love manifested in death for the believer ought to be all the incentive needed for him to exact the necessary discipline to keep the mind clean, pure and holy in absolute submission to His Word and Will.

The Bottom Line: Man's deeds are not mere accidents prompted by outside forces or chance happenings, but flow from the fountainhead in the mind which makes him responsible for his actions.[1229] The mind must be fortified, strongly guarded against all that would defile and destroy. With Jesus in us, controlling us, defending us, we will be more than conquerors with regard to the enemies' effort to take siege of our heart.

280
Self-control, in legitimate appetites and pleasures
Proverbs 25:16
"Hast thou found honey? eat so much as is sufficient for thee, lest thou be filled therewith, and vomit it."

Hast thou "found honey?" (honey is found in the hollow of trees or crevices of rocks[1230]) eat "so much as is sufficient" (eat only enough to satisfy) for thee, lest thou be "filled therewith" (stuffed due to overindulgence[1231]), and "vomit it" ("throw up" from the mouth the honey).

Eating honey is good and healthy unless eaten in excess, which is detrimental. As honey's sweetness is tasteful, just so are legitimate pleasures. Danger exists in overindulgence in both. H. A. Ironside explains, "What is legitimate and wholly proper in its place may prove very detrimental to all spiritual growth if it be permitted to become the supreme controlling power of the life."[1232]

The writer of Hebrews echoes the same truth: "Let us lay aside every weight, and the sin which doth so easily beset us, and let us run with patience the race that is set before us" (Hebrews 12:1). "Weights" in themselves are not sin but become sin when they begin to control one's life. Keep appetites for even *good* food and pleasures in check. Practice self-control (rigid restraint). Excessive consumption or participation in allowable things leads to physical or spiritual nausea (soul sickness, hindrance, interference to Christian walk and fellowship with God).

The lack of self-control, discipline is pictured in Proverbs 25:28 as a man whose heart is like a "city that is broken down, and without walls." The unwillingness to practice restraint is like a city exposed to the enemy's attack at their discretion. Vulnerability to Satan and his cohorts exists in such a man. W. A. Criswell remarks, "Without self-control, one is more susceptible to the tempter and his testing of the senses at every point."[1233] With it, Chuck Swindoll remarks, "[It] stops bad habits. It checks us. It halts us."[1234]

The Apostle Paul relates the imperative of self-control to an athlete training for a race. Its lessons are self-evident. "Do you not know that in a race all the runners run [their very best to win], but only one receives the prize? Run [your race] in such a way that you may seize the prize and make it yours! Now every athlete who [goes into training and] competes in the games is disciplined and exercises self-control in all things. They do it to win a crown that withers, but we [do it to receive] an imperishable [crown that cannot wither]. Therefore I do not run without a definite goal; I do not flail around like one beating the air [just shadow boxing]. But [like a boxer] I strictly discipline my body and make it my slave, so that, after I have preached [the gospel] to others, I myself will not somehow be disqualified [as unfit for service]" (1 Corinthians 9:24–27 AMP).

The Apostle Peter said, "For this very reason, make every effort to supplement your faith with virtue, and virtue with knowledge, and knowledge with self-control, and self-control with steadfastness" (2 Peter 1:5–6). Peter says *make every effort* to exhibit self-control (along with other things). It is God that provides the power for the discipline of restraint. That is undeniable (Philippians 4:13). However, the believer must make the effort to appropriate it (Romans 7:24–25). Chuck Swindoll explains, "The effort we make comes from a higher power. It doesn't come from ourselves. It comes from God."[1235]

A former alcohol addict in Swindoll's church shared insight from *The Recovery Study Bible* about developing self-control. "It goes on to say that self-control is not will power. It is not something we get by gritting our teeth and forcing ourselves to 'just say no.' Self-control is called a fruit. Fruit doesn't instantly pop out on a tree. As the tree grows and seasons pass, the fruit naturally develops. As we continue to follow God's guidance, taking one step at a time, our self-control will gradually grow. Our job is to stay connected to God. It is the Holy Spirit's job to produce the fruit of self-control in our life."[1236] (See Galatians 5:22–23)

The Bottom Line: An uncontrolled life leads to trouble. "Better to be patient than powerful; better to have self-control than to conquer a city" (Proverbs 16:32 NLT). Do you master the body (ruler of, dominion over, controller) or does it master you (its slave, prisoner, captive)?

281
Self-praise, arrogance on display
Proverbs 27:2
"Let another man praise thee, and not thine own mouth; a stranger, and not thine own lips."

Let "another man praise thee" (if "praise or commendation" is warranted, let it be both initiated and spoken by others) and not thine "own mouth" (don't be guilty of being "pompous"; arrogant or "full of self" telling others how good a person you are); a "stranger" (same as "another man"; Ross says, "A person who may speak more objectively about your accomplishments and abilities"[1237]), and not thine own lips.

"There is usually a motive behind the habit of self-praise, and, though this may be nothing worse than childish vanity, it carries with it a desire for exciting the admiration of others; it aims at reaping a harvest of laudation."[1238] Don't be given to self-praise (highly speaking, exaltation of one's self). "Self-praise stinks" (Arabic proverb). To highly speak of one's own achievements, possessions, talents or deeds is wrongfully and sinfully arrogant. It nauseates the person whom it is designed to impress and diminishes, if not destroying, the very reputation it seeks to instill.

The Proverb principle advises that "bragging," if it occurs at all, ought to be done by another ("not thine own lips"). Humility shrinks back into the shadow when praised; pride looms toward its limelight.

> Humility and knowledge in poor clothes excel
> pride and ignorance in costly attire.
> William Penn

Upon thoughts of self-praise, ponder 1 Corinthian 4:7, in which Paul says, "[For] Who says you are better than others [made you so important; or sees anything different in you]? What do you have that was not given to you? And if it was given to you, why do you brag [boast] as if you did not receive it as a gift [receive it]?" (EXB). And always keep in the forefront of the mind the words of Jesus: "Without me ye can do nothing" (John 15:5). Always apply the principle Jesus set forth to never choose the upper seat in the synagogue (Luke 11:43). And likewise remember His rules: "For whosoever exalteth himself shall be abased; and he that humbleth himself shall be exalted" (Luke 14:11), and, "So the last shall be first, and the first last" (Matthew 20:16). Matthew Henry remarks, "There may be a just occasion for us to vindicate ourselves, but it does not become us to applaud ourselves. *Proprio laus sordet in ore*—Self-praise defiles the mouth."[1239] "Self-praise silences the lips of admiration from others. The truly humble man will not crave such admiration."[1240]

The Bottom Line: Abstain from self-exaltation, leaving commendation to the Lord and others. "If I honour myself," said Jesus (John 8:54), "my honour is nothing." And Paul testifies, "Not he that commendeth himself is approved, but whom the Lord commendeth" (2 Corinthians 10:18).

282
Sexual Relationship, stick with your own mate
Proverbs 5:18
"Let thy fountain be blessed: and rejoice with the wife of thy youth."

"Let" (keep) "thy" (husband) "fountain" (his wife [Proverbs 5:15]) be "blessed" (joy, happiness): AND "rejoice" (be happy with her; the kind derived from romantic sexual relations with her;[1241] knowledge God has ordained her to be your wife, that of all the men in the world she belongs to you, brings the soul great delight[1242]) with the wife of thy "youth" (possibly refers to a youthful wife).

Ecclesiastes 9:9 states, "Live joyfully with the wife whom thou lovest all the days of [your] life." Marriage is to be enjoyed (a heavenly delight), not merely endured. Happiness and joy in marriage depend on fidelity. "Drink waters [sexual relations] out of thine own cistern [spouse]" (Proverbs 5:15). Adultery kills a marriage at worst and wrecks it at best.

Regarding the means of remaining true sexually to one's spouse, W. A. Criswell said, "Tender and loving affection between husband and wife is the best and surest defense against promiscuity."[1243] It depends on intoxicating ("ravished") endearment. "Let her be as the loving hind and pleasant roe; let her breasts satisfy thee at all times; and be thou ravished always with her love" (Proverbs 5:19). Spouses are to love each other supremely ("as the loving hind and pleasant roe") and "satisfy" one another sexually, lest they seek other outlets ("be ravished with a strange woman [or man], and embrace…a stranger" [Proverbs 5:20]). Solomon emphasizes the intoxicating love (crazy love) that spouses manifest to each other as well as their sexual fidelity and continuous sexual relationship is to be "at all times" and "always" (Proverbs 5:19).

What a husband/wife might do in secret (adultery), the "eyes of the Lord" sees (Proverbs 5:21). God not only sees the iniquity but will hold them accountable ("pondereth all his goings"). "For God shall bring every work into judgment, with every secret thing, whether it be good, or whether it be evil" (Ecclesiastes 12:14). The *King James Bible Commentary* states, "The Lord ponders all the goings of man and has assigned bitter and severe consequences to the sin of sexual promiscuity. Sexual sin ruthlessly incarcerates the participants. The cords of this sin wrap themselves around the very soul of the participant until he cannot free himself, even though he may desire freedom. His persistent lack of self-control has led him beyond the place where he might be instructed."[1244] See Proverbs 5:21–23. The writer of Hebrews states, "Marriage is to be held in honor among all [that is, regarded as something of great value], and the marriage bed undefiled [by immorality or by any sexual sin]; for God will judge the sexually immoral and adulterous" (Hebrews 13:4 AMP).

Children must be aware of sexual immorality's strong enticement (Proverbs 5:3); its devastating consequence (Proverbs 5:4–5, 11); and the way to avoid it (Proverbs 5:7–8).

The Bottom Line: The Christian home God instituted is to manifest rapturous love and ecstatic joy between husband and wife all the days of their lives. Find delight in one another, manifesting tender love and affection, not just in the bedroom but in *every room.*

283
Sickness, take a good dose of healing medicine
Proverbs 3:7–8
"Be not wise in thine own eyes: fear the LORD, and depart from evil. It shall be health to thy navel, and marrow to thy bones."

"Be not wise in thine own eyes" (admonition not to be conceited in thinking you have the intelligence to order your life better than God does; self-reliant): "fear the LORD" (to recognize God's holy character and submit life totally unto His control and live in adherence to Holy Scriptures), "depart from evil" (abandon the path of wickedness; immoral conduct). It shall be "health" (healing medicine, physically and spiritually) to thy "navel" (body) and "marrow" (strength) to thy bones.

As the prevention of physical sickness (like the influenza epidemic gripping many parts of our nation as I write) depends on avoiding exposure to the causes, just so, preventing spiritual sickness requires that certain people, places and practices be avoided. The Proverb states that to be spiritually healthy the believer must avoid conceit (being impressed with oneself; arrogance). Few things are as nauseating as being in the presence of a person who is beautiful or handsome who is *puffed up* with self-vanity. Paul warns of the sin of haughtiness ("arrogantly superior" attitude): "For I say, through the grace given unto me, to every man that is among you, not to think of himself more highly than he ought to think; but to think soberly, according as God hath dealt to every man the measure of faith" (Romans 12:3).

In addition to appearance, the causes of this sin include intelligence, skill, talents, ability and knowledge. To stay healthy, stay humble. To remain spiritually healthy, avoid wickedness ("evil"). "Let every one that nameth the name of Christ depart from iniquity" (2 Timothy 2:19). It goes without saying that to walk in spiritual health one must walk the path of righteousness (uprightness; purity; holiness; obedience; pleasing unto God). Jesus said, "Abide in me, and I in you. As the branch cannot bear fruit of itself, except it abide in the vine; no more can ye, except ye abide in me. I am the vine, ye are the branches: He that abideth in me, and I in him, the same bringeth forth much fruit: for without me ye can do nothing. If a man abide not in me, he is cast forth as a branch, and is withered; and men gather them, and cast them into the fire, and they are burned" (John 15:4–6).

Spiritual health hinges also upon avoidance of tempting places. "Neither give place [beachhead into your life] to the devil" (Ephesians 4:27). Proverbs 4:15 says, "Avoid it, pass not by it, turn from it, and pass away." Scripture strenuously exhorts the believer to consciously plan (order life) to go out of the way to avoid tempting situations. (If you have a problem with eating too many sweets, don't rent an apartment above a bakery.) Avoid scriptural ignorance and spiritual malnutrition. Receive heartedly and apply earnestly biblical instruction. "My son, attend to my words; incline thine ear unto my sayings. Let them not depart from thine eyes; keep them in the midst of thine heart. For they are life unto those that find them, and health to all their flesh" (Proverbs 4:20–22). Scriptural verses will keep you from spiritual reverses. Peter exhorts, "As newborn babes, desire the sincere milk of the word [holy Scripture], that ye may grow thereby" (1 Peter 2:2).

The Bottom Line: The "fear of the Lord" ("to recognize God's character and respond by revering, trusting, worshiping, obeying, and serving Him"[1245]) helps in the prevention of "evil" (wrongdoing; spiritual sickness).

284
Sin, the bitter consequence of just one sin
Proverbs 5:22
"His own iniquities shall take the wicked himself, and he shall be holden with the cords of his sins."

His "own iniquities" (transgression, wrongdoing, sin) shall take the "wicked" (ungodly) himself, AND he shall be "holden" (taken captive; ensnared as in a hunter's trap) with "the cords of his sins" (nets to capture birds were made with cords and ropes; the sinner's sin will be a "net" for his own demise and ruin).

Saul's failure to utterly destroy the Amalekites as God commanded led to his rejection as King of Israel (1 Samuel 15:23). Surely Saul had underestimated the consequences of just one sin, never dreaming it would cost him the throne of Israel. Most identify with Saul in that they equally are prone to overestimate the tolerance of God toward sin and underestimate its tragic consequences. What might the act of just one sin produce in your life?

It can color the rest of your life. Playing with sin is like playing with coal. It is impossible not to be colored with its nature. You may say, "Frank, this one wrong thing I do won't hurt me. Everybody is doing it. One beer won't hurt me. One snort won't hurt me. One visit to a pornographic website won't harm me. One act of sexual immorality won't injure me. Cheating one time on an exam won't hurt me." You are wrong. Sin, regardless of its size or the number of times it is committed, does hurt you, and it colors the rest of life. King Saul will attest to this as indisputable.

It can addict (enslave) for all of your life. A Kentucky farmer maintained his field like a garden. A young man, in anger, sneaked into the field at night and sowed Johnson grass seed. In time, the grass sprouted and spread throughout the farmer's field. The farmer never learned of the culprit who sowed it. Years passed, and the young man who sowed the seed in the field married the farmer's daughter. Upon the death of his father-in-law, he inherited the farm. This man fought the unending battle of digging up the roots of that Johnson grass he had sown in his youth.

Sowing the seeds of alcohol, drugs, pornography, dishonesty and immorality in the soul now may lead to a lifetime of digging them up by the roots. Youth is the planting stage of life; adulthood is the reaping stage. You will reap what you sow, perhaps for the rest of your life. "One sin," says C. H. Spurgeon, "can ruin a soul forever; it is not in the power of the human mind to grasp the infinity of evil that slumbereth in the bowels of one solitary sin."[1246]

It can alter God's plan for your life. Saul was God's choice to rule Israel, but one sin thwarted that from occurring. Moses was God's choice to lead the Israelites into the Promised Land, but one sin prevented it. Samson was God's man to judge Israel, but after twenty years, one sin forced him to step down. Likewise, only one sin can cause God to alter His perfect plan for your life. Don't possibly forfeit God's foremost plan by yielding to one sin.

It can spoil the testimony for life. It takes one sin only a few minutes to tear down the strong reputation and testimony that took years to construct.

It can shorten life. Ananias and Sapphira had life cut short due to one sin (Acts 5:10). Achan's one sin shortened his life (Joshua 7:20–25). The Apostle John states that there is a "sin unto death" (1 John 5:16). The consumption of alcohol shortens one's life; the use of drugs shortens life; tobacco use shortens life; perverted sexual lifestyles shorten life. Mark it down—one sin may lead to a life cut short.

It can condemn the soul to Hell for eternity. The only sin that separates man from God for eternity is that of unbelief. Jesus declared, "He that believeth on him is not condemned: but he that believeth not is condemned already, because he hath not believed in the name of the only begotten Son of God" (John 3:18). In order to go to Hell, one does not have to live a life of grave sin; he needs only to neglect Christ as Lord and Savior. If you are not a Christian, right now turn from sin and embrace Christ as your Lord and Savior (Romans 10:9–13).

One sin confessed may be forgiven. Solomon states, "He that covereth his sins shall not prosper: but whoso confesseth and forsaketh them shall have mercy" (Proverbs 28:13). Either you allow God to deal with your sin, or you will have to deal with it. He stands ever ready to forgive and cleanse of whatever sin you acknowledge with a repentant heart (1 John 1:9; Hebrews 8:12). Sin confessed is forgiven; however, its consequences may be unalterable. Never forget this truth!

The Bottom Line: As a little thorn causes a great blister, a little moth destroys a great garment, and a small fox destroys a great vine, what you count as a little sin, committed but one time, can bring irreparable damage to your life. Sin, as with some poisons, takes only one dose to destroy life or devastate all the rest of life.

285
Sin, the devil's barber shop
Proverbs 13:6

"Righteousness keepeth him that is upright in the way: but wickedness overthroweth the sinner."

"Righteousness" (state of being right and doing right; the upright) "keepeth" (guards, preserves) him that is "upright" (the Christian) in the "way" (concourse of life): BUT wickedness "overthroweth" (destroys; ruins) the sinner.

The principle stated is that sinfulness ruins or destroys ("overthroweth") a man. Samson's visit to the Devil's barber shop well illustrates the teaching (Judges 16:16–22). Samson, the strongest man who ever lived, became the weakest. As he slept on Delilah's lap, his hair (but much more than his hair) was clipped. The Devil clipped Samson's power, profession (testimony), potential and peace. All who visit the Devil's barber shop of pornography, alcohol, drugs, dishonesty, sexual immorality and gambling will likewise have these things clipped from their lives. In contrast, he that walks in "righteousness" (rightly, correctly, chastely) will be preserved from such ruin and devastation.

The Bottom Line: A person can choose which path to travel but cannot choose its destination. Travel on the broad road of sin always leads to despair, disaster, and doom—always.

286
Sin, the law of cause and effect
Proverbs 18:3

"When the wicked cometh, then cometh also contempt, and with ignominy reproach."

"The wicked cometh" (sin cometh with the sinner) brings "contempt" (disdain, sneers) which leads to "ignominy" (disgrace) that leads to "reproach" (shame; "'reproach" goes with shame. This reproach refers to the critical rebukes and taunts of the community against a wicked person[1247]). "Cause and effect" is always demonstrated with sin. Like a boomerang, it always returns, bearing bitter fruit. Sin brings contempt, which leads to disgrace, which leads to shame.

Sinful conduct ought to always be repugnant to and punished by the community, while they embrace the sinner (hate sin; love the sinner). Allen Ross says, "The disgrace, for example, would be the critical rebukes of the community against the wicked person."[1248] Regrettably, in some communities, *political correctness* prevents public outcry against horrendous acts of wickedness and the dishonor he that commits it deserves. The church must not side with the world or with its political correctness philosophy. Tactfully and lovingly she must always side with that which is right, honorable, correct and moral.

The words bear repeating over and over until they are heard: "That which is theologically wrong can never be politically correct." Scripture is clear that rebuke and reproof are to be given in a spirit of love to all who err from the truth in engaging in deeds of wrongdoing. It also outlines the manner for issuance of such reproof (Matthew 18:15; 1 Timothy 5:20). An example of contempt for the wicked is recorded in Malachi 2:8–9: "'But you priests have left God's paths. Your instructions have caused many to stumble into sin. You have corrupted the covenant I made with the Levites,' says the Lord of Heaven's Armies. 'So I have made you despised and humiliated in the eyes of all the people. For you have not obeyed me but have shown favoritism in the way you carry out my instructions'" (NLT).

The Bottom Line: Sin brings the punishment of man (disgrace, dishonor) and also of God (Isaiah 13:11; Matthew 10:28; Romans 1:18; Revelation 21:8). That which the wicked fears will "come upon him" (Proverbs 10:24) suddenly (Proverbs 24:22).

287
Single, the blessedness of singlehood
Proverbs 18:22

"Whoso findeth a wife findeth a good thing, and obtaineth favour of the LORD."

Whoso "findeth" (marries) a wife findeth a "good thing" (you have been blessed; most "fortunate"[1249]), and "obtaineth favor of the Lord" (the acceptance and approval of God; not saying those who don't marry cannot obtain His favor[1250]).

The Proverb is not condemning being single. It simply states that God sanctions (approves) marriage, and to marry a good woman (Proverbs 31) is a blessing or gift from God. "A virtuous woman [worthy and godly] is a crown to her husband: but she that maketh ashamed is as rottenness in his bones" (Proverbs 12:4). Obviously, it is not God's will for everyone to marry. In 1 Corinthians 7, the Apostle Paul, in counseling the unmarried, makes clear they are not unspiritual because they are single. He says, "It is perfectly proper, honorable, morally befitting for a man to live in strict celibacy" (1 Corinthians 7:1 WUEST). It's honorable to remain single. Not to marry is not to gain the disfavor of the Lord.

John Stott, bachelor throughout life, said, "If marriage is good, singleness is also good. It's an example of the balance of Scripture that, although Genesis 2:18 indicates that it is good to marry, 1 Corinthians 7:1 (in answer to a question posed by the Corinthians) says that 'it is good for a man not to marry.' So both the married and the single states are 'good'; neither is in itself better or worse than the other."[1251]

The population of singles is soaring in America [The Bureau of Labor Statistics (2014): 124.6 million sixteen years and older were single, or 50.2 percent of the population, compared with 37.4 percent of the population in 1976[1252]], necessitating the church to step up the pace in "engaging" them with the Gospel (evangelistic events; singles' ministry programs; soul-winning visitation). It is a field "white unto harvest."

The Bottom Line: Not to marry is not to gain the disfavor of the Lord, for singleness is honorable. Paul argued that remaining unmarried freed the person to be totally focused on life and service unto the Lord (1 Corinthians 7:32–33).

288
Sinlessness, its impossibility to attest
Proverbs 20:9
"Who can say, I have made my heart clean, I am pure from my sin?"

"Who can say" (a rhetorical question which implies the answer "nobody"), I have made my heart "clean" (pure), I am "pure" (clean) from my "sin" (transgression of God's law; not only conduct of disobedience or wrongdoing toward God and our fellowman, but attitudes, motives and inaction about things that ought to have been done).

All men are miserable, wretched sinners. No one can say he is without sin in thought and deed ("pure").

Solomon, in the dedication of the Temple, underscored this indisputable fact: "There is no man that sinneth not" (1 Kings 8:46). Paul attested: "All have sinned, and come short of the glory of God" (Romans 3:23). John said, "If we say that we have no sin, we deceive ourselves, and the truth is not in us" (1 John 1:8). Man may count himself sinless, but he is grossly deceived. In God's "sight shall no man living be justified" (Psalm 143:2) apart from His grace and mercy. The only person who can claim to be *pure* is he who has experienced divine forgiveness for sins committed whether in thought or deed (Psalm 51:7). "Blessed [happy] is he whose transgression is forgiven, whose sin is covered. Blessed is the man unto whom the LORD imputeth not iniquity, and in whose spirit there is no guile" (Psalm 32:1–2). See 1 Kings 8:46; Ecclesiastes 7:20.

McKane says that one "can never be certain that his mind is pure and that he is without alloy of sin. Even when he has no good reason to believe otherwise and might draw such a conclusion in good faith, he cannot be certain that he is not self-deceived and has failed to plumb unsuspected depths of duplicity and perversion which Yahweh will take into account."[1253] Paul was of the same mind, for he said, "My conscience is clear, but that does not make me innocent. It is the Lord who judges me" (1 Corinthians 4:4 NIV).

Believers therefore in deepest humility ought to pray regularly with David, "Search me, O God, and know my heart: try me, and know my thoughts: And see if there be any wicked way in me, and lead me in the way everlasting" (Psalm 139:23–24). The Christian will never arrive at a state of sinlessness in this life, but he is to strive to grow in grace that he may become less and less sinful. Until sinlessness is attained in Heaven, the believer must pray with Robert Murray McCheyne, "Lord, make me as holy as a pardoned sinner can be made."[1254]

The Bottom Line: He that claims to be without fault knows better. See Proverbs 21:2. God's judgment will fall upon sin and the sinner regardless of whether or not it is acknowledged. Refuge is to be found in the abounding forgiveness of sin through its confession (1 John 1:9). H. A. Ironside says, "When all pretense to purity in oneself is given up, it is found in Christ for those who receive Him."[1255] All men, regardless of face, race or place, are sinners who must humble themselves, saying, "Lord, be merciful to me, a sinner" (Luke 18:13).

289
Skill, its benefits
Proverbs 22:29

"Seest thou a man diligent in his business? he shall stand before kings; he shall not stand before mean men."

Seest thou a man "diligent" (skilled; experienced) in his "business" (work)? he shall stand before "kings" (he will serve rulers; the important); he shall "not stand before mean" (obscure; less important[1256]) men.

Opportunity for success and the best of jobs (and promotion, advancement in a job) is contingent upon skills possessed. The master workman is sought out by "kings," whereas he that is an ordinary laborer works for the lesser known in common labor. A person should train and study hard to be *exceptional* at what he does, not just *adequate*. Favor is found with laborers who do their job with diligence and excellence (not just doing enough to get by). "And whatsoever ye do, do it heartily, as to the Lord, and not unto men" (Colossians 3:23). "Not slothful in business" (Romans 12:11).

> The heights by great men reached and kept
> Were not attained by sudden flight,
> But that while their companions slept
> Were toiling upward through the night.
>
> ~ Henry Wadsworth Longfellow

Wolseley said, "I believe success in life is within the reach of all who set before them an aim and an ambition that is not beyond the talents and ability which God has bestowed upon them. The first step on the ladder that leads to success is the firm determination to succeed; the next is the possession of that moral and physical courage which will enable one to mount up, rung after rung, until the top is reached. The best men make a false step now and then, and some even have very bad falls. The weak and puling cry over their misfortunes and seek for the sympathy of others and do nothing further after their first or second failure, but the plucky and the courageous pick themselves up without a groan over their broken bones or their first failures and set to work to mount the ladder again, full of confidence in themselves and with faith in the results that always attend upon cheerful perseverance."[1257]

The Bottom Line: The lazy, slothful, unambitious and unskilled will be denied the best opportunities. Discover God's given *knack* and hone in on it, developing it to its fullest potential. The righteous diligent may not be summoned to work (position of a hired servant) for a king, but upon their death, they will be so summoned by the King of Kings to serve Him in Heaven (Revelation 7:15).

290
Slander, don't stoke it; smother it
Proverbs 26:20

"Where no wood is, there the fire goeth out: so where there is no talebearer, the strife ceaseth."

Where no "wood" (fuel for slander) is, there the "fire goeth out" (extinguished): so where there is no "talebearer" (gossiper, slanderer), the "strife" (quarrelling) "ceaseth" (stops).

The *Atlanta Constitution* printed this piece many years ago. "I am more deadly than the screaming shell of a howitzer. I win without killing. I tear down homes, break hearts and wreck lives. I travel on the wings of the wind. No innocence is strong enough to intimidate me, no purity pure enough to daunt me. I have no regard for truth, no respect for justice, no mercy for the defenseless. My victims are as numerous as the sands of the sea and often as innocent. I never forget and seldom forgive. My name is Gossip!"[1258]

Slanderous gossip, as a fire, needs fuel ("wood") to survive. To extinguish slander's devastating and destructive impact, all that is needed is to withhold its needed fuel (sharing, declaring and spreading). "We should form the habit of letting all slander and gossip go in one ear and out the other instead of letting it go out our mouths."[1259] Proverbs 26:20 simply states, don't stoke or fuel the slanderer's fire but attempt to smother it. The listening to and spreading of slanderous remarks makes one a co-conspirator with the talebearers in the destruction they precipitate. Martin Luther reminds us, "You are not only responsible for what you say, but also for what you do not say."[1260]

If slandered, respond as did Nehemiah (Nehemiah 6:5–8). When he refused to stop the rebuilding of the walls about Jerusalem, opponents fabricated the story of his desire to become king in Judah. Nehemiah nevertheless was immovable, refusing to allow slander to stop the work God ordained. He prayed, "O God, strengthen my hands" (Nehemiah 6:9) and pressed on.

Prayer is the saints' great weaponry against the missiles of slander. Pray for patience to endure the trial, protection from harm, and the silencing of the false reports by the truth springing forth to light. C. H. Spurgeon advised, "The best way to deal with slander is to pray about it. God will either remove it or remove the sting from it. Our own attempts at clearing ourselves are usually failures; we are like the boy who wished to remove the blot from his copy and by his bungling made it ten times worse."[1261]

The Bottom Line: Richard Cecil said, "If there is any person to whom you feel dislike, that is the person of whom you ought never to speak."[1262]

291
Slander, its warlike weapons upon another
Proverbs 25:18

"A man that beareth false witness against his neighbour is a maul, and a sword, and a sharp arrow."

"Do not spread false reports. Do not help a guilty person by being a malicious witness" (Exodus 23:1 NIV).

"Brothers, do not slander one another" (James 4:11 BSB).

A man that "beareth" (gives) "false witness" (lies) against his "neighbor" (companion or friend) is a "maul, and a sword, and a sharp arrow" (see explanation below).

A slanderous tongue (speaks an evil or untrue report) is like using warlike weapons upon another (sword, ax, arrow) to ruin his reputation, ministry, family and relationships while inflicting horrendous pain and grief to the soul. Matthew Henry elucidates, "A false testimony is everything that is dangerous; it is a maul (or club to knock a man's brains out with), a flail, which there is no fence against; it is a sword to wound near at hand and a sharp arrow to wound at a distance."[1263]

> Slander leaves a slur, even if it be wholly disproved. Once let an ill word get into men's mouths, and it is not easy to get it fully out again.
> C. H. Spurgeon

"When Solomon wrote the Proverbs," Chuck Swindoll states, "he included the seven things the Lord hates. Among them, 'a false witness who utters lies' (Proverbs 6:19 NASB). Nevertheless, liars are still on the loose. If you have been the brunt of someone's lying tongue, more specifically, if you have been falsely accused, you don't need me to describe real pain. You've not only been there, you've discovered how difficult it can be to defend yourself. You try, but folks are hard to convince once they've heard convincing lies. The venom from a poisoned tongue has already taken its toll. Tragically, churches can be a feeding ground for loose lips and lying tongues. It takes courage to stand up to liars."[1264]

As stated in the last section, the listening to and spreading of slanderous remarks makes one a co-conspirator with the talebearers in the destruction they precipitate. Solomon underscores the point: "Whoever goes about slandering reveals secrets; therefore do not associate with a simple babbler" (Proverbs 20:19 ESV) and "Where no wood is, there the fire goeth out: so where there is no talebearer, the strife ceaseth" (Proverbs 26:20). Again, don't stoke or fuel the slanderer's fire, but attempt to smother it.

The Bottom Line: "The slanderer wounds three at once—himself, him he speaks of, and him that hears."[1265]

292
Sleep, squandering precious time through excess time in bed
Proverbs 20:13

"Love not sleep, lest thou come to poverty; open thine eyes, and thou shalt be satisfied with bread."

"Slothfulness casteth into a deep sleep; and an idle soul shall suffer hunger" (Proverbs 19:15).

"Love not sleep" (Poole, "immoderate"[1266] time sleeping; "to sleep is a matter of necessity; to love sleep is the mark of indolence"[1267]), lest thou come to "poverty" (lose what you have for lack of work); "open thine eyes" (wake up and get to work), AND thou shalt be "satisfied with bread" (there will be more than enough on the table for you to satisfy your appetite).

In a lifespan of 75, years a person that sleeps eight hours a day will sleep a total of 9,125 days or one-third of his life.[1268] Don't "love" (overindulge) sleep. Get sufficient sleep (sleep deprivation is unhealthy), but then "open thine eyes." Upon awaking, be industrious; don't squander the time. Jumpstart the day with prayer, Scripture reading, and solitude with the Lord. Early rising also facilitates a distraction-free environment to write, more in-depth Bible study and uninterrupted praying, artistic painting, and exercise.

Doddridge explained that the reason he was able to write numerous books despite a busy schedule was rising early. He discovered a great difference between rising at five and rising at eight in the morning—the first adding several more years to the course of life.[1269] With time rapidly elapsing for us all, early rising is an excellent way to capture more of it to facilitate the accomplishment of more for God. In this writing project, I have risen many mornings at three or earlier.

Everybody is wired differently; early rising is easier for some than others. Solomon's point simply put is don't become addicted to sleep (loving it above responsibilities, obligations, communion with the Lord, and spiritual and secular work). Don't allow sleep to rob you of wondrous opportunities that bring great benefit spiritually, emotionally, physically and at times monetarily. Redeem the time (Ephesians 5:16). God will hold us accountable for how we used time on earth—even how much of it was allotted to sleep (Psalm 90:12).

The Bottom Line: It is unwise to sleep excessively, wasting away unproductive hours in bed while there is much to be done before life ends. Jesus cautions, "The night cometh, when no man can work" (John 9:4). May it be your determined purpose to so use time wisely that upon the night's arrival you may say, "I have finished the work which thou gavest me to do" (John 17:4). We will have plenty of time to rest in Heaven.

293

Sleep, the righteous sleep restfully and peacefully
Proverbs 3:24

"When thou liest down, thou shalt not be afraid: yea, thou shalt lie down, and thy sleep shall be sweet."

When thou "liest down" (go to bed), thou shalt not be "afraid" (of any fright, threat, terror; Deane and Taswell say, "No fear is to be apprehended where Jehovah is Protector [see Psalms 3:5, 6; 46:1–3; 91:1–5; 121:5–8]"[1270]): yea, thou shalt "lie down" (to bed), AND thy "sleep shall be sweet" (pleasant, peaceful, restful, sound[1271]). See Jeremiah 31:26 and contrast with Job 7:4.

Sleep is evasive for the wicked whose foolish and corrupt lifestyle often interrupts it. Not so with the righteous. He shall sleep like a baby (pleasant night sleep), for He knows the all-seeing and protective eye of the Lord is ever upon him. Neither cares nor calamities interfere with the sleep of the righteous ones when their mind is stayed on Him. David declared, "I laid me down and slept; I awaked; for the LORD sustained me" (Psalm 3:5). His sweet sleep hinged on knowing the God of "sleep."

C. H. Spurgeon remarks, "The sleep of the body is the gift of God. He rocks the cradle for us every night; He draws the curtain of darkness; He bids the sun shut up his burning eyes; and then He comes and says, 'Sleep, sleep, My child; I give thee sleep.'"[1272] He continues, "Not a man would close his eyes, did not God put His fingers on his eyelids; did not the Almighty send a soft and balmy influence over his frame which lulled his thoughts into quiescence, making him enter into that blissful state of rest which we call sleep."[1273]

The Bottom Line: A pleasant night's sleep is a blessing from the Lord which is reserved for the godly whose life is ordered by biblically sound wisdom and discretion. See Psalm 127:2.

294
Smile, a free gift to give to others
Proverbs 15:30
"The light of the eyes rejoiceth the heart."

"The light of the eyes" (radiant glow complexion,[1274] smiling face) makes others happy ("rejoices the heart"). R. E. Murphy says, "The expressiveness of the eyes betrays an inner joy which others can recognize and be affected by."[1275]

A smile has healthy medicine to make another's day better. It is a costless yet priceless gift. Mother Teresa of Calcutta said, "We shall never know all the good that a simple smile can do."[1276] The poet Emily Dickenson said, "They might not need me; but they might. I'll let my head be just in sight; a smile as small as mine might be precisely their necessity."[1277] In departing home each day, bear the attitude with regard to people encountered, "If you don't have a smile, I will give you one of mine." Washington Irving summarizes the power of gifting a smile, "A kind heart is a fountain of gladness, making everything in its vicinity freshen into smiles."[1278]

In dressing, one of the most important things to put on is a *smile.*

Give the world a smile each day,
Helping someone on life's way.
From the paths of sin bring the wanderer's in
To the master's fold to stay.
Help to cheer the lone and sad;
Help to make some pilgrim glad. ~ Otis Deaton (1924)

The Bottom Line: Mother Teresa said, "Every time you smile at someone, it is an action of love, a gift to that person, a beautiful thing." Denis Watley says, "A smile is the light in your window that tells others that there is a caring, sharing person inside."[1279]

295
Snare, escaping the sexual snare
Proverbs 7:8
"He went the way to her house."

"With her much fair speech [flattery] she caused him to yield, with the flattering of her lips she forced him" (Proverbs 7:21).

"And it came to pass, as she spake to Joseph day by day, that he hearkened not unto her, to lie by her, or to be with her" (Genesis 39:10).

"He" (the foolish young man void of understanding) "went the way" (intentionally or accidentally we are not told, but from the context it appears it was the former) "to her house" (the harlot's house where she would be on the street waiting to entice him to sin). Little did the young man know that a well-designed snare for his seduction had been set by the harlot. To summarize, Robert L. Alden wrote, "If you want to avoid the

Devil, stay away from his neighborhood. If you suspect you might be vulnerable to a particular sin, take steps to avoid it."[1280]

Joseph victoriously encountered the sexual snare laid out by Mrs. Potiphar, as all may if they follow his example (Genesis 39:12).

He had his eyes wide open all the time. Joseph had a predetermined response to the sex temptation. Determine in advance sure and firm responses to the seductive gestures and enticing appeals that will be hurled upon you (Proverbs 7:21).

He knew the right words to say. "For her unclean solicitation he returneth pure and wholesome words."[1281] In essence, Joseph said to Mrs. Potiphar, "This is morally wrong, a sin against God which I will not engage in" (Genesis 39:9).

He tried to keep his distance from her. This was a smart and strategic move by Joseph to avoid moral failure.

He had his feet ready to run at all times. Joseph literally ran from the sex temptation (Genesis 39:12). Paul exhorts, "Flee youthful lusts" (2 Timothy 2:22). Escape for thy life. Run from the *sex snare* promptly and swiftly.

He had his heart in the right place. Joseph's intimate love relationship with and allegiance to the Lord (Genesis 39:2) helped garrison him from the sin. The surest defense against sexual immorality is a personal in-depth relationship with Jesus Christ (John 15:5; 1 John 4:4).

The Bottom Line: Mightier men than you have been overtaken by a Mrs. Potiphar. "Let him that thinketh he standeth take heed lest he fall" (1 Corinthians 10:12). The snare is set, yet hidden from view, awaiting its chance to suddenly bring you down. E. Stanley Jones (twentieth-century missionary and theologian) stated, "The battle of life as a whole will probably not rise above the sex battle. Lose the sex battle and defeat spreads into every portion of your being. Win it and all of life is lifted by that victory."[1282]

296
Snare, the Devil has snares everywhere for everyone
Proverbs 22:25
"Lest thou learn his ways, and get a snare to thy soul."

"Lest" (so that you will not) thou "learn his ways" (take on the behavior of the angry man [verse 24] but applies to any sinful action), AND get a "snare to thy soul" (get trapped in sinful conduct; like the "angry man" unable to break free, to change).

"Satan hath snares," states Thomas Brooks, "for the wise and snares for the simple, snares for the hypocrites and snares for the upright, snares for generous souls and snares for timorous souls, snares for the rich and snares for the poor, snares for the aged and snares for youth. Happy are those souls that are not taken and held in the snares that he hath laid!"[1283] Various and numerous are the snares the enemy of the soul has prepared to trip every man up. Included among them is that of pornography, sexual immorality, alcohol, drugs, gambling and religious skepticism. Many a giant has fallen into these demoralizing and destructive traps. Paul advises, "Let him that thinketh he standeth take heed lest he fall" (1 Corinthians 10:12). All would be wise to pray continuously with David, "Keep me from the snares which they have laid for me, and the gins of the workers of iniquity" (Psalm 141:9). Why? "Greater is he that is in you, than he that is in the world." (1 John 4:4).

Amidst a thousand snares I stand,
Upheld and guarded by Thy hand;
That hand unseen shall hold me still
And lead me to Thy holy hill.[1284]

The Bottom line: Pray for divine protection against secret plots designed for your demise physically, emotionally and spiritually. If presently entrapped, look to the Lord for escape without delay. "If the Son therefore shall make you free, ye shall be free indeed" (John 8:36). See Psalm 141:9–10.

297
Soul, laziness brings ruin to the soul
Proverbs 24:30–31
"I went by the field of the slothful, and by the vineyard of the man void of understanding; And, lo, it was all grown over with thorns, and nettles had covered the face thereof, and the stone wall thereof was broken down."

"I" (the observer [sage,[1285] profoundly wise person]) "went by" (walked past) the "field of the slothful" (crop field of the lazy[1286]), and by the "vineyard of the man void of understanding" (grape vineyard of the foolish, insensible, stupid); AND, lo, it was "all grown over with thorns, and nettles had covered the face [ground] thereof" (overrun with weeds due to failure to work it) and the "stone wall thereof was broken down" (the fence that encircled the field to keep intruders and animals out was in disrepair[1287]).

The cause for the barren field (absence of food growth) overtaken by weeds was the man's laziness. He failed to broadcast seed into the sod or upon doing so neglected its cultivation. The grapeless vineyard overtaken with weeds was the result of a lack of common sense ("void of understanding"). "He also that is slothful in his work is brother to him that is a great waster" (Proverbs 18:9). "The sluggard will not plow by reason of the cold; therefore shall he beg in harvest, and have nothing" (Proverbs 20:4).

There is no fatigue so wearisome as that which comes from lack of work.
C. H. Spurgeon

A higher lesson to be gleaned from the Proverb is that the neglect of one's heart field or vineyard results in spiritual barrenness, emptiness and indifference. The lazy Christian is the stunted, stagnant Christian. "They made me the keeper of the vineyards; but mine own vineyard have I not kept" (Song of Solomon 1:6). The person speaking in this text had the responsibility for the upkeep (the pruning, plowing, planting) of vineyards that belonged unto others. It is clear that she was not negligent in this assignment but diligent and determined to cultivate them so that each would fulfill its purpose to the owner's pleasure. Such faithfulness to her employer and sacrificial work is commendable!

However, the passion that led her to serve so zealously in the vineyards of others precipitated neglect in her own, and for that she should be reprimanded. She testifies, "They made me the keeper of the vineyards; but mine own vineyard have I not kept." She enabled the vineyards of others to stay pruned and thus bear much fruit, while her own was overtaken with weeds and thorns yielding little or no fruit. Many Christians identify with the vineyard laborer. They promote the growth of others spiritually while neglecting their own.

S. D. Gordon stated, "A life of victory and power hinges upon three things: one, an act; two, a purpose; three, a habit—an initial act, a fixed purpose, a daily habit."[1288] In sequence as stated, Gordon was referencing surrender, obedience and quiet time. Gordon, in emphasizing the daily habit of quiet time, said, "After the initial act of surrender, the secret of a strong winsome Christian life is in spending time daily alone with God over His Word." Start today the great work of pruning, plowing and planting in the vineyard of *your* heart through disciplined resolve to daily study God's Word and pray, regularly prune the weeds of sin from your heart, and habitually attend church to receive biblical instruction and to be spurred forward by the saints in godliness.

The Bottom Line: Laziness is ruinous to the soul. The soul's vineyard must be diligently worked. "Its neglect," states Charles Bridges, "checks its every step of progress; so that 'the soul'—instead of being 'a well-watered garden' (Jeremiah 31:12), sending forth refreshing fragrance and grateful fruits—relapses into its former wilderness state, laid open to every temptation, and too often ultimately a prey to sensual appetites."[1289]

298
Soul Winning, he that winneth souls is wise
Proverbs 11:30
"The fruit of the righteous is a tree of life; and he that winneth souls is wise."

"And others save with fear, pulling them out of the fire; hating even the garment spotted by the flesh" (Jude 23).

The "fruit" (that which comes forth from a person's life, example, conduct) of the "righteous" (the upright; the Christian) is a "tree of life" (Buzzell says "a source of meaningful life to others"[1290]); he that "winneth souls is wise" (MacArthur says it means literally "to take lives" for their betterment and good or influencing them to embrace the ways of wisdom[1291]; Kemp says it is a military term used in the "taking" of towns by warfare and a fishing term used in "catching fish"[1292] [Matthew 4:19]). See Daniel 12:3 and Luke 5:10. Matthew Poole summarizes, he "that catcheth souls as a fowler doth birds, that maketh it his design and business and useth all his skill and diligence to gain souls to God and to pluck them out of the snare of the Devil, is wise."[1293] This interpretation is that of most conservative evangelicals.

Hebrew scholars share that the text is not in regard to evangelism or soul salvation but to the winning of men to wisdom (uprightness, godliness, "the straight and narrow path"). I contend that the only way the fool can be won to the way of uprightness and wisdom is through winning him to the saving knowledge of Jesus Christ. After all, Jesus Christ is the personification of Wisdom. Paul declared, "Christ the power of God, and the wisdom of God" (1 Corinthians 1:24). Man's reception of God's Wisdom, Jesus Christ, results in a change of paths (ungodly to the godly) and eternal life. Righteous living in keeping with God's standard is only possible through a personal relationship with Jesus Christ.

The *fruit a righteous life* is the germination of a *tree of life* in another. C. H. Spurgeon explains, "From the child of God there falls the fruit of holy living, even as an acorn drops itself from an oak; this holy living becomes influential and produces the best results in others, even as the acorn becomes itself an oak and lends its shade to the birds of the air. The Christian's holiness becomes a tree of life…a tree calculated to give life and sustain it in others. A fruit becomes a tree! A tree of life!"[1294]

How glorious and wondrous it is that the righteous Christian by his holy lifestyle in conduct and conversation through the divine work of the Holy Spirit produces *trees of life* (abundant and eternal life) like unto his own ("win souls"). This is the *chief fruit* of the righteous. Abiding in Jesus is the spiritual fertilizer that enables the believer to bear not only "fruit" but "much fruit" (John 15:4–5). To abide in Christ means to keep Him at the center of life, to obey Him without vacillating, to take cues from Him regarding decisions and conduct and to steadfastly walk in intimacy with Him (John 8:31).

Failure to abide in Christ results in impotency to bear fruit (John 15:6). He said, "Herein is my Father glorified, that ye bear much fruit; so shall ye be my disciples" (v. 8). Regardless of age, every believer who abides in Jesus and understands the simple basics in witnessing, the why (Romans 3:23; 5:8) and how (Romans 10:9–13), is capable of leading a soul to saving faith. Soul winning is often *more caught than taught*. As you win souls, teach others by precept and example to be soul winners.

The Bottom Line: Looking in depth into the text and the rearview mirror (New Testament: Acts 1:8; Matthew 28:19–20; Luke 19:10; Jude

23) back to Proverbs 11:30, it is overtly clear it refers to the winning of souls from the wicked path to that of the righteous in Jesus Christ. Spurgeon appeals, "If you have found life, proclaim it to the dead; if you have found liberty, publish it to the captives; if you have found Christ, tell of Him to others."[1295]

299
Soul Winning, its archenemies
Proverbs 24:11–12

"If thou forbear to deliver them that are drawn unto death, and those that are ready to be slain; If thou sayest, Behold, we knew it not; doth not he that pondereth the heart consider it? and he that keepeth thy soul, doth not he know it? and shall not he render to every man according to his works?"

If thou "forbear" (refuse) to "deliver them" (rescue) that are "drawn unto death" (in mortal danger unjustly), and those that are "ready to be slain" (people who are being dragged to their execution); if thou sayest, Behold, we "knew it not" (play ignorant regarding their plight); doth not he that "pondereth the heart" (God who weighs the heart knows the truth) consider it? AND he that "keepeth" (guards, overwatches you in protection), doth not he know it? AND shall not he "render to every man according to his works" (God will repay man for the good and bad which he does; it's inescapable). Allen Ross summarizes, "The general application would include any who are in mortal danger, through disease, hunger, war—we cannot dodge responsibility, even by ignorance."[1296]

I make application of the Proverb to those that are being led to the slaughter by Satan (ruination presently and Hell hereafter) and the need of their rescuing. We have been given orders to "deliver them that are drawn unto death" but are not obeying (Acts 1:8). The reason for not obeying is attributable to ten enemies to the task of evangelism.

The first enemy to soul winning is Worldliness. The separated Christian is the soul-winning Christian. Worldliness quenches soul-winning fire. If we are to be world changers, difference makers, winners of souls, we must have clean hands and a pure heart.

The second enemy to soul winning is Busyness (distractions). Ironically, doing "church" robs time that ought to be spent in witnessing. Bailey Smith said, "The other things we have to do may be called important by those around us, but there is nothing on earth more important to do than to win a person to Jesus Christ." Corrie ten Boom is credited with saying, "If the Devil cannot make us bad, he will make us busy."

A third enemy to soul winning is an Imperceptibility of Hell. One's perception of Hell defines his soul-winning effort. Therefore, be sure it's biblical, as revealed by Jesus in the story of the rich man and Lazarus (Luke 16:19–31).

A fourth enemy to soul winning is an Unbiblical Premise. To embrace the view that God has already determined who goes to Heaven and Hell will extinguish soul-winning fires. To believe man's destiny is already determined negates the need to witness. But that premise is biblically unsound. Peter didn't believe it. He declared, "The Lord is not slack concerning his promise, as some men count slackness; but is longsuffering to us-ward, not willing that any should perish, but that all should come to repentance" (2 Peter 3: 9). John didn't believe it. He said, "He died in our place to take away our sins, and not only our sins but the sins of all people" (1 John 2:2 NCV). Paul didn't believe it. He stated, "For whosoever shall call upon the name of the Lord shall be saved" (Romans 10:13). Jesus for sure didn't embrace it. He said, "The Son of man is come to seek and to save that which was lost" (Luke 19:10). Not until a Christian gets his mind settled on the fact that man has a choice with regard to his soul will he ever feel the urgent need to tell him of Jesus.

A fifth enemy to soul winning is Evangelistic Indifference. The problem of modern evangelism IS evangelistic apathy. It is the prevalent sin of the church. Without a love for God and concern for the lost, you won't go and tell.

A sixth enemy of soul winning is Transference. Thinking that somebody else will do it, we pass the buck to the next guy to tell of Jesus.

The seventh enemy of soul winning is an Unwillingness to Change Methods. We must be willing to adjust our method, not the message, to win more. Paul said that he sought to be all things to all men that he might win some. Tweak the method that it may be an effective means to bring the lost to Christ. Someone wrote a book entitled The Seven Last Words of the Church—"We never did it that way before." Think "outside the box."

The eighth enemy of soul winning is Fear. The basic fear most face that hinders them from being a witness is the fear of failure. Remember, witnessing is sharing Jesus in the power of the Holy Spirit, leaving the results to Him. There are no failures in soul winning.

The ninth enemy of soul winning is Christian Fellowship. Christians can become so attached to each other socially that they never connect with the lost. Though unintentional, many adapt a monastic type of lifestyle that prevents intermingling with those who need Christ.

The tenth enemy of soul winning is Absence of Its Push in the Church. The failure to keep soul winning prominent among the saints lessens engagement in it.

R. G. Lee said, "I fear that we as Christians treat our main business as an incidental. We should be like Whitefield who said, "I am willing to go to prison and to death for you, but I am not willing to go to Heaven without you." When fishermen are sent to the river, they fish. When nurses are sent to the hospital, they nurse. When painters are sent to a house, they paint. When soldiers are sent to the battle, they fight. But when our God sends us into the world to win souls, we sing "Throw Out the Lifeline" but do not throw. We sing "I Love to Tell the Story" and do not tell it. Our singing and our practice are so strangely at variance."[1297]

The Bottom Line: Satan will ever storm the believer and church with evangelistic enemies seeking to thwart the task of soul winning. The responsibility of rescuing souls on the road to eternal torment "cannot be dodged, even by ignorance."

300
Soul Winning, to sleep in harvest is deplorable
Proverbs 10:5
"He that gathereth in summer is a wise son: but he that sleepeth in harvest is a son that causeth shame."

He that "gathereth in summer" (harvester of crops) is a "wise" (sensible, smart, intelligent) son: BUT he that "sleepeth in harvest" (too lazy to get out of bed to bring in the ready crop) is a son that "causeth shame" (brings disgrace to the family).

The text applies to the harvesting of crops but is applicable to that of souls. The day in which we now live is "summer" (time of the harvest). Every believer is to be vigilant in the work of harvesting the lost before it ends. Why is sleeping in harvesttime a shame? R. G. Lee cites several reasons.

First, it is a shame because it shows a tragic lack of responsibility when fields are white unto harvest.

Second, it is a shame because the harvest will not wait. "Harvesttime is crisis time." The crisis must be met promptly and zealously. "Doors once opened but unentered may close again. Minds made susceptible but not won for Christ may turn away and become hardened. Truth resisted once is easier to resist next time. We must strike while the iron is hot."

Third, it is a shame to sleep in harvesttime because the harvest will not reap itself. It depends upon the soldiers of Christ of all ages, sexes and positions.

Lee concludes in saying, "Now a man asleep is useless. He toils not, neither does he spin. He cannot be used in any program of the church, for he is deaf to all the holier calls. He is blind to all the loftier visions. He is a spiritual nonentity. He does not count. He weighs nothing on God's scales of requirement. He is powerless as a tombstone—as impotent as spots of dried blood. The church needs him; God needs him; every good cause needs him. But he is asleep. Christ is saying with pathos indescribable to you and to me: 'Can you not arouse yourselves from your sleep, shake yourselves from this lethargy of death and watch with Me in this great harvest night?'"[1298]

> Jesus rose from the grave,
> And you!
> You can't even get out of bed!
> Oh, Jesus rose from the dead!
> Come on, get out of your bed! ~ Keith Green (Asleep in the Light)

Which of the two sons in the Proverb pictures you? Are you as the wise son who rolled up his sleeves and worked hard in reaping the harvest, or the foolish son (apathetic, lazy) who slept while souls were dying and going to Hell.

The Bottom Line: To *sleep* in harvesttime is not only a shame but a sin (Acts 1:8; Matthew 28:18–20).

301
Speech, divine enablement governing the believer's tongue
Proverbs 16:1

"The preparations of the heart in man, and the answer of the tongue, is from the LORD."

The "preparations of the heart" (the plans of the mind are of man) in man, AND the "answer of the tongue" (the Holy Spirit controls the Spirit-filled believer's tongue; what is said is not that which is intended at times, for the Holy Spirit alters it, but always He is ordering our speech) is from the Lord.

God sovereignly enables the righteous to speak persuasively what ought to be said whether in preaching, teaching, witnessing or in reply to man's inquiry. Buzzell interprets the Proverb, "God guides what comes out of the heart in man's words."[1299] Scott translates the text, "A man plans what he will say, but his tongue utters what the Lord wills."[1300] The Revised English Bible has it, "A mortal may order his thoughts, but the Lord inspires the words his tongue utters." What a most encouraging Proverb to all who speak in behalf of the Lord, whether lay person or clergy! We do due diligence in preparation to speak (study, prayer, meditation, research) only then to rely upon the Lord to direct its deliverance in accordance to His will. Matthew Henry comments, "We are not sufficient of ourselves to think or speak anything of ourselves that is wise and good, but that all our sufficiency is of God, who is with the heart and with the mouth and works in us both to will and to do."[1301]

James Smith writes, "Man's tongue must be directed, if he speaks to God's glory. To exalt ourselves or to honor our fellowmen is easy; it is natural; it is common. But to speak to honor God's great name, to exalt His rich grace, and to show forth His praise is what no man is prepared to do until God disposes him. Hence, the wise man's record, 'The preparations of the heart in man, and the answer of the tongue is from the LORD.'"[1302] My experience certainly testifies to the truth of the Proverb. In yielding my mouth to be His mouthpiece, I have evidenced His divine control in what was to be said and how. Occasionally, for reasons unknown at the moment, later to be gloriously revealed, God has directed my tongue to speak words unintended. Balaam is a biblical example of the Proverb (Numbers 23).

The Bottom Line: "If God does not govern our tongue, we shall not succeed in what we speak" (Challoner). With God controlling the tongue, we have confidence and boldness in speaking. Certainly if God could control the tongue of a mule to speak reprimand to Balaam, His use of ours poses no problem (Numbers 22:28–30). As an additional benefit, we will not suffer from "foot-in-mouth" disease.

302
Speech, instructing others in wisdom
Proverbs 10:31
"The mouth of the just bringeth forth wisdom."

"My mouth shall speak of wisdom; and the meditation of my heart shall be of understanding" (Psalm 49:3).

The "mouth of the just" (speech of the upright, righteous) "bringeth" ("to bear fruit"[1303] like a tree) forth "wisdom" (wisdom is discernment that only God gives that enables man to do that which is right and pleasing in His sight—and which is for the man's best good—in every course of action [Philippians 2:15]).

He who speaks wisdom (Reyburn and Fry say "wise, intelligent or skillful words"[1304]) receives it from lingering in the presence of God. Daniel said, "Blessed be the name of God for ever and ever: for wisdom and might are his: And he changeth the times and the seasons: he removeth kings, and setteth up kings: he giveth wisdom unto the wise, and knowledge to them that know understanding: He revealeth the deep and secret things: he knoweth what is in the darkness, and the light dwelleth with him. I thank thee, and praise thee, O thou God of my fathers, who hast given me wisdom and might, and hast made known unto me now what we desired of thee: for thou hast now made known unto us the king's matter" (Daniel 2:20–23).

"When we give," George Lawson says, "due attention to the Word of Truth, it will dwell in our minds, dispelling ignorance and error and communicating that light which is necessary to direct the whole of our conduct; in our memories, affording a constant supply for spiritual meditation ready for use in every emergency; in our wills, to guide their choice and inclination; in our affections, to direct their motions, to curb their extravagance, and to inflame their ardor towards spiritual objects; in our consciences, to preserve alive the impressions of the divine law and to direct them in judging of the spiritual state of the soul. The senses of the body minister to the soul. The ear must be inclined to wisdom, that we may learn it. The eye, surveying the wonders of God's hand, furnishes the soul with apprehensions of His power and wisdom. But the ear is that learning sense by which the richest treasures of spiritual knowledge are admitted into to the soul."[1305] What a good epitaph to have engraved upon a tombstone is "The mouth of this person brought forth wisdom." It certainly would have been proper for that to have been etched on my father-in-law's gravestone (Kenneth Pack), for wisdom flowed from his lips.

The Bottom Line: In Holy Scripture and in Jesus' wisdom is that which is to be searched out and utilized in all of life. Of Scripture, Paul states it will make a person wise unto salvation (2 Timothy 3:15); in Jesus Christ, he states, are all the treasures of wisdom hidden (Colossians 2:3). It is God who gives man the tongue of wisdom, so inquire of Him for it.

303
Speech, just say no
Proverbs 7:25
"Let not thine heart decline to her ways, go not astray in her paths."

"Let not" (don't consent; say no) thine "heart" (the seat of reason, emotions and thoughts) "decline to her ways" (refuse to be persuaded or enticed by the sensual desire of the flesh to yield to the request of the "immoral woman" [Proverbs 7:5] or to any other sinful act), "go not astray in her paths" (don't stray from the righteous path of morality to enter upon that which leads to "Nowheresville" whose end is ruin, suffering and destruction [Proverbs 7:26]).

The word "no" is a complete sentence in and of itself. In saying it, nothing more often has to be spoken. Especially is this true with regard to peer pressure to engage in wrong. Teach your child that saying a loud "no" to all the voices that beckon to evil is sufficient, that reasoning for saying it is not necessary (to others). Obviously, there are times when giving a reason for saying "no" is beneficial (witness, deterrent to others' doing wrong, to underscore the sin's destructive impact, etc.). Daniel knew how to say "no" probably more forcefully than any other person in Scripture and thus serves as a worthy pattern to imitate. "Daniel purposed in his heart that he would not defile himself" (Daniel 1:8). Not knowing how to say "no" has caused more shipwrecks among youth than books can record. Inhabitants of a country in Asia became slaves to another country for failure to pronounce one syllable: "no."

Pythagoras said, "The oldest, shortest words—'yes' and 'no'—are those which require the most thought."

The Bottom Line: To say "no" to wrong and those who pander it, one must first say a decisive "yes" to God.

304
Speech, speak graciously and kindly to all
Proverbs 31:26
"She openeth her mouth with wisdom; and in her tongue is the law of kindness."

"Death and life are in the power of the tongue: and they that love it shall eat the fruit thereof" (Proverbs 18:21).

"She" (the Proverbs 31 godly woman) "openeth her mouth" (when she speaks) with "wisdom" (not gossip or backbiting but sensible, godly, gracious speech that is pleasing unto the Lord); AND in her "tongue" (the instruction and advice she gives) is the "law of kindness" (she teaches biblical instruction and understanding [Proverbs 1:8] "lovingly, kindly and faithfully"[1306]; Walvoord and Zuck say, "The instruction probably refers to her teaching her children and her servant girls"[1307]).

Wise, gracious and kind words flow from lips that connect with a pure and godly heart. How blessed it is to sit and converse with the truly godly as they delightfully and profitably speak. It is rich medicine to the soul. Conversely, it is upsetting and nauseating to listen to a contentious woman or man. Solomon states, "A continual dropping in a very rainy day and a contentious woman are alike" (Proverbs 27:15). Dr. Thompson's description of a Palestine rainstorm illustrates its meaning. He says, "Such rains as we have had thoroughly soak through the flat earthen roofs of these mountain houses, and the water descends in numberless leaks all over the room. This continual dropping—*tuk, tuk*—all day and all night is the most annoying thing in the world, unless it be the ceaseless chatter of a contentious woman."[1308] The contentious (controversial, argumentative) are totally annoying, and all seek to avoid them.

Criticisms, maliciousness, backbiting, slander, negativity and ridicule flow from an impure and unholy life. James states that what's in the heart flows out the spout. "With it [tongue] we bless our God and Father, and with it we curse men, who have been made in the similitude of God. Out of the same mouth proceed blessing and cursing. My brethren, these things ought not to be so. Does a spring send forth fresh water and bitter from the same opening? Can a fig tree, my brethren, bear olives, or a grapevine bear figs? Thus no spring yields both salt water and fresh" (James 3:9–12 NKJV).

Paul admonishes, "Let your speech be alway with grace, seasoned with salt" (Colossians 4:6). All conversation must be enveloped with pleasantry and kindness, void of poisonous venom. Scripture allows no wiggle room with regard to gracious speech, for it states frankly, "Let no corrupt communication proceed out of your mouth, but that which is good to the use of edifying, that it may minister grace unto the hearers" (Ephesians 4:29). "No" in the Greek language means "no." Don't speak words that are corrosive or fail to "edify" (build up, cheer up) the hearer. He who speaks perversely "shall eat the fruit thereof" (Proverbs 18:21). Man will pay the price for the injurious words spoken. Consequences are inevitable; punishment will be inflicted.

The Bottom Line: Flavor speech with the "salt" of godly wisdom and piety. Bridle the tongue that it may speak appropriately, kindheartedly and gently to all, regardless of circumstance.

305
Speech, talk less to say more
Proverbs 13:3
"He that keepeth his mouth keepeth his life: but he that openeth wide his lips shall have destruction."

"A fool's mouth is his destruction, and his lips are the snare of his soul" (Proverbs 18:7).

He that "keepeth" (guards; to weigh what one says[1309]) his "mouth" (instrument of speech) "keepeth" (guards) his "life" (protects a person's very life): BUT he that "openeth wide his lips" (to speak without forethought; "reckless, thoughtless, hasty and rash talk"[1310]; "Tight control over what one says prevents trouble. Amenemope advises to 'sleep a night before speaking'"[1311]) shall have "destruction" (meets with ruin [Proverbs 10:8, 14]). To summarize, Allen Ross remarks, "The lesson is that a tight control over what one says prevents trouble."[1312]

Quaint sayings about the tongue:

"A silent man's words are not brought into court" (Danish)

"Let not the tongue say what the head shall pay for" (Spanish)

"The sheep that bleats is strangled by the wolf" (Italians)

"Silence was never written down" (Kelly)[1313]

"When I utter a word, it hath dominion over me; but when I utter it not, I have dominion over it" (Talmud)

"The silent man hath his shoulders covered with the garment of security" (Persian poet)

Xenocrates used to say that he sometimes was "sorry for having spoken, never for having kept silence."[1314]

James calls the tongue a fire, a world of iniquity, an unruly evil full of deadly poison that defiles the whole body that must be *bridled* (James 3:6, 8). Bridling the tongue however is extremely difficult, more so than steering a ship in a hurricane (verse 4). Scott Morgan uses a bicycle chain to illustrate what really controls ("bridles") the tongue. Imagine, he writes, "a bicycle chain connecting heart and mouth. Our mouth is driven by what preoccupies our heart. Bridling our tongue means dealing with our heart first—not merely avoiding blurting out unkind words."[1315]

Bridling the tongue involves being careful what you say, when you say it and how you say it. Sometimes silence is golden. To speak rashly often results in hurt to others and oneself. Mean, proud, obnoxious, deflating and debasing words *never* are to be spoken. Neither are you permitted to speak truthful words any way you want, to whomever you want. Even speaking truthfully about another must be done in an attitude and tone of love (Ephesians 4:15) and then only for their betterment, not disdain. "Set a watch, O LORD, before my mouth; keep the door of my lips" (Psalm 141:3).

A sharp tongue is the only edged tool that grows keener with constant use.
Washington Irving

On a windswept hill in an English country churchyard stands a drab, gray slate tombstone. The quaint stone bears an epitaph not easily seen unless you stoop over and look closely. The faint etchings read:

"Beneath this stone, a lump of clay, lies Arabella Young, who on the twenty-fourth of May began to hold her tongue."

The Bottom Line: "A fool uttereth all his mind: but a wise man keepeth it in till afterwards" (Proverbs 29:11). William Norris, the American journalist, wrote:

If your lips would keep from slips,
Five things observe with care:
To whom you speak; of whom you speak;
And how, and when, and where.

306
Stress, worrying and stressing damages health
Proverbs 14:30
"A sound heart is the life of the flesh: but envy the rottenness of the bones."

A "sound" (tranquil; peaceful) "heart" (here, "the emotional state of a person"[1316]) is the "life of the flesh" (gives health to the total body physically, emotionally and morally): BUT "envy" (the NLT says "jealousy") "the rottenness of the bones" (envy, as other sins, destroys, ruins, decays one's well-being mentally and physically; the person finds no tranquility or health in body or spirit[1317]).

Medically and psychologically it is known that stress damages health—something Solomon knew hundreds of years prior to its being revealed by research. Stress places a person in jeopardy of numerous health risks, including cardiovascular disease, digestive problems, sleep issues, headaches, weight gain, and memory and concentration impairment.[1318] The longevity of stress intensifies its potential negative impact. Worry (stress) also impacts the spiritual health. Worry wounds the heart of God in its distrust, harms the testimony and reputation, interferes with spiritual progress and may lead to overt sin (Psalm 37:8).

Several years ago a popular slogan spread like wildfire throughout the country. It stated, "Don't worry; be happy." Though simplistic, it indicates a major key to stress-free living that Jesus emphasized. He said, "Do not be anxious or worried about anything, but in everything [every circumstance and situation] by prayer and petition with thanksgiving, continue to make your [specific] requests known to God. And the peace of God [that peace which reassures the heart, that peace] which transcends all understanding, [that peace which] stands guard over your hearts and your minds in Christ Jesus [is yours]" (Philippians 4:6–7 AMP). The person who places difficulties, needs, challenges and concerns in the sovereign hand of Almighty God in prayer, trusting that He will do what's best, will be delivered from the clutches of stress and dwell in "peace." Isaiah declared of the Lord, "Thou wilt keep him in perfect peace, whose mind is stayed on thee: because he trusteth in thee" (Isaiah 26:3).

Chuck Swindoll summarizes the key to a tranquil heart: "Let's get six words clearly fixed in our minds. These six words form the foundation of God's therapeutic process for all worrywarts: WORRY ABOUT NOTHING; PRAY ABOUT EVERYTHING. Turn your worry list into your prayer list. Give each worry—one by one—to God."[1319] And this is exactly what Peter instructed us to do: "Casting all your care upon him; for he careth for you" (1 Peter 5:7).

The Bottom Line: Adrian Rogers states, "Worry is a sign that we are not focusing on our Father. Matthew 6:33 says, "But seek ye first the kingdom of God, and his righteousness; and all these things shall be added unto you." What things? Finanes, food, fitness, fashion and a hope-filled future (see Jeremiah 29:11–13). Tomorrow has two handles—fear and faith—and you can take it by either."[1320]

307
Stubborn, it is futile to stand against God
Proverbs 21:30

"There is no wisdom nor understanding nor counsel against the LORD.*"*

"Therefore, behold, I will proceed to do a marvellous work among this people, even a marvellous work and a wonder: for the wisdom of their wise men shall perish, and the understanding of their prudent men shall be hid" (Isaiah 29:14).

There is no "wisdom" (here the word bears different meaning from its use in Proverbs at large; Scott says "the arrogant claim of secular wisdom"[1321]) nor "understanding" (intelligence; insight; discernment) nor "counsel" (plans) "against the LORD" (can succeed or avail against the Lord). See Psalm 33:10–11.

To fight against God's commands, plans and counsels will not succeed. To mock and attack God's sacred Book is an empty endeavor. No effort to thwart God's supremacy in the universe will prevail. No army, nation, politician, atheist, theologian or movement can wage battle against the Almighty successfully. No human or satanic schemes developed with the greatest wisdom, intellect and strategy can counter the domination and plan of God. The masteries of man are overmastered by God. "The LORD bringeth the counsel of the heathen to nought: he maketh the devices of the people of none effect. The counsel of the LORD standeth for ever" (Psalm 33:10–11).

Three life lessons emerge. There can be no success without dependence upon God.[1322] "Trust in the LORD with all thine heart; and lean not unto thine own understanding" (Proverbs 3:5). Second, God and His Word are unconquerable despite the venomous effort of the wicked. "They will make war against the Lamb. But the Lamb will have victory over them. That's because he is the most powerful Lord of all and the greatest King of all" (Revelation 17:14 NIRV). Third, the child of God will never be defeated or put to shame by the scoffers or mockers for relying upon the wisdom of God dispensed by the Holy Spirit or Holy Scriptures. Let all the forces of Hell assail, yet the saint will remain "unshaken." "He will never allow the righteous to be shaken" (Psalm 55:22 NASB). "Though an host," says David, "should encamp against me, my heart shall not fear: though war should rise against me, in this will I be confident" (Psalm 27:3). Jeremiah attests, "And they shall fight against thee; but they shall not prevail against thee; for I am with thee, saith the LORD, to deliver thee" (Jeremiah 1:19).

John Gill summarizes, "No human schemes whatever, formed with the greatest wisdom and prudence, can ever prevail against God or set aside or hinder the execution of any design of His; nothing that is pointed against His church, His cause and interest, His truths and ordinances in the issue shall succeed; all that are found fighters against Him shall not prosper, let them be men of ever so much sagacity and wisdom; though there may be ever so many devices in a man's heart, and these ever so well planned, they shall never defeat the counsel of the Lord."[1323]

The Bottom Line: It is vain to oppose God, for such effort is futile and meets with destruction. There can be no success against God or without God. Isaiah states, "For the LORD of hosts hath purposed, and who shall disannul it? and his hand is stretched out, and who shall turn it back?" (Isaiah 14:27). "May each tried saint cast himself upon the omnipotent Savior-God in every time of apparently overwhelming trouble, and thus prove for himself that 'safety is of the Lord.'"[1324]

308
Stubborn, stop being stubborn-headed
Proverbs 7:11
"She is loud and stubborn; her feet abide not in her house."

"She" (the harlot identified in the previous verse) is "loud and stubborn" (Deane and Taswell say "boisterous and ungovernable like an animal that will not bear the yoke"[1325] [Hosea 4:16]); her "feet abide not in her house" (she never stays at home, always on the go unlike the godly woman that is described in Titus 2:5).

The dictionary defines "stubborn" as "having or showing dogged determination not to change one's attitude or position on something, especially in spite of good arguments or reasons to do so." In Scripture it relates to the "hardness of heart" (man's obstinate refusal to obey the Lord). Zedekiah is a keen example of stubbornness. "Zedekiah turned against King Nebuchadnezzar, who had forced him to swear [vow; take an oath] in God's name to be loyal to him. But Zedekiah became stubborn [stiffened his neck] and refused to obey [hardened his heart against seeking] the LORD, the God of Israel" (2 Chronicles 36:13 EXB). All who are tenaciously stubborn toward conversion and/or compliance with God's Word can be brought to "sudden" (instant) calamity or destruction. "If you get more stubborn every time you are corrected, one day you will be crushed and never recover" (Proverbs 29:1 GNT).

Billy Graham offers godly counsel on dealing with stubbornness. "Don't let your stubbornness keep you from dealing honestly with your stubbornness! And don't excuse it or conclude you can't (or won't) do anything about it, because God wants to help you overcome it—both for your sake and the sake of those around you. What's wrong with a stubborn, unyielding attitude that always insists it must be right? For one thing, it comes from pride—the kind of pride that refuses to see another person's point of view and is blind to our own faults. But this kind of pride is a sin in God's eyes, and it leads inevitably to His judgment. The Bible says, 'I hate pride and arrogance, evil behavior and perverse speech'" (Proverbs 8:13 NIV). A prideful, stubborn attitude also cuts us off from other people and ultimately from God. Who likes to be around someone who never listens to advice and claims they alone are right? Probably no one—and when you get two stubborn people together, the sparks begin to fly. The Bible warns, 'Where there is strife, there is pride, but wisdom is found in those who take advice' (Proverbs 13:10 NIV)."[1326]

The Bottom Line: John Maxwell says, "When you are full of pride on the inside, it makes you stiff, stubborn and creates strife with others."[1327]

309
Stumbling Block, being a stumbling block, not a stepping stone
Proverbs 25:26

"A righteous man falling down before the wicked is as a troubled fountain, and a corrupt spring."

A "righteous man" (the upright, Christian) "falling down" (overcome by temptation; engages in sinful conduct) before the "wicked" (ungodly, unsaved witness it or are aware of it[1328]) is as a "troubled fountain" (fountain of water that is defiled, unfit to consume[1329]), AND a "corrupt" (murky) "spring" (water that should be fresh and healthy to drink is undrinkable due to pollution[1330]). Deane and Taswell summarize, "The mouth of the righteous should be 'a well of life,' wholesome, refreshing, helpful; his conduct should be consistent and straightforward, fearless in upholding the right (Isaiah 51:12), uncompromising in opposing sin. When such a man, for fear or favor or weakness or weariness, yields to the wicked, compromises principle, no longer makes a stand for truth and purity and virtue, he loses his high character, brings a scandal on religion and lowers his own spiritual nature."[1331]

Contamination with that which is filthy and unwholesome prevents a fountain (well) from fulfilling its purpose for existence (supply life-sustaining water). The drinking of its water (when polluted) destroys life rather than sustaining it. Charles Bridges remarks, "The well is therefore a blessing or a curse, according to the purity or impurity of its waters."[1332] Solomon uses the Proverb to picture the Christian who falters (engages in sinful conduct). Instead of being a stepping stone to faith for the lost, he is their stumbling block. "The righteous one," states John MacArthur, "who sins muddies the water for the wicked who see him and for whom he should serve as an example of righteousness."[1333] To fall into sin defiles the fountain (heart), hindering it from providing the life-sustaining "Water of Life" to the spiritually thirsty. Further, it ceases to give water that satisfies the longing of the soul and is a curse to others instead of a blessing. David's sin with Bathsheba contaminated his "fountain," quenching God's use of him to witness. He prays, "Purge me with hyssop, and I shall be clean: wash me, and I shall be whiter than snow....*Then* will I teach transgressors thy ways; and sinners shall be converted unto thee" (Psalm 51:7;13).

The inconsistent lifestyle of the righteous tarnishes their reputation and testimony to the glee of Satan and injury of the lost (they are driven back from the faith). It even gives incentive to others who are righteous to follow in their wanton path. Charles Bridges elucidates, "Principles and practices are sanctioned that wound our Divine Master. The consciences of the ungodly are lulled. 'The lame,' instead of being 'healed,' are 'turned out of the way' (Hebrews 12:13). Thus 'scandalous falls of good men are like a bag of poison cast by Satan into the spring, from whence the whole town is supplied with water.'"[1334]

The Bottom Line: The righteous are either a pure or a corrupted fountain. If your fountain is impure, ask God to thrust into the well of your heart *heavenly salt* like He did at Jericho that that it may be purified. "And he went forth unto the spring of the waters, and cast the salt in there, and said, Thus saith the LORD, I have healed these waters" (2 Kings 2:21).[1335] "Hold up my goings in thy paths, that my footsteps slip not" (Psalm 17:5).

310
Suicide, the wrong way to cope with depression
Proverbs 31:7
"Let him drink, and forget his poverty, and remember his misery no more."

Let "him" (points back to the previous verse) "drink" (beer and wine), and forget his "poverty" (misfortune), AND remember his "misery no more" (trouble, heartache, suffering, depression). The Proverb addresses the use of beer and wine for medicinal purposes, not recreational. The discovery of better and more effective medications for depression are now available, negating the need of strong drink.

Tragically, the way many youth "remember [their] misery no more," in addition to alcohol consumption, is through suicide. It is the second-leading cause of adolescents' death (after accidents) in the United States (52 percent by firearms, 22 percent by hanging or suffocation, and 18 percent by poisons).[1336]

Suicide is not the solution to agonizing emotional pain. It's not a sedative like drugs or alcohol that numbs the pain; it is death to life forever. Every suicide is a mad rush to end "unbearable pain" without thought to its ultimate end of permanent separation from family and friends. Life is difficult. It always will be difficult. Part and parcel of growing up are certain heartaches, sorrows, failures, disappointments and frustrations, from which none are exempt.

While I was a college student, a chapel speaker said something I have never forgotten, something I hope you will etch upon the walls of your mind. He simply said, "There's a tolerable solution for every intolerable problem you face." I have proved that statement to be true time and again. Life is hard, but God is good. He promises to walk through every storm, sorrow, bitter disappointment, lonely moment and failure with you. He can do anything but fail you. Therefore, fear not that which happens to or around you, relying upon Him who will not "fail thee, nor forsake thee."

Days of emotional and physical upheaval will come, but they will PASS. The darkness eventually must give way to the light. God promises to still the boisterous winds and waves beating upon the vessel of your life, saying, "Peace, be still." Don't panic. Wait on Him. Trust in Him. Soon the raging sea will become as a sheet of glass, and tranquility will reign again. "In his favour is life: weeping may endure for a night, but joy cometh in the morning" (Psalm 30:5).

Helpful strategies to cope with and conquer depression. Draw near unto the Lord. Meditate upon God's Word, allowing the Holy Spirit to renew the soul. Focus on others, and minister to their needs. Don't become isolated; press yourself to be socially involved. Stay physically active (walking, running, swimming). Absolutely avoid alcohol and drug consumption. Confide in a trusted companion; vent feelings and emotional pain. Consult with a Christian licensed therapist/doctor. And in all and through all, fully understand that God loves you unconditionally.

Dr. Timothy Faulk, clinical psychological therapist, stated, "Remember, people who are feeling suicidal isolate themselves, so reaching out to them is vital. They need you to encourage them to talk, and then they need you to listen carefully. Talk openly and directly about suicide. Use the words 'suicide,' 'kill yourself,' and 'dead' in a matter-of-fact way."[1337] Faulk continues, "Be nonjudgmental and accept the person's feelings, even if you disagree with them. Show your interest and support. Don't let the person swear you to secrecy. As a person tells you that he or she is thinking about suicide, start thinking about people you can ask for help (ministers, school counselors, teachers, mental health professionals and psychologists). You can do a lot to help the person initially, but the situation is too dangerous to handle entirely on your own."[1338] Never hesitate to call for help in dealing with the suicidal. Encourage at the outset that the suicidal call the suicide hotline where their identity need not be revealed (1-800-SUICIDE or Billy Graham Ministries, 877-247-2426).

The Bottom Line: Help others handle the wrenching pain of a broken relationship, a busted dream, disappointment in a friend, and the consequence of a sin, protecting them from suicide.

311
Suretyship, what wisdom says about being a cosigner on notes
Proverbs 11:15
"He that is surety for a stranger shall smart for it: and he that hateth suretiship is sure."

"It's poor judgment to guarantee another person's debt or put up security for a friend" (Proverbs 17:18 NLT).

He that is a "surety" (cosigner on a note) for a "stranger" (someone he doesn't know or know well; other Proverbs include "friends" [Proverbs 6:1; 17:18; 22:26]) shall "smart" (pay the price for it; get hurt or get "burned") for it: AND he that "hateth" (avoids it; refrains from it) "suretyship" (a pledge to make good another's debt) is "sure" (secure— the cosigner will not be "hounded by creditors"[1339] for the money the borrower defaulted on that he agreed to pay, or risk financial loss, collapse due to making good the note). See Proverbs 6:1–5; 17:18; 22:26–27.

Forthrightly, the Bible speaks against surety. "A man void of understanding striketh hands, and becometh surety in the presence of his friend" (Proverbs 17:18). "Don't agree to guarantee another person's debt or put up security for someone else" (Proverbs 22:26 NLT). A surety is a contractual or other commitment to guarantee another person's loan (for example, by cosigning). *The Free Dictionary* gives this succinct definition of surety: "A person who agrees to take legal responsibility for someone else's debts or obligations if that person defaults." In being a cosigner on a loan for a friend, there is the risk of jeopardizing the relationship, especially in the event he or she defaults. Being a surety is bad in the sense that you may have to sell treasured possessions or utilize retirement savings to settle it if the person defaults (it could so drain finances as to make you destitute). It may present hardship upon family members in the event of your death.[1340]

It is further a bad idea to be a surety, for it *helps* another be in debt. Suretyship may also injure creditworthiness, credit score and favor with lenders. Solomon above all emphasizes that a person should never be a surety for a stranger. "Take his garment, for he has put up security for a stranger; get collateral if it is for foreigners" (Proverbs 20:16 HCSB).

CreditCards.com reports that of the 1 in 6 American adults that have cosigned a loan for a friend or a relative "38 percent got stuck with at least part of the bill, 28 percent saw their credit score take a hit and 26 percent of cosigners said their relationship with the other person was damaged."[1341]

Try honorably to be released from being a surety. Solomon advises "My child, be careful about giving a guarantee for somebody else's loan, about promising to pay what someone else owes. You might get trapped by what you say; you might be caught by your own words. My child, if you have done this and are under your neighbor's control, here is how to get free. Don't be proud. Go to your neighbor and beg to be free from your promise. Don't go to sleep or even rest your eyes, but free yourself like a deer running from a hunter, like a bird flying away from a trapper" (Proverbs 6:1–5 NCV).

What ought to be the response when a friend requests that you be a cosigner for a loan? Graciously refuse, stating your policy never to be a cosigner. Instead, offer an interest-free loan or, if possible, give him financial assistance without expectation of its return. "Being a reliable friend in times of adversity (Proverbs 17:17) is different from a foolhardy agreement to provide financial security for a high-interest loan."[1342] Charles Bridges admonishes us to understand the "repeated warning against suretyship is intended to inculcate [instill by repetitious instruction] considerateness; not to excuse selfishness or to dry up the sources of helpful sympathy."[1343]

Jesus was man's surety. H. A. Ironside observes that Jesus became our surety when we were "strangers and foreigners," something that He "smarted" for gravely in being bruised and wounded for our sins to pay its full debt. He died, "the just for the unjust, that he might bring us to God" (1 Pet. 3:18). He freely paid a debt He did not owe to deliver (save, rescue, free) us from its payment obligation without harm to His own estate. "All we owed was exacted from Him when He suffered upon the tree for sins not His own. He could then say, 'I restored that which I took not away' (Psa. 69:4). Bishop Lowth's beautiful rendering of Isa. 53:7 reads, 'It was exacted, and He became answerable.' This is the very pith and marrow of the Gospel."[1344] Hallelujah, Jesus paid the sin debt in full.

> Jesus paid it all;
> All to Him I owe.
> Sin had left a crimson stain;
> He washed it white as snow. ~ Elvina M. Hall (1865)

The Bottom Line: Instruct students that when asked to be a surety for a loan or purchase, to kindly state their policy is never to be a cosigner. A fast-clad rule now will save heartache and perhaps financial loss later. Likewise, instruct them never to ask another to be a surety for them (with parental exception).

312

Surrender, absolute surrender of everything to Christ
Proverbs 23:26

"My son, give me thine heart, and let thine eyes observe my ways."

"My son" (the teacher, sage to his student) "give me thine heart" (give me your devotion and careful attention[1345] that I might biblically instruct and advise you), AND "let thine eyes" (watch my example; follow what I do[1346]) "observe" (Hubbard and Ogilvie say "to watch over something with the vigilance of a sentinel"[1347]) "my ways" (lifestyle; manner of living day in and day out; but also to walk in the same path of purity and righteousness as well[1348]).

God, the supreme Teacher, desires a submissive, devoted and affectionate heart that observes (follows, keeps) His ways. Jonathan Edwards declared, "I claim no right to myself, no right to this understanding, this will, these affections that are in me. Neither do I have any right to this body or its members, no right to this tongue, to these hands, feet, ears or eyes. I have given myself clear away and not retained anything of my own." Absolute surrender is the placing of the body and its members at God's disposal for Him to do with what He wishes, when He wishes, and however He wishes. It is the laying of oneself upon the altar of sacrifice in total submission to God's will and plan (Romans 12:1–2).

I surrender all;
I surrender all.
All to Thee, my blessed Savior,
I surrender all.

Andrew Murray states, "God is ready to assume full responsibility for the life wholly yielded to Him."[1349]

The Bottom Line: A. W. Tozer remarks, "The man or woman who is wholly or joyously surrendered to Christ can't make a wrong choice—any choice will be the right one."[1350]

313
Teachable, receptivity to godly instruction
Proverbs 15:31–32
"The ear that heareth the reproof of life abideth among the wise. He that refuseth instruction despiseth his own soul."

A teachable person ("ear that heareth") that receives the "reproof of life" (Reyburn and Fry say "whatever promotes health or well-being of body, mind or spirit"[1351]) "abideth" (at home among the wise).

Proverbs at large emphasizes that to possess biblical knowledge and understanding, a man must be teachable, possess "ears to hear" godly instruction (Proverbs 1:2–3; 2:1–2; 4:1–2; 5:1–2; 8:10; 10:8; 12:1). To acquire divine wisdom (discernment as to what to do in every life situation that honors and pleases God and leads to man's best good) requires a heart that abides in fellowship with the Lord. The Book of Proverbs is candid in stating that "fools hate knowledge" (Proverbs 1:22) and "despise wisdom" (v. 7), which leads to "shame" and 'dishonor' (Proverbs 13:18).

J. I. Packer remarks, "Not until we have become humble and teachable, standing in awe of God's holiness and sovereignty…acknowledging our own littleness, distrusting our own thoughts, and willing to have our minds turned upside down, can divine wisdom become ours."[1352] Chuck Swindoll said, "Someone has said, 'Education is going from an unconscious to conscious awareness of one's ignorance.' No one has a corner on wisdom. Our acute need is to cultivate a willingness to learn and to remain teachable."[1353]

The Bottom Line: "Hear counsel [godly advice], and receive instruction, that thou mayest be wise" (Proverbs 19:20). "That ye might walk worthy of the Lord unto all pleasing, being fruitful in every good work, and *increasing in the knowledge of God;* Strengthened with all might, according to his glorious power, unto all patience and longsuffering with joyfulness" (Colossians 1:10–11). The benefit of biblical knowledge and wisdom vastly outweighs the discipline exercised in their acquisition. The sanest thing a person can do to make the best of life (outside of knowing Jesus Christ personally as Lord and Savior) is to be "teachable," receiving godly instruction from parents, preachers, peers and personal study of God's Word, seeking the wisdom of the Lord.

314
Teachers, avoid instructors peddling liberal, corrupt theology
Proverbs 19:27

"Cease, my son, to hear the instruction that causeth to err from the words of knowledge."

"Cease" (an imperative: "stop listening to and heeding!"[1354]), "my son" (sage to his pupil or father to his son; only place it is used between 7:1 and 23:15[1355]), to "hear" (listen to; give place to; consent) the "instruction" (of the foolish) that "causeth to err" (stray away from biblical instruction and belief) from the "words of knowledge" (the wisdom of God as revealed in His Word; godly instruction).

A similar instruction is shared by Jesus: "Beware of false prophets" (Matthew 7:15); "Take heed what ye hear" (Mark 4:24). The Apostle Paul likewise reprimanded the Galatians for listening to teachers causing them to err from the truth: "I marvel that ye are so soon removed from him that called you into the grace of Christ unto another gospel: Which is not another; but there be some that trouble you, and would pervert the gospel of Christ" (Galatians 1:6–7).

Commenting on such heretical instruction, Charles Bridges states, "And their *instruction, causing to err from the words of knowledge,* is more palatable to the perverseness of the heart, more alluring to the inexperience of the young, than scriptural teaching. Insinuating infidels who endeavor to shake the principles of young persons under the pretense of removing heedless scruples and enlarging their minds and delivering them from the shackles of bigotry—such persons, shun them as the plague."[1356] Matthew Henry remarked, "It is the wisdom of young men to dread hearing such talk as puts loose and evil principles into the mind."[1357]

The words of knowledge. John Gill interprets this to mean: "The wholesome words of our Lord Jesus, the salutary doctrines of the Gospel, may be here meant; those words of grace, wisdom and knowledge which come from Him and give knowledge of His Person, offices, relations, incarnation, and blessings of grace by Him; from whence they are called the word of peace and reconciliation, the word of righteousness, the word of life, and the word of salvation. Now these are all words of knowledge and are the means of a spiritual, experimental and fiducial [trusting] knowledge of Christ, which is preferable to all other knowledge, and even to everything in the world; and therefore care should be taken and everything avoided that tends to cause to err from these words and doctrines which convey, promote and improve this knowledge."[1358]

A second meaning of the Proverb is found in the interpretation of the Hebrew word for instruction: *musar*. It "is used in a good sense throughout this book; it is better to regard the injunction as warning against listening to wise teaching with no intention of profiting by it: "Cease to hear instruction in order to err," etc.; i.e., if you are only going to continue your evil doings.[1359] Such "listening" without "heeding" brings dangerous consequences.

The only sure preservation from corrupt and erroneous teaching is sound instruction from the pulpit and classroom and personal study. If in danger of being led to err from the truth, immediately "escape for thy life" from him that dangles its poisonous bait, whether preacher, teacher or friend.

The Bottom Line: Cease from hearing heretics—to listen is to err. All their cunning enticement and deceptive words are the framework which conceals unbiblical principles.[1360] "Weigh them in the balances of the sanctuary, and they shall be found wanting. Trace them to their source, and it will be found to be a corrupt fountain."[1361]

315
Teaching, the instruction of the righteous benefits the unsaved
Proverbs 13:14
"The law of the wise is a fountain of life, to depart from the snares of death."

The "law" (Murphy says "to the teaching of the sage, not to the Decalogue"[1362]; of the godly wise based on Holy Scriptures) is a "fountain of life" (imparts, infuses real life [Proverbs 10:11]), "to depart" (to turn away from; forsake) from the "snares of death" (picture of a trap for an animal that springs suddenly and surprisingly; here the unexpected trap of premature death which sin easily may precipitate [Proverbs 2:11]). To summarize, the biblical instruction of the righteous wise is a preventative against premature death and a host of other destructive consequences precipitated by foolishness. In preventing spiritual and moral decadence, it lifts man to a higher plane of life (John 10:10).

Godly wise believers possess knowledge that may save man from the snares of satanic deception and captivity, indescribable havoc and heartache, an ill-spent life and an eternal Hell. Don't be silent; keep sharing insight and instruction gleaned from Holy Scriptures and your walk with God "whether they will hear, or whether they will forbear" (Ezekiel 2:5). A word to the unbeliever: The biblical instruction and advice of the righteous is purposed by God for your own good. In addition to being a "fountain of life" (source of a real and meaningful life), its obedience will protect you from the snares of Satan and their devastating and destructive consequences. "Then they will come to their senses and escape from the devil's trap. For they have been held captive by him to do whatever he wants" (2 Timothy 2:26 NLT). See Proverbs 10:11.

The Bottom Line: The sanest thing that any man may do is to clutch tightly the biblical instruction of the godly, making it a 'lamp unto their feet and a light unto their path' (Psalm 119:105).

316
Temptation, its "modus operandi"
Proverbs 5:5
"Her feet go down to death; her steps take hold on hell."

"Her" (the adulteress woman) "feet" (manner of life; Reyburn and Fry say "her leading a victim where she goes"[1363]) go down to "death" (the grave); "her steps" (her conduct ever moves in the direction of death[1364] or destruction); take hold on "hell" (her behavior drags you down to the grave[1365]; ruin; Hindson and Kroll say, "Sheol is the place of those dying without the blessing of God, a place reserved for all who refuse to ponder the path of life"[1366]).

Temptation is pictured as a man walking in the steps of an adulterous woman to her bed. He arrives by taking a series of "steps." It matters not if he takes two steps forward and one back, small or big ones, as long as he keeps walking in her steps.

According to tradition, this is how an Eskimo hunter kills a wolf. First, he coats the blade of a sharp knife with animal blood and allows it to freeze. Next, he adds layer upon layer of animal blood on the blade until the blade is completely concealed with frozen blood. The hunter then places the knife into the snow-covered ground with blade pointing upward.

A wolf, picking up the scent of blood, locates the knife and licks it faster and faster, harder and harder, until its keen razor-sharp edge is bare. His craving for blood masks the sting of the blade cutting into the mouth and the realization that the blood it now is licking is its own. Ultimately the wolf's carnivorous appetite for more and more blood ends in its death.

Man turns to alcohol, drugs, sexual encounters, pornography, gambling, theft, and dishonesty for the same reason the wolf licks the knife blade. It is appealing and appears to be pleasurable and harmless. But soon the law of diminishing returns sets in, requiring more and more of the same to be satisfied. It's not one drink but three drinks; not three drinks but a case. Faster and harder one licks the deceptive bait blade of alcohol until a crisis develops or even death. The wolf didn't see coming what resulted, nor do those who take that first drink and second drink and...It's just the baiting scheme Satan uses to lure one into a snare, only then to destroy body, mind and soul. The law of sowing and reaping not only applies to seed planted in the soil but to that planted in the heart (Galatians 6:7). This law clearly teaches that a person may choose the seed he plants in the sod of the soul, but he cannot choose its outcome. A person always reaps what is sown, whether desired or detested.

The Bottom Line: Don't be a simpleton, ignorant of the "modus operandi" of temptation. Study it and learn from it so that you may be spared from yielding to its persuasion and experiencing its crushing consequence. Sin always begins with a first step.

317
Temptation, overcome it, not be overthrown by it
Proverbs 1:11

"If they say, Come with us, let us lay wait for blood, let us lurk privily for the innocent without cause."

If "they" (sinners) say, "come with us" (an invitation for the young man to participate in their evil conduct), "let us lay wait for blood" (our plan is to ambush a person, take his belongings and kill him[1367]), "let us lurk privily" (ambush) for "the innocent" (someone that is helpless, inapt to defend himself[1368]) "without cause" (just because we want to).

Satan always attacks and tempts ("Come with us") at a person's most vulnerable spot. Focus thereupon by continuous fortification. Success over temptation hinges upon the believer's use of the *Helmet of Salvation* to protect from domination by carnal and sensual thoughts and the fiery darts of temptation; *the Sword of the Spirit,* the power of Holy Scripture that thwarts satanic efforts to overthrow God's rule, will and work; and *Knees of Prayer,* the believer's source of power, protection and provision (Ephesians 6:10–18). Upon being tempted, rely upon the Scripture, as Jesus did in the wilderness temptations, striking back immediately and forcefully with the power words of victory: "Get thee behind me, Satan" (Luke 4:8); "Greater is he that is in [me], than he that is in the world" (1 John 4:4) and other such verses. Pray earnestly for strength to resist and a way of to escape it. "No temptation has overtaken you except such as is common to man; but God is faithful, who will not allow you to be tempted beyond what you are able, but with the temptation will also make the way of escape, that you may be able to bear it" (1 Corinthians 10:13 NKJV). In seeing the way of escape, take it immediately.

Regardless of numerous failures to thwart the temptation, never lose hope. Jesus' victory at the cross over the Devil assures your own victory in Him. With Paul, believe and say determinedly, "I can do all things [including thwarting temptation] through Christ which strengtheneth me" (Philippians 4:13). Freedom from defeat is waiting in the authority and power of Jesus Christ. Cease allowing Satan to intimidate and dominate. It's time to say, "Enough is enough."

The Bottom Line: Tony Evans states, "The way you get rid of sin is not simply dealing with or focusing on the sin. It's like being on a diet and deciding to focus on food all the time—it won't work. Instead, to deal with temptation we must shift our focus. Rather than keeping our eyes on our sin, we need to turn our eyes to our Savior. As we focus on Him and not on our Romans 7 experience, we find the freedom to overcome. Don't look at your sin. Look to your Savior."[1369]

318
Testing, the purpose of divine testing
Proverbs 17:3

"The fining pot is for silver, and the furnace for gold: but the LORD trieth the hearts."

The "fining pot is for silver" (a crucible; intense heat is used to smelt silver placed within it, removing its impurities), and the "furnace for gold" (similarly a hot furnace is used to remove the impurities from gold): BUT the Lord "trieth the hearts" (God tests the heart for impurity).

"The fining pot" is a container that melts metals into liquid form under intense heat. A "furnace" would likewise be used to melt metal. Both removed the impurities from the silver and gold. Likewise, Solomon states, God tests, refines or judges ("trieth") man's heart. As the furnace of fire determines the purity of gold, removing any impurities if present, just so, righteous God by intense testing of man purges out the dross of sin. Job testified, "But he knoweth the way that I take: when he hath tried me, I shall come forth as gold" (Job 23:10). Peter states, "Pure gold put in the fire comes out of it proved pure; genuine faith put through this suffering comes out proved genuine" (1Peter 1:7 MSG).

In Jeremiah the Lord elucidates the testing, saying, "I the LORD search the heart, I try the reins, even to give every man according to his ways, and according to the fruit of his doings" (Jeremiah 17:10). The Lord examines (tests) man's heart, detecting its darkest secrets, most darling sin, deviating defiance and devotional deficiency to reveal all such impurities, that through confession and repentance the person may be pure inside and out (holy, sanctified vessel). Malachi explains, "For He is like a refiner's fire and like fullers' soap. He will sit as a smelter and purifier of silver, and He will purify the sons of Levi and refine them like gold and silver, so that they may present to the LORD offerings in righteousness. Then the offering of Judah and Jerusalem will be pleasing to the LORD as in the days of old and as in former years" (Malachi 3:2–4).

The testing or refining is to make the believer more like Jesus (righteousness) that he may live "pleasing to the Lord" in every dimension of life. "We have all read how they try the great guns before they use them in the Queen's service. So God tries us, to prove whether we are fit for the service of Christ's militant here on earth. As the brightest jewels have to be cut and ground, and some tried in a fierce fire, so the brightest gems, on the day when God makes up His jewels, will be those people who have suffered and passed through the fire of affliction, of whom it can be said, 'Blessed is the man that endureth temptation [testing].'"[1370]

W. A. Criswell further explains, "Now when Satan tries you, he tries to ruin you, to destroy you, to plow you up, to bury you deep. But when God tries you, what God is doing is like a refiner's fire, to make pure gold out of you. Any trial that comes from God—if it's from Heaven, if it's providence, there's in it some great and blessed thing. It's not a vicious thing, and it's not a wicked thing, but it is a holy and heavenly thing. The providential trials of our life are to make true sons of us, to reveal the gold of God that is in us; a refiner's fire."[1371]

C. H. Spurgeon, in the sermon "Whither Goest Thou?" says, "God appoints the weight and number of all our adversities—if He declares the number ten, they cannot be eleven. If He wills that we bear a certain weight, no one can add half an ounce more. Every trial comes from God. Take courage. The rod is one of the tokens of the child of God. If you were not God's child, you might be left unchastised; but inasmuch as you are dear to Him, He will whip you when you disobey. If you were only a bit of 'common clay,' God would not put you into the furnace. But as you are 'gold' and He knows it, you must be refined; and to be refined it is needful that the fire should exercise its power upon you. Because you are bound for Heaven, you will meet with storms on your voyage to Glory. I cannot tell what troubles may come, nor what temptations may arise. But I know in whose hands I am, and I am persuaded that He is able to preserve me, so that when He has tried me, I shall come forth as GOLD. I go into the fire, but I shall not be burned up in it; 'I shall come forth.'"[1372]

The man that endures the testing will be rewarded ("blessed") in at least six ways: "Blessedness of thankfulness for being sustained; of holy dependence under conscious weakness; of peace and submission under God's hand; of fearlessness as to result of further trial; of familiarity with God enjoyed in the affliction; of growth in grace through the trial. He who, being tested, is supported in the ordeal, and comes out of the trial approved, is the blessed man."[1373]

The Bottom Line: C. H. Spurgeon says, "Trials teach us what we are; they dig up the soil and let us see what we are made of."[1374] Jeremy Taylor states, "By trials God is shaping us for higher things."[1375]

319
Theft, thou shalt not steal
Proverbs 29:24

"Whoso is partner with a thief hateth his own soul: he heareth cursing, and bewrayeth it not."

Whoso is "partner" (accomplice to a thief; Reyburn and Fry say "someone who helps a thief steal and so is rewarded by receiving some of the thief's stolen goods"[1376]) with a thief "hateth" (becomes his own enemy, for the act brings harsh consequences he will have to bear[1377]) his own "soul" (life): he "heareth cursing, and bewrayeth it not" (the accomplice being persuaded to join in the theft now must conceal it by perjury before police, judges and him whose possessions were taken; the accomplice's failure to identify the master thief makes him personally accountable for the crime[1378] [Leviticus 5:1]).

The accomplice of a thief is as guilty as the "thief." Such complicity brings dishonor and destruction. Proverbs warns against the company of all that violate the law: thieves (Proverbs 29:24), fools (Proverbs 13:20), slanderers (Proverbs 20:19), the "shamelessly immoral"[1379] (Proverbs 28:7) and sinners in general (Proverbs 1:10–16).

The eighth commandment expressly states, "Thou shalt not steal." There are six ways in which a person may break this commandment.

There is *theft of property*, the taking of something that belongs to another regardless of its value or size. Stealing a piece of bubble gum is just as much theft as stealing a CD. Cheating on exams and in athletic contests is a form of stealing.

There is *theft of reputation*. In this case it's not the hands that do the stealing but the tongue. The tongue steals a person's reputation by uttering slanderous and injurious remarks.

There is the *theft of purity*. The sexual seduction of another violates this commandment in that one steals the other's treasure. Solomon states, "Stolen waters are sweet...[b]ut...her guests are in the depths of hell" (Proverbs 9:17–18)

There is the *theft of faith*. Jeremiah said, "'Is not my word like fire?' declares the LORD, 'and like a hammer which shatters a rock? Therefore behold, I am against the prophets...who steal my words from each other'" (Jeremiah 23:29–30 NASB). The person (professor, teacher, pastor or friend) who takes the scissors of skepticism to clip the faith of another will be held accountable by God.

There is the *theft from God*. How do we steal from God? Malachi answers that it is by withholding from God our tithes and offerings (Malachi 3:8–10). Failure to give God His tithe is as much stealing as entering a neighbor's house and taking a television set.

There is *time theft*. To receive pay for time not spent in the workplace or work not actually done is an act of thievery. Weekly the average employee steals four hours and five minutes from his or her employer, according to the American Payroll Association.[1380]

The Bottom Line: Honesty is not just the best policy; it's the only policy. The price for theft vastly outweighs the income it brings. There are no degrees of honesty. Either you are honest or dishonest.

320
Thoughts, don't accept bad thoughts others plant in your mind
Proverbs 4:23
"Keep thy heart with all diligence; for out of it are the issues of life."

"Keep" ("more than all guarding," "with all vigilance"[1381]) thy "heart" (mind) with all "diligence" (guard it above all other things); for out of it are the "issues of life" (values that govern all of life).

Charles Spurgeon had a prolonged battle with blasphemous assaults upon his mind that led almost to the point of despair. He even began questioning his salvation. After all, no Christian would think such thoughts. In desperation, he confided in an elderly godly saint that which he was experiencing. The man inquired, "Do you hate these thoughts?" Young Spurgeon replied, "I do." The man replied, "Then they are not yours;...Groan over them, repent of them, and send them on to the Devil, the father of them to whom they belong—for they are not yours." It is part of Satan's cruel and conniving scheme to plant a wanton thought in our mind, making it appear that it is our own. Don't accept it or own it. With the same advice that Spurgeon received, I say be sorry over them, get cleansing of them and then send them to their originator and owner, the Devil.

The Bottom Line: Don't let Satan badger and beat you down over thoughts not your own. Dismiss them in prayer. Give no place to them. Transfer them back to Hell to their owner.

321
Thoughts, effect of foolish thinking
Proverbs 24:9

"The thought of foolishness is sin."

The scheming or devising ("thought") of an evil act ("foolishness" or "folly") is sin (transgression against God).

Note that the Proverb states that merely entertaining thoughts of doing wrong is *sin*. Matthew Henry remarks, "We contract guilt, not only by the act of foolishness, but by the thought of it, though it go no further; the first risings of sin in the heart are sin, offensive to God, and must be repented of or we are undone. Not only malicious, unclean, proud thoughts, but even foolish thoughts are sinful thoughts."[1382] "O Jerusalem, wash thine heart from wickedness, that thou mayest be saved. How long shall thy vain [evil] thoughts lodge within thee?" (Jeremiah 4:14). Pray for divine forgiveness, cleansing of and release from evil thoughts. "Casting down imaginations, and every high thing that exalteth itself against the knowledge of God, and *bringing into captivity every thought to the obedience of Christ*" (2 Corinthians 10:5).

"Keep thy heart [thoughts; the wellspring of conduct] with all diligence; for out of it are the issues of life" (Proverbs 4:23). Evil conduct flows from the wellspring of corrupted thought.

The Bottom Line: Refuse to allow thoughts to control you; you control them. Adrian Rogers said, "When God is in the heart, then we think right, live right, do right. When God is absent, we think wrong, do wrong, live wrong."[1383] God gives mastery of the thought life through His Word (Psalm 119:9–11), His holy indwelling presence (Light expels darkness— John 1:5; 8:12) and liberating power (John 8:36).

322
Tolerance, the need for Christian intolerance
Proverbs 8:13

"The fear of the LORD is to hate evil: pride, and arrogancy, and the evil way, and the froward mouth, do I hate."

The "fear of the Lord" (to honor, revere and obey God) is to "hate" (count as an enemy) "evil" (all forms of unrighteousness; sin): "pride and arrogance" (the haughty, conceited, egotistical), and the "evil way" (wickedness), and the "froward mouth" (perverse speech).

Josh McDowell states, "Tolerance has been so cleverly promoted that when anyone advocates moral values in a community or school, that person is criticized for opposing personal rights. It is no virtue to tolerate behavior that threatens the morality or safety of our children."[1384] Billy Graham elucidates upon the issue: "In the realm of Christian experience there is a need for intolerance. In some things Christ was the most tolerant, broad-minded Man who ever lived, but in other things He was one of the most intolerant. The word *tolerant* means "liberal and broad-minded." In one sense, it implies the compromise of one's convictions, a yielding of ground upon important issues."[1385] Graham continues, "We have become tolerant about divorce, the use of alcohol, delinquency, wickedness in high places, immorality, crime and godlessness. We have been sapped of conviction, drained of our beliefs, and we are bereft of our faith."[1386]

"The world needs Christians," writes John MacArthur, "who embrace an antithetical worldview, a biblical mindset that answers questions of truth and morality in terms of black and white. Why? Because there is no salvation without absolute, unshakeable truth. Compromising, changing, tolerant opinions don't provide answers for the 'crazy and confusing and painful' issues."[1387]

The Bottom Line: Embrace a biblical worldview which views morality, religion and lifestyle not in "shades of gray" but "black and white" based upon the Word of God. See 1 Timothy 6:3–5.

323
Tongue, put a bridle on the tongue
Proverbs 29:11
"A fool uttereth all his mind: but a wise man keepeth it in till afterwards."

"Whoso keepeth his mouth and his tongue keepeth his soul from troubles" (Proverbs 21:23).

A fool "uttereth all his mind" (the fool gives full expression of what he thinks, due to the absence of self-control, whether it's anger, bitterness or any other emotion[1388]): BUT a "wise man keepeth it in till afterwards" (literally "holds it back;" practices restraint and self-control[1389]). To summarize, the disposition of fools is to "speak their mind" (truth or not) without thought or concern about the effect, good or bad. He speaks rashly (off the cuff) holding nothing back, especially is this the case when provoked. In contrast, the wise man thinks ("keepeth it in") before he speaks and then speaks reservedly and profitability.

James counsels, "Wherefore, my beloved brethren, let every man be swift to hear, slow to speak" (James 1:19). Be "slow to speak" with regard to commitments to tasks of which you are incapable. Reneging on promises is extremely embarrassing and injurious to your Christian witness. Be "slow to speak" with regard to providing counsel; think through the advice to be shared, lest later it prove to be wrong or injurious. Be "slow to speak" with regard to matters that will bear horrendous consequences within the home, church and world (weigh carefully the impact of what you will say to ascertain if it's necessary or the time to say it). Be "slow to speak" about the faults and failures of others. When provoked to anger, always be "slow to speak," lest words said be later regretted (Proverbs 12:16). Be "slow to speak" just to be saying something (Proverbs 10:19). Be "slow to speak" until you know the whole story. Speaking hastily results often in mistakes, offending others, bad decisions, injury to the cause of Christ (witness), strife, shame and diminishment of character in the eyes of friends.

The Bottom Line: Over the years all have heard the saying, "Count to ten before you speak." Simplistic as that is, it would do great good if practiced.

324
Tongue, the wrong uses of the tongue
Proverbs 12:18
"There is that speaketh like the piercings of a sword: but the tongue of the wise is health."

"Even so the tongue is a little member, and boasteth great things. Behold, how great a matter a little fire kindleth! And the tongue is a fire, a world of iniquity: so is the tongue among our members, that it defileth the whole body, and setteth on fire the course of nature; and it is set on fire of hell" (James 3:5–6).

There is that "speaketh" (rash, reckless words that are not thought through, not intended to hurt but are extremely painful[1390]) like the "piercings of a sword" (cuttingly painful): BUT the tongue of the "wise" (righteous, godly, and sensible) is "health" (Ross says, "They are healing because they are faithful and true, gentle and kind, and uplifting and encouraging"[1391]). Matthew Henry summarizes, "The tongue is death or life, poison or medicine, as it is used."[1392]

There is power in words to help or hurt; uplift or deflate; encourage or discourage; unite or divide; conceal or reveal; forgive or condemn. God delights in him who possesses righteous lips (Proverbs 16:13). Multiple and various types of wrong uses of the tongue are indicated in Proverbs, providing an excellent resource for instruction for children.

Lying Tongue. "The lip of truth shall be established for ever: but a lying tongue is but for a moment" (Proverbs 12:19).

Gossiping Tongue. "A gossip goes around telling secrets, but those who are trustworthy can keep a confidence" (Proverbs 11:13 NLT). "A perverse person stirs up conflict, and a gossip separates close friends" (Proverbs 16:28 NIV).

Harsh Tongue. "A soft answer turns away wrath, but a harsh word stirs up anger" (Proverbs 15:1 ESV).

Lying Tongue. "The getting of treasures by a lying tongue is a vanity tossed to and fro of them that seek death" (Proverbs 21:6).

Belittling Tongue. "It is foolish to belittle one's neighbor; a sensible person keeps quiet" (Proverbs 11:12 NLT).

Betraying Tongue. "A gossip goes around telling secrets, but those who are trustworthy can keep a confidence" (Proverbs 11:13 NLT).

Retaliating Tongue. "Do not say, 'I'll pay you back for this wrong!' Wait for the LORD, and he will avenge you" (Proverbs 20:22 NIV).

Hasty Tongue. "Seest thou a man that is hasty in his words? there is more hope of a fool than of him" (Proverbs 29:20). "He that refraineth his lips is wise" (Proverbs 10:19).

Grumbling Tongue. "People's own foolishness ruins their lives, but in their minds they blame the LORD" (Proverbs 19:3 NCV).

Hollow Tongue. "A flattering mouth worketh ruin" (Proverbs 26:28).

Divisive Tongue. "[God hates him] that soweth discord among brethren" (Proverbs 6:19).

Profane Tongue. "A wholesome tongue is a tree of life: but perverseness therein is a breach in the spirit" (Proverbs 15:4). "Put away from thee a froward mouth, and perverse lips put far from thee" (Proverbs 4:24).

Foolish Tongue. "A fool's mouth is his destruction, and his lips are the snare of his soul" (Proverbs 18:7).

> The true test of a man's spirituality is not his ability to speak, as we are apt to think, but rather his ability to bridle his tongue.
> R. Kent Hughes

Pray with the psalmist, "Set a watch [guard], O LORD, before my mouth; keep the door of my lips" (Psalm 141:3).

The Bottom Line: The undisciplined tongue is gravely injurious to others and to oneself, necessitating conquest at all cost. "Mind what you say, or you might say whatever comes to mind."

325
Trials, their benefits
Proverbs 27:21

"As the fining pot for silver, and the furnace for gold; so is a man to his praise."

As the "fining pot for silver" (a crucible in which silver was placed over intense fire to remove its impurities), and "the furnace for gold" (a hot burning furnace on which gold was placed to remove its impurities); so is a man to "his praise" (the manner in which a man handles personal praise and commendation *tests* his true character[1393] [1 Samuel 18:7]).

In James 1:2 NIV, it says to "consider it pure joy…whenever you face trials of many kinds." Trials are "pure joy" only in knowing their benefactor and blessing. Otherwise they are viewed as obstacles to our joy and peace. Trials are sovereignly allowed to enhance the believer's growth and maturity in the faith. Sometimes their design is discipline. "No discipline seems enjoyable at the time, but painful. Later on, however, it yields the fruit of peace and righteousness to those who have been trained by it" (Hebrews 12:11 HCSB). At other times they simply are allowed to affirm adoption into His family and approval. It is helpful to remember that trials are not always the result of wrongdoing. "We also boast of our troubles, because we know that trouble produces endurance, endurance brings God's approval, and his approval creates hope" (Romans 5:3–4 GNT).

A. C. Dixon states, "Reason is a servant, not a master. It is the most abject slave in the world. It does the bidding of ignorance, of sin, of virtue, of knowledge, of faith or of unbelief. It has little or no moral sense. It works for those who assert their mastery over it. I am sick. Unbelief says, 'Therefore God does not treat me kindly; life is a failure.' Faith says, 'God has in this sickness a message of love for me. He may be laying me aside for repairs; He is making a need that He delights to supply.' I have lost by death my dearest friend. Unbelief says, 'Therefore God made a mistake.' Faith says, 'Heaven is now more attractive; I have a treasure there. My friend has been saved from the evil to come. Out of this death may come more good than out of life.' Calamity sweeps away my property. Unbelief says, 'Therefore God has forsaken me.' Faith says, 'God is trying me in the furnace. He wants to get rid of the dross and make the gold in me pure.'"[1394]

Realizing the promise of faith in adversity, no wonder Paul declared, "Most gladly therefore will I rather glory in my infirmities, that the power of Christ may rest upon me" (2 Corinthians 12:9). Vincent states, "The compound verb [*may rest upon*] here means to fix a tent or a habitation upon; and the figure is that of Christ abiding upon him as a tent spread over him during his temporary stay on earth."[1395] To know that in fierce trials Christ spreads a tent over you in protection and power provides comfort and hope. "It is a poor faith," states C. H. Spurgeon, "which can trust God only when friends are true, the body full of health, and the business profitable; but that is true faith which holds by the Lord's faithfulness when friends are gone, when the body is sick, when spirits are depressed, and the light of our Father's countenance is hidden. A faith which can say, in the direst trouble, 'Though he slay me, yet will I trust in him,' is Heaven-born faith."[1396]

B. R. Lakin states, "Perhaps God has allowed a crushing blow to fall upon your life. It may seem, for the moment, to be an appalling mistake. But it isn't. You are 'in His hand,' and no man can take you out. In His infinite wisdom and love, He may allow you to suffer for a season, but He will bring you out as gold 'tried by fire.' More eloquent than the ministry of preaching, singing or teaching is the ministry of suffering. If you are in the 'furnace of affliction,' then rejoice that He considered you strong enough to endure such a difficult ministry and serve Him faithfully."[1397] "Like the growth of a muscle lifting weights, the resistance of the trial causes the muscle of faith to grow stronger. It is in the heat of trials where these deficiencies in faith and character surface. It is only when they surface that God can begin to purify our hearts and motives and actions."[1398]

The Bottom Line: Leo Tolstoy said "Truth, like gold, is to be obtained not by its growth, but by washing away from it all that is not gold."[1399]

326

Troublemaker, inciting trouble in the family
Proverbs 11:29
"He that troubleth his own house shall inherit the wind."

He that "troubleth" (troublemaker) his "own house" (personal family) shall "inherit the wind" (gets nothing out of it, no profit; at the father's death the troublesome son will learn he was "disinherited"[1400]).

There are numerous ways in which a family member may trouble the household. A father troubles his family through uncontrolled anger, adultery, greed (withholding from members what is needed), alcohol abuse, gambling (robbing food off the table to play the lottery, etc.), slothfulness, temperament, violence, irritability, bad example and irreligion. A child troubles the home through an unruly disposition, rebellious attitude, selfishness, idleness (refusal to get a job), party lifestyle, alcohol or drug addiction and temper. He "shall inherit the wind." There is no profit or gain in creating trouble in the home, only horrendous personal disappointment, sorrow and loss (may be disinherited). The father/husband who mismanages the household certainly will pay the highest toll.

To cause continual vexation to the household is a serious sin that God will judge. Each member's role in the family is to promote unity, love and peace. Shakespeare said, "How sharper than a serpent's tooth it is to have a thankless child."[1401] A child that shows disrespect and ingratitude toward a parent, creating turmoil in the home, is more venomous than the bite of a rattlesnake unto them.

A young man was just this to his mother, ungrateful and defiant. One night when he arrived home past curfew again, his dad waited with a shotgun in hand. As the boy entered the house, the father tossed the gun to him, saying, "Go upstairs, put the barrel to your mother's head and pull the trigger." The boy, set back by the instruction, replied, "Dad, what are you asking me to do?" The father repeated the instructions, to which the son asked, "Why?" The father told him that to shoot his mother would be the merciful way to kill her, in contrast to the gradual, slow way he was killing her with rebellious behavior. Shakespeare is so right—disrespect, deviant and disobedient behavior to one's parents is sharp fangs mightier than that of a serpent, gradually killing them. Pillows are wet continuously with the tears of hurting parents over the defiance and ill-respect of their children. Such a wounded spirit may be healed only by reconciliation between the parent and child.

The Bottom Line: Nothing is gained from the pain undertaken to trouble (creating chaos in) your home. Much that is treasured is lost.

327
Trust, self-reliance is an imposter that will deceive you
Proverbs 28:26
"He that trusteth in his own heart is a fool: but whoso walketh wisely, he shall be delivered."

The man that "trusteth" (self-reliance) in his own "heart" (in his own cleverness, intelligence) is a "fool" (lack of sense; stupid): BUT whoso "walketh wisely" (travels the path of righteousness), he shall be "delivered" (will escape from trouble, for he orders life by wisdom, unlike the one who trusts in himself and will therefore experience much trouble[1402]).

Charles Bridges remarks, "To trust an imposter who has deceived us a hundred times, or a traitor who has proved himself false to our most important interests, is surely to deserve the name of *fool*."[1403] The Proverb ascribes the name to him that "trusteth in his own heart" (allows his heart that is untrustworthy to betray him by relying upon it to control decisions and directions of life). The mature know from experience "that the way of man is not in himself: it is not in man that walketh to direct his steps" (Jeremiah 10:23).

Presumptuous dependence upon self, to the exclusion of the Lord and others, again and again has proved detrimental if not ruinous. The heart of man *above all else* is deceitful (liar; deceiver; evil schemer) and desperately wicked, incapable of making judgments in keeping with the best good for others and self (Jeremiah 17:9). It has lied to us time and again, proving its untrustworthiness. But God is "greater than our heart" providing the wisest of guidance in every facet of life (1 John 3:20). His counsel is safe and sure (Proverbs 8:14; 19:21). The wise man, in contrast to the fool, looks outside himself, to God primarily and then to the godly, for direction ("whoso walketh wisely"). He acknowledges the truth of Jeremiah 10:23 and applies Proverbs 3:5 to life.

The Bottom Line: Throughout life do not place too much stock in your own judgment; look unto the Lord primarily for guidance and then to the *godly wise* (Psalm 37:30; Proverbs 11:14*)*. Don't neglect the counsel of the Lord, as the fool does (Proverbs 1:25); so doing, you will avert mistakes, failures, loss and shipwreck. "Let not the wise man glory in his wisdom, neither let the mighty man glory in his might, let not the rich man glory in his riches: But let him that glorieth glory in this, that he understandeth and knoweth me, that I am the LORD which exercise lovingkindness, judgment, and righteousness, in the earth: for in these things I delight, saith the LORD" (Jeremiah 9:23–24).

328
Truth, buy it and never sell it
Proverbs 23:23
"Buy the truth, and sell it not; also wisdom, and instruction, and understanding."

"Buy the truth" (acquire biblical knowledge regardless of cost; expend whatever strength, time and treasure necessary to get it[1404]), and "sell it not" (don't part with it for any reason); also "wisdom" (wisdom is divine discernment that enables man to do that which is right and pleasing unto the Lord—which is for his best good—in every course of action), and "instruction" (moral discipline[1405]) and "understanding" (ability to discern[1406]).

"So justice is driven back, and righteousness stands at a distance; truth has stumbled in the streets, honesty cannot enter" (Isaiah 59:14 NIV).

447

The prophet Isaiah is right. Truth has fallen in the streets, and honesty is prevented from entering. Your children are being reared in such an environment where *truth is not what it used to be* (according to the evildoer) and honesty and integrity are unwelcomed guests. Solomon gives great counsel for combating this heresy in saying, "Buy the truth, and sell it not." Value truth above the riches and prestige of the world. Truth is so to be prized that one ought to go to the greatest measures (no cost too much, no sacrifice too great) to gain it. And once he finds it, he is never to put it up for sale (depart from it), regardless of the bidder.

C. H. Spurgeon, in the sermon "Buying the Truth" (Proverbs 23:23), states, "The text seems to tell us that truth is the one pearl beneath the skies that is worth having, and whatever else we buy not, we must buy the truth, and whatever else we may have to sell, yet we must never sell the truth, but hold it fast as a treasure that will last us when gold has cankered and silver has rusted and the moth has eaten up all goodly garments, and when all the riches of men have gone like a puff of smoke or melted in the heat of the judgment day like the dew in the beams of the morning sun. Buy the truth. Here is the treasure. Cost it what it may, buy you it. Here is the piece of merchandise which you must buy but must not sell. You may give all for it, but you may take nothing in exchange for it, since there is nothing that can be likened unto it."[1407]

The Bottom Line: Obtain the truth and then never allow others to reason or scorn or laugh you out of it. Someone has said, "It is not enough that one hold the truth if the truth hold not him."

329
Truthfulness, answering man honestly is like a kiss on the lips
Proverbs 24:26
"Every man shall kiss his lips that giveth a right answer."

Every man shall "kiss his lips" ("signifies love, devotion, sincerity and commitment."[1408] Ironside says, "The kiss, among Eastern nations, was a symbolical act, denoting affection and esteem."[1409] Bühlmann says "a sign of trusting affection"[1410]; only time the phrase is used in Scripture) him that "giveth a right" (honest, straightforward) answer. Allen Ross says that the practice of placing a "kiss on the lips" among friends was observed by the Persians.[1411]

The man who gives an "honest" answer to that which is asked, regardless of consequence, is respected, honored and admired ("kiss his lips"). He is counted a righteous man. *The Pulpit Commentary* explains, "An answer that is fair and suitable to the circumstances is as pleasant and assuring to the hearers as a kiss on the lips."[1412] S. S. Buzell remarks, "How are honest words and kisses alike? As a sincere kiss shows affection and is desirable, so an honest (and perhaps straightforward) answer shows a person's concern and therefore is welcomed."[1413] Another interpretation of the expression "kiss his lips" is that a person who speaks straightforward and honestly to you (doesn't skirt the truth) is a *real friend* (sign of true friendship). Kisses are a sign of affection, approval and allegiance. Honest but tactful and loving speech is also. Warren Wiersbe cautions, "Truth without love is brutality, and love without truth is hypocrisy."[1414]

Thomas Fuller said, "If I speak what is false, I must answer for it; if truth, it will answer for me."[1415]

The Bottom Line: Speak honestly in every arena and audience of life. Honest speech is a sweet-smelling fragrance that attracts and wins the respect and admiration of others (Ephesians 4:15).

330
Unity, they will know we are Christians by our love
Proverbs 30:27
"The locusts have no king, yet go they forth all of them by bands."

Locusts, without ("no") a "king" (leader, commander) march as soldiers in regimental formation, methodically and in unison to accomplish tasks ("bands"). See Joel 2:7–8. In this regard they mirror (or should) the church, the body of Christ.

There was a man who was shipwrecked on a deserted island. He built a nice house, and being the religious man he was, a church. In time the man constructed several more buildings. Rescuers, upon their arrival, made inquiry about the buildings. "What is that big building?" they asked. He replied, "My home." Then they asked, "What is that magnificent building?" to which he answered, "My church." At the last they inquired, "What are all those other buildings?" The man replied, "Those are other churches I built. I kept having arguments in each of them and kept moving my membership."

Throughout Scripture unity among the saints is insisted on. The psalmist said, "Behold, how good and how pleasant it is for brethren to dwell together in unity!" (Psalm 133:1). The Apostle Paul spoke much about unity among the saints: "Now I beseech [appeal to] you, brethren, by the name [authority] of our Lord Jesus Christ, that ye all speak the same thing, and that there be no divisions among you [live in harmony]; but that ye be perfectly joined together in the same mind and in the same judgment" (1 Corinthians 1:10). In Philippians 1:27 (KJB2000), he urged harmony among believers in saying, "Only let your manner of life be as it becomes the gospel of Christ: that whether I come and see you, or else be absent, I may hear of your affairs, that you stand fast in one spirit, *with one mind striving together for the faith of the gospel.*"

And in Ephesians 4:3 (ESV) Paul tells believers to be "eager to maintain the unity of the Spirit in the bond of peace." God causes believers to have "unity" (Greek noun for "unity"; from the word "one"); to be knitted together; to be at peace with one another by the indwelling work of the Holy Spirit in them.[1416]

Vance Havner said, "We are not to be wired together by organization, frozen together by formalism, rusted together by tradition, but melted together by one Spirit."[1417] The foundation of unity in the church is its members walking in harmony with God personally ("Whatever disunites man from God, also disunites man from man."[1418]); embracing and adhering to sound biblical doctrine; and the refusal to allow disagreements to create divisions, schisms and strife (to disagree agreeably without its harming fellowship, the advancement of the Gospel or, most importantly, the glory and honor of God).

A. T. Pierson summarizes, "To a true child of God, the invisible bond that unites all believers to Christ is far more tender and lasting and precious; and as we come to recognize and realize that we are all dwelling in one sphere of life in Him, we learn to look on every believer as our brother in a sense that is infinitely higher than all human relationships. This is the one and only way to bring disciples permanently together. All other plans for promoting the unity of the church have failed."[1419]

Of all that Jesus could have said was the telltale sign of a Christian, He chose that of unifying love. In John 13:35, He says, "By this shall all men know that ye are my disciples, if ye have love one to another." It's high time the church stop her *fussing and fighting,* damaging the name of

Christ in the community, and genuinely practice Christian love one to another and to those without.

> We will walk with each other; we will walk hand in hand,
> And they'll know we are Christians by our love, by our love;
> Yes, they'll know we are Christians by our love.[1420] ~ Peter Schools

The Bottom Line: Charles Hodge remarks, "The church is everywhere represented as one. It is one body, one family, one fold, one kingdom. It is one because pervaded by one Spirit. We are all baptized into one Spirit so as to become, says the apostle, one body."[1421]

331
Unsaved, their heavy unseen burden
Proverbs 27:3

"A stone is heavy, and the sand weighty; but a fool's wrath is heavier than them both."

A "fool's" (rebellious, unrighteous) "wrath" (provocation; irritation or trouble resultant from his sinful conduct[1422]; grief or vexation) exceeds the weightiness of a heavy stone and a bag of wet sand (the burden to bear is heavier). R. E. Murphy comments, "The physical fatigue caused by bearing heavy burdens is obvious, but worse is the mental and spiritual pain that a fool provokes."[1423]

Despite the portrayal that life is a blast, the fool inwardly bears a heavier burden of grief and vexation resultant from sinful conduct than either a large stone or heap of sand *figuratively possesses.* "The way of transgressors is hard" (Proverbs 13:15); much more so than perhaps imagined. The foolish dig a pit, fall into it and don't know how to get out (Proverbs 26:27). Frustrated and irritated with sin's undoing, secretly he envies the righteous—their peace, hope, joy, safety and success. With the very fabric of life torn apart, he's impotent to do anything about it. Most sadly, many such fools opt for suicide. It is only then that the heaviness of the burden of their guilt and sin's consequence is revealed openly. With this in mind, Solomon certainly had good cause to instruct the righteous not to envy the wicked. "Be not thou envious against [of] evil men" (Proverbs 24:1), as did David also who said not to be envious of those who do wrong (Psalm 37:1).

The righteous surely knows about soul burden and its weightiness. Job attests that his grief was "heavier than the sand of the sea" (Job 6:3). But unlike the fool or the ungodly, the righteous know to whom to resort for its alleviation and comfort (Proverbs 18:10). Look beyond the appearance of the foolish to see how their heart aches with trouble, grief and frustration. Helen Smith Shoemaker wrote, "People are lost and need to be found. They search for God, ultimate reality and faith, but they cannot by themselves find 'the most important door in the world,' which is 'the door through which people walk when they find God.'" Poetically, Shoemaker describes this truth.

> People crave to know where the door is,
> And all that so many ever find
> Is only a wall where a door ought to be.
>
> They creep along the wall like blind men,
> With outstretched, groping hands,
> Feeling for a door, knowing there must be a door,
> Yet they never find it.
>
> Men die outside that door, as starving beggars die
> On cold nights in cruel cities in the dead of winter—
> Die for want of what is within their grasp.
> They live on the other side of it—
> Live because they have not found it.[1424]

Sir Humphrey Davy said, "I envy no quality of mind or intellect in others—not genius, power, wit, or fancy; but if I could choose what would be most delightful, and I believe most useful to me, I should prefer a firm religious belief to every other blessing; for it makes life a discipline of goodness, creates new hopes when all earthly hopes vanish, and throws over the decay, the destruction of existence, the most gorgeous of all lights; calling in the most delightful visions where the sensualist and the sceptic view only gloom, decay, and annihilation."[1425]

The Bottom Line: Nobody knows the trouble the sinner bears as a result of life lived apart from God in sin—that is, nobody but the Lord. Show them the "door" into His presence.

332
Unstable, avoid vacillators in convictions and conduct
Proverbs 24:21

"My son, fear thou the LORD and the king: and meddle not with them that are given to change."

My son, "fear thou the Lord" (revere, honor, trust and obey) and the king (don't disobey either the Lord or the king): AND "meddle not with" (don't associate with[1426]; TEV says "have nothing to do with") them that are "given to change" (unstable, vacillating in belief and behavior).

People whose convictions and conduct change as it were with the wind are to be avoided. The principle is never truer than with regard to the Christian faith, morality and governmental politics. "Flip-floppers" may embrace you and your stance on issues today only to "change" their mind tomorrow. Such vacillators are unreliable and potentially destructive to all who associate with them.

The Bottom Line: The mentally and spiritually stable are surefooted in their beliefs and practice, only changing either for the better when necessary. Associate, align, partner, consult, date or marry people of this mindset.

333
Vengeance, avoid retaliation—extend forgiveness
Proverbs 24:29

"Say not, I will do so to him as he hath done to me: I will render to the man according to his work."

Say not, "I will do so to him as he hath done to me" (do not desire vengeance; retaliation): "I" (the offended man says) will "render" (get even) with the man according to his "work" (the wrong deed he did to me).

Choke down the emotion to get even. Paul cautions, "Never take your own revenge, beloved, but leave room for the wrath of God, for it is written, 'VENGEANCE IS MINE, I WILL REPAY,' says the Lord" (Romans 12:9 NASB). Charles Stanley says, "We are to forgive so that we may enjoy God's goodness without feeling the weight of anger burning deep within our hearts. Forgiveness does not mean we recant the fact that what happened to us was wrong. Instead, we roll our burdens onto the Lord and allow Him to carry them for us."[1427]

You have been hurt sorely, and it's like a blanket that constantly envelopes your life with ever changing emotions of anger, bitterness, resentment and vengeance. God is aware of the hurt and promises healing and blessing if handled in His prescribed way. In fact, He pledges to work good out of the bad that occurred (Romans 8:28). All in all, the good that God brings out of our hurt from the hand of others enables us to say with Joseph, "You intended to harm me, but God intended it for good to accomplish what is now being done, the saving of many lives" (Genesis 50:20 NIV). Embracing such an attitude is momentous in exhibiting forgiveness (pardoning and releasing the offender of their infliction of pain).

"There is one eternal principal," states William Barclay, "which will be valid as long as the world lasts. The principle is: Forgiveness is a costly thing. Human forgiveness is costly. A son or a daughter may go wrong; a father or a mother may forgive; but that forgiveness has brought tears; it has brought whiteness to the hair, lines to the face, a cutting anguish and then a long dull ache to the heart. It did not cost nothing. There was a price of a broken heart to pay." "Divine forgiveness is costly. God is love, but God is holiness. God, least of all, can break the great moral laws on which the universe is built. Sin must have its punishment, or the very structure of life disintegrates. And God alone can pay the terrible price that is necessary before men can be forgiven. Forgiveness is never a case of saying: 'It's all right; it doesn't matter.' Forgiveness is the most costly thing in the world....Where there is forgiveness, someone must be crucified on a cross."[1428]

Yes, forgiveness is costly! It costs the horrendous pain and grief you experience as a result of the hurtful word or act—the tears, sleepless nights, despair, shame and hollowness in the soul. It costs death to pride ("I will never speak to him again") and heightened humility. It costs rendering blessing instead of cursing (1 Peter 3:9). It costs turning the cheek to him who hits it and giving your shirt to him who steals your coat (Luke 6:29). It costs death to vengeance ("I will make him pay for what he did") and submission to the Lord to handle as He deems best (Romans 12:19). It costs going contrary to popular opinion ("You have every right to be angry, bitter and unforgiving") to do the Christian thing. In 1988, shortly before her death, Marghanita Laski, one of our best-known secular humanists and novelists, said, "What I envy most about you Christians is your forgiveness; I have nobody to forgive me."[1429]

In pondering the great cost of forgiveness, you must agree with Barclay, "Where there is forgiveness, someone must be crucified." And that someone is you. Recall the words of Paul: "And they that are Christ's have crucified the flesh with the affections and lusts" (Galatians 5:24) and "I die daily" (1 Corinthians 15:31). Death must occur to the "Big I," as Bertha Smith used to called it, if forgiveness is to be manifested. The idea of death to the flesh encompasses a willingness to sacrifice your rights, desires and deserts so that the guilty (he who hurt you) may be fully forgiven and placed in right standing with you. Though costly, forgiving others pays us back in the weight of gold.

The Bottom Line: "To be a Christian," states C. S. Lewis, "means to forgive the inexcusable, because God has forgiven the inexcusable in you."[1430]

334
Vision, the effect when God's Word is not proclaimed
Proverbs 29:18
"Where there is no vision, the people perish."

Where there is no "vision" (revelation from God; the expounded truth of God's Word), the people "perish" (they live without restraint).

The Proverb is not referencing the absence of a vision as commonly known (plan or goal for the future) but of the expounded Word of God by His messengers. Where the Bible is not proclaimed, the people know nothing of the grace, mercy or knowledge of God. And they "perish" (unrestrained conduct that leads to spiritual ruin—Hosea 4:6). Untold millions yet are perishing for lack of a vision. There are 6,741 *Unreached People Groups* in the world (groups that are less than 2 percent evangelical Christian), which make up 42.2 percent of the world's population, and 2,792 *Unevangelized People Groups* (groups that are greater than 2 percent evangelical Christian but still with great numbers of unsaved) which make up 11 percent of the world's population.[1431] The Barna Research *State of the Bible* Survey (2015) revealed that 72 percent of Christians believe the Gospel is available in all the world's languages. However, this is not the case, for 1,859 different languages (31 percent) don't even have a Bible translation in process while 2,195 (26 percent) do, but with no completed Scripture as yet.[1432] An estimated 160 million people remain without one verse of Scripture translated into their heart language.[1433]

Pray for *laborers* to be thrust into the harvest field (especially where there is no or little vision) by the Lord. Jesus instructs: "Pray ye therefore the Lord of the harvest, that he will send forth labourers into his harvest" (Matthew 9:38). E. M. Bounds states, "Missionaries, like ministers, are born of praying people. A praying church begets laborers in the harvest field of the world. The scarcity of missionaries argues a non-praying church."[1434] Pray for pastors, associate ministers, musicians and singers, evangelists and missionaries to be raised up and utilized in fulfilling the Great Commission. Likewise, pray for laymen to be raised up to teach, testify, train and preach at home and abroad. Pray more of them into "volunteer missions" and the work of soul winning.

The Bottom Line: Without a vision from God, man remains in spiritual darkness and ignorance. We must pray laborers into the unevangelized places of our world. "Happy" is the person who hears and receives the gospel message unto salvation (Proverbs 29:18).

335
Vocational, the divine call to gospel ministry
Proverbs 19:21
"There are many devices in a man's heart; nevertheless the counsel of the LORD, that shall stand."

There are many "devices" (plans) in a man's heart (mind); nevertheless the "counsel of the LORD" (the purpose or will of the Lord), that "shall stand" (prevail, succeed, win out). Allen Ross summarizes "that only those plans that God approves will succeed."[1435]

Every Christian is "called" to serve God in a general sense, while some are "called" to serve Him in a specific sense as vocational servants. Paul states in Ephesians 4:11–12, "And he gave some, apostles; and some, prophets; and some, evangelists; and some, pastors and teachers; For the perfecting of the saints, for the work of the ministry, for the edifying of the body of Christ."

How can a believer know if God is extending a call into full-time Christian service? How does it come? How do you know when it comes? When does it come? How do you say yes to it when it comes? God's will is neither vague nor hidden but readily knowable. Discovery of God's will is pivotal to living in the arena of maximum usefulness, happiness and peace. Paul admonishes, "See then that you walk circumspectly, not as fools but as wise, redeeming the time, because the days are evil. Therefore do not be unwise, but understand what the will of the Lord is" (Ephesians 5:15–17 NKJV).

Alice in Wonderland, when asking the cat for directions, was asked, "Where do you want to go?" She replied, "It doesn't matter." The cat responded, "Then it doesn't matter which way you go." Direction in life matters to the Christian, or at least it ought to. It matters enormously which way you go.

God promises divine guidance to help His children know "which way to go." "The God of our fathers has chosen you that you should know His will, and see the Just One, and hear the voice of His mouth" (Acts 22:14 NKJV). "For I know the plans I have for you," declares the Lord, "plans to prosper you and not to harm you, plans to give you hope and a future" (Jeremiah 29:11 NIV).

Spiritual Markers

After living in Egypt, Abraham returned to the place where he had previously called upon the name of the Lord (Genesis 13:3–4). This was a spiritual marker in his life. Spiritual markers are places, reference points which identify a transition, decision or direction when God clearly gave guidance.[1436] In looking at these markers, one can readily see the direction God is moving his life. These markers are important in understanding God's guidance. They're like the "yellow brick road"; each marker (brick) builds upon the other, moving you in God's designed direction. To gain assurance that you have not deviated off the road (God's will), it is helpful to look at the previous markers upon encountering a new one (for instance a call to vocational Christian ministry). If they all seem to point in the same direction as the new marker, then it is most likely that you are moving in the right direction. Review the spiritual markers of your life in sequence and see how God may or may not be guiding to vocational ministry.

The Bottom Line: God has a plan for every life; for some it includes vocational Christian ministry. If divinely given the assignment to serve as a vocational minister, respond with Isaiah in saying, "Here am I; send me" (Isaiah 6:8).

336
Vows, fulfill pledges made to the Lord
Proverbs 20:25

"It is a snare to the man who devoureth that which is holy, and after vows to make enquiry."

It is a "snare" (a snare is a trap hunters prepared to capture animals; a forewarning that unkept promises to God leads to dangerous ground) to the man who "devoureth" (to act rashly without forethought) that which is "holy" (Reyburn and Fry say it means to "dedicate something to God"[1437]), AND after "vows" (promises made to God) to make "inquiry" (to reflect upon the vow made; to only consider the vow or promise made seriously after the fact with the view of escaping it). To summarize, man is prone in time of distress and emotional inspiration to rashly and spontaneously pledge the Lord fuller surrender, greater sacrifice or specific service, only to ponder its weightiness in its aftermath, followed by reneging.

Prior to making a pledge or vow unto the Lord, man is to consider its cost and his means to fulfill it. The Lord nowhere in Scripture orders a vow to be made; it is always to be voluntary. But when it is promised, it is required that it be fulfilled, or else dire consequences will result (Deuteronomy 23:21–23). Beware of momentary bursts of religious impression or excitement that prompt insincere hasty promises to the Lord. See Acts 5:1–10 (vow of Ananias and Sapphira).

The serious blunder of making a vow to God that is not kept is addressed by Solomon also in Ecclesiastes: "When thou vowest a vow unto God, defer not to pay it; for he hath no pleasure in fools: pay that which thou hast vowed. Better is it that thou shouldest not vow, than that thou shouldest vow and not pay. Suffer not thy mouth to cause thy flesh to sin; neither say thou before the angel, that it was an error: wherefore should God be angry at thy voice, and destroy the work of thine hands?" (Ecclesiastes 5:4–6).

Matthew Henry explains, "It is a snare to a man, after he has made vows to God, to enquire how he may evade them or get dispensed with, and to contrive excuses for the violating of them. If the matter of them was

458

doubtful, and the expressions were ambiguous, that was his fault; he should have made them with more caution and consideration."[1438] Upon opening your mouth unto the Lord with *vows* (commitments), it becomes too late to take them back. Scripture says, "Don't let your words cause you to sin, and don't say to the priest at the Temple, 'I didn't mean what I promised.' If you do, God will become angry with your words and will destroy everything you have worked for" (Ecclesiastes 5:6 NCV).

The story of Jephthah illustrates the foolishness of making rash vows without "counting the cost." This king, prior to leading the Israelites to battle against the Ammonites, made a vow stipulating that if he returned home the victor, whoever first came out the doors to meet him would be slain. He was victor in the battle, and the first one to meet him upon his arrival home was his daughter. Jephthah, though greatly distressed and grieved, kept the vow (Judges 11:29–40). The account serves well to teach the foolishness of rash vows. W. A. Criswell remarks, "In no sense was Jephthah's tragic vow, or his foolish action [in keeping it], pleasing to God."[1439]

In the story of the two sons, the one who at the first declined to work in the vineyard, only later to work, was commended. The other son who agreed to work changed his mind. See Mathew 21:28–32. The lesson is clear. It is far better to say "No" only later to say "Yes" than to rashly say "Yes" only later to say "No" to that which the Lord summons.

The Bottom Line: J. Vernon McGee summarizes, "Don't make a vow until you are sure of what you can do. [For example, d]on't publicly dedicate your life to God until you have thought it through. God doesn't want that kind of a sentimental decision."[1440] Jesus warned, "No man, having put his hand to the plough, and looking back, is fit for the kingdom of God" (Luke 9:62).

337
Warning, you had better not mess with the righteous
Proverbs 24:15
"Lay not wait, O wicked man, against the dwelling of the righteous; spoil not his resting place."

"Who delivered us from so great a death, and doth deliver: in whom we trust that he will yet deliver us" (2 Corinthians 1:10).

"Lay not wait" (to ambush the righteous without warning), O "wicked man" (the ungodly, foolish; those who stubbornly refuse to "acknowledge or obey God"[1441]), against the "dwelling" (place of abode) of the "righteous" (the upright and God-fearing); "spoil" (to rob or harm) not his "resting place" (home).

The wicked in heart hate the righteous. "If the world hate you [righteous], ye know that it hated me [Jesus] before it hated you" (John 15:18). All too often Christians are assaulted, ridiculed, imprisoned and their homes robbed, vandalized or destroyed. But the evil plots of the wicked are futile. The saint is relentless in his faith and though knocked down seven times always rebounds (Proverbs 24:16). "Persecuted, but not forsaken; *cast down, but not destroyed*; Always bearing about in the body the dying of the Lord Jesus, that the life also of Jesus might be made manifest in our body. For we which live are alway delivered unto death for Jesus' sake, that the life also of Jesus might be made manifest in our mortal flesh" (2 Corinthians 4:9–11). "For a just man falleth seven times, and riseth up again" (Proverbs 24:16). The Christian may get knocked down, but never is he knocked out. In Jesus Christ he is resilient.

The Bottom Line: The wicked had better realize that to touch the righteous is extremely dangerous and hazardous. "For he that toucheth you toucheth the apple of his eye" (Zechariah 2:8). God promises to bring down (harsh but righteous judgment; ruin) the wicked that mistreats His people (Proverbs 24:16). God will vindicate the righteous. See Psalm 105:15.

338
Wealth, money can't buy your way into Heaven
Proverbs 11:4
"Riches profit not in the day of wrath: but righteousness delivereth from death."

"Riches" (wealth gained unjustly[1442]; but one's money gained lawfully or not will not justify him when judged by the Lord) "profit not" (bears no advantage or value[1443]) in the "day of wrath" (the Day of Judgment; retribution for the sinner): BUT "righteousness" (to be right through the Lord Jesus Christ and do right) "delivereth" (rescues) from "death" (the unhappy and premature death of the wicked; looking back from the New Testament, it includes "eternal death" in the lake of fire).

King Solomon was one of the wealthiest kings of Israel. Abraham, David and Job were wealthy. Each in their wealth had favor with God. Wealth in general is not condemned, only its acquisition by deceitful and unethical means and placement above God. "Treasures of wickedness profit nothing" (Proverbs 10:2). Riches may protect man from due justice for wrongdoing at present, but not forever. Divine judgment will come ("day of wrath") surely and perhaps suddenly.

A second truth of the principle is that at the Judgment a rich man's money will be of no avail. He will stand as the poorest on earth stripped naked of earthly possessions to give account of life lived and relationship to Jesus Christ. Money may buy fancy clothes, nice homes, expensive jewelry, and cars, but it cannot purchase entrance into Heaven. Heaven is acquired by "righteousness"—not man's, but God's. "For they being ignorant of God's righteousness, and going about to establish their own righteousness, have not submitted themselves unto the righteousness of God" (Romans 10:3). Upon man's repentance (contrition for and turning from sin) and faith in Jesus Christ, God imputes His righteousness unto him. "For he hath made him [Jesus] to be sin for us, who knew no sin; that we might be made the righteousness of God in him" (2 Corinthians 5:21). "And therefore it was imputed to him [Abraham] for righteousness. Now it was not written for his sake alone, that it was imputed to him; But for us also, to whom it shall be imputed, if we believe on him that raised up Jesus our Lord from the dead" (Romans 4:22–24). Abraham wasn't saved by his own merit or good works, but rather by Christ's righteousness which was imputed to him by God. The word *impute* means "to attribute to another, to pass to one's account."

In pointing out the futility of self-righteousness and the must of divine imputation of Christ's righteousness as a means of salvation, the apostle Paul declared, "That I may gain Christ, and may be found in Him, not having a righteousness of my own derived from the Law, but that which is through faith in Christ, the righteousness which comes from God on the basis of faith" (Philippians 3:8–9 NASB). Paul says a person must have the righteousness of God that comes by faith in Christ in order to enter Heaven. At the moment of salvation, God covers a person with the canopy of Christ's perfected righteousness (imputes); and from that moment forward, when He looks at that person, He sees Christ's righteousness (2

Corinthians 5:21), not any righteousness that the person might claim. We refer to this as the judicial forgiveness of God. What an awesome and glorious truth!

The apostle Paul gives yet another beautiful picture of judicial forgiveness when he says, "When you were spiritually dead because of your sins and because you were not free from the power of your sinful self, God made you alive with Christ, and he forgave all our sins. He canceled the debt, which listed all the rules we failed to follow. He took away that record with its rules and nailed it to the cross" (Colossians 2:13–14 NCV). In ancient days, a list of the crime(s) of the executed were hung on the cross with them. God took every sin we would ever commit and nailed it to Jesus' cross. Jesus paid the full payment for our sin so that we might be reconciled to God. The Christian is no longer in bondage to the debt of sin (its penalty), because Jesus paid it once and for all.

The Bottom Line: Don't place trust or happiness in riches nor make it the driving force of life. It cannot compensate for the "emptiness" in the soul that only Christ can satisfy, or buy entrance into Heaven.

339
Wicked, memory will bring mourning for the sinner
Proverbs 5:11

"And thou mourn at the last."

And thou "mourn" (Deane and Taswell say, "It is not the plaintive wailing or the subdued grief of heart which is signified, but the loud wail of lamentation, the groaning indicative of intense mental suffering called forth by the remembrance of past folly, and which sees no remedy in the future"[1444]) at the "last" ("when all is said and done"; at the ending of life).

The wicked with joy and frivolity engage in wanton conduct, mocking and laughing at the very One who gave them life. But the day is coming when the laughing will turn to mourning. God will have the final word, as will the effects of the sins committed. A life of sin always ends horrifically, sadly and regretfully, despite its glamourous and promising portrayal. H. A. Ironside with excellence states, "To learn by painful experience, if the Word of God is not bowed to, is a bitter and solemn thing. God is not mocked; what is sown must be reaped. The unsteady hand, the confused brain, the bleared eye, premature age, and weakened powers, with days and nights of folly to look back on with regret that can never be banished from the memory: such are a few of the results of failing to heed the advice of wisdom in the natural world."[1445] Bitter regrets "at the last" (old age or hour of death) will occupy the mind of the wicked, eroding peace and hope for the future and prompting *mourning* ("groaning indicative of intense mental suffering"[1446]). Groaning is a word used to describe the *roaring* of the sea (Isaiah 5:30).[1447] The wicked groaning as the roaring of the ocean continuously will wail, "How have I hated instruction, and my heart despised reproof; And have not obeyed the voice of my teachers, nor inclined mine ear to them that instructed me!" (Proverbs 5:12–13). Remorse, remorse, remorse for disregard for God, His Word, parents and preachers—what a horrid and awful end!

> For all sad words of tongue and pen,
> The saddest are these: "It might have been."
> ~ John Greenleaf Whittier

A sermon in *The American National Preacher* cited the following story. An eminent statesman who died furnished in his last hours an affecting illustration of the power of an awakened conscience. He had led a thoughtless life, and his highest ambition was to be esteemed a man of genius and honor, true to his friends, and a cordial hater of his enemies. At length, he was brought to a sick and dying bed. A clergyman visited him in the hope that he might be induced, in the eleventh hour, to flee to Christ for pardon and salvation. He questioned him in relation to his feelings, but his only reply was in tones of agony: *"Remorse, remorse."* And when his voice was silenced and his limbs were stiffening, he made another effort to express the hopelessness of his misery by motioning for a card and tracing with his hand, quivering in death, the same significant word: *"Remorse, remorse."*[1448]

What a wrenching end for the wretched on earth. It is but a faint shadow of the awfulness of Hell that awaits. But there is yet hope for the most ungodly who may be reading this entry. With all within me I urge you to flee the wrath of God which is yet to come. Flee the tormenting conscience presently and eternally. With the two angels, I say what they said to Lot, "Escape for thy life" (Genesis 19:17). Run into the outstretched arms of Jesus Christ who promises to receive the vilest, blackest sinner upon his return to Him through repentance and faith (Romans 10:9–13). At death invitation closes, and the riches of the Gospel in Christ Jesus are unavailable.

The Bottom Line: In the end the conscience deadened by sinful depravity shall be awakened by Holy God to bear witness to the truth of God's Word as stated in Proverbs and the rest of Holy Scriptures, inflicting the heart with the raging fury of remorse. "Remorse is the last witness to Wisdom and her claims."[1449]

340
Wicked, sinners' ploy to allure saints into sin
Proverbs 1:10
"My son, if sinners entice thee, consent thou not."

"My son" (the sage's parental-type address to his student or father's to his son), "if" (when) "sinners" (the foolish, ungodly, transgressors of God's law; the immoral) "entice thee" (to beckon persuasively, tempt, allure), "consent thou not" (don't do it; practice restraint, refuse).

Satan has "sinners" to target the unstable and innocent soul, seeking their participation in their sin. Be "street smart" (about flattery, first impressions, deceptive human manipulation and persuasive words designed to lure to alcohol, drugs, pornography, sex). Matthew Henry well states, "How industrious wicked people are to seduce others into the paths of the destroyer: they will entice."[1450]

The Bottom Line: Saying "no" to temptation and tempters, though at times difficult, protects from sin's sure injurious consequence, which may be irreversible. "And be sure your sin will find you out" (Numbers 32:23).

341
Wicked, the wicked will face a payday someday
Proverbs 12:7
"The wicked are overthrown, and are not: but the house of the righteous shall stand."

The "wicked" (the ungodly and foolish; those who do not acknowledge God or obey Him) are "overthrown" (their destruction is coming; Maclaren says in plotting to overthrow others, they are overthrown, "their mischief comes back, like the Australian boomerang, to the hand that flings it"[1451]), and are not: BUT the "house of the righteous" (the righteous himself and his family[1452]) shall "stand" (remain safe and secure; ever victorious whether in life's battles or in death's end; Deane and Taswell say, "The house of the righteous, being founded on a secure foundation, shall stand"[1453] [Matthew 7:24]).

The wicked may appear to be winning, but in time they will be "overthrown." *Overthrown* is the same Hebrew word used in reference to the sudden destruction of Sodom (Lamentations 4:6). It means destruction or ruin.[1454] Solomon is stating that God will bring the wicked to a sudden end; they will cease to be on earth, only to experience eternal consequences for their sin in Hell forever. As R. G. Lee said in his famous sermon, there will be a "Payday Someday." Man will give a divine accounting for life lived and rejection of God. But the "righteous shall stand." Christians shall endure ("stand") the trials and tribulations of life victoriously, and though death may remove them, their end is Heaven. And once removed, yet they will be remembered, unlike the wicked.

The Bottom Line: The ungodly will face a "payday someday." They will not escape the divine retribution of a Holy God for their hideous conduct and stubborn unbelief.

342
Widow, the church's task to care for widows
Proverbs 15:25
"The LORD will destroy the house of the proud: but he will establish the border of the widow."

The Lord will "destroy" ("uproots violently") the "house of the proud" (Reyburn and Fry say "powerfully arrogant or ruthless people"[1455] that steal land [by moving the boundary marker that defines one's ownership of property] from defenseless widows): BUT "he" (God) will "establish the border" (make sure her property boundary is secure) of the "widow" (the wife whose husband has died and has no one to look out for her interests; Deane and Taswell remark that the widow is often seen in Scripture as "symbolic" of "weakness and desolation"[1456] [Deuteronomy 10:18; Psalm 146:9]).

The principle assures the widow that God cares for and overwatches her with protection. David underscores the truth: "The Lord watches over the sojourners; he upholds the widow and the fatherless, but the way of the wicked he brings to ruin" (Psalm 146:9 ESV). Our gracious and compassionate Lord draws a circle of fire about the confines of the widow, keeping injurious intruders out. The widow can assuredly depend upon the Lord for help (Jeremiah 49:11). None who seek to take advantage of a defenseless widow (unjust dealings, robbery, and deceit) will escape God's fury; he will be brought to "ruin."

Caring for the widow is the believer's task. James 1:27 says, "Pure religion and undefiled before God and the Father is this, To visit the fatherless and widows in their affliction." In 1 Timothy 5:3–16 the Lord gives specific guidelines for their care. Moses stood up for the widow: "You shall not afflict any widow or orphan" (Exodus 22:22 NASB). He also warned, "Cursed is he who distorts the justice due an alien, orphan, and widow" (Deuteronomy 27:19 NASB). J. Vernon McGee cautions, "The early church took care of widows, but they didn't do it in some haphazard, sentimental way. The deacons were to make an investigation to see who were truly widows, where the need was, and how much need there was."[1457] W. D. Mounce clarifies that a true widow "is not simply a woman whose husband is dead but one who deserves to be supported by the church."[1458]

The Bottom Line: A mark of spirituality is the care one gives to widows and orphans.

343
Wife, husbands ought to praise their wives
Proverbs 31:28–29
"Her children arise up, and call her blessed; her husband also, and he praiseth her. Many daughters have done virtuously, but thou excellest them all."

"A man's greatest treasure is his wife" (Proverbs 18:22 CEV).

"Her" (the godly woman) children "arise up" (they "stand up and proclaim"[1459]), and "call her blessed" (like saying, ''Hooray, hooray for our mother"[1460]); her husband also, and he "praiseth her" (he speaks highly of her[1461]). "Many daughters have done virtuously, but thou excellest them all" (the husband's actual praise to his wife; though there are many wives and mothers that are awesome, she excels them all).

The husband "praiseth her" (honors; speaks highly of his wife) as one of the best and godliest women on earth. Likewise, every husband is to show honor to his wife. Gary Smalley states, "Honor is a decision to view our spouse as a priceless treasure—a person of high worth and value. This is what King Solomon encouraged as well: "A man's greatest treasure is his wife" (Proverbs 18:22 CEV). Honor isn't based on behavior or subject to emotion.[1462]

Honor her by not demeaning her. H. A. Ironside said, "The Lord never does anything to tear down or put down His chosen bride! Even when He must discipline us, He does it in love that we may share His holiness. The application for Christian husbands is obvious. Any thoughts, words or deeds that put down your wife, ridicule her, attack her, or tear her down are not in line with your God-given purpose."[1463]

Honor by focusing on her needs. Ironside continues, "A husband may say, 'I'd die for my wife if it ever came down to it. I'd fight to the death in order to protect her.' That's tremendous, and I hope you would! But here's the real question: 'Are you crucifying self on a daily basis on behalf of your wife?' Is your focus on using her to meet your needs or on setting aside your selfish desires in order to meet her needs?"[1464] Be ever sensitive to your wife's needs. Tone down the rhetoric. Speak kindly and gently to her. Unintentionally men speak to their wives at times in a way that is demeaning and degrading, not honoring.

Express affection constantly. Let her know that she has captured your heart forever. Affirm your love by actions and *words*. Remember special occasions (birthday, anniversary, and Mother's Day), making a big deal out of them.

Exhibit openness. Let her interrupt your schedule personally or call on the phone whenever the need arises. Your wife's contact should be far more important than that of the CEO of the company. Listen when she speaks. Pay attention. Get engaged in the conversation.

Thou shalt not compare her with other women. Accept her for who she is as she does you. Don't poke stabs at her by stating you wish she was talented or gifted as other women. Voice approval and praise of her actions, appearance, attributes and godliness. *Defend her honor* when others assault. Live up to her trust. Make her feel important.

The Bottom Line: Gary Smalley says, "You grant your spouse value whether they want it or deserve it. Honor is a decision you make and a gift you give."[1465] Martin Luther well said, "Let the wife make the husband glad to come home, and let him make her sorry to see him leave."[1466]

344
Wife, the gracious and virtuous woman
Proverbs 11:16
"A gracious woman retaineth honour: and strong men retain riches."

A "gracious woman" ("appearance is lovely, graceful and attractive"[1467]) "retaineth" (maintains) "honor" (receives praise and respect): AND "strong men" (violently aggressive men or energetic strong men[1468]) "riches" (wealth). Matthew Henry summarizes, "The *gracious woman* is as solicitous to retain that which is honorable (virtue, modesty, wisdom, humility, prudence, godliness and other graces) as *strong men* are to "retain" (secure) their estates."[1469]

This is the only Proverb that makes a contrast between man and woman.

Ruth is a classic example of a gracious woman. In a foreign land and in need, she retained her honor. Boaz could say to her, "[F]or all the city of my people doth know that thou art a virtuous woman" (Ruth 3:11). The entire city ("all of my people") of Bethlehem knew Ruth was honorable in her relationship with Boaz (sexually) and in every other detail of her life.[1470] Even amidst difficult circumstance she maintained her reputation as being honorable.

The secret of a virtuous, honorable woman is also seen in Proverbs 31:30, which in the Amplified Bible reads: "Charm and grace are deceptive, and beauty is vain [because it is not lasting], but a woman who reverently and worshipfully fears the Lord, she shall be praised!" Francis Dixon states of the Proverbs 31 woman that "she loved the Lord (Psalm 116:1); she desired in all things to please Him (Hebrews 11:5); she endeavored to obey Him (Acts 5:29); she served Him faithfully (Mark 14:8); she gave herself and her all to Him (Romans 12:1–2); and she knew the meaning of 1 Thessalonians 5:16–18."[1471]

The Bottom Line: A virtuous and honorable woman doesn't just happen; it takes conviction and dedication to biblical core values and intimate fellowship with the Lord without swaying. The gracious woman is diligent to maintain a good reputation.

345
Wife, traits of the good bride
Proverbs 31:11–12

"The heart of her husband doth safely trust in her, so that he shall have no need of spoil. She will do him good and not evil all the days of her life."

The "heart" (seat of intelligence, understanding, decision-making; the mind) of "her" (the good wife) husband doth "safely trust in her" (confidence in her ability to manage the household[1472]), so that he shall have no need of "spoil" (he possesses no fear that his hard-earned money will be squandered frivolously, and through her industriousness in making garments and the income it provides he is assured of having everything that is needed). She will do him "good" (she "deals out"[1473] nothing but good to him) and "not evil" (always be the best thing that ever happened to him, humanly speaking) "all the days of her life" (she is committed to the marital vow that only at "death do we part," and to always bring nothing but good into his life).

The character traits of love unrivaled, marital fidelity, prudent housekeeping and spending and dependability enables "the heart of her husband to safely trust in her." Spousal trust protects from jealousy, fear, and worry, injurious false accusations and suspicion. It creates an atmosphere of peace, tranquility, confidence and assurance in the home. The home where the heart of husband and wife are knitted together with "a cord that cannot be broken" is not only secure and satisfying but successful.

It is not a trust but a *safe* trust (not partial but full confidence) the husband places in his wife. He counts her worthy of it based upon actions and attitude. Trustworthiness only is obtained and then maintained by the demonstration of being worthy of trust. Wives are to avoid all that diminishes that trust, bolstering it constantly (and vice-versa). "Trusting you is my decision. Proving me right is your choice." The honorable wife does her husband "good, not harm, all the days of her life" (NIV) (always, constantly until death). She always seeks "how she may please her husband" (1 Corinthians 7:34). Charles Bridges states, "Her husband's comfort is her interest and her rest. To live for him is her highest happiness."[1474]

The Bottom Line: Trustworthiness is an essential foundation pillar of a happy marriage. Protect it from erosion.

346
Wink, the contemptuous and deceitful wink
Proverbs 10:10
"He that winketh with the eye causeth sorrow."

He that "winketh with the eye" (a gesture that indicates deceit or insincerity[1475]) "causeth" (precipitates) "sorrow" (trouble).

The "wink" is likely a sign of insincerity and deceit. The man who winks with the eye following something he said indicates it wasn't meant (fraud, deceptive, cunning). It is a gesture to allure another to join him in something wrong, to scorn or mock others. "This is a sign of craft, malice, and complicity with other wicked comrades."[1476] The small gesture may cause great sorrow (injury, trouble, hurt, damage). Charles Bridges states, "Mischievous sport indeed is it to cause sorrow for selfish gratification; to make the eye an instrument of wanton sin."[1477]

The Bottom Line: H. A. Ironside summarizes, "He whose words and intentions are opposed [opposite] is a source of grief to others, and shall fall himself. The kiss of Judas was an action of this nature."[1478]

347
Wisdom, divine wisdom ignored and unwanted by fools
Proverbs 17:16
"Wherefore is there a price in the hand of a fool to get wisdom, seeing he hath no heart to it?"

Wherefore is there a "price in the hand" (he thinks he can buy it with money; only desires it for reputation's sake) of a "fool to get wisdom" ("the simpleton," he that has not the ability or desire to comprehend wisdom; Ptahhotep says, "A fool sees knowledge in ignorance, usefulness in harmfulness....He lives on that by which one dies; his food is distortion of speech"[1479]), "seeing he hath no heart to it?" (empty of desire or want for wisdom). To summarize, the fool is not interested in the acquisition of biblical knowledge and understanding, but if he were, it would be under his terms [price in the hand], not the Lord's.

A child may have the tuition paid ("price in the hand") for a university education, but if he has no desire to study, learn and avail himself of the opportunity, it was supplied in vain. Within the hand of every fool is the "price" (means to freely acquire) to gain wisdom. He has the Book of Knowledge and Truth (the Holy Bible), the godly, opportunity, church, time and most importantly, the Lord God to steep him in wise and righteous living. But he simply, stubbornly, stupidly, sinfully has "no heart to it" (no desire, thirst, hunger for it).

George Lawson aptly states, "Does he not know that wisdom is infinitely more precious than land or gold? No; this is the reason of his carelessness. He has no heart to wisdom; he knows not its value and has no relish of its pleasures. That which is more precious than rubies is to him more worthless than a pebble. That which is more sweet than honey is tasteless as the white of an egg."[1480] "Wisdom is before him that hath understanding; but the eyes of a fool are in the ends of the earth" (Proverbs 17:24).

Endeavor to reach the fool, but in "seeing he hath no heart" for wisdom (godly instruction and direction; personal relationship with Jesus Christ), move onward to others who do. Though wealth cannot purchase wisdom for those who love it not, wisdom procures wealth (Proverbs 3:16).[1481]

The Bottom Line: You can lead a horse to water, but you cannot make him drink. Jesus warned, "Don't cast your pearls before swine" (Matthew 7:8 VOICE).

348
Wisdom, its benefits far exceed human reasoning
Proverbs 9:12
"If thou be wise, thou shalt be wise for thyself: but if thou scornest, thou alone shalt bear it."

If thou be "wise" (spiritually and morally sensible; receives biblical instruction and advice), thou shalt be "wise for thyself" (your wisdom will benefit you [Job 22:2]): BUT if thou "scornest" (a mocker), thou alone shalt "bear it" (you alone will pay the price, suffer). Wisdom is the impartation by God to man of the understanding or discernment to know the right and most prudent thing to do in any given situation in life.

Wisdom benefits life, whereas mockery of God's instruction brings suffering. Though it might be counted "risky" to lay aside human reasoning and rationale to order life by God's wisdom, all that do are the clear winners. Its many rewards (benefits) are set forth by J. Wash Watts in *Old Testament Teaching*. "Increase in learning and sound counsels (1:5); security and quietness (1:33); preservation (2:8); understanding in righteousness and justice and equity (2:9); yea, every good path (2:9); pleasure in knowledge (2:10); deliverance from the evil way and evil men (2:12); deliverance from the strange woman (2:16); dwelling in the land (3:2); favor in the sight of God and man (3:4); providential guidance (3:6); health (3:8); prosperity (3:10); happiness (3:13); riches and honor (3:16); peace (3:17); life unto thy soul (3:22); confidence (3:26); grace (4:9); wisdom in ruling (19:12); atonement (21:18); life, righteousness, and honor (21:21); a good name (22:1); riches, honor, and life (22:4); mercy (28:13); a prudent wife (18:22; 31:10–31)."[1482] With the list I include success (Proverbs 15:22). Watts says that "in many instances wisdom is the reward of wisdom."[1483]

In light of the multitudinous benefits of wisdom, why is it that it is despised by most? It is because "there is no fear of God before his eyes" (Psalm 36:1) which "is the beginning of knowledge: but fools despise wisdom and instruction" (Proverbs 1:7). Satan has blinded man to its value and deceived them as to its need. "In whom the god of this world hath blinded the minds of them which believe not, lest the light of the glorious gospel of Christ, who is the image of God, should shine unto them" (2 Corinthians 4:4).

Biblical truth, its understanding and application, is so invaluable and imperative to a victorious life that C. H. Spurgeon forthrightly said, "Let everything else go, but do not part with a particle of truth. You are so much the richer by every truth you know; you will be so much the poorer by every truth you forget. Hold it then, and hide it in your heart."[1484] With David, *hide* (store it up through memorization and meditation) the Word of God in the heart (Psalm 119:11).

The Bottom Line: The truth is that God's wisdom (counted foolishness to man) is far wiser than the reasoning or intelligence of man. "Even the foolishness of God is wiser than human wisdom" (1 Corinthians 1:25 NCV).

349
Wisdom, its boot camp
Proverbs 19:20

"Hear counsel, and receive instruction, that thou mayest be wise in thy latter end."

"Hear" (Reyburn and Fry say, "Heed or pay attention to"[1485] [Proverbs 2:1; 4:10; 10:8]) "counsel" (godly advice), and receive "instruction" (Buzzell says "moral correction and discipline"[1486]), that thou mayest be "wise in thy latter end" (in old age; preachers and teachers lament over the young with the words of Deuteronomy 32:29, "O that they were wise, that they understood this, that they would consider their latter end!"). See Isaiah 1:3.

Each stage of life contains new challenges and conflicts, requiring new wisdom (wisdom is divine discernment that enables man to do that which is right and pleasing unto the Lord—which is for man's best good—in every course of action). Not even one as wise as Solomon outgrows the need for more of its treasure. A person is to "hear counsel, and receive instruction" (listening; to pay close attention and soak it in) progressively through life, though its initial training school is in youth. James Montgomery Boice says, "God says, 'If you are going to live for Me, you must begin at the earliest possible moment, without delay, preferably when you are very young (Psalm 119:9). If you do not live for me when you are young, you will probably not live for me when you are older either, and the end of your life will be ruinous.'"[1487]

The acquisition and application of wisdom early in life is the sure foundation for the building of a strong, sound, sturdy, scriptural and successful *house* (Matthew 7:24–25). "Wisdom gathered and digested in youth is seen in the prudence and intelligence of manhood and old age."[1488] He that starts with little wisdom accumulates much "in the end" (old age). This underscores why the godly aged are to be sought for wisdom.

Job states, "With the ancient [aged; elderly] is wisdom; and in length of days [long life] understanding" (Job 12:12). Daniel, wisely instructed in youth (Daniel 1:4), found *wisdom in the latter end* to govern 120 provinces in the kingdom during the reign of King Darius (Daniel 6:1–3). Timothy's biblical instruction while a child (2 Timothy 3:14–15) enabled him to find *wisdom in the latter end* to assist the Apostle Paul in various ministry endeavors. Children of all ages need to understand that wise, sound biblical instruction and counsel heeded today brings *wisdom in the latter end,* as it was for Daniel and Timothy. Bruce Waltke says that wisdom is "inseparable from knowledge," that a person could memorize the entire Book of Proverbs and yet lack wisdom if it failed to impact his heart.[1489] Wisdom guides man in the right use of knowledge in every facet of life.

The Bottom Line: Wisdom's "Bootcamp" ("hear counsel...receive instruction") occurs in childhood and adolescence, at which time parents, grandparents, ministers and teachers (religious and academic) instill biblical values, knowledge, understanding, and moral instruction (Deuteronomy 11:19). The child that readily, willingly hears and heeds the advice, reproof and instruction (ruled, governed by it) has a secure foundation on which to erect the rest of life.

350
Wisdom, its finding is worth the search
Proverbs 3:17
"Her ways are ways of pleasantness, and all her paths are peace."

"Her ways" (wisdom's guidance, direction[1490]) are ways of "pleasantness" (delightful, enjoyable, agreeable[1491]), and all her "paths" (everywhere wisdom leads you) are "peace" ("shalom"; safety and security). To summarize, he that embraces wisdom, allowing her to order all the details of life, will be blessed beyond measure with untold benefits from righteous living.

He who embraces wise and godly instruction possesses the purest and most consistent happiness. It is a transcendent "pleasantness" enveloped in peace (tranquility, security, well-being and safety[1492]) and inner quietness of soul despite the circumstance. In contrast, the happiness gained by accumulation of wealth ("silver and fine gold"), earthly possessions, and sinful pleasures is transient and incomplete, lacking the ability to bring inner peace (Proverbs 3:14–15). It is no wonder that Solomon strenuously exhorts man to diligently search (Proverbs 2:4) for wisdom (biblical knowledge and its understanding and application that one may know how to live to please the Lord). He says, "Happy is the man that *findeth* wisdom" (Proverbs 3:13). "All her paths" are pleasantry enveloped in peace.

There is pleasantry in Christian sacrifice, self-denial, cross-bearing, confession and restoration, worship, abstinence from evil, chastening, persecution, spiritual warfare and service. The conquering of a personal sin (mortification; putting it to death) also is a pleasantry for it only heightens the Christian's joy and happiness. The believer is never as happy as when the final death blow is delivered to a besetting sin and it is buried forever. "For if ye live after the flesh, ye shall die: but if ye through the Spirit do mortify the deeds of the body, ye shall live" (Romans 8:13). George Lawson eloquently states, "More exquisite is that *pleasure which the mortification of one sinful desire produces than that which results from the gratification of a thousand.*"[1493]

I'd rather have Jesus than silver or gold;
I'd rather be His than have riches untold;
I'd rather have Jesus than houses or lands;
I'd rather be led by His nail-pierced hand

Than to be the king of a vast domain
Or be held in sin's dread sway;
I'd rather have Jesus than anything
This world affords today. ~ Oscar C. A. Bernadotte, (1888)

Alexander Maclaren remarks, "Calm pleasures there abide. The only complete peace which fills and quiets the whole man comes from obeying Wisdom, or what is the same thing, from following Christ. There is no other way of bringing all our nature into accord with itself, ending the war between the conscience and inclination, between the flesh and spirit. There is no other way of bringing us into amity [accord; harmony] with all circumstances, so that fortunate or adverse shall be recognized as good, and nothing be able to agitate us very much. Peace with ourselves, the world, and God, is always the consequence of listening to Wisdom."[1494]

The Bottom Line: K. T. Aitken says, "For the things which make a man and woman truly rich and bring real joy and happiness, money is a worthless currency. Their price is wisdom."[1495]

351
Wisdom, makes powerful its possessor
Proverbs 24:5
"A wise man is strong; yea, a man of knowledge increaseth strength."

"Wisdom is better than weapons of war" (Ecclesiastes 9:18).

A "wise man" (biblical knowledge and understanding from the Lord; spiritually sensible, intelligent, in contrast to the fool that is emptyheaded of truth) "increaseth strength" (Deane and Taswell say "in strength, full of strength, because, however feeble in body, he is wise in counsel, firm in purpose, brave in conduct, thoroughly to be depended upon, and supported by his perfect trust in God"[1496]; the wise though physically frail is mightier than Hercules without wisdom); yea, a man of "knowledge increaseth strength" (gains power).

Wisdom makes strong, powerful its possessor; the more of it that is gained, the greater will be the strength (Colossians 1:9–11). Matthew Henry comments, "A wise man will compass that by his wisdom which a strong man cannot effect by force of arms. The spirit is strengthened both for the spiritual work and the spiritual warfare by true wisdom."[1497] Godly wisdom makes the believer (or nation) stronger than his adversaries, however inferior he may be in other respects.[1498] "Knowledge is power" is a much known saying. I amend it to say, godly knowledge and its application is power. When man operates under the instruction and guidance of Almighty God, he is stronger "than weapons of war" (bombs, cannons, nuclear missiles). Paul undoubtedly understood this truth in saying, "Nay, in all these things [whatever comes against us] we are more than conquerors through him that loved us" (Romans 8:37). Therefore, press for more knowledge and understanding of God's Word and will, for the more that is acquired, the stronger in the faith you become. The Book of Proverbs is in itself a source for growth in wisdom.

The Bottom Line: A wise man is mightier than and superior to a strong man who is void of wisdom.

352
Wisdom, portrait of the wise man
Proverbs 1:5

"A wise man will hear, and will increase learning; and a man of understanding shall attain unto wise counsels."

A wise man "will hear" (Murphy says "an active listening; an obedience"[1499]), AND "increase learning" (the instructions in the Book of Proverbs are not just for the "simple or foolish" but for the wise as well to learn more [Proverbs 9:9]); AND a man of "understanding" (Aitken says "understand" and "insight" are derived from the same Hebrew root. "Both 'insight' and its sister noun 'understanding' are used interchangeably with 'wisdom' [see Proverbs 2:2–3, 'wisdom…understanding… insight']; thus the wise man is the 'man of understanding [1:5]'"[1500]; that is, he is a man of wise discernment) shall attain unto "wise counsels" (refers to moral guidance; the Hebrew word is related to that which refers to "cord; rope" which "meant directing a ship by pulling ropes on the mast." It refers to the ability to steer a right course through life[1501]).

The Proverb is in miniature what the Book of Proverbs is at large in that it encapsulates man's need for divine wisdom and understanding (discernment) to live morally, ethically, socially and theologically right in a world that for the most part does not, and does not make it easy for others to do so. The Book of Proverbs makes clear that Wisdom comes from God (the "Root" of all wisdom) and paints a distinctive picture via traits and characteristics (the fruit of wisdom) of the truly wise man in contrast to the foolish.

Distinguishing marks of the wise cited in Proverbs include the following.

He fears (honors, reveres, obeys) the Lord; he is a born-again believer (Proverbs 1:7). He is virtuous, abstaining from sexual immorality (Proverbs 5:15). He is respectfully obedient to his parents (Proverbs 1:8; 6:20). He avoids foolish companions (Proverbs 14:7) choosing rather to associate with the godly (Proverbs 13:20). He is industrious, not lazy (Proverbs 18:9; 26:14). He is a loyal and loving friend (Proverbs 17:17; 18:24; 19:4; 27:6). He refrains from strong drink (Proverbs 23:31; 31:4). He bridles the tongue (Proverbs 21:23). He exhibits deep humility, not a self-inflated ego (Proverbs 8:13; 11:2; 16:5). He readily is open to and seeks advice from the wise (Proverbs 4:13; 11:14; 12:15; 13:10; 19:20).

He is teachable, understanding his ignorance about the theological, moral and practical (Proverbs 1:2–5; 13:1; 23:9). He practices mental restraint (discipline), keeping the impure out while concentrating on the good and holy (Proverbs 4:23; 25:28). He discerns right from wrong and walks accordingly (Proverbs 4:25; 5:1–2). He treasures the Word of God, storing it in the heart for meditation, gestation and protection (Proverbs 7:1–3). He understands personal sinfulness, accountability to God and the constant need for confession and repentance (Proverbs 20:9). He bears witness to the unregenerate in an effort to bring them to redemption (Proverbs 11:30) while assuming responsibility for the innocent unjustly treated (Proverbs 24:12). He has tunnel vision, a focus on God's plan for life (Proverbs 3:5–6; 4:25–27). He is a person that shows good judgment in decisions and choices (Proverbs 10:13; 13:15). He controls the wanton appetites of the flesh through steadfast resistance (Proverbs 1:10; 13:6). He keeps anger in check (Proverbs 15:18; 29:11).

Is the portrait in some measure a picture of the life that you live? Continuously press onward to the fuller realization and manifestation of wisdom and its fruit. Not even the wisest man that ever lived (King Solomon) outgrew the need for more of the riches of God's wisdom. No king or president or peasant does. As wisdom cries out for you, cry out for wisdom (Proverbs 1:20–23; James 1:5)! Luke's Gospel tells us that "Jesus increased in wisdom and stature, and in favour with God and man" (Luke 2:52).

Perhaps the portrait in no wise depicts you, although it is desired that it might. I have good news! Proverbs is written not only to increase the wisdom of the wise (Proverbs 1:5) but to instruct the "simple" (he that is void of wisdom) in its acquisition and application. Alexander Maclaren says, "He is on the way to become wise whose seeking heart turns away from evil and evil men and feels [seeks] after God as the vine tendrils after a stay or as the sunflower turns to the light. For such wholehearted desire after the one supreme good there must be a resolute averting of desire from 'sinners.'"[1502] Wisdom's foundation is the acknowledgement of and the submission to Jesus Christ as Lord and Savior.

The Bottom Line: Wisdom is a lifelong journey whose destination will never be fully realized until one reaches Heaven (Proverbs 4:18). Stay in hot pursuit of wisdom.

353
Wisdom, the ability to handle life with skill and success
Proverbs 1:2

"To know wisdom..."

To "know" (acquire, gain at any price) "wisdom" (divine discernment to know the most prudent direction to go or decision to make; spiritual insights from the Lord for living a successful and happy life pleasing to Him; Reyburn and Fry say "sound judgment"[1503]).

Throughout Proverbs wisdom is presented as a spiritual quality, not secular or worldly. It's only source of acquisition is in a personal relationship with God made possible through Jesus Christ, His Son. "The fear of the LORD is the beginning of knowledge (wisdom)" (Proverbs 1:7). The placement of trust and allegiance in Jesus Christ is foundational to the possession of wisdom. Its work primarily has to do with the development of character. Its fountainhead is God who through Holy Scripture instills in the heart the core governing principles of life, granting knowledge in their application in day-to-day life and challenges so one may have happiness and success both in the spiritual and physical realms. Wisdom is "the skill of living in a way that honors God."[1504]

Haddon W. Robinson, in his foreword to Robert L. Alden's book *Proverbs: A Commentary on an Ancient Book of Timeless Advice,* states, "Men and women educated to earn a living often don't know anything about handling life itself. Alumni from noted universities have mastered information about a narrow slice of life but couldn't make it out of the first grade when it comes to living successfully with family and friends. Let's face it. Knowledge is not enough to meet life's problems. We need wisdom, the ability to handle life with skill."[1505]

Adrian Rogers masterfully differentiates between knowledge and wisdom. "Knowledge is learned; wisdom is given. Knowledge comes by looking around; wisdom comes by looking up. Knowledge comes from study; wisdom comes from meditation. Wisdom is the way to apply your knowledge. You see, a man can have knowledge, but he needs understanding—he needs wisdom."[1506] Man may acquire knowledge apart from the Holy Spirit but never acquire true wisdom apart from Him.[1507]

Paul says, "In [Jesus Christ] are hid all the treasures of wisdom and knowledge" (Colossians 2:3). It is impossible for man to know true wisdom apart from knowing Jesus Christ. Daniel underscores the source of wisdom: "Blessed be the name of God for ever and ever: for wisdom and might are his: And he changeth the times and the seasons: he removeth kings, and setteth up kings: he giveth wisdom unto the wise, and knowledge to them that know understanding: He revealeth the deep and secret things: he knoweth what is in the darkness, and the light dwelleth with him. I thank thee, and praise thee, O thou God of my fathers, who hast given me wisdom and might, and hast made known unto me now what we desired of thee: for thou hast now made known unto us the king's matter" (Daniel 2:20–23).

George Lawson clarifies how wisdom is acquired. He states, "Experience, however long, observation, however close, human teaching, however skillful, can do nothing to supply us with true knowledge, without the influence of that Spirit which rested upon Christ as a Spirit of wisdom and understanding, and which is given by Him to all His followers in their measure."[1508] One acquires wisdom through a relationship with God (Proverbs 1:7; 2:6); trust, dependence upon God to order life (Proverbs 3:5–6); and by request of God (Proverbs 2:2–5; James 1:5).

Wisdom is important to acquire, for it clarifies right from wrong; truth from falsities; best from better; the pleasing in God's sight from the woeful; and the expedient from the less important. Wisdom benefits life with happiness, success, safety, confidence, peace, contentment and added days (Proverbs 3:16–26).

In a nutshell, wisdom helps us make right choices. No wonder Solomon states that its possession is better than that of gold (Proverbs 16:16) and to be desired above that of rubies (Proverbs 3:14; 8:11). Conversely, Solomon candidly says that one who refuses to walk in the wisdom of the Lord "wrongeth his own soul: all they that hate me [wisdom] love death" (Proverbs 8:36).

The Bottom Line: Perhaps the greatest quality of life is wisdom. Proverbs 19:8 says, "He who gets wisdom loves himself" (RSV). In other words, if you really love yourself, help yourself out: Get Wisdom! It's not elusive but readily available upon diligent search (Proverbs 8:17).

354
Wisdom, the embodiment of wisdom is Jesus Christ
Proverbs 8:17
"I love them that love me; and those that seek me early shall find me."

"And David behaved himself wisely in all his ways; and the LORD was with him" (1 Samuel 18:14).

"I" (wisdom) "love them that love me" (those who desire her will in return be profited by her); AND those that "seek me early" (pursue diligently at the earliest possible time, preferably in youth) shall "find me" (wisdom will make itself available).

It is wisdom that man should seek "early" (strenuously, earnestly in youthfulness), for she has great gifts to bestow. Only in loving (attaining, prizing) wisdom will man profit ("love them") from her knowledge and understanding about life issues. "Her profit is better than silver, and her gain better than gold" (Proverbs 3:14 CEB). Wisdom enables man to understand knowledge rightly and apply it properly.

Solomon, aware of wisdom's value, requested it above the riches and treasures of the world. Solomon says, "Give therefore thy servant an understanding heart to judge thy people, that I may discern between good and bad: for who is able to judge this thy so great a people? And the speech pleased the Lord, that Solomon had asked this thing. And God said unto him, Because thou hast asked this thing, and hast not asked for thyself long life; neither hast asked riches for thyself, nor hast asked the life of thine enemies; but hast asked for thyself understanding to discern judgment; Behold, I have done according to thy words: lo, I have given thee a wise and an understanding heart; so that there was none like thee before thee, neither after thee shall any arise like unto thee" (1 Kings 3:9–12). The promise of wisdom is that she will be discovered if diligently sought ("shall find me"), regardless of status or education.

A second application of the principle refers to Jesus Christ, who is the personification of wisdom. All that is true of wisdom is true of Him. He is the very embodiment of wisdom's virtues and traits. Paul states in 1 Corinthians 1:24, "Christ [is] the power of God, and the wisdom of God." Man apart from Christ cannot know true wisdom, for He is its conduit. In the final note of Romans, Paul exclaims, "God alone is wise. Glory belongs to him through Jesus Christ forever! Amen" (Romans 16:27 GW). Colossians 2:3 declares that in Christ "are hid all the treasures of wisdom and knowledge." Proverbs 8 depicts wisdom as a Person.

C. H. Spurgeon, in the sermon "Christ—The Power and Wisdom of God," said, "[Jesus] is equally 'the wisdom of God.' The great things that He did before all worlds were proofs of His wisdom. He planned the way of salvation; He devised the system of atonement and substitution; He laid the foundations of the great plan of salvation. There was wisdom. But He built the heavens by wisdom, and He laid the pillars of light, whereon the firmament is balanced, by His skill and wisdom. Mark the world; and learn, as ye see all its multitudinous proofs of the wisdom of God, and there you have the wisdom of Christ; for He was the Creator of it. And when He became a Man, He gave proofs enough of wisdom. Even in childhood, when He made the doctors sit abashed by the questions that He asked, He showed that He was more than mortal. And when the Pharisee and Sadducee and Herodian were all at last defeated and their nets were broken, He proved again the superlative wisdom of the Son of God. And when those who came to take Him stood enchained by His eloquence, spellbound by His marvelous oratory, there was again a proof that He was the wisdom of God, who could so enchain the minds of men."[1509]

Wisdom is the right use of knowledge, and the Word of Christ (Holy Scriptures) helps in its proper application. Spurgeon continues, "Christ is the great Pilot who puts His hand on the tiller and makes him wise to steer through the shoals of temptation and the rocks of sin. Get the Gospel, and you are a wise man. 'The fear of the Lord is the beginning of wisdom,' and right understanding have they who keep His commandments."[1510] Jesus assures that all who seek Him will find Him if they seek diligently (not halfheartedly). Hebrews 11:6 says, "For he that cometh to God must believe that He is, and that He is a rewarder of them that *diligently* seek Him."

The Bottom Line: Wisdom is the key to success, meaning and happiness in life, and is found only in a personal relationship to Jesus Christ. Find Christ, and you find wisdom, for He is the treasure chest of wisdom. Read His Word under the illumination of the Holy Spirit's guidance to understand how to navigate life without shipwreck. Growth in wisdom occurs over time; it takes time to develop and cultivate. The more you become like Jesus, the more wisdom is gained.

355
Witness, proclaim the wisest words that may be spoken
Proverbs 10:31
"The mouth of the just bringeth forth wisdom: but the froward tongue shall be cut out."

"The mouth of a righteous man is a well of life: but violence covereth the mouth of the wicked" (Proverbs 10:11).

The "mouth" (speech) of the "just" (the righteous, Christian) "bringeth forth" (bears fruit like a tree,[1511] the fruit is good and beneficial) "wisdom" (wise words from God based upon sound biblical theology and instruction skillfully uttered): BUT the "froward tongue" (perverse; perverts what is right[1512]) shall be "cut off" (Reyburn and Fry say, "Deceitful liars will be punished"[1513]).

The righteous ("just") bear profitable and pleasant fruit through wise (godly, scriptural, skillful) speech (witness, advice). A tree bears fruit in keeping with its nature; just so, wise words are the fruit of godliness (Luke 6:43–45). "A man shall be satisfied with good by the fruit of his mouth" (Proverbs 12:14). The wisest words that may be spoken are those which Jesus spoke to Nicodemus recorded in John 3. "Marvel not that I said unto thee, Ye must be born again....For God so loved the world, that he gave his only begotten Son, that whosoever believeth in him should not perish, but have everlasting life" (verses 7, 16). The fruit of the righteous (in part) is their witness to the eternally damned in an effort to rescue them.

A lost and dying world needs the Good News more than "Good Advice." Henry Martyn said, "The spirit of Christ is the spirit of missions. The nearer we get to Him, the more intensely missionary we become."[1514] C. H. Spurgeon remarks, "Soul winning is the chief business of the Christian minister; it should be the main pursuit of every true believer."[1515]

C. E. Autrey writes, "Our sick and frustrated world needs a depth of therapy rather than an application of a skin ointment. Our problem is not one of nerves and psychological symptoms, but it is of the heart. It is sin eating away at the vitals of men. Men need forgiveness of sins. They need a real fellowship with the Creator."[1516] Speak the words of gospel truth to all that might listen. The truly wise understand this is imperatively urgent.

The Bottom Line: Speak the wisest words that ever man may speak consistently and regularly unto him who needs them sorely.

356
Woman, the inner disposition is what counts
Proverbs 11:16
"A gracious woman retaineth honour: and strong men retain riches."

The "gracious woman" (full of God's grace) is known for her internal beauty (humility, kindheartedness, modesty, charm and uprightness, and moral and godly excellence). Such "ornaments" obtain and retain her "honor" (respect, praise). The New Testament version of the Proverb is 1 Peter 3:3–4: "What matters is not your outer appearance—the styling of your hair, the jewelry you wear, the cut of your clothes—but your inner disposition. Cultivate inner beauty, the gentle, gracious kind that God delights in. The holy women of old were beautiful before God that way, and were good, loyal wives to their husbands" (MSG).

As a strong man fights to retain the riches obtained from men who would take them from him, so the gracious woman fights as tenaciously to retain honor and glory for her godly ornaments (purity, modesty, godly disposition, etc.).

Joseph Parker comments, "Men should endeavor to cultivate grace, tenderness, all that is charmful in spirit, disposition and action. This cannot be done by mere mimicry; it is to be done by living continually with Christ, studying His spirit, entering into all His purposes, and reproducing, not mechanically, but spiritually, as much as possible of all that was distinctive of His infinite character. The Bible has ever given honor to woman. He is a fool and an unjust man who wishes to keep women in silence, obscurity and in a state of unimportance; and she is a foolish woman who imagines that she cannot be gracious without being strong, and who wishes to sacrifice her graciousness to some empty reputation for worthless energy."[1517]

The Bottom Line: Matthew Henry summarizes, "A pious and discreet woman will keep esteem and respect, as strong men keep possession of wealth."[1518] Ladies, the strength in your graciousness outweighs men's in their wealth.

357
Women, a warning to men about prostitutes
Proverbs 23:27
"For a whore is a deep ditch; and a strange woman is a narrow pit."

For a "whore" (prostitute) is a "deep ditch" (a figure of speech alluding to something that is dangerous[1519] and ensnaring; requires help to get out of); AND a "strange woman" (immoral woman, perhaps a prostitute) is a "narrow pit" (literally "a narrow well"[1520] which is more dangerous than the deep pit for its narrowness; you get stuck and cannot move, thus cannot escape).

Prostitutes and other immoral women seek to decoy man from the path of righteousness (purity, wholesomeness, virtue and honor). Be forewarned that their deadly trap (deep pit and narrow well) is unforeseen, unseen and inescapable to its captives (without assistance) and filled with heart-wrenching pain and guilt. In the following verse Solomon likens the wayward woman (prostitute or wife of another) to a *robber* lurking for a victim (only time the analogy is used in Proverbs). As a robber she steals from young men their purity, virtue and innocence. From the married men she robs marital fidelity (faithfulness), trust, harmony and happiness, creating chaos in the marriage and home (Proverbs 7:27). Sadly, the immoral woman has much success in the seduction of men, for Solomon says, "She...*increaseth* the transgressors among men" (Proverbs 23:28). Stay far away from this kind of woman. Don't consort with them. Strictly count them "off limits." Live righteously, keeping the eye fixed upon Jesus, ever depending upon Him for strength to conquer the temptation of the immoral.

The Bottom Line: Many are the "giants" that the wayward woman has slain. "Let him that thinketh he standeth take heed lest he fall" (1 Corinthians 10:12).

358
Words, harsh words stab like a sword
Proverbs 15:4

"A wholesome tongue is a tree of life: but perverseness therein is a breach in the spirit."

A "wholesome tongue" (a healing tongue, that soothes by its words[1521]) is a "tree of life" (McKane says the tree of life signifies a source of vitality to others[1522]; her fruit is luscious, nourishing, strength-enhancing; MacArthur says "a metaphor referring to temporal and spiritual renewal and refreshment"[1523]): BUT "perverseness" therein [in the tongue] (untruth, deceitfulness, falsehood, lying) is a "breach in the spirit" (it brings ruin, despair to him and the person deceived[1524]). George Lawson summarizes, "Unmerited rebukes, reproaches, unkind words, and cruel mockings, are perverseness in that little member, which boasteth and can really effect great things. The advantages derived from a healing tongue are like the fruits of the tree of life—the erring are reclaimed; the dejected are comforted; the weak are animated and invigorated by it."[1525]

Harsh words are but an invisible sharp razor that cuts and pains their recipient deeply (Psalm 52:2). I have been on the receiving end of venomous words from a friend while other "friends" sat by without interruption. Though what was said hurt, the manner in which it was spoken and its condoning by friends exacted a pain indescribable. A physical stabbing with a knife would have been less painful. My spirit was wounded, and my heart was broken. I learned that day: "Careless words stab like a sword, but wise words bring healing" (Proverbs 12:18 NCB). "An insincere and evil friend is more to be feared than a wild beast; a wild beast may wound your body, but an evil friend will wound your mind." Rick Warren is on target in stating, "People need to know that their words have consequences."[1526]

If you have been wounded by harsh and critical words or by the silence of family or friends when assaulted verbally, or with disappointment over the treatment rendered by a friend, then as I did, you must release the deep, abiding emotional pain unto the Lord by exhibiting forgiveness to all who caused the hurt. This may not be easy. It may take time to get to this point, but with God's help, it can and must be done for your own personal well-being and the glory of God. Chuck Swindoll remarks, "Regardless of the level of maturity you've reached in your walk with Christ, you are not immune to hurt. Sharp words strike like shrapnel, and they get imbedded in the brain. The result is the inflicting of a wound that's slow to heal. Sometimes, regrettably, it never heals."[1527]

The Bottom Line: "Wise words bring healing" (Proverbs 12:18 NCV). "Wise words" from God's Word and the godly (implemented) are the antidote to the poison of harsh words. Part of the "wise words" in Scripture instruct you to forgive the offender, not to seek vindication, and bring the pain to the Lord.

359
Words, power of right words spoken at right moments
Proverbs 15:23
"A word spoken in due season, how good is it!"

"A man shall be satisfied with good by the fruit of his mouth" (Proverbs 12:14).

A "word spoken in due season" (a fitting word shared at the choicest of times), how "good it is" (Buzzell says, "It delights not only the hearer but him that speaks them"[1528]). To summarize, appropriate words (of encouragement, comfort, hope, peace, concern, correction) spoken with knowledge, care and wisdom precisely at the right time benefit both the recipient and their speaker.

The right word spoken at the right time is powerful to convict, correct, comfort, convert and change the course of one's day or life. "A word fitly spoken is like apples of gold in pictures of silver" (Proverbs 25:11). Never underestimate the power of words to build up or tear down. Let us be on the lookout for the "due season" in a person's life (suitable, advantageous moments) to speak that *special* word which is needed. "Due seasons" are times of sorrow when the heart is softened by grief, times of crisis when it is not known where to turn, times of rejection when others abandon, times of utter despondency when life hits the bottom, times of moral failure when correction is needed, times of disappointment when the heart is discouraged, times of doubting to which the mind and soul are held captive, times of a new direction when special guidance is needed, times of bad news when the heart searches for answers, times of good news when joy lifts the spirit, times of dying when the heart needs hope and assurance, and times of Holy Spirit conviction of sin when the soul is open to salvation. Such are the moments the choicest of words fitting the occasion ought to be spoken thoughtfully, prayerfully, courageously, sympathically and personally to obtain maximum results.

Solomon cautions that there is a time to speak and a time to be silent (Ecclesiastes 3:7). Don't speak until the Holy Spirit impresses you to. All err occasionally in saying the right thing at the wrong time, reducing, if not negating, its desired impact. Abigail did not tell Nabal of his danger until he was sober (1 Samuel 25:36–37). The *soil* must be ready to receive the seed, or else it will be wasted. Allen Ross agrees, "Even to say the right thing at the wrong time is counterproductive."[1529]

The Bottom Line: Don't underestimate the power of your words when they hit home in a person's life. Stay alert and sensitive to whom you should speak, what you should speak, and when you should speak it. You will be a difference-maker in people's lives simply by speaking a word in "due season."

360
Words, the harm of off-the-cuff remarks
Proverbs 29:20

"Seest thou a man that is hasty in his words? there is more hope of a fool than of him."

"The heart of the righteous studieth [thinks carefully, thoroughly] to answer: but the mouth of the wicked poureth out evil things" (Proverbs 15:28).

Seest thou a man that is "hasty in his words" (he gushes out words without forethought; Walvoord and Zuck say, "He blurts out thoughtless, insensitive remarks"[1530]; rashly, carelessly not considering whom they may hurt). There is more "hope of a fool than of him" (he is worse than a fool[1531]).

Mind what you say. Chew over in the solitude of the heart the proper words to say prior to speaking. Don't speak before you think. To blurt out ("hasty") words thoughtlessly and recklessly more times than not is injurious. He that speaks *hastily* upon every subject as a know-it-all (without need to consult with God, the Scriptures and the more knowledgeable) is puffed up with pride and conceit. In contrast to him who speaks rashly is the godly wise who "studieth to answer" (meditates, ponders, reflects, thinks). Obviously, the more serious the inquiry or circumstance, the longer it ought to be considered and its answer or advice weighed prior to responding.

The Bottom Line: H. A. Ironside summarizes, "The man who walks in the fear of God will weigh his words, lest by a hasty utterance he dishonor his Lord and hinder where he desires to help. The wicked has no such consideration and speaks whatever comes to his lips, let it do what harm it may."[1532]

361
Words, the incalculable value of deep counsel
Proverbs 18:4

"The words of a man's mouth are as deep waters, and the wellspring of wisdom as a flowing brook."

The "words of a man's mouth" (the ideal man, as the ideal woman in Proverbs 31[1533]; the man of utter righteousness, uprightness, honorable, just, godly and wise) are as "deep waters" (that is, Buzzell says, they are "hidden" or "difficult" to access[1534]; but deep in profound and wise thoughts[1535]) and the "wellspring of wisdom" (inexhaustible supply); as a "flowing brook" (a "gushing" stream freely accessible to all that desire to drink her refreshing waters[1536]).

D. A. Garrett states that Proverbs speaks much about the value of words because "it views words as the index to the soul. By paying attention to what a person says (and indeed to how much he or she says), one can determine whether a person is wise or a fool. Words are the fruit that show the quality of the heart."[1537] There is imprecise speech (incomprehensible); speech void of theological and godly substance (wisdom), clarity and understanding. Such speech is as a *shallow stream* that fails to benefit the listener. In contrast, the words of the ideal man (wise, godly, and intelligent) are as "deep waters" which cannot be fully tapped or exhausted ("well-spring"). This speech (treasure of wisdom) is as a "flowing brook" that continuously bubbles up with wise insight, knowledge and discernment that are easily accessible, readily understandable and highly helpful.

The godly speak out of their treasure of wisdom gathered from intimacy with the Lord, absorption of Holy Scriptures, experience and insight gained from others. It is a wellspring that splashes out wisdom time and time again in being "pumped." The man may be dressed in overalls, speak in plain and simple terms and have a limited education, but what he says supersedes in "depth," importance and help what the man says who is attired in an executive suit and speaks eloquently and has a university degree, but who speaks from an empty tank spiritually. Take advantage of the free invaluable insight and wisdom to be gained at the feet of the godly wise. Lower the bucket into their well and draw it out. "ounsel in the heart of man is like deep water; but a man of understanding will draw it out" (Proverbs 20:5).

The Bottom Line: Don't waste time listening to people (preachers, teachers, friends, theologians) who are spiritually bankrupt or destitute in soul. They have nothing of benefit. Identify the godly wise and converse with them often, for therein will your soul be refreshed, renewed, and instructed.

362
Worldliness, the four generations of corruptness
Proverbs 30:11–14

"There is a generation that curseth their father, and doth not bless their mother. There is a generation that are pure in their own eyes, and yet is not washed from their filthiness. There is a generation, O how lofty are their eyes! and their eyelids are lifted up. There is a generation, whose teeth are as swords, and their jaw teeth as knives, to devour the poor from off the earth, and the needy from among men."

The word "generation" refers to a *class* of people that share certain characteristics in common (not to a 30- to 40-year period). There are four evil generations (classes of people) cited in this Proverb: (1) one that shows disdain for parental authority (v. 11); one that is self-righteous with no need of God (v. 12); one that exhibits arrogant smugness (v. 13), and one that is mean and injurious to the poor (v. 14). Isaiah adds a fifth "generation." He says, "Woe unto them that call evil good, and good evil; that put darkness for light, and light for darkness; that put bitter for sweet, and sweet for bitter" (Isaiah 5:20)! These "generations" coexist presently.[1538]

Agur warns the innocent against being overtaken by the deplorable and injurious attitudes and actions of the "generation" which these traits vividly describe. Guard against prideful conceit which will justify such conduct (though a professing Christian). Jesus warns against self-delusion with regard to genuine salvation and/or holiness of life. "Thou blind Pharisee, cleanse first that which is within the cup and platter, that the outside of them may be clean also" (Matthew 23:26). Pray that they which are of the "generation" Agur and Isaiah depict will be illuminated to their error in thinking, sinful estate, deplorable arrogance, and wicked conduct. Oh, that it may be that a greater "generation" that fears God, obeys and serves God will populate the earth to counteract that generation of the ungodly.

The Bottom Line: Don't be swallowed up blindly into the culture that advocates and practices such conduct as manifested in these "generations."

363
Worship, the only worship God accepts
Proverbs 21:27
"The sacrifice of the wicked is abomination: how much more, when he bringeth it with a wicked mind?"

The "sacrifice of the wicked" ("the ritual acts of worship"[1539]) is "abomination" (the Lord hates, detests it because it is hypocritical; they practice sanctuary ritual without knowing God or walking in righteousness[1540]): "how much more" (it is even more deplorable when made with an evil intent[1541]) when he "bringeth it with a wicked mind" (evil intent, a bad motive; the wicked [unsaved] think the sacrifice, though void of any repentance, can buy the continued acceptance of God[1542]).

Worship without righteousness and repentance (hypocritical worship) is detestable and thus unacceptable to the Lord. To religiously attend church, pray, sing, testify, give an offering and lift up your head in expressing adoration to Christ when the heart is obstinate, sinful and rebellious is sordid hypocrisy of the worst sort. It is an "abomination" (atrocity; abhorrence) that only intensifies when the *hypocrisy* is couched with a "wicked mind" (evil intent to appease God with sacrifices for sins of which he is unrepentant).

The attempt to buy God's favor, though utterly deplorable, is practiced in religious circles presently. Regarding *hypocritical and conniving worship,* God says, "This people draw near me with their mouth, and with their lips do honour me, but have removed their heart far from me" (Isaiah 29:13). Rejecting and detesting their empty and theatrical worship, He states, "I have no pleasure in you, saith the LORD of hosts, neither will I accept an offering at your hand" (Malachi 1:10). "And when ye spread forth your hands, I will hide mine eyes from you: yea, when ye make many prayers, I will not hear" (Isaiah 1:15).

Acceptable worship is based upon *confession* (repentance), *cleansing* (removal of sin), *conduct* (righteousness; conformity to God's standards) and *cause* (right motives) as delineated by our Lord in Isaiah 1:12–18.

Stop with the religious rituals (stop going through the motions of worship without worshipping). "When ye come to appear before me, who hath required this at your hand, to tread my courts? Bring no more vain oblations; incense is an abomination unto me" (Isaiah 1:12–13).

Turn from evil doings (repentance). "Put away the evil of your doings from before mine eyes; cease to do evil" (Isaiah 1:16).

Get right, get clean with "me." "Wash you, make you clean....Come now, and let us reason together, saith the LORD: though your sins be as scarlet, they shall be as white as snow; though they be red like crimson, they shall be as wool" (Isaiah 1:16, 18).

Live righteously. "Learn to do well; seek judgment, relieve the oppressed, judge the fatherless, plead for the widow" (Isaiah 1:17). Acceptable worship includes a resolution to live a life aligned with the teachings of the Bible.

I'm coming back to the heart of worship,
And it's all about You.
It's all about You, Jesus.
I'm sorry, Lord, for the thing I've made it
When it's all about You.
It's all about You, Jesus. ~ Michael W. Smith

The Bottom Line: "God is a Spirit: and they that worship him must worship him in spirit and in *truth*" (John 4:24). "Let the words of my mouth, and the meditation of my heart, be acceptable in thy sight, O LORD, my strength, and my redeemer" (Psalm 19:14).

364
Wounded, the emotional trauma of a crushed spirit
Proverbs 18:14

"The spirit of a man will sustain his infirmity; but a wounded spirit who can bear?"

The "spirit of a man" (Murphy says, "It stands for the strength and determination of a person that can deal with physical sickness"[1543]) will sustain his infirmity; BUT a "wounded spirit" (a crushed spirit that is so deeply depressed[1544] and distressed it literally can destroy a person

[Proverbs 15:13; 17:22]) who can "bear"? (What person can withstand that kind of emotional upheaval, carry that load).

Every person sooner or later will experience the wounded, broken spirit.

What it is. A wounded spirit is the injury to the emotions that manifests such horrendous pain and misery that it may feel as if one has been torn open and is bleeding from every orifice of the body. It is fueled by many things, including the unrelenting focus on the injuries, unforgiveness toward the offender and a desire to make them pay. Medical personnel talk of "weeping wounds," wounds which continue to fester, discharge and ooze, refusing to heal, due to noxious matter. Emotionally, many people have "weeping wounds," wounds inflicted years earlier that refuse to heal due to the toxins of an unforgiving spirit, retaliatory spirit, bitterness, anger, blaming of God, fear, and pride. In the same way that doctors can close up wounds that have not healed, we are good at doing the same with emotional or spirit wounds. The wound may be closed, but it is yet unhealed deep inside the body or mind, bearing grievous impact.

How it originates. It occurs from cruel hands that maliciously and rashly attack or accuse (Proverbs 11:9); rebuking and correcting hands (parents, ministers and friends) that lovingly point out wrong (Proverbs 27:6); merciful and gracious hands (God) that wound in order to heal (Proverbs 20:30; Psalm 119:71); adversarial hands (Satan) that injure in spiritual warfare (Luke 22:31; 1 Peter 5:8–9); innocent hands (parents, ministers, others) that unwittingly and unintentionally wound (2 Corinthians 2:1–10; Luke 22:61) and personal hands (one's own self) that inflict emotional distress and grief due to sin (Psalm 38:4–6; 1 Peter 5:7).

Its telltale signs. Symptoms of a wounded spirit may be exhibited by diminishing of mental, spiritual and emotional stamina; lashing out; bitterness; blaming God; paralyzing guilt; cutting remarks; withdrawal from others; diminished hopes; indifference; inferiority; defeatism; irritability; anger; depression; feelings of hopelessness; pain and hurt; grave sensitivity to something in the past; restraint of love for fear of rejection; an unforgiving spirit; retaliatory spirit; poor self-image; suicidal thoughts; self-denunciation; escapism through alcohol, drugs, food, and materialism; absence of peace inwardly; restlessness; sleeplessness; the spewing out of old injuries portraying others badly "out of the blue" in conversations; and obsession with the pain inflicted and him who caused it.

> It is a terrible wounding when he who should have been your friend becomes your foe, and when, like your Lord, you also have your Judas Iscariot. It is not easy to bear misrepresentation and falsehood, to have your purest motives misjudged. This is a very painful kind of wounded spirit.
> C. H. Spurgeon, *The Cause and Cure of a Wounded Spirit*

Its healing means.[1545] David, from experience, could wholeheartedly say, "He [God] healeth the broken in heart, and bindeth up their wounds" (Psalm 147:3). "Hope sees," declares R. G. Lee, "beyond the cloud, beyond the obstacle, beyond the hardship, beyond the weakness, beyond the failure, beyond the difficulty. Hope says to us, 'Never accept the verdict of your defeat, the verdict of your melancholy, the verdict of your sickness, the verdict of your disaster, the verdict of your disappointment.' The psalmist says, 'Thou hast made me to hope.'"[1546]

The Bottom Line: Healing ultimately arrives from the hand of Jesus Christ, the Great Physician who may use godly counselors, ministers, parents and friends to bring it.

365
Wounds, the cause of a locked iron gate about the heart
Proverbs 18:19

"A brother offended is harder to be won than a strong city: and their contentions are like the bars of a castle."

A "brother" (Buzzell says "can mean either blood relative or friend"[1547]) "offended" (emotionally wounded or injured by actions of another) is "harder to be won than a strong city" (he that is mistreated is most difficult to reclaim as a brother or friend; Reyburn and Fry paraphrase, "A brother we have injured closes his door to us"[1548]): AND "their contentions" (disputes, disagreements or quarreling) are like the "bars of a castle" (like a closed locked gate of iron at the entrance of a castle).

A friend or blood relative, when offended and hurt by deceit, cruelty, slanderous talk and/or disdain, is most difficult to be restored, for the offense erects a *locked gate of iron* at the entrance of their heart, forbidding entrance to the offender. Kidner observes that these barrier walls erected by the offense are easy to erect and hard to demolish.[1549] MacArthur remarks, "There are no feuds as difficult to resolve as those with relatives, no barriers are so hard to bring down. Hence, great care should be taken to avoid such conflicts."[1550] Lawson says, "Contentions between brethren are generally more irremediable than any others. It is therefore our duty to guard against those mischiefs which are so much easier prevented than removed; and with this view, we must not wantonly provoke our friends nor be ready to take offence at their conduct."[1551]

Who would have thought it? A sharp disagreement developed between the two premier missionaries of the early church regarding John Mark. Barnabas wanted to take him on the next missionary journey, but perhaps to your surprise, Paul didn't (Acts 15:37–41). John Mark's desertion while in the heat of ministry with them in Pamphylia caused Paul's trust to turn to distrust in him. Paul may have been thinking of Solomon's words: "Confidence in an unfaithful man in time of trouble is like a broken tooth, and a foot out of joint" (Proverbs 25:19), which will hardly be used again. Who was right? The great New Testament scholar A. T. Robertson provides this insight: "No one can rightly blame Barnabas for giving his cousin John Mark a second chance, nor Paul for fearing to risk him again. One's judgment may go with Paul, but one's heart goes with Barnabas."[1552]

The real question though is not "Who was right?" but "Was it right?" In one word, the biblical answer is no. John Pollock states, "There must have been serious wrong in the situation which made the lovable, even-tempered Barnabas use angry words, and Paul had far to go before he could write, 'Love is patient and kind; love... does not insist on its own way.'[1553] Bitter disagreement that leads to heated contention and conflict is always to be avoided. It's okay to disagree; just disagree agreeably, kindly and lovingly.

The contention resulted in Paul and Barnabas going in separate directions in ministry. They would never again reunite in ministry. The conflict inflicted a deep heart wound that would never completely heal. The "Paul-Barnabas dispute" scenario sadly unfolds in businesses, families, churches and other ministries, routinely resulting in people going their separate ways never to speak or meet again over what they count irreconcilable differences. Offenses that wound deeply a friend's spirit erect impenetrable barriers to access. Reconciliatory efforts to restore the breached relationship nonetheless are to be attempted.

"A few hot words may undo the love of years, as a few blows of the axe cuts down the oak of a century's growth."[1554] The deep and meaningful relationship of Paul and Barnabas shouldn't have ended so abruptly, but it sadly did due to their bitter argument. If relationships are imperiled, may it not be due to hot and venomous words. Matthew Henry insightfully states, "Paul and Barnabas, who were not separated by the persecutions of the unbelieving Jews, nor the impositions of the believing Jews, were yet separated by an unhappy disagreement between themselves. Oh, the mischief that even the poor and weak remainders of pride and passion that are found even in good men do in the world, do in the church! No wonder the consequences are so fatal where they reign."[1555]

The Bottom Line: Preventative steps to avoid contention are extremely prudent should a friendship be valued. In the final analysis, the loss of a treasured friend may not be worth the dispute or confrontation. Weigh options carefully; act prudently and wisely prior to engaging in conflict with a friend. Murphy advises the application of the wisdom of Proverbs 17:14: "Squelch a dispute before it begins."[1556]

366
Yoked, the biblical mandate not to be unequally yoked
Proverbs 6:23
"For the commandment is a lamp; and the law is light; and reproofs of instruction are the way of life."

For the "commandment" (that which harmonizes with God's will as to what is to be done and not done[1557]) is a "lamp" (God's commandments are a guiding light—illuminate the way for conduct); and the "law is light" (Torah; the law of God also gives guidance to conduct) and "reproofs of instruction" (provides correction; Buzzell says, "Discipline, though painful, helps keep a person on the right path"[1558]) are the "way of life" (will show you how to live a happy and successful life). "Thy word is a lamp unto my feet, and a light unto my path" (Psalm 119:105). Deane and Taswell say, "The 'commandment' and the 'law' may stand for the whole revelation of God without reference to any particular precept, but they have here a specific bearing on a particular form of human conduct, as appears from the following verses."[1559]

Throughout Proverbs man is repeatedly instructed to avoid fellowship with the wicked and fools. To mingle socially or enter into partnerships or marriage with the ungodly is forbidden. Solomon frankly says, "Keep thee from the evil woman" (or any ungodly person). Paul commands, "Do not be unequally yoked together with unbelievers" (2 Corinthians 6:14 NKJV). A yoke is a wooden bar that couples two oxen to each other and to a pulling beam so they can plow or pull a wagon. An "unequally yoked" team consisted of two different sorts of oxen (e.g., a strong ox joined to a weak ox). Instead of getting the task done, unequally yoked oxen would go around in circles. One can but imagine the frustration that arose between such a team.

The biblical truth is clear. Christians are not to be united (coupled) with unbelievers in friendship, faith, dating, marriage or business partnership, for the two have completely different natures, values, convictions, worldviews and purposes that would cause inevitable conflict. *The Message* paraphrase of Paul's text may enable its better comprehension: "Don't become partners with those who reject God. How can you make a partnership out of right and wrong? That's not partnership; that's war. Is light best friends with dark? Does Christ go strolling with the Devil? Do trust and mistrust hold hands?" Violation of the mandate is to court disaster.

The Bottom Line: Maintain not only separation from sin (mixing with it) but from the ungodly with which you are spiritually and morally incompatible. "Come out from among them, and be ye separate, saith the Lord" (2 Corinthians 6:17).

367
Youth, the secret to a full and meaningful life
Proverbs 7:1–3
"My son, keep my words, and lay up my commandments with thee. Keep my commandments, and live; and my law as the apple of thine eye. Bind them upon thy fingers, write them upon the table of thine heart."

"My son" (the sage, teacher of profound wisdom to his pupil), "keep" (observe, adhere to) my "words" (teaching), and "lay up" (store up like a treasure) my "commandments" (Murphy says, "'Teaching' and 'command' are parallel"[1560]; the whole of Holy Scriptures[1561]) with thee.

"Keep" (observe) my "commandments" (the instructions cited in Proverbs regarding righteous living; the entirety of the Holy Scriptures), and "live" (in obeying, the youth would experience a "full and meaningful life"[1562]; abundant life [John 10:10]); AND my "law" (not just the "Torah" but the entirety of Holy Scripture) as the "apple of thine eye" (MacArthur says it refers to the pupil of the eye which is carefully protected, for it is the source of light...the youth is to safely guard, treasure the sage's instruction, for they give him moral and spiritual sight[1563]). "Bind them upon thy fingers" (wear them, i.e., take them with you constantly, and never be without them as one wears the "wedding ring"[1564]; MacArthur says, "Give the truth of divine wisdom a permanent place in the mind and in conduct"[1565]), "write them upon the table of thine heart" (Simeon says, "We should have them 'inscribed on the tablet of our hearts,' so that they may be always at hand, ready to direct and regulate our ways. Conscience, by looking inward, should be able to see them in an instant and to suggest the line of conduct conformable to them"[1566]). H. A. Ironside observes, "It is this constant dwelling upon the Word of God that preserves from sin. Notice how upon both hand and heart that Word is to be bound and written. This involves far more than cursory reading of the Scriptures. It is the making it one's own, the daily feeding upon it, that preserves the soul."[1567]

Throughout the Book of Proverbs, youth are instructed regarding wisdom and foolishness, submissive obedience and stubborn disobedience to God, right and wrong paths, good and bad companions, clean and corrupt tongues, respect and disdain to parents, work and waste (laziness), purity and immorality, honesty and deceit, integrity and hypocrisy, humility and pride, sin and judgment, saints and fools, truth and lies, righteous teachers and heretics, generosity and greed, discretion and imprudence, reward and punishment, divine guidance and man's, discord and harmony, admiration and jealousy, love and envy, depression and peace, the Holy Scriptures and human reasoning. He is told to embrace the one and avoid the other that he may live pleasing unto the Lord in every course of action and enjoy a full and meaningful life void of misery.

The benefits of wise instruction in biblical knowledge and understanding (including ethics and morality) and its adherence are exceedingly numerous (Proverbs 1:33; 2:9, 11, 20–22; 3:2, 4, 13, 18, 22, 26, 33, 35; 8:18–19, 35; 10:2–3, 6, 27–30; 11:3, 30; 12:28; 13:6, 20, 25; 14:11, 27; 15:24, 29, 32; 16:17; 18:10, 15; 19:23; 21:21; 22:11; 28:6, 14, 18, 26; 29:25). Most assuredly if a youth earnestly and honestly would weigh such gain of wisdom and biblical instruction over against the temporal pleasure of sin and its consequence, he would embrace both without hesitation. But that's just the problem Solomon wrestled with in the Book. Youth, for the most part, simply will not.

In Proverbs 1:22, 25, he says, "How long, ye simple ones [Buzzell says "refers to a person who is naive and untaught," the gullible, easily persuaded or influenced[1568]], will ye love simplicity? And the scorners [mockers of God and His Word] delight in their scorning, and fools [the fool, Toy says, "loves ignorance, and deliberately refuses to listen to instruction in right living and refers to a person who is insensible to moral truth and acts without regard to it"[1569]] hate knowledge?...But ye have set at nought [to ignore; *Merriam-Webster:* "to refuse to take notice of"] all my counsel, and would none [have nothing to do with] of my reproof [correction]." In retrospect, the sinner will say, "How have I hated instruction, and my heart despised reproof; And have not obeyed the voice of my teachers, nor inclined mine ear to them that instructed me! I was almost in all evil in the midst of the congregation and assembly" (Proverbs 5:12–14).

And great is their ruin presently and damnation eternally for their disdainful response. "Therefore shall they eat of the fruit of their own way [reap what they sow; calamity, trouble (Galatians 6:7)], and be filled with their own devices [consumed with ungodly conduct]" (Proverbs 1:31). See Romans 1:24–28.

C. S. Lewis, in *The Great Divorce,* summarizes, "There are only two kinds of people in the end: those who say to God, 'Thy will be done,' and those to whom God says, in the end, 'Thy will be done.' All that are in Hell choose it. Without that self-choice, there could be no Hell. No soul that seriously and constantly desires joy will ever miss it. Those who seek find. To those who knock it is opened." See John 5:40; Revelation 3:20; 22:17.

The Bottom Line: Life comes with a "Handbook" complete with instructions as to how it may be lived to its utmost in every facet. The "Handbook" is the Holy Bible, which is a "lamp unto my feet, and a light unto my path" (Psalm 119:105). Man is lost without its Light to show the way out of the darkness of evil that shrouds the world. But he must avail himself of it to be delivered. Imagine being hopelessly lost in the deep forest at midnight when a light appears. Acting upon the light, you discover its source—the burning headlamps of a jeep. Upon the hood of the jeep is a detailed map showing the way out of the forest. Immediately you tear the map into small pieces and demolish the headlamps of the jeep. Sounds absurd, does it not? In this scenario, what person would be responsible for your remaining lost? Certainly not the one who provided the jeep, headlamps and map! Sadly, this is often man's response to the light God provides through His sacred Word communicated by parents, teachers, missionaries, evangelists and pastors. By rejection of the gospel light, man chooses his own ruin presently and destiny in Hell. "The foolishness of man [his own undoing] perverteth [ruins, devastates, destroys] his way" (Proverbs 19:3). The sanest thing for a person (child, youth or adult) to do is to turn from a life of self-rule or self-governing to the rule of the Lord Jesus Christ, embracing Him as Lord (ruler, authority of life) and personal Savior (John 10:9–10; Romans 10:9–13).

[1] Henry, Matthew. *Matthew Henry's Commentary on the Whole Bible: Complete and Unabridged in One Volume.* (Peabody: Hendrickson, 1994), 954.

[2] Lawson, George. *Exposition of the Book of Proverbs.* (Edinburgh, 1821), Proverbs 1:4.

[3] Jamieson, Robert, A. R. Fausset, & David Brown. *Commentary Critical and Explanatory on the Whole Bible,* (Vol. 1). (Oak Harbor, WA: Logos Research Systems, Inc., 1997), 389.

[4] Exell, Joseph, Ed. *The Biblical Illustrator: Proverbs.* (Grand Rapids: Baker Book House)

[5] Bridges, Charles. *A Commentary on Proverbs.* (Carlisle, PA: The Banner of Truth Trust, 2008 [first published, 1846]), xv.

[6] Lawson, George. *Exposition of the Book of Proverbs.* (Edinburgh, 1821), preface.

[7] *Strong's Concordance* #4910/4911.

[8] Crowder, J. W., Ed. *An Interpretation of the English Bible: The Poetical Books of the Bible.* (Nashville: Broadman Press, 1948), 146.

[9] Bullock, G. Hassell. *An Introduction to the Old Testament Poetic Books.* (Chicago: Moody, 1976), 159.

[10] Maclaren, Alexander. *Exposition of Holy Scripture, Proverbs.* (Grand Rapids: Baker Book House, 1977), 88.

[11] Exell, Joseph, Ed. *The Biblical Illustrator: Proverbs.* (Grand Rapids: Baker Book House)

[12] Bridges, Charles. *A Commentary on Proverbs.* (Carlisle, PA: The Banner of Truth Trust, 2008), preface, v.

[13] Gray, James M. *The Christians Workers Commentary.* (New York: Fleming H. Revell Company, 1915), 228.

[14] Ibid.

[15] Ibid.

[16] Rice, John R. *The John R. Rice Study Bible.* (Nashville: Thomas Nelson Publishers, 1981), 682.

[17] Swindoll, Chuck. *Overview of Proverbs.* www.insight.org, accessed December 5, 2017.

[18] Packer, J. I. *Knowing God.* (Madison, Wisconsin: Intervarsity Press, 1977), 211.

[19] Crowder, J. W., Ed. *An Interpretation of the English Bible: The Poetical Books of the Bible.* (Nashville: Broadman Press, 1948), 148.

[20] Ibid., 149.

21 Waltke, Bruce K. *The Book of Proverbs* (Vol. 1). (Grand Rapids: William B. Eerdmans Publishing Company, 2004), 76.

22 Jeremiah, David. *The David Jeremiah Study Bible.* (Nashville: Worthy Publishing, 2016), 805.

23 Whitlock, L. G., R. C. Sproul, B. K. Waltke, and M. Silva. *The Reformation Study Bible: Bringing the Light of the Reformation to Scripture: New King James Version.* (Nashville: T. Nelson, 1995), Proverbs 1:2.

24 Wiersbe, W. W. *Wiersbe's Expository Outlines on the Old Testament.* (Wheaton, IL: Victor Books, 1993), Proverbs.

25 Waltke, Bruce K. *The Book of Proverbs* (Vol. 1). (Grand Rapids: William B. Eerdmans Publishing Company, 2004), 55.

26 Newheiser, J. *Opening Up Proverbs.* (Leominster: Day One Publications, 2008), 11.

27 Waltke, Bruce K. *The Book of Proverbs* (Vol. 1). (Grand Rapids: William B. Eerdmans Publishing Company, 2004), 67.

28 Maclaren, Alexander. *Exposition of Holy Scripture, Proverbs.* (Grand Rapids: Baker Book House, 1977), 72.

29 Spence-Jones, H. D. M. (Ed.). *Proverbs.* (London; New York: Funk & Wagnalls Company, 1909), 56.

30 Ibid.

31 Bobgan, Martin and Deidre. *Psycho Heresy.* (Santa Barbara, CA: EastGate Publishers, 1987), 7.

32 Criswell, W. A., P. Patterson, E. R. Clendenen, D. L. Akin, M. Chamberlin, D. K. Patterson, & J. Pogue, (Eds.). *Believer's Study Bible* (electronic ed.). (Nashville: Thomas Nelson, 1991), 1 Kings 4:31.

33 Based upon an average speed of 20 miles per day. Camels can travel in a caravan, such as that of the Queen of Sheba, at a pace of 18–25 miles per day. http://news.softpedia. com/news/10-Amazing-Facts-About-Camels-68843.shtml, accessed February 9, 2018.

34 Wiseman, Donald J. *Tyndale Old Testament Commentaries: I and 2 Kings.* (Downers Grove, IL: InterVarsity Press, 1993), 139.

35 *The NET Bible First Edition Notes.* (Biblical Studies Press, 2006), Proverbs 6:17.

36 Reyburn, W. D. and E. M. Fry. *A Handbook on Proverbs.* (New York: United Bible Societies, 2000), 146.

37 Spence-Jones, H. D. M. (Ed.). *Proverbs.* (London; New York: Funk & Wagnalls Company, 1909), 131.

38 *The NET Bible First Edition Notes.* (Biblical Studies Press, 2006), Proverbs 6:17.

39 Gill, John. *Gill's Exposition of the Whole Bible.* Proverbs 6:17.

[40] Reyburn, W. D. and E. M. Fry. *A Handbook on Proverbs*. (New York: United Bible Societies, 2000), 145.

[41] http://www.azquotes.com/author/14373-Charles_R_Swindoll/tag/mother, accessed October 22, 2017.

[42] Morris, Henry M. *The New Defender's Study Bible*. (World Publishing, 2005), Exodus 20:11.

[43] Roberts, Alexander and James Donaldson, Ed., *The Ante-Nicene Fathers*. (New York: Charles Scribner's Sons, 1905), 148.

[44] www.christianquotes.info/quotes-by-topic/quotes-about-abortion/#ixzz4tDYQcueD, accessed September 20, 2017.

[45] Adrian Rogers. "The Sin of Silence, Part Two." www.oneplace.com/ministries/love-worth-finding/read/articles/the-sin-of-silence-part-2-15982.html, accessed September 20, 2017.

[46] www.christianquotes.info/quotes-by-topic/quotes-about-abortion/#ixzz4tDXIRUls, accessed September 20, 2017.

[47] Buzzell, S. S. in J. F. Walvoord and R. B. Zuck (Eds.). *The Bible Knowledge Commentary: An Exposition of the Scriptures* (Vol. 1). (Wheaton, IL: Victor Books, 1985), 945.

[48] Reyburn, W. D. and E. M. Fry. *A Handbook on Proverbs*. (New York: United Bible Societies, 2000), 398.

[49] Ibid.

[50] Bridges, Charles. *A Commentary on Proverbs*. (Carlisle, PA: The Banner of Truth Trust, 2008), 307–308.

[51] https://www.brainyquote.com/topics/adultery, accessed February 3, 2018.

[52] Spence-Jones, H. D. M. (Ed.). *Proverbs*. (London; New York: Funk & Wagnalls Company, 1909), 137.

[53] Ibid.

[54] Reyburn, W. D. and E. M. Fry. *A Handbook on Proverbs*. (New York: United Bible Societies, 2000), 156.

[55] Murphy, R. E. *Proverbs* (Vol. 22). (Dallas: Word, Incorporated, 1998), 39.

[56] Reyburn, W. D. and E. M. Fry. *A Handbook on Proverbs*. (New York: United Bible Societies, 2000), 156.

[57] Spence-Jones, H. D. M. (Ed.). *Proverbs*. (London; New York: Funk & Wagnalls Company, 1909), 138.

[58] Ibid.

[59] MacDonald, W. (A. Farstad, Ed.). *Believer's Bible Commentary: Old and New Testaments*. (Nashville: Thomas Nelson, 1995), 804.

[60] Greg Holt. "A Sin Against the Home," January 14, 2017. https://inspirationalchristians fortoday.com/2017/01/14/a-sin-against-the-home/, accessed January 4, 2018.

[61] *The NET Bible First Edition Notes.* (Biblical Studies Press, 2006), Proverbs 20:29.

[62] Spence-Jones, H. D. M. (Ed.). *Proverbs.* (London; New York: Funk & Wagnalls Company, 1909), 390.

[63] *The NET Bible First Edition Notes.* (Biblical Studies Press, 2006), Proverbs 20:29.

[64] Reyburn, W. D. and E. M. Fry. *A Handbook on Proverbs.* (New York: United Bible Societies, 2000), 435.

[65] *The NET Bible First Edition Notes.* (Biblical Studies Press, 2006), Proverbs 20:29.

[66] http://www.thoughts-about-god.com/quotes/quotes-aging.html, accessed February 4, 2017.

[67] Lucado, Max. *Lucado Devotional Bible, NCV.* "Abundant Life."

[68] "Habit Formation." www.psychologytoday.com/basics/habit-formation, accessed September 1, 2017.

[69] www.brainyquote.com/quotes/keywords/habits.html, accessed September 1, 2017.

[70] Ibid.

[71] www.christianquotes.info/quotes-by-topic/quotes-about-habits/#ixzz4rRi4m7wp, accessed September 1, 2017.

[72] http://www2.gracenotes.info/topics/old-age.html, accessed September 1, 2017.

[73] MacArthur, J., Jr. (Ed.). *The MacArthur Study Bible* (electronic ed.). (Nashville, TN: Word Pub., 1997), 904.

[74] Reyburn, W. D. and E. M. Fry. *A Handbook on Proverbs.* (New York: United Bible Societies, 2000), 413–414.

[75] Waltke, Bruce K. *The Book of Proverbs* (Vol. 2). (Grand Rapids: William B. Eerdmans Publishing Company, 2004), 126.

[76] MacArthur, J., Jr. (Ed.). *The MacArthur Study Bible* (electronic ed.). (Nashville, TN: Word Pub., 1997), 904.

[77] Rogers, Adrian. "The Battle of the Bottle" (sermon).

[78] Ironside, H. A. *Notes on the Book of Proverbs.* (Neptune, NJ: Loizeaux Bros., 1908), 259–260.

[79] McGee, J. V. *Thru the Bible Commentary* (electronic ed., Vol. 3). (Nashville: Thomas Nelson, 1997), 67.

[80] Spence-Jones, H. D. M. (Ed.). *Proverbs.* (London; New York: Funk & Wagnalls Company, 1909), 290.

[81] McKane, William. *Proverbs: A New Approach. Old Testament Library.* (Philadelphia: Westminster, 1970), 477.

[82] Reyburn, W. D. and E. M. Fry. *A Handbook on Proverbs*. (New York: United Bible Societies, 2000), 328.

[83] Ibid., 325.

[84] Buzzell, S. S. in J. F. Walvoord and R. B. Zuck (Eds.). *The Bible Knowledge Commentary: An Exposition of the Scriptures* (Vol. 1). (Wheaton, IL: Victor Books, 1985), 935.

[85] http://www.christianity.com/christian-life/christian-living-faq/how-should-i-deal-with-my-anger-11555743.html, accessed March 5, 2016.

[86] Ibid.

[87] Piper, John. "Kill Anger Before It Kills You or Your Marriage." http://www.desiringgod. org/articles/kill-anger-before-it-kills-you-or-your-marriage, April 23, 2003. Accessed July 20, 2015.

[88] https://www.brainyquote.com/topics/anger, accessed January 28, 2018.

[89] http://www.focusonthefamily.com/parenting/your-childs-emotions/when-children-become-angry/uncovering-the-pain-behind-your-childs-anger, accessed October 16, 2017.

[90] http://www.christianity.com/christian-life/christian-living-faq/how-should-i-deal-with-my-anger-11555743.html, accessed March 5, 2016.

[91] Attributed to Abraham Lincoln, and one similar to Dale Carnegie.

[92] Ross, Allen P. *The Expositor's Bible Commentary*. (Grand Rapids: Zondervan, 1991), 969.

[93] https://www.aspca.org/animal-cruelty/dog-fighting, accessed February 2, 2018.

[94] https://www.aspca.org/animal-cruelty/dog-fighting/closer-look-dog-fighting, accessed February 2, 2018.

[95] Bridges, Charles. *A Commentary on Proverbs*. (Carlisle, PA: The Banner of Truth Trust, 2008), 137.

[96] Ibid.

[97] Lawson, G. *Exposition of the Book of Proverbs* (Vol. 1). (Edinburgh; Glasgow; London: David Brown; W. Oliphant; F. Pillans; M. Ogle; Ogle, Duncan, and Co.; J. Nisbet, 1821), 233–234.

[98] *The NET Bible First Edition Notes*. (Biblical Studies Press, 2006), Proverbs 12:25.

[99] "40 Charles Spurgeon Quotes on Anxiety, Fear, and Worry." http://www.cross-points.org/charles-spurgeon-quotes-on-anxiety-fear-and-worry/, accessed November 1, 2017.

[100] Henry, Matthew. *Matthew Henry's Commentary on the Whole Bible: Complete and Unabridged in One Volume*. (Peabody: Hendrickson, 1994), 2328.

[101] Ibid.

[102] Barclay, W. (Ed.). *The Letters to the Philippians, Colossians, and Thessalonians* (electronic ed.). (Philadelphia: The Westminster John Knox Press, 1975), 77.

[103] Ibid., 78.

[104] Mcgee, J. V. *Thru the Bible Commentary* (electronic ed., Vol. 5). (Nashville: Thomas Nelson, 1997), 322–323.

[105] "40 Charles Spurgeon Quotes on Anxiety, Fear, and Worry." http://www.cross-points.org/charles-spurgeon-quotes-on-anxiety-fear-and-worry/, accessed November 1, 2017.

[106] Henry, Matthew. *Matthew Henry's Commentary on the Whole Bible: Complete and Unabridged in One Volume.* (Peabody: Hendrickson, 1994), 981.

[107] Lucado, Max. "A Worry-Slapper," May 8, 2012. https://maxlucado.com/listen/a-worry-slapper/, accessed November 1, 2017.

[108] Spence-Jones, H. D. M. (Ed.). *Proverbs.* (London; New York: Funk & Wagnalls Company, 1909), 426.

[109] Bridges, Charles. *A Commentary on Proverbs.* (Carlisle, PA: The Banner of Truth Trust, 2008), 418.

[110] Lawson, George. *Exposition of the Book of Proverbs.* (Edinburgh, 1821), Proverbs 22:21.

[111] Clark Pinnock, cited by www.defendingyourfaith.org/Apologetics.htm, accessed May 20, 2011.

[112] Murphy, R. E. *Proverbs* (Vol. 22). (Dallas: Word, Incorporated, 1998), 223.

[113] Spence-Jones, H. D. M. (Ed.). *Proverbs.* (London; New York: Funk & Wagnalls Company, 1909), 557.

[114] *The NET Bible First Edition Notes.* (Biblical Studies Press, 2006), Proverbs 29:25.

[115] Ibid.

[116] Ibid. Proverbs 13:20.

[117] Henry, Matthew. *Matthew Henry's Commentary on the Whole Bible: Complete and Unabridged in One Volume.* (Peabody: Hendrickson, 1994), 983.

[118] Lawson, George. *Exposition of the Book of Proverbs.* (Edinburgh, 1821), Proverbs 22:24.

[119] Reyburn, W. D. and E. M. Fry. *A Handbook on Proverbs.* (New York: United Bible Societies, 2000), 306.

[120] Spence-Jones, H. D. M. (Ed.). *Proverbs.* (London; New York: Funk & Wagnalls Company, 1909), 268.

[121] Comfort, Ray. *Think on These Things.* (Racine, Wisconsin: Broad Street, 2017), 125.

[122] Huxley, Aldous. *Ends and Means*. (Garland Publishers), 270, 273, cited in James Boice, *Genesis* (Zondervan), 1:236. https://bible.org/seriespage/lesson-18-why-people-reject-christ-john-319-21, accessed December 14, 2017.

[123] Henry, Matthew. *Matthew Henry's Commentary on the Whole Bible: Complete and Unabridged in One Volume*. (Peabody: Hendrickson, 1994), 2123.

[124] Lawson, G. *Exposition of the Book of Proverbs* (Vol. 1). (Edinburgh; Glasgow; London: David Brown; W. Oliphant; F. Pillans; M. Ogle; Ogle, Duncan, and Co.; J. Nisbet, 1821), 278.

[125] Morris, Leon. *The Gospel According to John*. (Eerdmans), 233.

[126] Reyburn, W. D. and E. M. Fry. *A Handbook on Proverbs*. (New York: United Bible Societies, 2000), 377.

[127] Spence-Jones, H. D. M. (Ed.). *Proverbs*. (London; New York: Funk & Wagnalls Company, 1909), 335.

[128] Ross, Allen P. *The Expositor's Bible Commentary*. (Grand Rapids: Zondervan, 1991), 1020.

[129] Swindoll, Charles R. *Strengthening Your Grip*. (Waco, TX: Word Books, 1982), 207.

[130] https://www.brainyquote.com/topics/attitude, accessed November 27, 2017.

[131] Waltke, Bruce K. *The Book of Proverbs* (Vol. 1). (Grand Rapids: William B. Eerdmans Publishing Company, 2004), 614.

[132] Spurgeon, C. H. "The Immutability of God" (Sermon), January 7, 1855.

[133] Henry, Matthew. *Matthew Henry's Commentary on the Whole Bible: Complete and Unabridged in One Volume*. (Peabody: Hendrickson, 1994), 987.

[134] Spurgeon, C. H. "The Immutability of God," (Malachi 3:6). June 7, 1855.

[135] Lewis, C. S. *Mere Christianity*. (Harper One, 1980).

[136] Hamilton, William W. *Sermons on the Books of the Bible,* Vol. II, 45.

[137] https://www.blueletterbible.org/faq/attributes.cfm, accessed October 13, 2017.

[138] Packer, J. I. *Knowing God*. (Madison, Wisconsin: Intervarsity Press, 1977).

[139] Waltke, Bruce K. *The Book of Proverbs* (Vol. 1). (Grand Rapids: William B. Eerdmans Publishing Company, 2004), 101.

[140] *The NET Bible First Edition Notes*. (Biblical Studies Press, 2006), Proverbs 16:6.

[141] Henry, Matthew. *Matthew Henry's Commentary on the Whole Bible: Complete and Unabridged in One Volume*. (Peabody: Hendrickson, 1994), 990.

[142] Buzzell, S. S. in J. F. Walvoord and R. B. Zuck (Eds.). *The Bible Knowledge Commentary: An Exposition of the Scriptures* (Vol. 1). (Wheaton, IL: Victor Books, 1985), 907–908.

[143] Bridges, Charles. *A Commentary on Proverbs*. (Carlisle, PA: The Banner of Truth Trust, 2008), 230.

[144] *The NET Bible First Edition Notes*. (Biblical Studies Press, 2006), Proverbs 14:14.

[145] Ibid.

[146] Rice, John R. *The Backslider* (Pamphlet). Murfreesboro, TN: Sword of the Lord Publishers, October 1944), Chapter 1.

[147] http://christian-quotes.ochristian.com/Backsliding-Quotes/, accessed August 11, 2017.

[148] Ibid.

[149] Bridges, Charles. *A Commentary on Proverbs*. (Carlisle, PA: The Banner of Truth Trust, 2008), 179.

[150] Ibid.

[151] https://gracequotes.org/quote/remember-that-if-you-are-a-child-of-god-you-wil, accessed October 19, 2017.

[152] http://christian-quotes.ochristian.com/Backsliding-Quotes/, accessed August 11, 2017.

[153] *The NET Bible First Edition Notes*. (Biblical Studies Press, 2006), Proverbs 11:22.

[154] Spence-Jones, H. D. M. (Ed.). *Proverbs*. (London; New York: Funk & Wagnalls Company, 1909), 217.

[155] Henry, Matthew. *Matthew Henry's Commentary on the Whole Bible: Complete and Unabridged in One Volume*. (Peabody: Hendrickson, 1994), 979.

[156] Ibid.

[157] Bridges, Charles. *A Commentary on Proverbs*. (Carlisle, PA: The Banner of Truth Trust, 2008), Proverbs 11:22.

[158] Pfeiffer, C. F. *The Wycliffe Bible Commentary: Old Testament*. (Chicago: Moody Press, 1962). Proverbs 22:28.

[159] Reyburn, W. D. and E. M. Fry. *A Handbook on Proverbs*. (New York: United Bible Societies, 2000), 483.

[160] *The NET Bible First Edition Notes*. (Biblical Studies Press, 2006), Proverbs 22:28.

[161] Lawson, G. *Exposition of the Book of Proverbs* (Vol. 1). (Edinburgh; Glasgow; London: David Brown; W. Oliphant; F. Pillans; M. Ogle; Ogle, Duncan, and Co.; J. Nisbet, 1821), 447.

[162] Reyburn, W. D. and E. M. Fry. *A Handbook on Proverbs*. (New York: United Bible Societies, 2000), 391.

[163] Spurgeon, C. H. *Lectures to My Students.*

[164] Reyburn, W. D. and E. M. Fry. *A Handbook on Proverbs*. (New York: United Bible Societies, 2000), 123.

[165] *The NET Bible First Edition Notes.* (Biblical Studies Press, 2006), Proverbs 5:12–13.

[166] Alden, Robert L. *Proverbs: A Commentary on an Ancient Book of Timeless Advice.* (Grand Rapids: Baker, 1984), 51.

[167] Simeon, C. *Horae Homileticae: Proverbs to Isaiah XXVI* (Vol. 7). (London: Holdsworth and Ball, 1833), 60.

[168] Hubbard, D. A. and L. J. Ogilvie. *Proverbs* (Vol. 15). (Nashville, TN: Thomas Nelson Inc.1989), 92.

[169] Lawson, George. *Exposition of the Book of Proverbs.* (Edinburgh, 1821), Proverbs 5:12–14.

[170] Aitken, K. T. *Proverbs.* (Louisville, KY: Westminster John Knox Press, 1986), 64.

[171] Reyburn, W. D. and E. M. Fry. *A Handbook on Proverbs.* (New York: United Bible Societies, 2000), 71.

[172] Ibid.

[173] Ibid.

[174] Spence-Jones, H. D. M. (Ed.). *Proverbs.* (London; New York: Funk & Wagnalls Company, 1909), 54.

[175] Buzzell, S. S. in J. F. Walvoord and R. B. Zuck (Eds.). *The Bible Knowledge Commentary: An Exposition of the Scriptures* (Vol. 1). (Wheaton, IL: Victor Books, 1985), 911.

[176] Wiersbe, W. W. *Wiersbe's Expository Outlines on the Old Testament.* (Wheaton, IL: Victor Books, 1993), Proverbs 3.

[177] Bratcher, R. G., and E. A. Nida. *A Handbook on Paul's Letters to the Colossians and to Philemon.* (New York: United Bible Societies, 1993), 89.

[178] Murphy, R. E. *Proverbs* (Vol. 22). (Dallas: Word, Incorporated, 1998), 229.

[179] Ironside, H. A. *Notes on the Book of Proverbs.* (Neptune, NJ: Loizeaux Bros., 1908), 439.

[180] Spence-Jones, H. D. M. (Ed.). *Proverbs.* (London; New York: Funk & Wagnalls Company, 1909), 572.

[181] Waltke, Bruce K. *The Book of Proverbs* (Vol. 2). (Grand Rapids: William B. Eerdmans Publishing Company, 2004), 476.

[182] Ibid.

[183] Criswell, W. A. *The Criswell Study Bible.* (Nashville: Thomas Nelson Publishing Company, 1979), 1459.

[184] www.christianquotes.info/top-quotes/19-awesome-quotes-from-the-book-of-proverbs/, accessed December 11, 2017.

[185] Criswell, W. A. *Why I Preach the Bible Is Literally True.* (Nashville: Broadman Press, 1969), 19–20.

[186] Henry, Matthew. *Matthew Henry's Commentary on the Whole Bible: Complete and Unabridged in One Volume.* (Peabody: Hendrickson, 1994), 1023.

[187] Reyburn, W. D. and E. M. Fry. *A Handbook on Proverbs.* (New York: United Bible Societies, 2000), 311.

[188] *The NET Bible First Edition Notes.* (Biblical Studies Press, 2006), Proverbs 14:10.

[189] Murphy, R. E. *Proverbs* (Vol. 22). (Dallas: Word, Incorporated, 1998), 104.

[190] Spence-Jones, H. D. M. (Ed.). *Proverbs.* (London; New York: Funk & Wagnalls Company, 1909), 270.

[191] Ibid.

[192] *Fraser's Magazine for Town and Country,* Volume 34. (London: printed by George Barclay, 1846), 131.

[193] Henry, Matthew. *Matthew Henry's Commentary on the Whole Bible: Complete and Unabridged in One Volume.* (Peabody: Hendrickson, 1994), 985.

[194] Simeon, C. *Horae Homileticae: Proverbs to Isaiah XXVI* (Vol. 7). (London: Holdsworth and Ball, 1833), 133.

[195] Ibid.

[196] Author unknown.

[197] Murphy, R. E. *Proverbs* (Vol. 22). (Dallas: Word, Incorporated, 1998), 206.

[198] McKane, William. *Proverbs: A New Approach. Old Testament Library.* (Philadelphia: Westminster, 1970), 607.

[199] Ironside, H. A. *Notes on the Book of Proverbs.* (Neptune, NJ: Loizeaux Bros., 1908), 377.

[200] Reyburn, W. D. and E. M. Fry. *A Handbook on Proverbs.* (New York: United Bible Societies, 2000), 465.

[201] Henry, Matthew. *Matthew Henry's Commentary on the Whole Bible: Complete and Unabridged in One Volume.* (Peabody: Hendrickson, 1994), 1004.

[202] Vogel, Arielle. "What Does the Bible Say About Credit Cards?," July 10, 2017, www.crown.org/what-does-the-bible-say-about-credit-cards, accessed August 23, 2017.

[203] Spence-Jones, H. D. M. (Ed.). *Proverbs.* (London; New York: Funk & Wagnalls Company, 1909), 423.

[204] Men's Manual Vol. 2. *The Dangers of Going into Debt.* (Institute in Basic Life Principles), 78–81.

[205] Pacheco, Megan. "What Does the Bible Say about Lending and Borrowing?" (Sept. 18, 2013), https://www.crosswalk.com/home-page/todays-features/lending-borrowing-and-the-bible.html, accessed January 23, 2018.

[206] Morris, Leon. *The Epistle to the Romans.* (Grand Rapids, MI; Leicester, England: W. B. Eerdmans; Inter-Varsity Press,1988), 467.

[207] Reyburn, W. D. and E. M. Fry. *A Handbook on Proverbs*. (New York: United Bible Societies, 2000), 157.

[208] *The NET Bible First Edition Notes*. (Biblical Studies Press, 2006), Proverbs 6:35.

[209] www.desiringgod.org/articles/the-wickedness-of-bribery-and-the-hope-of-the-gospel, accessed September 1, 2017.

[210] www.forbes.com/sites/alexandrawrage/2017/01/25/bribery-is-bad-for-business/#28cce0204a42, accessed September 1, 2017.

[211] Spurgeon, C. H. *The Treasury of David*, Psalm 26:10.

[212] Garrett, D. A. *Proverbs, Ecclesiastes, Song of Songs* (Vol. 14). (Nashville: Broadman & Holman Publishers, 1993), 233.

[213] Walvoord, J. F. and R. B. Zuck. *The Bible Knowledge Commentary: An Exposition of the Scriptures* (Vol. 1). (Wheaton, IL: Victor Books, 1985), 969.

[214] Garrett, D. A. *Proverbs, Ecclesiastes, Song of Songs* (Vol. 14). (Nashville: Broadman & Holman Publishers, 1993), 233.

[215] Cohn, Andrea and Andrea Canter, Ph.D. "Bullying: Facts for Schools and Parents." NASP Fact Sheet. Accessed February 9, 2014. http://www.nasponline.org/resources/factsheets/ bullying_fs.aspx.

[216] The National Education Association. "Nation's educators continue push for safe, bully-free environments." NEA. Accessed February 10, 2014, http://www.nea.org/home/ 53298.htm.

[217] Cohn, Andrea and Andrea Canter, Ph.D. "Bullying: Facts for Schools and Parents." NASP Fact Sheet. Accessed February 9, 2014, http://www.nasponline.org/resources/factsheets/ bullying_fs.aspx.

[218] Coughlin, Paul. "A Faith-Based Response to Adolescent Bullying," http://www. cbn.com/family/parenting/coughlin_bully1.aspx, accessed July 29, 2014.

[219] Mayer, Bill, General Editor. *Help! My Child Is Being Bullied*. (Carol Stream, Illinois: Tyndale House Publishers, 2006), 8.

[220] "Warning Signs of Bullying." https://www.stopbullying.gov/at-risk/warning-signs/index.html, accessed August 7, 2017.

[221] www.wikihow.com/Deal-With-Workplace-Bullying-and-Harrassment.

[222] Spence-Jones, H. D. M. (Ed.). *Proverbs*. (London; New York: Funk & Wagnalls Company, 1909), 561.

[223] *The NET Bible First Edition Notes*. (Biblical Studies Press, 2006), Proverbs 27:23.

[224] Ross, Allen P. *The Expositor's Bible Commentary*. (Grand Rapids: Zondervan, 1991), 1101.

[225] Henry, Matthew. *Matthew Henry's Commentary on the Whole Bible: Complete and Unabridged in One Volume*. (Peabody: Hendrickson, 1994), 1017.

226 Reyburn, W. D. and E. M. Fry. *A Handbook on Proverbs*. (New York: United Bible Societies, 2000), 533.

227 Ibid.

228 Ibid.

229 MacArthur, J., Jr. (Ed.). *The MacArthur Study Bible* (electronic ed.). (Nashville, TN: Word Pub., 1997), 912.

230 Murphy, R. E. *Proverbs* (Vol. 22). (Dallas: Word, Incorporated, 1998), 186.

231 Ross, Allen P. *The Expositor's Bible Commentary*. (Grand Rapids: Zondervan, 1991), 1077.

232 Buzzell, S. S. in J. F. Walvoord and R. B. Zuck (Eds.). *The Bible Knowledge Commentary: An Exposition of the Scriptures* (Vol. 1). (Wheaton, IL: Victor Books, 1985), 959.

233 Spence-Jones, H. D. M. (Ed.). *Proverbs*. (London; New York: Funk & Wagnalls Company, 1909), 198.

234 https://www.brainyquote.com/authors/ving_rhames, accessed November 30, 2017.

235 Reyburn, W. D. and E. M. Fry. *A Handbook on Proverbs*. (New York: United Bible Societies, 2000), 314.

236 Garrett, D. A. *Proverbs, Ecclesiastes, Song of Songs* (Vol. 14). (Nashville: Broadman & Holman Publishers, 1993), 143.

237 *The NET Bible First Edition Notes*. (Biblical Studies Press, 2006), Proverbs 14:16.

238 Henry, Matthew. *Matthew Henry's Commentary on the Whole Bible: Complete and Unabridged in One Volume*. (Peabody: Hendrickson, 1994), 985.

239 Bridges, Charles. *A Commentary on Proverbs*. (Carlisle, PA: The Banner of Truth Trust, 2008), 181.

240 C. H. Spurgeon. "A Caution for the Presumptuous," (New Park Street Pulpit: Volume 1, Sermon # 22), May 13, 1855.

241 Reyburn, W. D. and E. M. Fry. *A Handbook on Proverbs*. (New York: United Bible Societies, 2000), 131.

242 Murphy, R. E. *Proverbs* (Vol. 22). (Dallas: Word, Incorporated, 1998), 33.

243 braineyquote.com, accessed April 7, 2015.

244 Reyburn, W. D. and E. M. Fry. *A Handbook on Proverbs*. (New York: United Bible Societies, 2000), 77.

245 Ibid.

246 Ortlund, R. C., Jr., (R. K. Hughes, Ed.). *Preaching the Word: Proverbs—Wisdom That Works*. (Wheaton, IL: Crossway, 2012), 124.

247 Ironside, H. A. *Notes on the Book of Proverbs*. (Neptune, NJ: Loizeaux Bros., 1908), 26.

[248] Bridges, Charles. *A Commentary on Proverbs.* (Carlisle, PA: The Banner of Truth Trust, 2008), 27.

[249] Allen, Kerry James. *Exploring the Mind and Heart of the Prince of Preachers.* (Oswego, IL: Fox River Press, 2005), 57.

[250] Ibid.

[251] McGee, J. V. *Thru the Bible Commentary* (electronic ed., Vol. 3). (Nashville: Thomas Nelson, 1997), 50.

[252] Ironside, H. A. *Notes on the Book of Proverbs.* (Neptune, NJ: Loizeaux Bros., 1908), 158.

[253] Ibid.

[254] Ross, Allen P. *The Expositor's Bible Commentary.* (Grand Rapids: Zondervan, 1991), 940.

[255] Henry, Matthew. *Matthew Henry's Commentary on the Whole Bible: Complete and Unabridged in One Volume.* (Peabody: Hendrickson, 1994), 969.

[256] Walvoord, J. F. and R. B. Zuck. *The Bible Knowledge Commentary: An Exposition of the Scriptures* (Vol. 1). (Wheaton, IL: Victor Books, 1985), 961.

[257] Ibid.

[258] Criswell, W. A. "Taking Hold of God's Ableness" (sermon). December 13, 1970.

[259] Ibid.

[260] Buzzell, S. S. in J. F. Walvoord and R. B. Zuck (Eds.). *The Bible Knowledge Commentary: An Exposition of the Scriptures* (Vol. 1). (Wheaton, IL: Victor Books, 1985), 926.

[261] Spence-Jones, H. D. M. (Ed.). *Proverbs.* (London; New York: Funk & Wagnalls Company, 1909), 196.

[262] Ironside, H. A. *Notes on the Book of Proverbs.* (Neptune, NJ: Loizeaux Bros., 1908), 97.

[263] Exell, Joseph, Ed. *The Biblical Illustrator: Proverbs.* (Grand Rapids: Baker Book House), Proverbs 10:8.

[264] Henry, Matthew. *Matthew Henry's Commentary on the Whole Bible: Complete and Unabridged in One Volume.* (Peabody: Hendrickson, 1994), 975.

[265] Buzzell, S. S. in J. F. Walvoord and R. B. Zuck (Eds.). *The Bible Knowledge Commentary: An Exposition of the Scriptures* (Vol. 1). (Wheaton, IL: Victor Books, 1985), 931.

[266] Murphy, R. E. *Proverbs* (Vol. 22). (Dallas: Word, Incorporated, 1998), 90.

[267] Bridges, Charles. *A Commentary on Proverbs.* (Carlisle, PA: The Banner of Truth Trust, 2008), 135.

[268] Ibid.

[269] /www.goodreads.com/quotes/tag/commendation, accessed October 26, 2017.

270 http://www.azquotes.com/quotes/topics/praise.html, accessed October 26, 2017.

271 Ross, Allen P. *The Expositor's Bible Commentary.* (Grand Rapids: Zondervan, 1991), 1079.

272 Murphy, R. E. *Proverbs* (Vol. 22). (Dallas: Word, Incorporated, 1998), 191.

273 McKane, William. *Proverbs: A New Approach. Old Testament Library.* (Philadelphia: Westminster, 1970), 579.

274 Ironside, H. A. *Notes on the Book of Proverbs.* (Neptune, NJ: Loizeaux Bros., 1908), 345.

275 Exell, Joseph S. *The Biblical Illustrator.* Commentary on Proverbs 25:2. https://www.studylight.org/commentaries/tbi/proverbs-25.html. 1905–1909. New York.

276 Jamieson, Robert, A. R. Fausset, & David Brown. *Commentary Critical and Explanatory on the Whole Bible,* (Vol. 1). (Oak Harbor, WA: Logos Research Systems, Inc., 1997), Proverbs 25:2.

277 Murphy, R. E. *Proverbs* (Vol. 22). (Dallas: Word, Incorporated, 1998), 28.

278 Ross, Allen P. *The Expositor's Bible Commentary.* (Grand Rapids: Zondervan, 1991), 926.

279 Ibid.

280 Truett, George W. *A Quest for Souls.* (New York and London: Harper & Brothers Publishers, 1917), 45.

281 Ibid., 47. Italics added.

282 https://www.brainyquote.com/topics/focus, accessed December 4, 2017.

283 https://examinedexistence.com/12-fantastic-quotes-one-thing-not-multi-tasking/, accessed December 4, 2017.

284 https://examinedexistence.com/12-fantastic-quotes-one-thing-not-multi-tasking/, accessed December 4, 2017.

285 Ross, Allen P. *The Expositor's Bible Commentary.* (Grand Rapids: Zondervan, 1991), 1106.

286 Plaut, Gunther, quoted in Allen Ross. *The Expositors Bible Commentary, Proverbs,* 1106.

287 Henry, Matthew. *Matthew Henry's Commentary on the Whole Bible: Complete and Unabridged in One Volume.* (Peabody: Hendrickson, 1994), 1018.

288 Waltke, Bruce K. *The Book of Proverbs* (Vol. 2). (Grand Rapids: William B. Eerdmans Publishing Company, 2004), 418.

289 Spence-Jones, H. D. M. (Ed.). *Proverbs.* (London; New York: Funk & Wagnalls Company, 1909), 64.

290 *The NET Bible First Edition Notes.* (Biblical Studies Press, 2006), Proverbs 3:26.

291 Spurgeon, C. H. *Morning and Evening,* May 23.

[292] Ibid.

[293] http://www.azquotes.com/quotes/topics/confidence-in-god.html, accessed December 9, 2017.

[294] Cowman, L. B. *Streams in the Desert.* (Grand Rapids: Zondervan, 1997), March 10 entry.

[295] *The NET Bible First Edition Notes.* (Biblical Studies Press, 2006), Proverb 3:25.

[296] Reyburn, W. D. and E. M. Fry. *A Handbook on Proverbs.* (New York: United Bible Societies, 2000), 88.

[297] Spence-Jones, H. D. M. (Ed.). *Proverbs.* (London; New York: Funk & Wagnalls Company, 1909), 64.

[298] Ibid.

[299] Ibid.

[300] Wiersbe, W. W. *Be Skillful.* (Wheaton, IL: Victor Books, 1996), 40.

[301] Ibid.

[302] https://www.goodreads.com/author/quotes/4215981.John_Ortberg, accessed January 22, 2018.

[303] Spurgeon, C. H. *My Sermon Notes.* (New York: Funk & Wagnalls, 1891), 52–53.

[304] Reyburn, W. D. and E. M. Fry. *A Handbook on Proverbs.* (New York: United Bible Societies, 2000), 550.

[305] Ibid.

[306] Ibid.

[307] Ibid., 433.

[308] Adrian Rogers. "How to Have a Good Conscience" (sermon), www.oneplace.com/ ministries/love-worth-finding/read/articles/how-to-have-a-good-conscience-11482.html, accessed October 27, 2017.

[309] Spence-Jones, H. D. M. (Ed.). *Proverbs.* (London; New York: Funk & Wagnalls Company, 1909), 533.

[310] Ibid.

[311] Kidner, Derek. *The Proverbs: An Introduction and Commentary. Tyndale Old Testament Commentary.* (Downers Grove: InterVarsity, 1964), 168.

[312] Spence-Jones, H. D. M. (Ed.). *Proverbs.* (London; New York: Funk & Wagnalls Company, 1909), 533.

[313] Chambers, Oswald. *My Utmost for His Highest.* May 13.

[314] Spence-Jones, H. D. M. (Ed.). *Proverbs.* (London; New York: Funk & Wagnalls Company, 1909), 533.

[315] Buzzell, S. S. in J. F. Walvoord and R. B. Zuck (Eds.). *The Bible Knowledge Commentary: An Exposition of the Scriptures* (Vol. 1). (Wheaton, IL: Victor Books, 1985), 929.

316 Reyburn, W. D. and E. M. Fry. *A Handbook on Proverbs*. (New York: United Bible Societies, 2000), 251.

317 Ross, Allen P. *The Expositor's Bible Commentary*. (Grand Rapids: Zondervan, 1991), 963.

318 Murphy, R. E. *Proverbs* (Vol. 22). (Dallas: Word, Incorporated, 1998), 83.

319 Spence-Jones, H. D. M. (Ed.). *Galatians*. (London; New York: Funk & Wagnalls Company, 1909), 299.

320 "The Law of Small Potatoes." (Murfreesboro, Tenn: The Sword of the Lord Publishers, January 12, 2018), 5. Adapted.

321 From The Gospel Herald as cited at http://www.moreillustrations.com/Illustrations/sowing%20and%20reaping%201.html, accessed August 24, 2017.

322 Reyburn, W. D. and E. M. Fry. *A Handbook on Proverbs*. (New York: United Bible Societies, 2000), 363.

323 Murphy, R. E. *Proverbs* (Vol. 22). (Dallas: Word, Incorporated, 1998), 124.

324 Ibid.

325 Gill, John. *Gill's Exposition of the Whole Bible*. Proverbs 16:33.

326 Ironside, H. A. *Notes on the Book of Proverbs*. (Neptune, NJ: Loizeaux Bros., 1908), 204.

327 https://billygraham.org/answer/a-christian-friend-of-mine-doesnt-use-words-like-luck-or-lucky/, accessed August 13, 2017.

328 Spence-Jones, H. D. M. (Ed.). *Proverbs*. (London; New York: Funk & Wagnalls Company, 1909), 316.

329 Maclaren, Alexander. *Exposition of Holy Scripture, Proverbs*. (Grand Rapids: Baker Book House, 1977), 210.

330 Reyburn, W. D. and E. M. Fry. *A Handbook on Proverbs*. (New York: United Bible Societies, 2000), 576.

331 Ross, Allen P. *The Expositor's Bible Commentary*. (Grand Rapids: Zondervan, 1991), 1097.

332 Murphy, R. E. *Proverbs* (Vol. 22). (Dallas: Word, Incorporated, 1998), 207.

333 Today's Insight—Feb. 4, 2015, http://www.christianity.com/devotionals/todays-insight-chuck-swindoll/today-s-insight-feb-4-2015.html, accessed October 29, 2017.

334 This saying entered circulation by 1861 and the earliest instances were anonymous. https://quoteinvestigator.com/2013/10/26/kindness-see/, accessed January 29, 2018.

335 *The NET Bible First Edition Notes*. (Biblical Studies Press, 2006), Proverbs 19:21.

336 Criswell, W. A., P. Patterson, E. R. Clendenen, D. L. Akin, M. Chamberlin, D. K. Patterson, & J. Pogue, (Eds.). *Believer's Study Bible* (electronic ed.). (Nashville: Thomas Nelson, 1991), Proverbs 19:21.

[337] Henry, Matthew. *Matthew Henry's Commentary on the Whole Bible: Complete and Unabridged in One Volume.* (Peabody: Hendrickson, 1994), 998.

[338] *Geneva Study Bible,* Proverbs 19:21.

[339] Criswell, W. A., P. Patterson, E. R. Clendenen, D. L. Akin, M. Chamberlin, D. K. Patterson, & J. Pogue, (Eds.). *Believer's Study Bible* (electronic ed.). (Nashville: Thomas Nelson, 1991), Proverbs 19:21.

[340] C. H. Spurgeon, (1993). *Psalms.* Crossway Classic Commentaries (Wheaton, Illinois: Crossway Books), 126.

[341] Spence-Jones, H. D. M. (Ed.). *Proverbs.* (London; New York: Funk & Wagnalls Company, 1909), 216.

[342] *The NET Bible First Edition Notes.* (Biblical Studies Press, 2006), Proverbs 11:14.

[343] Reyburn, W. D. and E. M. Fry. *A Handbook on Proverbs.* (New York: United Bible Societies, 2000), 248.

[344] Ibid.

[345] Henry, Matthew. *Matthew Henry's Commentary on the Whole Bible: Complete and Unabridged in One Volume.* (Peabody: Hendrickson, 1994), 978.

[346] Lawson, George. *Exposition of the Book of Proverbs.* (Edinburgh, 1821), Proverbs 24:5.

[347] Henry, Matthew. *Matthew Henry's Commentary on the Whole Bible: Complete and Unabridged in One Volume.* (Peabody: Hendrickson, 1994), 978.

[348] Elliot, Elisabeth. "Discipline: The Glad Surrender."

[349] Ironside, H. A. *Notes on the Book of Proverbs.* (Neptune, NJ: Loizeaux Bros., 1908), 119–120.

[350] *The NET Bible First Edition Notes.* (Biblical Studies Press, 2006), Proverbs 12:5.

[351] Buzzell, S. S. in J. F. Walvoord and R. B. Zuck (Eds.). *The Bible Knowledge Commentary: An Exposition of the Scriptures* (Vol. 1). (Wheaton, IL: Victor Books, 1985), 931.

[352] https://www.brainyquote.com/topics/advice, accessed November 27, 2017.

[353] Henry, Matthew. *Matthew Henry's Commentary on the Whole Bible: Complete and Unabridged in One Volume.* (Peabody: Hendrickson, 1994), 1015.

[354] MacArthur, J., Jr. (Ed.). *The MacArthur Study Bible* (electronic ed.). (Nashville, TN: Word Pub., 1997), 915.

[355] Ironside, H. A. *Notes on the Book of Proverbs.* (Neptune, NJ: Loizeaux Bros., 1908), 374–375.

[356] Barnes, Albert. *Barnes' Notes on the Bible,* Proverbs 26:23.

[357] *The NET Bible First Edition Notes.* (Biblical Studies Press, 2006), Proverbs 28:1.

[358] "Christian Quotes on Courage." dailychristianquote.com/dcqcourage.html, accessed November 29, 2011.

[359] www.brainyquote.com/quotes/topics/topic_courage.html, accessed September 4, 2017.

[360] William Francis Collier. *History of the British Empire (1870)*. (Edinburg and New York: T. Nelson & Sons, 1876), 124.

[361] www.brainyquote.com/quotes/quotes/c/cslewis100842.html?src=t_courage, accessed September 4, 2017.

[362] www.whatchristianswanttoknow.com/bible-verses-about-worry-20-comforting-scripture-quotes, accessed September 4, 2017.

[363] Ross, Allen P. *The Expositor's Bible Commentary*. (Grand Rapids: Zondervan, 1991), 919.

[364] Bridges, Charles. *A Commentary on Proverbs*. (Carlisle, PA: The Banner of Truth Trust, 2008), 35.

[365] Henry, Matthew. *Matthew Henry's Commentary on the Whole Bible: Complete and Unabridged in One Volume*. (Peabody: Hendrickson, 1994), 961.

[366] Spence-Jones, H. D. M. (Ed.). *Proverbs*. (London; New York: Funk & Wagnalls Company, 1909), 481.

[367] Reyburn, W. D. and E. M. Fry. *A Handbook on Proverbs*. (New York: United Bible Societies, 2000), 547.

[368] Ibid.

[369] https://www.brainyquote.com/topics/criticism, accessed December 11, 2017.

[370] Henry, Matthew. *Matthew Henry's Commentary on the Whole Bible: Complete and Unabridged in One Volume*. (Peabody: Hendrickson, 1994), 1012.

[371] https://www.brainyquote.com/topics/criticism, accessed December 11, 2017.

[372] Bridges, Charles. *A Commentary on Proverbs*. (Carlisle, PA: The Banner of Truth Trust, 2008), 468.

[373] *The NET Bible First Edition Notes*. (Biblical Studies Press, 2006), Proverbs 20:20.

[374] Ibid.

[375] Spence-Jones, H. D. M. (Ed.). *Proverbs*. (London; New York: Funk & Wagnalls Company, 1909), 387.

[376] Henry, Matthew. *Matthew Henry's Commentary on the Whole Bible: Complete and Unabridged in One Volume*. (Peabody: Hendrickson, 1994), 1000.

[377] Ibid.

[378] Criswell, W. A., P. Patterson, E. R. Clendenen, D. L. Akin, M. Chamberlin, D. K. Patterson, & J. Pogue, (Eds.). *Believer's Study Bible* (electronic ed.). (Nashville: Thomas Nelson, 1991), Proverbs 20:20.

379 https://www.brainyquote.com/topics/cursing, accessed January 29, 2018.
380 http://www.spurgeon.us/mind_and_heart/quotes/p4.htm, accessed November 23, 2017.
381 Ibid.
382 Reyburn, W. D. and E. M. Fry. *A Handbook on Proverbs.* (New York: United Bible Societies, 2000), 104.
383 Ross, Allen P. *The Expositor's Bible Commentary.* (Grand Rapids: Zondervan, 1991), 1082.
384 MacDonald, W. (A. Farstad, Ed.). *Believer's Bible Commentary: Old and New Testaments.* (Nashville: Thomas Nelson, 1995), 855.
385 Ibid.
386 https://www.brainyquote.com/topics/arrogance, accessed January 29, 2018.
387 Chambers, Oswald. *My Utmost for His Highest,* May 13.
388 Reyburn, W. D. and E. M. Fry. *A Handbook on Proverbs.* (New York: United Bible Societies, 2000), 426.
389 *The NET Bible First Edition Notes.* (Biblical Studies Press, 2006), Proverbs 20:18.
390 Murphy, R. E. *Proverbs* (Vol. 22). (Dallas: Word, Incorporated, 1998), 152.
391 Reyburn, W. D. and E. M. Fry. *A Handbook on Proverbs.* (New York: United Bible Societies, 2000), 427.
392 Ironside, H. A. *Notes on the Book of Proverbs.* (Neptune, NJ: Loizeaux Bros., 1908), 266.
393 Henry, Matthew. *Matthew Henry's Commentary on the Whole Bible: Complete and Unabridged in One Volume.* (Peabody: Hendrickson, 1994), 1000.
394 Reyburn, W. D. and E. M. Fry. *A Handbook on Proverbs.* (New York: United Bible Societies, 2000), 279.
395 Ross, Allen P. *The Expositor's Bible Commentary.* (Grand Rapids: Zondervan, 1991), 973.
396 Davis, Gregson (ed.). *A Companion to Horace.* (Chichester, West Sussex: Blackwell Publishing, 2010), 255–256.
397 Ibid.
398 Ironside, H. A. *Notes on the Book of Proverbs.* (Neptune, NJ: Loizeaux Bros., 1908), 139–140.
399 Murphy, R. E. *Proverbs* (Vol. 22). (Dallas: Word, Incorporated, 1998), 105.
400 Rice, John R. "All Satan's Apples Have Worms" (sermon).
401 Ironside, H. A. *Notes on the Book of Proverbs.* (Neptune, NJ: Loizeaux Bros., 1908), 163–164.
402 Henry, Matthew. *Matthew Henry's Commentary on the Whole Bible: Complete and Unabridged in One Volume.* (Peabody: Hendrickson, 1994), 985.

[403] Spence-Jones, H. D. M. (Ed.). *Proverbs*. (London; New York: Funk & Wagnalls Company, 1909), 90.

[404] Barclay, W. (Ed.). *The Letter to the Hebrews*. (Philadelphia: The Westminster John Knox Press, 1975), 157.

[405] Ibid.

[406] Ibid., 157–158.

[407] Ibid., 158.

[408] Ross, Allen P. *The Expositor's Bible Commentary*. (Grand Rapids: Zondervan, 1991), 913.

[409] Spence-Jones, H. D. M. (Ed.). *Proverbs*. (London; New York: Funk & Wagnalls Company, 1909), 37.

[410] Henry, Matthew. *Matthew Henry's Commentary on the Whole Bible: Complete and Unabridged in One Volume*. (Peabody: Hendrickson, 1994), 958.

[411] Ross, Allen P. *The Expositor's Bible Commentary*. (Grand Rapids: Zondervan, 1991), 913. (The author added the bracket notations.)

[412] Buzzell, S. S. in J. F. Walvoord and R. B. Zuck (Eds.). *The Bible Knowledge Commentary: An Exposition of the Scriptures* (Vol. 1). (Wheaton, IL: Victor Books, 1985), 910.

[413] Robertson, A. T. *Paul's Joy in Christ: Studies in Philippians*. (Grand Rapids, MI: Baker Book House, 1980), 70.

[414] Spence-Jones, H. D. M. (ed.). *Proverbs*. (London; New York: Funk & Wagnalls Company, 1909), 38.

[415] *The NET Bible First Edition Notes*. (Biblical Studies Press, 2006), Proverbs 2:11.

[416] Spence-Jones, H. D. M. (Ed.). *Proverbs*. (London; New York: Funk & Wagnalls Company, 1909), 38.

[417] Lawson, G. *Exposition of the Book of Proverbs* (Vol. 1). (Edinburgh; Glasgow; London: David Brown; W. Oliphant; F. Pillans; M. Ogle; Ogle, Duncan, and Co.; J. Nisbet, 1821), 38.

[418] Simeon, C. *Horae Homileticae: Proverbs to Isaiah XXVI* (Vol. 7). (London: Holdsworth and Ball, 1833), 38.

[419] Murray, Andrew. *The New Life*. (New York: A.D.F. Randolph & Company, 1891), 216.

[420] https://www.brainyquote.com/topics/discretion, accessed December 5, 2017.

[421] Ironside, H. A. *Notes on the Book of Proverbs*. (Neptune, NJ: Loizeaux Bros., 1908), 235.

[422] Spence-Jones, H. D. M. (Ed.). *Proverbs*. (London; New York: Funk & Wagnalls Company, 1909), 91.

423 Hubbard, D. A. and L. J. Ogilvie. *Proverbs* (Vol. 15). (Nashville, TN: Thomas Nelson Inc.1989), 88.

424 The author was inspired to write from this angle by Steve Brown's secular article, "Overcoming Squirrels & Other Distractions," sharpeningleaders.com accessed January 20, 2018.

425 Spence-Jones, H. D. M. (Ed.). *Proverbs.* (London; New York: Funk & Wagnalls Company, 1909), 92.

426 Reyburn, W. D. and E. M. Fry. *A Handbook on Proverbs.* (New York: United Bible Societies, 2000), 390.

427 Ibid.

428 Ross, Allen P. *The Expositor's Bible Commentary.* (Grand Rapids: Zondervan, 1991), 1027.

429 Ibid.

430 https://www.deseretnews.com/top/2752/0/40-inspiring-quotes-about-education-in-the-classroom-education-in-life.html, accessed October 11, 2017.

431 Kidner, Derek. *The Proverbs: An Introduction and Commentary. Tyndale Old Testament Commentary.* (Downers Grove: InterVarsity, 1964), 129.

432 https://www.deseretnews.com/top/2752/0/40-inspiring-quotes-about-education-in-the-classroom-education-in-life.html, accessed October 11, 2017.

433 https://www.goodreads.com/quotes/177520-what-does-education-often-do-it-makes-a-straight-cut-ditch, accessed October 11, 2017.

434 Reyburn, W. D. and E. M. Fry. *A Handbook on Proverbs.* (New York: United Bible Societies, 2000), 435.

435 Waltke, Bruce K. *The Book of Proverbs* (Vol. 2). (Grand Rapids: William B. Eerdmans Publishing Company, 2004), 166.

436 Spence-Jones, H. D. M. (Ed.). *Proverbs.* (London; New York: Funk & Wagnalls Company, 1909), 335.

437 Ibid.

438 Reyburn, W. D. and E. M. Fry. *A Handbook on Proverbs.* (New York: United Bible Societies, 2000), 377.

439 Bridges, Charles. *A Commentary on Proverbs.* (Carlisle, PA: The Banner of Truth Trust, 2008), 273.

440 Spence-Jones, H. D. M. (Ed.). *Proverbs.* (London; New York: Funk & Wagnalls Company, 1909), 335.

441 Lawson, G. *Exposition of the Book of Proverbs* (Vol. 1). (Edinburgh; Glasgow; London: David Brown; W. Oliphant; F. Pillans; M. Ogle; Ogle, Duncan, and Co.; J. Nisbet, 1821), 421.

442 Walvoord, J. F. and R. B. Zuck. *The Bible Knowledge Commentary: An Exposition of the Scriptures* (Vol. 1). (Wheaton, IL: Victor Books, 1985), 962.

[443] *The NET Bible First Edition Notes.* (Biblical Studies Press, 2006), Proverbs 26:10.

[444] Reyburn, W. D. and E. M. Fry. *A Handbook on Proverbs.* (New York: United Bible Societies, 2000), 562.

[445] Walvoord, J. F. and R. B. Zuck. *The Bible Knowledge Commentary: An Exposition of the Scriptures* (Vol. 1). (Wheaton, IL: Victor Books, 1985), 962.

[446] Reyburn, W. D. and E. M. Fry. *A Handbook on Proverbs.* (New York: United Bible Societies, 2000), 220.

[447] Ibid.

[448] Chambers, Oswald. *My Utmost for His Highest,* April 25 entry.

[449] Walvoord, J. F. and R. B. Zuck. *The Bible Knowledge Commentary: An Exposition of the Scriptures* (Vol. 1). (Wheaton, IL: Victor Books, 1985), 964.

[450] Yates, Kyle M. *Preaching From the Prophets,* 30.

[451] Ironside, H. A. *Notes on the Book of Proverbs.* (Neptune, NJ: Loizeaux Bros., 1908), 383.

[452] Henry, Matthew. *Matthew Henry's Commentary on the Whole Bible: Complete and Unabridged in One Volume.* (Peabody: Hendrickson, 1994), 1016.

[453] Spurgeon, C. H. "The Wandering Bird" (Sermon #3453), Proverbs 27:8.

[454] Ibid.

[455] Reyburn, W. D. and E. M. Fry. *A Handbook on Proverbs.* (New York: United Bible Societies, 2000), 552.

[456] MacArthur, J., Jr. (Ed.). *The MacArthur Study Bible* (electronic ed.). (Nashville, TN: Word Pub., 1997), 913.

[457] Henry, Matthew. *Matthew Henry's Commentary on the Whole Bible: Complete and Unabridged in One Volume.* (Peabody: Hendrickson, 1994), 1012.

[458] Spence-Jones, H. D. M. (Ed.). *Proverbs.* (London; New York: Funk & Wagnalls Company, 1909), 484.

[459] Buzzell, S. S. in J. F. Walvoord and R. B. Zuck (Eds.). *The Bible Knowledge Commentary: An Exposition of the Scriptures* (Vol. 1). (Wheaton, IL: Victor Books, 1985), 916.

[460] Spence-Jones, H. D. M. (Ed.). *Proverbs.* (London; New York: Funk & Wagnalls Company, 1909), 125.

[461] Henry, Matthew. *Matthew Henry's Commentary on the Whole Bible: Complete and Unabridged in One Volume.* (Peabody: Hendrickson, 1994), 966.

[462] Reyburn, W. D. and E. M. Fry. *A Handbook on Proverbs.* (New York: United Bible Societies, 2000), 92.

[463] Henry, Matthew. *Matthew Henry's Commentary on the Whole Bible: Complete and Unabridged in One Volume.* (Peabody: Hendrickson, 1994), 849.

[464] Ibid.

[465] Stalker, J. *The Seven Deadly Sins.* (London: Hodder and Stoughton, 1901), 67.

466 Morgan, R. J. *Nelson's Annual Preacher's Sourcebook* (2002 Edition). (Nashville: Thomas Nelson Publishers, 2001), 232.

467 Chambers, Oswald. *He Shall Glorify Me: Talks on the Holy Spirit and Other Themes.* (Grand Rapids: Discovery House, 1946).

468 Stalker, J. *The Seven Deadly Sins.* (London: Hodder and Stoughton, 1901), 80.

469 Lawson, G. *Exposition of the Book of Proverbs* (Vol. 1). (Edinburgh; Glasgow; London: David Brown; W. Oliphant; F. Pillans; M. Ogle; Ogle, Duncan, and Co.; J. Nisbet, 1821), 308.

470 Spurgeon, C. H. *Faith's Checkbook.* May 6.

471 Murray, Andrew. *Humility* (Chapter 6). http://www.worldinvisible.com/library/murray/ 5f00.0565/5f00.0565.06.htm, accessed August 9, 2017.

472 Bridges, Jerry. *The Pursuit of Holiness.* (Colorado Springs: NavPress, 1996), 120.

473 Spence-Jones, H. D. M. (Ed.). *Proverbs.* (London; New York: Funk & Wagnalls Company, 1909), 425.

474 Murphy, R. E. *Proverbs* (Vol. 22). (Dallas: Word, Incorporated, 1998), 170.

475 Spence-Jones, H. D. M. (Ed.). *Proverbs.* (London; New York: Funk & Wagnalls Company, 1909), 425.

476 Ibid.

477 Google.com, accessed October 29, 2017.

478 Packer J. I. "Situation Ethics." https://www.the-highway.com/articleJan02.html, accessed October 29, 2017.

479 Reyburn, W. D. and E. M. Fry. *A Handbook on Proverbs.* (New York: United Bible Societies, 2000), 543.

480 Spence-Jones, H. D. M. (Ed.). *Proverbs.* (London; New York: Funk & Wagnalls Company, 1909), 479.

481 Ironside, H. A. *Notes on the Book of Proverbs.* (Neptune, NJ: Loizeaux Bros., 1908), 347.

482 *John Trapp Complete Commentary,* Proverbs 14:22.

483 *The NET Bible First Edition Notes.* (Biblical Studies Press, 2006), Proverbs 14:21–22.

484 Buzzell, S. S. in J. F. Walvoord and R. B. Zuck (Eds.). *The Bible Knowledge Commentary: An Exposition of the Scriptures* (Vol. 1). (Wheaton, IL: Victor Books, 1985), 936.

485 Henry, Matthew. *Matthew Henry's Commentary on the Whole Bible: Complete and Unabridged in One Volume.* (Peabody: Hendrickson, 1994), 985.

486 Lawson, G. *Exposition of the Book of Proverbs* (Vol. 1). (Edinburgh; Glasgow; London: David Brown; W. Oliphant; F. Pillans; M. Ogle; Ogle, Duncan, and Co.; J. Nisbet, 1821), 299.

487 Exell, Joseph, Ed. *The Biblical Illustrator: Proverbs.* (Grand Rapids: Baker Book House), Proverbs 14:22.
488 Peter Kreeft. *The Reasons to Believe.* www.catholiceducation.com, accessed March 25, 2011.
489 Olford, Stephen. *Basics for Believers.* (Colorado Springs, CO: Victor, 2003), 13.
490 https://www.brainyquote.com/topics/experience, December 9, 2017.
491 Ibid.
492 Spence-Jones, H. D. M. (Ed.). *Proverbs.* (London; New York: Funk & Wagnalls Company, 1909), 575.
493 Murphy, R. E. *Proverbs* (Vol. 22). (Dallas: Word, Incorporated, 1998), 73.
494 Hubbard, D. A. and L. J. Ogilvie. *Proverbs* (Vol. 15). (Nashville, TN: Thomas Nelson Inc.1989), 477.
495 Spence-Jones, H. D. M. (Ed.). *Proverbs.* (London; New York: Funk & Wagnalls Company, 1909), 575.
496 Bridges, Charles. *A Commentary on Proverbs.* (Carlisle, PA: The Banner of Truth Trust, 2008), 605.
497 Ibid., 606 (paraphrased statement by Bridges).
498 Ironside, H. A. *Notes on the Book of Proverbs.* (Neptune, NJ: Loizeaux Bros., 1908), 448.
499 Henry, Matthew. *Matthew Henry's Commentary on the Whole Bible: Complete and Unabridged in One Volume.* (Peabody: Hendrickson, 1994), 1024.
500 Spence-Jones, H. D. M. (Ed.). *Proverbs.* (London; New York: Funk & Wagnalls Company, 1909), 459.
501 Reyburn, W. D. and E. M. Fry. *A Handbook on Proverbs.* (New York: United Bible Societies, 2000), 519.
502 DeHaan, Richard. https://odb.org/2006/10/20/peace-in-the-storm/, accessed October 30, 2017.
503 Spence-Jones, H. D. M. (Ed.). *Proverbs.* (London; New York: Funk & Wagnalls Company, 1909), 271.
504 Reyburn, W. D. and E. M. Fry. *A Handbook on Proverbs.* (New York: United Bible Societies, 2000), 314.
505 http://nypost.com/2017/10/18/italian-schools-newest-class-detecting-fake-news/, accessed October 31, 2017.
506 http://nypost.com/2017/10/06/fake-news-is-here-forever-study-says/, accessed October 31, 2017.
507 Reyburn, W. D. and E. M. Fry. *A Handbook on Proverbs.* (New York: United Bible Societies, 2000), 403.
508 Spence-Jones, H. D. M. (Ed.). *Proverbs.* (London; New York: Funk & Wagnalls Company, 1909), 367.

[509] Walvoord, J. F. and R. B. Zuck. *The Bible Knowledge Commentary: An Exposition of the Scriptures* (Vol. 1). (Wheaton, IL: Victor Books, 1985), 969.

[510] Spence-Jones, H. D. M. (Ed.). *Proverbs*. (London; New York: Funk & Wagnalls Company, 1909), 557.

[511] Fuller, David Otis (ed.). *Spurgeon's Sermon Notes*. (Grand Rapids: Kregel Publications, 1990), 92.

[512] Spurgeon, C. H. "Two Ancient Proverbs" (Sermon #3080).

[513] Ibid.

[514] Fuller, David Otis (ed.). *Spurgeon's Sermon Notes*. (Grand Rapids: Kregel Publications, 1990), 92.

[515] Murphy, R. E. *Proverbs* (Vol. 22). (Dallas: Word, Incorporated, 1998), 216.

[516] Ross, Allen P. *The Expositor's Bible Commentary*. (Grand Rapids: Zondervan, 1991), 1106.

[517] Bridges, Charles. *A Commentary on Proverbs*. (Carlisle, PA: The Banner of Truth Trust, 2008), 552.

[518] Ross, Allen P. *The Expositor's Bible Commentary*. (Grand Rapids: Zondervan, 1991), 907.

[519] Waltke, Bruce K. *The Book of Proverbs* (Vol. 1). (Grand Rapids: William B. Eerdmans Publishing Company, 2004), 112.

[520] Ibid. (Waltke discusses two words for *fool* which are here included.)

[521] MacArthur, J., Jr. (Ed.). *The MacArthur Study Bible* (electronic ed.). (Nashville, TN: Word Pub., 1997), 877.

[522] Spence-Jones, H. D. M. (Ed.). *Proverbs*. (London; New York: Funk & Wagnalls Company, 1909), 5.

[523] Buzzell, S. S. in J. F. Walvoord and R. B. Zuck (Eds.). *The Bible Knowledge Commentary: An Exposition of the Scriptures* (Vol. 1). (Wheaton, IL: Victor Books, 1985), 907–908.

[524] Spence-Jones, H. D. M. (Ed.). *Proverbs*. (London; New York: Funk & Wagnalls Company, 1909), 514.

[525] http://www.spurgeon.us/mind_and_heart/quotes/f2.htm, accessed October 29, 2017.

[526] Ibid.

[527] Reyburn, W. D. and E. M. Fry. *A Handbook on Proverbs*. (New York: United Bible Societies, 2000), 113.

[528] *The NET Bible First Edition Notes*. (Biblical Studies Press, 2006), Proverbs 4:26.

[529] Alden, Robert L. *Proverbs: A Commentary on an Ancient Book of Timeless Advice*. (Grand Rapids: Baker, 1984), 48.

[530] Murphy, R. E. *Proverbs* (Vol. 22). (Dallas: Word, Incorporated, 1998), 28.

531 Ironside, H. A. *Notes on the Book of Proverbs*. (Neptune, NJ: Loizeaux Bros., 1908), 54.

532 Exell, Joseph, Ed. *The Biblical Illustrator: Proverbs*. (Grand Rapids: Baker Book House), Proverbs 4:26.

533 Spurgeon, C. H. *Sermons That Have Won Souls*, 189–190.

534 Mcduff, John Ross. *Sunsets on the Hebrew Mountains*. (New York: Robert Carter and Brothers, 1862), 201.

535 Murphy, R. E. *Proverbs* (Vol. 22). (Dallas: Word, Incorporated, 1998), 175.

536 *The NET Bible First Edition Notes*. (Biblical Studies Press, 2006), Proverbs 15:21.

537 Reyburn, W. D. and E. M. Fry. *A Handbook on Proverbs*. (New York: United Bible Societies, 2000), 338.

538 Henry, Matthew. *Matthew Henry's Commentary on the Whole Bible: Complete and Unabridged in One Volume*. (Peabody: Hendrickson, 1994), 988.

539 Bridges, Charles. *A Commentary on Proverbs*. (Carlisle, PA: The Banner of Truth Trust, 2008), 212.

540 *The NET Bible First Edition Notes*. (Biblical Studies Press, 2006), Proverbs 10:23.

541 Ibid. Proverbs 10:23.

542 Henry, Matthew. *Matthew Henry's Concise Commentary*. Proverbs 16:27–28.

543 Henry, Matthew. *Matthew Henry's Commentary on the Whole Bible: Complete and Unabridged in One Volume*. (Peabody: Hendrickson, 1994), 976.

544 Ironside, H. A. *Notes on the Book of Proverbs*. (Neptune, NJ: Loizeaux Bros., 1908), 106.

545 Reyburn, W. D. and E. M. Fry. *A Handbook on Proverbs*. (New York: United Bible Societies, 2000), 232.

546 Maclaren, Alexander. *Exposition of Holy Scripture, Proverbs*. (Grand Rapids: Baker Book House, 1977), 181.

547 Ibid., 182–184. The author summarized and adapted Maclaren's three points for brevity and conciseness.

548 Spurgeon, C. H. (T. Carter, Ed.). *2,200 Quotations from the Writings of Charles H. Spurgeon: Arranged Topically or Textually and Indexed by Subject, Scripture, and People*. (Grand Rapids, MI: Baker Books, 1995), 171.

549 Reyburn, W. D. and E. M. Fry. *A Handbook on Proverbs*. (New York: United Bible Societies, 2000), 541.

550 Clarke, Adam. *Clarke's Commentary*, Proverbs 25:2.

551 Poole, Matthew. *Matthew Poole's English Annotations on the Holy Bible*. "Commentary on Proverbs 25:2."

552 Ibid., 265.

[553] Henry, Matthew. *Matthew Henry's Commentary on the Whole Bible: Complete and Unabridged in One Volume.* (Peabody: Hendrickson, 1994), 980.

[554] The song is credited by *The Traditional Ballad Index* to Alfred Henry Ackley (1887–1960). http://www.stephengriffith.com/folksongindex/i-shall-not-be-moved/, accessed February 4, 2018.

[555] Reyburn, W. D. and E. M. Fry. *A Handbook on Proverbs.* (New York: United Bible Societies, 2000), 426.

[556] *The NET Bible First Edition Notes.* (Biblical Studies Press, 2006), Proverbs 20:17.

[557] Ross, Allen P. *The Expositor's Bible Commentary.* (Grand Rapids: Zondervan, 1991), 1045.

[558] Buzzell, S. S. in J. F. Walvoord and R. B. Zuck (Eds.). *The Bible Knowledge Commentary: An Exposition of the Scriptures* (Vol. 1). (Wheaton, IL: Victor Books, 1985), 949.

[559] https://www.brainyquote.com/topics/fraud, accessed November 21, 2017.

[560] Maclaren, *Exposition to the Holy Scripture,* Proverbs 20:17, 237.

[561] Ibid, 239.

[562] https://www.brainyquote.com/topics/fraud, accessed November 21, 2017.

[563] Reyburn, W. D. and E. M. Fry. *A Handbook on Proverbs.* (New York: United Bible Societies, 2000), 514.

[564] Debt Article by Ron Blue. http://www.stewardshipmatters.net/Blog.aspx?acId=139133, accessed September 2, 2017.

[565] Smith, Clay. "Take Action," sermon January 7, 2018. Alice Drive Baptist Church, Sumter, SC.

[566] Ibid.

[567] *The NET Bible First Edition Notes.* (Biblical Studies Press, 2006), Proverbs 19:3.

[568] Ibid.

[569] Ibid.

[570] MacDonald, W. (A. Farstad, Ed.). *Believer's Bible Commentary: Old and New Testaments.* (Nashville: Thomas Nelson, 1995), 840.

[571] Bridges, Charles. *A Commentary on Proverbs.* (Carlisle, PA: The Banner of Truth Trust, 2008), 308.

[572] Henry, Matthew. *Matthew Henry's Commentary on the Whole Bible: Complete and Unabridged in One Volume.* (Peabody: Hendrickson, 1994), 996.

[573] Simeon, C. *Horae Homileticae: Proverbs to Isaiah XXVI* (Vol. 7). (London: Holdsworth and Ball, 1833), 204.

[574] Spence-Jones, H. D. M. (Ed.). *Proverbs.* (London; New York: Funk & Wagnalls Company, 1909), 461.

[575] Grace Quotes. https://gracequotes.org/quote/worry-is-the-sin-of-distrusting-the-promise-and-pr/, accessed January 11, 2018.

[576] Ibid.

[577] www.brainyquote.com/quotes/keywords/anxiety.html, accessed September 4, 2017.

[578] https://www.scrapbook.com/quotes/doc/26631.html, accessed January 11, 2018.

[579] Rogers, Adrian. "Two Days That Will Steal Your Joy" (devotional). http://www.lwf.org, accessed July 25, 2014.

[580] Cowman, L. B. *Streams in the Desert.* (Grand Rapids: Zondervan, 1997), October 7.

[581] Graham, Billy. *The Holy Spirit.* (Nashville: Thomas Nelson, 1978), 255.

[582] Lord, Peter. *The 2959 Plan.* (Titusville, FL).

[583] Reyburn, W. D. and E. M. Fry. *A Handbook on Proverbs.* (New York: United Bible Societies, 2000), 40.

[584] Lawson, George. *Exposition of the Book of Proverbs.* (Edinburgh, 1821), Proverbs 4:14–16.

[585] Reyburn, W. D. and E. M. Fry. *A Handbook on Proverbs.* (New York: United Bible Societies, 2000), 576.

[586] Ibid.

[587] Spence-Jones, H. D. M. (Ed.). *Proverbs.* (London; New York: Funk & Wagnalls Company, 1909), 516.

[588] Gill, John. *Gill's Exposition of the Whole Bible.* Proverbs 27:9.

[589] Bridges, Charles. *A Commentary on Proverbs.* (Carlisle, PA: The Banner of Truth Trust, 2008), 510.

[590] Cicero, *De Amicitia*, XXI. 80. (Adapted).

[591] Thomas, D. W. "Notes on Some Passages in the Book of Proverbs," VT 15 [1965]: 275.

[592] *The NET Bible First Edition Notes.* (Biblical Studies Press, 2006), Proverbs 19:4.

[593] https://www.goodreads.com/quotes/232403-friendship-is-one-of-the-sweetest-joys-of-life-many, accessed October 19, 2017.

[594] Spurgeon, C. H. "The Best Friend" (Proverbs 27:10). Excerpt from the Biblical Museum. http://www.preceptaustin.org/index.php/spurgeon_on_proverbs, accessed February 1, 2018.

[595] Black, Hugo. *Friendship.* (London: Hodder and Stoughton, 1897), 191.

[596] Buzzell, S. S. in J. F. Walvoord and R. B. Zuck (Eds.). *The Bible Knowledge Commentary: An Exposition of the Scriptures* (Vol. 1). (Wheaton, IL: Victor Books, 1985), 945.

[597] Ibid.

[598] Lawson, George. *Exposition of the Book of Proverbs*. (Edinburgh, 1821), Proverbs 11:13.

[599] Spence-Jones, H. D. M. (Ed.). *Proverbs*. (London; New York: Funk & Wagnalls Company, 1909), 359.

[600] Lawson, George. *Exposition of the Book of Proverbs*. (Edinburgh, 1821), Proverbs 18:24.

[601] Spence-Jones, H. D. M. (Ed.). *1 Samuel*. (London; New York: Funk & Wagnalls Company, 1909), 339.

[602] *Matthew Henry's Concise Commentary*, 1 Samuel 18:1–5.

[603] Morgan, G. Campbell. *Searchlights*, 204.

[604] Murphy, R. E. *Proverbs* (Vol. 22). (Dallas: Word, Incorporated, 1998), 82.

[605] Ironside, H. A. *Notes on the Book of Proverbs*. (Neptune, NJ: Loizeaux Bros., 1908), 202.

[606] Bridges, Charles. *A Commentary on Proverbs*. (Carlisle, PA: The Banner of Truth Trust, 2008), 352–353.

[607] Ibid., 117.

[608] Spence-Jones, H. D. M. (Ed.). *Proverbs*. (London; New York: Funk & Wagnalls Company, 1909), 334.

[609] MacDonald, W. (A. Farstad, Ed.). *Believer's Bible Commentary: Old and New Testaments*. (Nashville: Thomas Nelson, 1995), 835.

[610] Keller, Timothy. *God's Wisdom for Navigating Life*. (New York, New York: Viking, 2017), 167.

[611] Chuck Gallozzi. "Saddest Words." www.personal-development.com/chuck/saddest. htm, accessed October 16, 2011.

[612] https://www.goodreads.com/quotes/232963-a-true-friend-unbosoms-freely-advises-justly-assists-readily-adventures, accessed December 8, 2017.

[613] Walvoord, J. F. and R. B. Zuck. *The Bible Knowledge Commentary: An Exposition of the Scriptures* (Vol. 1). (Wheaton, IL: Victor Books, 1985), 961.

[614] Murphy, R. E. *Proverbs* (Vol. 22). (Dallas: Word, Incorporated, 1998), 193.

[615] Henry, Matthew. *Matthew Henry's Commentary on the Whole Bible: Complete and Unabridged in One Volume*. (Peabody: Hendrickson, 1994), 1012.

[616] Ross, Allen P. *The Expositor's Bible Commentary*. (Grand Rapids: Zondervan, 1991), 973.

[617] Ibid.

[618] *The NET Bible First Edition Notes*. (Biblical Studies Press, 2006), Proverbs 27:6.

[619] Reyburn, W. D. and E. M. Fry. *A Handbook on Proverbs*. (New York: United Bible Societies, 2000), 575.

[620] Spence-Jones, H. D. M. (Ed.). *Proverbs*. (London; New York: Funk & Wagnalls Company, 1909), 515.

[621] Pearson, C. Ridley. *Counsels of the Wise King or Proverbs of Solomon Applied to Daily Life,* Vol. 2. (London: W. Skeffington & Son, 1881), 152.

[622] Ibid.

[623] Ironside, H. A. *Notes on the Book of Proverbs.* (Neptune, NJ: Loizeaux Bros., 1908), 382.

[624] Criswell, W. A. *The Criswell Study Bible.* (Nashville: Thomas Nelson Publishing Company, 1979), Proverbs 27:5–6.

[625] Ibid.

[626] Bridges, Charles. *A Commentary on Proverbs.* (Carlisle, PA: The Banner of Truth Trust, 2008), 505.

[627] Spence-Jones, H. D. M. (Ed.). *Proverbs.* (London; New York: Funk & Wagnalls Company, 1909), 252.

[628] MacArthur, John. "Gambling: The Seductive Fantasy," Part I. (GC 90-164), www.biblebb.com/files/MAC/90-164.HTM, accessed March 5, 2011. [This sermon depicts the biblical reasons why gambling is a sin.]

[629] http://lifeofgoodnews.blogspot.com/2011/07/truth-about-gambling-from-adrian-rogers.html, accessed November 18, 2017.

[630] https://thedailyhatch.org/2013/07/18/adrian-rogers-on-gambling/, accessed November 18, 2017.

[631] Harvard Medical School Division on Addictions, cited in *The Oklahoma Association of Gambling Awareness.* www.oagaa.org/html/statistics.htm, accessed March 5, 2011.

[632] Stinchfield, R. *Problem and Pathological Gambling Among College Students.* (www.edst.purdue.edu/faculty.../GamblingChapterStinchHanOls.pdf), 64.

[633] "Teen Gambling." Teenhelp.com. (www.teenhelp.com), accessed March 5, 2011.

[634] Stinchfield, R. *Problem and Pathological Gambling Among College Students.* (www.edst.purdue.edu/faculty.../GamblingChapterStinchHanOls.pdf), 64.

[635] Keller, Timothy. *God's Wisdom for Navigating Life.* (New York, New York: Viking, 2017), 301.

[636] https://www.brainyquote.com/topics/gambling, accessed November 18, 2017.

[637] *The NET Bible First Edition Notes.* (Biblical Studies Press, 2006), Proverbs 11:25.

[638] MacDonald, W. (A. Farstad, Ed.). *Believer's Bible Commentary: Old and New Testaments.* (Nashville: Thomas Nelson, 1995), 2 Corinthians 8:9.

[639] MacArthur, John. 2 Corinthians 8:9.

[640] Wilson, Catherine. "Raising a Cheerful Giver: Teaching Children to Give Generously." http://www.focusonthefamily.ca/parenting/school-age/raising-a-cheerful-giver-teaching-children-to-give-generously, accessed August 4, 2017.

[641] Ibid.

[642] Maclaren, Alexander. *Exposition of Holy Scripture, Proverbs.* (Grand Rapids: Baker Book House, 1977), 175. (The paragraph is an adaptation from Maclaren.)

[643] Ibid. (The author paraphrased Maclaren.)

[644] Reyburn, W. D. and E. M. Fry. *A Handbook on Proverbs.* (New York: United Bible Societies, 2000), 370.

[645] Ross, Allen P. *The Expositor's Bible Commentary.* (Grand Rapids: Zondervan, 1991), 1016.

[646] Spence-Jones, H. D. M. (Ed.). *Proverbs.* (London; New York: Funk & Wagnalls Company, 1909), 332.

[647] Spence-Jones, H. D. M. (Ed.). *The Pulpit Commentary.* (London; New York: Funk & Wagnalls Company, 1909), Proverbs, 332.

[648] Ironside, H. A. *Notes on the Book of Proverbs.* (Neptune, NJ: Loizeaux Bros., 1908), 210.

[649] Ibid.

[650] Spence-Jones, H. D. M. (Ed.). *Proverbs.* (London; New York: Funk & Wagnalls Company, 1909), 351.

[651] Ibid.

[652] Reyburn, W. D. and E. M. Fry. *A Handbook on Proverbs.* (New York: United Bible Societies, 2000), 390.

[653] Spurgeon, Charles. "Good News" (sermon #2866). Proverbs 25:25.

[654] MacArthur, J., Jr. (Ed.). *The MacArthur Study Bible* (electronic ed.). (Nashville, TN: Word Pub., 1997), 911.

[655] Gill, John. *Gill's Exposition of the Whole Bible.* Proverbs 24:17.

[656] Spence-Jones, H. D. M. (Ed.). *The Pulpit Commentary.* (London; New York: Funk & Wagnalls Company, 1909), Proverbs, 332.

[657] Willard, C. R. In H. F. Paschall and H. H. Hobbs (Eds.), *The Teacher's Bible Commentary.* (Nashville: Broadman and Holman Publishers, 1972), Proverbs, 371.

[658] Hubbard, D. A. and L. J. Ogilvie. *Proverbs* (Vol. 15). (Nashville, TN: Thomas Nelson Inc. 1989), 366.

[659] Buzzell, S. S. in J. F. Walvoord and R. B. Zuck (Eds.). *The Bible Knowledge Commentary: An Exposition of the Scriptures* (Vol. 1). (Wheaton, IL: Victor Books, 1985), 956.

[660] Ibid.

[661] Yates, Kyle M. *Preaching From the Prophets,* 160.

[662] Spence-Jones, H. D. M. (Ed.). *Proverbs.* (London; New York: Funk & Wagnalls Company, 1909), 321.

[663] Spurgeon, C. H. *Morning and Evening,* December 19 (morning).

664 Reyburn, W. D. and E. M. Fry. *A Handbook on Proverbs*. (New York: United Bible Societies, 2000), 355.

665 https://www.christianquotes.info/quotes-by-topic/quotes-about-godliness/#ixzz4xOwE5rfL, accessed October 30, 2017.

666 Reyburn, W. D. and E. M. Fry. *A Handbook on Proverbs*. (New York: United Bible Societies, 2000), 258.

667 Ibid.

668 Ibid.

669 www.brainyquote.com/quotes/keywords/doing_good.html, accessed October 25, 2017.

670 Swindoll, Chuck. *Job: A Man of Heroic Endurance*. (Nashville: WPublishing Group, 2004), 180.

671 https://www.christianquotes.info/quotes-by-topic/quotes-about-gossip/#ixzz4zegLcOMN, accessed November 27, 2017.

672 Bridges, Charles. *A Commentary on Proverbs*. (Carlisle, PA: The Banner of Truth Trust, 2008), 573.

673 Garrett, D. A. *Proverbs, Ecclesiastes, Song of Songs* (Vol. 14). (Nashville: Broadman & Holman Publishers, 1993), 231.

674 Ross, Allen P. *The Expositor's Bible Commentary*. (Grand Rapids: Zondervan, 1991), 1115.

675 Henry, Matthew. *Matthew Henry's Commentary on the Whole Bible: Complete and Unabridged in One Volume*. (Peabody: Hendrickson, 1994), 1021.

676 Reyburn, W. D. and E. M. Fry. *A Handbook on Proverbs*. (New York: United Bible Societies, 2000), 419.

677 Buzzell, S. S. in J. F. Walvoord and R. B. Zuck (Eds.). *The Bible Knowledge Commentary: An Exposition of the Scriptures* (Vol. 1). (Wheaton, IL: Victor Books, 1985), 948.

678 Henry, Matthew. *Matthew Henry's Commentary on the Whole Bible: Complete and Unabridged in One Volume*. (Peabody: Hendrickson, 1994), 999.

679 Reyburn, W. D. and E. M. Fry. *A Handbook on Proverbs*. (New York: United Bible Societies, 2000), 368–369.

680 Collins, Gary. *Family Shock,* 27.

681 Ibid.

682 Anderson, Jeff. "10 Best Things About Growing Old," posted 20 Sep 2016. http://www. aplaceformom.com/blog/best-things-about-growing-old-9-4-13, accessed March 11, 2017.

683 Rivers, Charles (Ed.). *American Legends: The Life of Billy Graham*. (CreateSpace Independent Publishing Platform, 2015), Introduction.

684 Myers, David. *The Pursuit of Happiness,* 44.

[685] Buzzell, S. S. in J. F. Walvoord and R. B. Zuck (Eds.). *The Bible Knowledge Commentary: An Exposition of the Scriptures* (Vol. 1). (Wheaton, IL: Victor Books, 1985), 938.

[686] Ironside, H. A. *Notes on the Book of Proverbs*. (Neptune, NJ: Loizeaux Bros., 1908), 181.

[687] Dobson, James. "Helping Children Deal With Death." http://drjamesdobson.org/blogs/ dr-dobson-blog/dr-dobson-blog/2015/12/18/helping-children-deal-with-death, accessed February 28, 2016

[688] Ibid.

[689] Malphurs, Aubrey and Keith Willhite. *A Contemporary Handbook for Weddings and Funerals and Other Occasions*. (Grand Rapids, Michigan: Kregal Publications, 2006), 238. (adapted)

[690] Reyburn, W. D. and E. M. Fry. *A Handbook on Proverbs*. (New York: United Bible Societies, 2000), 225.

[691] Ibid., 226.

[692] MacDonald, W. (A. Farstad, Ed.). *Believer's Bible Commentary: Old and New Testaments*. (Nashville: Thomas Nelson, 1995), 815.

[693] MacArthur, John. "Answering the Hard Questions About Forgiveness." http://www. gty.org, accessed July 30, 2014.

[694] Adams, Jay. *From Forgiven to Forgiving*. (Amityville, NY: Calvary, 1994), 25.

[695] http://www.brainyquote.com/quotes/authors/l/lewis_b_smedes. html#QsYP5fSelHoXbSF5.99, accessed July 24, 2014.

[696] Rogers, Adrian. "Haunted by The Ghost Of Guilt," (Bible Study: October 1, 2014). https://www.lwf.org/bible-study/posts/haunted-by-the-ghost-of-guilt-13335, accessed December 1, 2017.

[697] Tozer A. W., *I Talk Back to the Devil,* 12–13.

[698] Henry, Matthew. *Matthew Henry's Commentary on the Whole Bible: Complete and Unabridged in One Volume*. (Peabody: Hendrickson, 1994), 990.

[699] Spence-Jones, H. D. M. (Ed.). *Proverbs*. (London; New York: Funk & Wagnalls Company, 1909), 271.

[700] Waltke, Bruce K. *The Book of Proverbs* (Vol. 1). (Grand Rapids: William B. Eerdmans Publishing Company, 2004), 111.

[701] Murphy, R. E. *Proverbs* (Vol. 22). (Dallas: Word, Incorporated, 1998), 105.

[702] Lawson, G. *Exposition of the Book of Proverbs* (Vol. 1). (Edinburgh; Glasgow; London: David Brown; W. Oliphant; F. Pillans; M. Ogle; Ogle, Duncan, and Co.; J. Nisbet, 1821), 291–292.

[703] Murphy, R. E. *Proverbs* (Vol. 22). (Dallas: Word, Incorporated, 1998), 105.

[704] Ibid., 22.

[705] Lewis, C. S. The Case for Christianity, 43.

[706] Reyburn, W. D. and E. M. Fry. *A Handbook on Proverbs.* (New York: United Bible Societies, 2000), 335.

[707] Ibid.

[708] Murphy, R. E. *Proverbs* (Vol. 22). (Dallas: Word, Incorporated, 1998), 113.

[709] http://www.insight.org/resources/daily-devotional/individual/the-value-of-a-positive-attitude, accessed November 27, 2017.

[710] Cowman, L. B. *Streams in the Desert.* (Grand Rapids: Zondervan, 1997), October 4.

[711] https://www.brainyquote.com/topics/husband, accessed November 26, 2017.

[712] Unknown.

[713] *The NET Bible First Edition Notes.* (Biblical Studies Press, 2006), Proverbs 21:5.

[714] *The NET Bible First Edition Notes.* (Biblical Studies Press, 2006), Proverbs 21:5.

[715] Hogan, Meghan. "The Dangers of Impulsive Decision Making, http://www.goodchoices goodlife.org/choices-for-real-life-real-living/the-dangers-of-impulsive-decision-making/, accessed October 24, 2017.

[716] Henry, Matthew. *Matthew Henry's Commentary on the Whole Bible: Complete and Unabridged in One Volume.* (Peabody: Hendrickson, 1994), 967.

[717] Ironside, H. A. *Notes on the Book of Proverbs.* (Neptune, NJ: Loizeaux Bros., 1908), 67.

[718] McGee, J. V. *Thru the Bible Commentary: Poetry (Proverbs).* (electronic ed., Vol. 20). (Nashville: Thomas Nelson, 1997), 69.

[719] Dixon, Francis. "Seven Things God Hates." (Bournemouth, England: Lansdowne Bible School and Postal Fellowship, October 29, 1974).

[720] Ibid.

[721] Ross, Allen P. *The Expositor's Bible Commentary.* (Grand Rapids: Zondervan, 1991), 935.

[722] Reyburn, W. D. and E. M. Fry. *A Handbook on Proverbs.* (New York: United Bible Societies, 2000), 381–382.

[723] Ross, Allen P. *The Expositor's Bible Commentary.* (Grand Rapids: Zondervan, 1991), 1022.

[724] Ironside, H. A. *Notes on the Book of Proverbs.* (Neptune, NJ: Loizeaux Bros., 1908), 227. (Note: The author essentially summarized Ironside's commentary on the text since it was impossible to improve on.)

[725] Ibid.

[726] Reyburn, W. D. and E. M. Fry. *A Handbook on Proverbs.* (New York: United Bible Societies, 2000), 75.

[727] Criswell, W. A., P. Patterson, E. R. Clendenen, D. L. Akin, M. Chamberlin, D. K. Patterson, & J. Pogue, (Eds.). *Believer's Study Bible* (electronic ed.). (Nashville: Thomas Nelson, 1991), Proverbs 3:2.

[728] MacDonald, W. (A. Farstad, Ed.). *Believer's Bible Commentary: Old and New Testaments.* (Nashville: Thomas Nelson, 1995), 798.

[729] Reyburn, W. D. and E. M. Fry. *A Handbook on Proverbs.* (New York: United Bible Societies, 2000), 504.

[730] Ironside, H. A. *Notes on the Book of Proverbs.* (Neptune, NJ: Loizeaux Bros., 1908), 326–327.

[731] Spurgeon, C. H. "Wisdom's Request to Her Son" (Proverbs 23:26). http://www. preceptaustin.org/index.php/spurgeon_on_proverbs, accessed February 1, 2018.

[732] https://www.brainyquote.com/quotes/martin_luther_king_jr_101472, accessed January 13, 2018.

[733] Reyburn, W. D. and E. M. Fry. *A Handbook on Proverbs.* (New York: United Bible Societies, 2000), 347.

[734] Spurgeon Sermon Notes on Proverbs, "Pondering Hearts" (Proverbs 21:2). http://www. preceptaustin.org/spurgeon_on_proverbs, accessed January 12, 2018.

[735] *The NET Bible First Edition Notes.* (Biblical Studies Press, 2006), Proverbs 21:17.

[736] MacArthur, J., Jr. (Ed.). *The MacArthur Study Bible* (electronic ed.). (Nashville, TN: Word Pub., 1997), 907.

[737] Ibid.

[738] Spence-Jones, H. D. M. (Ed.). *Proverbs.* (London; New York: Funk & Wagnalls Company, 1909), 461.

[739] Buzzell, S. S. in J. F. Walvoord and R. B. Zuck (Eds.). *The Bible Knowledge Commentary: An Exposition of the Scriptures* (Vol. 1). (Wheaton, IL: Victor Books, 1985), 959.

[740] Spence-Jones, H. D. M. (Ed.). *Proverbs.* (London; New York: Funk & Wagnalls Company, 1909), 88.

[741] Spurgeon, C. H. "The Holdfast" (sermon N0. 418), June 9, 1878. http://www.biblebb. com/files/spurgeon/1418.htm, accessed December 6, 2017.

[742] Ross, Allen P. *The Expositor's Bible Commentary.* (Grand Rapids: Zondervan, 1991), 976.

[743] Lawson, G. *Exposition of the Book of Proverbs* (Vol. 1). (Edinburgh; Glasgow; London: David Brown; W. Oliphant; F. Pillans; M. Ogle; Ogle, Duncan, and Co.; J. Nisbet, 1821), 259.

[744] Maclaren, Alexander. *Exposition of Holy Scripture, Proverbs.* (Grand Rapids: Baker Book House, 1977), 170.

[745] Henry, Matthew. *Matthew Henry's Commentary on the Whole Bible: Complete and Unabridged in One Volume.* (Peabody: Hendrickson, 1994), 982.

[746] http://ministry127.com/resources/illustration/skipping-school, accessed August 22, 2017.

[747] www.brainyquote.com/quotes/quotes/n/nathanielh120248.html?src=t_honesty, accessed August 22, 2017.

[748] Ibid., 977.

[749] https://www.moodymedia.org/articles/i-worked-cobbler/, accessed January 21, 2018 [author paraphrased and adapted].

[750] Jamieson, Robert, A. R. Fausset, & David Brown. *Commentary Critical and Explanatory on the Whole Bible,* (Vol. 1). (Oak Harbor, WA: Logos Research Systems, Inc., 1997), 396.

[751] Reyburn, W. D. and E. M. Fry. *A Handbook on Proverbs.* (New York: United Bible Societies, 2000), 323.

[752] Curtis Hutson, Ed., *Great Preaching on Heaven.* (Murfreesboro, TN: Sword of the Lord Publishers, 1987), 15.

[753] https://www.christianquotes.info/top-quotes/14-inspiring-quotes-about-heaven/ #ixzz51YBkAmjf, accessed December 17, 2017.

[754] Henry, Matthew. *Matthew Henry's Commentary on the Whole Bible: Complete and Unabridged in One Volume.* (Peabody: Hendrickson, 1994), 986.

[755] https://www.christianquotes.info/top-quotes/14-inspiring-quotes-about-heaven/#ixzz51YCaEkKP, accessed December 17, 2017.

[756] MacDonald, W. (A. Farstad, Ed.). *Believer's Bible Commentary: Old and New Testaments.* (Nashville: Thomas Nelson, 1995), 827–828.

[757] The Hemphills, "He's Still Working on Me" (song). Released 1980.

[758] Spence-Jones, H. D. M. (Ed.). *Proverbs.* (London; New York: Funk & Wagnalls Company, 1909), 458.

[759] Carroll, B. H. *Old Testament Teaching,* 167.

[760] Reyburn, W. D. and E. M. Fry. *A Handbook on Proverbs.* (New York: United Bible Societies, 2000), 201.

[761] Henry, Matthew. *Matthew Henry's Commentary on the Whole Bible: Complete and Unabridged in One Volume.* (Peabody: Hendrickson, 1994), 973.

[762] Spence-Jones, H. D. M. (Ed.). *Proverbs.* (London; New York: Funk & Wagnalls Company, 1909), 181.

[763] MacDonald, W. (A. Farstad, Ed.). *Believer's Bible Commentary: Old and New Testaments.* (Nashville: Thomas Nelson, 1995), 812.

[764] Henry, Matthew. *Matthew Henry's Commentary on the Whole Bible: Complete and Unabridged in One Volume.* (Peabody: Hendrickson, 1994), 987.

[765] Spence-Jones, H. D. M. (Ed.). *Proverbs.* (London; New York: Funk & Wagnalls Company, 1909), 270.

[766] Ironside, H. A. *Notes on the Book of Proverbs.* (Neptune, NJ: Loizeaux Bros., 1908), 163.

[767] Gill, John. *Gill's Exposition of the Whole Bible.* Proverbs 14:11.

[768] Reyburn, W. D. and E. M. Fry. *A Handbook on Proverbs.* (New York: United Bible Societies, 2000), 388.

[769] Murray, Andrew. *Humility: The Beauty of Holiness.* (Aneko Christian Classics), chapter 8.

[770] B. E. B. *Holy Meditations for Every Day.* (London: Frederick Warne & Co., 1867), 15.

[771] Ibid., 114.

[772] Murray, Andrew. *Humility: The Beauty of Holiness.* (Aneko Christian Classics), chapter 2.

[773] Rogers, Adrian. "A Word for Wives." https://www.oneplace.com/ministries/love-worth-finding/read/articles/a-word-for-wives-8720.html, accessed January 22, 2018.

[774] Henry, Matthew. *Matthew Henry's Commentary on the Whole Bible: Complete and Unabridged in One Volume.* (Peabody: Hendrickson, 1994), 999.

[775] Spurgeon, C. H. "Do Not Sin Against the Child." (Sermon delivered November 8, 1868). Genesis 42:22.

[776] Bridges, Charles. *A Commentary on Proverbs.* (Carlisle, PA: The Banner of Truth Trust, 2008), 340.

[777] Ross, Allen P. *The Expositor's Bible Commentary.* (Grand Rapids: Zondervan, 1991), 1090.

[778] Spence-Jones, H. D. M. (Ed.). *Proverbs.* (London; New York: Funk & Wagnalls Company, 1909), 215.

[779] Ibid.

[780] Henry, Matthew. *Matthew Henry's Commentary on the Whole Bible: Complete and Unabridged in One Volume.* (Peabody: Hendrickson, 1994), 977.

[781] Reyburn, W. D. and E. M. Fry. *A Handbook on Proverbs.* (New York: United Bible Societies, 2000), 90.

[782] Lawson, G. *Exposition of the Book of Proverbs* (Vol. 1). (Edinburgh; Glasgow; London: David Brown; W. Oliphant; F. Pillans; M. Ogle; Ogle, Duncan, and Co.; J. Nisbet, 1821), 198–199.

[783] Waltke, Bruce K. *The Book of Proverbs* (Vol. 1). (Grand Rapids: William B. Eerdmans Publishing Company, 2004), 545.

[784] Maclaren, *Exposition to the Holy Scriptures,* Proverbs 23:17-18, 249.

[785] Ironside, H. A. *Notes on the Book of Proverbs.* (Neptune, NJ: Loizeaux Bros., 1908), 323.

[786] Ibid., 248.

[787] Spence-Jones, H. D. M. (Ed.). *Proverbs.* (London; New York: Funk & Wagnalls Company, 1909), 443.

[788] Lawson, G. *Exposition of the Book of Proverbs* (Vol. 1). (Edinburgh; Glasgow; London: David Brown; W. Oliphant; F. Pillans; M. Ogle; Ogle, Duncan, and Co.; J. Nisbet, 1821), 254.

[789] http://christian-quotes.ochristian.com/Death-Quotes, accessed March 26, 2013.

[790] Reyburn, W. D. and E. M. Fry. *A Handbook on Proverbs.* (New York: United Bible Societies, 2000), 520.

[791] Ibid.

[792] Maclaren, Alexander. *Exposition of Holy Scripture, Proverbs.* (Grand Rapids: Baker Book House, 1977), 264.

[793] Ibid., 265.

[794] Ibid., 266.

[795] Scarborough, L. R. "Lost!" *The Sword of the Lord,* April 13, 1973, 1.

[796] Maclaren, Alexander. *Exposition of Holy Scripture, Proverbs.* (Grand Rapids: Baker Book House, 1977), 268–269.

[797] *The NET Bible First Edition Notes.* (Biblical Studies Press, 2006), Proverbs 8:20–21.

[798] Henry, Matthew. *Matthew Henry's Commentary on the Whole Bible: Complete and Unabridged in One Volume.* (Peabody: Hendrickson, 1994), 971.

[799] Gill, John. *The New John Gill Exposition of the Entire Bible.* Proverbs 8:21.

[800] Exell, Joseph, Ed. *The Biblical Illustrator: Proverbs.* (Grand Rapids: Baker Book House), Proverbs 8:21.

[801] Maclaren, Alexander. *Exposition of Holy Scripture, Proverbs.* (Grand Rapids: Baker Book House, 1977), Proverbs 8:21.

[802] Reyburn, W. D. and E. M. Fry. *A Handbook on Proverbs.* (New York: United Bible Societies, 2000), 343.

[803] Spence-Jones, H. D. M. (Ed.). *Proverbs.* (London; New York: Funk & Wagnalls Company, 1909), 296.

[804] Bridges, Charles. *A Commentary on Proverbs.* (Carlisle, PA: The Banner of Truth Trust, 2008), 446.

[805] Ironside, H. A. *Notes on the Book of Proverbs.* (Neptune, NJ: Loizeaux Bros., 1908), 452–453.

[806] *The NET Bible First Edition Notes.* (Biblical Studies Press, 2006), Proverbs 19:27.

[807] Ironside, H. A. *Notes on the Book of Proverbs.* (Neptune, NJ: Loizeaux Bros., 1908), 256.

[808] Waltke, Bruce K. *The Book of Proverbs* (Vol. 2). (Grand Rapids: William B. Eerdmans Publishing Company, 2004), 36.

[809] Spence-Jones, H. D. M. (Ed.). *Proverbs*. (London; New York: Funk & Wagnalls Company, 1909), 371.

[810] *The NET Bible First Edition Notes*. (Biblical Studies Press, 2006), Proverbs 12:16.

[811] Warren, Rick. "6 Biblical Ways to Handle Disunity." (January 13, 2012), http://pastors.com/6-biblical-ways-to-handle-disunity/2/, accessed October 3, 2014.

[812] Swindoll, Chuck. *Paul: A Man of Grace and Grit*. (Nashville: Word Publishing, 2002), 173.

[813] Henry, Matthew. *Matthew Henry's Commentary on the Whole Bible: Complete and Unabridged in One Volume*. (Peabody: Hendrickson, 1994), 981.

[814] Murphy, R. E. *Proverbs* (Vol. 22). (Dallas: Word, Incorporated, 1998), 91.

[815] Ibid., 385

[816] Reyburn, W. D. and E. M. Fry. *A Handbook on Proverbs*. (New York: United Bible Societies, 2000), 157.

[817] Insight for Today, August 5, 2017. www.insight.org/resources/daily-devotional/individual/jealousy, accessed September 4, 2017.

[818] Ibid.

[819] https://www.christianquotes.info/quotes-by-topic/quotes-about-jealousy/#ixzz5462HfEIN, accessed January 13, 2018.

[820] Henry, Matthew. *Matthew Henry's Commentary on the Whole Bible: Complete and Unabridged in One Volume*. (Peabody: Hendrickson, 1994), 984.

[821] Ironside, H. A. *Notes on the Book of Proverbs*. (Neptune, NJ: Loizeaux Bros., 1908), 155.

[822] Jennings, C. F. *Studies in Isaiah*. (Eugene, Oregon: Wipf & Stock, 1966), 645.

[823] Henry, Matthew. *Matthew Henry's Commentary on the Whole Bible: Complete and Unabridged in One Volume*. (Peabody: Hendrickson, 1994), 984.

[824] Stevens, Marsha. lyrics.christiansunite.com, accessed April 19, 2013.

[825] Spurgeon, C. H. *Morning and Evening*, May 18,

[826] Spence-Jones, H. D. M. (Ed.). *Proverbs*. (London; New York: Funk & Wagnalls Company, 1909), 502.

[827] Ibid.

[828] Ironside, H. A. *Notes on the Book of Proverbs*. (Neptune, NJ: Loizeaux Bros., 1908), 372.

[829] *The NET Bible First Edition Notes*. (Biblical Studies Press, 2006), Proverbs 12:25.

[830] Reyburn, W. D. and E. M. Fry. *A Handbook on Proverbs*. (New York: United Bible Societies, 2000), 280.

831 *The NET Bible First Edition Notes.* (Biblical Studies Press, 2006), Proverbs 12:25.

832 https://www.brainyquote.com/quotes/quotes/m/mothertere133195.html, accessed September 3, 2017.

833 Reyburn, W. D. and E. M. Fry. *A Handbook on Proverbs.* (New York: United Bible Societies, 2000), 242.

834 Lawson, George. *Exposition of the Book of Proverbs.* (Edinburgh, 1821), Proverbs 16:12.

835 Henry, Matthew. *Matthew Henry's Commentary on the Whole Bible: Complete and Unabridged in One Volume.* (Peabody: Hendrickson, 1994), Proverbs 16:12.

836 Buzzell, S. S. in J. F. Walvoord and R. B. Zuck (Eds.). *The Bible Knowledge Commentary: An Exposition of the Scriptures* (Vol. 1). (Wheaton, IL: Victor Books, 1985), 932.

837 Reyburn, W. D. and E. M. Fry. *A Handbook on Proverbs.* (New York: United Bible Societies, 2000), 279.

838 Henry, Matthew. *Matthew Henry's Commentary on the Whole Bible: Complete and Unabridged in One Volume.* (Peabody: Hendrickson, 1994), 981.

839 Reyburn, W. D. and E. M. Fry. *A Handbook on Proverbs.* (New York: United Bible Societies, 2000), 359.

840 Ibid.

841 Ross, Allen P. *The Expositor's Bible Commentary.* (Grand Rapids: Zondervan, 1991), 1009.

842 Murphy, R. E. *Proverbs* (Vol. 22). (Dallas: Word, Incorporated, 1998), 123.

843 Bridges, Charles. *A Commentary on Proverbs.* (Carlisle, PA: The Banner of Truth Trust, 2008), 242.

844 Ibid.

845 Reyburn, W. D. and E. M. Fry. *A Handbook on Proverbs.* (New York: United Bible Societies, 2000), 331.

846 Henry, Matthew. *Matthew Henry's Commentary on the Whole Bible: Complete and Unabridged in One Volume.* (Peabody: Hendrickson, 1994), 987.

847 Hartford, Charles F. *The Keswick Convention,* 158. https://books.google.com, accessed February 28, 2015.

848 Buzzell, S. S. in J. F. Walvoord and R. B. Zuck (Eds.). *The Bible Knowledge Commentary: An Exposition of the Scriptures* (Vol. 1). (Wheaton, IL: Victor Books, 1985), 932.

849 Ibid.

850 Spence-Jones, H. D. M. (Ed.). *Proverbs.* (London; New York: Funk & Wagnalls Company, 1909), 237.

851 Ibid.

852 Spurgeon, C. H. *Faith's Checkbook*. (New Kensington, Pennsylvania: Whitaker House, 2002), November 23 entry.

853 Ironside, H. A. *Notes on the Book of Proverbs*. (Neptune, NJ: Loizeaux Bros., 1908), 315.

854 Maclaren, Alexander. *Exposition of Holy Scripture, Proverbs*. (Grand Rapids: Baker Book House, 1977), 189.

855 www.christianquotes.info/quotes-by-topic/quotes-about-work/#ixzz4oXbe5MrI, accessed August 1, 2017.

856 https://www.brainyquote.com/authors/john_c_maxwell, accessed October 30, 2017.

857 Carroll, B. H. *Old Testament Teaching,* 150.

858 Murphy, R. E. *Proverbs* (Vol. 22). (Dallas: Word, Incorporated, 1998), 4.

859 Reyburn, W. D. and E. M. Fry. *A Handbook on Proverbs*. (New York: United Bible Societies, 2000), 27.

860 Ross, Allen P. *The Expositor's Bible Commentary*. (Grand Rapids: Zondervan, 1991), 1060.

861 Ibid.

862 Reyburn, W. D. and E. M. Fry. *A Handbook on Proverbs*. (New York: United Bible Societies, 2000), 381–382.

863 Warden, Michael. "The Transformed Heart" (Lulu.com, 2008), 80.

864 https://www.brainyquote.com/quotes/keywords/solitude.html, accessed February 18, 2017.

865 Rogers, Adrian. "God's Answer to Loneliness," http://www.oneplace.com/ministries/ love-worth-finding/read/articles/gods-answer-to-loneliness-9028.html, accessed February 18, 2017.

866 Dobson, James C. "Life on the Edge: The Next Generation's Guide to a Meaningful Future." https://www.goodreads.com/quotes/7951819-29-most-loneliness-results-from-insulation-rather-than-isolation-in, accessed February 17, 2017.

867 Bratcher, R. G. and W. D. Reyburn. *A Translator's Handbook on the Book of Psalms*. (New York: United Bible Societies, 1991), 863.

868 Spence-Jones, H. D. M. (Ed.). *The Pulpit Commentary*. (London; New York: Funk & Wagnalls Company, 1909), Psalm 102:6–7.

869 https://www.brainyquote.com/quotes/quotes/l/lordbyron150314.html, accessed February 25, 2017.

870 http://www.oneplace.com/ministries/love-worth-finding/read/articles/gods-answer-to-loneliness-9028.html, accessed February 18, 2017.

871 "Why Did Jesus Cry, 'My God, My God, Why Have You Forsaken Me?,'"
https://www.gty.org/library/print/bible-qna/BQ032913, accessed February 18, 2017.

872 Reyburn, W. D. and E. M. Fry. *A Handbook on Proverbs*. (New York: United Bible Societies, 2000), 225.

873 Bridges, Charles. *A Commentary on Proverbs*. (Carlisle, PA: The Banner of Truth Trust, 2008), 97.

874 Henry, Matthew. *Matthew Henry's Commentary on the Whole Bible: Complete and Unabridged in One Volume*. (Peabody: Hendrickson, 1994), 975.

875 https://www.goodreads.com/quotes/137205-though-our-feelings-come-and-go-god-s-love-for-us, accessed January 24, 2018.

876 Murphy, R. E. *Proverbs* (Vol. 22). (Dallas: Word, Incorporated, 1998), 51.

877 Ironside, H. A. *Notes on the Book of Proverbs*. (Neptune, NJ: Loizeaux Bros., 1908), 81.

878 Newheiser, J. *Opening Up Proverbs*. (Leominster: Day One Publications, 2008), 90.

879 Fuller, Thomas. cited by Lust Quotes, christian-quotes.ochristian.com, accessed November 17, 2011.

880 Reyburn, W. D. and E. M. Fry. *A Handbook on Proverbs*. (New York: United Bible Societies, 2000), 278.

881 Ironside, H. A. *Notes on the Book of Proverbs*. (Neptune, NJ: Loizeaux Bros., 1908), 138–139.

882 Ibid.

883 "The Six Types of Dishonesty." honestyexperiment.wordpress.com /2013/06/25/types-of-dishonesty, accessed August 22, 2017.

884 Ibid.

885 Wiersbe, W. W. *Wiersbe's Expository Outlines on the Old Testament*. (Wheaton, IL: Victor Books, 1993), Proverbs 12:17–22.

886 Ibid.

887 Ironside, H. A. *Notes on the Book of Proverbs*. (Neptune, NJ: Loizeaux Bros., 1908), 138.

888 Spence-Jones, H. D. M. (Ed.). *Proverbs*. (London; New York: Funk & Wagnalls Company, 1909), 237.

889 "Teaching Children the Virtues of the Truth." http://www.washingtontimes.com/news/ 2015/feb/9/family-talk-teach-children-virtues-truth/, accessed August 1, 2017.

890 McGee, J. V. *Thru the Bible Commentary* (electronic ed., Vol. 3). (Nashville: Thomas Nelson, 1997), 45.

891 Lawson, George. *Exposition of the Book of Proverbs*. (Edinburgh, 1821), Proverbs 12:29.

[892] Spence-Jones, H. D. M. (Ed.). *Proverbs.* (London; New York: Funk & Wagnalls Company, 1909), 503.

[893] Ibid.

[894] Ross, Allen P. *The Expositor's Bible Commentary.* (Grand Rapids: Zondervan, 1991), 1029.

[895] Lucado, Max & T. A. Gibbs. *Grace for the Moment: Inspirational Thoughts for Each Day of the Year.* (Nashville, Tennessee: J. Countryman, 2000), 218.

[896] Packer, J. I. *Knowing God.* (Madison, Wisconsin: Intervarsity Press, 1977), 211.

[897] Wesley, John. in Dan Hayes, "Motivating Reasons to Pray" (www.startingwithgod.com), accessed January 8, 2008.

[898] Packer, J. I. *Knowing God.* (Madison, Wisconsin: Intervarsity Press, 1977), 214.

[899] Ross, Allen P. *The Expositor's Bible Commentary.* (Grand Rapids: Zondervan, 1991), 1029.

[900] Jamieson, Robert, A. R. Fausset, & David Brown. *Commentary Critical and Explanatory on the Whole Bible,* (Vol. 1). (Oak Harbor, WA: Logos Research Systems, Inc., 1997), 402.

[901] Reyburn, W. D. and E. M. Fry. *A Handbook on Proverbs.* (New York: United Bible Societies, 2000), 661.

[902] Spence-Jones, H. D. M. (Ed.). *Proverbs.* (London; New York: Funk & Wagnalls Company, 1909), 600.

[903] Ibid.

[904] Dodds, Abigail. "Every Woman's Call to Work," https://www.desiringgod.org/articles/every-woman-s-call-to-work, accessed December 11, 2017.

[905] Reyburn, W. D. and E. M. Fry. *A Handbook on Proverbs.* (New York: United Bible Societies, 2000), 565.

[906] Ibid.

[907] Henry, Matthew. *Matthew Henry's Commentary on the Whole Bible: Complete and Unabridged in One Volume.* (Peabody: Hendrickson, 1994), 1014.

[908] Waltke, Bruce K. *The Book of Proverbs* (Vol. 2). (Grand Rapids: William B. Eerdmans Publishing Company, 2004), 126.

[909] MacArthur, J., Jr. (Ed.). *The MacArthur Study Bible* (electronic ed.). (Nashville, TN: Word Pub., 1997), 904.

[910] Walvoord, J. F. and R. B. Zuck. *The Bible Knowledge Commentary: An Exposition of the Scriptures* (Vol. 1). (Wheaton, IL: Victor Books, 1985), Proverbs 31:6–7.

[911] Pfeiffer, C. F. *The Wycliffe Bible Commentary: Old Testament.* (Chicago: Moody Press, 1962), Proverbs 31:6.

[912] Ironside, H. A. *Notes on the Book of Proverbs*. (Neptune, NJ: Loizeaux Bros., 1908), 471.

[913] Spence-Jones, H. D. M. (Ed.). *Proverbs*. (London; New York: Funk & Wagnalls Company, 1909), 335.

[914] Rogers, Adrian. "Laughter—A Merry Heart (Devotional, October 17, 2017). https:// www.lwf.org/daily-treasures/laughter-a-merry-heart, accessed October 12, 2018.

[915] Fairchild, Mary. "The Healing Power of Laughter," http://christianity.about.com, accessed August 11, 2014.

[916] Ibid.

[917] Ibid.

[918] Bridges, Charles. *A Commentary on Proverbs*. (Carlisle, PA: The Banner of Truth Trust, 2008), 274.

[919] Reyburn, W. D. and E. M. Fry. *A Handbook on Proverbs*. (New York: United Bible Societies, 2000), 70.

[920] Ibid.

[921] Insight for Today. "Memorizing Scripture," September 26, 2015. www.insight.org/ resources/daily-devotional/individual/memorizing-scripture, accessed August 13, 2017.

[922] Reyburn, W. D. and E. M. Fry. *A Handbook on Proverbs*. (New York: United Bible Societies, 2000), 222.

[923] Ibid.

[924] Henry, Matthew. *Matthew Henry's Commentary on the Whole Bible: Complete and Unabridged in One Volume*. (Peabody: Hendrickson, 1994), 975.

[925] Ibid.

[926] Ibid.

[927] Lawson, G. *Exposition of the Book of Proverbs* (Vol. 1). (Edinburgh; Glasgow; London: David Brown; W. Oliphant; F. Pillans; M. Ogle; Ogle, Duncan, and Co.; J. Nisbet, 1821), 173.

[928] Bridges, Charles. *A Commentary on Proverbs*. (Carlisle, PA: The Banner of Truth Trust, 2008), 515.

[929] Ross, Allen P. *The Expositor's Bible Commentary*. (Grand Rapids: Zondervan, 1991), 1099.

[930] Barclay, William. *New Testament Words*. (Louisville, KY: Westminster John Knox Press, 1974), 221.

[931] Reyburn, W. D. and E. M. Fry. *A Handbook on Proverbs*. (New York: United Bible Societies, 2000), 656.

[932] Ibid.

[933] Spence-Jones, H. D. M. (Ed.). *Proverbs*. (London; New York: Funk & Wagnalls Company, 1909), 598.

[934] Spence-Jones, H. D. M. (Ed.). *Proverbs.* (London; New York: Funk & Wagnalls Company, 1909), 216.

[935] Ibid.

[936] Hodge, Charles. *Systematic Theology,* 471.

[937] Barclay, W. (Ed.). *The Gospel of Matthew* (Vol. 1). (Philadelphia, PA: The Westminster John Knox Press, 1976), 103.

[938] http://www.azquotes.com/author/13978-Charles_Spurgeon/tag/mercy, accessed November 30, 2017.

[939] Pfeiffer, C. F. *The Wycliffe Bible Commentary: Old Testament.* (Chicago: Moody Press, 1962), Proverbs 25:11.

[940] Greenstone, Julius H. *Proverbs with Commentary.* (Philadelphia: The Jewish Publication Society of America, 1960), 266.

[941] Ross, Allen P. *The Expositor's Bible Commentary.* (Grand Rapids: Zondervan, 1991), 1082.

[942] Larsen, David. *The Company of the Preachers,* 578.

[943] Spence-Jones, H. D. M. (Ed.). *Proverbs.* (London; New York: Funk & Wagnalls Company, 1909), 518.

[944] Ross, Allen P. *The Expositor's Bible Commentary.* (Grand Rapids: Zondervan, 1991), 1100.

[945] *The NET Bible First Edition Notes.* (Biblical Studies Press, 2006), Proverbs 27:19.

[946] Reyburn, W. D. and E. M. Fry. *A Handbook on Proverbs.* (New York: United Bible Societies, 2000), 452.

[947] MacDonald, W. (A. Farstad, Ed.). *Believer's Bible Commentary: Old and New Testaments.* (Nashville: Thomas Nelson, 1995), 846.

[948] Blue, Ron and Judy. http://www.focusonthefamily.com/parenting/schoolage-children/money-lessons/teaching-your-kids-about-money, accessed October 11, 2017.

[949] https://www.umass.edu/aesop/content.php?n=0&i=1, accessed October 11, 2017.

[950] Blue, Ron and Judy. http://www.focusonthefamily.com/parenting/schoolage-children/money-lessons/teaching-your-kids-about-money, accessed October 11, 2017.

[951] Ramsey, Dave. "Teach Kids About Money," http://www.focusonthefamily.com/ parenting/schoolage-children/money-lessons/teach-kids-about-money, accessed October 11, 2017.

[952] Ironside, H. A. *Notes on the Book of Proverbs.* (Neptune, NJ: Loizeaux Bros., 1908), 324.

[953] Henry, Matthew. *Matthew Henry's Commentary on the Whole Bible: Complete and Unabridged in One Volume.* (Peabody: Hendrickson, 1994), 1007.

[954] http://www.crosswalk.com/devotionals/loveworthfinding/what-are-your-plans-for-mothers-day-love-worth-finding-may-8-2010-11631323.html, accessed October 22, 2017.

[955] Rogers, Adrian. "Is Capital Punishment Contrary to the Word of God?," https://www. lwf.org/questions-and-answers/is-capital-punishment-contrary-to-the-word-of-god, accessed December 31, 2017.

[956] MacArthur, John. "Bible Questions and Answers, Part 59." https://www.gty.org/ library/sermons-library/70-31/bible-questions-and-answers-part-59, accessed December 31, 2017.

[957] Reyburn, W. D. and E. M. Fry. *A Handbook on Proverbs.* (New York: United Bible Societies, 2000), 461.

[958] Ross, Allen P. *The Expositor's Bible Commentary.* (Grand Rapids: Zondervan, 1991), 1059.

[959] Bridges, Charles. *A Commentary on Proverbs.* (Carlisle, PA: The Banner of Truth Trust, 2008), 395.

[960] Bridges, Charles. *A Commentary on Proverbs.* (Carlisle, PA: The Banner of Truth Trust, 2008), 395.

[961] Ironside, H. A. *Notes on the Book of Proverbs.* (Neptune, NJ: Loizeaux Bros., 1908), 298.

[962] Henry, Matthew. *Matthew Henry's Commentary on the Whole Bible: Complete and Unabridged in One Volume.* (Peabody: Hendrickson, 1994), 961.

[963] Reyburn, W. D. and E. M. Fry. *A Handbook on Proverbs.* (New York: United Bible Societies, 2000), 90.

[964] Wuest, K. S. *Wuest's Word Studies from the Greek New Testament: For the English Reader.* (Grand Rapids: Eerdmans, 1997), Galatians 6:10.

[965] http://www.whatchristianswanttoknow.com/20-amazing-quotes-about-serving, accessed November 18, 2013.

[966] Ortberg, John. *The Life You've Always Wanted: Spiritual Disciplines for Ordinary People.* (Grand Rapids: Zondervan; Revised edition, September 17, 2002), 250.

[967] Murphy, R. E. *Proverbs* (Vol. 22). (Dallas: Word, Incorporated, 1998), 194.

[968] Ironside, H. A. *Notes on the Book of Proverbs.* (Neptune, NJ: Loizeaux Bros., 1908), 359.

[969] Spurgeon, C. H. "Good News" (Sermon # 2866; Proverbs 25:25), at the Metropolitan Tabernacle, Newington.

[970] Ibid.

[971] Reyburn, W. D. and E. M. Fry. *A Handbook on Proverbs.* (New York: United Bible Societies, 2000), 439.

[972] *The NET Bible First Edition Notes.* (Biblical Studies Press, 2006), Proverbs 21:3.

[973] Henry, Matthew. *Matthew Henry's Commentary on the Whole Bible: Complete and Unabridged in One Volume.* (Peabody: Hendrickson, 1994), 1001.

[974] Spence-Jones, H. D. M. (Ed.). *Proverbs.* (London; New York: Funk & Wagnalls Company, 1909), 6.

[975] https://www.josh.org/answers-for-teens-detail/, accessed January 25, 2018.

[976] Reyburn, W. D. and E. M. Fry. *A Handbook on Proverbs.* (New York: United Bible Societies, 2000), 604.

[977] Elwell, Walter A. *Evangelical Dictionary of Theology.* (1997), entry for "Hardening, Hardness of Heart."

[978] Ironside, H. A. *Notes on the Book of Proverbs.* (Neptune, NJ: Loizeaux Bros., 1908), 414–415.

[979] Lawson, George. *Exposition of the Book of Proverbs.* (Edinburgh, 1821), Proverbs 29:1.

[980] Bridges, Charles. *A Commentary on Proverbs.* (Carlisle, PA: The Banner of Truth Trust, 2008), 556.

[981] Kidner, Derek. *The Proverbs: An Introduction and Commentary. Tyndale Old Testament Commentary.* (Downers Grove: InterVarsity, 1964), 127.

[982] *The NET Bible First Edition Notes.* (Biblical Studies Press, 2006), Proverbs 18:2.

[983] McKane, William. *Proverbs: A New Approach. Old Testament Library.* (Philadelphia: Westminster, 1970), 515.

[984] Garrett, D. A. *Proverbs, Ecclesiastes, Song of Songs* (Vol. 14). (Nashville: Broadman & Holman Publishers, 1993), 163.

[985] Ironside, H. A. *Notes on the Book of Proverbs.* (Neptune, NJ: Loizeaux Bros., 1908), 181.

[986] Buzzell, S. S. in J. F. Walvoord and R. B. Zuck (Eds.). *The Bible Knowledge Commentary: An Exposition of the Scriptures* (Vol. 1). (Wheaton, IL: Victor Books, 1985), 926.

[987] Reyburn, W. D. and E. M. Fry. *A Handbook on Proverbs.* (New York: United Bible Societies, 2000), 221.

[988] Sanders, J. Oswald. *Divine Art of Soul winning,* 68.

[989] Anonymous. https://quoteinvestigator.com/2012/08/13/overalls-work/, accessed January 15, 2018.

[990] Twain, Mark. *Autobiography.*

[991] Reyburn, W. D. and E. M. Fry. *A Handbook on Proverbs.* (New York: United Bible Societies, 2000), 492.

[992] Ibid.

[993] Henry, Matthew. *Matthew Henry's Commentary on the Whole Bible: Complete and Unabridged in One Volume.* (Peabody: Hendrickson, 1994), 1007.

[994] Spence-Jones, H. D. M. (Ed.). *Proverbs.* (London; New York: Funk & Wagnalls Company, 1909), 451.

[995] https://www.brainyquote.com/topics/orphan, accessed November 16, 2017.

[996] Spence-Jones, H. D. M. (Ed.). *Proverbs.* (London; New York: Funk & Wagnalls Company, 1909), 64.

[997] Henry, Matthew. *Matthew Henry's Commentary on the Whole Bible: Complete and Unabridged in One Volume.* (Peabody: Hendrickson, 1994), 961.

[998] Reyburn, W. D. and E. M. Fry. *A Handbook on Proverbs.* (New York: United Bible Societies, 2000), 226.

[999] Spence-Jones, H. D. M. (Ed.). *Proverbs.* (London; New York: Funk & Wagnalls Company, 1909), 555.

[1000] Carroll, B. H. *Old Testament Teaching,* 173.

[1001] Buzzell, S. S. in J. F. Walvoord and R. B. Zuck (Eds.). *The Bible Knowledge Commentary: An Exposition of the Scriptures* (Vol. 1). (Wheaton, IL: Victor Books, 1985), 948.

[1002] Pearson, C. Ridley. *Counsels of the Wise King or Proverbs of Solomon Applied to Daily Life,* Vol. 2. (London: W. Skeffington & Son, 1881), 11.

[1003] Ibid.

[1004] Criswell, W. A., P. Patterson, E. R. Clendenen, D. L. Akin, M. Chamberlin, D. K. Patterson, & J. Pogue, (Eds.). *Believer's Study Bible* (electronic ed.). (Nashville: Thomas Nelson, 1991), Proverbs 22:6.

[1005] Waltke, Bruce K. *The Book of Proverbs* (Vol. 2). (Grand Rapids: William B. Eerdmans Publishing Company, 2004), 205.

[1006] McCready, Amy. "Avoid Raising an Entitled Child: 5 Strategies That Really Work" (November 4, 2016), www.today.com/parents/avoid-raising-entitled-child-5-strategies-really-work-t44576, accessed September 29, 2017.

[1007] *The NET Bible First Edition Notes.* (Biblical Studies Press, 2006), Proverbs 22:6.

[1008] Spence-Jones, H. D. M. (Ed.). *Proverbs.* (London; New York: Funk & Wagnalls Company, 1909), 422.

[1009] MacArthur, J., Jr. (Ed.). *The MacArthur Study Bible* (electronic ed.). (Nashville, TN: Word Pub., 1997), 908.

[1010] Spence-Jones, H. D. M. (Ed.). *Proverbs.* (London; New York: Funk & Wagnalls Company, 1909), 199.

[1011] Buzzell, S. S. in J. F. Walvoord and R. B. Zuck (Eds.). *The Bible Knowledge Commentary: An Exposition of the Scriptures* (Vol. 1). (Wheaton, IL: Victor Books, 1985), 947.

[1012] Reyburn, W. D. and E. M. Fry. *A Handbook on Proverbs.* (New York: United Bible Societies, 2000), 410.

[1013] Unknown.

[1014] *Baker's Evangelical Dictionary of Bible Theology.* http://www.biblestudytools.com/ dictionaries/bakers-evangelical-dictionary/honor.html, accessed August 5, 2017.

[1015] *The NET Bible First Edition Notes.* (Biblical Studies Press, 2006), Proverbs 24:2.

[1016] Reyburn, W. D. and E. M. Fry. *A Handbook on Proverbs.* (New York: United Bible Societies, 2000), 531.

[1017] Henry, Matthew. *Matthew Henry's Commentary on the Whole Bible: Complete and Unabridged in One Volume.* (Peabody: Hendrickson, 1994), 1010.

[1018] Arichea, D. C. and H. Hatton. *A Handbook on Paul's Letters to Timothy and to Titus.* (New York: United Bible Societies, 1995), 131.

[1019] Barclay, W. (Ed.). *The Letters to Timothy, Titus, and Philemon.* (Philadelphia: Westminster John Knox Press, 1975), 117.

[1020] *The NET Bible First Edition Notes.* (Biblical Studies Press, 2006), Proverbs 16:27.

[1021] Toy, C. H. *Proverbs* [ICC], 125–26.

[1022] Henry, Matthew. *Matthew Henry's Commentary on the Whole Bible: Complete and Unabridged in One Volume.* (Peabody: Hendrickson, 1994), 991.

[1023] Reyburn, W. D. and E. M. Fry. *A Handbook on Proverbs.* (New York: United Bible Societies, 2000), 360.

[1024] http://www.mainlesson.com/display.php?author=kaufman&book=plutarch&story=themistocles, November 29, 2017.

[1025] Maclaren, Alexander. *Exposition of Holy Scripture, Proverbs.* (Grand Rapids: Baker Book House, 1977), 108.

[1026] Ibid., 109.

[1027] Spence-Jones, H. D. M. (Ed.). *Proverbs.* (London; New York: Funk & Wagnalls Company, 1909), 482.

[1028] Garrett, D. A. *Proverbs, Ecclesiastes, Song of Songs* (Vol. 14). (Nashville: Broadman & Holman Publishers, 1993), 207.

[1029] Spence-Jones, H. D. M. (Ed.). *Proverbs.* (London; New York: Funk & Wagnalls Company, 1909), 482.

[1030] Ironside, H. A. *Notes on the Book of Proverbs.* (Neptune, NJ: Loizeaux Bros., 1908), 352.

[1031] Walvoord, J. F. and R. B. Zuck. *The Bible Knowledge Commentary: An Exposition of the Scriptures* (Vol. 1). (Wheaton, IL: Victor Books, 1985), 960.

[1032] Spence-Jones, H. D. M. (Ed.). *Proverbs.* (London; New York: Funk & Wagnalls Company, 1909), 482.

[1033] Reyburn, W. D. and E. M. Fry. *A Handbook on Proverbs*. (New York: United Bible Societies, 2000), 51–52.

[1034] Spence-Jones, H. D. M. (Ed.). *Proverbs*. (London; New York: Funk & Wagnalls Company, 1909), 17.

[1035] Spurgeon, C. H. "The Anchor" (sermon #1294). May 21, 1876.

[1036] Ten Boom, Corrie. *Jesus Is Victor*. (Fleming H. Revell Company, 1985).

[1037] Ironside, H. A. *Notes on the Book of Proverbs*. (Neptune, NJ: Loizeaux Bros., 1908), Proverbs 16:7.

[1038] Henry, Matthew. *Matthew Henry's Commentary on the Whole Bible: Complete and Unabridged in One Volume*. (Peabody: Hendrickson, 1994), 990.

[1039] Criswell, W. A., P. Patterson, E. R. Clendenen, D. L. Akin, M. Chamberlin, D. K. Patterson, & J. Pogue, (Eds.). *Believer's Study Bible* (electronic ed.). (Nashville: Thomas Nelson, 1991), Proverbs 16:7.

[1040] MacArthur, J., Jr. (Ed.). *The MacArthur Study Bible* (electronic ed.). (Nashville, TN: Word Pub., 1997), 899.

[1041] Smith, J. E. *The Wisdom Literature and Psalms*. (Joplin, MO: College Press Pub. Co., 1996), Proverbs 1:10–14.

[1042] Maclaren, Alexander. *Exposition of Holy Scripture, Proverbs*. (Grand Rapids: Baker Book House, 1977), 75.

[1043] Reyburn, W. D. and E. M. Fry. *A Handbook on Proverbs*. (New York: United Bible Societies, 2000), 399.

[1044] Jamieson, Robert, A. R. Fausset, & David Brown. *Commentary Critical and Explanatory on the Whole Bible,* (Vol. 1). (Oak Harbor, WA: Logos Research Systems, Inc., 1997), Proverbs 19:5.

[1045] MacArthur, John. "The Blasphemous Sin of Defaming Others," Part 2, http://www.gty. org/resources/sermons/59-27, accessed August 2, 2014.

[1046] Reyburn, W. D. and E. M. Fry. *A Handbook on Proverbs*. (New York: United Bible Societies, 2000), 38.

[1047] Ibid.

[1048] Henry, Matthew. *Matthew Henry's Commentary on the Whole Bible: Complete and Unabridged in One Volume*. (Peabody: Hendrickson, 1994), 956.

[1049] Gill, John. *Gill's Exposition of the Whole Bible*. Proverbs 1:10.

[1050] Reyburn, W. D. and E. M. Fry. *A Handbook on Proverbs*. (New York: United Bible Societies, 2000), 224.

[1051] Ford, W. Herschel. *Simple Sermons for Special Days and Occassions*. (Nashville: Zondervan Publishing House, 1967), Foreword.

[1052] Vines, Jerry and Jim Shaddix. *Progress in the Pulpit: How to Grow in Your Preaching*. (Chicago: Moody Publishers, 2017), chapter 2.

[1053] Spence-Jones, H. D. M. (Ed.). *Proverbs*. (London; New York: Funk & Wagnalls Company, 1909), 55.

[1054] Murphy, R. E. *Proverbs* (Vol. 22). (Dallas: Word, Incorporated, 1998), 21.

[1055] Ibid.

[1056] Buzzell, S. S. in J. F. Walvoord and R. B. Zuck (Eds.). *The Bible Knowledge Commentary: An Exposition of the Scriptures* (Vol. 1). (Wheaton, IL: Victor Books, 1985), 911.

[1057] Maclaren, Alexander. *Exposition of Holy Scripture, Proverbs.* (Grand Rapids: Baker Book House, 1977), 87.

[1058] Ross, Allen P. *The Expositor's Bible Commentary.* (Grand Rapids: Zondervan, 1991), 1002.

[1059] Reyburn, W. D. and E. M. Fry. *A Handbook on Proverbs.* (New York: United Bible Societies, 2000), 348.

[1060] Spence-Jones, H. D. M. (Ed.). *The Pulpit Commentary.* (London; New York: Funk & Wagnalls Company, 1909), Proverbs, 309.

[1061] Maclaren, Alexander. *Exposition of Holy Scripture, Proverbs.* (Grand Rapids: Baker Book House, 1977), 202.

[1062] Bridges, Charles. *A Commentary on Proverbs.* (Carlisle, PA: The Banner of Truth Trust, 2008), 226.

[1063] Ironside, H. A. *Notes on the Book of Proverbs.* (Neptune, NJ: Loizeaux Bros., 1908), 193.

[1064] Buzzell, S. S. in J. F. Walvoord and R. B. Zuck (Eds.). *The Bible Knowledge Commentary: An Exposition of the Scriptures* (Vol. 1). (Wheaton, IL: Victor Books, 1985), 957.

[1065] Spence-Jones, H. D. M. (Ed.). *Proverbs.* (London; New York: Funk & Wagnalls Company, 1909), 443.

[1066] Ibid.

[1067] Graham, Franklin. "Political Correctness Gone Amok," February 20, 2012. https:// billygraham.org/story/franklin-graham-political-correctness-gone-amok/, accessed December 15, 2017.

[1068] The quote, though attributed to President Abraham Lincoln, has also been credited to William Gladstone.

[1069] Ironside, H. A. *Notes on the Book of Proverbs.* (Neptune, NJ: Loizeaux Bros., 1908), 415.

[1070] Ibid.

[1071] Reyburn, W. D. and E. M. Fry. *A Handbook on Proverbs.* (New York: United Bible Societies, 2000), 601.

[1072] Ross, Allen P. *The Expositor's Bible Commentary.* (Grand Rapids: Zondervan, 1991), 1110.

[1073] Spence-Jones, H. D. M. (Ed.). *Proverbs.* (London; New York: Funk & Wagnalls Company, 1909), 539.

[1074] Ibid., 218

[1075] Ibid.

[1076] Reyburn, W. D. and E. M. Fry. *A Handbook on Proverbs*. (New York: United Bible Societies, 2000), 257.

[1077] Spence-Jones, H. D. M. (Ed.). *Proverbs*. (London; New York: Funk & Wagnalls Company, 1909), 218.

[1078] Criswell, W. A. *The Criswell Study Bible*. (Nashville: Thomas Nelson Publishing Company, 1979), Proverbs 11:26.

[1079] *The NET Bible First Edition Notes*. (Biblical Studies Press, 2006), Proverbs 4:25.

[1080] Spence-Jones, H. D. M. (Ed.). *Proverbs*. (London; New York: Funk & Wagnalls Company, 1909), 92.

[1081] Study jointly commissioned by Covenant Eyes, Josh McDowell Ministry, and the Barna Group.

[1082] Jackson, Rob. "When Children View Pornography." http://www.focusonthefamily. com/parenting/sexuality/when-children-use-pornography/when-children-view-pornography, accessed August 1, 2017.

[1083] "Symantec survey reveals more than 80 percent of children using e-mail receive inappropriate spam daily," Business Wire, June 9, 2003.

[1084] "The Poison of Pornography." https://www.oneplace.com/ministries/love-worth-finding/read/articles/the-poison-of-pornography-15292.html, accessed January 30, 2018.

[1085] Spence-Jones, H. D. M. (Ed.). *Proverbs*. (London; New York: Funk & Wagnalls Company, 1909), 195.

[1086] Ross, Allen P. *The Expositor's Bible Commentary*. (Grand Rapids: Zondervan, 1991), 953.

[1087] Henry, Matthew. *Matthew Henry's Commentary on the Whole Bible: Complete and Unabridged in One Volume*. (Peabody: Hendrickson, 1994), 974.

[1088] Ross, Allen P. *The Expositor's Bible Commentary*. (Grand Rapids: Zondervan, 1991), 1103.

[1089] Bridges, Charles. *A Commentary on Proverbs*. (Carlisle, PA: The Banner of Truth Trust, 2008), 528.

[1090] Franklin Graham on the National Day of Prayer—2010.

[1091] https://gracequotes.org/quote/the-coming-revival-must-begin-with-a-great-revival/, accessed January 25, 2018.

[1092] www.whatchristianswanttoknow.com/27-christian-quotes-about-revival/ #ixzz4x5KnmLjG, accessed October 31, 2017.

[1093] Wiersbe, W. W. (1996). The Bible Exposition Commentary (Wheaton, Ill.: Victor Books), Luke 18:1.

[1094] Swindoll, Chuck. *The Quest for Character*. (Grand Rapids: Zondervan Publishing House, 1982), 38.

[1095] Reyburn, W. D. and E. M. Fry. *A Handbook on Proverbs*. (New York: United Bible Societies, 2000), 592.

[1096] *The NET Bible First Edition Notes*. (Biblical Studies Press, 2006), Proverbs 30:8.

[1097] Ibid.

[1098] Henry, Matthew. *Matthew Henry's Commentary on the Whole Bible: Complete and Unabridged in One Volume*. (Peabody: Hendrickson, 1994), 1023.

[1099] Spence-Jones, H. D. M. (Ed.). *Proverbs*. (London; New York: Funk & Wagnalls Company, 1909), 573.

[1100] Reyburn, W. D. and E. M. Fry. *A Handbook on Proverbs*. (New York: United Bible Societies, 2000), 626.

[1101] Gill, John. *Gill's Exposition of the Whole Bible*. Proverbs 30:8.

[1102] Poole, Matthew. *Matthew Poole's English Annotations on the Holy Bible*. "Commentary on Proverbs 30:8."

[1103] Spence-Jones, H. D. M. (Ed.). *Proverbs*. (London; New York: Funk & Wagnalls Company, 1909), 573.

[1104] Murphy, R. E. *Proverbs* (Vol. 22). (Dallas: Word, Incorporated, 1998), 229.

[1105] Ross, Allen P. *The Expositor's Bible Commentary*. (Grand Rapids: Zondervan, 1991), 1120.

[1106] Ibid.

[1107] Dallas Theological Seminary podcast. Charles Swindoll, "Finishing Well." December 11, 2012.

[1108] Henry, Matthew. *Matthew Henry's Commentary on the Whole Bible: Complete and Unabridged in One Volume*. (Peabody: Hendrickson, 1994), 2319.

[1109] Ibid.

[1110] Wiersbe, W. W. *Wiersbe's Expository Outlines on the Old Testament*. (Wheaton, IL: Victor Books, 1993), Proverbs 18:13.

[1111] Ibid.

[1112] Ibid.

[1113] Henry, Matthew. *Matthew Henry's Commentary on the Whole Bible: Complete and Unabridged in One Volume*. (Peabody: Hendrickson, 1994), 995.

[1114] McKane, William. *Proverbs: A New Approach. Old Testament Library*. (Philadelphia: Westminster, 1970).

[1115] http://izquotes.com/quote/319561, accessed October 25, 2017.

[1116] Spurgeon, C. H. *The Salt Cellars: Being a Collection of Proverbs, Together with Homily Notes Thereon,* Vol. 2. (Bellingham, WA: Logos Bible Software, 2009), 17.

[1117] Law, William. *A Serious Call to a Devout and Holy Life*. (1728), Chapter XV.

[1118] Nee, Watchman. *The Spiritual Man,* Part 6, Chapter 2.

[1119] http://www.cslewisinstitute.org/Pride_and_Humility_Page1, accessed September 3, 2017.

[1120] Lewis, C. S. *Mere Christianity.* (Harper One, 1980), 123.

[1121] Exell, Joseph, Ed. *The Biblical Illustrator: Proverbs.* (Grand Rapids: Baker Book House), Proverbs 16:18

[1122] Henry, Matthew. *Matthew Henry's Commentary on the Whole Bible: Complete and Unabridged in One Volume.* (Peabody: Hendrickson, 1994), 991.

[1123] Keller, Timothy. *God's Wisdom for Navigating Life.* (New York, New York: Viking, 2017), 287.

[1124] Spurgeon, C. H.Exposition of Luke 15 included in "The Prodigal's Climax." Metropolitan Tabernacle Pulpit (sermon #2414), May 19, 1887.

[1125] *The NET Bible First Edition Notes.* (Biblical Studies Press, 2006), Proverbs 25:14.

[1126] http://www.wiseoldsayings.com/promises-quotes/, accessed December 8, 2017.

[1127] https://www.brainyquote.com/topics/promises, accessed December 8, 2017.

[1128] Ibid.

[1129] Ross, Allen P. *The Expositor's Bible Commentary.* (Grand Rapids: Zondervan, 1991), 958.

[1130] Henry, Matthew. *Matthew Henry's Commentary on the Whole Bible: Complete and Unabridged in One Volume.* (Peabody: Hendrickson, 1994), 1176.

[1131] Exell, Joseph, Ed. *The Biblical Illustrator: Isaiah,* Vol. 3. (Grand Rapids: Baker Book House), 21.

[1132] Ibid.

[1133] Pardington, Dr. cited by L. B. Cowper. *Streams in the Desert,* October 6.

[1134] Wiersbe, W. W. *Be Comforted,* "Be" Commentary Series. (Wheaton, IL: Victor Books, 1996), 126.

[1135] Reyburn, W. D. and E. M. Fry. *A Handbook on Proverbs.* (New York: United Bible Societies, 2000), 463.

[1136] Ibid.

[1137] Spence-Jones, H. D. M. (Ed.). *Proverbs.* (London; New York: Funk & Wagnalls Company, 1909), 254.

[1138] Buzzell, S. S. in J. F. Walvoord and R. B. Zuck (Eds.). *The Bible Knowledge Commentary: An Exposition of the Scriptures* (Vol. 1). (Wheaton, IL: Victor Books, 1985), 934.

[1139] Reyburn, W. D. and E. M. Fry. *A Handbook on Proverbs.* (New York: United Bible Societies, 2000), 299.

[1140] Henry, Matthew. *Matthew Henry's Commentary on the Whole Bible: Complete and Unabridged in One Volume.* (Peabody: Hendrickson, 1994), 983.

[1141] Spence-Jones, H. D. M. (Ed.). *Proverbs.* (London; New York: Funk & Wagnalls Company, 1909), 254.

[1142] Reyburn, W. D. and E. M. Fry. *A Handbook on Proverbs.* (New York: United Bible Societies, 2000), 432.

[1143] Ibid.

[1144] Maclaren, Alexander. *Exposition of Holy Scripture, Proverbs.* (Grand Rapids: Baker Book House, 1977), 199.

[1145] Bennett, Arthur, Ed. *The Valley of Vision.* (Carlisle, PA: Banner of Truth, 1975/2002), 217.

[1146] Ross, Allen P. *The Expositor's Bible Commentary.* (Grand Rapids: Zondervan, 1991), 1030.

[1147] Simeon, C. *Horae Homileticae: Proverbs to Isaiah XXVI* (Vol. 7). (London: Holdsworth and Ball, 1833), 198.

[1148] Spence-Jones, H. D. M. (Ed.). *Proverbs.* (London; New York: Funk & Wagnalls Company, 1909), 364.

[1149] Ironside, H. A. *Notes on the Book of Proverbs.* (Neptune, NJ: Loizeaux Bros., 1908), 242.

[1150] Maclaren, Alexander. *Exposition of Holy Scripture, Proverbs.* (Grand Rapids: Baker Book House, 1977), 79.

[1151] http://drjamesdobson.org/popupplayer?broadcastId=5403fdae-2d54-4fd1-a678-b0e3c57cc810, accessed June 21, 2016.

[1152] Maclaren, Alexander. *Exposition on the Holy Scripture,* Proverbs 18:10, 211.

[1153] Ibid., 213.

[1154] Buzzell, S. S. in J. F. Walvoord and R. B. Zuck (Eds.). *The Bible Knowledge Commentary: An Exposition of the Scriptures* (Vol. 1). (Wheaton, IL: Victor Books, 1985), 944.

[1155] Maclaren, Alexander. *Exposition on the Holy Scripture,* Proverbs 18:10, 213.

[1156] Ibid., 215.

[1157] Buzzell, S. S. in J. F. Walvoord and R. B. Zuck (Eds.). *The Bible Knowledge Commentary: An Exposition of the Scriptures* (Vol. 1). (Wheaton, IL: Victor Books, 1985), 909.

[1158] Lawson, George. *Exposition of the Book of Proverbs.* (Edinburgh, 1821), Proverbs 1:28.

[1159] Henry, Matthew. *Matthew Henry's Commentary on the Whole Bible: Complete and Unabridged in One Volume.* (Peabody: Hendrickson, 1994), 957.

[1160] Reyburn, W. D. and E. M. Fry. *A Handbook on Proverbs.* (New York: United Bible Societies, 2000), 599.

[1161] Ibid., 72.

[1162] Ross, Allen P. *The Expositor's Bible Commentary.* (Grand Rapids: Zondervan, 1991), 1109.

[1163] Bonhoeffer, Dietrich. "Life Together: The Classic Exploration of Christian Community."

[1164] Henry, Matthew. *Matthew Henry's Commentary on the Whole Bible: Complete and Unabridged in One Volume.* (Peabody: Hendrickson, 1994), 1019.

[1165] MacArthur, J., Jr. (Ed.). *The MacArthur Study Bible* (electronic ed.). (Nashville, TN: Word Pub., 1997), 917.

[1166] Spence-Jones, H. D. M. (Ed.). *Proverbs.* (London; New York: Funk & Wagnalls Company, 1909), 460.

[1167] Murphy, R. E. *Proverbs* (Vol. 22). (Dallas: Word, Incorporated, 1998), 182.

[1168] Ironside, H. A. *Notes on the Book of Proverbs.* (Neptune, NJ: Loizeaux Bros., 1908), 336.

[1169] Whybray, R. N. *Proverbs.* [CBC], 140.

[1170] Reyburn, W. D. and E. M. Fry. *A Handbook on Proverbs.* (New York: United Bible Societies, 2000), 47.

[1171] Ironside, H. A. *Notes on the Book of Proverbs.* (Neptune, NJ: Loizeaux Bros., 1908), 24–25.

[1172] Rice, John. *Revival Appeals.* (Murfressboro: Sword of the Lord Publishers, 1945), 168.

[1173] Spence-Jones, H. D. M. (Ed.). *Proverbs.* (London; New York: Funk & Wagnalls Company, 1909), 218.

[1174] Ibid.

[1175] Ironside, H. A. *Notes on the Book of Proverbs.* (Neptune, NJ: Loizeaux Bros., 1908), 124.

[1176] Henry, Matthew. *Matthew Henry's Commentary on the Whole Bible: Complete and Unabridged in One Volume.* (Peabody: Hendrickson, 1994), 979.

[1177] *The NET Bible First Edition Notes.* (Biblical Studies Press, 2006), Proverbs 20:29.

[1178] Spence-Jones, H. D. M. (Ed.). *Proverbs.* (London; New York: Funk & Wagnalls Company, 1909), 390.

[1179] *The NET Bible First Edition Notes.* (Biblical Studies Press, 2006), Proverbs 20:29.

[1180] Reyburn, W. D. and E. M. Fry. *A Handbook on Proverbs.* (New York: United Bible Societies, 2000), 435.

[1181] *The NET Bible First Edition Notes.* (Biblical Studies Press, 2006), Proverbs 20:29.

[1182] Bridges, Charles. *A Commentary on Proverbs.* (Carlisle, PA: The Banner of Truth Trust, 2008), 362–363.

[1183] http://vancehavner.com/biography/, accessed October 23, 2016.

[1184] *Lives of the Artists: Michelangelo.* (Milwaukee, Wisconsin: Garth Stevens Publishing, 2004), 41–42.

1185 http://www.gty.org/resources/sermons/56-13/gods-plan-for-older-men-and-older-women, accessed October 24, 2016.

1186 Spence-Jones, H. D. M. (Ed.). *Proverbs.* (London; New York: Funk & Wagnalls Company, 1909), 388.

1187 Ironside, H. A. *Notes on the Book of Proverbs.* (Neptune, NJ: Loizeaux Bros., 1908), 271.

1188 Lucado, Max. *In the Eye of the Storm* and *Applause of Heaven.* (Two classics in one volume). Chapter 11.

1189 Henry, Matthew. *Matthew Henry's Commentary on the Whole Bible: Complete and Unabridged in One Volume.* (Peabody: Hendrickson, 1994), 1000.

1190 McGee, J. V. *Thru the Bible Commentary: History of Israel (1 and 2 Chronicles)* (electronic ed., Vol. 14). (Nashville: Thomas Nelson, 1991), 149.

1191 Morgan, R. J. *Nelson's Annual Preacher's Sourcebook (2004 Edition).* (Nashville, TN: Thomas Nelson Publishers, 2004), 17.

1192 www.vitalchristianity.org/docs/New%20Articles/Revivial-Requirement2.pdf, accessed May 10, 2014.

1193 Duewel, Wesley L. *Revival Fire.* (Grand Rapids: Zondervan Publishing House, 1995), 277.

1194 https://www.christianquotes.info/quotes-by-topic/quotes-about-revival/#ixzz4qTZ2P6T5, accessed August 22, 2017.

1195 Spence-Jones, H. D. M. (Ed.). *Proverbs.* (London; New York: Funk & Wagnalls Company, 1909), 553.

1196 Reyburn, W. D. and E. M. Fry. *A Handbook on Proverbs.* (New York: United Bible Societies, 2000), 606.

1197 Ibid., 394.

1198 MacArthur, J., Jr. (Ed.). *The MacArthur Study Bible* (electronic ed.). (Nashville, TN: Word Pub., 1997), 902.

1199 *Precept Austin.* 1 Corinthians 13:5-6 Commentary, http://www.preceptaustin.org/ 1corinthians_135-6, accessed December 5, 2017.

1200 https://www.brainyquote.com/topics/rude, accessed December 5, 2017.

1201 Spence-Jones, H. D. M. (Ed.). *Proverbs.* (London; New York: Funk & Wagnalls Company, 1909), 409.

1202 Henry, Matthew. *Matthew Henry's Commentary on the Whole Bible: Complete and Unabridged in One Volume.* (Peabody: Hendrickson, 1994), 1003.

1203 Lawson, George. *Exposition of the Book of Proverbs.* (Edinburgh, 1821), Proverbs 21:31.

1204 Ironside, H. A. *Notes on the Book of Proverbs.* (Neptune, NJ: Loizeaux Bros., 1908), 296.

[1205] Spence-Jones, H. D. M. (Ed.). *Proverbs.* (London; New York: Funk & Wagnalls Company, 1909), 409.

[1206] Reyburn, W. D. and E. M. Fry. *A Handbook on Proverbs.* (New York: United Bible Societies, 2000), 228.

[1207] Ibid.

[1208] Spurgeon, C. H. *Morning and Evening,* May 23.

[1209] https://www.christianquotes.info/top-quotes/20-awesome-quotes-salvation/ #ixzz50m1vi2ED, accessed December 9, 2017.

[1210] https://www.christianquotes.info/top-quotes/20-awesome-quotes-salvation/ #ixzz50m1vi2ED, accessed December 9, 2017.

[1211] Ironside, H. A. *Notes on the Book of Proverbs.* (Neptune, NJ: Loizeaux Bros., 1908), 437.

[1212] Barclay, W., Ed. *The Letter to the Hebrews, The Daily Study Bible Series,* Rev. ed. (Philadelphia: The Westminster Press, 2000), 104.

[1213] Spence-Jones, H. D. M. (Ed.). *Proverbs.* (London; New York: Funk & Wagnalls Company, 1909), 292.

[1214] Ironside, H. A. *Notes on the Book of Proverbs.* (Neptune, NJ: Loizeaux Bros., 1908), 180.

[1215] Ross, Allen P. *The Expositor's Bible Commentary.* (Grand Rapids: Zondervan, 1991), 965.

[1216] https://www.gty.org/library/sermons-library/45-22/false-security-part-1, accessed October 20, 2017.

[1217] Ibid.

[1218] Pink, A. W. *Studies in the Scriptures.* (Sovereign Grace Publishers, 1926–27), 114–115.

[1219] Ibid.

[1220] Hamilton, William W. *Sermons on the Books of the Bible*, Vol. V, 249.

[1221] Reyburn, W. D. and E. M. Fry. *A Handbook on Proverbs.* (New York: United Bible Societies, 2000), 236.

[1222] MacArthur, J., Jr. (Ed.). *The MacArthur Study Bible* (electronic ed.). (Nashville, TN: Word Pub., 1997), 882.

[1223] Maclaren, Alexander. *Exposition of Holy Scripture, Proverbs.* (Grand Rapids: Baker Book House, 1977), 117.

[1224] Reyburn, W. D. and E. M. Fry. *A Handbook on Proverbs.* (New York: United Bible Societies, 2000), 112.

[1225] Spence-Jones, H. D. M. (Ed.). *Proverbs.* (London; New York: Funk & Wagnalls Company, 1909), 91.

[1226] Ibid.

[1227] Henry, Matthew. *Matthew Henry's Commentary on the Whole Bible: Complete and Unabridged in One Volume.* (Peabody: Hendrickson, 1994), 964.

[1228] Maclaren, Alexander. *Exposition of Holy Scripture, Proverbs.* (Grand Rapids: Baker Book House, 1977), 123.

[1229] Ibid., 117.

[1230] Spence-Jones, H. D. M. (Ed.). *Proverbs.* (London; New York: Funk & Wagnalls Company, 1909), 482.

[1231] Ibid.

[1232] Ironside, H. A. *Notes on the Book of Proverbs.* (Neptune, NJ: Loizeaux Bros., 1908), 353.

[1233] Criswell, W. A. *The Criswell Study Bible.* (Nashville: Thomas Nelson Publishing Company, 1979), Proverbs 25:28.

[1234] Crosswalk. "Self-Control Is Inner Strength." Today's Insight, March 14, 2013.

[1235] Chuck Swindoll. "Self-Control." http://www.valleyviewseek.org/self-control, accessed August 6, 2017.

[1236] Ibid.

[1237] Ross, Allen P. *The Expositor's Bible Commentary.* (Grand Rapids: Zondervan, 1991), 1094–1095.

[1238] Spence-Jones, H. D. M. (Ed.). *Proverbs.* (London; New York: Funk & Wagnalls Company, 1909), 521.

[1239] Henry, Matthew. *Matthew Henry's Commentary on the Whole Bible: Complete and Unabridged in One Volume.* (Peabody: Hendrickson, 1994), 1015.

[1240] Spence-Jones, H. D. M. (Ed.). *Proverbs.* (London; New York: Funk & Wagnalls Company, 1909), 522.

[1241] Reyburn, W. D. and E. M. Fry. *A Handbook on Proverbs.* (New York: United Bible Societies, 2000), 127.

[1242] Henry, Matthew. *Matthew Henry's Commentary on the Whole Bible: Complete and Unabridged in One Volume.* (Peabody: Hendrickson, 1994), 965.

[1243] Criswell, W. A., P. Patterson, E. R. Clendenen, D. L. Akin, M. Chamberlin, D. K. Patterson, & J. Pogue, (Eds.). *Believer's Study Bible* (electronic ed.). (Nashville: Thomas Nelson, 1991), Proverbs 5:19.

[1244] Hindson, E. E., and W. M. Kroll, (Eds.). *KJV Bible Commentary.* (Nashville: Thomas Nelson, 1994), 1207.

[1245] Buzzell, S. S. in J. F. Walvoord and R. B. Zuck (Eds.). *The Bible Knowledge Commentary: An Exposition of the Scriptures* (Vol. 1). (Wheaton, IL: Victor Books, 1985), 907–908.

[1246] Spurgeon, *Metropolitan Tabernacle Pulpit,* "Particular Redemption," February 28, 1858.

[1247] *The NET Bible First Edition Notes.* (Biblical Studies Press, 2006), Proverbs 18:3.

[1248] Ross, Allen P. *The Expositor's Bible Commentary.* (Grand Rapids: Zondervan, 1991), 1023.

[1249] Reyburn, W. D. and E. M. Fry. *A Handbook on Proverbs.* (New York: United Bible Societies, 2000), 394.

[1250] Ibid.

[1251] John Stott. *John Stott on Singleness* (August 17, 2011). http://www.christianitytoday.com/ct/2011/augustweb-only/johnstottsingleness.html, accessed December 11, 2017.

[1252] The Bureau of Labor Statistics, 2014.

[1253] Ross, Allen P. *The Expositor's Bible Commentary.* (Grand Rapids: Zondervan, 1991), 1042–1043.

[1254] *New Englander,* Vol. VI-1848. (New Haven: A. H. Maltby, 1848), 229.

[1255] Ironside, H. A. *Notes on the Book of Proverbs.* (Neptune, NJ: Loizeaux Bros., 1908), 264.

[1256] Spence-Jones, H. D. M. (Ed.). *Proverbs.* (London; New York: Funk & Wagnalls Company, 1909), 427.

[1257] Exell, Joseph S. *The Biblical Illustrator.* Commentary on Proverbs 22:29. https://www.studylight.org/commentaries/tbi/proverbs-22.html. 1905–1909. New York.

[1258] MacDonald, W. (A. Farstad, Ed.). *Believer's Bible Commentary: Old and New Testaments.* (Nashville: Thomas Nelson, 1995), 858.

[1259] Baggarly, H. M. *Tulia Herald,* Tulia, Texas, Feb. 4, 1954.

[1260] https://www.christianquotes.info/quotes-by-topic/quotes-about-gossip/ #ixzz50tOdGqoL, accessed December 10, 2017.

[1261] https://www.christianquotes.info/quotes-by-topic/quotes-about-gossip / #ixzz50tMXjyPh, accessed December 10, 2017.

[1262] https://www.christianquotes.info/quotes-by-topic/quotes-about-gossip/ #ixzz50tNqhuOK, accessed December 10, 2017.

[1263] Henry, Matthew. *Matthew Henry's Commentary on the Whole Bible: Complete and Unabridged in One Volume.* (Peabody: Hendrickson, 1994), 1012.

[1264] Swindoll, Chuck. *Job: A Man of Heroic Endurance.* (Nashville: WPublishing Group, 2004), 163.

[1265] Spence-Jones, H. D. M. (Ed.). *Proverbs.* (London; New York: Funk & Wagnalls Company, 1909), 492.

[1266] Poole, Matthew. *Matthew Poole's English Annotations on the Holy Bible.* "Commentary on Proverbs 20:13".

[1267] Jamieson, Robert, A. R. Fausset, & David Brown. *Commentary Critical and Explanatory on the Whole Bible,* (Vol. 1). (Oak Harbor, WA: Logos Research Systems, Inc., 1997), Proverbs 20:13.

[1268] https://www.theguardian.com/notesandqueries/query/0,5753,-50504,00.html, accessed February 6, 2018.

[1269] Lawson, George. *Exposition of the Book of Proverbs.* (Edinburgh, 1821), Proverbs 20:13.

[1270] Spence-Jones, H. D. M. (Ed.). *Proverbs.* (London; New York: Funk & Wagnalls Company, 1909), 63.

[1271] Reyburn, W. D. and E. M. Fry. *A Handbook on Proverbs.* (New York: United Bible Societies, 2000), 87.

[1272] Spurgeon, C. H. "The Peculiar Sleep of the Beloved," March 4, 1855 (Sermon).

[1273] Ibid.

[1274] Reyburn, W. D. and E. M. Fry. *A Handbook on Proverbs.* (New York: United Bible Societies, 2000), 342.

[1275] Murphy, R. E. *Proverbs* (Vol. 22). (Dallas: Word, Incorporated, 1998), 115.

[1276] https://www.brainyquote.com/topics/smile, accessed December 15, 2017.

[1277] Ibid.

[1278] Ibid.

[1279] https://www.brainyquote.com/topics/smile, accessed January 26, 2018.

[1280] Alden, Robert L. *Proverbs: A Commentary on an Ancient Book of Timeless Advice.* (Grand Rapids: Baker, 1984), 63.

[1281] Spence-Jones, H. D. M. (Ed.). *The Pulpit Commentary.* (London: C. Kegan Paul & Company, 1881), Genesis, 449.

[1282] Stanley Jones, E. *Abundant Living.* (Nashville: Abingdon-Cokesbury Press, 1942), 130.

[1283] Brooks, Thomas and Alexander Balloch Grosart. *The Complete Works of Thomas Brooks.* (Edinburgh: J. Nichol, 1866), 12.

[1284] Spurgeon, *Faith's Checkbook,* November 10.

[1285] Murphy, R. E. *Proverbs* (Vol. 22). (Dallas: Word, Incorporated, 1998), 186.

[1286] Reyburn, W. D. and E. M. Fry. *A Handbook on Proverbs.* (New York: United Bible Societies, 2000), 535.

[1287] Ibid., 536.

[1288] Cited in "Preach the Word: Back to the Basics Part I: The Morning Watch," www. preachtheword.com/sermon/b2b01.shtml, accessed December 6, 2011.

[1289] Bridges, Charles. *A Commentary on Proverbs.* (Carlisle, PA: The Banner of Truth Trust, 2008), 461.

[1290] Buzzell, S. S. in J. F. Walvoord and R. B. Zuck (Eds.). *The Bible Knowledge Commentary: An Exposition of the Scriptures* (Vol. 1). (Wheaton, IL: Victor Books, 1985), 930.

[1291] MacArthur, J., Jr. (Ed.). *The MacArthur Study Bible* (electronic ed.). (Nashville, TN: Word Pub., 1997), 892.

1292 Kemp, Joseph W. *The Soulwinner and Soulwinning.* (New York: George H. Doran Company, 1916), 26–28. www.archive.org/stream/MN41613ucmf.../MN41613ucmf_8_djvu.txt. accessed April 13, 2010

1293 Poole, Matthew. *Matthew Poole's English Annotations on the Holy Bible.* "Commentary on Proverbs 11:30."

1294 Spurgeon, C. H. *Sermons for Evangelistic Occasions.* (Grand Rapids: Zondervan Publishing House, 1962), 11.

1295 Ibid., 19.

1296 Ross, Allen P. *The Expositor's Bible Commentary.* (Grand Rapids: Zondervan, 1991), 1075.

1297 Lee, Robert G. "Is Hell a Myth?" (sermon). https://fundamentalbaptistsermons. net/RGLee/LeeRGIsHellAMyth.htm, accessed January 26, 2018.

1298 Lee, R. G. *Sermonic Library: From Feet to Fathoms,* (Orlando, Florida: Christ for the World Publishers, 1981), 52–55.

1298 Ironside, H. A. *Notes on the Book of Proverbs.* (Neptune, NJ: Loizeaux Bros., 1908), 195.

1299 Buzzell, S. S. in J. F. Walvoord and R. B. Zuck (Eds.). *The Bible Knowledge Commentary: An Exposition of the Scriptures* (Vol. 1). (Wheaton, IL: Victor Books, 1985), 940.

1300 Reyburn, W. D. and E. M. Fry. *A Handbook on Proverbs.* (New York: United Bible Societies, 2000), 347.

1301 Henry, Matthew. *Matthew Henry's Commentary on the Whole Bible: Complete and Unabridged in One Volume.* (Peabody: Hendrickson, 1994), 989.

1302 Smith, James. "The Preparation of the Heart," 1861. https://www.gracegems.org/ Smith3/preparation_of_the_heart.htm

1303 *The NET Bible First Edition Notes.* (Biblical Studies Press, 2006), Proverbs 10:31.

1304 Reyburn, W. D. and E. M. Fry. *A Handbook on Proverbs.* (New York: United Bible Societies, 2000), 237.

1305 Lawson, G. *Exposition of the Book of Proverbs* (Vol. 1). (Edinburgh; Glasgow; London: David Brown; W. Oliphant; F. Pillans; M. Ogle; Ogle, Duncan, and Co.; J. Nisbet, 1821).

1306 Reyburn, W. D. and E. M. Fry. *A Handbook on Proverbs.* (New York: United Bible Societies, 2000), 662.

1307 Walvoord, J. F. and R. B. Zuck. *The Bible Knowledge Commentary: An Exposition of the Scriptures* (Vol. 1). (Wheaton, IL: Victor Books, 1985), 973.

1308 Ironside, H. A. *Notes on the Book of Proverbs.* (Neptune, NJ: Loizeaux Bros., 1908), 387.

[1309] Reyburn, W. D. and E. M. Fry. *A Handbook on Proverbs*. (New York: United Bible Societies, 2000), 286.

[1310] Buzzell, S. S. in J. F. Walvoord and R. B. Zuck (Eds.). *The Bible Knowledge Commentary: An Exposition of the Scriptures* (Vol. 1). (Wheaton, IL: Victor Books, 1985), 932.

[1311] *The NET Bible First Edition Notes*. (Biblical Studies Press, 2006), Proverbs 13:3.

[1312] Ross, Allen P. *The Expositor's Bible Commentary*. (Grand Rapids: Zondervan, 1991), 975.

[1313] Spence-Jones, H. D. M. (Ed.). *Proverbs*. (London; New York: Funk & Wagnalls Company, 1909), 251.

[1314] Ibid., 387.

[1315] Morgan, Scott. "How to Tame the Tongue," January 5, 2011. billygraham.org/decision-magazine/january-2011/how-to-tame-the-tongue, accessed August 21, 2017.

[1316] *The NET Bible First Edition Notes*. (Biblical Studies Press, 2006), Proverbs 14:30.

[1317] *The NET Bible First Edition Notes*. (Biblical Studies Press, 2006), Proverbs 14:30.

[1318] Mayo Clinic Staff. "Stress Management," www.mayoclinic.org/healthy-lifestyle/stress-management/in-depth/stress/art-20046037, accessed October 26, 2017.

[1319] Swindoll, Chuck. Insight for Today: A Daily Devotional. "Give God Your Worries," March 17, 2017.

[1320] Rogers, Adrian. "A Word for Worriers" (sermon). www.oneplace.com/ministries/love-worth-finding/read/articles/a-word-for-worriers-9900.html, accessed October 26, 2017.

[1321] Reyburn, W. D. and E. M. Fry. *A Handbook on Proverbs*. (New York: United Bible Societies, 2000), 459.

[1322] Henry, Matthew. *Matthew Henry's Commentary on the Whole Bible: Complete and Unabridged in One Volume*. (Peabody: Hendrickson, 1994), 1003.

[1323] Gill, John. *Gill's Exposition of the Whole Bible*. Proverbs 21:30.

[1324] Ironside, H. A. *Notes on the Book of Proverbs*. (Neptune, NJ: Loizeaux Bros., 1908), 297.

[1325] Spence-Jones, H. D. M. (Ed.). *Proverbs*. (London; New York: Funk & Wagnalls Company, 1909), 155.

[1326] Graham, Billy. *My Answer*. "Can God Help Me to Stop Being So Stubborn?," Tribune Media Services on Jan 26, 2011.

[1327] https://www.brainyquote.com/topics/stubborn

[1328] MacArthur, J., Jr. (Ed.). *The MacArthur Study Bible* (electronic ed.). (Nashville, TN: Word Pub., 1997), 913.

[1329] Reyburn, W. D. and E. M. Fry. *A Handbook on Proverbs*. (New York: United Bible Societies, 2000), 554.

[1330] Ibid.

[1331] Spence-Jones, H. D. M. (Ed.). *Proverbs*. (London; New York: Funk & Wagnalls Company, 1909), 485.

[1332] Bridges, Charles. *A Commentary on Proverbs*. (Carlisle, PA: The Banner of Truth Trust, 2008), 481.

[1333] MacArthur, J., Jr. (Ed.). *The MacArthur Study Bible* (electronic ed.). (Nashville, TN: Word Pub., 1997), 913.

[1334] Bridges, Charles. *A Commentary on Proverbs*. (Carlisle, PA: The Banner of Truth Trust, 2008), 482.

[1335] Ibid.

[1336] Scalise, Dr. Eric. "Faith to Face Depression," http://drjamesdobson.org/blogs/dr-eric-scalise/dr.-eric-scalise/2017/03/15/faith-to-face-depression, accessed October 15, 2017.

[1337] Faulk, Timothy. personal correspondence. December 15, 2012.

[1338] Ibid., (bracket content added).

[1339] Reyburn, W. D. and E. M. Fry. *A Handbook on Proverbs*. (New York: United Bible Societies, 2000), 249.

[1340] Henry, Matthew. *Matthew Henry's Commentary on the Whole Bible: Complete and Unabridged in One Volume*. (Peabody: Hendrickson, 1994), 978.

[1341] Schultz, Matt. "The Dangers of Cosigning a Loan for Friends or Relatives," (August 2, 2016). http://www.nydailynews.com/life-style/dangers-co-signing-loan-friends-relatives-article-1.2736065, accessed February 7, 2018.

[1342] Buzzell, S. S. in J. F. Walvoord and R. B. Zuck (Eds.). *The Bible Knowledge Commentary: An Exposition of the Scriptures* (Vol. 1). (Wheaton, IL: Victor Books, 1985), 943.

[1343] Bridges, Charles. *A Commentary on Proverbs*. (Carlisle, PA: The Banner of Truth Trust, 2008), 118.

[1344] Ironside, H. A. *Notes on the Book of Proverbs*. (Neptune, NJ: Loizeaux Bros., 1908), 120–121.

[1345] Reyburn, W. D. and E. M. Fry. *A Handbook on Proverbs*. (New York: United Bible Societies, 2000), 503.

[1346] Ibid., 504.

[1347] Hubbard, D. A. and L. J. Ogilvie. *Proverbs* (Vol. 15). (Nashville, TN: Thomas Nelson Inc.1989), 374.

[1348] Ibid.

[1349] https://www.christianquotes.info/top-quotes/16-awesome-quotes-about-surrendering-to-god/#ixzz4xml75iiH, accessed November 7, 2017.

[1350] https://www.christianquotes.info/top-quotes/16-awesome-quotes-about-surrendering-to-god/#ixzz4xmHHJoum, accessed November 7, 2017.

[1351] Reyburn, W. D. and E. M. Fry. *A Handbook on Proverbs*. (New York: United Bible Societies, 2000), 343.

[1352] http://www.azquotes.com/quotes/topics/teachable.html, accessed January 1, 2018.

[1353] http://www.azquotes.com/quotes/topics/teachable.html, accessed January 1, 2018.

[1354] *The NET Bible First Edition Notes*. (Biblical Studies Press, 2006), Proverbs 19:27.

[1355] Buzzell, S. S. in J. F. Walvoord and R. B. Zuck (Eds.). *The Bible Knowledge Commentary: An Exposition of the Scriptures* (Vol. 1). (Wheaton, IL: Victor Books, 1985), 948.

[1356] Bridges, Charles. *Exposition of the Book of Proverbs*. (Edinburgh: Banner of Truth Trust, 1968), 331.

[1357] Henry, Matthew. *Matthew Henry's Commentary on the Whole Bible: Complete and Unabridged in One Volume*. (Peabody: Hendrickson, 1994), Proverbs 19:27.

[1358] Gill, John. *Gill's Exposition of the Whole Bible*. Proverbs 19:27.

[1359] Spence-Jones, H. D. M. (Ed.). *Proverbs*. (London; New York: Funk & Wagnalls Company, 1909), 371.

[1360] Bridges, Charles. *Exposition of the Book of Proverbs*. (Edinburgh: Banner of Truth Trust, 1968), 332.

[1361] Ibid.

[1362] Murphy, R. E. *Proverbs* (Vol. 22). (Dallas: Word, Incorporated, 1998), 97.

[1363] Reyburn, W. D. and E. M. Fry. *A Handbook on Proverbs*. (New York: United Bible Societies, 2000), 119.

[1364] Ibid.

[1365] Ibid.

[1366] Hindson, E. E., and W. M. Kroll (Eds.). *KJV Bible Commentary*. (Nashville: Thomas Nelson, 1994), 1206.

[1367] Reyburn, W. D. and E. M. Fry. *A Handbook on Proverbs*. (New York: United Bible Societies, 2000), 38.

[1368] Ibid.

[1369] Evans, Tony. "Overcoming Temptation." http://tonyevans.org/overcoming-temptation/, accessed December 7, 2017.

[1370] Buxton. *The Biblical Illustrator*, "Divine Testing," Electronic Database. James 1:12.

[1371] Criswell, W. A. "Trusting God." *Daily Word,* November 22, 2017. W. A. Criswell Sermon Library.

[1372] http://www.gracegems.org/15/pure_gold.htm, accessed November 17, 2017.

[1373] Spurgeon, C. H. *Sermon Notes,* "The Tried Man the Blessed Man" (James 1:12).

[1374] https://www.christianquotes.info/top-quotes/20-encouraging-quotes-trials-struggles/#ixzz4yi1xkUxD, accessed November 17, 2017.

[1375] https://www.christianquotes.info/top-quotes/20-encouraging-quotes-trials-struggles/#ixzz4yi1xkUxD, accessed November 17, 2017.

[1376] Reyburn, W. D. and E. M. Fry. *A Handbook on Proverbs.* (New York: United Bible Societies, 2000), 615.

[1377] Walvoord, J. F. and R. B. Zuck. *The Bible Knowledge Commentary: An Exposition of the Scriptures* (Vol. 1). (Wheaton, IL: Victor Books, 1985), 969.

[1378] Spence-Jones, H. D. M. (Ed.). *Proverbs.* (London; New York: Funk & Wagnalls Company, 1909), 557.

[1379] Reyburn, W. D. and E. M. Fry. *A Handbook on Proverbs.* (New York: United Bible Societies, 2000), 591.

[1380] www.americanpayroll.org, accessed October 17, 2017.

[1381] *The NET Bible First Edition Notes.* (Biblical Studies Press, 2006), Proverbs 4:23.

[1382] Henry, Matthew. *Matthew Henry's Commentary on the Whole Bible: Complete and Unabridged in One Volume.* (Peabody: Hendrickson, 1994), 1009.

[1383] Rogers, Adrian. "Guard Your Heart." https://www.oneplace.com/ministries/love-worth-finding/read/articles/guard-your-heart-15291.html, accessed January 2, 2018.

[1384] Dawson, Scott. *Evangelism Today.* (Grand Rapids: Baker Books, 2009), 29.

[1385] Graham, Billy. "The Sin of Tolerance," October 3, 2012. billygraham.org/story/the-sin-of-tolerance/, accessed August 12, 2017.

[1386] Ibid.

[1387] MacArthur, John. "The Rise of Extreme Tolerance," October 27, 2009. www.gty.org/ library/articles/A305/the-rise-of-extreme-tolerance, accessed August 12, 2017.

[1388] *The NET Bible First Edition Notes.* (Biblical Studies Press, 2006), Proverbs 29:11.

[1389] Ibid.

[1390] Buzzell, S. S. in J. F. Walvoord and R. B. Zuck (Eds.). *The Bible Knowledge Commentary: An Exposition of the Scriptures* (Vol. 1). (Wheaton, IL: Victor Books, 1985), 931.

[1391] Ross, Allen P. *The Expositor's Bible Commentary.* (Grand Rapids: Zondervan, 1991), 971.

[1392] Henry, Matthew. *Matthew Henry's Commentary on the Whole Bible: Complete and Unabridged in One Volume.* (Peabody: Hendrickson, 1994), 981.

[1393] Reyburn, W. D. and E. M. Fry. *A Handbook on Proverbs.* (New York: United Bible Societies, 2000), 583.

[1394] Hutson, Curtis, Editor. *Great Preaching on Comfort.* (Murfreesboro, Tennessee: Sword of the Lord Publishers, 1990), 88.

[1395] Vincent, M. R. *Word Studies in the New Testament.* (New York: Charles Scribner's Sons, 1887), 2 Corinthians 12:9.

[1396] Spurgeon, C. H. *Morning and Evening,* October 7.

[1397] Ibid. 98.

[1398] https://www.cru.org/train-and-grow/life-and-relationships/hardships/the-significance-of-trials.html, accessed October 20, 2017.

[1399] https://www.goodreads.com/quotes/tag/refinement, accessed October 19, 2017.

[1400] Buzzell, S. S. in J. F. Walvoord and R. B. Zuck (Eds.). *The Bible Knowledge Commentary: An Exposition of the Scriptures* (Vol. 1). (Wheaton, IL: Victor Books, 1985), 930.

[1401] Shakespeare, William. *King Lear.* (Act I, Scene IV, 13). nfs.sparknotes.com, accessed May 25, 2011.

[1402] *The NET Bible First Edition Notes.* (Biblical Studies Press, 2006), Proverbs 28:26.

[1403] Bridges, Charles. *A Commentary on Proverbs.* (Carlisle, PA: The Banner of Truth Trust, 2008), 552.

[1404] Spence-Jones, H. D. M. (Ed.). *Proverbs.* (London; New York: Funk & Wagnalls Company, 1909), 443.

[1405] Ibid.

[1406] Ibid.

[1407] Spurgeon, C. H. "Buying the Truth," (sermon # 3449) delivered June 26, 1870. The introduction of the sermon provides a great illustration that might be shared with children with great effect.

[1408] *The NET Bible First Edition Notes.* (Biblical Studies Press, 2006), Proverbs 24:26.

[1409] Ironside, H. A. *Notes on the Book of Proverbs.* (Neptune, NJ: Loizeaux Bros., 1908), 340.

[1410] Murphy, R. E. *Proverbs* (Vol. 22). (Dallas: Word, Incorporated, 1998), 186d

[1411] Ross, Allen P. *The Expositor's Bible Commentary.* (Grand Rapids: Zondervan, 1991), 1077.

[1412] Spence-Jones, H. D. M. (Ed.). *Proverbs.* (London; New York: Funk & Wagnalls Company, 1909), 462.

[1413] Buzzell, S. S. in J. F. Walvoord and R. B. Zuck (Eds.). *The Bible Knowledge Commentary: An Exposition of the Scriptures* (Vol. 1). (Wheaton, IL: Victor Books, 1985), 959.

[1414] https://www.goodreads.com/quotes/tag/truth-telling, accessed November 26, 2017.

[1415] https://www.christianquotes.info/quotes-by-topic/quotes-about-truth/#ixzz4zYebmZEm, accessed November 26, 2017.

[1416] Bratcher, R. G., and E. A. Nida. *A Handbook on Paul's Letters to the Colossians and to Philemon.* (New York: United Bible Societies, 1993), 94.

[1417] http://www.thischristianjourney.com/thischristianjourney/GeneralPages/Outlines/ A_Unified_Church.htm, accessed January 26, 2018.

[1418] Burke, Edmund. https://www.christianquotes.info/top-quotes/15-powerful-quotes-about-unity/#ixzz50NxAGAji, accessed December 5, 2017.

[1419] https://www.christianquotes.info/top-quotes/15-powerful-quotes-about-unity/ #ixzz50NyhVvZw, accessed December 5, 2017.

[1420] Words and Music: 1966 F.E.L. Publications. Assigned 1991 Lorenz Publishing Company (Admin. by Lorenz Corporation)

[1421] https://www.christianquotes.info/top-quotes/15-powerful-quotes-about-unity/ #ixzz50NxAGAji, accessed December 5, 2017.

[1422] Reyburn, W. D. and E. M. Fry. *A Handbook on Proverbs.* (New York: United Bible Societies, 2000), 573.

[1423] Murphy, R. E. *Proverbs* (Vol. 22). (Dallas: Word, Incorporated, 1998), 206.

[1424] Hunter, George III. *How to Reach Secular People.* (Nashville, TN: Abingdon Press, 1992), 53–54

[1425] Exell, Joseph S. *The Biblical Illustrator.* Commentary on Jude 1:3. https://www. studylight.org/commentaries/tbi/jude-1.html. 1905–1909. New York.

[1426] Reyburn, W. D. and E. M. Fry. *A Handbook on Proverbs.* (New York: United Bible Societies, 2000), 528.

[1427] Stanley, Charles. *Landmines in the Path of the Believer.* (Nashville: Thomas Nelson, 2007).

[1428] Barclay, William. *The Letter to the Hebrews.* (Philadelphia: Westminster Press, 1957), 120.

[1429] Stott, John. "The Contemporary Christian." http://www.sermonillustrations.com/a-z/f/forgiveness.htm, accessed July 25, 2014.

[1430] *Promises and Prayers,* 87.

[1431] http://www.thetravelingteam.org/stats/, accessed May 4, 2017.

[1432] http://www.christianpost.com/news/bible-not-available-in-57-of-world-languages-most-americans-believe-the-bible-is-available-in-every-language-137423/, accessed June 27, 2017.

[1433] https://www.wycliffe.org.uk/about/our-impact/, accessed July 18, 2017.

[1434] Bounds, E. M. *The Essentials of Prayer: Prayer and Missions.* (Dallas: Gideon House Books, 2016), Chapter 13.

[1435] Ross, Allen P. *The Expositor's Bible Commentary.* (Grand Rapids: Zondervan, 1991), 1036.

[1436] Blackaby, Henry. *Experiencing God,* 194

[1437] Reyburn, W. D. and E. M. Fry. *A Handbook on Proverbs.* (New York: United Bible Societies, 2000), 431.

[1438] Henry, Matthew. *Matthew Henry's Commentary on the Whole Bible: Complete and Unabridged in One Volume.* (Peabody: Hendrickson, 1994), 1000.

[1439] Criswell, W. A. *The Criswell Study Bible.* (Nashville: Thomas Nelson Publishing Company, 1979), Judges 11:30–31.

[1440] McGee, J. V. *Thru the Bible Commentary* (electronic ed., Vol. 3). (Nashville: Thomas Nelson, 1997), 70.

[1441] Reyburn, W. D. and E. M. Fry. *A Handbook on Proverbs.* (New York: United Bible Societies, 2000), 67.

[1442] Ibid., 242.

[1443] Ibid.

[1444] Spence-Jones, H. D. M. (Ed.). *Proverbs.* (London; New York: Funk & Wagnalls Company, 1909), 110.

[1445] Ironside, H. A. *Notes on the Book of Proverbs.* (Neptune, NJ: Loizeaux Bros., 1908), 58.

[1446] Spence-Jones, H. D. M. (Ed.). *Proverbs.* (London; New York: Funk & Wagnalls Company, 1909), 110.

[1447] Ibid.

[1448] Bidwell, W.H. Ed. *The American National Preacher.* (New York: Living Ministers of the United States, 1843), 103.

[1449] Spence-Jones, H. D. M. (Ed.). *Proverbs.* (London; New York: Funk & Wagnalls Company, 1909), 110.

[1450] Henry, Matthew. *Matthew Henry's Commentary on the Whole Bible: Complete and Unabridged in One Volume.* (Peabody: Hendrickson, 1994), 956.

[1451] Maclaren, Alexander. *Exposition of Holy Scripture, Proverbs.* (Grand Rapids: Baker Book House, 1977), 159.

[1452] Ibid.

[1453] Spence-Jones, H. D. M. (Ed.). *Proverbs.* (London; New York: Funk & Wagnalls Company, 1909), 234. ("sure foundation" [Matthew 7:24]).

[1454] Reyburn, W. D. and E. M. Fry. *A Handbook on Proverbs.* (New York: United Bible Societies, 2000), 268.

[1455] Ibid., 340.

[1456] Spence-Jones, H. D. M. (Ed.). *Proverbs.* (London; New York: Funk & Wagnalls Company, 1909), 295.

[1457] McGee, J. V. *Thru the Bible Commentary: The Epistles (1 and 2 Timothy/Titus/ Philemon)* (electronic ed., Vol. 50). (Nashville: Thomas Nelson, 1991), 70–71.

[1458] Mounce, W. D. *Pastoral Epistles* (Vol. 46). (Dallas: Word, Incorporated, 2000), 278.

[1459] Reyburn, W. D. and E. M. Fry. *A Handbook on Proverbs.* (New York: United Bible Societies, 2000), 663.

[1460] Ibid.

[1461] Ibid.

[1462] Smalley, Greg. "Cherish: Recognize Your Spouse's Value." www.focusonthe family.com/marriage/ communication-and-conflict/the-power-of-healthy-conflict/cherish-recognize-your-spouses-value, accessed November 21, 2017.

[1463] Ironside, H. A. "Lesson 49: Do You Really Love Your Wife?" Part I. (Ephesians 5:25–33).

[1464] https://bible.org/book/export/html/22068, accessed November 21, 2017.

[1465] Ibid.

[1466] https://www.brainyquote.com/topics/wife, accessed November 21, 2017.

[1467] Reyburn, W. D. and E. M. Fry. *A Handbook on Proverbs.* (New York: United Bible Societies, 2000), 250.

[1468] Ibid.

[1469] Henry, Matthew. *Matthew Henry's Commentary on the Whole Bible: Complete and Unabridged in One Volume.* (Peabody: Hendrickson, 1994), 978.

[1470] McGee, J. V. *Thru the Bible Commentary* (electronic ed., Vol. 3). (Nashville: Thomas Nelson, 1997), 42.

[1471] Dixon, Francis. *Ten Studies in Proverbs.* "Portrait of a Virtuous Woman: Study 10," Words of Life Ministries. http://www.wordsoflife.co.uk/bible-studies/study-10-portrait-of-a-virtuous-woman, accessed August 29, 2017.

[1472] Reyburn, W. D. and E. M. Fry. *A Handbook on Proverbs.* (New York: United Bible Societies, 2000), 654.

[1473] Ibid.

[1474] Bridges, Charles. *A Commentary on Proverbs.* (Carlisle, PA: The Banner of Truth Trust, 2008), 621.

[1475] *The NET Bible First Edition Notes.* (Biblical Studies Press, 2006), Proverbs 10:10.

[1476] Spence-Jones, H. D. M. (Ed.). *Proverbs*. (London; New York: Funk & Wagnalls Company, 1909), 196.

[1477] Bridges, Charles. *A Commentary on Proverbs*. (Carlisle, PA: The Banner of Truth Trust, 2008), 97.

[1478] Ironside, H. A. *Notes on the Book of Proverbs*. (Neptune, NJ: Loizeaux Bros., 1908), 98.

[1479] Waltke, Bruce K. *The Book of Proverbs* (Vol. 1). (Grand Rapids: William B. Eerdmans Publishing Company, 2004), 112.

[1480] Lawson, G. *Exposition of the Book of Proverbs* (Vol. 1). (Edinburgh; Glasgow; London: David Brown; W. Oliphant; F. Pillans; M. Ogle; Ogle, Duncan, and Co.; J. Nisbet, 1821), 413.

[1481] Jamieson, Robert, A. R. Fausset, & David Brown. *Commentary Critical and Explanatory on the Whole Bible*, (Vol. 1). (Oak Harbor, WA: Logos Research Systems, Inc., 1997), Proverbs 17:16.

[1482] Watts, J. Wash. *Old Testament Teaching*. (Nashville: Broadman Press, 1967), 214.

[1483] Ibid.

[1484] C. H. Spurgeon, "The Holdfast," sermon #1418 (June 9, 1878).

[1485] Reyburn, W. D. and E. M. Fry. *A Handbook on Proverbs*. (New York: United Bible Societies, 2000), 407.

[1486] Buzzell, S. S. in J. F. Walvoord and R. B. Zuck (Eds.). *The Bible Knowledge Commentary: An Exposition of the Scriptures* (Vol. 1). (Wheaton, IL: Victor Books, 1985), 947.

[1487] Boice, J. M. *Psalms 107–150: An Expositional Commentary*. (Grand Rapids, MI: Baker Books, 2005), 977.

[1488] Spence-Jones, H. D. M. (Ed.). *Proverbs*. (London; New York: Funk & Wagnalls Company, 1909), 369.

[1489] Waltke, Bruce K. *The Book of Proverbs* (Vol. 1). (Grand Rapids: William B. Eerdmans Publishing Company, 2004), 77.

[1490] Reyburn, W. D. and E. M. Fry. *A Handbook on Proverbs*. (New York: United Bible Societies, 2000), 82.

[1491] Ibid.

[1492] Ibid.

[1493] Lawson, George. *Exposition of the Book of Proverbs*. (Edinburgh, 1821), Proverbs 3:17.

[1494] Maclaren, Alexander. *Exposition of Holy Scripture, Proverbs*. (Grand Rapids: Baker Book House, 1977), 93.

[1495] Aitken, K. T. *Proverbs*. (Louisville, KY: Westminster John Knox Press, 1986), 46.

[1496] Spence-Jones, H. D. M. (Ed.). *Proverbs.* (London; New York: Funk & Wagnalls Company, 1909), 458.

[1497] Henry, Matthew. *Matthew Henry's Commentary on the Whole Bible: Complete and Unabridged in One Volume.* (Peabody: Hendrickson, 1994), 1009.

[1498] Ironside, H. A. *Notes on the Book of Proverbs.* (Neptune, NJ: Loizeaux Bros., 1908), 331.

[1499] Murphy, R. E. *Proverbs* (Vol. 22). (Dallas: Word, Incorporated, 1998), 4.

[1500] Aitken, K. T. *Proverbs.* (Louisville, KY: Westminster John Knox Press, 1986), 11.

[1501] *The NET Bible First Edition Notes.* (Biblical Studies Press, 2006), Proverbs 1:5.

[1502] Maclaren, Alexander. *Expositions of Holy Scriptures.* Proverbs 23:15–23, 243.

[1503] Reyburn, W. D. and E. M. Fry. *A Handbook on Proverbs.* (New York: United Bible Societies, 2000), 23.

[1504] *The Quest Study Bible.* (Grand Rapids: Zondervan, 2011), 907.

[1505] Alden, Robert L. *Proverbs: A Commentary on an Ancient Book of Timeless Advice.* (Grand Rapids: Baker, 1984), 7.

[1506] Rogers, Adrian. "The Difference Between Knowledge and Wisdom." *Daily Treasures,* September 11, 2017. www.lwf.org/, accessed October 23, 2017.

[1507] Ibid.

[1508] Lawson, George. *Exposition of the Book of Proverbs.* (Edinburgh, 1821), Proverbs 1:2.

[1509] Spurgeon, C. H. "Christ—The Power and Wisdom of God," sermon # 132.

[1510] Ibid.

[1511] *The NET Bible First Edition Notes.* (Biblical Studies Press, 2006), Proverbs 10:31.

[1512] Ibid.

[1513] Reyburn, W. D. and E. M. Fry. *A Handbook on Proverbs.* (New York: United Bible Societies, 2000), 237.

[1514] http://www.azquotes.com/quotes/topics/soul-winning.html, accessed December 14, 2017.

[1515] Ibid.

[1516] Autrey, C. E. *Evangelistic Sermons,* 46.

[1517] Exell, Joseph, Ed. *The Biblical Illustrator: Proverbs.* (Grand Rapids: Baker Book House), Proverbs 11:16.

[1518] *Matthew Henry Concise Commentary,* Proverbs 11:16.

[1519] Reyburn, W. D. and E. M. Fry. *A Handbook on Proverbs.* (New York: United Bible Societies, 2000), 504.

[1520] Ibid.

[1521] Spence-Jones, H. D. M. (Ed.). *Proverbs*. (London; New York: Funk & Wagnalls Company, 1909), 291.

[1522] Ross, Allen P. *The Expositor's Bible Commentary*. (Grand Rapids: Zondervan, 1991), 993.

[1523] MacArthur, J., Jr. (Ed.). *The MacArthur Study Bible* (electronic ed.). (Nashville, TN: Word Pub., 1997), 880.

[1524] Reyburn, W. D. and E. M. Fry. *A Handbook on Proverbs*. (New York: United Bible Societies, 2000), 329.

[1525] Lawson, G. *Exposition of the Book of Proverbs* (Vol. 1). (Edinburgh; Glasgow; London: David Brown; W. Oliphant; F. Pillans; M. Ogle; Ogle, Duncan, and Co.; J. Nisbet, 1821), 317–318.

[1526] Warren, Rick. "6 Biblical Ways to Handle Disunity" (January 13, 2012), http://pastors.com/6-biblical-ways-to-handle-disunity/2/, accessed October 3, 2014.

[1527] Swindoll, Chuck. *Paul: A Man of Grace and Grit*. (Nashville: Word Publishing, 2002), 173.

[1528] Buzzell, S. S. in J. F. Walvoord and R. B. Zuck (Eds.). *The Bible Knowledge Commentary: An Exposition of the Scriptures* (Vol. 1). (Wheaton, IL: Victor Books, 1985), 939.

[1529] Ross, Allen P. *The Expositor's Bible Commentary*. (Grand Rapids: Zondervan, 1991), 998.

[1530] Walvoord, J. F. and R. B. Zuck. *The Bible Knowledge Commentary: An Exposition of the Scriptures* (Vol. 1). (Wheaton, IL: Victor Books, 1985), 968.

[1531] Ibid.

[1532] Ironside, H. A. *Notes on the Book of Proverbs*. (Neptune, NJ: Loizeaux Bros., 1908), 188.

[1533] Spence-Jones, H. D. M. (Ed.). *Proverbs*. (London; New York: Funk & Wagnalls Company, 1909), 348.

[1534] Buzzell, S. S. in J. F. Walvoord and R. B. Zuck (Eds.). *The Bible Knowledge Commentary: An Exposition of the Scriptures* (Vol. 1). (Wheaton, IL: Victor Books, 1985), 944.

[1535] Reyburn, W. D. and E. M. Fry. *A Handbook on Proverbs*. (New York: United Bible Societies, 2000), 384.

[1536] Ibid.

[1537] Garrett, D. A. *Proverbs, Ecclesiastes, Song of Songs* (Vol. 14). (Nashville: Broadman & Holman Publishers, 1993), 163.

[1538] Criswell, W. A., P. Patterson, E. R. Clendenen, D. L. Akin, M. Chamberlin, D. K. Patterson, & J. Pogue, (Eds.). *Believer's Study Bible* (electronic ed.). (Nashville: Thomas Nelson, 1991), Proverbs 30:11–14. (The author adapted Criswell's interpretation in the description of each generation.)

[1539] *The NET Bible First Edition Notes.* (Biblical Studies Press, 2006), Proverbs 21:27.

[1540] Ibid.

[1541] Ross, Allen P. *The Expositor's Bible Commentary.* (Grand Rapids: Zondervan, 1991), 1058.

[1542] Ibid.

[1543] Ibid., 136.

[1544] Ibid.

[1545] The author's book *The Wounded Spirit* provides clear, concise and in-depth spiritual guidance regarding cure for the wounded spirit.

[1546] Hutson, Curtis, Ed. *Great Preaching on Comfort.* (Murfreesboro, TN: Sword of the Lord Publishers, 1990), 164–165.

[1547] Buzzell, S. S. in J. F. Walvoord and R. B. Zuck (Eds.). *The Bible Knowledge Commentary: An Exposition of the Scriptures* (Vol. 1). (Wheaton, IL: Victor Books, 1985), 945.

[1548] Reyburn, W. D. and E. M. Fry. *A Handbook on Proverbs.* (New York: United Bible Societies, 2000), 392.

[1549] Ross, Allen P. *The Expositor's Bible Commentary.* (Grand Rapids: Zondervan, 1991), 1028.

[1550] MacArthur, J., Jr. (Ed.). *The MacArthur Study Bible* (electronic ed.). (Nashville, TN: Word Pub., 1997), 902.

[1551] Lawson, G. *Exposition of the Book of Proverbs* (Vol. 1). (Edinburgh; Glasgow; London: David Brown; W. Oliphant; F. Pillans; M. Ogle; Ogle, Duncan, and Co.; J. Nisbet, 1821), 449–450.

[1552] Swindoll, Chuck. *Paul: A Man of Grace and Grit.* (Nashville: Word Publishing, 2002), 176.

[1553] Ibid.

[1554] Exell, Joseph, Ed. *The Biblical Illustrator: Acts,* Vol. 15. (Grand Rapids: Baker Book House, undated), 450.

[1555] Henry, Matthew. *Matthew Henry's Commentary on the Whole Bible: Complete and Unabridged in One Volume.* (Peabody: Hendrickson, 1994), 2133.

[1556] Murphy, R. E. *Proverbs* (Vol. 22). (Dallas: Word, Incorporated, 1998), 137.

[1557] Spence-Jones, H. D. M. (Ed.). *Proverbs.* (London; New York: Funk & Wagnalls Company, 1909), 133.

[1558] Buzzell, S. S. in J. F. Walvoord and R. B. Zuck (Eds.). *The Bible Knowledge Commentary: An Exposition of the Scriptures* (Vol. 1). (Wheaton, IL: Victor Books, 1985), 917.

[1559] Spence-Jones, H. D. M. (Ed.). *Proverbs.* (London; New York: Funk & Wagnalls Company, 1909), 133.

[1560] Murphy, R. E. *Proverbs* (Vol. 22). (Dallas: Word, Incorporated, 1998), 42.

[1561] Simeon, C. *Horae Homileticae: Proverbs to Isaiah XXVI* (Vol. 7). (London: Holdsworth and Ball, 1833), 72.

[1562] Buzzell, S. S. in J. F. Walvoord and R. B. Zuck (Eds.). *The Bible Knowledge Commentary: An Exposition of the Scriptures* (Vol. 1). (Wheaton, IL: Victor Books, 1985), 919.

[1563] MacArthur, J., Jr. (Ed.). *The MacArthur Study Bible* (electronic ed.). (Nashville, TN: Word Pub., 1997), 886.

[1564] Henry, Matthew. *Matthew Henry's Commentary on the Whole Bible: Complete and Unabridged in One Volume.* (Peabody: Hendrickson, 1994), 968.

[1565] MacArthur, J., Jr. (Ed.). *The MacArthur Study Bible* (electronic ed.). (Nashville, TN: Word Pub., 1997), 886.

[1566] Simeon, C. *Horae Homileticae: Proverbs to Isaiah XXVI* (Vol. 7). (London: Holdsworth and Ball, 1833), 74.

[1567] Ironside, H. A. *Notes on the Book of Proverbs.* (Neptune, NJ: Loizeaux Bros., 1908), 73.

[1568] Buzzell, S. S. in J. F. Walvoord and R. B. Zuck (Eds.). *The Bible Knowledge Commentary: An Exposition of the Scriptures* (Vol. 1). (Wheaton, IL: Victor Books, 1985), 907.

[1569] Reyburn, W. D. and E. M. Fry. *A Handbook on Proverbs.* (New York: United Bible Societies, 2000), 46.